Microsoft® Certified Professional

Windows® NT Workstation 4.0 Exam Guide

Microsoft® Certified Professional

Windows® NT Workstation 4.0 Exam Guide

Written by Steve Kaczmarek

que®

Windows NT Workstation 4.0 Exam Guide

Copyright© 1997 by Que® Corporation.

Library of Congress Catalog No.: 96-77218

ISBN: 0-7897-0989-9

99 98 97   6 5 4 3 2 1

Interpretation of the printing code: the rightmost double-digit number is the year of the book's printing; the rightmost single-digit number, the number of the book's printing. For example, a printing code of 97-1 shows that the first printing of the book occurred in 1997.

All terms mentioned in this book that are known to be trademarks or service marks have been appropriately capitalized. Que cannot attest to the accuracy of this information. Use of a term in this book should not be regarded as affecting the validity of any trademark or service mark.

Screen reproductions in this book were created using Collage Plus from Inner Media, Inc., Hollis, NH.

Credits

President
Roland Elgey

Publisher
Joe Wikert

Publishing Director
Brad R. Koch

Editorial Services Director
Elizabeth Keaffaber

Managing Editor
Thomas F. Hayes

Director of Marketing
Lynn E. Zingraf

Senior Acquisitions Editor
Elizabeth South

Product Director
Kevin Kloss

Product Development Specialist
Teri Guendling

Production Editor
Julie A. McNamee

Editors
Elizabeth Barrett
Kelli Brooks
Lisa M. Gebken
Kate Givens

Strategic Marketing Manager
Barry Pruett

Technical Editor
Robert Bogue

Technical Support Specialist
Nadeem Muhammed

Acquisitions Coordinator
Tracy Williams

Software Relations Coordinator
Patty Brooks

Editorial Assistant
Virginia Stoller

Book Designer
Ruth Harvey

Cover Designer
Ruth Harvey

Production Team
Michael Beaty
Amy Gornik
Bob LaRoche
Angela Perry

Indexers
Bruce Clingaman
Tim Wright

Composed in **Bembo** and *Avenir* by Que Corporation.

Dedication

To my partner, Bill Glewicz, who has supported and encouraged me throughout this and many other efforts; my Cairn Scruffy, who contentedly warmed my feet while I typed away at my computer; and to my parents, Donald and Pearl Kaczmarek, who fostered in me the pursuit of knowledge and a determination to succeed.

Acknowledgments

The author would like to thank the following for their support during this project:

***Elizabeth South**, **Lisa Wagner**, and **Julie McNamee** at Que Corporation who made this book possible.*

***Pam Bernard**, **Pam Riter**, and **Elaine Avros** at Productivity Point International for their support and assistance, especially when balancing training and writing schedules.*

My fellow partners and trainers at Productivity Point International for their assistance and expertise when my mental active RAM failed to work properly.

Productivity Point International, a truly world-class training organization, for its ongoing investment and conviction in me and for offering me such an exciting career opportunity.

About the Author

Steven D. Kaczmarek, MCSE, MCT, has been associated with Productivity Point as a training consultant since October of 1991. During that time he has focused on providing operating system, network management, and personal computer support training to its clients. Since January of 1996, he has also provided independent consulting services. He holds training and professional certifications (MCT and MCP) from Microsoft Corporation for Windows 3.1, Windows for Workgroups 3.11, Windows 95, Windows NT 3.51 and Windows NT 4.0, Microsoft Systems Management Server 1.2 and TCP/IP, as well as the Microsoft Certified Systems Engineer (MCSE) certification for both Windows NT 3.51 and Windows NT 4.0. He is currently coauthoring another in this line of exam guides *Windows NT Server 4.0 Enterprise Exam Guide*.

Prior to joining Productivity Point, Steve provided a variety of client personal computer support services through the IS departments of Heller International, McDonald's Corporation, and Continental Bank, which included purchasing and installation of personal computer hardware and software, network management, maintenance and help desk support, and customized training. He jokes that he started working with personal computers when they were in their "terrible twos" and has survived them into their "teen years."

Steve has a Master of Science degree from Loyola University with a specialization in computational mathematics. Steve can be reached through e-mail at **SDKACZ@AOL.COM** (America Online) or **105000,1756@COMPUSERVE.COM** (CompuServe).

Productivity Point International (PPI) provides integrated training and support services to the corporate market. PPI has the largest North American network of Microsoft Authorized Technical Education Centers, with the ability to provide technical or end-user training for nationwide roll outs through its Enterprise Wide Solutions program.

We'd Like to Hear from You!

As part of our continuing effort to produce books of the highest possible quality, Que would like to hear your comments. To stay competitive, we *really* want you, as a computer book reader and user, to let us know what you like or dislike most about this book or other Que products.

You can mail comments, ideas, or suggestions for improving future editions to the address below, or send us a fax at (317) 581-4663. For the online inclined, Macmillan Computer Publishing has a forum on CompuServe (type **GO QUEBOOKS** at any prompt) through which our staff and authors are available for questions and comments. The address of our Internet site is **http://www.quecorp.com** (World Wide Web).

In addition to exploring our forum, please feel free to contact me personally to discuss your opinions of this book: I'm **74404,3307** on CompuServe, and **lwagner@que.mcp.com** on the Internet.

Thanks in advance—your comments will help us to continue publishing the best books available on computer topics in today's market.

Lisa Wagner
Senior Product Development Specialist
Que Corporation
201 W. 103rd Street
Indianapolis, Indiana 46290
USA

Contents at a Glance

Table of Contents

Introduction

This book was written by Microsoft Certified Professionals, for Microsoft Certified Professionals, and MCP Candidates. It is designed, in combination with your real-world experience, to prepare you to pass the **Windows NT Workstation 4.0 Exam (70-73)**, as well as give you a background in general knowledge of Windows NT Workstation 4.0. Most of the concepts discussed in this book apply also to Windows NT Server 4.0 and will give you a foundation for that product as well.

The reader should already have a strong working knowledge of the following subjects before beginning a study of this product:

- ◆ *Windows 3.1.*
- ◆ *Windows 95.* Although an overview of the interface will be provided in Chapter 4, it is strongly suggested that you be well acquainted with the look and feel of Windows 95.

◆ *Basic networking concepts.* Appendix G is designed to provide you with the basic concepts and terminology essential as a foundation for understanding Windows NT 4.0.

As of this writing, the exams cost $100 each. Each exam consists of 50 to 100 questions and are timed from one to two hours each. Depending on the certification level, you may have to take as many as six exams, covering Microsoft operating systems, application programs, networking, and software development. Each test involves preparation, study, and, for some of us, heavy doses of test anxiety. Is certification worth the trouble?

Microsoft has cosponsored research that provides some answers.

Benefits for Your Organization

At companies participating in a 1994 Dataquest survey, a majority of corporate managers stated that certification is an *important factor* to the overall success of their companies because:

◆ *Certification increases customer satisfaction.* Customers look for indications that their suppliers understand the industry and have the ability to respond to their technical problems. Having Microsoft Certified Professionals on staff reassures customers; it tells them that your employees have used and mastered Microsoft products.

◆ *Certification maximizes training investment.* The certification process specifically identifies skills that an employee is lacking or areas where additional training is needed. By so doing, it validates training and eliminates the costs and loss of productivity associated with unnecessary training. In addition, certification records enable a company to verify an employee's technical knowledge and track retention of skills over time.

Benefits Up Close and Personal

Microsoft also cites a number of benefits for the certified individual:

- Industry recognition of expertise, enhanced by Microsoft's promotion of the Certified Professional community to the industry and potential clients.

- Access to technical information directly from Microsoft.

- Dedicated CompuServe and The Microsoft Network forums that enable Microsoft Certified Professionals to communicate directly with Microsoft and with one another.

- A complimentary one-year subscription to *Microsoft Certified Professional Magazine*.

- Microsoft Certified Professional logos and other materials to publicize MCP status to colleagues and clients.

- An MCP newsletter to provide regular information on changes and advances in the program and exams.

- Invitations to Microsoft conferences, technical training sessions, and a special events program newsletter from the MCP program.

Additional benefits, depending upon the certification, include:

- Microsoft TechNet or Microsoft Developer Network membership or discounts.

- Free product support incidents with the Microsoft Support Network seven days a week, 24 hours a day.

- One-year subscription to the Microsoft Beta Evaluation program, providing up to 12 monthly CD-ROMs containing beta software for upcoming Microsoft software products.

- Eligibility to join the Network Professional Association, a worldwide independent association of computer professionals.

Some intangible benefits of certification are:

- Enhanced marketability with current or potential employers and customers, along with an increase in earnings potential.

◆ Methodology for objectively assessing current skills, individual strengths, and specific areas where training is required.

How Does This Book Fit In?

One of the challenges that has always faced the would-be Microsoft Certified Professional is to decide how to best prepare for an examination. In doing so, there are always conflicting goals, such as how to prepare for the exam as quickly as possible, and yet, still actually learn how to do the work that passing the exam qualifies you to do.

Our goal for this book is to make your studying job easier by filtering through the reams of Windows NT 4.0 technical material, and presenting in the chapters and lab exercises only the information that you actually need to *know* to pass the Windows NT 4.0 Certification Exam (plus a little bit extra). Other information that we think is important for you to have available while you're working has been relegated to the appendixes, sidebars, and notes.

How to Study with This Book

This book is designed to be used in a variety of ways. Rather than lock you into one particular method of studying, force you to read through sections you're already intimately familiar with, or tie you to your computer, we've made it possible for you to read the chapters at one time, and do the labs at another. We've also made it easy for you to decide whether you need to read a chapter or not by giving you a list of the topics and skills covered at the beginning of each chapter, and describing how the chapter relates to previous material.

Labs are arranged topically, not chapter-by-chapter, so that you can use them to explore the areas and concepts of Windows NT 4.0 that are new to you, or that you need reinforcement in. We've also decided not to intermix them with the text of the chapter, since nothing is more frustrating than not being able to continue reading a chapter because your child is doing his homework on the computer, and you can't use it until the weekend.

The chapters are written in a modular fashion, so that you don't necessarily have to read all the chapters preceding a certain chapter to be able to follow a particular chapter's discussion. Chapter 2 provides a basic overview of Windows NT and its architecture and should be read first as other chapters refer to this material. All chapters, with the exception of Chapter 4, contain material likely to be found on the Windows NT Workstation 4.0 exam, so be sure to read them all eventually.

Don't skip the lab exercises, either. You certainly can practice what you read on your PC while you are reading. Some of the knowledge and skills you need to pass the Windows NT 4.0 MCP exam can only be acquired by working with Windows NT 4.0. Lots of practice and the lab exercises help you acquire these skills.

How This Book Is Organized

The book is broken up into 12 chapters, each focusing on a particular topic that is an important piece of the overall picture.

- Chapter 1, "Microsoft Certified Professional Program," gives you an overview of the Microsoft Certified Professional program, what certifications are available to you, and where Windows NT 4.0 and this book fit in.
- Chapter 2, "Understanding Microsoft Windows NT 4.0," provides an overview of the features and functionality of Windows NT 4.0, including discussions of the operating system architecture, virtual memory, workgroups, and domains.
- Chapter 3, "Installing Windows NT Workstation 4.0," discusses the installation process step-by-step from computer requirements to troubleshooting suggestions, including an examination of the Windows NT boot process.
- Chapter 4, "An Overview of the Windows NT 4.0 Interface," reviews the new Windows NT interface and highlights certain useful utilities and programs.

◆ Chapter 5, "Configuration and the Registry," explores various means of configuring and customizing Windows NT Workstation 4.0 through the Control Panel and through the Windows NT Registry. A discussion of hardware profiles is also included.

◆ Chapter 6, "Managing Users and Accounts," discusses the creation and management of accounts on Windows NT Workstation 4.0.

◆ Chapter 7, "Windows NT 4.0 Security Model," explores Windows NT's security model in detail, focusing on the login process and file, folder, and share-level permissions.

◆ Chapter 8, "Managing Disk Resources," covers the creation and management of disk partitions, volume sets, and stripe sets using the Disk Administrator utility as well as reviews the NTFS file system characteristics.

◆ Chapter 9, "Managing Printers," discusses the wonderful world of network printing and introduces Windows NT's printing process, including sharing and setting permissions on network printers.

◆ Chapter 10, "Running Applications Under Windows NT 4.0," provides an overview of how the Windows NT subsystems support applications running under Windows NT. In particular, we review the subsystem architecture and some key points about application support, and give particular focus to MS-DOS and Windows 16-bit applications and how they are supported under Windows NT 4.0.

◆ Chapter 11, "Network Connectivity and Remote Support," reviews the protocols that are supported by Windows NT 4.0, including a brief overview of TCP/IP, and what has been added in this release. We also discuss the function of services related to network activity, client support for NetWare networks, and remote access support.

◆ Chapter 12, "Tuning, Optimizing, and Other Troubleshooting Tips," explores the Virtual Memory Manager more closely and the use of pagefiles. We examine the use of Event Viewer and Windows Diagnostics as troubleshooting tools. We introduce the Performance Monitor utility and discuss how it can be used to track system performance.

Following these chapters are the Lab Exercises. As mentioned earlier, you can do these exercises at your own pace, when you want to— you're not tied down to the computer for every chapter.

All of the Windows NT Workstation 4.0 exam objectives are covered in the material contained in the text of the chapters and the lab exercises. Information contained in sidebars is provided to give history, extend the topic into Windows NT 4.0 Server, expound on a related procedure, or provide other details. It is useful information, but not primary exam material.

Finally, the many appendixes in this book provide you with additional advice, resources, and information that can be helpful to you as you prepare and take the Windows NT Workstation 4.0 Certified Professional exam, and later as you work as a Windows NT 4.0 Certified Professional:

◆ Appendix A, "Glossary," provides you with definitions of terms that you need to be familiar with as a Windows NT 4.0 MCP.

◆ Appendix B, "Certification Checklist," provides an overview of the certification process in the form of a to-do list, with milestones you can check off on your way to certification.

◆ Appendix C, "How Do I Get There from Here?" provides step-by-step guidelines for successfully navigating from initial interest to final certification.

◆ Appendix D, "Testing Tips," gives you tips and pointers for maximizing your performance when you take the certification exam.

◆ Appendix E, "Contacting Microsoft," lists contact information for certification exam resources at Microsoft and at Sylvan Prometric testing centers.

◆ Appendix F, "Suggested Reading," presents a list of reading resources that can help you prepare for the certification exam.

◆ Appendix G, "Networking Basics," provides material designed to give you an understanding of basic networking concepts and terms, a foundation you will need before reading this book.

◆ Appendix H, "Internet Resources for Windows NT," is a list of places to visit on the Internet related to Windows NT

◆ Appendix I, "Using the CD-ROM," gives you the basics of how to install and use the CD-ROM included with this book, which includes skill self-assessment tests and simulated versions of the Microsoft exam, and the Microsoft TechNet sampler, with over 400M of Microsoft technical information, including the Microsoft KnowledgeBase.

◆ Appendix J, "Sample Tests," provides performance-based questions designed to test your problem-solving capabilities.

Special Features of This Book

There are many features in this book to make it easier to read and make the information more accessible. Those features are described in the following sections.

Chapter Overview

Each chapter begins with an overview of the material covered in that chapter. The chapter topics are described in the context of material already covered, and material coming up.

Notes

Notes present interesting or useful information that isn't necessarily essential to the discussion, but will enhance your understanding of Windows. Notes look like this:

Note Microsoft posts beta exam notices on the Internet (**http://www.microsoft.com**), and mails notices to certification development volunteers, past certification candidates, and product beta participants. ▨

Tips

Tips present short advice on quick or often-overlooked procedures. These include shortcuts that save you time. A tip looks like this:

Tip

Use the Windows NT Taskbar to quickly switch between open programs and windows.

Key Concepts

Key Concepts present particularly significant information about a Windows NT function or concept. Count on this material being on the test. Here's an example of a key concept:

 Key Concept

When you share a resource in Windows NT, the default is to provide everyone with complete access to the resource. If you want additional security, you must add it yourself by restricting access with permissions.

Sidebar

Sidebars are used to provide additional information and enhance the discussion at hand. If a particular topic has a different twist in Windows NT server, it will be discussed in a sidebar. A sidebar looks like this (but longer):

Network Monitor on NT Server

Another useful performance tracking tool is packaged in with Windows NT Server 4.0. It is called the Network Monitor and provides network packet analysis to the administrator.

Caution

A Caution is meant to draw your attention to a particularly tricky twist in a concept, or to point out potential pitfalls. Cautions look like this:

> **Caution**
> If you do not keep your Emergency Repair Disk up to date, and you use it to restore Registry information, you can wipe out your existing account database by overwriting it with the old information.

In addition to these special features, there are several conventions used in this book to make it easier to read and understand. These conventions are described in the following sections.

Underlined Hotkeys, or Mnemonics

Hotkeys in this book appear underlined, like they appear on-screen. In Windows, many menus, commands, buttons, and other options have these hotkeys. To use a hotkey shortcut, press Alt and the key for the underlined character. For instance, to choose the Properties button, press Alt and then R. You should not study for the MCP exam by using the hotkeys, however. Windows is a mouse-centric environment, and you will be expected to know how to navigate it using the mouse—clicking, right-clicking, and using drag and drop.

Shortcut Key Combinations

In this book, shortcut key combinations are joined with plus signs (+). For example, Ctrl+V means hold down the Ctrl key, while you press the V key.

Menu Commands

Instructions for choosing menu commands have this form:

Choose <u>F</u>ile, <u>N</u>ew.

This example means open the File menu and select New, which in this case opens a new file.

This book also has the following typeface enhancements to indicate special text, as indicated in the following table.

Typeface	Description
Italic	Italics are used to indicate new terms and variables in commands or addresses.
Boldface	Bold is used to indicate text you type, and Internet addresses and other locators in the online world.
`Computer type`	This command is used for on-screen messages and commands (such as DOS copy or UNIX commands).
My Filename.doc	File names and folders are set in a mixture of upper-and lowercase characters, just as they appear in Windows NT 4.0.

Chapter Prerequisite

This chapter has no prerequisites, only a desire to become a Microsoft Certified Professional.

1

Microsoft Certified Professional Program

As Microsoft products take an increasing share of the marketplace, the demand for trained personnel grows, and the number of certifications follows suit. As of April of 1996, the team of Microsoft Certified Professionals increased in number, up to over 40,000 product specialists, over 8,000 engineers, and over 1,600 solution developers. There were also over 4,900 certified trainers of Microsoft products.

This chapter covers the Microsoft Certified Professional Program and describes each certification in more detail. Microsoft certifications include:

- ◆ Microsoft Certified Professional
- ◆ Microsoft Certified Systems Engineer (MCSE)
- ◆ Microsoft Certified Product Specialist (MCPS)
- ◆ Microsoft Certified Solutions Developer (MCSD)
- ◆ Microsoft Certified Trainer (MCT)

Exploring Available Certifications

When Microsoft started certifying people to install and support its products, there was only one certification available, the Microsoft Certified Professional (MCP). As time went on, demand by employers and prospective customers of consulting firms for more specialized certifications grew.

There are now four certifications available in the MCP program, as described in the following sections.

Microsoft Certified Systems Engineers (MCSE)

Microsoft Certified Systems Engineers are qualified to plan, implement, maintain, and support information systems based on Microsoft Windows NT and the BackOffice family of client/server software. The MCSE is a widely respected certification because it does not focus on just one aspect of computing, such as networking. Instead, the MCSE has demonstrated skills and abilities on the full range of software, from client operating systems to server operating systems to client/server applications.

Microsoft Certified Solution Developers (MCSD)

Microsoft Certified Solution Developers are qualified to design and develop custom business solutions with Microsoft development tools, platforms, and technologies, such as Microsoft BackOffice and Microsoft Office.

Microsoft Certified Product Specialists (MCPS)

Microsoft Certified Product Specialists have demonstrated in-depth knowledge of at least one Microsoft operating system. Candidates may pass additional Microsoft certification exams to further qualify their skills with Microsoft BackOffice products, development tools, or desktop applications.

The Microsoft Certified Product Specialist Areas of Specialization (AOS) that lead to the MCSE certification include:

- *Networking.* This AOS requires the candidate to pass the Windows NT Server exam, one desktop operating system exam, such as the Windows NT 4.0 exam, and one networking exam, such as the Networking Essentials for BackOffice exam.
- *TCP/IP.* This AOS requires the candidate to pass the Windows NT Server exam and the Internetworking TCP/IP on Windows NT exam.
- *Mail.* This AOS requires the candidate to pass the Windows NT Server exam and the Microsoft Mail (Enterprise) exam.
- *SQL Server.* This AOS requires the candidate to pass the Windows NT Server exam and both SQL Server exams.
- *Systems Management Server.* This AOS requires the candidate to pass the Windows NT Server exam and the SMS exam.
- *SNA Server.* This AOS requires the candidate to pass the Windows NT Server exam and the SNA Server exam.

The Microsoft Certified Product Specialist product-specific exams are your first steps into the world of Microsoft certification. After establishing a specialty, you can work toward additional certification goals at the MCSE or MCSD level.

Microsoft Certified Trainers (MCT)

Microsoft Certified Trainers are instructionally and technically qualified to deliver Microsoft Official Curriculum through Microsoft authorized education sites.

Understanding the Exam Requirements

The exams are computer-administered tests that measure your ability to implement and administer Microsoft products or systems, troubleshoot problems with installation, operation or customization, and provide technical support to users. The exams do more than test your ability to define terminology and recite facts. Product knowledge is an important foundation for superior job performance, but definitions and feature lists are just the beginning. In the real world, you need hands-on skills and the ability to apply your knowledge—to understand confusing situations, solve thorny problems, and optimize solutions to minimize downtime and maximize current and future productivity.

To develop exams that test for the right competence factors, Microsoft follows an eight-phase exam development process:

◆ In the first phase, experts analyze the tasks that make up the job being tested. This job analysis phase identifies the knowledge, skills, and abilities relating specifically to the performance area to be certified.

◆ The next phase develops objectives by building on the framework provided by the job analysis. That means translating the job function tasks into specific and measurable units of knowledge, skills, and abilities. The resulting list of objectives (the *objective domain*, in educational theory-speak) is the basis for developing certification exams and training materials.

◆ Selected contributors rate the objectives developed in the previous phase. The reviewers are technology professionals who are currently performing the applicable job function. After prioritization and weighting based on the contributors' input, the objectives become the blueprint for the exam items.

◆ During the fourth phase, exam items are reviewed and revised to ensure that they are technically accurate, clear, unambiguous, plausible, free of cultural bias, and not misleading or tricky. Items also are evaluated to confirm that they test for high-level, useful knowledge, rather than obscure or trivial facts.

◆ During alpha review, technical and job function experts review each item for technical accuracy, reach consensus on all technical issues, and edit the reviewed items for clarity of expression.

♦ The next step is the beta exam. Beta exam participants take the test to gauge its effectiveness. Microsoft performs a statistical analysis, based on the responses of the beta participants, including information about difficulty and relevance, to verify the validity of the exam items and to determine which items are used in the final certification exam.

♦ When the statistical analysis is complete, the items are distributed into multiple parallel forms, or versions, of the final certification exam.

Note Microsoft posts beta exam notices on the Internet (**http://www.microsoft.com**), and mails notices to certification development volunteers, past certification candidates, and product beta participants. █

Tip

If you participate in a beta exam, you may take it at a cost that is lower than the cost of the final certification exam, but it should not be taken lightly. Beta exams actually contain the entire pool of possible questions, of which about 30 percent are dropped after the beta. The remaining questions are divided into the different forms of the final exam. If you decide to take a beta exam, you should review and study as seriously as you would for a final certification exam. Passing a beta exam counts as passing the final exam—you receive full credit for passing a beta exam.

Also, because you will be taking *all* of the questions that will be used for the exam, expect a beta to take significantly longer than the final exam. For example, the beta tests for Windows NT 4.0 have so far had a time limit of four hours each, and more than three times as many questions as the final versions of the exams!

Also during this phase, a group of job function experts determines the cut, or minimum passing score for the exam. (The cut score differs from exam to exam because it is based on an item-by-item determination of the percentage of candidates who answered the item correctly.)

◆ The final phase—Exam Live!—is administered by Sylvan Prometric™, an independent testing company. The exams are always available at Sylvan Prometric testing centers worldwide.

Note If you're interested in participating in any of the exam development phases (including the beta exam), contact the Microsoft Certification Development Team by sending a fax to (206) 936-1311. Include the following information about yourself: name, complete address, company, job title, phone number, fax number, e-mail or Internet address, and product areas of interest or expertise. ■

Microsoft Certified Systems Engineer Core Exams

To achieve the Microsoft Certified Systems Engineer certification, a candidate must pass four required "core" exams, plus two elective exams. There are two possible paths, or tracks, that lead to an MCSE certification—the Windows NT 4.0 track and the Windows NT 3.51 track.

Microsoft Windows NT 4.0 Track to an MCSE

The Microsoft Windows NT 4.0 track to an MCSE is significantly different from the earlier Windows NT 3.51 track, although there are still four core exams. These first two exams are required:

◆ Implementing and Supporting Microsoft Windows NT 4.0 Server (70-67). This exam covers installing and supporting Windows NT 4.0 in a single-domain environment. This exam also qualifies a candidate as an MCPS.

◆ Implementing and Supporting Microsoft Windows NT 4.0 Server in the Enterprise (70-68). This exam covers installing and supporting Windows NT 4.0 in an enterprise computing environment with mission critical applications and tasks. This exam does *not* qualify a candidate as an MCPS.

The third required core exam can be fulfilled by one of four different exams:

◈ Microsoft Windows 3.1 (70–30). Legacy support.

◈ Microsoft Windows for Workgroups 3.11 (70-48). Legacy support.

◈ Implementing and Supporting Microsoft Windows 95 (70-63). Tests a candidate's ability to implement and support Microsoft Windows NT 4.0 in a variety of environments, including as a network client on Novell NetWare. This exam qualifies a candidate as an MCPS.

◈ Implementing and Supporting Microsoft Windows NT Workstation 4.0 (70-73). Tests a candidate's ability to implement and support Microsoft Windows NT Workstation 4.0. This exam qualifies a candidate as an MCPS.

The fourth core exam can be fulfilled by one of the following:

Note This exam is waived for those candidates who also are Novell Certified NetWare Engineers (CNE) or Banyan Certified Banyan Engineers (CBE). ▦

◈ Networking with Windows for Workgroups 3.11 (70-46). Legacy support.

◈ Networking with Windows 3.1 (70-47). Legacy support.

◈ Networking Essentials (70-58). Tests the candidate's networking skills required for implementing, administrating, and troubleshooting systems that incorporate Windows NT 4.0 and BackOffice.

Windows NT 3.51 Track to the MCSE Certification

Most current Microsoft Certified Systems Engineers followed, or are following, this track, which will continue to be a valid track.

There are four core exams. The first two, the Windows NT 3.51 exams, are required:

◈ Implementing and Supporting Microsoft Windows NT Server 3.51 (70-43). This exam covers installing and supporting Windows NT Server 3.51 in a variety of environments. This exam also qualifies a candidate as an MCPS.

◆ Implementing and Supporting Microsoft Windows NT Workstation 3.51 (70-42). This exam covers installing and supporting Windows NT Workstation 3.51. This exam qualifies a candidate as an MCPS.

The third required core exam can be fulfilled by one of three different exams:

◆ Microsoft Windows 3.1 (70-30). Legacy support.

◆ Microsoft Windows for Workgroups 3.11 (70-48). Legacy support.

◆ Implementing and Supporting Microsoft Windows 95 (70-63). Tests a candidate's ability to implement and support Microsoft Windows 95 in a variety of environments, including as a network client on Novell NetWare. This exam qualifies a candidate as an MCPS.

The fourth core exam can be fulfilled by one of the following:

Note This exam is waived for those candidates who also are Novell Certified NetWare Engineers (CNE) or Banyan Certified Banyan Engineers (CBE).

◆ Networking with Windows for Workgroups 3.11 (70-46). Legacy support.

◆ Networking with Windows 3.1 (70-47). Legacy support.

◆ Networking Essentials (70-58). Tests the candidate's networking skills required for implementing, administrating, and troubleshooting systems that incorporate Windows NT 4.0 and BackOffice.

Electives for the Microsoft Certified Systems Engineers

Besides the core exam requirements, you must pass two elective exams to complete a Microsoft Certified Systems Engineer certification. The list of electives in Table 1.1 was current as of March 1996.

Ch
1

Table 1.1   Microsoft Certified Systems Engineer Electives

Exam	Number
Microsoft SNA Server	70-12
Implementing and Supporting Microsoft Systems Management Server 1.0	70-14
System Administration of Microsoft SQL Server 6.0	70-26
Implementing a Database Design on Microsoft SQL Server 6.0	70-27
Microsoft Mail for PC Networks—Enterprise	70-37
Internetworking Microsoft TCP/IP on Microsoft Windows NT 3.51	70-53

Continuing Certification Requirements

After you gain an MCP certification, such as the Microsoft Certified Systems Engineer certification, your work isn't over. Microsoft requires you to maintain your certification by updating your exam credits as new products are released and old ones are withdrawn.

A Microsoft Certified Trainer is required to pass the exam for a new product within three months of the exam's release. For example, the Windows 95 exam (70-63) was released on October 9, 1995. All MCTs, including the authors of this book, were required to pass exam 70-63 by January 9, 1996, or lose certification to teach the course.

Holders of the other MCP certifications (MCPS, MCSD, MCSE) are required to replace an exam that gives them qualifying credit within six months of the withdrawal of that exam. For example, the Windows for Workgroups 3.10 exam was one of the original electives for the MCSE certification. When it was withdrawn, MCSEs had six months to replace it with another elective exam, such as the TCP/IP exam.

Chapter Prerequisite

You should be familiar with the basic operation of either Windows 3.x or Windows 95. It would be optimal for the reader to already have a comfortable grasp of the Windows NT interface. It is essential that you have a strong working knowledge of basic networking concepts.

Understanding Microsoft Windows NT 4.0

Before we begin a detailed discussion of Microsoft Windows NT Workstation 4.0, allow me to provide a clearer understanding of what the Windows NT product line provides and how it can be used within an organization. While this book concentrates on Windows NT Workstation 4.0, where applicable to more fully develop a concept, draw a comparison, or whet your appetite, I provide information relating to Windows NT 4.0 Server. This chapter provides an overview of the features and functionality of Microsoft Windows NT Workstation 4.0 and Server.

Topics discussed in this chapter include:

◆ Providing a list of features and functionality common to the Windows NT product line past and present and exploring certain specific characteristics in more detail.

◆ Understanding when an installation of Windows NT Workstation or Server is appropriate given the needs of the clients involved, the level of administration desired, and the level of security required.

◆ Introducing the basic architecture of the Windows NT operating system and explaining the features and functions that are new to version 4.0.

◆ Comparing Microsoft's workgroup model with its enterprise model of network communication.

Exploring Windows NT 4.0's New Features

Microsoft Windows NT is a 32-bit operating system designed to provide fast and efficient performance for power computer users such as software developers, CAD programmers, and design engineers. Figure 2.1 displays the features common to both Windows NT Workstation and Server (versions 3.51 and 4.0). Because it provides better performance for existing 16-bit applications (both MS-DOS and Windows), as well as 32-bit applications developed specifically for the operating system, Windows NT is increasingly found on the desk of the business user. These performance enhancements include:

◆ Multiple platform support

◆ Preemptive multitasking

◆ Expanded processing support

◆ Expanded memory support

◆ Expanded file system support

◆ Enhanced security

◆ Network and communications support

FIG. 2.1 ⇒

These features are common to both Windows NT Workstation and Server.

Windows NT Features and Functions

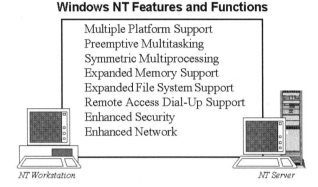

Multiple Platform Support
Preemptive Multitasking
Symmetric Multiprocessing
Expanded Memory Support
Expanded File System Support
Remote Access Dial-Up Support
Enhanced Security
Enhanced Network

NT Workstation   *NT Server*

Ch

2

Multiple Platform Support

Microsoft Windows NT is engineered to run on several hardware platforms. The *Hardware Abstraction Layer*, or *HAL*, component of the Windows NT architecture isolates platform-specific information for the operating system; for example, how to interact with a RISC-based processor as opposed to an Intel x86 processor. This makes Windows NT a highly portable system through the recompilation of only a few pieces of code such as the HAL. Windows NT supports Intel x86 and Pentium-based computers and RISC-based computers such as MIPS R4000, DEC Alpha AXP, and PowerPC.

Preemptive Multitasking

All processes in Windows NT are given at least one thread of operation. A thread represents a piece of code relating to a process. For example, loading a file may require several "threads" to carry out the process, such as locating the file on disk, allocating RAM for the file, moving it into that allocated memory space, and so on. Many processes and applications written for Windows and Windows NT have multiple threads associated with them. Windows NT can treat each thread of a process independently of the others, providing a greater degree of control over the overall performance of the system. Each thread also is given a processing priority based on its function.

For example, an operating system process such as memory allocation receives a higher priority for its threads than a file save process. Each thread is given a specific amount of time with the processor. This is sometimes called *time-slicing*. Higher priority threads are processed ahead of lower priority threads. All the threads of one priority are processed first before those of the next priority, and so on. This process is called *preemptive multitasking*. In addition, certain threads, primarily those that are system related, are processed in the protected mode of the processor (known as ring 0) and thus are protected from other processes and crashes. Other threads, those relating to application functions, such as file printing, run in the unprotected mode of the processor. This means that while they may be given their own memory space, other "poorly written" applications (and their threads) might try to "butt in" and result in what is generally referred to as a "General Protection" or "GP" fault. Microsoft and Windows NT have taken several precautions to ensure that this does not happen in Windows NT. We will explore these in more detail later in this book. Supporting both multitasking and multithreading gives applications excellent processing support and protection against system hangs and crashes.

Expanded Processing Support

Microsoft Windows NT provides *symmetric multiprocessing* with support for OEM implementations of up to 32 processors. Every process that runs under Windows NT has at least one thread of operation or programming code associated with it. A process might be user generated, such as the writing of a file to disk or printing a document, or system generated, such as validating a user logon or providing read access to a file.

Symmetric multiprocessing enables the Windows NT operating system to load balance process threads across all available processors in the computer as opposed to *asymmetric multiprocessing* in which the operating system takes control of one processor and directs application threads to other available processors.

Expanded Memory Support

Windows NT supports computers with up to 4 gigabytes of RAM and theoretic file or partition sizes of up to 16 exabytes (though this number will vary depending on the type of hardware you have). An exabyte is one billion gigabytes. You might consider that to be a theoretical number, and to a certain extent it is. However, it was not that long ago that MIS departments debated the wisdom of purchasing 10-megabyte disk drives for their users' computers because they felt that the drives would never be filled up.

Ch
2

Expanded File System Support

Windows NT provides support for the MS-DOS FAT (File Allocation Table) file system as well as its own NTFS (New Technology file system). Previous versions of Windows NT also supported OS/2's HPFS (High Performance file system). Version 4.0 no longer provides support for HPFS.

NTFS provides a high level of security in the form of file- and directory-level permissions similar to those found in other network operating systems such as trustee rights used in Novell's NetWare. NTFS also provides transaction tracking to help recover data in the event of system failure and sector sparing which identifies potentially bad disk storage space and moves data to good storage. NTFS also provides data compression implemented as a file or directory property. For more information on NTFS see Chapter 7, "Windows NT 4.0 Security Model."

Enhanced Security

Security begins with Windows NT's WINLOGON and NETLOGON processes which authenticate a user's access to a computer, workgroup, or enterprise by validating their username and password and assigning each with its own security identifier. In addition to this mandatory logon, Windows NT offers share-level resource control, security auditing functions, and file- and directory-level permissions (in NTFS partitions). A more detailed discussion of Windows NT security is in Chapter 6, "Managing Users and Accounts."

Network and Communications Support

Windows NT is designed to provide several inter-networking options. The NetBEUI, NWLINK (IPX/SPX), TCP/IP, AppleTalk, and DLC protocols are all supported and included. Windows NT also is supported on Novell NetWare networks, Microsoft LAN Manager, IBM LAN Server and SNA networks, Banyan VINES, and DEC PATHWORKS.

Through Remote Access Service (RAS), Windows NT offers a secure dial-up option for clients and servers. RAS clients can remotely access any shared network resource to which they have been given access through RAS' gateway functions, such as shared folders and printers.

In a Windows NT network, valid workstation clients include Microsoft Windows NT workstations and servers, Windows 3.x, MS-DOS, Windows for Workgroups, Windows 95, OS/2, Novell NetWare (client/server), and Macintosh.

Choosing Windows NT Workstation or Server

The difference in choosing when to use Windows NT Workstation or Windows NT Server is not necessarily the difference between desktop and enterprise computing. Both Windows NT Workstation and Windows NT Server provide the capability to make resources available on the network and thus act as a "server." For that matter, a Windows NT server could be made part of a workgroup of Windows NT workstations to act as the resource server for that workgroup. Choosing Windows NT Workstation or Windows NT Server really comes down to the features specific to each product and the type of network model that will be implemented. The following sections discuss the differences between Windows NT Workstation and Windows NT Server.

Microsoft Windows NT Workstation

Microsoft Windows NT Workstation is designed for the so-called power user, such as developers or CAD designers, but increasingly is becoming the desktop operating system of choice for end-user business computing because of its robust feature set as described in the last section. In addition to those features and functions which are common to both Windows NT Workstation and Windows NT Server, Windows NT Workstation offers the following specific characteristics (see Figure 2.2 also):

- ◆ Unlimited outbound peer-to-peer connections.
- ◆ Ten inbound client connections for resource access.
- ◆ Can be a RAS client or server, but supports only one remote dial-in session.
- ◆ Retail installation supports two processors for symmetric multiprocessing.
- ◆ Acts as an import server for Directory Replication Services.

FIG. 2.2 ⇒
Windows NT
Workstation
features and
functions.

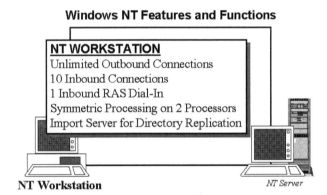

Windows NT Features and Functions

NT WORKSTATION
Unlimited Outbound Connections
10 Inbound Connections
1 Inbound RAS Dial-In
Symmetric Processing on 2 Processors
Import Server for Directory Replication

NT Workstation   *NT Server*

Microsoft Windows NT Server

Windows NT Server is designed to provide file, print, and application service support within a given network model. Figure 2.3 illustrates specific characteristics of Windows NT Server. While it also can be used as a desktop system, it is engineered to provide optimum performance when providing network services, for example, by optimizing memory differently for application servers than for domain controllers. In addition to the features and functions described previously, Windows NT Server offers the following:

◆ As many inbound connections to resources as there are valid client licenses (virtually unlimited).

◆ Support for as many as 256 remote dial-in RAS sessions.

◆ Retail installation supports as many as four processors for symmetric multiprocessing.

◆ A full set of services for application and network support such as:

   • Services for Macintosh allowing client support for Macintosh computers

   • Gateway Service for NetWare allowing Windows NT clients to access Novell NetWare file and print resources

   • Directory Replication Service for copying of directory structures and files from a source Windows NT server computer to a target Windows NT server or workstation computer

◆ Full integration into the Microsoft BackOffice suite including System Management Server, SNA Server, SQL Server

FIG. 2.3 ⇒
Windows NT
Server features
and functions.

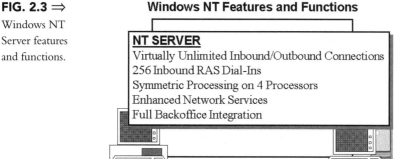

Windows NT Features and Functions

NT SERVER
Virtually Unlimited Inbound/Outbound Connections
256 Inbound RAS Dial-Ins
Symmetric Processing on 4 Processors
Enhanced Network Services
Full Backoffice Integration

NT Workstation

NT Server

The Microsoft Windows NT Server product can be installed as either a server only providing network accessible resources or as a domain controller additionally providing centralized administration of user accounts and resource access. These concepts will be reviewed later in this chapter.

New Features and Functions in Windows NT 4.0

This newest version of Windows NT continues Microsoft's commitment to reliable, performance-driven, network-ready, operating systems by incorporating the power, features, and functions of the Windows NT operating system with the object-oriented Windows 95 user interface. Enhanced features and functions common to both Windows NT Workstation 4.0 and Server include:

- ◆ Windows 95 user interface
- ◆ Windows Explorer
- ◆ Hardware profiles
- ◆ Enhanced dial-up networking support
- ◆ NDS-aware client services for Novell NetWare 4.x
- ◆ Integrated Microsoft Exchange Client
- ◆ Internet Explorer 2.0
- ◆ Web services

Windows 95 User Interface

All the basic features of Microsoft's Windows 95 interface have been integrated into Windows NT 4.0. This includes updated or enhanced system utilities like the Performance Monitor (called the System Monitor in Windows 95), as well as additional utilities such as the Windows Explorer, Network Neighborhood, Briefcase, desktop shortcuts, Microsoft Network support, and the Recycle Bin.

Note Chapter 3 provides a general overview of the new Windows NT 4.0 interface. The reader is advised to also study Windows 95 for a complete understanding of the interface and its functionality. There are several good books to help you acquire this additional information. One such book is entitled *Platinum Edition Using Windows 95*, published by Que. ▤

Windows Explorer

This feature of the interface replaces the File Manager utility. It provides excellent browsing capabilities for management of drives, directories, files, and network connections. Explorer presents the user's data access information as a hierarchy of drives, desktop, network connections, folders, and files. The browsing capabilities of Explorer offer not only browsing of file and directory names, but also of data strings within files. Throughout this book and its labs, you will use Windows Explorer to access files and folders, set permissions, create and manage shared folders, and so on.

 Note Though Windows Explorer replaces the File Manager utility by default, File Manager is still available and can be launched by the user.

File Manager can be run by following these simple steps:

1. Choose Start from the taskbar.

2. Choose Run from the Start menu.

3. Enter in the File Manager file name: **winfile.exe**

4. Click OK.

Microsoft recommends using File Manager only until you become comfortable with Windows Explorer. File Manager is still available for transition purposes only. ▪

Hardware Profiles

Perhaps one of the most useful enhancements to Windows NT 4.0 is the support for multiple hardware profiles. First introduced in Windows 95, this feature enables you to create hardware profiles to fit various computing needs. The most common example for using hardware profiles would be with portable computers. You can create separate profiles to support the portable when it is in use by itself, and for when it is positioned in a docking station.

> **Note** Plug and Play is a much appreciated feature of Windows 95.
> Note that while the Plug and Play service has been included
> with Windows NT 4.0, "hot" plug and play, that is to say the ability for the
> operating system to recognize a configuration change on-the-fly and
> implement it, will not be fully supported until the next major release of
> Windows NT. Windows NT 4.0 does, however, recognize some hardware
> changes when it restarts. For example, additional memory or a new hard
> disk will be automatically detected by Windows NT the next time you
> boot up. ▇

Enhanced Dial-Up Networking Support

The RAS Client service now is installed as Dial-Up Networking. In
addition, Windows NT 4.0 provides the Dial-Up Networking Monitor
for monitoring user connections and devices as well as Remote Access
Admin for monitoring remote user access to a RAS Server.

Windows NT 4.0 also offers Telephony API version 2.0 (TAPI) and
universal modem driver (Unimodem) support which provides communications technology for fax applications, the Microsoft Exchange client, The Microsoft Network (MSN), and Internet Explorer.

API provides access to the signaling for setting up calls and managing
them, as well as preserving existing media stream functionality to manipulate the information carried over the connection TAPI establishes.
This allows applications to not only dial and transfer calls, but also to
support fax, desktop conferencing, or applications that use the telephone dial pad to access voice-prompted menus.

NDS-Aware Client Service for Novell NetWare 4.x

Microsoft provides an enhanced version of its Client Services for
NetWare (CSNW) with Windows NT 4.0 which supplies compatibility with Novell NetWare servers (versions 3.x and higher) running
NetWare Directory Services (NDS). This allows users to view NetWare
shared resources organized in an hierarchical tree format.

Integrated Microsoft Windows Messaging

Microsoft Windows Messaging is Microsoft's newest electronic mail product. Windows Messaging has been included with Windows NT 4.0 and enables users to send and receive mail, embed objects in mail messages, and integrate mail functionality into Microsoft applications.

Internet Explorer 2.0

Microsoft's Internet Explorer 2.0 is included with Windows NT 4.0 to enable users access to the Internet. However, Microsoft now has Internet Explorer 3.0 available through its various Internet sights (**www.microsoft.com**, for example). Watch for Microsoft to continue to enhance this product and make upgrades widely (and cheaply) available.

 Note Internet Explorer requires that the TCP/IP protocol be installed and a connection made to the Internet. ▨

Web Publishing

Microsoft includes Web publishing services in Windows NT 4.0 which allow you to develop, publish, and manage Web pages, FTP, and Gopher services for your company's intranet or for smaller peer-to-peer networks. With Windows NT Workstation 4.0, Microsoft provides Peer Web Services (PWS) for smaller workgroup-based Web publishing. With Windows NT 4.0 Server, Microsoft provides Internet Information Services (IIS) designed for heavy Intranet and Internet usage.

Integrated Network Monitor Agent

Windows NT 4.0 includes a version of the Network Monitor utility which is included with Microsoft's System Management Server Back-Office product. Network Monitor provides a full range of network analysis tools for tracking and interpreting network traffic, frames, and so forth.

Last But Certainly Not Least

Of all the features contained in Windows NT 4.0, there is one from which you will obtain the most productivity. It also is an example of enhancements made to Windows NT's Open GL and direct draw video support. This is of course, PINBALL! Yes, there is a new game added to Windows NT 4.0 and it is quite an addition. As mentioned, it does take full advantage of changes to Windows NT's architecture and enhancements for video support. Try it out!

> **Note** Pinball is installed in the Games folder which can be found by choosing Start, Programs, Accessories, Games. If you have not installed your games, you can use the Add/Remove Programs applet in Control Panel to add them. In the applet, choose the Windows Setup tab, highlight Accessories, choose Details and select Games. Choose OK. Be sure to have your source files or CD handy because Windows NT will prompt you for them. ▪

In addition to these features which Windows NT Workstation 4.0 and Server share, Windows NT 4.0 Server offers the following specific list of features and functions:

- ◆ Microsoft Internet Information Server
- ◆ DNS Name Server and enhanced support
- ◆ Integrated Support for Multi-Protocol Routing
- ◆ Enhanced support for BOOTP and DHCP Routing
- ◆ Remote Reboot Support for Windows 95 clients
- ◆ New remote server administration tools for Windows 95 clients
- ◆ Installation wizards for most utility program installations

Comparing the Workgroup and Enterprise Models of Network Communication

This section explores two networking models that can be adopted within a Microsoft network—the Workgroup model, designed for small groups of computers connected in a peer-to-peer configuration and the Enterprise model, designed for large networks in which computers are grouped in one or more domains.

Workgroup Model

The Workgroup model of networking is more commonly referred to as the Peer-to-Peer model. Figure 2.4 provides a more graphic illustration of this model. In this model, all Windows NT workstations participate in a networking group. They all can make resources available to members of the workgroup and access each other's resources as well. In other words, each Windows NT workstation acts as both a workstation and a server.

FIG. 2.4 ⇒

Workgroup model.

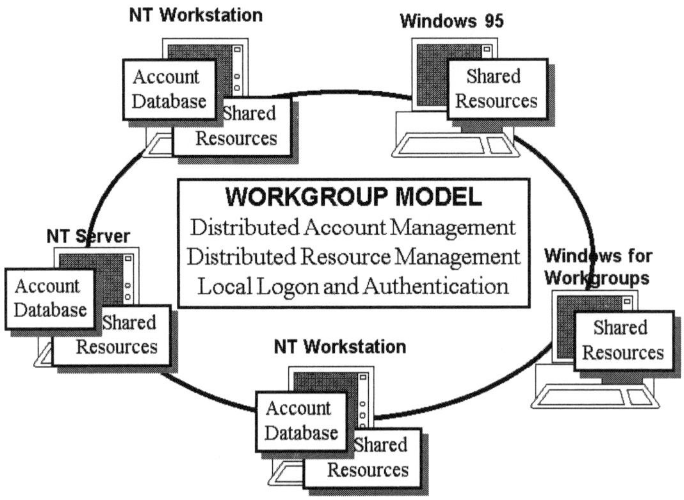

Recall that Windows NT workstations support a total of 10 inbound connections. These connections include access to resources by other workgroup members. Access to resources is provided by authenticating the inbound user at the resource computer. Thus, each computer participating in a workgroup must maintain a list of users that will be accessing the resources on that computer.

Potentially, this means that each computer will have at least as many user accounts as there are participating members in the workgroup. Account administration in a workgroup is considered to be distributed as is resource administration. Furthermore, the responsibility for maintaining the integrity of user accounts and resource access generally falls to the owner of the computer. A Workgroup model then might be construed to have limited security potential if the users are not fully aware of the security decisions they need to make (unique passwords, adding permissions to shares, files and folders, and so on).

The Workgroup model works well within smaller networks where the number of users requiring access to workgroup resources is small and easily managed. This number has been suggested to be between 10 and 20 computers/users. As mentioned before, a Windows NT server can participate in a workgroup. If a larger number of computers or users is required within a Workgroup model, the more heavily used resources might be located in a Windows NT server participating in the work-group. This could help to simplify the management of larger groups of users accessing resources because the responsibility for securing these resources is not shifted from the individual workstations to the server (and the server's administrator).

The Enterprise Model

The Enterprise model of networking, also known as the Domain model, was introduced by Microsoft as a response to the management challenges presented by the growing Workgroup model. Figure 2.5 presents a graphic illustration of this model.

FIG. 2.5 ⇒
Enterprise model.

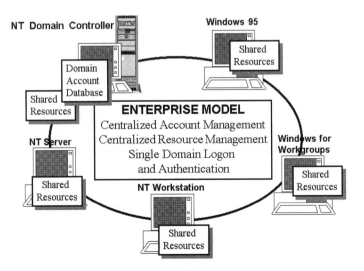

The hallmarks of the Enterprise model include:

- Single user logon
- Centralized administration of user and group accounts
- Centralized administration of resource access
- A mechanism for synchronizing account information within the domain and across domains
- Integration with other network systems

Unlike the Workgroup model, the Enterprise model centralizes account management by maintaining a centralized database of user and group account information at the domain level. When a user logs on to the domain, his or her user account is passed on to an available authenticating server in the enterprise called a domain controller. Because the user's account is centralized at the enterprise level rather than the local level, the user can theoretically log on to the domain from any workstation participating in the domain.

Likewise, resource access is provided by adding users from the domain database to resource access control lists. Thus, only one account database is necessary to manage any resource available within the enterprise domain. Recall that in the Workgroup model, each computer maintains its own account database which is used for managing resource access at that computer. Resources may actually reside on various server and workstation computers throughout the enterprise. By their participation in the domain, the resources utilize the same central account database for managing user access.

Often, there may be multiple Enterprise models within an organization, each consisting of one or more domains with their own resources and in some cases with their own account database as well. Users from one domain can be given access to the resources at another domain by means of a security relationship called a *trust* (see Figure 2.6).

FIG. 2.6 ⟹
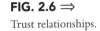

Trust relationships.

TRUST RELATIONSHIPS

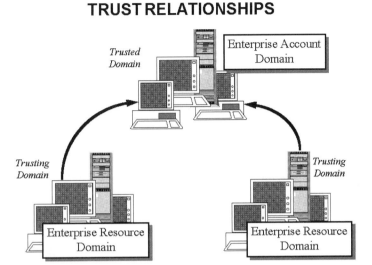

Trusts are created between the primary domain controller servers for each domain. The primary domain controller manages and maintains the master account database for its domain. The domain that has the resources needed by the users in another domain is referred to as the *trusting domain* because it trusts the users to use the resources responsibly. The domain that contains the users that need access to the resources in the trusting domain is referred to as the *trusted domain* because the users are trusted to use the resources responsibly. An easy way to remember the distinction is to consider yourself the resource holder. As the resource holder, you can point to the people you trust to use your resources. They are "trusted" by you to use the resources responsibly.

When a resource domain trusts an account domain, in addition to the account database from its own domain, those resources also have access to the account database in the trusted domain. Thus, a user can log on from the trusted or the trusting domain and have access to any resource that has given the user access.

There are four types of Enterprise Domain models:

◆ Single

◆ Master

◆ Multiple Master

◆ Complete Trust

Single Domain Model

In the Single Domain model, there are no trust relationships. All users and all resources are contained within one enterprise domain. Figure 2.7 illustrates a Single Domain model.

FIG. 2.7 ⇒
Single Domain model.

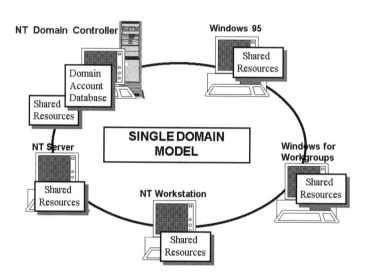

This model is common for small businesses, or where the computers do not participate in a larger WAN environment.

Master Domain Model

In this model, there is one domain that maintains the account database, and one or more domains that administer resources (see Figure 2.8). The account database contains all the users, groups, and Windows NT computer accounts that are members of or participate in this domain. Resource domains generally do not contain lists of users and groups.

Instead, they identify who can use their resources by obtaining the list of users and groups from the account domain through the creation of a trust relationship between the resource and account domains.

FIG. 2.8 ⇒
Master Domain model.

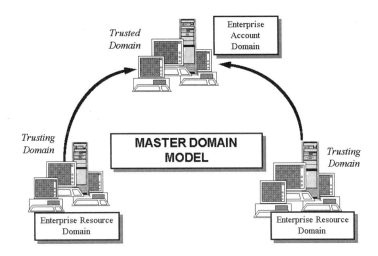

This model is common in organizations where resources belong to various departments, and those departments maintain authority over their resource access. They need not maintain user accounts, only access to their resources. They would then populate their resource access control lists with users from the account domain's database.

Multiple Master Domain Model

This model is similar to the Master Domain model. The difference is that the account database may be distributed between two or more account domains. This may be a result of the way users are distributed through a WAN (wide area network), the size of the databases, or the type of server computers, and so on. Figure 2.9 illustrates a Multiple Master Domain model with its trust relationships.

In this model, each resource domain trusts each account domain. In addition, the account domains trust each other. In this way, any resource manager can provide resource access to any account domain user.

FIG. 2.9 ⇒
Multiple Master
Domain model.

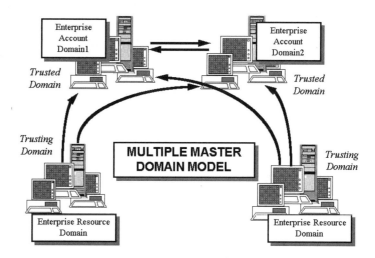

Complete Trust Model

This model is perhaps the simplest to describe, though it provides the least amount of security. It is graphically displayed in Figure 2.10. In this model, every domain trusts every other domain. Every domain maintains a copy of its own account database. Resource administrators can provide resource access to users from any other domain. However, resource access is potentially only as secure as the "worst" administrator. This is not to say that this model has not been successfully implemented in several large organizations. It does, however, require a greater degree of control to remain secure.

FIG. 2.10 ⇒
Complete Trust
model.

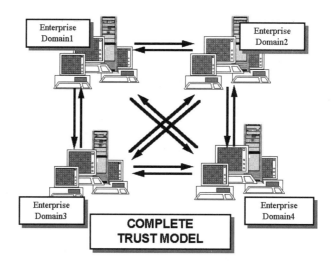

> **Note**   Trusts and domain models are Windows NT Server concepts and are covered extensively in books dedicated to Windows NT Server. Nevertheless, the basic information presented here is sufficient for the reader to field any questions related to domain relationships that should appear on the Windows NT Workstation 4.0 certification test.

Which Model Is Best?

Windows NT Workstation offers a high-performance 32-bit pre-emptive multitasking operating system for the desktop that can share resources with other users. It provides a robust set of features, utilities, security, and services which make it an appropriate choice for either the Workgroup or Enterprise model of networking.

Nevertheless, it is not meant to provide the power, access, and efficiency of the Windows NT Server product for providing resource access across a network. Windows NT Server is the best choice for managing network resources in larger workgroups or for administering access in a company-wide network.

Similarly, choose your networking model according to the number of users and the type, frequency, and so forth, of the resources the network will provide. Networks with relatively small numbers of users accessing specific resources on specific computers will be easily accommodated and administered by the Workgroup model. Recall that in this model, both account administration and resource management are distributed to each member of the workgroup. Each computer maintains its own accounts database. As the workgroup grows, the number of users in each computer's database will grow proportionately.

Networks with large numbers of users that require a single point of logon, centralized account administration, and centralized resource management benefit from the Enterprise model. The type of domain model that you choose for the enterprise will depend on how those users and resources are distributed within your organization.

Basic Architecture of Windows NT 4.0

An integral part of any understanding of Windows NT is a discussion of the internal architecture of the Windows NT operating system (see Figure 2.11). There are several resources available for an in-depth coverage of this topic. However, this basic overview will provide the building blocks and concepts needed to comprehend Windows NT security, service support, and other topics covered in this book.

FIG. 2.11 ⇒

Basic Architectural model.

WINDOWS NT 4.0 BASIC ARCHITECTURAL MODEL

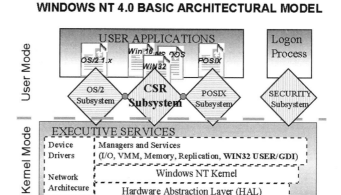

The Windows NT 4.0 architecture consists of two primary processing areas: User or Application mode and Kernel or Privileged Processor mode. The User mode, as it implies, provides operating system support primarily for user applications and the environment.

The Kernel mode provides operating system support services for just about everything else including Kernel processing, memory management, hardware access, and so forth. These kernel mode services are referred to as the *Executive Services.*

User (Application) Mode

The User mode of the operating system provides application processing support. Applications in Windows NT run in one of three subsystems provided by the operating system. These are the WIN32, OS/2, and

POSIX subsystems. The primary subsystem, and that which is loaded at boot time, is WIN32. Win32 supports both 32-bit Windows and Win95 applications as well as 16-bit DOS and Windows applications. A more detailed discussion of how these applications run under Windows NT is provided in Chapter 9, "Managing Printers."

Note OS/2 was designed and implemented by IBM to support 32-bit applications in an object-oriented environment. POSIX stands for "Portable Operating System Interface for UNIX" and was originally an IEEE effort to standardize portability of applications across UNIX-based environments. ■

The OS/2 subsystem provides support for 1.x character-based OS/2 applications. POSIX provides support for POSIX-based applications. Any application program calls from these two subsystems that read/write to the display are forwarded to the WIN32 subsystem. Any other calls to drivers, or other executive services are communicated directly to the Kernel mode.

In Windows NT version 3.51, the USER and GDI (Graphics Device Interface) portions of the operating system were included in the WIN32 subsystem, thus in User mode. The USER is the window manager and responds to user input on-screen. The GDI processes graphics primitives such as pixels, lines, fills, and so on. The GDI also performs graphics rendering for print files.

If an application needed either the USER or GDI for processing, it would have to create an IPC (InterProcess Communication) to it. This would involve a context switch from User mode to Kernel mode (ring 0 to ring 3 of the processor) as well as 64K buffering. Then, another context switch would take place back to User mode. This, obviously, involves some time and decreases overall performance.

Windows NT version 4.0 moves the USER and GDI into the Kernel mode. This move significantly improves application performance by eliminating the 64K buffer, and leaving only a kernel transition. The benefit can be seen particularly in those applications that involve direct draw to the screen, such as Pinball, as well as in multimedia applications such as QuickTime.

Kernel (Privileged Processor) Mode

Kernel mode provides support for all major operating system functions. It controls access to memory and the execution of privileged instructions. All Kernel mode processes run in the protected mode of the processor, ring 0. As such, the applications running in User mode are effectively buffered from direct access to hardware. Thus, 16-bit applications that are designed to access hardware directly will not run successfully under Windows NT. These would have to be rewritten to "talk" to the Windows NT Kernel mode services.

The Kernel mode consists of three parts: Executive Services, Hardware Abstraction Layer (HAL), and Windows NT kernel.

Executive Services

This is the largest part of Kernel mode. The Executive Services provide support for processes, threads, memory management, I/O, IPC, and security. It is here that most Windows NT services and process managers execute. It also is here where device driver support is provided, including Windows NT's network architecture support drivers, protocols, and so forth. It is written mostly in portable C code which helps make Windows NT portable across platforms. It is this C code which needs to be recompiled in order to accommodate different platforms such as Dec Alpha, PowerPC, and MIPS.

Windows NT Kernel

The Windows NT kernel provides support for thread management and context switching, synchronization among services and processes in the Executive, multiprocessor load balancing, and exception and interrupt handling.

HAL (Hardware Abstraction Layer)

The HAL provides hardware platform support. It isolates specific platform details from the Executive and the Windows NT kernel. It is largely due to the HAL that those 16-bit applications that like to talk directly to hardware are unable to run. It can be said, therefore, that users applications are effectively isolated from base hardware interaction under Windows NT. HAL does it for you. Shades of *2001*!

Windows NT Virtual Memory Management

One of the Executive Services managers is the Virtual Memory Manager (see Figure 2.12). The memory architecture of Windows NT is a 32-bit, demand-based flat model. This model allows the Virtual Memory Manager to access up to 4G of RAM—generally far more than the amount of physical RAM installed in most computers.

FIG. 2.12 ⟹

Virtual Memory
Manager.

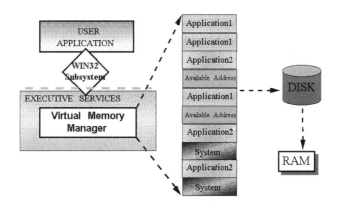

Those readers who recall Windows' swap file model will recall that there were two types of swap files: permanent and temporary. Both swap files managed available RAM in 4K pieces using an internal Windows algorithm called the LRU (Least Recently Used). Essentially, the LRU said that the piece of code in memory that was least recently accessed by a process was liable to be swapped to disk when more RAM was needed for a current process. On computers with the minimal required RAM for Windows, there could be a considerable amount of swapping that takes place. The main difference between permanent and temporary swap files is that a permanent swap file has a preallocated amount of space reserved on the disk. Temporary swap files begin at 2M and then "grow" as needed to a predetermined amount. Thus, while a permanent swap file actually provided better swap performance because the space was always there and available, it also reduced the amount of available disk storage. Similarly, while temporary swap files did not reduce the amount of disk storage available up front, more resource was expended in finding additional storage space when the swap file needed to "grow."

Windows NT combines the "best" of these swap files. The Windows NT pagefile (PAGEFILE.SYS) is created when Windows NT is installed and generally defaults to an initial, preallocated size (ala permanent swap files) of 12 plus physical RAM and a maximum size of three times physical RAM (depending on the amount of disk space available). So, on a computer with 16M of physical RAM, the default initial pagefile size would be 28M (12+16M) and the maximum size would be about 48M (3*16M). Windows NT will boot with the initial size pagefile available. The pagefile subsequently grows as applications are loaded and demands for physical RAM increase.

It is important to realize that while Windows NT allows addressing of up to 4G of physical RAM, the virtual memory manager can allocate up to 2G of *virtual* storage for *each* application. Another 2G is allocated for all system (Kernel mode) processing.

The Virtual Memory Manager addresses application memory as follows:

1. When an application is loaded, the Virtual Memory Manager assigns it virtual memory addresses in physical RAM.

2. The data is then moved in pages out of physical RAM and into the pagefile.

3. As the data is needed by the application, it calls for the virtual memory addresses.

4. The Virtual Memory Manager moves those pages on demand into available locations in physical RAM.

This process of assigning virtual addresses to the application effectively hides the organization of physical RAM from the application. The various pages of the application may wind up in noncontiguous space in physical RAM (that is, in sectors which may be distributed at different locations on the disk rather than next to each other), but as the Virtual Memory Manager is providing it with its addresses, it really doesn't care—because it doesn't know. This allows Windows NT to make the most efficient use of available physical RAM, and provide an overall performance increase for application processing.

Windows NT Cache Manager

The final aspect of the Windows NT Architecture that we will discuss is the Windows NT Cache Manager. As one might expect by now, the tried and true Windows and DOS SMARTDrive disk cache manager is no more. It has been replaced by an operating system-driven Cache Manager that runs as part of the Executive services, and thus in kernel mode. Its actual physical size depends on the amount of physical RAM installed. Windows NT's cache competes for RAM with other applications and processes and thus is automatically sized by the Cache Manager working in synch with the Memory Manager.

The Cache Manager provides an intelligent read-ahead/write-back operation. It predicts the next read location based on the history and locations of the last three reads. It also performs lazy writes; that is, using the processor, when it is not being accessed by any other process, to update the file on disk while maintaining data in memory for quick access.

From Here...

The next chapter discusses the system requirements for Windows NT 4.0 and the installation procedures. Before you proceed, test your knowledge with the review questions on the CD.

Taking the Disc Test

 If you have read and understood the material in the chapter, you are ready to test your knowledge. Insert the CD-ROM that comes with this book and run the self-test software as described in Appendix I, "Using the CD-ROM."

Chapter Prerequisite

You should already be familiar with the basic workings of your computer system, particularly how to boot it, its current operating system, and the basics of BIOS, memory, hard disks, CPU types, serial and parallel ports, network adapters, video adapters, and the mouse.

Installing Windows NT Workstation 4.0

In this chapter we will explore the Windows NT Workstation 4.0 installation process. We will concentrate on three primary components of the installation process: preparation, execution, and completion. The following specific topics will be addressed:

- ◆ Understanding Windows NT Workstation 4.0's system requirements as well as other data you will need for a complete installation

- ◆ Exploring the Windows NT Workstation 4.0 Setup Program and Installation Wizard

- ◆ Completing the setup process and starting Windows NT Workstation 4.0

◆ The process of performing an unattended installation

◆ Installation and uninstallation troubleshooting tips and techniques

◆ Exploring how to migrate applications and settings from earlier versions of Windows to Windows NT Workstation 4.0

◆ Exploring the Windows NT 4.0 Boot Process

Preparing to Install Windows NT Workstation 4.0

The installation of Windows NT Workstation 4.0 is actually pretty straightforward and relatively painless. However, there is some information that you should have collected ahead of time to make installation even smoother. Before you begin your installation of Windows NT Workstation 4.0, do some detective work. There are basically two questions that you need to ask yourself:

1. What is the system configuration of the computer that I am installing Windows NT Workstation 4.0 on?

2. What kind of installation am I implementing?

System configuration includes such information as the make and model of the computer, the BIOS type and date, bus architecture, video card and monitor, network adapter, modem, memory, processor type, disk controller and drive, sound card, and so on. It also includes the current operating system, installed applications, available disk space, and so on.

Beyond deciding from among the Typical, Custom, Portable, and Compact options, you will also need to know what kind of network model, if any, the computer will be participating in, the location of the installation files, the number of blank formatted disks you need to have ready, and so on. A more exhaustive checklist will follow later in this chapter.

It sounds like a lot of detective work. But if you think about it, you probably know the answer to most of these questions right off the top of your head. Windows NT does an excellent job of detecting most of this information for itself. What we are most concerned with here is discovering the nuances of a specific configuration that can throw a speed bump into the installation process. For example, if you have MS-DOS 5.0 or higher installed on your system, you might use the Microsoft Diagnostics utility to provide some of the more subtle details such as interrupt and DMA settings. After you have installed Windows NT Workstation a few times within your own organization, you will begin to understand and appreciate the nuances that your particular computer and network configurations bring to the installation process.

Windows NT Workstation 4.0 System Requirements

The following table outlines the basic hardware requirements for a successful installation of Windows NT Workstation 4.0.

Ch
3

Table 3.1 Windows NT Workstation 4.0 Hardware Requirements

Component	Description
CPU	32-bit Intel 486/25 or higher, Intel Pentium, Pentium Pro, or supported RISC-based processors such as MIPS, Digital Alpha AXP, Power PC
Disk	118M free disk space required for Windows NT System file partition (149M for RISC-Based computers)
Memory	12M RAM minimum required; 16M suggested (16M for RISC-based computers)
Video	Display adapter with VGA resolution or higher
Drives	CD-ROM drive and 3.5" disk drive if installing locally
Network	One or more supported adapter cards if member of a network and/or if installing over the network
File System	A FAT partition (recommended, but not necessary) on an Intel-based computer; a minimum 2M required FAT partition on RISC-based computers

The most important characteristic of the computer's configuration, and the one that you will pay the closest attention to, is the hardware's compatibility with Windows NT Workstation 4.0. For most organizations, the compatibility of the hardware will probably not be a big issue. However, if one piece of hardware is incompatible, expect your installation to have problems. In fact, if you have a hardware failure during installation, your first thought should be "incompatible hardware," probably followed by some sort of stress-reducing phraseology.

Microsoft works very closely with most major hardware manufacturers to ensure the compatibility of its products with Windows NT. To this end, Microsoft regularly publishes and updates a Hardware Compatibility List (HCL). If you have any doubt at all about the compatibility of the hardware, consult this list. Pay particularly close attention to network adapters, SCSI adapters and drives, especially CD-ROM drives, video drivers, and sound and game cards. For example, video driver support has changed significantly with Windows NT 4.0 rendering earlier version drivers inoperative. Also, do not take it for granted that just because your computer model is BrandName TurboX and it appears on the HCL that all the internal components (especially those mentioned earlier) are also supported. It is reasonable to assume that all internal components are supported. However, if your installation fails due to a hardware problem, check the failed component against the HCL as your first troubleshooting step.

Note There are several ways of accessing the HCL. If you subscribe to Microsoft TechNet, you will find a copy of the HCL there by searching for "Hardware Compatibility List." You can also find the most up-to-date versions by accessing Microsoft's World Wide Web site at **http://www.microsoft.com/ntserver/hcl/hclintro.htm** or Microsoft's FTP server at **ftp://microsoft.com/bussys/winnt/winnt_docs/hcl**.

The second most important consideration regards third party devices and drivers. Once again, Microsoft provides a tremendous list of support drivers for most major third party products. Even though Microsoft provides most of the drivers you will need, if there is any doubt, be sure to have a Windows NT-compatible driver available just in case.

You can generally obtain these relatively easily from the device manufacturer.

Tip

If you are installing Windows NT Workstation 4.0 as part of a major roll-out within your organization, you should consider performing a test installation on sample computer configurations from within your organization. At the very least, perform test installations on those computers that can be identified as "iffy" in regard to their compatibility.

Choosing Windows NT Workstation 4.0 or Windows 95

There are some considerations you should take into account when deciding between installing Windows NT Workstation 4.0 or Windows 95 on your computer. As you have seen in the section titled Windows NT Workstation 4.0 System Requirements, Windows NT Workstation 4.0 has higher hardware requirements than Windows 95. Windows 95 can be installed on a computer with a minimum 386DX processor, 4M of memory (though 8 is recommended), a VGA or higher monitor, and 35-40M of disk space. By contrast, Windows NT Workstation 4.0 requires a minimum 486/33 processor, 12M of memory (16M recommended), 120M or more of disk space, and a CD-ROM drive or some other access to source files.

Other considerations include the feature set of each product. Windows NT Workstation 4.0 offers a greater number of security options, multiple platform support, symmetric multiprocessing and full 32-bit processing. Windows 95 does not provide these features, but does offer a wider scope of device driver support, and it fully supports Plug and Play.

Your choice of operating system ultimately will depend on the hardware configuration of your computers, the features you desire in an operating system, the role your computer will play (does it contain data that needs a higher level of security, for example), and, of course, your budget.

Ch
3

Preparation Checklist

After collecting the computer's hardware information, ensuring its compatibility with Windows NT Workstation 4.0 and that it meets the minimum installation requirements, there is some additional information that you need to know before executing the setup process. As we explore the setup process itself, we will expound on each of these in more detail. For future reference, however, use this checklist as a guide for preparation. With the exception of the first four items, it represents the information that will be requested during the setup process.

- Read all Windows NT documentation files.
- Assess system requirements. See Table 3.1.
- Assess hardware compatibility. Verify by consulting the Hardware Compatibility List.
- Gather device driver and configuration data:
  - Video   Display Type, Adapter and chipset type
  - Network   Card type, IRQ, I/O Address, DMA, Connector, and so on
  - SCSI Controller Adapter and chipset type, IRQ, bus type
  - Sound/Media   IRQ, I/O Address, DMA
  - I/O Ports   IRQ, I/O Address, DMA
  - Modems   Port, IRQ, I/O Address, modem type
- Back up your current configuration and data files.
- Determine which type of initial setup will be performed. (You may need three blank formatted disks before running setup.)
- Determine the location of the source files for performing this installation. (Are they on CD-ROM, on a shared network location?)
- Determine on which partition the Windows NT system files will be installed.
- Determine which file system you will install.
- Determine whether you will create an Emergency Repair Disk. (If so, you need one blank disk available before running setup.)
- Identify your installation CD Key.

◆ Decide on a unique name for your computer.

◆ Determine which workgroup or domain name that the computer will join.

◆ Identify network connection data: IP addresses, IPX card numbers, and so on.

◆ Identify in which time zone the computer is located?

Tip

There are well over 90 text files that contain additional information specific to individual devices like network cards and video drivers. These can be found by browsing for .TXT files in the subdirectories for your specific platform. For example, on an Intel computer, look in the I386 platform directory on your Windows NT Workstation 4.0 installation CD-ROM under the DRVLIB.NIC subdirectory for a subdirectory with your network card's name, and in that directory look for and read the files with a .TXT extension.

There are certain other files that bear close examination. In the platform directory, for example I386, look for SETUP.TXT. It contains general information regarding devices and drivers used and required during installation. There are also three compressed files that contain release specific information: readme.wr_, printer.wr_, and network.wr_. These can be expanded and read with the Windows Write program or the Windows 95 WordPad program. From a DOS prompt, switch to the platform directory and enter the command using the following syntax: expand file.wr_ c:\target directory\file.wri. For example, if you've created a directory called readme on the C: drive, expand the network.wr_ file there by typing: expand network.wr_ c:\readme\network.wri.

Executing the Windows NT Workstation 4.0 Startup Process

So far we have concentrated on preinstallation detective work and preparation. Let's now turn our attention to the actual setup process and begin by discussing the five major phases that occur during this process.

1. The setup will begin in what is referred to as DOS or text mode. If you have installed Windows before, this blue text screen format will look familiar to you. During this mode, several screens will appear asking for various pieces of information about the computer configuration for Windows NT Workstation 4.0. The screens will include:

   - A menu of startup options
   - Detection and configuration of storage devices such as SCSI drives
   - Initial hardware verification
   - Choice of the installation disk partition
   - Choice of file system for the installation partition
   - Installation directory name

2. This information is used to reboot the computer and load a mini-version of Windows NT 4.0. This is a 32-bit multi-threaded kernel that enhances and supports the setup process.

3. As the computer reboots, Windows NT hardware detection takes place. This event discovers and initializes hardware devices for use by Windows NT. These devices include:

   - SCSI adapter
   - Video adapter
   - Mouse and Keyboard
   - Disk drives
   - CD-ROM drive(s)
   - Comm and Parallel ports
   - Memory configuration
   - Bus adapter

4. A GUI interface is installed and the Windows NT 4.0 Setup Wizard is displayed. The Wizard will walk you through the rest of the installation process asking for information such as:

   - Personal information
   - Unique computer name

- Network card information
- Network configuration information such as protocols
- Workgroup or Domain membership
- First user account and administration information
- Whether to create an Emergency Repair Disk
- Time Zone
- Video display setup

5. Finally, any additional support files are copied to the Windows NT system directory, configuration information is saved in the Windows NT Registry, and the setup process completes and restarts the computer.

The following sections discuss each of these phases in more detail by walking through an actual installation of Windows NT Workstation 4.0. Read through the process carefully and then try it yourself in the lab.

Note The setup process is essentially the same for Intel-based and RISC-based computers. The process described here will apply to Intel-based computers. Any variation that applies to RISC-based computers will be noted as it occurs in the process. ▨

Ch
3

Beginning Setup

The setup process begins by locating the installation files. If you intend to install Windows NT locally, you will need at the very minimum a compatible CD-ROM drive and optionally a 3.5 inch disk drive. If you are installing Windows NT over the network, which will largely be the case in most organizations, you will need to have an active network connection and at least read access to the location of the installation files.

It is interesting to note—to me anyway—that it is not necessary that the installation files be on an existing Windows NT computer, or that the network you are running is necessarily The Microsoft Network. Indeed, the installation files could be loaded on a Novell Netware server and the computer that is to have Windows NT installed is running the Netware client software. So long as the Windows NT computer-to-be can access a network drive, the setup process can be initiated.

The first phase of the setup process by default requires the creation of three startup disks. Windows NT copies all the basic boot configuration information as well as the mini–Windows NT kernel to these disks and uses these to start the process. If you are installing Windows NT locally, and have the original setup disks and CD-ROM, you probably have a set of startup disks in the Windows NT box. You can use these or let Windows NT create a new set for you. If your computer does not have a compatible CD-ROM drive, you will need to use these disks to begin the setup process.

Note According to Microsoft's technical documentation for Windows NT Workstation 4.0, if the BIOS of your computer supports the El Torito Bootable CD-ROM (no emulation mode) format, you can begin setup from the Windows NT CD-ROM directly and let Windows NT prompt you to create the startup disks. However, problems have been reported with various compatible CD-ROM drives that may require you to use the packaged setup disks to begin setup. ▪

Generally, if you are installing Windows NT over the network, you will not have access to the disks that come in the box and will want Windows NT to create them for you.

Another purpose of the startup disks is to provide a means of starting Windows NT for repair or recovery purposes if you cannot later boot. If you intend to create and keep current an Emergency Repair Disk, you can only use this disk if you first boot using the startup disks.

However, it is not essential that you create these disks during the startup process. You can save some time by performing a diskless installation of Windows NT. This is particularly useful when performing an over-the-network installation, or rolling out Windows NT on a large scale.

The Windows NT Setup executable on the Intel platform is named *WINNT.EXE*. If you are installing Windows NT for the first time on a computer, you will use this executable. If you already have a copy of Windows NT installed on the computer, for example Windows NT Workstation 3.51, and intend to upgrade to Windows NT 4.0 or install a new copy of Windows NT 4.0, you can use an alternative executable called *WINNT32.EXE*. This is a 32-bit version of the setup program and will run with increased performance.

Setting Up Windows NT Workstation 4.0 on RISC-Based Systems

On RISC-based systems, the setup process begins a little differently. Remember that on RISC-based computers, you must have a minimum 2M FAT partition created before proceeding with Windows NT setup. This partition will hold the two hardware-specific Windows NT boot files: *OSLOADER.EXE* and *HAL.DLL*. If you do not have a FAT partition, you must run the *ARCINST.EXE* utility located on the Windows NT Installation CD-ROM in the \MIPS subdirectory. When you boot your computer, choose RUN A PROGRAM from the ARC menu and enter the path to the ARCINSTALL.EXE utility. After the utility starts, choose Configure System Partition and follow the screens. The rest of the setup will proceed generally as described in this book.

WINNT.EXE and WINNT32.EXE offer a variety of setup option switches that give you more control over how the installation proceeds. The syntax for using either executable is as follows:

```
[WINNT¦WINNT32] [/S:sourcepath] [/T:tempdrive] [/I:inffile]
[/O or /OX] [/F] [/C] [/B] [/U[:scriptfile]] [/R or /
RX:directory]
```

Table 3.2 outlines these switches.

Table 3.2 WINNT.EXE Option Switches

Switch	Explanation
/B	Performs setup without creating startup disks. Instead, it creates a temporary directory on the hard disk with the most free space called *WIN_NT.~BK*. This requires an additional 4-5M of free disk space above the 114M installation minimum.
/O	Creates the three installation startup disks. Note that with this switch these disks can be created at any time. This switch would be used for the network installations of Windows NT.

continues

Table 3.2 Continued

Switch	Explanation
/OX	Performs the same action as /O, but for local CD-ROM installation.
/S:	Specifies the full drive or network path of the Windows NT sourcepath installation files.
/U[:script]	Used with /S, provides an unattended installation by skipping the screen that asks for the installation file location. With an optional script file, will not prompt the installer for any information during setup.
/T:tempdrive	Allows you to specify the location of the temporary files. If not specified, Windows NT will choose a drive for you.
/I:inffile	Specifies the file name of the setup information file. The default file is DOSNET.INF.
/C	Skips the free-space check on the startup disks. This can save a little time.
/F	Skips file verification as they are copied to the startup disks. This can save a little more time.
/R	Specifies an optional directory to be installed.
/RX	Specifies an optional directory to be copied.

We are now ready to start the setup process. As stated at the beginning of this section, setup begins by locating the installation files.

1. If you have access to your CD-ROM drive on your computer, switch to the CD-ROM drive and locate the directory that pertains to your system type (I386, MIPS, ALPHA, PPC) or connect to the network location of the installation files using your DOS client connection software.

   If you do not have access to your CD-ROM drive, try booting from the startup disk provided in the Windows NT Workstation 4.0 box.

2. Type **WINNT** with any desired option switches. The text mode phase of the setup process will initiate.

Note If you are installing Windows NT Workstation 4.0 from an existing installation of Windows NT, simply choose File, Run in Program Manager or File Manager and enter **WINNT32** followed by any desired option switches. ▪

Text Mode Phase

Recall that the DOS or Text Mode phase of setup has six basic events:

- ◆ A menu of startup options
- ◆ Detection and configuration of storage devices such as SCSI drives
- ◆ Initial hardware verification
- ◆ Choice of the installation disk partition
- ◆ Choice of file system for the installation partition
- ◆ Installation directory name

We will explore each now in more detail.

Startup Menu

The first screen that appears welcomes you to the Setup process and presents four different ways to proceed.

Tip
On all setup screens, a pretty useful help dialog box is available by pressing F1. Also, you can exit setup at any time by pressing F3.

1. To learn more about Windows NT Setup before continuing, press F1.
2. To set up Windows NT now, press Enter.
3. To repair a damaged Windows NT version 4.0 installation, press R.
4. To quit Setup without installing Windows NT, press F3.

Ch
3

These are fairly straightforward options, and are mirrored in the white status bar at the bottom of the screen with their keyboard shortcuts.

Of these four options, the one which may raise a question is the third, repairing a damaged installation of Windows NT. This is the option that you use with the Emergency Repair Disk to restore configuration information. The Emergency Repair Disk contains data from the Windows NT Registry—more about that later.

Mass Storage Device Configuration

The next step in the setup process is the detection of mass storage devices such as CD-ROMs, SCSI adapters, and so on. The detected devices are displayed on the screen. IDE (Integrated Device Electronics) and ESDI (Enhanced Small Device Interface) drives are also detected, but generally not displayed in the list.

If you have a device installed that is not shown on the screen, you can choose to add it by pressing **S**. Otherwise, press Enter to continue with setup. Of course, you can always add the additional devices after setup has completed from the Windows NT Control Panel. If you do press **S**, be sure to have your drivers disk available. (Refer to the Preparation Checklist.)

License Agreement

Setup will present you with a multi-page license agreement. This is the standard type of software agreement that Microsoft presents warning you to install a valid copy of Windows NT and not a borrowed copy from somebody else. You will need to page down through the license screens to accept the agreement and get to the next step in installation.

Verifying Hardware

The setup process next displays the basic list of hardware and software components that it detected including:

- Computer
- Display
- Keyboard
- Keyboard Layout
- Pointing Device

If the list matches what you have in the computer, press Enter. If you need to make a change, use the up- or down-arrow to highlight the component that needs to be changed, press Enter, and choose the appropriate item from the list.

Partition Configuration

The next screen involves choosing the disk partition on which the Windows NT system files will be installed. This is referred to as the system partition. The system partition can be an existing formatted or unformatted partition, or it may be an area of free space on the hard disk. Setup will display the partitions and free space that it detects on all physical disks. Use your up- and down-arrows to select the partition or free space where you want to install Windows NT.

If you select an area of free space, you will need to press **C** to Create the partition. A new screen will display telling you how large the partition can be, and asking you for your desired size. Enter in the desired size of the partition and press Enter. Windows NT will create the partition for you, return you to the Partition Configuration screen and display the new partition in the list. Select the new partition and press Enter to continue.

If you are using an existing partition as the Windows NT system partition, select it and press Enter.

You can also select and delete partitions from this screen. This can be useful if you need to free up some space and then create a larger partition for Windows NT.

Note In either case, be sure that there is at least 118M of free space available on the selected partition. This is a *minimum* value; more free space will help performance. For example, you will need space for a pagefile for virtual memory management. Recall that the default initial size for a pagefile is 12+the amount of physical RAM installed in your computer.

Do not install Windows NT on a compressed partition. Disable compression before Setup begins.

If the partition is mirrored, disable mirroring before Setup begins.

If any partition is labeled as Windows NT Fault Tolerance, do not delete these as they represent stripe sets, volume sets, and mirrors that could result in significant loss of data.

Ch
3

Formatting the Partition

The system partition contains all the Windows NT system drivers, hardware configuration, security information, the Registry, and so on. There is also a primary or boot partition into which Windows NT copies its boot files. The next screen allows you to choose which file system—FAT or NTFS—you would like to format the proposed system partition with. If you selected the wrong partition, just press Escape to return to the previous screen.

Your choice of file system depends on several factors. Here is a list of considerations for choosing NTFS:

♦ NTFS supports Windows NT file and directory permissions security and access auditing; FAT supports only the Read Only, System, Hidden, and Archive attributes.

♦ NTFS supports transaction tracking and sector sparing for data recovery; FAT does not.

♦ NTFS supports partition sizes of up to 16E and file sizes of 4–64G depending on cluster sizes; FAT supports a maximum file size of 4G and is inefficient for partition sizes greater than 250M.

♦ NTFS provides file and directory compression implemented as a property; FAT does not.

♦ NTFS is recognized only by Windows NT on that computer; FAT is recognized by NTFS, MS-DOS, or OS/2.

If you are installing Windows NT on a new computer, and do not intend to also run MS-DOS or Windows 95 on that computer (called "dual-booting"), then you can simply create the partition and format it as NTFS or FAT.

If you do intend to dual-boot with MS-DOS or Windows 95, be sure that it is already installed and that the boot partition is already formatted as FAT. If you install Windows NT on the boot partition, Windows NT will modify the master boot record (MBR) with its boot information and maintain a boot pointer to the MS-DOS system files. If you install NT first, format the partition as FAT, and *then* install MS-DOS, the MBR will be altered and you will not be able to boot Windows NT successfully.

RISC Partition Formats

NTFS can be used on RISC-based computers. However, Windows NT requires at least one FAT system partition of 2M minimum size for its boot file information. Create this partition, as well as another system partition of appropriate size, for NTFS following your RISC-based computer's documentation.

Dual Booting Windows NT Workstation 4.0 and OS/2

Windows NT and OS/2 can coexist on the same computer. If you have installed OS/2 and MS-DOS on the computer and use the OS/2 boot command to switch between operating systems, Windows NT will configure its boot up to dual boot between itself and whichever of the two operating systems you had running when you installed Windows NT.

As Windows NT 4.0 no longer supports the HPFS file system, if you intend to keep OS/2 on HPFS, you must install Windows NT in another partition. Similarly, if you are using the OS/2 Boot Manager, the Windows NT installation process will disable it upon completion. You must re-enable it by marking the Boot Manager partition as the active partition using Windows NT's Disk Administrator utility. If after working in OS/2 you choose to boot to Windows NT, use OS/2's Boot Manager to mark the Windows NT partition as active and then reboot the computer.

Dual Booting Windows NT Workstation 4.0 and Windows NT 4.0 Server

For testing, instruction, or development purposes, you may choose to have both Windows NT Workstation 4.0 and Server installed on your computer, or perhaps even different versions of Windows NT. The setup program detects the existence of another installation of Windows NT, Windows 95, Windows for Workgroups, or Windows 3.1 and displays that installation's system directory as an upgrade directory for your current installation. Simply press **N** for "New Directory" as offered on the screen to install this version of Windows NT in a different directory. The setup program will keep the other version(s) intact and install this version in its own directory. Setup will also modify the boot menu to display this new version at the top of the boot menu and as the default boot up operating system.

Ch

3

Installation Directory

Setup will next ask for the name and location of the Windows NT system files. Windows NT will display the path and default name of the directory for you on the selected partition. The default directory name is WINNT. You may change the name to whatever you want, but it is recommended that you keep the name recognizable, such as WINNT40, especially if you have other versions of Windows or Windows NT on the computer.

If you do have an existing version of Windows, Windows 95, or Windows NT on the selected partition, setup will detect that and display that directory as the installation choice. Setup assumes that you will want to upgrade the existing operating system.

If you choose to upgrade Windows, setup will migrate most INI settings, such as those contained in the win.ini, system.ini, and application ini files from the previous installation over to Windows NT 4.0. When you boot, you will still be able to choose MS-DOS and start Windows.

If you choose to upgrade an existing installation of Windows NT, setup will migrate all registry settings to Windows NT 4.0. However, you will lose the ability to boot to the older installation.

You may not install Windows NT Workstation 4.0 in the same directory as Windows 95. You must choose a new directory for installation. Consequently, no migration of settings will take place, and you will need to reinstall your Windows 95 applications under Windows NT.

Final Screens

The next screen of the text mode phase informs you that setup will examine the disk for corruption. It offers two types of exams: basic and exhaustive. The basic exam, initiated by pressing Escape, is best used on new partitions that do not already have data stored. The exhaustive exam, initiated by pressing Enter, runs slightly longer depending on the size of the partition and the amount of data stored. Even though the exhaustive exam does take a little extra time, it is highly recommended if you are installing Windows NT Workstation 4.0 on an existing partition with existing data.

After you make your selection, setup displays a dialog showing the status of the process as it copies files to the new Windows NT system directory.

When the files have been copied and the directory structure created, setup informs you that the text mode portion has completed and that you should press Enter to restart the computer. At this point you can press Enter, or if it is getting late, you could just turn off your computer. Actually, it is often suggested that you do power off the computer and then power back on so as to reset all the hardware devices, particularly network cards, for Windows NT.

Restart, Lock, and Load!

When the computer reboots, if you watch very closely, you will see the Windows NT boot menu appear briefly with a choice for Windows NT installation. This is the default and will start automatically. If you are quick with your fingers, you can press the up or down arrow keys to disable the default time and boot to MS-DOS or Windows 95. There will be a menu entry for either MS-DOS or Windows 95 depending on which operating system has been installed. Otherwise, just let Windows NT take over.

It is during this phase that Windows NT loads its 32-bit multithreaded kernel that enhances and supports the setup process. As the computer reboots, Windows NT hardware detection takes place. This event discovers and initializes hardware devices for use by Windows NT such as SCSI adapters, video adapter, mouse and keyboard drivers, CD-ROM drives, comm and parallel ports, memory configuration, and bus adapter.

You will see what will become a familiar set of boot-up screens. The first will be a black screen that loads system drivers (white consecutive dots), followed by the infamous blue screen. Infamous because it is here that you will see screen dumps related to unsuccessful boots of Windows NT. Most of the time, however, this screen simply outlines the progress of various boot tasks. If you have chosen to format or convert a partition to NTFS, you will see messages to that effect as conversion takes place. Also, Windows NT will reboot the system once again for the file system to be recognized and take effect.

Once this process completes, Windows NT loads the GUI portion of setup called the Windows NT Setup Wizard.

Ch
3

Windows NT Setup Wizard

The Setup Wizard is a much streamlined and intuitive interface for gathering information pertinent to the configuration of Windows NT on the computer. Essentially, the wizard will ask you configuration option questions during the display of several Windows GUI dialog boxes. After you have made your selections and provided the appropriate information, the wizard will load the necessary drivers, update the registry, and complete the installation.

Tip

Each Setup Wizard dialog box has Back, Next, and Help buttons to make it easy to move back and forth among the screens and reselect options before committing yourself.

The very first screen that you will see will outline the standard Microsoft client license agreement. You must select OK to this agreement before continuing with setup.

The next dialog box outlines how the wizard will proceed. There are three parts to the wizard setup:

1. Gathering information about your computer.
2. Installing Windows NT Networking.
3. Finishing Setup.

Gathering Information About Your Computer

The Setup Options dialog box offers four installation option choices: Typical, Portable, Compact, and Custom. Table 3.3 highlights which components are installed by default for each setup option.

Table 3.3 Default Components Installed by Each Setup Option

Component	Typical	Portable	Compact	Custom
Accessibility Options	Yes	Yes	No	Selectable
Accessories	Yes	Yes	No	Selectable

Component	Typical	Portable	Compact	Custom
Communication Options	Yes	Yes	No	Selectable
Games	No	No	No	Selectable
Windows Messaging	No	No	No	Selectable
Multimedia	Yes	Yes	No	Selectable

Typical and Custom are very much the same as the Express and Custom options that most of us have encountered when installing Windows and most Windows applications. The two setup options new to Windows NT 4.0 are Portable and Compact.

Typical Setup is the default as well as the recommended option. It installs all optional Windows components including Microsoft Exchange and of course, the games. It asks few questions and automatically configures component settings.

Custom, on the other hand, gives the most control over the installation and configuration of options.

Portable is designed to accommodate the increasing number of users running Windows NT Workstation on their portable computers. This installation offers options that are geared toward portable use, including support for PCCARD (previously referred to as PCMCIA).

Compact is designed for computer systems that have limited disk space available and will not install any optional components. Only the minimum components necessary will be installed. This can reduce the space required by 10-20M.

The next two dialog boxes will prompt you for a user name and company name for registration purposes as well as a Product Identification number or CD Key. The number is usually included on the CD case or in your Windows NT installation manual. In some organizations, depending on the type of installation being performed, you may not need this number because your organization has negotiated a company-wide license for distributing the software. You must enter something in both

Ch
3

these dialogs in order to proceed to the next dialog box. Contact your MIS department for the appropriate number.

The next dialog box asks for the computer name. This is the name that Windows NT will use to identify this computer internally and for network and remote communication. It must be a unique name if the computer will be a member of a workgroup or domain. This name can be up to 15 characters long.

Tip

While a computer name can contain spaces, it is not recommended. In a large network, users connecting to computers can become confused as to the presence or absence of spaces in a name. In fact, in a large corporate network, a standard naming convention for computer, workgroup, and domain names will greatly simplify the configuration and maintenance of your network.

The next screen references the Administrator Account and asks for a password for that account. The administrator account is a built-in account that Windows NT creates for managing the configuration of the computer including security and account information. The name of the administrator account is ADMINISTRATOR and the password can be up to 14 characters. You will need to enter the password twice, once to confirm it.

Caution

Passwords in Windows NT are *case-sensitive* so be sure that you type it in correctly and then remember it! If you forget your password during the course of installation, *you will not be able to access Windows NT.*

You may have read recently that certain Pentium-based computers have a faulty *floating point* module. In very specific circumstances this can sometimes produce inaccurate results when dividing certain values. If setup has detected that your computer has such a problem, the next screen will give you the option to disable the module and let Windows NT perform the math. This will result in a decrease in performance for floating point operations. However, if your applications rely heavily on floating point arithmetic, such as complex Excel macros and SQL database queries and sorts, then you may prefer to choose Yes to this option.

The next screen involves the option of creating an *Emergency Repair Disk*. The Emergency Repair Disk contains setup information relevant to this installation of Windows NT including the location of source files and computer configuration and security information from the Registry. It can be used to replace corrupted or missing boot files, recover account information, and restore Windows NT to the master boot record of the computer boot partition if it has been modified. In order to use this disk, you must have a startup disk to boot with and then press **R** for repair from the startup menu.

If you choose to create an Emergency Repair Disk, be sure to have a blank disk handy, and choose Yes.

Tip

If you choose not to create an Emergency Repair Disk at this time, you can always create one later. Windows NT provides a command prompt command called RDISK.EXE, which is used to create a new Emergency Repair Disk and to update an existing disk.

Depending on the type of installation you choose at the start of the wizard, you may see a dialog box that lets you choose which Optional Components to install. You may choose one of two options: Most Common or Show a List.

If you choose Most Common, setup will proceed to the next portion of the Setup Wizard process. If you choose to Show a List, you will see a new dialog box with a list of options. This is the same dialog box that you see when selecting optional components in Windows 95.

The truly fine thing about this dialog box is the way that it presents you with component information. You will see a list of five or six main components. Most of these are actually component areas that are composed of a list of component items from which you can choose. As you select each main component, a description box to the right explains what functionality each provides, as well as how many of the component items have been selected for installation. If you select the Details button, another dialog box will display the checklist of component items. You may select or deselect them as you wish and then return to the main dialog box. As you select items, the description screen will note how many items you selected, such as "12 of 14 items selected." You will also see just how much additional disk space will be required for the items in question.

As you select Next, the wizard takes you to part two of its setup process: Installing Windows NT Networking.

Installing Windows NT Networking

The next few dialog boxes reference information regarding the configuration of network related functions and components. Your first choice will be to indicate whether you are implementing network features at all, and if so, whether you will be Wired to the Network through a local interface such as a network card, or if you have Remote Access to the Network through a modem connection, or both.

If you have chosen Wired to the Network, the next dialog box will prompt you to detect and install the network card. Choose Start Search to begin setup's detection process. The dialog box will display a list of all detected network cards. You can choose to configure any combination of cards by selecting or deselecting their check boxes.

If setup cannot detect the card, or you have a driver disk available, you can install the card from your disk by choosing Select from List, and then the Have Disk button.

Note Remember to check the Hardware Compatibility List to be sure that your network card is supported by Windows NT. (See the Preparation Checklist.)

You can install additional cards or change card settings later from Windows NT's Control Panel. ▨

The Setup Wizard will most likely next display a configuration option dialog box for the specific card(s) you selected. This dialog box, or series of dialog boxes, ask for the correct IRQ, I/O base port address, and memory buffer address settings, as well as any other card specific settings such as on–board transceivers, thin versus thick coax, and so on.

> **Note** Please note that Windows NT will display the manufacturer's proposed or factory settings in these dialog boxes. As some cards are software-configurable, the actual settings on the cards may not match the manufacturer's settings. To avoid conflicts, especially the failure of Windows NT to initialize the card and network settings on your computer, be sure to know your card settings ahead of time. (See the Preparation Checklist found in the section titled " Preparing to Install Windows NT Workstation 4.0—Preparation Checklist".)

The next dialog box asks for *Network Protocol* choices. By default, Windows NT selects *TCP/IP* and *NWLINK IPX/SPX* as your protocol. However, you may select any combination of TCP/IP, *NWLINK* (Windows NT's 32-bit implementation of IPX/SPX) and *NETBEUI*. Additional protocols may be added by choosing Select from List. Other protocols that can be installed include Appletalk, DLC, and Point to Point Tunneling, or, if you have a protocol disk, you may select Have Disk.

The next step is to select the *Network Services* that are appropriate for your computer. By default, five services are installed with Windows NT networking and cannot be deselected. They are *Computer Browser, RPC Configuration, NetBIOS Interface, Workstation,* and *Server.* Again, additional services such as Client Service for Netware, Microsoft Peer Web Services, Remote Access Services, and so on can be installed by selecting Select from Disk, or from disk by choosing Have Disk. Network services will be discussed in Chapter 11 "Network Connectivity and Remote Support."

At this point, you have made all appropriate choices and the wizard gives you a choice to continue on and install the network components, or go back and alter your selections. Choose Back to make changes and Next, of course, to continue.

The next dialog box displays the *Network Bindings.* Think of bindings as being the network "paths" that determine how services, protocols, and

Ch
3

adapters interact to effect network communications. You can adjust the bindings by changing their order, enabling, or disabling them. Windows NT has selected the optimum bindings based on your network component settings. If you need to adjust them later, you can do so from Windows NT's Control Panel. A further discussion of bindings will be offered in Chapter 11 "Network Connectivity and Remote Support."

The final piece of information required for you to complete the network portion of the wizard setup is the *Network Model*. The dialog box will display the Computer Name that you entered earlier (giving you a last chance during setup to change it), and ask whether you will be joining a workgroup or domain. If you are joining a workgroup, or creating a new workgroup, enter the workgroup's name (up to 15 characters).

If you are joining an existing domain, enter the name of the domain that you are joining. Before you join a domain, you must have a computer account created for your computer name in the domain that you are joining. The domain administrator must set this up for you ahead of time. Do not wait until you get to this point in the installation to ask your domain administrator for a computer account. He or she will probably not be amused. If you are the domain administrator, or have been given appropriate administrative privileges in the domain, you can create this account during installation by specifying the computer name, and the account name and password that have the appropriate privileges.

You cannot create a new domain during the installation of Windows NT Workstation 4.0. Domains are created from Domain Controller servers. Also, before you can log on to the domain after installation, you will need a valid user account for that domain as well.

Each card that you install may have protocol-specific information that is required. For example, if you choose TCP/IP, you will need to specify a local address, router information, WINS address information, and so on, or specify DCHP configuration. These dialog boxes will display at this time as the wizard completes the setup of network components.

Note If you began your installation as an over the network type, and you did not power off your computer after the text mode, you may see a message to the effect that Windows NT cannot verify the card settings and should it use them anyway. The answer is YES use the settings. The reason for this message is that in a warm boot such as Windows NT performs after the text mode setup, all device settings, particularly network card settings, are not reset. Thus Windows NT is detecting that those settings are already in use. A cold boot, on the other hand, involves powering off the computer. This, of course, resets all device settings, including the network card settings that triggered the message in the first place. ▪

If Windows NT is unable to initiate network communication, you will have the option to go back and check your settings, or continue on without configuring the network.

As you select Next, the wizard takes you to part three of its setup process: Finishing Setup.

Finishing Setup

There are just two more dialog boxes to consider before the Setup Wizard can complete the installation. The first dialog box displays the *Date and Time* utility. Adjust the settings to reflect the time zone of the computer, as well as to ensure that the system time is correct.

Note Several interprocess mechanisms as well as certain applications and Microsoft BackOffice products rely on time stamps and time synchronization among computers. Inaccurate time zones or time values can result in process failures and in some cases, an incomplete processing of data. ▪

Finally, the Display Properties dialog box pops up. This one allows you to configure your video display by changing settings such as pixel resolution, color palette, refresh frequency and font size, as well as changing your video driver information. Before you complete this screen, choose Test to see whether you can actually read your display with the settings you chose. After testing, you can choose OK.

A status dialog box now displays showing the progress of files copied from the temporary directory (WIN_NT.~LS). When this is

Ch
3

complete, the wizard asks you to remove any floppy disks and press the Restart button to reboot the computer. As before, at this point you could safely turn your computer off.

If you let the computer restart, and have chosen a dual-boot configuration for your installation, you will see the Windows NT boot loader menu. Your new installation of Windows NT Workstation 4.0 will be first in the list, and it will be the default operating system unless you choose the other operating system option within 30 seconds. If you choose Windows NT, it will load with all the options you chose, and present you with the Welcome screen.

Troubleshooting Installation and Setup

If you have carefully read this chapter, you will have relatively little problem, if any, with your installation of Windows NT Workstation 4.0. In fact, installing Windows NT 4.0 is rarely troublesome if you have done your detective work. It is designed to detect and configure as much on its own as possible. Nevertheless, let's run through a couple of tips, suggestions, and reminders beginning with the Preparation Checklist.

◈ Read all Windows NT documentation files.

◈ Assess system requirements. See Table 3.1.

◈ Assess hardware compatibility. Verify by consulting the Hardware Compatibility List.

◈ Gather device driver and configuration data.

• Video	Display Type, Adapter and chipset type
• Network	Card type, IRQ, I/O Address, DMA, Connector, and so on.
• SCSI Controller	Adapter and chipset type, IRQ, bus type
• Sound/Media	IRQ, I/O Address, DMA
• I/O Ports	IRQ, I/O Address, DMA
• Modems	Port, IRQ, I/O Address, modem type

◆ Back up your current configuration and data files.

◆ Determine which type of initial setup will be performed. (You may need three blank formatted disks before running setup.)

◆ Determine the location of the source files for performing this installation. (Are they on CD-ROM, on a shared network location?)

◆ Determine on which partition the Windows NT system files will be installed.

◆ Determine which file system you will install.

◆ Determine whether you will create an Emergency Repair Disk. (If so, you need one blank disk available before running setup.)

◆ Identify your installation CD Key.

◆ Decide on a unique name for your computer.

◆ Determine which workgroup or domain name that the computer will join.

◆ Identify network connection data: IP addresses, IPX card numbers, and so on.

◆ Identify in which time zone the computer is located?

Perhaps most critical to a successful installation of Windows NT Workstation 4.0 is the compatibility of your computer's hardware. There are two reminders that I offer here:

1. Be sure that your computer meets the minimum requirements necessary for installing and running Windows NT Workstation 4.0.

2. Be sure that you have checked *all* hardware components in your computer against the Hardware Compatibility List for Windows NT Workstation 4.0.

These two actions alone will significantly increase your success rate.

Next, become familiar with the hardware settings for installed devices, particularly network cards. This includes not only IRQ, DMA, I/O address and connector data, but also network protocol settings such as IP address, DNS location, router address, DHCP information, IPX card address, and so on.

Finally, follow a naming convention for your computers and work-groups that ensures uniqueness, recognizability, and ease of maintenance. If becoming a member of a domain, be sure that your computer already has a computer account in the domain you are joining (as well as a user account for you).

Occasionally, you may encounter unusual errors relating to your hard disk. If installation should fail due to disk-related problems, here are a few areas to explore:

1. Is the hard disk supported (on the HCL)?

2. Do you have a valid boot sector available on the disk. Recall that especially for RISC-based systems, Windows NT requires a minimum 2M FAT system partition.

3. Are your SCSI drives being detected correctly by Windows NT? You may need to check physical settings such as termination.

4. Check for viruses in the Master Boot Record (MBR). If there is a virus that alters the MBR either before, during, or after installation, Windows NT will not be able to boot successfully. A likely message you may receive is: "Bad or missing NTLDR."

5. If, when Windows NT reboots to start the GUI Setup Wizard it fails, usually with the message: "Bad or missing NTOSKRNL," this could be due to a misdetection of the SCSI drive. Boot to DOS and use the DOS Editor to modify the BOOT.INI file. This read-only system file is created by Windows NT during installation and used to display the boot menu. It is stored in the root directory of the system partition. Use the DOS ATTRIB command to turn off the Read Only (R) and System (S) attributes before editing the file. Change all references of SCSI for this installation to MULTI. Also check that the partition numbers listed in the BOOT.INI file for Windows NT match the partition number of the Windows NT system file directory. Be sure to save your changes and set the attributes back.

Note The syntax for using the DOS ATTRIB command to turn off attributes is as follows:

C:>**ATTRIB -S -R BOOT.INI**

Set the attributes back by typing:

C:>**ATTRIB +S +R BOOT.INI** ■

 Note Windows NT counts partitions starting with "0" as follows:

1. Hidden system partitions.

2. The first primary partition on each drive.

3. Additional primary partitions on each drive.

4. Logical partitions on each drive.

So, if the physical disk has a hidden system partition (like a COMPAQ BIOS partition), a C: drive primary partition, and a D: drive logical partition, and you are installing Windows NT on drive D:, you are installing Windows NT on partition 2 (hidden-0, C:-1, D:-2). ■

Ch
3

Using NTHQ to Troubleshoot

Windows NT also supplies a troubleshooting utility that may be of use for both Windows NT Workstation 4.0 and Server in discovering how Windows NT is detecting your hardware configuration. It is called NTHQ and can be found in the \SUPPORT\HQTOOL directory on the installation CD.

To use this utility, boot to DOS, place a blank disk in the A: drive, switch to the directory on the CD, and run MAKEDISK.BAT. This will create a bootable disk that you can use to run NTHQ. Reboot the computer with this disk and follow the directions.

NTHQ creates an on-screen report that can be saved to a log file on disk, as well as printed out. It performs a hardware detection on the computer similar to that performed by Windows NT during setup and can be used to determine your hardware settings and specifically which ones are causing setup to fail. It includes data about the motherboard such as I/O, DMA, and IRQ settings for CMOS, Memory Access

Controller, Comm and Printer Ports, Plug and Play BIOS, data about the Network Card, Video, Storage Devices, and a Summary of all device configuration settings. It also shows what is questionable regarding the Hardware Compatibility List.

NTHQ Sample Report

Here is an example of the kinds of data that NTHQ captures and reports.

```
Hardware Detection Tool For Windows NT 4.0

Master Boot Sector Virus Protection Check
Hard Disk Boot Sector Protection: Off.
No problem to write to MBR

ISA Plug and Play Add-in cards detection Summary Report

No ISA Plug and Play cards found in the system
ISA PnP Detection: Complete

EISA Add-in card detection Summary Report
Scan Range: Slot 0 - 16
Slot 0: EISA System Board
EISA Bus Detected: No
EISA Detection: Complete

Legacy Detection Summary Report

System Information
Device: System board
Can't locate Computername
Machine Type: IBM PC/AT
Machine Model: fc
Machine Revision: 00
Microprocessor: Pentium
Conventional memory: 655360
Available memory: 32 MB
BIOS Name: Phoenix
BIOS Version:
BIOS Date: 06/12/96
Bus Type: ISA

Enumerate all IDE devices

IDE Devices Detection Summary Report
Primary Channel: master drive detected
Model Number: TOSHIBA MK2720FC
```

```
Firmware Revision: S1.16 J
Serial Number: 66D70208
Type of Drive: Fixed Drive
Disk Transfer Rate: >10Mbs
Number of Cylinders: 2633
Number of Heads: 16
Number of Sectors Per Track: 63
Number of unformatted bytes per sector Per Track: 639
LBA Support: Yes
DMA Support: Yes
PIO Transfer Cycle Time Mode 2
DMA Transfer Cycle Time Mode 2

IDE/ATAPI: Complete

=============End of Detection Report============
Adapter Description: Cirrus Logic VGA
Listed in Hardware Compatibility List: Yes

Adapter Description: Creative Labs Sound Blaster 16 or AWE-32
Adapter Device ID: *PNPB003
Listed in Hardware Compatibility List: Not found-check the
latest HCL

Adapter Description: Gameport Joystick
Adapter Device ID: *PNPB02F
Listed in Hardware Compatibility List: Not found-check the
latest HCL

Adapter Description: Unknown Cirrus Logic chipset, report!
Adapter Device ID: 12021013
Listed in Hardware Compatibility List: Not found-check the
latest HCL
```

Ch

3

Performing an Unattended Setup of Windows NT Workstation 4.0

It is possible to automate the setup process so as to provide some or all of the information needed during setup and thus allow for little or no additional user input. This can be especially helpful when installing a large number of computers with similar configurations, such as having the same domain name, monitor settings, network card drivers and setting, and so on.

There are five basic steps involved in implementing an unattended setup of Windows NT Workstation 4.0.

◆ Create a distribution server by placing the Windows NT Workstation 4.0 installation files for the appropriate computer platform in a shared directory on a file server.

◆ Create an answer file that supplies information common to all the computers being installed.

◆ Create a uniqueness data file that supplies information specific to each computer's installation.

◆ Provide access to the installation files on the distribution server for the computers that are being installed.

◆ Run Windows NT setup referencing the location of the setup files, answer files, and uniqueness data files.

Each of these steps will now be discussed in more detail.

Create a Distribution Server

It is a relatively simple task to copy the installation files to a shared directory on a file server. Simply identify which Windows NT server you wish to use. This should be a server that the target computers will be able to access easily, preferably a server on the same subnet, and one that is not already being used to capacity by other applications or processes. It also should have its own CD-ROM, or be able to access a CD-ROM drive.

Next, create an installation folder on that server. Into that folder, copy the installation files for the target computers' hardware platform from the appropriate platform directory on the Windows NT Workstation 4.0 installation CD-ROM (i386, MIPS, ALPHA, or PPc). You could use the MD-DOS xcopy command with the /S switch (to copy all subdirectories) from a command prompt, or use Windows Explorer.

Finally, share the newly created directory. (See Chapter 7, "Windows NT 4.0 Security Model," for information about sharing folders in Windows NT.)

Create an Answer File

Answer files (unattend.txt) are used to supply setup information that is common to all the computers using that file. The kind of information that would be common to the computers would include network settings such as card driver, interrupts, DMA, protocols to be installed, and services to be installed, which workgroup or domain the computers are joining, modem types, and organization name. Here is a copy of the sample unattend.txt file for an Intel-based computer that can be found on the Windows NT Workstation 4.0 CD-ROM. Each platform directory contains its own version of this file.

```
; Microsoft Windows NT Workstation Version 4.0 and

; Windows NT Server Version 4.0

; (c) 1994 - 1996 Microsoft Corporation. All rights reserved.

;

; Sample Unattended Setup Answer File

;

; This file contains information about how to automate the installation

; or upgrade of Windows NT Workstation and Windows NT Server so the

; Setup program runs without requiring user input.

;

; For information on how to use this file, read the appropriate sections

; of the Windows NT 4.0 Resource Kit.


[Unattended]

OemPreinstall = no

ConfirmHardware = no
```

```
NtUpgrade = no

Win31Upgrade = no

TargetPath = WINNT

OverwriteOemFilesOnUpgrade = no


[UserData]

FullName = "Your User Name"

OrgName = "Your Organization Name"

ComputerName = COMPUTER_NAME


[GuiUnattended]

TimeZone = "(GMT-08:00) Pacific Time (US & Canada);
Tijuana"


[Display]

ConfigureAtLogon = 0

BitsPerPel = 16

XResolution = 640

YResolution = 480

VRefresh = 70

AutoConfirm = 1


[Network]

Attend = yes

DetectAdapters = ""

InstallProtocols = ProtocolsSection
```

JoinDomain = Domain_To_Join

[ProtocolsSection]

TC = TCParameters

[TCParameters]

DHCP = yes

As you can see, this text file looks very much like a Windows .INI file. It can be created by simply copying and modifying the sample file, creating your own using any text editor, or by running the Setup Manager utility, also found on the Windows NT 4.0 installation CD-ROM. While it is usually called "unattend.txt" you can give it any legal file name so long as you refer to it correctly when running setup. The Setup Manager utility provides a graphical interface for creating and modifying the unattend.txt file(s). A complete treatment of the unattend.txt file and using Setup Manager can be found in the Windows NT Workstation Resource Kit Version 4.0.

Once created, this file should be placed in the same location as the Windows NT 4.0 installation source files on the distribution server.

Create a Uniqueness Data File

The unattend.txt file creates a setup data file that contains information that is common to all the computers being installed. However, this will not completely automate the process when installing more than one computer. Recall that each computer's computer name, for example, must be unique. That sort of information cannot be supplied in the unattend.txt file alone.

A uniqueness data file (UDF) can be created to supply the more detailed and machine specific information required to more fully automate the setup process. The UDF file identifies specific sections that should be merged into the answer file. Here is a sample UDF file.

;This section lists all unique ids that are supported by this database.

;The left hand side is a unique id, which can be any string but

; must not contain the asterisk (*), space, comma, or equals character.

;The right hand side is a list of sections, each of which should match the name

; of a section in unattend.txt. See below.

;

id1 = section1,section2

id2 = section1,section3,section4

[section1]

;This is a section whose name should match the name of a section in unattend.txt.

; Each line in this section is written into the same section in unattend.txt,

; via the profile APIs. A line here thus replaces a line in unattend.txt with the

; same left hand side. (If a matching line does not exist in unattend.txt, the line will

; be added.) A line that just has a left hand side and does not have a value will delete

; the same line in unattend.txt.

;

;To make this section specific to a particular unique id, precede its name with id:.

;This allows specification of different sections in this file that map to the same

; section in unattend.txt. See below.

;

key1 = value

key2 = value

[id2:section2]

; This section is merged into [section2] in unattend.txt for unique id2.

;

key5 = value

The sections contained in the UDF are the same sections used in the unattend.txt file. A section's entries in the UDF are merged into the corresponding section in the unattend.txt file. The unique id referred to in the sample represents an id that you assign for each computer you are installing. By assigning a unique id to each section, you can create copies of the same section, each of which modifies the installation slightly from computer to computer. For example, the [UserData] section can provide a different user name and computer name for each subsequent computer installation by creating multiple copies of the [UserData] section, modifying each accordingly, and assigning each a different unique id correspondent to that computer.

Let's say that I am installing three computers. Each should have a unique computer name: ComputerA, ComputerB, and ComputerC. I will assign each computer a unique id: ID1, ID2, ID3. The attend.txt section that modifies the computer name is [UserData]. The UDF would then look like this:

ID1=[UserData]

ID2=[UserData]

ID3=[UserData]

Ch

3

```
[ID1:UserData]

Computername=ComputerA

[ID2:UserData]

Computername=ComputerB

[ID3:UserData]

Computername=ComputerC
```

Connect to the Distribution Server

The computers on which Windows NT Workstation 4.0 will be installed must be able to connect to and access the shared folder containing the installation, answer, and UDF files. This is generally accomplished by installing the DOS Network Client 3.0 software on the computer if there is no other means of connecting to the distribution server, such as through Windows for Workgroups network connectivity options, Windows 95, or an existing installation of Windows NT Workstation. Chapter 16, "MS Network Client Version 3.0 for MS-DOS," of the MS Windows NT 4.0 Server Resource Kit provides the steps for creating a network setup disk for your MS-DOS computers.

Once network connection has been established, a simple "net" command can be used at a command prompt to access the installation source files using the command syntax: net use d: \\distribution_server\ shared_folder. This net command maps a logical drive letter on your computer to the shared folder on the distribution server. Switching to that drive letter at a command prompt, or through File Manager or Windows Explorer will effectively point you to the files in the shared folder. For example, if the Windows NT Workstation 4.0 installation files have been installed in a shared folder called "INSTALL" on a distribution server called "SOURCE1," connect to the folder by typing the following command at a command prompt: net use E: \\SOURCE1\ INSTALL. The E: drive is now mapped to the Windows NT 4.0 source file directory on the distribution server.

Run Setup

The final step is to run Windows NT setup by referring to the source directory, answer files, and UDFs that you created. This is accomplished by using several of the boot switches that were outlined in Table 3.2 earlier in this chapter. After you map a drive to the shared folder containing the Windows NT Workstation 4.0 installation files on the distribution server, switch to that drive. At a command prompt, enter the following command syntax: **winnt /u:answer_filename / s:source_drive /UDF:ID[,UDF_filename]**.

For example, let's say I have created an answer file called unattend.txt that contains common setup information for my computers, as well as a uniqueness data file called unique.txt that contains specific setup in-structions for each computer. Each computer is identified by a unique id following the convention "ID1, ID2, and so on." At the first com-puter, corresponding to ID1, I would map a drive (E:, for example) to the distribution server. At a command prompt, I would enter the fol-lowing command: winnt /u:unattend.txt /s:e: /UDF:ID1[,unique.txt].

At the next computer, I would do the same thing, changing the ID reference to one appropriate to that computer, and so on until I have completed my installation.

Tip

The command to map the drive and the setup command can be placed together in a batch file along with any other batch commands you may want to include, such as disconnecting from the mapped drive. The batch file could be sent to users to run on their computers through e-mail, or through a package delivery system such as Microsoft's System Manage-ment Server, a BackOffice product.

Understanding the Windows NT Boot Process

The Windows NT 4.0 boot process, while a bit more complicated dur-ing the operating system load phase, is still pretty much like booting most any other operating system. There are five basic steps:

1. Power On Self Test (POST). This occurs with every computer when you first power it on. This is the BIOS check of installed hardware, interrupts, I/O, memory, and so on.

2. Next, the Master Boot Record (MBR) is read to determine which operating system (OS) will govern the boot process.

3. The OS system file recorded in the MBR is loaded, and the operating system is initialized, hardware is initialized, and drivers and configuration files are loaded.

4. The OS kernel is loaded.

5. Environment settings are initialized.

Windows NT 4.0 follows these same basic steps with some variation for steps 3, 4, and 5.

The Windows NT boot process has two primary phases: Boot and Load.

The *BOOT PHASE* consists of the pre-boot sequence during which the operating system is initialized, hardware is detected, and the Executive Services is loaded. When Windows NT is installed, it replaces the MS-DOS entries in the Master Boot Record with its own system file *NTLDR*. Along with NTLDR, the following boot files are read during the Boot Phase: BOOT.INI, NTDETECT.COM, NTOSKRNL.EXE, and NTBOOTDD.SYS (all some combination of the hidden, read only, and system file attributes and stored in the root directory of the boot partition), NTOSKRNL.EXE and HAL.DLL (stored in the Windows NT system directory), and the HKEY_LOCAL_MACHINE\ SYSTEM hive.

1. NTLDR loads a mini-OS and changes memory to a flat 32-bit model.

2. NTLDR next reads the BOOT.INI file to display the Operating System Menu on the screen.

3. If the user chooses "NT" or that is the default, NTLDR loads NTDETECT.COM. NTDETECT.COM determines what hardware is installed in the computer and uses this information to build the HKEY_LOCAL_MACHINE\HARDWARE hive.

If the system boots Windows NT from a SCSI drive whose SCSI adapter BIOS is disabled, NTLDR will load NTBOOTDD.SYS to initialize and access that device.

If the user chooses MS-DOS or Microsoft Windows (for Windows 95), NTLDR loads BOOTSECT.DOS, which records the boot sector location of the alternative OS system files and loads them. OS initialization then proceeds as normal for that OS.

4. NTLDR next loads NTOSKRNL.EXE, which initializes the Executive Services of the operating system. Think of this as Windows NT's COMMAND.COM.

5. NTLDR then loads the HAL.DLL and the SYSTEM hive and any drivers that need to initialize at boot time to continue the building of the Executive Services.

6. At this point, the screen displays progress dots across the top indicating the loading and initialization of drivers. At this time, the user is also prompted to press the spacebar to invoke the Last Known Good boot configuration. Control is passed to NTOSKRNL.EXE and the LOAD PHASE begins.

   During the *LOAD PHASE*, the rest of the kernel and user modes of the operating system are set up. The kernel is initialized, control sets information, Windows NT services are loaded, and the WIN32 subsystem starts.

7. The blue screen is displayed indicating the kernel is initializing, drivers are initialized, and the CurrentControlSet is created and copied to the CLONE control set.

8. The Services Load Phase begins with the starting of SMSS.EXE, the session manager. The session manager runs the programs listed in HKEY_LOCAL_MACHINE\SYSTEM\ CURRENTCONTROLSET\CONTROL\ SESSION MANAGER\BootExecute, usually AUTOCHK.EXE, which performs a CHKDSK of each partition. If a drive has been flagged to be converted to NTFS, this will also have been added to BootExecute and conversion takes place at this time as well.

Ch
3

Next, the pagefile is configured as defined in KEY_LOCAL_ MACHINE\SYSTEM\CURRENT CONTROLSET\ CONTROL\ SESSIONMANAGER\ MEMORY MAN- AGEMENT parameters.

Finally, the required subsystem defined in HKEY_LOCAL_MACHINE\SYSTEM\CURRENT CONTROLSET\CONTROL\ SESSIONMANAGER\ SUBSYSTEMS\REQUIRED is loaded. The only required subsystem at this time is WIN32.

9. With the loading of the WIN32 subsystem, WINLOGON. EXE, the service that governs the logon process, is loaded and started. WINLOGON in turn starts the Local Security Authority (LSASS.EXE), which displays the Ctrl+Alt+Del screen, and the Service Controller (SCREG.EXE), which starts services which are configured to start automatically such as Computer Browser, Workstation, and Server.

10. Finally, the user enters the username and password and logs in to the computer or domain. If the logon is successful, the CLONE control set is copied to Last Known Good. If the boot is not successful, the user can power off or shut down and choose Last Known Good to load the last values that resulted in a successful logon.

The Boot Process for RISC-Based Computers

The boot process for RISC-based computers is essentially the same. During the Boot Phase, the resident ROM firmware of the system selects the boot device from a preference table stored in RAM and controls the selection of the boot partition and the appropriate OS file. In this case, the firmware finds and loads OSLOADER.EXE, which is Windows NT's operating system file for RISC-based computers.

OSLOADER in turn finds and loads NTOSKRNL.EXE, HAL.DLL, .RAL files (for ALPHA systems) and the system hive, and the Load Phase continues as usual.

Note that because the computer's firmware controls the initialization of hardware and the selection of the boot partition, there is no need for the NTLDR, NTDETECT.COM, BOOT.INI, or BOOTSECT.DOS files on a RISC-based computer.

BOOT.INI

The BOOT.INI file is a read only, system, ASCII text file created by Windows NT during installation. It is stored in the root directory of the primary boot partition of the computer. It contains the information that Windows NT uses to display the Boot Menu when the computer is booted (see step 2 earlier). It is divided into two sections: Boot Loader and Operating System. The Boot Loader section contains the default operating system and timeout values, and the Operating System section displays operating system choices and the location of the system files. It can be modified using any ASCII text editor after first turning off the system and read only properties.

> **Note**   You can locate the BOOT.INI, using Windows Explorer, Windows Find, or My Computer. To change its properties, right-click on the file and choose Properties. Deselect Read-only and System. Be sure to re-select these attributes again when you have finished modifying the file. ▪

In the following example, we see that the default timeout value is 30 seconds. If the user does not make a selection during that time, the default operating system will be loaded. Notice that the unusual looking path to the WINNT40 directory matches a line under the Operating Systems section.

```
[Boot Loader]
Timeout=30
Default=multi(0)disk(0)rdisk(0)partition(4)\WINNT40
[Operating Systems]
multi(0)disk(0)rdisk(0)partition(4)\WINNT40="Windows NT
➡Workstation Version 4.00"
multi(0)disk(0)rdisk(0)partition(4)\WINNT40="Windows NT
➡Workstation Version 4.00 [VGA mode]"
   /basevideo /sos
C:\="Microsoft Windows"
```

That unusual looking path is called an *ARC path* (Advanced RISC Computer). The best way to think of an ARC path is as a hardware path. By now, everyone has used a DOS path. It indicates the drive and directory location of a specific file. An ARC path indicates the *physical* disk location of the Windows NT system files—the specific partition on a specific physical disk connected to a specific physical controller.

Ch
3

Referring to the example, the ARC path `multi(0)disk(0)rdisk(0)partition(4)\WINNT40` can be interpreted as follows:

The first value can be either *multi* or *scsi*. This really has no direct relation as to whether the controller is a SCSI controller. Windows NT will choose SCSI if the controller does *not* have its card BIOS enabled. Otherwise, the choice will be MULTI. The number that appears in parentheses is the ordinal number of the controller.

The next two values are *disk* and *rdisk*. If the first value choice was *SCSI*, then the *disk* number will represent the SCSI bus number and will be incremented accordingly (the physical disk attached to the card), and the *rdisk* value will be ignored. If the first value is *multi*, then the *disk* value will be ignored and the *rdisk* value representing the physical disk on the adapter will be incremented accordingly.

Next, the *partition* value indicates on which partition on the disk the directory *\WINNT40* can be found. Recall that this is the Windows NT system directory that you selected during installation.

So, putting it all together for our example, during boot, if the user lets the timeout value expire, or specifically selects Windows NT from the menu, Windows NT can find the Windows NT system files (specifically the location of the NTOSKRNL.EXE file) in the WINNT40 directory on the 4th partition of the first disk attached to the first controller in this computer. If the user selects "Microsoft Windows" from the menu, then NTLDR will load BOOTSECT.DOS and proceed to boot (in this case) Windows 95.

The Boot Menu

The Operating Systems section values are what build the boot menu that you see during startup. Each ARC path has a text menu selection associated with it that is enclosed in quotes. By default there are always two entries for Windows NT, and one for the other operating system, usually MS-DOS (C:\=M MS-DOS")or Windows 95 (C:\="Microsoft Windows"). The second entry for Windows NT represents a fall-back entry that loads Windows NT with a generic VGA driver. If you make changes to the display settings that make it difficult or impossible to read the screen, selecting this choice during startup ignores those settings and loads a generic VGA driver so that you can see the screen and rectify the problem. This is accomplished through the \basevideo switch that you see at the end of that line in the sample BOOT.INI file displayed in the last section.

Tip

Windows NT provides a variety of switched that can be added to these or additional Windows NT boot entries to modify the way Windows NT boots. For example, I might want to create another entry in my boot menu that displays all the driver files that are loaded during boot. I could copy the first line in the Operating Systems section to a new line, modify the text to read "Windows NT Workstation 4.0 Driver Load," and add the /SOS switch to the end of the line. Thus, if I was having trouble booting, or wasn't sure whether a particular driver was being found, I could select this choice and they would be displayed during the Load Phase (step 6 earlier).

Here is a table of the more practical boot switches that can be used in the Boot.ini file.

Table 3.4   Windows NT Boot Switches for BOOT.INI

Switch	Description
/Basevideo	Boots Windows NT with the standard VGA display driver in 640 by 480 resolution.
/SOS	Displays driver file names instead of progress dots during the Load Phase.
/Crashdebug	Used for troubleshooting, enables Automatic Recovery and Restart mode for the Windows NT boot process, and displays a system memory dump during the blue screen portion of the Load Phase.

continues

Ch
3

Table 3.4 Continued	
Switch	Description
/Maxmem:n	Specifies the maximum amount of RAM in megabytes that Windows NT will recognize and work with. This is helpful when you suspect a bad SIMM or memory chip and you are trying to pinpoint its location.

Understanding Control Sets and the Last Known Good Option

In the HKEY_LOCAL_MACHINE\System hive there are several control set subkeys. These are used by Windows NT to boot the system, keep track of configuration changes, and provide an audit trail of failed boot attempts. In general there are four control sets: Clone, ControlSet001, ControlSet002, and CurrentControlSet. There is also a subkey called Select whose parameter values point out which control set is being used for the current settings, default settings, failed settings, and Last Known Good settings. For example, if the value for Current is 0x1, the "1" indicates that CurrentControlSet is being derived from or mapped to ControlSet001.

Clone is used by Windows NT during the boot process (step 7 earlier) as a temporary storage area for the boot configuration. Settings from CurrentControlSet are copied into Clone during the Load Phase. When a user logon results in a successful boot, the configuration settings in Clone are copied to another control set such as ControlSet002 and is referred to as the Last Known Good. If the boot attempt is unsuccessful, these values are copied to a different control set number.

ControlSet001 is generally the default control set and produces the CurrentControlSet. As such, it also by default contains the Windows NT boot configuration.

ControlSet00x represents other control sets. The control set with the highest number increment is usually pointed to in the Select subkey as the Last Known Good configuration. Other control set numbers invariably refer to failed boot configurations.

CurrentControlSet is mapped back to ControlSet001. These settings are copied to Clone during the Load Phase of the boot process. Whenever an administrator makes a change to the configuration of the computer, such as modifying the virtual memory parameters, adding a new driver, or creating a hardware profile, those changes are saved to CurrentControlSet (and thus to ControlSet001 if that control set is set as the Default in the Select subkey).

Key Concept

So during the Load Phase, the settings in CurrentControlSet (derived from ControlSet001) are copied to Clone and used to determine service order, driver files to load, startup configurations, hardware profiles, and so on. If boot is successful (for example, logs in to Windows NT successfully) Clone is copied to the control set designated as the Last Known Good, say ControlSet002. If changes made by the administrator result in a failed boot attempt, the failed configuration in Clone is copied to ControlSet002, what used to be the Last Known Good control set becomes ControlSet003, and the user has the option of selecting to boot with the Last Known Good control set.

Ch
3

The Last Known Good control set contains the last boot configuration that resulted in a successful logon to the computer. The user is given the option to use Last Known Good when the Load Phase begins and the progress dots are displayed on the screen. The user has five seconds within which to press the spacebar to invoke the Last Known Good.

Caution

If the system itself detects a severe or critical device initialization or load error, it will display a message asking the user whether choosing Last Known Good might not be a good option. Users can choose to bypass this message, but do so at their own risk.

Tip
The Last Known Good helps to recover in the event of a failed boot. But remember that a failed boot is one in which a user cannot successfully log on to Windows NT. The user *may be able to* log on successfully and still have a system that fails to run correctly due to a configuration error. The Last Known Good will not be helpful in this situation because it is created as soon as the boot is successful (for example, you log on successfully).

Troubleshooting the Boot Process

The most common errors that you are likely to encounter during the boot process will be due to corrupt or missing boot files. Recall the boot files needed by Windows NT:

```
NTLDR
BOOT.INI
BOOTSECT.DOS
NTDETECT.COM
NTOSKRNL.EXE
```

If the NTLDR file is missing or corrupt, the following message will be displayed after the POST:

```
BOOT: Couldn't find NTLDR
Please insert another disk.
```

While there are a variety of reasons for this file to become missing or corrupt, the most common are viruses that attack the MBR (Master Boot Record), and a user inadvertently reinstalling MS-DOS onto the computer. If the problem involves a virus, use a virus protection program to restore the MBR. If this is unsuccessful, you can use the Emergency Repair Disk to reestablish NTLDR in the MBR. The worst case will be to reinstall Windows NT from scratch—which you should try to avoid.

If the problem involves a user reinstalling MS-DOS, or "sys-ing" the hard drive, again, use the Emergency Repair Disk to reestablish the NTLDR. The worst case, again will be to reinstall Windows NT.

If BOOT.INI is missing or corrupt, Windows NT will look for the default Windows NT system directory name (usually WINNT) on the boot partition. If Windows NT is installed in a directory other than the default name, or if Windows NT cannot locate it, the following message is displayed after the prompt for Last Known Good:

```
Windows NT could not start because the following file is
missing or corrupt:
\winnt root\system32\ntoskrnl.exe
Please reinstall a copy of the above file.
```

If the ARC path to the Windows NT system file directory is incorrect in the Boot.ini file NTLDR may display this message:

```
Windows NT could not start because of a computer disk hardware
configuration problem. Could not read from the selected boot
disk. Check boot path and disk hardware. Please check Windows
NT (TM) documentation about hardware disk configuration and
your hardware reference manuals for additional information.
```

Incorrect paths are relatively easy to fix. Because BOOT.INI is a text file, turn off its System and Read Only attributes and edit the ARC path using your favorite text editor.

> **Caution**
>
> The ARC path indicated in the Default parameter in the Boot Loader section of the BOOT.INI *must match* an ARC path for a parameter under Operating Systems section. If it does not, the menu will display a phantom selection option called "NT (default)," which may result in the same error message discussed for a missing Boot.ini file.

If BOOTSECT.DOS is missing, NTLDR displays this error message when the user tries to select the other operating system from the boot menu:

```
I/O Error accessing boot sector file
multi(0)disk(0)rdisk(0)partition(1):\bootsect.dos
```

Because this file is unique to each computer, the best way to recover it would be to restore it from that backup you create regularly (!), or use the Emergency Repair Disk.

If NTDETECT.COM is missing or corrupt, expect the following message after the user selects Windows NT from the boot menu, or the menu times out to Windows NT:

Ch

3

```
NTDETECT v1.0 Checking Hardware...
NTDETECT v1.0 Checking Hardware...
```

Again, recover using the Emergency Repair Disk or from a backup.

If NTOSKRNL.EXE is missing or corrupt, NTLDR displays this message after the prompt for Last Known Good:

```
Windows NT could not start because the following file is
missing or corrupt:
\winnt root\system32\ntoskrnl.exe
Please reinstall a copy of the above file.
```

As before, this file can be recovered using the Emergency Repair Disk, or from a file backup.

The Emergency Repair Disk

The Emergency Repair Disk is usually created during the Windows NT installation process (see Chapter 3, "Installing Windows NT Workstation 4.0"). However, it can be created (and updated) at any time by running the Windows NT command RDISK.EXE at a Windows NT DOS prompt.

To use the Emergency Repair disk you must first boot the computer using a Windows NT Startup disk.

Tip

If you do not have one, but have access to the original installation files, you can create one by typing the command: WINNT /O. Be sure to have three disks available.

From the Startup menu, choose <u>R</u>epair. The repair process offers four options:

1. *Inspect Registry Files.* This option prompts the user for replacement of each Registry file, including System and SAM.

Caution

The files on the Emergency Repair Disk overwrite the files in the Registry. For this reason, this is *not* the best way to recover damaged security or account information. A backup will be much more useful in maintaining the integrity of existing account entries.

2. *Inspect Startup Environment.* This option checks the BOOT.INI file for an entry for Windows NT. If it doesn't find one, it adds one for the next boot attempt.

3. *Verify Windows NT System Files.* This option verifies whether the Windows NT system files match those of the original installation files. For this option you will need to have access to the original installation files. This option also looks for and verifies the integrity of the boot files.

Tip

If you updated Windows NT with a service pack, you will need to reinstall the service pack after initiating a repair.

Ch
3

4. *Inspect Boot Sector.* This option checks the MBR for NTLDR. If it is missing or corrupt, it will restore the boot sector.

If you know specifically which file is missing or corrupt, you can replace the file directly from the source files using the Windows NT EXPAND utility. At a Windows NT prompt type **EXPAND -R** followed by the compressed file name. If Windows NT is inoperable on your system, use another Windows NT system to expand the file and then copy it to your computer.

Windows NT Boot Disk

Another useful tool to have in your toolkit is a Windows NT boot disk. This is not a diskette formatted with NTFS. Rather, it is a disk that has been formatted under Windows NT that has copies of the boot files on it.

When you format a diskette under Windows NT, Windows NT creates a boot sector on that disk that references NTLDR. Simply copy the five boot files to this disk and *voilà*, you have a Windows NT boot disk. This disk can be used in a variety of Windows NT computers because it is not unique to each installation. The only file you may need to modify for obvious reasons is the BOOT.INI file. This makes it much easier to replace missing or corrupt boot files.

Tip
You can format a disk from My Computer. Right-click the A: Drive icon and select *F*ormat. Make the appropriate selections and choose OK.

Uninstalling Windows NT Workstation 4.0

It is possible that you may encounter a need to uninstall Windows NT Workstation 4.0 from your computer. For example, if you were testing it and the evaluation period has completed, if you want to install a different operating system entirely, or if you want to change the computer from a Windows NT Workstation 4.0 to a Windows NT 4.0 Server. The steps required to remove Windows NT Workstation 4.0 from your computer depend on the file system your computer uses when booting.

FAT Partition

If you dual boot between MS-DOS or Windows 95 and Windows NT Workstation 4.0, then your system partition is using the FAT file system. You can remove Windows NT Workstation 4.0 and restore the bootup operating system back to what it was before (MS-DOS or Windows 95).

1. Boot your computer to start either MS-DOS or Windows 95.
2. Create a boot disk, also called a system disk.
    a) Place an unformatted disk in the A: drive of your computer.
    b) At a DOS prompt enter the command: **FORMAT A: /S**. This command transfers the MS-DOS or Windows 95 system files used for booting to the disk.
    c) Answer Yes to the prompt and proceed.
3. Copy the SYS.COM file from the DOS directory on your computer to the disk you just formatted.

4. Reboot your computer from the system disk you just created by leaving it in the A: drive and restarting your computer.

5. At the A: prompt, enter the command: **SYS C:**. This command will transfer the MS-DOS or Windows 95 system files from the system disk to the master boot record of the computer.

6. Remove the system disk from the A: drive and restart the computer. The computer should now boot directly to MS-DOS or Windows 95 and no longer display the Windows NT boot menu.

7. Remove the Windows NT-related files from the hard disk.

    a) C:\pagefile.sys (this file may be located on a different partition if Windows NT was installed in a different partition)

    b) C:\boot.ini (marked with the attributes system and read-only)

    c) C:\nt*.* (marked with the attributes hidden, system, and read-only—these files include ntldr, ntdetect.com, and possibly ntbootdd.sys)

    d) C:\bootsect.dos (marked with the attributes hidden and system)

    e) \winnt system file folder (found on whichever partition you installed Windows NT Workstation 4.0)

    f) \program files\Windows NT (found on whichever partition you installed Windows NT Workstation 4.0)

Ch
3

NTFS Partition

If you chose to install Windows NT in the system partition and formatted the partition to use the NTFS file system, you do not have a dual-boot system. Subsequently, you cannot boot to either MS-DOS or Windows 95 as they require a FAT partition to boot. In this case, you must essentially remove the partition to remove Windows NT Workstation 4.0. You can use the MS-DOS FDISK utility from MS-DOS versions 6.0 and higher to remove the partition and repartition it for MS-DOS, or you can use the Windows NT Setup program to remove the NTFS partition.

Using FDISK

1. Create a system disk from an MS-DOS or Windows 95-based computer. (See the steps outlined in the previous section "FAT Partition.")

2. Copy the file fdisk.exe from the DOS directory on that computer to the system disk.

3. Boot the Windows NT Workstation 4.0 from the system disk by placing it in the A: drive and then restarting the computer.

4. At the A: prompt, enter the command: **FDISK**.

5. Choose option 3   Delete Partition or Logical DOS Drive from the FDISK menu.

6. Choose option 4—Delete Non-DOS Partition from the Delete Partition menu.

7. Select the partition number of the partition you want to delete. This will likely be partition number 1.

8. Confirm your intent to delete the partition.

Using Windows NT 4.0 Setup

1. Restart the computer with the Windows NT startup disk in the A: drive. (Refer to the section titled "Executing the Windows NT Workstation 4.0 Setup Process—Beginning Setup," as well as Table 3.2 for information about using and creating a startup disk.)

2. Proceed through setup to the screen prompting you to choose or create a partition.

3. Select the NTFS partition that you wish to delete.

4. Press **D** on the keyboard to delete the partition.

5. Press F3 to exit Windows NT setup and the partition will be deleted.

There are other utilities which can also be used to delete the NTFS partition. The Windows NT and Windows' Resource Kits include a utility called DELPART which can be used to remove partitions. Partition Magic™ manufactured by Power Quest and Norton Utilities for Windows NT™ manufactured by Symantec also provide partition management utilities which provide options for deleting NTFS partitions.

Upgrading to Windows NT Workstation 4.0

In this section we will discuss some of the considerations for upgrading existing versions of Windows and Windows NT Workstation to Windows NT Workstation 4.0.

Windows NT Workstation

When upgrading from earlier versions of Windows NT Workstation, setup will migrate all account information, network settings, and most other registry settings. It will migrate environment settings to the extent that the new interface supports them. By this I mean that color sets, cursors schemes, and the like will be migrated. Program Manager settings will not because Program Manager does not exist in the new interface. Program Groups will appear under the Programs selection on the Start menu.

If you choose to install Windows NT Workstation 4.0 in a new directory, you are in effect installing a new version of Windows NT on your computer. Consequently, previous settings, account information, and so on will not be migrated. Also, if this installation of Windows NT will participate in the same workgroup or domain as the current installation, and you plan to switch between them, you must assign a new, unique computer name for this installation and create a separate computer account for the installation in the domain.

Windows 95

Recall that the Windows NT Workstation 4.0 setup program does not allow you to upgrade over Windows 95. Therefore, there will be no automatic migration of settings from Windows 95 to Windows NT Workstation 4.0. You must reinstall applications and reset environment settings after installation is complete.

Windows 3.1 and Windows for Workgroups 3.11

Just as we saw with Windows NT Workstation, during the installation process, the Windows NT 4.0 setup program will detect an earlier version of Windows and offer to upgrade it by installing it in the existing Windows directory. If you choose to do so, you will be able to boot to DOS and run Windows or boot to Windows NT and run Windows NT with most of the same settings.

When Windows NT boots and displays the Welcome screen for the first time after installation, it will automatically migrate existing program groups other than those that have a Windows NT counterpart such as MAIN, ACCESSORIES, and GAMES. The program groups will appear under Programs on the Start menu. In addition, Windows NT will migrate Startup Group programs, file associations and OLE information from the Windows Registry (REG.DAT), application settings, and any WIN.INI, SYSTEM.INI, and CONTROL.INI parameter values that do not conflict with similar or changed settings contained in the Windows NT Workstation 4.0 Registry.

When a user (not the Administrator account) logs on to Windows NT Workstation for the first time, Windows NT will automatically migrate those user environment settings which do not conflict with the new Windows NT 4.0 interface. For example, the user's color schemes, wallpaper, and mouse setup would be migrated, desktop arrangement of program groups would not.

Persistent network connections are not migrated. Persistent connections are network mappings that the user created through File Manager or at the command prompt that, by default, are saved in the WIN.INI file. Windows NT 4.0 creates and saves these connections differently. If you do have existing drive connections that you want to preserve, you should note those and reestablish them under Windows NT. Default domain names and user names from Windows for Workgroups are also not migrated.

If you choose to install Windows NT 4.0 in its own directory, no Windows settings will be migrated. However, you can manually cause

Windows NT to migrate the Windows settings as described above. Simply copy the INI and GRP files from the Windows root directory into the Windows NT root directory (by default called \WINNT). When Windows NT is next booted and a user logs on, the migration process will occur as outlined earlier.

If for some reason migration does not take place, or you need to execute the migration process again, you will need to make a modification to the Windows NT Registry. Working with the Registry is covered in Chapter 5, "Configuration and the Registry." Briefly, you will need to find the Registry key \HKEY_CURRENT_USER\Windows Migration Status and remove it. Then restart Windows NT and migration should proceed as before.

From Here...

This chapter discussed in some detail the installation and setup process for Windows NT Workstation 4.0. Now that we have it installed, we need to become familiar with the new Windows 95 Interface. Those of you who are already Windows 95 literate will have no trouble adjusting to Windows NT Workstation 4.0. Those of you coming from a Program Manager background will want to spend a little more time playing with the new interface to find all your favorite utilities, explore the enhancements that the new interface brings to the desktop, and perhaps play the new pinball game.

The next two chapters, entitled "An Overview of the Windows NT 4.0 Interface" and "Configuration and the Registry," are designed to help you become familiar with the new interface and explore how to modify the configuration.

Taking the Disc Test

If you have read and understood the material in the chapter, you are ready to test your knowledge. Insert the CD-ROM that comes with this book and run the self-test software as described in Appendix I, "Using the CD-ROM."

4

An Overview of the Windows NT 4.0 Interface

In this chapter, we will review the new Windows NT 4.0 user interface. This interface incorporates the Windows 95 object-oriented look and feel into Windows NT 4.0's 32-bit architecture. This chapter is not designed to detail the Windows NT look and feel to the reader. It will, however, provide an overview of the interface, particularly as it applies to Windows NT 4.0 utilities, configuration, and so on, which will be more than sufficient knowledge to pass the exam. The following topics will be addressed:

◆ The Logon/Logoff process

◆ The desktop, new icons and concepts such as what happened to File Manager, and how to launch programs

◆ Taskbar, Network Neighborhood, Recycle Bin, Briefcase, and My Computer

◆ Windows Explorer and how to use it to navigate your computer

◆ Windows NT Help program and how to use it to your best advantage

Logging On to Windows NT Workstation 4.0

Before we can begin a discussion of the new Windows NT 4.0 user interface, we need to log on to Windows NT 4.0. The logon process really hasn't changed from previous versions of Windows NT. When Windows NT is booted, you are presented with an animated Begin Logon dialog box encouraging you to press Ctrl+Alt+Del to log on.

Pressing Ctrl+Alt+Del is really the first Windows NT security function. Traditionally, this sequence terminated all open applications and rebooted your MS-DOS computer. Similarly, the same sequence at this point of the logon process sends a terminate interrupt to the processor. It is designed, however, to terminate any "stealth" program that might record your user name and password and otherwise breach logon security.

After pressing Ctrl+Alt+Del, Windows NT displays the Logon Information dialog box. You are prompted to enter a valid user name and password and then click OK. This dialog box also features a Shutdown button allowing you to shut your computer down at this point without logging on.

Note It is interesting to note that while this button appears in the Logon Information dialog box on Windows NT Workstation computers, it does **not** appear in the same window on an installation of Windows NT Server. This should make good sense because while it can be a convenience for the user not to have to wait for the logon process to complete before the system can be shut down, it would not be advisable for just *anyone* to be able to do the same for a network server. ▨

At this point, you can log on either with the Administrator account that you created, or with the user account created during installation. After the Windows NT Security Subsystem authenticates your account, the Windows NT 4.0 desktop will appear. On top of the desktop, Windows NT will display its Welcome dialog box (see Figure 4.1).

FIG. 4.1 ⟹

You'll see this Welcome screen when you first start Windows NT Workstation 4.0.

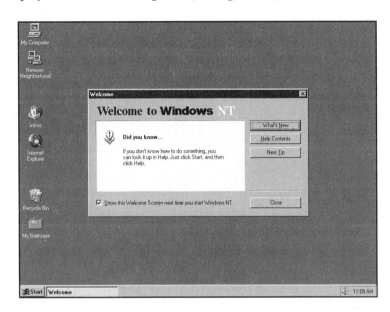

Ch

4

From the Welcome dialog box you can choose to get a quick overview of the new features of the desktop and how to get around, open the Windows NT Help program, or display a Windows NT working tip. The Welcome dialog box is displayed each time you log on. This dialog can be configured to **not** display by deselecting the check box in its lower-left corner. The dialog box can always be reopened through the Help program using the following steps:

1. Select Start, Help from the taskbar.
2. Select the Contents tab in the Help dialog box.
3. Open the topic Tips and Tricks.
4. Open the subtopic Tips of the Day.
5. Open the document Viewing the Welcome Screen.
6. Follow the instructions to reopen the Welcome Screen.

Among the first things you will notice about the desktop is the Start button on the taskbar in the lower-left corner of the screen. This is the point of origin for all your installed applications and utilities. You will also notice some default objects along the left side of your screen. We will discuss all this in more detail in just a moment. First, now that we have logged on to Windows NT, we also need to know how to log off properly.

As in previous versions of Windows NT, as well as Windows 95 and Windows, it is very important that you exit the operating system in the appropriate manner. This means performing a proper shutdown of your system before powering off the computer. A proper shutdown closes all open applications, writes cached information to the disk, closes all system files, stops all services, and notifies the network that you are coming offline. Unfortunately, many users have developed the bad habit of simply powering off the computer when they are finished. That may have had minimal consequences on the Windows-based systems, but is far more serious on a Windows NT-based computer. Improperly shutting down your Windows NT workstation may be result in a mildly annoying loss of data files to a more serious corruption of system files resulting in a failed attempt to reboot Windows NT.

The proper steps for shutting down your Windows NT Workstation 4.0 are as follows:

1. Click the Start button on the taskbar

2. From the Start menu that appears, choose the last menu option, Shut Down. A dialog box appears with three options:

   - Choose Shut Down the Computer to prepare Windows NT for being powered off. An orderly shut down will occur, and Windows NT will display a message asking whether you wish to restart your computer when shutdown is complete. If your computer supports power management, Windows NT may also be enabled to power off the computer when shutdown completes.

   - Choose Restart the Computer to reboot the computer after shutdown is complete. This performs a warm boot of the computer.

- Choose <u>C</u>lose All Programs and Log On as a Different User to close down open applications and save data, log off the current user, and display the Begin Logon dialog box for the next user.

3. Choose the appropriate option from the list and click Yes or press Enter on the keyboard.

Windows NT Security Dialog Box

Another option for shutting down or logging off your system is the Windows NT Security dialog box. It can be accessed by pressing Ctrl+Alt+Del on your keyboard. From this dialog box, you can shut down the system, log off, change your password (provided you know the original), access the Task Manager, and lock the workstation. Locking the workstation password protects the screen so that only the user who locked it, or an administrator can unlock the desktop.

Exploring the Windows NT 4.0 Desktop

Responding to the suggestions and needs of its Windows NT clients, Microsoft has incorporated the Windows 95 interface into the default desktop of Windows NT 4.0. This makes it easier to use, customize, and manage than the Program Manager interface. The desktop consists of two basic elements: objects and the taskbar.

Objects

Objects provide the user with a unified way of dealing with icons on the screen. Objects include files, folders, programs, printers, modems, and so on. All objects have properties, settings, and parameters that can be accessed with a right-mouse click. These settings and parameters are displayed in a properties sheet and will vary depending on the type of object and the program it is accessing.

The sample properties sheet in Figure 4.2 was displayed by selecting a folder, pressing the right mouse button, and choosing <u>P</u>roperties from the menu. This one shows us the name of the folder (read: directory), its location, its size and contents, when it was created, and any attributes that have been assigned to it. The sharing tab displays a second page that lets us share the folder with other members of the workgroup or domain that your computer might participate in. The concept and process of sharing is covered in much detail in Chapter 7, "Windows NT 4.0 Security Model."

FIG. 4.2 ⇒

Sample Properties sheet.

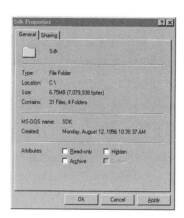

Taskbar

The Windows NT taskbar appears by default on the bottom of the desktop screen. It consists of the Start button at the far left and clock at the far right. The taskbar also acts as your task manager by maintaining a row of open program titles. This makes moving from one window to another as easy as a click of the mouse on the taskbar and eliminates the need for resizing, tiling, or cascading your open applications into a confusing array of windows. It also minimizes the possibility of opening multiple versions of the same application. A quick scan of the taskbar can confirm that a program is already running, and a quick mouse click will take you there. Alt+Tab is still available to task switch between programs as well. Also, a right-click on the taskbar will display a pop-up from which you can select Task Manager and switch between programs.

The taskbar is also an object and as such has properties. Right-clicking the taskbar displays a menu which looks a lot like the Program Manager menu option <u>W</u>indow. From here, you can cascade, tile (horizontally or vertically), and minimize all windows, as well as access the new Windows NT Task Manager and the properties sheet.

Taskbar Properties

The taskbar properties sheet has two tabs (see Figure 4.3). The first, Taskbar Options, allows control over how the taskbar appears on the screen.

FIG. 4.3 ⇒

Right-clicking the taskbar displays its properties sheet.

Option choices are outlined in Table 4.1.

Table 4.1   Taskbar Options

Selection	Description
Always on <u>T</u>op	Default. Always displays the taskbar on the desktop regardless of whether a window is maximized.
A<u>u</u>to Hide	Hides the taskbar so as not to detract from the desktop real estate. Taskbar reappears when the cursor is moved over last location of taskbar.
Show Small <u>I</u>cons in Start Menu	Displays a smaller version of Smart menu icons useful for lower resolution screens.
Show <u>C</u>lock	Default. Toggles the taskbar clock on and off.

The second tab of the taskbar Properties dialog box called *Start Menu Programs* offers a means of customizing the Start Menu itself (see Figure 4.4). For example, you could place your favorite program directly on the Start Menu so that you would not have to browse through several other folders to find it.

FIG. 4.4 ⇒

You can customize the Start menu from the taskbar properties sheet by selecting the Start Menu Programs tab.

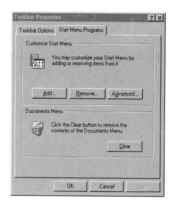

1. From the Start Menu Programs tab choose <u>A</u>dd. This displays a wizard for changing the Start Menu.

2. Either type in the path and file name of the application you want to add, or browse for it by clicking the B<u>r</u>owse button (see Figure 4.5). This is called a shortcut because it represents the file location, not the actual file. Then click <u>N</u>ext.

FIG. 4.5 ⇒

The Add Program Wizard makes it easy to add a program to the Start menu. First, tell it what you want to add.

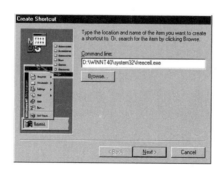

3. The next screen of the wizard prompts you to select the folder in which you'll add the shortcut (see Figure 4.6). You can click the Start Menu itself, any folder within the Start Menu, create a

new folder for the shortcut with the New Folder button, or even choose to place the shortcut on the desktop. Make your choice and click Next.

4. Enter a name for the shortcut (see Figure 4.7).

FIG. 4.6 ⟹
Next, tell the wizard where you want to add it.

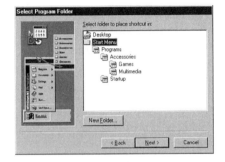

FIG. 4.7 ⟹
Finally, tell the wizard what you want to call the program (called a shortcut).

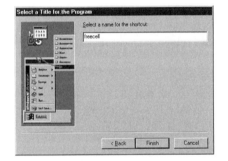

5. Choose Finish, and then OK. Click Start, Menu on the taskbar and see your new shortcut.

The taskbar itself can be dragged to any side of the screen. Just click and drag it with the mouse to the sides, top, or bottom of the screen to change its position.

Starting Programs

All programs can be accessed through the Start menu on the taskbar. The Start menu effectively replaces the Program Manager for application access.

Ch

4

Where Is My Favorite Windows Program?

If you are new to this interface, but a long-time Windows user, you will probably be initially flustered by not being able to find your favorite programs or utilities. The two most obvious examples are Program Manager and File Manager. These have been replaced by leaner, meaner utilities. However, to ease you into the transition over to Windows NT's new interface, you can still run these two old favorites by clicking Start and then choosing Run. Enter **Progman.exe** or **Winfile.exe** to start Program Manager and File Manager, respectively. This requires additional resource management on Windows NT's part, so use this only as long as it takes for you to get used to Windows NT's alternatives.

Use Table 4.2 to help you find your way:

Table 4.2 Where Is It?

Program Manager	Choose Start on the taskbar.
File Manager	Choose the Windows Explorer.
DOS Prompt	Choose Start, then Programs, then MS-DOS Prompt.
Control Panel	Choose Start, then Settings.
Print Manager	Choose Start, then Settings.
File\Run	Choose Start, then Run.
Task Switching	Click the application title on the taskbar that you wish to switch to, or right-click the taskbar and choose Task Manager.

When you click the Start Menu, Windows NT displays a menu of choices for finding and running programs (see Figure 4.8).

Programs

Programs (see Figure 4.9) displays a list of programs and program folders including *Accessories*, the *Startup* folder, the *Command Prompt*, and the *Windows NT Explorer*. Any new program groups created as a result of installing an application or migrating from previous Windows versions

will also be displayed here. The Games folder can be found under
Applications. On the lower portion of this menu you will find the
Windows NT *Administrative Tools* group.

FIG. 4.8 ⇒

The Start menu
substitutes for Pro-
gram Manager and
is used for launch-
ing your Windows
NT applications.

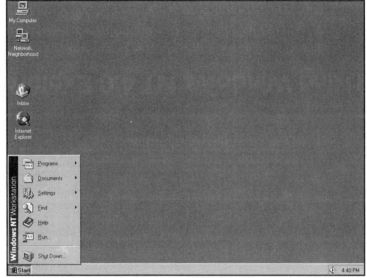

FIG. 4.9 ⇒

Use Programs
on the Start Menu
to open the major-
ity of your
Windows NT
applications.

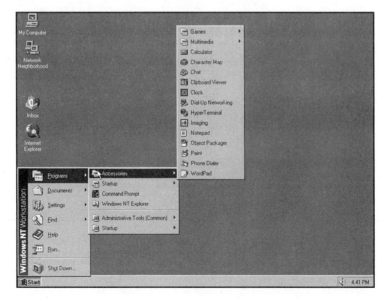

Ch

4

Documents

Documents displays the last 15 documents that were opened. This provides an efficient and productive way to get started quickly.

Settings

Settings offers access to configuration utilities through Control Panel and Printers, as well as another way to change the properties of the taskbar (see Figure 4.10).

FIG. 4.10 ⇒

Select Settings from the Start menu to access Control Panel, Printers, and Taskbar.

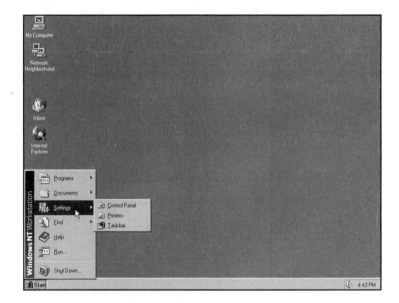

Find

This new utility allows you to search the computer for files and folders, as well as the network for shared computers. This find utility will also search for text contained within documents providing a truly robust search utility for Windows NT 4.0. We will discuss this utility in more detail later in this chapter.

Help

This menu choice starts the Windows NT Help program. Windows NT 4.0 Help has been greatly enhanced making an already helpful program even better. Help can always be accessed by pressing F1 on the keyboard, or clicking the numerous Help buttons that now show up in almost every dialog box. Help is now also linked directly to many dialog boxes so that when you find help on a certain topic, you can click a button and have Windows NT display the appropriate dialog box for you to fill in *while you are reading the Help information.* A thorough discussion of how to use this program will follow later in this chapter.

Run

Run takes the place of Program Manager and File Manager's File\Run menu option. When you select Run, Windows NT displays a text box in which you may enter the path and name of the program you wish to execute (see Figure 4.11). There is also a Browse button that lets you look for the program.

FIG. 4.11 ⇒

The Run box allows you to enter the path and name of a program you want to execute.

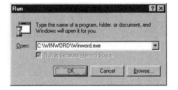

Shut Down

Finally, *Shut Down*, as we have seen earlier, provides the appropriate way to shut down the computer or log off.

Shortcuts

Another way to customize your desktop is to create a shortcut to an application or file and place it on your desktop to facilitate access and loading. Moving a file actually changes its location and file pointer in Windows NT. Copying a file creates another file object—twice the space. A shortcut is simply a pointer to the file. The shortcut is given a file name of Shortc~x.lnk where x represents the number of this shortcut, for example, 1st, 2nd, and so on. It is stored in the WINNT40\ Profiles\Username\Desktop folder, Username being the login name of the user who created the shortcut.

To create a shortcut:

1. Find the application or file using My Computer, or the Windows Explorer.

2. Right-click its icon and drag it to the desktop. Windows NT will respond with a menu of choices:

> Move Here
>
> Copy Here
>
> Create Shortcut(s) Here

3. Choose Create Shortcut(s) Here. Windows NT will create a shortcut object on the desktop that you can use to access the file or application directly.

My Computer

No, this is not what your child might cry out when you need to bump them off of their favorite dinosaur program. Well, maybe it is, but what I am referring to here is one of the new default objects that you see on your desktop.

This icon displays all resources that are available on your computer (see Figure 4.12) and in a way resembles File Manager in the way you can drill down through folders to find what you want. You can also switch to a directory as shown in the figure. Note that in addition to directories, folders can also represent printers, Control Panel, network members, and so on.

FIG. 4.12 ⇒

Selecting My Computer opens a window that shows three drives: A:, C:, D:, and icons to open Dial-Up Networking, Control Panel, and Printers.

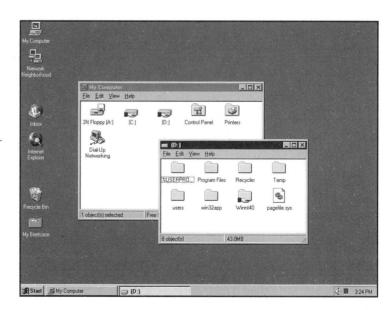

You can see at a glance each drive, including CD-ROM, any network drive mappings, as well as access Control Panel and Printers for configuring Windows NT.

The windows opened through My Computer also feature a menu bar with File (from which you can create new folders and shortcuts), Edit (for copy, paste, and undo operations), View (to modify the window display, arrange icons, and refresh the screen) and Help options.

Network Neighborhood

This icon represents access to the network in which your computer participates. This might include members of a workgroup, domain, or enterprise (see Figure 4.13). As with My Computer, clicking the various icons in each window will take you further into the network relationship that your computer is a part of. This makes it relatively easy to navigate through the enterprise. In addition to the usual File, Edit, View, and Help menu options, right-clicking a computer's shared resource will give you the option to either map a network drive to that resource or create a shortcut for that resource on the desktop.

Ch

4

FIG. 4.13 ⇒

Selecting Network Neighborhood opens a window that displays your network at a glance. In this example, you can see that this computer is using Microsoft's networking and is a member of a workgroup called Studygroup.

Opening up the properties screen of Network Neighborhood actually displays the Network dialog box from Control Panel. We will explore that utility program in more detail in Chapter 11, "Network Connectivity and Remote Support." You will find that there are often multiple ways of viewing properties screens.

Recycle Bin

The *Recycle Bin* provides a handy way of dealing with deleted files. When a file is deleted through the interface, for example, through Windows Explorer, it is placed in the Recycle Bin (see Figure 4.14). If you need to recover the file for any reason, open the Recycle Bin, select the file(s) to recover, choose Eile from the menu, and then Recover.

FIG. 4.14 ⇒

This example of opening Recycle Bin shows many files have been deleted but not yet purged from the computer's hard disk.

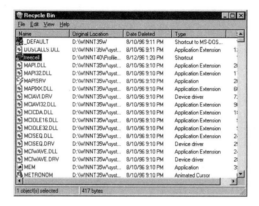

The File menu choice also offers an option to clear out the Recycle Bin or delete selected files. This in effect purges the files and makes the disk space formerly occupied by the files immediately available to the system.

FIG. 4.15 ⇒

The Recycle Bin's properties sheet on this computer shows that it is using the default 10% of the hard disk for storing deleted files.

A quick look at the properties of the Recycle Bin (see Figure 4.15) shows us that by default, Windows NT reserves 10% of the hard disk space on all or selected drives for storage of deleted files. Once this space fills up, the oldest files are automatically purged to make room for newer files. While this happens automatically, you may want more control over how much disk storage is reserved, and just when the files are purged. Modifying these properties and regularly maintaining the Recycle Bin provide that control.

My Briefcase

My Briefcase is a unique utility designed primarily for laptop use, but adaptable for the desktop computer as well. It allows you to take copies of files with you on the laptop or on disk and work on them in another location or while on the road. When you return to your office computer, or dock your laptop, My Briefcase can synchronize the files you worked on while away with the files located on the desktop computer (or on the office network, and so on) by overwriting the original files with the changes you made to the copies. Thus, you need not concern yourself with which copy is the most recent, as it will keep track of versions by modification date.

As you can see from Figure 4.16, it is relatively easy to set up and use My Briefcase.

Ch
4

FIG. 4.16 ⇒

This example shows both the Welcome screen and the contents window that displays when opening My Briefcase.

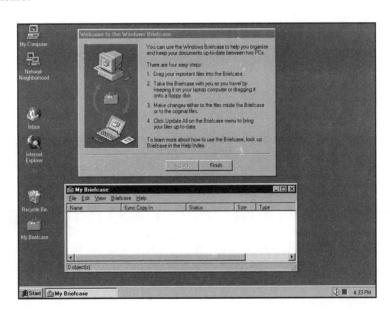

Steps for Using Up My Briefcase

1. Drag the files you want into the briefcase.

2. Keep it on your laptop, or drag the entire briefcase to a disk.

3. Work with either set of files.

4. Update all or selected files by opening My Briefcase, choosing Briefcase from the menu, and then Update All or Update Selection.

Note When you copy a file into My Briefcase, you are creating a separate file rather than a shortcut. A 2M file will require 2M storage space. Consequently, all files may not fit on a floppy disk. Check your storage space before using My Briefcase. ▪

Other Icons

Depending on the additional Windows NT 4.0 services or programs that you install, additional icons may be displayed on the desktop. For example, if the Microsoft Exchange client is installed, Windows NT will add an inbox and Exchange icon to your screen. If you have added the Internet Explorer, an icon for that utility will also be installed. If you choose to set up The Microsoft Network, you will see an icon for that program also.

Of course, you can add your own shortcut icons to the screen to more effectively customize your environment and keep you most productive. For example, you could create a shortcut for your printer, and shortcuts for the documents you work on frequently. When you need to print a document, you need only drag the document shortcut onto the printer shortcut to start the print process.

Using Windows NT 4.0 Explorer

The *Windows NT Explorer* is the closest utility in look and function to Windows File Manager. It is the primary navigation tool for your system. When you open an object such as My Computer, Windows NT displays a window with the contents of My Computer. As you open an icon in this window, another window opens, and then another, and…well, it can get messy, not to mention confusing, to have all those windows open on the desktop—and then have to close them all. My Computer and Network Neighborhood do have the option of replacing each previous window with the succeeding window. However, then you lose the path back from where you came.

Changing the Open Window Option for My Computer and Network Neighborhood

When you open My Computer and Network Neighborhood, Windows NT displays a window with the contents of the object. When you open one of the contents objects, another window opens, and so on. This can fill your desktop quickly with multiple windows and make it harder to find your way around.

These two objects have a view option which will replace each open window with a new window as you open each icon. You can set this option as follows:

1. Open My Computer (or Network Neighborhood).
2. Choose View, then Options.
3. On the folder tab, select the radio button option: Browse Folders By Using a Single Window that Changes as You Open Each Folder.
4. Choose OK.

If you set this option for either object, it will take effect for both.

Other View options include the ability to hide certain file types, display file extensions, display compressed files, and add, remove, or modify the settings of file types.

Ch
4

Windows Explorer, like File Manager, lets you drill down through drives, folders, and so on. The left pane of the window displays the object's folders and files. As each folder is selected here, the right pane displays the contents of the folder.

You can use Windows Explorer to browse your desktop, drives, CD-ROM, Recycle Bin, and Network Neighborhood as shown in Figure 4.17. In addition, Windows Explorer includes all your network connections and shared resources. You can browse these as well, all from the same interface. So, think of Windows Explorer not as a replacement for File Manager, but more like File Manager Deluxe!

You can start Windows Explorer by clicking Start, selecting Programs, and then choosing Windows Explorer. This will open Explorer for the entire desktop. However, you could also right-click a desktop object such as Network Neighborhood or My Computer and choose Explore. This will open Windows Explorer and set the focus on that particular object.

FIG. 4.17 ⇒

When Windows NT Explorer was started on this computer, the default directory focus was on the D: drive, so that drive is expanded. Note that besides files and directories, you can also see desktop objects such as Network Neighborhood and disk drives.

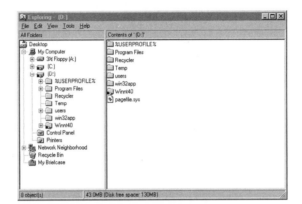

Quick Tour of the Windows Explorer Menu

Windows Explorer is easily used and configured by selecting the appropriate option from its menu.

File

Use options from the File menu to create new folders or shortcuts (and other objects), delete or rename folders and files, and to look at or modify the properties of an object.

Edit

Use Edit options to cut, copy, or paste folders and files and to make selections.

View

View provides most of the configuration options for Windows Explorer. Use View to display a toolbar to help you navigate Explorer and facilitate its use. You can also display a status bar which gives a quick one-line description of your selection. Choose whether to display items listed with large or small icons, and with or without showing all file details. Arrange the icons by name, type, size, or date, or automatically by Explorer. Select Options to display a property sheet that lets you further refine how the file items are displayed, and add, modify, or delete file types. Use Refresh to refresh the panes and be sure you are seeing the most current information.

For example, to display files with their file extensions, choose View, Options to display the Options dialog box. In the Options dialog box deselect the Hide File Extensions for Known File Types option.

Tools

Tools lets you use the Windows Find program to search for files, folders, or computers on your system. From this menu choice, you can also map and disconnect network drives to shared resources. It also features a Go To option that lets you type in the name of the folder you would like to open and takes you there directly.

Help

Help, of course, opens the Windows NT 4.0 Help program.

Viewing Documents

Another convenient feature that Microsoft has brought over to Windows NT 4.0 from Windows 95 is the ability to display most documents with a document viewer utility called *Quick View*. Quick View works off the program association that a document may have. For example, if a document is a bitmap with a .BMP extension, it is already associated with the *Paint* program. If I right-click it from within Windows Explorer (or from any other window), I can choose the Quick View option to open Paint and display the bitmap. If a file has no program association, then right-click the file and choose Open With. This option displays a dialog box asking you to choose a program to use to view the file. You can also associate all files of the same type with the specified viewer.

Ch

4

Searching Your Computer with the Windows NT 4.0 Find Program

Microsoft has added a new search function to Windows NT 4.0 called *Find*. This utility lets you search for files, folders, and computers on the network (see Figure 4.18).

FIG. 4.18 ⟹

Here we are asking Find to locate the file Freecell in all the directories (folders) on the D: drive.

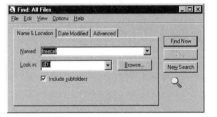

This utility is quite intuitive to use. A quick look at the properties sheet for Find shows that you can search by name and location of the file, or based on specific date and time modification parameters such as between a range of dates or in the last specified number of days. You can even specify the kind of file types within which to narrow your search, their size, and perhaps most usefully, by files which contain a specified string of text.

Your search criteria can be saved and reused or modified later. From the Options menu, you can make your search case-sensitive.

When the search is completed, Find displays an expanded results pane showing all of the files that matched the criteria specified (see Figure 4.19). From here, you can copy files, open files, create shortcuts, delete files, and so on.

FIG. 4.19 ⇒
Find completed
our search for
Freecell and dis-
plays five related
files in its results
window.

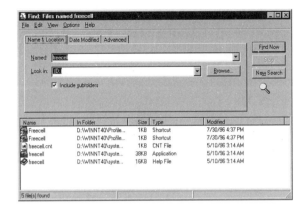

Exploring Windows NT 4.0 Help

Microsoft has greatly enhanced the Help program available in Windows NT. Windows NT Help is now both context-sensitive and task-based. *Context-sensitive* of course means that by choosing the help button in a dialog box or properties sheet, or pressing **F1** with a particular item selected, Windows NT will display a help window for that item. It might be a pop-up description box or it might be the Help program itself with more detailed directions. Windows NT Help also features a *What's This* button. At the top-right corner of most dialog boxes and properties sheets is a ? button. Click this and then on an item in the screen and Windows NT will display a pop-up about that item.

Task-based help follows a "how to" approach. Task-based help screens include button links back to the appropriate dialog boxes for accomplishing a specific task. By clicking the button, you can stay in Help and read the step-by-step directions for completing a task, while actually working in the dialog box. For example, if I wanted to know how to change the computer's date and time, I would look that up in Help.

When I opened the corresponding help document (see Figure 4.20), I could click the link (arrow) button and Windows NT will open the Date/Time Properties dialog box for me to work in.

Ch

4

FIG. 4.20 ⟹

Here we see both the NT Help screen and the NT dialog box it opens when clicking the arrow button for task-based help.

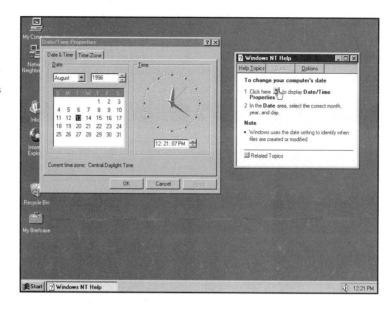

Using Windows NT Help

You can start Windows NT Help from most menu bars, and from the Start menu. The Help screen consists of three tabs: Contents, Index, and Find. Each lets you navigate Help a little differently depending on your needs and what you want to look up.

Contents

Contents as shown in Figure 4.21 focuses on subjects or topics such as *Tips and Tricks*, and *How To*. It also contains a complete list of Windows NT Command Prompt commands, their syntax, and suggested usage.

FIG. 4.21 ⟹

Windows NT Help: Contents Tab.

Index

The *Index* tab, shown in Figure 4.22, displays certain selected topics alphabetically. You can scroll through to find the topic you are looking for, or type in the first few letters in the text box. Optionally, if you do not find what you have typed, enter in a synonym to see related topics.

FIG. 4.22 ⟹

Windows NT
Help: Index Tab.

Find

The *Find* tab, shown in Figure 4.23, contains a search engine that lets you enter a word or phrase. Windows NT Help displays a list of matching words to help you narrow the search, then you select the appropriate topic from the third list.

The <u>O</u>ptions button (shown in Figure 4.23) lets you further refine the search by specifying how Windows NT should make the match against what you typed.

Help Topics

Once you have determined which topic to open, simply double-click the topic or click <u>D</u>isplay at the bottom of the Help screen.

Windows NT Help will display the topic for you. Each topic screen will be a little different. For example, the sample screen in Figure 4.24 presents us with three buttons each of which will display additional information. Selecting Command List opened another window with a choice of Windows NT commands listed alphabetically. Each of these can be further explored by clicking its button.

Ch

4

FIG. 4.23 ⇒

Windows Help:
Find Tab

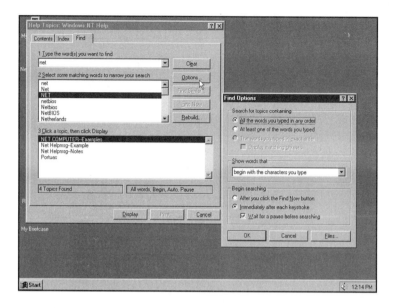

FIG. 4.24 ⇒

This Help screen
was displayed by
selecting Windows
NT Commands
from the Contents
tab of Windows NT
Help.

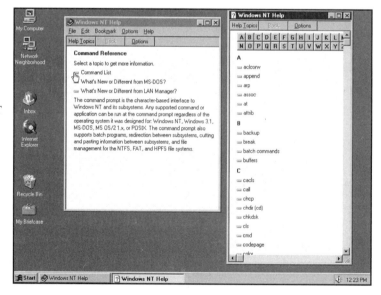

At the top of the Help screen are buttons to take you back to the main
Help screen, or, if you have drilled through several subtopics and related
topics, to take you to the previous topic, or to select various options
such as printing the topic, annotating it, copying it, changing the font,
etc. Annotate is particularly useful as it allows you to add your own
comments and notes to the help topic for future reference.

On the menu bar is the *Bookmark* menu choice. As in Windows, bookmark lets you mark this selection for easy and direct access in the future.

From Here...

So far we have installed Windows NT Workstation 4.0 and become familiar with some of the more significant features of its new interface. There is certainly a lot more to the interface and I encourage you to explore these on your own. The next step for us is to discuss how to configure Windows NT—changing settings, adding drivers, modifying the registry and so on.

Taking the Disc Test

If you have read and understood the material in the chapter, you are ready to test your knowledge. Insert the CD-ROM that comes with this book and run the self-test software as described in Appendix I, "Using the CD-ROM."

Ch

4

Chapter Prerequisite

Before reading this chapter,
you should be familiar with
the Windows NT Workstation
4.0 interface (introduced in
Chapter 4.

5

Configuration and the Registry

This chapter explores various means of configuring and customizing Windows NT Workstation 4.0. Customization includes something as simple as changing the color of the desktop. Configuration includes tasks like installing new device drivers. The Registry maintains the configuration information for Windows NT and provides Windows NT with the data it needs to boot successfully.

Windows NT provides several utilities for accomplishing these tasks. This chapter introduces you to these utilities and the Registry. Certain utilities, such as User Manager, Disk Administrator, and Network, while introduced here, are discussed in more detail in separate chapters.

Topics discussed in this chapter include:

   ◆ Personalizing the desktop environment through the display
     properties sheet

◆ Exploring the many Control Panel applets through which you make the majority of your configuration choices

◆ Reviewing the Windows NT administrative tools unique to Windows NT Workstation

◆ Examining the Windows NT 4.0 Registry to see how Windows NT maintains the system configuration, and how and when you can modify it

◆ The Windows NT 4.0 boot-up process and how Windows NT uses the Registry to start your system

Personalizing Your Desktop Environment

One of the first things most users want to do when they get Windows, Windows 95, or now Windows NT 4.0 is change things. Usually the first thing to go is the default color set, or the desktop background becomes a picture of the grandkids. Everyone likes to have control over their working space.

Windows NT Workstation 4.0 offers several ways to customize your desktop environment. The first that we discuss here is the Display Properties sheet.

Display Properties

Access the Display Properties sheet by right-clicking anywhere on the desktop background and then choosing Properties.

The Display Properties sheet, as shown in Figure 5.1, has five tabs, each corresponding to one of the more popular changes users like to make: Background, Screen Saver, Appearance, Plus!, and Settings. A nice addition to this and many other properties sheets is the Apply button. This lets you apply a change without closing the dialog box.

The Background tab lets you change the desktop wallpaper and pattern. These are the same types of changes you may have made in Windows when using the Desktop applet in Control Panel. A wallpaper can be any bitmap image and can be stored anywhere on your computer. The <u>B</u>rowse button lets you easily find the bitmap you like.

FIG. 5.1 ⇒

In this example of the Display Properties sheet, a new wallpaper bitmap has been chosen to replace the default background.

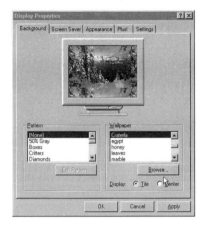

Screen savers, of course, are designed to protect your monitor from "burning in" an image of what's on the screen by displaying a moving image on the screen after a predetermined time period of inactivity on the keyboard or mouse. They can also be fun to look at. Most new monitors today are designed to prevent burn in.

Because it conforms to the OpenGL standard (direct draw to the screen, 3D graphics support, and so on), Windows NT 4.0 supports some pretty cool screen savers. Among the new screen savers included in Windows NT Workstation is the 3D Maze. This one displays a three-dimensional maze (à la Doom) and proceeds to maneuver you through it.

Most of the screen savers have additional customization options that can be accessed through the Se<u>t</u>tings button. You can also determine the period of inactivity before it kicks in, preview it in full screen, and password protect it. Password protecting is a good idea, especially if you are in the habit of walking away from your workstation with important stuff on your screen. You have to know the password before you can release the screen saver and return to your screen. However, screen savers can use a lot of processor time. If you have an application that requires extensive calculations or other processor-intensive processes, you may want to disable the screen saver while the application performs.

Ch
5

If you walk away, and the screen saver engages, it can actually "steal" processor time away from the application.

Having Fun with a Screen Saver!

Many software manufacturers build in little surprises or hidden features in their products. No, I'm not talking about bugs (which I like to call eccentricities). No, these hidden features are fun things and are usually referred to as *easter eggs*. Here are a couple that are built in to the Windows NT screen savers.

Open the Display Properties sheet and select the 3D Pipes screen saver. Change its settings so that the joint type is Ball. When the screen saver kicks in, look at the ball joints. Occasionally, one of them becomes a teapot. This is easier to spot on a 486 than a Pentium.

Another easter egg can be found by selecting the 3D Text screen saver. In its settings, change the text to "i love nt." The screen saver displays a surprise response. I leave it to you to determine whether it is "good?"

Through the Appearance tab, you can change your color schemes or set color, size, and sometimes font settings for individual items, including icons.

The Plus! tab gives you the option of using different icons for some of your desktop objects, as well as refining visual settings. For example, a visually impaired person might use large icons. If you have a high resolution monitor, you can have Windows NT smooth the edges of screen fonts and display icons using the full color range available.

Settings lets you make changes to the monitor settings. From this tab, you can modify the display type, screen resolution, refresh frequency, color palette, and font size. Before applying a change, Microsoft suggests clicking the Test button and previewing the screen to be sure that it is viewable.

Exploring Control Panel

If you have worked with previous versions of Windows, you have spent some time in Control Panel. Control Panel offers a variety of applets that modify your system configuration. Microsoft has reworked most of the Control Panel applets in Windows NT 4.0 to provide you with a much greater degree of granularity when making your selections.

Control Panel, shown in Figure 5.2, can be opened in a variety of ways. You will most commonly open it from the Settings option on the Start menu. However, you can also access it through My Computer, Windows Explorer, and by creating a shortcut to it or any of its applets on your desktop. There are 25 applets in Control Panel.

FIG. 5.2 ⇒

Windows NT
Workstation 4.0
Control Panel.

Note   As you add applications or Windows NT services to your computer, additional applets are likely added to the Control Panel. For example, when you add Client Services for Netware, which allows your Windows NT workstation to connect to a Netware server, an additional Client Services icon is added to the Control Panel, from which you can select your preferred Netware logon server. ■

Ch
5

Whenever you need to change a system parameter, your first stop should be Control Panel. Here is a list of the applets provided in Control Panel:

- ◆ Accessibility Options
- ◆ Add\Remove Programs
- ◆ DOS Console
- ◆ Printers
- ◆ Date\Time
- ◆ Devices
- ◆ Display

- ◆ Network
- ◆ PC Card
- ◆ Ports
- ◆ Regional Settings
- ◆ SCSI Adapters
- ◆ Server
- ◆ Services

- ◆ Fonts
- ◆ Internet
- ◆ Keyboard
- ◆ Modems
- ◆ Mouse
- ◆ Multimedia

- ◆ Sounds
- ◆ System
- ◆ Tape Devices
- ◆ Telephony
- ◆ UPS

Let's briefly review what functions each applet provides.

Accessibility Options is new to Windows NT 4.0. It is designed for those individuals with visual, hearing, or movement challenges. It offers several modifications including making the keyboard easier to use, visualizing computer sounds, and using the keyboard to control the mouse.

Add/Remove Programs lets you install and remove Windows NT components, such as games and accessories. It also provides a built-in procedure for automatically installing or uninstalling applications from disk or CD-ROM. If the application that is being installed is set up using either a Setup.exe or Install.exe file Add/Remove Programs will record the setup process, display the application in its list of installed applications, and let you remove the application using its Uninstall Wizard.

MS-DOS Console is often confused with the MS-DOS Prompt accessed through the Start menu. MS-DOS Console provides a means of modifying the way a DOS window appears on the desktop. You can alter screen colors, window size, font style and size, cursor size, and command history buffer.

Date/Time, of course, modifies the computer's internal date and time values. There is really nothing remarkable here except that the screens are far more graphic and easy to use than ever before. It even shows you what part of the world your time zone is in.

Devices shows you all the device drivers detected and installed by Windows NT, and which devices are currently running. It offers you the ability to start, stop, and configure startup types for device drivers.

Display produces exactly the same Display Properties sheet we discussed earlier. This is just another place to access it.

Fonts lets you view fonts installed on your system, add new fonts, and remove fonts that are no longer needed. You can also find the option to only display TrueType fonts in applications.

Internet is installed in Control Panel if you have installed the Internet Explorer. It lets you set the proxy server on your network through which you access the Internet. The proxy server is usually the firewall filtering who from your network can access the Internet and who from the Internet can access your network.

Keyboard allows adjustment of the delay and repeat rates of your keyboard and lets you change the keyboard type. It also lets you specify alternative language keyboards to include foreign language symbol sets.

Modems displays the properties of any modems installed on your computer. From here, you can add and remove modems and modify modem settings. Choosing Add starts the Install Modem Wizard. This wizard walks you through detecting, selecting, and setting up your system's modem.

Mouse lets you customize many characteristics of your mouse device. You can switch button usage for left-handed persons, modify the double-click speed (test it on the jack-in-the-box!), and change the pointer speed. There is also a tab for changing the various mouse pointers. This is where you find more interesting visual representations for the select, wait, working, and other pointers (see Figure 5.3). Clicking Browse displays all the neat pointer files that Windows NT supplies, including the infamous animated cursors. Look for the files with an .ANI extension. You can preview them before applying.

Multimedia provides configuration options for audio, video, MIDI, CD music, and any other multimedia-related devices.

Network identifies the computer, its relationship to the rest of the network, and all service, protocol, adapter, and bindings settings. This applet can also be accessed by selecting the properties for Network Neighborhood. This is where the majority of your network configuration takes place and is covered in more detail in Chapter 11, "Network Connectivity and Remote Support."

Ch

5

FIG. 5.3 ⇒

The Browse button displays a list of mouse pointer files that can be used to customize the pointers. You can change the mouse pointer for Working from the default hourglass with arrow to a dinosaur.

PC Card (PCMCIA) displays whether you have PC Card support on your computer, which cards are currently in use, and the resources they are using.

Ports lets you add, modify, and delete parameters for your computer's COM ports. For example, if you add a new COM port adapter card to your computer, or connect a serial printer to an existing port, you may want to configure it for a certain speed and parity.

Printers replaces Print Manager and displays icons related to each printer installed on your computer or connected through the network. From these, you can manage the printing devices and print jobs. There is also an Add Printer Wizard that walks you through the process of installing, configuring, and sharing your printing device. This applet can also be accessed from the taskbar by choosing Start, Settings, Printers.

Regional Settings displays current settings for number symbols, currency format, date and time values, and input locales based on world regions. This used to be called International and has been greatly enhanced.

SCSI Adapters displays SCSI adapters and drivers that have been installed on your computer and their resource settings (I/O, interrupt, and so on).

Server opens a dialog box that offers statistics relating to the server-based activities of your computer. It shows which network users are currently connected to your Windows NT workstation, which shared resources are being used and by whom, and any replication settings that may have been configured. It also lets you set administrative alerts, delivering system message pop-ups to a specified user or computer.

Services displays a list of all services that have been installed on your computer and their current running status. Windows NT services are functions or applications that are loaded as part of the Windows NT Executive. Thus, they run as part of the operating system rather than as a background or resident program (TSR).

As you see in Figure 5.4, this applet also gives you the ability to start and stop services, and to modify their startup configuration.

FIG. 5.4 ⇒

Here you see the Services dialog box showing the status of several Windows NT services running on this computer, as well as the startup options box for one of the services, displayed by selecting Startup.

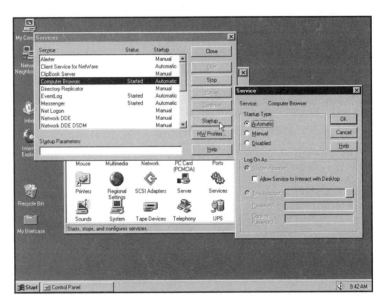

You can also set services based on hardware profiles so that only certain services run given a specific hardware installation. For example, a laptop that is not connected remotely to a network while the user is on the road may have certain network-related services turned off. This makes additional resources available to other applications. When docked at the user's desk at a station that is wired to the network, those network services would be turned back on.

Ch

5

Sounds lets you assign different types of sounds to system and application events such as warning beeps, opening a program, doing what you shouldn't, and so on.

System displays the System Properties sheet through which you can define the default operating system at boot time, set recovery options for Stop errors, determine which hardware profiles to use during startup, view and delete user profiles stored on your computer, view and define environment variables, modify application performance, and configure and customize pagefile parameters.

Tape Devices displays a dialog box to view, add, or delete tape devices and their driver settings that are installed on your computer.

Telephony opens the Dialing Properties dialog box that lets you view, add, or remove telephony drivers, and modify dialing parameters such as pressing 9 to get an outside line or disabling call waiting. You can create a different set of dialing parameters for different situations or locations. For example, dialing out through your modem at work may require no additional settings, whereas dialing out from a hotel room may require dialing one or more numbers in sequence to access a local or long distance line.

UPS lets you set configuration parameters for your uninterruptable power supply connected to the computer. Parameters include setting interface voltages for power failure and low battery signals, specifying a command file to be executed when the UPS is activated, and other UPS-specific characteristics, such as expected battery life.

Exploring the Administrative Tools

The Administrative Tools group contains utilities that are specific to your installation of either Windows NT Workstation 4.0 or Windows NT 4.0 Server.

There are seven tools that are installed on Windows NT Workstation 4.0 as shown in Figure 5.5: Backup, Disk Administrator, Event Viewer, Performance Monitor, Remote Access Administrator, User Manager, and Windows NT Diagnostics. These tools are discussed in more detail in later chapters.

FIG. 5.5 ⇒

You can find the Administrative Tools by selecting Programs from the Start Menu.

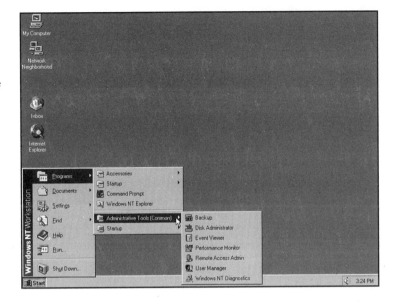

The *Backup* utility gives you considerable control over what data you want to back up and where you are backing it up to. It also controls the restore process. You can back up entire disks or directories or specific files, including the Registry. It keeps summary logs indicating what was backed up or restored and when, as well as any files that it determined were corrupted.

The *Disk Administrator* can best be described as a much improved and GUI FDISK utility. From here, you can easily create and format disk partitions, create volume sets and extended volumes, and create stripe sets. On the server version, you can also enable software fault tolerance (also known as RAID—Redundant Array of Inexpensive Disks) such as striping with parity and mirrored disk partitions.

The *Event Viewer* is a great troubleshooting utility. It records system events such as services that failed to start or devices that could not be initialized. When various audit functions are enabled in Windows NT, Event Viewer provides logs that record the audit information and display it for your review.

Performance Monitor is still receiving rave reviews from Windows NT administrators for the sheer amount of system performance data that

Ch

5

can be charted, saved, and reviewed. This utility is used to help determine performance bottlenecks on your system, processor utilization, server access, and so on. It is covered in more detail, along with Event Viewer, in Chapter 12, "Tuning, Optimizing, and Other Troubleshooting Tips."

After Remote Access Service (RAS) has been installed and configured on your computer, the *Remote Access Administrator* utility offers you management functions for your RAS client, such as defining which network users can access your computer through a dial-in connection, who is currently connected, which ports are in use, and whether the service is running. This utility is reviewed again in Chapter 11.

You create and manage user and group accounts through *User Manager*. Password policy information, location of user profiles and login scripts, users' functional rights, and user access auditing are all configured through User Manager. This utility is examined thoroughly in the next chapter, "Managing Users and Accounts."

Windows NT Diagnostics is an enhanced and GUI version of Microsoft's MS-DOS-based MSD (Microsoft Diagnostics). This cool utility gives detailed information culled directly from the Windows NT Registry relating to the system, display, disk drives, memory and pagefile usage, network statistics, environment variable values, resources in use and their settings, and services installed and their state. This version actually provides a far greater level of detail than previous Windows NT versions. You can even print out the information screens.

Creating and Managing Hardware Profiles

Hardware Profiles offer a way for you to create and maintain different hardware configurations—including which services and devices are initialized—for different computing scenarios. The most common use for hardware profiles is with laptop computers that are sometimes placed in a docking station. While elsewhere, the user can use the laptop's modem to dial in to the company network. When docked, that user can access the network through the network card installed in the docking station.

These are two different methods of connecting to the network that are used in two different scenarios and require different hardware. You can certainly maintain the same profile for both scenarios. However, when portable, you are likely to receive event or system messages relating to the "missing" network card. Likewise, if the docking station disables the laptop's modem, you can receive similar messages when the computer is docked. If you maintain two hardware profiles, you can customize which device is activated during which scenario.

Creating a Hardware Profile

To create a Hardware Profile, you must first access the System Properties dialog box as shown in Figure 5.6. The System Properties dialog box can be opened in one of two ways:

❖ Right-click My Computer on the desktop and then choose Properties.

❖ Open Control Panel and start the System applet.

FIG. 5.6 ⇒

The System Properties dialog box with the Hardware Profiles tab selected.

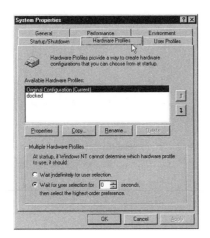

Ch

5

After the System Properties dialog box is displayed, follow these steps to create a new Hardware Profile:

1. Select the Hardware Profiles tab.

2. Choose an existing or original profile from the Available Hardware Profiles list box and choose Copy.

3. Enter the name of the new profile and choose OK.

4. Use the arrow buttons to the right of the profile list to determine the order preference of the profiles. This determines which order Windows NT uses to load the profiles during system startup.

5. Use the Properties button to indicate whether the computer is a portable and its docking state, and also whether this profile should disable all network functions (see Figure 5.7).

FIG. 5.7 ⇒
This Hardware Profile has been designated as a portable computer that is undocked.

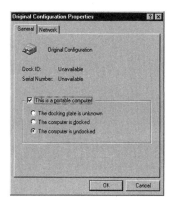

6. Specify what Windows NT should do during startup. If you want Windows NT to display a list of profiles at startup, choose Wait Indefinitely for Use Selection. Windows NT does not continue with the startup operation until a profile selection is made. Profiles are displayed after you are prompted to press the spacebar for the Last Known Good Configuration.

If you want to set a timeout value for selecting a profile before Windows NT selects the first profile in the list, choose Wait for User Selection for xx Seconds, Then Select the Highest-Order Preference. If you set the timeout value to 0, Windows NT simply boots with the highest order profile on startup. Pressing the spacebar when prompted for the Last Known Good Configuration re-displays the profile list.

Now that the Hardware Profile has been created, you need to identify which services and devices to enable and disable for each profile. This is accomplished through the Services and Devices applets, respectively, in Control Panel.

To define a specific Service or Device to the Hardware Profile, follow these steps:

1. Select the service or device from the list.

2. Click the HW Profiles button. This displays a new dialog box, as shown in Figure 5.8.

3. Select the profile that you are modifying from the list.

4. Choose Enable or Disable to turn the service or device on or off, respectively, for that profile.

5. Choose OK and close the Services or Devices applet.

When you start Windows NT and choose your hardware profile, the services and devices start as you configured them.

FIG. 5.8 ⇒

In this example, the Computer Browser service, while enabled normally, has been set to disabled for the profile called DOCKED.

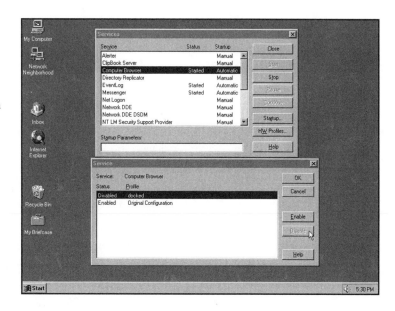

Examining the Windows NT Workstation 4.0 Registry

The Windows NT 4.0 *Registry* is perhaps the single most important element of the Windows NT operating system architecture. The Registry is an encrypted database of configuration and environment information relating to the successful booting of Windows NT 4.0. Think of this file as being the DOS AUTOEXEC.BAT and CONFIG.SYS files rolled into one—and then some.

Key Concept

The Registry is central to the operation of Windows NT 4.0. User environment settings are stored here. Driver information, services, hardware profile information, security objects and their permissions, and account information are all stored in the Registry. Microsoft considers the Registry so integral a part of Windows NT that it strongly discourages you from making changes to it.

In fact, the Control Panel, Administrative Tools group, and various properties sheets give you all the utilities you need to modify and customize your installation of Windows NT 4.0 for normal maintenance. All of these utilities modify one or more Registry entries. Therefore, there are only limited and specific reasons for you to make changes to the Registry directly.

Caution

A good rule of thumb for modifying the Registry: If there is a utility that can do the modification, *use the utility*! If you make substantial changes to the Registry that result in problems during boot-up or execution, Microsoft will *disallow* your support call.

That said, there *are* specific instances when you have to modify the Registry directly. These usually have to do with the absence of a utility to make a necessary change, or troubleshooting purposes. Some of the more common of these are discussed later in this chapter in the section titled "Using the Registry to Configure Windows NT Workstation 4.0."

Navigating with the Registry Editor

The Registry can be accessed by starting the Registry Editor utility. This utility can be accessed in several ways. Here are two:

- ◆ Open the Windows Explorer and select the SYSTEM32 folder under the Windows NT system folder (usually called WINNT or WINNT40). Double-click the file REGEDT32.EXE.

- ◆ Choose RUN from the Start menu and type in **REGEDT32.EXE**. Then choose OK.

If you will access the Registry often, you can also create a shortcut to REGEDT32.EXE on your desktop.

 Note   Throughout the remainder of this book, I refer to the Windows NT system directory as WINNT40. ▨

The Registry Editor displays the five main windows, called subtrees, of the Windows NT 4.0 Registry for the local computer as shown in Figure 5.9. They are:

- ◆ HKEY_LOCAL_MACHINE
- ◆ HKEY_CURRENT_CONFIG
- ◆ HKEY_USERS
- ◆ HKEY_CURRENT_USER
- ◆ HKEY_CLASSES_ROOT

By default, only users with Administrator access can make modifications to the Registry. Other users can only view the information contained there.

Ch
5

 Tip

I recommend setting the View option to Read Only, even for administrators. This guards against any accidental modifications that can lead to serious boot and operation problems. Enable it by selecting Read Only Mode from the Options menu in Registry Editor.

From Options, choose Font to change the font style and size to facilitate viewing, and Confirm on Delete to guard against accidental deletions.

FIG. 5.9 ⇒

This screen shows
the five subtrees of
the Windows NT
registry, tiled for
better viewing.

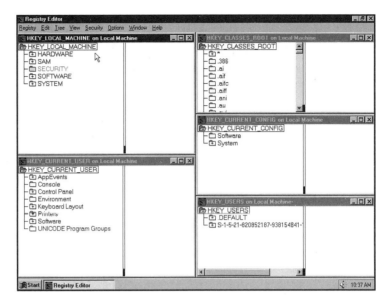

At first glance, these windows look a lot like File Manager or Windows
Explorer, and, in fact, you can navigate them in much the same way.
The left pane of each subtree window displays the keys pertinent to
that subtree. As each key is selected, the parameters and values assigned
to that key are displayed in the right pane. You can think of a key as
being a more sophisticated .INI file.

You may recall that an .INI file consists of section headings, each section containing one or more parameters unique to that section, and
each parameter having an appropriate value or values assigned to it.
The values can be text strings, file names, or simple "yes" or "no" or "1"
or "0" values.

A Registry key is quite similar. Think of it as a "nested" .INI file (see
Figure 5.10). A key can consist of parameters with assigned values, or it
can consist of one or more subkeys, each with its own parameters.

HKEY_LOCAL_MACHINE contains all the system configuration data
needed to boot and run the operating system successfully. This includes
services that need to be run, device drivers, hardware profiles, including
what is currently loaded, login parameters, and so on. It is composed
of five primary keys called hives, each of which can contain subtrees

several folders deep (see Figure 5.11). Each of the hives relates to a corresponding Registry file saved in the WINNT40\SYSTEM32\ CONFIG directory except for the Hardware hive which is built when the computer is booted. The five hives are:

- HARDWARE (properly called a "key")
- SOFTWARE
- SYSTEM
- SAM
- SECURITY

The *HARDWARE* hive, or key, contains data related to detected hardware devices installed on your computer.

FIG. 5.10 ⇒

Here is an example of a Windows .INI file. Notice the section headings in square brackets. Each section has at least one parameter. The values assigned to each parameter represent what the parameter "expects."

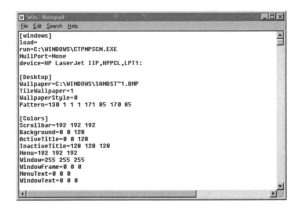

Ch

5

Key Concept

The HARDWARE key is built during the startup process. This information is *not* written down anywhere or stored permanently on the system. Instead, Windows NT "detects" this information each time it boots. Thus, it is referred to as a "volatile" hive or key since it is created during the boot process, can change as hardware changes, and is not written to disk.

FIG. 5.11 ⇒
A Windows NT
Registry key can
go several levels
deep before finally
displaying param-
eter values.

It includes information such as processor type and power, keyboard
class, port information, SCSI adapter information, drive data, video, and
memory. This information is primarily stored as binary data, and because it is built during startup, is useless to modify. The Windows NT
Diagnostics utility is the best tool to use to view this data.

The *SAM* and *SECURITY* hives contain security-related information.
SAM stands for *Security Account Manager* and, as you may suspect, contains user and group account information as well as workgroup or
domain membership information. The SECURITY hive contains Local
Security Account (*LSA*) policy information such as specific user rights
assigned to user and group accounts.

Neither of these hives nor their subtrees are viewable. It is part of
Microsoft's security policy to hide this information even from the system administrator. Even if you could look at it, it probably would not
make a lot of sense or give you any insight into violating account information.

Unlike the HARDWARE key, SAM and SECURITY *are* written to
files on the hard disk. Each has a registry and log file associated with
it—SAM and SAM.LOG, and SECURITY and SECURITY.LOG,

respectively. You can find them in the WINNT40\SYSTEM32\ CONFIG subdirectory on the Windows NT system partition.

The *SOFTWARE* hive consists of computer-specific software installed on your computer, as opposed to user-specific settings. This includes manufacturer and version; installed driver files; descriptive and default information for Windows NT-specific services and functions such as the Browser, NetDDE, Windows NT version information; and the WINLOGON service. This hive also has two files associated with it that can be found in the WINNT40\SYSTEM32\CONFIG subdirectory: SOFTWARE and SOFTWARE.LOG.

While the SOFTWARE hive contains more descriptive information regarding the installation of applications, drivers, and so forth on your computer, the *SYSTEM* hive provides configuration and parameter settings necessary for Windows NT to boot successfully and correctly maintain your computer's configuration. A quick look at the subtrees below SYSTEM shows at least three *control set* entries, as shown in Figure 5.12.

FIG. 5.12 ⇒
HKEY_LOCAL_
MACHINE with
the SYSTEM hive
expanded to show
the boot control
sets.

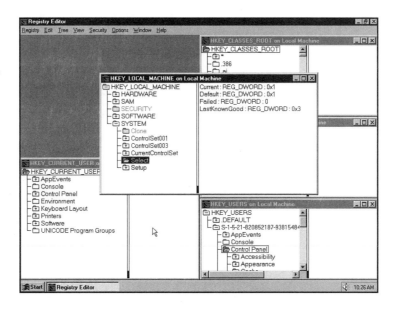

Ch
5

These are used to control the startup process, indicating which services should load, which drivers to load and initialize, and so on. Any changes you make to existing driver settings, or any new drivers you install and configure are added to a control set in the SYSTEM hive. Its corresponding files in the WINNT40\SYSTEM32\CONFIG subdirectory are SYSTEM and SYSTEM.ALT.

HKEY_CURRENT_CONFIG is a new subtree added to Windows NT 4.0. It is a subset of HKEY_LOCAL_MACHINE and reflects only the current software and system modifications made during the current session, as well as the current startup settings. This is useful for isolating data specific to a hardware profile from other data stored in the Registry.

HKEY_CLASSES_ROOT will look familiar to administrators of previous versions of Windows. It represents OLE and file association data specific to file extensions. This is information that was stored in Windows' REG.DAT file. This subtree is also a subset of HKEY_LOCAL_MACHINE and can be found there under the SOFTWARE hive.

HKEY_USERS consists of two subkeys relating to user settings. DEFAULT contains system default settings used when the LOGON screen is first displayed. The second entry represents the user who is currently logged on to the system. The long alphanumeric value you see is the user's Security Identifier, hereafter called the SID of the user.

Tip

All the entries you see under the SID subkey represent changes that can be made to the user's environment, primarily through Control Panel. If the user changes his color scheme, cursor pointers, wallpaper, and so on, the values can be found in his respective keys here. If you need to modify a user's entries, perhaps remotely, you can do so here as well. The values stored here correspond to an actual file like the HKEY_LOCAL_MACHINE hives do. Windows NT creates a subfolder in WINNT40/Profile for each user that logs on and changes their profile. This subfolder contains two files that correspond to the Registry entries for that user's profile: NTUSER.DAT.LOG and NTUSER.DAT.

HKEY_CURRENT_USER represents a subset of HKEY_USERS, and points back to the settings of the current user (the SID entry in HKEY_USERS).

Using the Registry to Configure Windows NT Workstation 4.0

This section is designed with two purposes in mind. The first is to introduce you to the method for looking up keys and making changes to them. The second is to point out some specific modifications that you can *only* accomplish by changing the Registry.

Let me begin by stating the not-so-obvious. As you navigate through the Registry and select various keys, you may or may not see parameter values displayed in the windows. That does not necessarily mean that there are *no values* present. It may simply mean that Windows NT is using the *default* values for that entry.

For example, if you select the HKEY_CURRENT_USER\ CONTROL PANEL\CURSORS subkey, and you have made no changes to your mouse pointers, you will see no entries here. However, it is obvious that you do, in fact, have default mouse pointers displayed on your screen. In this case, Windows NT does use parameter values— the default values.

Tip

Here is the general rule of thumb: If the Registry does not display parameter values when you select a subkey, assume that Windows NT is using the defaults for that subkey, realizing that a default can be to have *no* values loaded at all.

Let's use the example of changing the cursor pointer. A user has selected the peeling banana to replace the hourglass "wait" cursor, and wants to change it to the running horse. Also, this user wants to change the application starting cursor (hourglass with an arrow) to the lumber-

Ch
5

ing dinosaur. You can simply and easily do this through the Mouse applet in Control Panel, but you feel particularly bold today.

There are basically three pieces of information that you need to know before modifying this particular entry, and in general for changing any Registry entry. These three pieces of information are:

◆ Know which Registry entry you are going to change, what subkey or subkeys are involved (yes, there might be more than one!), and where they are located.

◆ Know which parameter needs to be added, modified, or deleted to affect your change.

◆ Know what value needs to be assigned to the parameter and its type.

Now, let's look at this step-by-step.

First, it is not always easy to determine what the subkey is and where it is. If the change you are making modifies the way the system operates (new device driver, changing the video display, adding a new hardware profile), those subkeys are most likely found under HKEY_LOCAL_MACHINE in the SYSTEM hive under one of the control set entries. If the change you are making affects the working environment of a particular user (desktop wallpaper, cursors, colors, window properties), those subkeys are most likely found under HKEY_USERS in the current user's subkey identified by the user's SID.

Also, sometimes the subkeys that need to be modified are easy to identify, like "cursors." Sometimes they are not. Who knew that the HKEY_LOCAL_MACHINE\SYSTEM\CURRENTCONTROLSET\ SERVICES\CE2NDIS31 entry refers to the driver settings for the Credit Card Ethernet Adapter installed in my laptop? So how do you find out? Sometimes your documentation tells you. Most times, you find them by exploration, trial, and error. But remember, Microsoft recommends that you *not* affect configuration changes through the Registry directly, especially when there is a utility that can do it for you. In the case of my network adapter, I don't really need to know where its configuration values are stored in the Registry because I can configure it through the Network applet in Control Panel or through the Properties sheet of the Network Neighborhood.

Finding Subkey Names in the Registry

If you are not sure of the subkey name you are looking for, but know what it might be called, or a category that it might fall into, you can use the Registry's *FIND KEY* function to look it up. Follow these steps:

1. Place your cursor at the top (root) of the directory structure in the subtree where you think the key is located.

2. Choose View, Find Key.

3. Type in the key name you are looking for.

4. Choose Match Whole Word Only or Match Case if you are relatively sure of the key entry; otherwise, deselect these options.

5. Choose Find Next.

FIND KEY places a box around the first subkey entry that matches the text string you entered. You can move the Find window out of the way if it blocks your view. Choose FIND NEXT again until you locate the appropriate subkey.

FIND KEY only works with key entries. It does not work on parameter entries.

Getting back to our example, because this is a user environment change, you know you can find the subkey in the HKEY_USERS subtree, under the user's SID entry. You can also select the HKEY_CURRENT_USER subtree because it points to the same location in the Registry.

From there, because you are modifying cursors, you want to look for a subkey called cursors. Because you modify cursors through the Control Panel, it is a pretty safe bet that you will find a Cursors subkey under the Control Panel subkey. You now know the location and the subkey to modify: HKEY_CURRENT_USER\CONTROL PANEL\ CURSORS.

Ch
5

The second thing you should know is which parameter needs to be added, modified, or deleted to effect your change.

Once again, finding out which parameter value is difficult unless someone gives you the parameter and value to enter. In this example, the parameter corresponding to the working hourglass is called WAIT, and the parameter corresponding to the application start hourglass with arrow is called APPSTARTING.

Finally, you need to know what value needs to be assigned to the parameter and its type.

By now, you get the idea. Again, in this example, the file names that correspond to the various cursors either have a .CUR or .ANI extension. You can find these listed in the WINNT40\SYSTEM32 subdirectory. Recall that the WAIT cursor needs to change from the banana (BANANA.ANI) to the running horse (HORSE.ANI), and that the APPSTARTING cursor needs to be the lumbering dinosaur (DINOSAUR.ANI).

There are five data types that can be applied to a parameter value. Again, you usually know which one to use, either because it is obvious or because someone has told you. Table 5.1 lists the value types and a brief description of each.

Table 5.1 Parameter Value Data Types

Data Type	Description
REG_SZ	Expects one text string data value
REG_DWORD	Expects one hexadecimal string of one to eight digits
REG_BINARY	Expects one string of hexadecimal digits, each pair of which is considered a byte value
REG_EXPAND_SZ	Expects one text string value that contains a replaceable parameter such as %USERNAME% or %SYSTEMROOT%

Data Type	Description
REG_MULTI_SZ	Expects multiple string values separated by a NULL character

In our example, cursors can only be associated with one file name (a text string). Therefore, our parameter value will have a data type of REG_SZ and their value will be the file name. Now we can modify the Registry. Just follow these steps:

1. Open the Registry Editor. From <u>O</u>ptions, deselect <u>R</u>ead Only Mode, if it is selected.

2. Maximize the HKEY_CURRENT_USER subtree window to make it easier to work with.

3. Expand the Control Panel key.

4. Highlight the Cursors key. In the right pane, because the WAIT cursor has already been modified once, there is an entry called WAIT, of data type REG_SZ and value BANANA.ANI.

5. Double-click the parameter entry (WAIT) to display the String Editor (see Figure 5.13).

FIG. 5.13 ⇒

The WAIT cursor currently has the value BANANA.ANI. Double-click it to display the String Editor and change the value to HORSE.ANI.

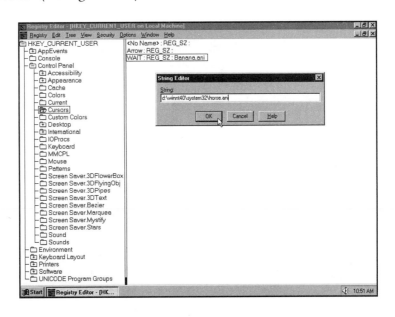

Ch

5

6. Enter the new parameter value (**D:\WINNT40\ SYSTEM32\HORSE.ANI**).

7. To add a new parameter and value, choose <u>E</u>dit from the Registry Editor menu bar, then Add <u>V</u>alue.

8. In the Add Value dialog box, enter the Value Name (APPSTARTING) and choose the appropriate Data Type (REG_SZ). Then choose OK (see Figure 5.14).

FIG. 5.14 ⇒
Choose <u>E</u>dit, Add <u>V</u>alue to add the new cursor parameter APPSTARING with a data type of REG_SZ, and click OK. In the String Editor, type **DINOSAUR.ANI**.

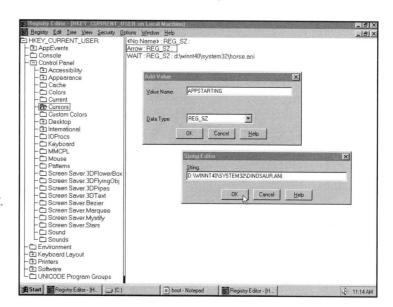

9. In the String Editor dialog box, enter the appropriate parameter value (**D:\WINNT40\SYSTEM32\DINOSAUR.ANI**), and click OK.

10. Select <u>R</u>ead Only Mode from the <u>O</u>ptions menu again, then close the Registry Editor.

The change does not take effect immediately.

Tip

In general, if this is a user environment change, the user has to log off and log back on before the change takes effect. If this is a system change, the computer has to be shut down and restarted before the change takes effect.

> **Caution**
>
> Parameter names are *not* case-sensitive. However, because they can be quite lengthy, Microsoft uses proper case when displaying these values to make them easier to read.
>
> If you misspell a parameter name, the result may simply be that Windows NT ignores it, or it can result in a service stopping altogether. This is also true with parameter values. If in doubt, look it up in the Windows NT Resource Kit, or test it first. Before testing, back up your original Registry or, at the least, save the original subkey.

Following are some other modifications that you can make to the Registry for which a utility does not exist.

Legal Notices

Legal notices are dialog boxes that pop up before a user can log on and usually indicate who is authorized to access that computer. You generally see these while logging into enterprise networks. You can change these in the Registry by modifying the following subkey and parameter values:

HKEY_LOCAL_MACHINE\SOFTWARE\MICROSOFT\
WINDOWS NT\CURRENTVERSION\WINLOGON*Legal NoticeCaption* and *LegalNoticeText.*

LegalNoticeCaption modifies the title bar of the dialog box that displays during logon, and *LegalNoticeText* is the text that is displayed in the dialog box.

For example, modify *LegalNoticeCaption* to display `Legal Notice for Computer SDK`. Modify *LegalNoticeText* to display `Unauthorized users will be shot on sight!`

To see this change, log off and log back on.

Shutdown Options

You may notice that the logon dialog box displays an option button to shut down the computer. On Windows NT Workstation 4.0, you are

Ch

5

allowed, by default, to shut down the computer without logging on to the system. This is a convenience for the user so that she does not have to wait for Windows NT to load (two or more minutes on lower performance computers) before she can effect a shutdown. You want to avoid having users just power off at all costs. So this is a good thing.

It is interesting to note, however, that for installations of Windows NT 4.0 Server, the Shutdown button does *not* appear in the logon dialog box. Therefore, a user, preferably an administrator, must log on to the server computer before effecting a shutdown. Again, as you don't necessarily want just anybody to be able to walk up to a server and shut it down, this is also a good thing.

The display or hiding of the Shutdown button is controlled through a Registry entry. If you want to modify this value to hide the Shutdown button on your workstation (or display it on a server—but why?), modify the following entry:

HKEY_LOCAL_MACHINE\SOFTWARE\MICROSOFT\
WINDOWS NT\CURRENTVERSION\WINLOGON\
ShutdownWithoutLogon

A "1" means "Yes, display the SHUTDOWN button," while a "0" means "No, do not display the SHUTDOWN button."

If your computer's BIOS supports a powering off of the computer when the operating system shuts down, modify the following entry from "0" (not supported) to "1" (supported):

HKEY_LOCAL_MACHINE\SOFTWARE\MICROSOFT\
WINDOWS NT\CURRENTVERSION\WINLOGON\
PowerdownAfterShutdown

Logon User Names

By default, Windows NT remembers the last user who logged on to a system and records this information (along with the workgroup or domain that the user logged in to) in the Registry. You can view this information in the following entries:

> HKEY_LOCAL_MACHINE\SOFTWARE\MICROSOFT\
> WINDOWS NT\CURRENT VERSION\WINLOGON\
> *DefaultUserName* and *DefaultDomainName*

For added security, you can hide the display of the last user who logged on so that no one can try guessing the password to get on to the system. As we all know, users tend to use passwords that are easily guessed. If a potential hacker must also guess at the username, that makes the computer less desirable to hack (kind of like putting the Club® on your steering wheel). If you would rather not display the last user who logged on to a computer, you need to *add* the following parameter name and value:

> HKEY_LOCAL_MACHINE\SOFTWARE\MICROSOFT\
> WINDOWS NT\CURRENT VERSION\WINLOGON\
> *DontDisplayLastUserName*

DontDisplayLastUserName expects a data type of REG_SZ and a value of either "1" (Yes, *don't* display the last user name) or "0" (No, *do* display the last user name). This is an example of a parameter that does not display in the right pane, but whose default value is loaded by the Registry.

The System Policy Editor

Windows NT 4.0 Server includes a configuration management utility called the System Policy Editor. This utility is not included with the Workstation version. It is intended for managing server-based workstation and user policies—that is, configuration information that is stored on a login server (domain controller) and downloaded to the user's workstation when the user logs on to the network. Most of the Registry changes that have been discussed in this chapter so far can be made more safely through the System Policy Editor. Also, the configuration is assured to "follow" the user and, thus, be consistent and standard.

In Figure 5.15, for example, a system policy has been created for user SDKACZ. Note that simply by pointing and clicking through a variety of intuitive screens, the user's access and environment can be fixed. In this example, the user's ability to modify the screen is reduced, a wallpaper has been selected, and the RUN and Settings Folders have been removed. This policy affects the user wherever SDKACZ logs on.

Ch
5

FIG. 5.15 ⇒

Sample System Policy Editor screen from Windows NT 4.0 Server.

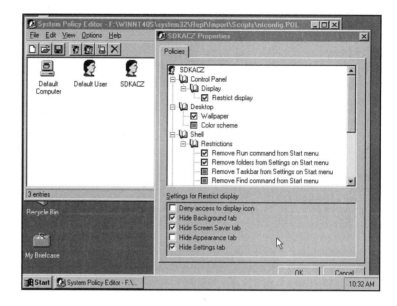

Similarly, a system policy can be established by workstation name, thus regulating a user's environment and access by workstation. For example, you could disable the last user name from displaying, or modify the legal notice dialog box again by simply pointing and clicking the appropriate check box. These settings then would affect every user who logged on to this specific workstation.

The workstation and user policies are saved in a file called NTCONFIG.POL and stored in the WINNT40\SYSTEM32\REPL\IMPORT\SCRIPTS subdirectory of each domain controller. This directory is also known by the share name *NETLOGON*.

Changing the Default Startup Screen

The default startup screen is the Ctrl-Alt-Del screen that is displayed when you log off or boot Windows NT. You can modify how this screen looks by modifying entries in the DEFAULT subkey of HKEY_USERS. For example, if you have created a company logo called XYZ.BMP that you want all your computers to display during startup, you need to modify the default desktop wallpaper. Access the following Registry entry:

HKEY_USERS\DEFAULT\DESKTOP*Wallpaper*

Change the Wallpaper entry from (DEFAULT) to "XYZ.BMP." The change takes effect when you log off, and displays the logo centered on the desktop.

If you want your bitmap to be tiled, change the TileWallpaper value in the same subkey from "0" to "1."

Through a little experimentation, you will find other changes that can be made here. For example, try changing the cursor pointers!

Accessing the Registry Remotely

It can happen that a computer's Registry has been modified either through a utility or directly, and now the computer is not quite functioning as it should. The Registry Editor provides a facility for accessing the computer's registry remotely. If you have an administrator account on your computer that matches one on the other machine (including password), you can access the other computer's Registry. Just follow these steps:

1. Open your Registry Editor.
2. From the menu, choose Select Computer.
3. In the Select Computer dialog box, enter the name of the computer or select it from the browse list, and then click OK.
4. The Registry Editor now displays the HKEY_LOCAL_MACHINE and HKEY_USERS subtrees from that computer. The title bar of each window displays the remote computer's name.
5. When you have finished working with the remote Registry, choose Close from the Registry menu option, *being sure that the remote Registry window is highlighted.*

If you do not close the remote Registry windows, they reappear the next time you start the Registry Editor on your computer.

Ch
5

From Here...

In this chapter, we explored how to configure your Windows NT installation. We reviewed the Control Panel applets and examined the Registry. But we were configuring the computer and environment settings. Another way to configure, or administer, your computer is to create and manage user accounts. This is what we discuss next in Chapter 6, "Managing Users and Accounts."

Taking the Disc Test

 If you have read and understood the material in the chapter, you are ready to test your knowledge. Insert the CD-ROM that comes with this book and run the self-test software as described in Appendix I, "Using the CD-ROM."

Managing Users and Accounts

This chapter discusses the creation and management of accounts on Windows NT Workstation 4.0. While we do not ordinarily think of creating multiple user accounts on a workstation computer, there are some compelling reasons for creating both user and group accounts on a Windows NT workstation. The information that you will learn in this section is also directly applicable to basic account management on Windows NT 4.0 Server. Throughout this chapter I will make reference to account management on a server to help compare and contrast that from the workstation.

Topics covered in this chapter include:

◆ Exploring user and group accounts

◆ Creating user and group accounts

◆ The uniqueness of account identification

◆ Managing users through group accounts

◆ Exploring account policies and system rights

◆ Creating and managing user profiles

◆ Troubleshooting account management issues

Understanding User and Group Accounts

As you recall from previous chapters, the first screen that you see after booting and pressing Ctrl+Alt+Del is the Logon Security dialog box. It is here that you must enter your username and password in order to gain access to the workstation either through local or network authentication.

Key Concept

You should therefore consider the user account as the first and foremost security object for access to your local and network resources.

Each user and group account that is created is unique to Windows NT and as such has a *unique* security identifier associated with it. This identifier is called the Windows NT Security Identifier, more commonly referred to as the SID. All references made by Windows NT to any account, especially those dealing with security access and permissions, are linked to the SID. If you delete the user account and re-create it *using exactly the same information*, Windows NT will create a *new* SID for that user and all security access and permissions will have to be reestablished. The account information is stored in the Security Accounts Manager database (SAM) which you will recall is part of the Windows NT 4.0 Registry. If the account is a local account—in other words, an account that a user uses to log on to a specific workstation at the workstation—the account is included in the SAM database of that workstation's Registry. If the account is a network account, meaning an account that is used to log on to the enterprise network from any given workstation, the account is included in the SAM database of the Primary Domain Controller for the account domain of the enterprise.

Key Concept

A local account, in general, will only have access to resources on the local workstation. A network account will have access as provided to network resources such as shared printers, files, and folders.

Note   Refer to Chapter 2, "Understanding Microsoft Windows NT 4.0," for a review of domain controllers and enterprise network models. ▪

Default User Accounts

When you first install Windows NT Workstation 4.0, two default accounts are created for you: the Administrator and Guest accounts. Neither of these accounts can be deleted. For this reason, care must be taken to preserve the integrity of these accounts.

The Guest account provides the least amount of access for the user and is, in fact, disabled by default on both Windows NT Workstation and Server to prevent inadvertent access to resources. It is strongly recommended that you assign a password to this account and for additional security, rename the account.

The Administrator account, as you might expect, provides the greatest amount of access and complete functional rights to the workstation (or the enterprise). Since this account is created by Windows NT by default, it also is the first account that a user has to log on to the workstation with. In reality, it is highly unlikely that the average user will need to log on to the workstation with full administrative privileges to do most everyday activities. Therefore, it is strongly recommended that this account be password-protected (with a unique, though memorable, password), and for additional security, it should also be renamed. After all, if you were a hacker trying to break in with administrative access, the first account name you would try would probably be "administrator," and then perhaps "supervisor" or "admin" or "XYZadmin" where XYZ is your company name. If I have exhausted your choices for alternate administrator account names, good! With Internet access especially prevalent, enterprise security has become an extremely significant and sensitive issue.

Ch

6

Another suggestion that Microsoft makes is to create a separate user account for everyday access. The user would then use this account to access his or her workstation and only log on as Administrator when that level of access is required. This eliminates a potential security "hole," i.e., being logged in as administrator and leaving for lunch without locking the workstation or logging out. This may not be quite so significant when logged on as a local administrator, but becomes far more disconcerting when logged on to a domain as a network administrator.

In some organizations, the Administrator account is not only renamed, but is randomly assigned one of several different passwords. Also, the user is often *not* told the new name or password. Administrative tasks that must take place on the workstation must be performed by a designated workgroup administrator. This is not quite as limiting to the user as one might think as you will discern later in this chapter.

Default Group Accounts

When you first install Windows NT Workstation 4.0, six default groups are created for you: Administrators, Power Users, Users, Guests, Backup Operators, and Replicator. These groups are considered *local* groups in that they are used to provide a certain level of functional access for that local workstation. Any additional groups that you create will also be local and will be used primarily for administering access to resources on that local workstation. Table 6.1 describes the types of functional access associated with each group.

Table 6.1   Built-in Local Groups

Group	Description
Administrators	Members of this group can fully administer the computer, or the domain. The Administrator account is automatically made a member of this group. Administrators, while not automatically having access to all files and resources, can gain access at any time.

Group	Description
Power Users	Members of this group have some of the same privileges that Administrators do, but cannot fully administer the workstation or domain.
Users	Members of this group have the necessary level of access to operate the computer for daily tasks such as word processing, database access, and so forth. Every new user that you create becomes a member of this group.
Guests	Members of this group have the least level of access to resources. The Guest account is automatically a member of this group. Anyone in the network can potentially access a computer's resources through this group, so it is important that resource permissions be appropriately set. (See Chapter 7, "Windows NT 4.0 Security Model.")
Backup Operators	Members of this group have only enough access to files and folders as is needed to back them up or restore them on this workstation.
Replicator	When Directory Replication is configured, this group is used to identify the specific user account, often called a *service* account that Windows NT uses to perform the replication function.

Table 6.2 lists functions and tasks, and the groups that can perform them.

Ch
6

Table 6.2 Functional Tasks Assigned to Default Groups

Function	Groups Assigned
Assign user rights	Administrators
Create and manage users	Administrators, Power Users, Users
Create and manage groups	Administrators, Power Users
Create and manage shares	Administrators, Power Users
Create common groups	Administrators, Power Users
Format the hard disk	Administrators
Keep a local profile	Administrators, Power Users, Backup Operators
Lock the workstation	Administrators, Power Users, Everyone
Override the lock	Administrators
Share\stop sharing printers	Administrators, Power Users

There are also four groups created and managed by Windows NT to "place" a user for accessing resources called internal or system groups. They are: Everyone, Interactive, Network, and Creator Owner.

Everyone, of course, means just that. Every user that logs on to the workstation or accesses a resource on the workstation (or server) locally or remotely becomes a member of the internal group Everyone. It is interesting to note that Windows NT's philosophy for securing resources is *not* to secure them at all. By default, the group Everyone has full access to resources. It is up to the administrator to restrict that access and *add* security.

Interactive represents to Windows NT the user who has logged on at the workstation itself and accesses resources on that workstation. This is also referred to as logging on locally.

Network represents to Windows NT any user who has connected to a resource on the workstation from another computer (remotely).

Creator Owner represents the user who is the owner or has taken ownership of a resource. This group can, for example, be used to assign file
access only to the owner of a file. While Everyone may have read access
to files in a directory, Creator Owner will have full access; thus, while
other users can read a file, only the owner of the file can make changes
to it.

The membership of these internal groups is fixed by the Windows NT
operating system and cannot be altered. For example, if you create a file,
you are the owner of that file, and Windows NT places you in the Creator Owner group for that file.

Group Management in Domains

This book is geared toward Windows NT Workstation 4.0 management
issues. However, as your workstation is apt to be a member of a larger
enterprise network, you should know a bit about domain group management as well.

When user accounts are created for participation in an enterprise network, these accounts are created and stored in the SAM database on a
primary domain controller. This special Windows NT server acts as the
authenticating server for users requesting logon and resource access
throughout the network.

Group accounts are created and maintained there as well. However,
there are two types of group accounts that can be created in a domain:

◆ *Local* groups in a domain are local to the domain controller(s)
   in that domain and are used to manage resources local to the
   domain controller(s) just like they are used to manage resources
   local to a workstation. Local groups can be created on workstations, servers, and domain controllers.

◆ *Global* groups, on the other hand, are global to the *domain*. They
   can be used by any workstation or server that is a member of
   the domain to manage *local* resources. In other words, you don't
   have to create individual local groups of domain users on
   individual computers. You can use the same global groups of

Ch

6

domain users that are available to all resource managers in the network. Global groups can only be created and maintained on domain controllers.

There are three built-in global groups and three additional local groups created on the domain controller. The Power Users group is not created for a domain controller. Table 6.3 describes each.

Table 6.3 Global and Local Groups on the Domain Controller

Group	Type	Description
Domain Admins	Global	This global group is used to assign its members administrative privileges on local computers by making it a member of the local Administrators group. It automatically becomes a member of the Administrators local group on the domain controller.
Domain Users	Global	This global group contains all domain user accounts that are created and is itself a member of the Users local group on the domain controller. If made a member of a workstation's local Users group, its members will assume the user privileges that the local Users group has been given on that workstation.
Domain Guests	Global	This global group contains the domain Guest account. If made a member of a workstation's local Guests group, the domain guest account will also have guest access to the workstation resources.

Group	Type	Description
Account Operators	Local	Members of this local group gain the ability to create and manage users, local groups, and global groups in the domain and to shut down the system.
Print Operators	Local	Members of this local group gain the ability to share and stop sharing printers, and to shut down the system.
Server Operators	Local	Members of this local group gain the ability to create and manage shared directories, share and stop sharing printers, lock and unlock the server, format the hard disk, shut down the system locally and remotely, change the system time, and backup and restore files and directories.

Local groups can have as their members any local users, domain users, and global groups. They cannot have another local group as a member.

Global groups can only have users from their own domain as a valid member.

Microsoft's group strategy for domains recommends that domain users be grouped into as many global groups as is appropriate. Local resource managers should then create local groups for maintaining access to the resources. The global groups are then used as members of the local groups. Whichever domain users are members of the global group will get whatever level of access was given to the local group. While this may at first seem to be a bit of over-management, in large networks with hundreds or thousands of users, this strategy makes much sense and can actually facilitate user management and resource access.

Ch

6

Planning for New User Accounts

Setting up new user accounts, especially on a domain controller, involves some planning. Here are four basic areas to consider before creating new accounts:

◆ Account naming conventions

◆ How to deal with passwords

◆ Group membership

◆ Profile information

If you are creating user accounts on a domain controller, you must also consider the following:

◆ Logon hours (when logon is possible)

◆ Which workstations the user can log on from

Naming Conventions

The choice of username determines how the user will be identified on the network. In all lists of users and groups, the account names will be displayed alphabetically, so the choice of username can be significant. For example, if your naming convention is FirstnameLastinitial, your usernames for the following users would look like this:

User	Username
Charlie Brown	CharlieB
Lucy VanPelt	LucyvanP
Beetle Bailey	BeetleB
Dagwood Bumstead	DagwoodB
Dilbert	Dilbert

Now, what if you had several Charlies or Lucys, and so on. In a large corporation, it would not be uncommon to have 20 or 30 persons with the same first name. Looking through a list of users with the same first name and only a last initial to go by could become not only confusing, but irritating as well.

A more effective convention might be LastnameFirstInitial, like so:

User	Username
Charlie Brown	BrownC
Lucy VanPelt	VanpeltL
Beetle Bailey	BaileyB
Dagwood Bumstead	BumsteadD
Dilbert	Dilbert

Finding the appropriate user in a list will be easier. Many organizations will already have a network ID naming convention in place and it would be perfectly acceptable to follow that.

Usernames must be unique both locally and to the enterprise. Therefore, your naming convention must plan for duplicate names. Charlie Brown and Chuck Brown would both have the username BrownC according to the second convention suggested above. So perhaps the convention could be altered to include middle initials in the event of a "tie," i.e., BrownCA and BrownCB, or include extra letters from the first name until uniqueness is achieved, i.e., BrownCha and BrownChu. Usernames are not case-sensitive and can contain up to 20 characters, including spaces, except the following: """ / \ { } : ; | = , + ★ ? < >.

You might also consider creating user accounts based on function rather than the user's name. For example, if the role of administrative assistant is assigned from a pool of employees, then it may make more sense to create an account called AdminAsst or FrontDesk, and so on. This will ensure that the assistant of the day will have access to everything that person should have access to—as well as minimize your administrative setup for that person.

Considerations Regarding Passwords

Besides the obvious consideration that requiring a password provides the greater level of security, there are some other things to think about. One of these is who controls the password.

Ch
6

When you create a new user account, you have three password-related options to determine:

- User Must Change Password at Next Logon
- User Cannot Change Password
- Password Never Expires

Selecting *User Must Change Password at Next Logon* allows you to set a blank or "dummy" password for the user. When the user logs on for the first time, Windows NT will require the user to change the password.

Key Concept

It is important to set company policy and educate the user in the importance of protecting the integrity of their accounts by using unique and "unguessable" passwords. Among the most common choices for passwords are children's names, pet's names, favorite sports teams, or team members. Try to avoid the obvious association when choosing a password.

User Cannot Change Password provides the most control to the administrator. This option is particularly useful for temporary employees, or the administrative assistant pool account.

Password Never Expires ensures that the password will not need to be changed, even if the overall password policy requires changes after a set period of time has elapsed. Again, this is useful for the types of accounts just mentioned or for service accounts.

Passwords are *case-sensitive* and can be up to 14 characters in length. It is generally suggested among network administrators to require a minimum password length of eight characters, using alphanumeric characters and a combination of upper- and lowercase. For example, I might use as my password a combination of my initials and the last four digits of my Social Security number—two things I am not likely to forget, but not obvious to anyone else. Thus my password might be SDK4532, or it might be sdk4532, SdK4532, 4532sdK, 45sdk32, and, oh well, you get the idea.

Group Membership

The easiest way to manage large numbers of users is to group them together logically, functionally, departmentally, and so forth. Creating local groups for local resource access control is the most common use for creating groups on the workstation. You do not have to decide how to group users before creating the groups, but if you have already planned your groups, you can include the user's group membership right up front while creating the account.

Determining User Profile Information

When referring to User Profiles on a Windows NT workstation, we are usually referring to a local logon script or the location of the user's personal folder (directory). In the larger workgroup or enterprise, however, the user profile might be a file of environment settings that is stored on a specific computer and downloaded to whatever Windows NT-based computer that the user is logging in from. The location of the logon script and personal folder might also be located on a remote computer rather than on the local workstation, especially useful if the user moves around a lot (like our pool of administrative assistants).

It is helpful, though not necessary, to determine ahead of time where this information will be kept, and how much will be used. Will you need a user profile stored on a server for every user, or only for administrative assistants? Does everyone need a logon script? Should personal files be stored on the local workstation, or on a central computer? (Again, this is useful for users who move around.)

A more thorough discussion of user profile files and login scripts will be undertaken later in this chapter.

Ch

6

Understanding User Manager

User and group accounts are created and managed through an administrative tool called User Manager. Account policies are also created and maintained through this utility, as well as the assignment of functional user rights and the enabling of security auditing. Functional rights define what functions a user can perform on a Windows NT computer. For example, shutting down the computer, changing the system time, formatting the hard disk, and installing device drivers are all functional rights.

Note   On a domain controller, the User Manager utility is called User Manager for Domains and includes additional management options appropriate for enterprise account management, such as logon hours, valid logon workstations, and trust relationships.

User Manager acts as the database manager for user and group accounts stored in the SAM database as shown in Figure 6.1. There are four menu options:

◆ *User* creates and modifies user and group accounts.

◆ *Policies* sets account policies, assigns functional user rights, and enables security auditing.

◆ *Options* enables\disables confirmation and save settings, and sets display fonts for User Manager.

◆ *Help* displays the Windows NT help files specific to User Manager.

FIG. 6.1 ⇒

User Manager displays the account database showing all user group accounts. Here we see the two default users and six default groups that are created during installation.

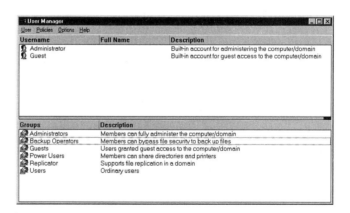

Creating a New User

Selecting New User from the User menu option displays the New User dialog box shown in Figure 6.2. This is a fairly intuitive screen and is described in the following list:

FIG. 6.2 ⇒

The New User
dialog box filled in,
with the Group
Memberships
window showing
the default mem-
bership in the
Users local group.

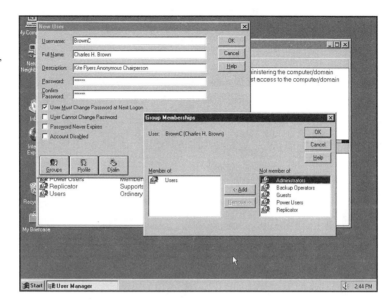

Username	This is the logon ID that you have chosen for the user. Recall that this name must be unique in the database (or in the enterprise when creating the account on a domain controller), up to 20 characters including spaces, but excluding "" / \ [ ] : ; | = , + ★ ? < >.
Full Name	This will be the user's full name. As with usernames, it is recommended that you determine a convention for entering this name (such as "Charles H. Brown") as the full name is used by Windows NT for determining the user account sort order.
Description	A simple description of the account or user, such as "Admin Assistant Account" or "Project Manager."
Password	The password is case-sensitive and can be up to 14 characters in length. Recall our discussion of password integrity earlier.
Confirm Password	You must confirm the password here before Windows NT can create the account.

Ch

6

User Must Change Password At Next Logon	This password option forces the users to change their password the next time they log on.
User Cannot Change Password	This password option prevents the users from being able to change their password. As mentioned earlier, this setting is useful for accounts for which the password should remain the same, such as temporary employee accounts.
Password Never Expires	This password option prevents the password from expiring and overrides the Maximum Password Age set in the Account Policy as well as User Must Change Password at Next Logon.
Account Disabled	Prevents the use of the account. This is a useful setting for users who are on vacation, on extended leave, or whose accounts otherwise should not be available for logging in to the network. It is always more appropriate to disable an account if there is any possibility of the user returning. Remember that deleting a user account also deletes the user's SID, and thus removes all previous network resource access for that user.
Groups	This button displays the Group Memberships dialog box which displays the user's group membership and from which group membership can be modified.
Profile	This button displays the User Environment Profile dialog box from which a server-based profile can be referenced, logon script defined, and home folder (directory) identified.
Dialin	This button displays the Dialin Information dialog box which is used to grant permission to use Dial-Up Networking to the user account and set Call Back options.

As you can see, it is a fairly straightforward process to create user accounts. By double-clicking the account name in the User Manager window, or highlighting the username and choosing Properties from User on the menu, you can view these settings for each user and modify them as is appropriate.

User Manager for Domains—New User Options

When creating and managing users in the enterprise account domain, there are some additional options available for the user accounts.

Hours	This button displays the Logon Hours dialog box from which you can determine what times of the day the user can log on to the network. This is useful for shift employees, or for backup times.
Logon To	This button displays the Logon Workstations dialog box and allows you to identify by computer name the computers at which this account can log on to the network. You can identify up to eight workstations.
Account	This button displays the Account Information dialog box in which you can specify an expiration date for the account and identify whether the account is a global domain account (default) or for a user from another untrusted domain who needs occasional access to your domain.

Creating a New Local Group

The process of creating a new local group is even more straightforward as you can see by the New Local Group dialog box displayed in Figure 6.3.

Group Name	This is the name you have chosen for the local group. It can have up to 256 characters except the backslash (\) which, while descriptive, would be somewhat confusing in display lists of groups. Group names, unlike usernames, *cannot* be changed.
Description	A simple description of the group such as Administrative Assistants or Project Managers.

Ch

6

FIG. 6.3 ⇒

This example of the New Local Group dialog box shows the new group name and description filled in, and the Add Users and Groups dialog box displayed.

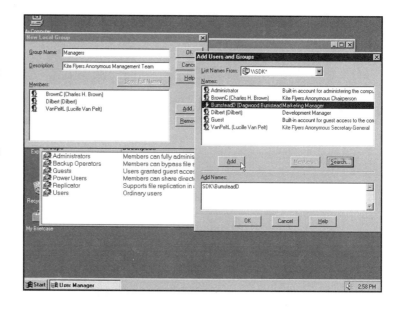

Show Full Names	This button displays the full name associated with each user account displayed in the *Members* list box.
Members	Displays all the current user accounts (or domain user and global group accounts) that are members of this local group.
Add	This button displays the Add Users and Groups dialog box from which you can select user accounts from your workstation SAM database, or domain user and global group accounts from the enterprise SAM database on a domain controller. An example of this dialog box is also shown in Figure 6.3. Select the workstation or account domain that has the desired user accounts from the List Names From list box, click the user you want to add to the group in the Names list box, and choose Add, then OK. Use the Search button to look for an account among all possible account databases. If you have selected a global

| | group in the <u>N</u>ames list box, use <u>M</u>embers to display the members of that global group. You can select multiple accounts at one time by Ctrl-clicking the additional accounts. |
| Remove | This button deletes the selected account from group membership. |

> **Note**　Here's a shortcut to populating a group. Before you create the group, select all the usernames you want in the group from the User Manager Username screen by Ctrl-clicking the additional accounts. Then create the group. The Members list box will display any user account that has been highlighted before the group was created. ▪

User Manager for Domains—Group Options

Creating a group in the enterprise account domain is pretty much the same as creating groups on the workstation. The difference is that in addition to creating local groups, you can also create global groups. Recall that a global group is one that can be used by any workstation or server that participates in the enterprise for managing resource access.

When you create a new global group, you can only select user accounts from the account domain database and these are the only accounts that are displayed for you.

Renaming, Copying, and Deleting Accounts

Recall from our discussion of the default Administrator and Guest accounts that for a higher level of security, you can rename these accounts. Renaming an account does not affect the account's SID in any way. This makes it relatively easy to change a username without affecting any of that user's access—whether it be changing the Administrator account to enhance its security, or reflecting a name change due to marriage or the Witness Protection Program. Simply highlight the username in User Manager, choose <u>R</u>ename from the <u>U</u>ser menu option, then enter in the new username in the box provided. Group names *cannot* be renamed.

Ch

6

Key Concept

If you choose to delete an account, remember that the account's SID will also be deleted and all resource access and user rights will be lost. This means that if you re-create the account even *exactly* as it was before, the SAM database will generate a new SID for the account and you will have to reestablish resource access and user rights for that account.

To delete the account, highlight it and press DEL on the keyboard, or choose <u>D</u>elete from <u>U</u>ser. Windows NT will warn you that the SID will be lost. Choose OK and the account will be deleted.

Note   You cannot delete built-in user or group accounts. ▓

The <u>C</u>opy option under <u>U</u>ser is useful for duplicating user account information that is the same for a group of users. Since you cannot rename a group, copying a group to a new name also duplicates its membership list and is the next best thing to renaming. Copying user and group accounts results in new accounts being created. As such, each new account will have its own new SID assigned to it.

When you copy a user account, the following settings are maintained: the Description, the password options that have been checked off, and if Account Disabled has been selected, it will be unchecked for the copy. Also, group membership and profile information are maintained for the copied account. This greatly simplifies the task of creating large numbers of similar users.

Note   In User Manager for Domains, Logon Hours, Logon To workstations, and account expiration and type are also copied to the new account. ▓

Creating and Managing Account Policies, System Rights, and Auditing

Account Policy information and User Rights are considered part of account management and as such are administered through User

Manager. Account Policy information includes password specific information such as password age and minimum length, and account lockout options. User rights represent the functional rights that a user acquires for a given workstation when logging in. Auditing for file and directory access, print access, and so forth is accomplished by specifying the users or groups whose access you wish to audit and is done at the file, directory, and print level. However, auditing for those security events must first be enabled for user and group accounts; that is done through User Manager as well.

Account Policy

Figure 6.4 shows a typical Account Policy. The options presented in this dialog box should be very familiar to network administrators.

FIG. 6.4 ⇒

The password must be at least six characters long and expires every 45 days. Also, if the user forgets the password in three consecutive tries within 30 minutes, the account will be locked out until an administrator releases it.

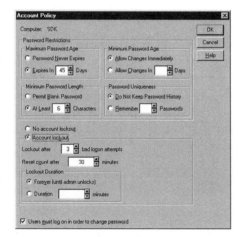

Maximum Password Age	The password may be set to never expire, or you may select a set number of days after which the user will be prompted to change the password. The default is set to 42 days.
Minimum Password Age	The default here is to allow users to change their password any time they want. Many organizations now prefer that passwords cannot be changed whenever the user wants. The user must

Ch

6

	wait a specified number of days before the password can be changed. This helps to maintain password uniqueness.
Minimum Password Length	The default, oddly enough, is to allow blank passwords. As discussed earlier, you will probably want to define a minimum length for the password. Most network administrators use eight as the minimum length. The maximum length can be fourteen.
Password Uniqueness	The default is to not maintain a history of past passwords. This allows a user to reuse passwords when they expire. While being able to reuse a password is convenient for the user, it is not always the most secure way to deal with passwords. Many organizations require passwords to be unique. This is accomplished by specifying the number of passwords to be "remembered" by the system for each user (up to 24), requiring a maximum password age and a minimum password age. For example, by setting the maximum and minimum password age to 30 days, and uniqueness to 24, the user would not be able to reuse the first password for 2 years. This in effect accomplishes uniqueness simply because the user is not likely to be able to remember that far back.
Account Lockout	The default is to not enable account lockout. Since this does add additional resource overhead to the system, it is probably not truly necessary except on workstations which contain particularly sensitive data. Nevertheless, in the enterprise, where security is essential, this option will probably be enabled and in fact is recommended.
Lockout After…	Specifies the number of bad logon attempts (incorrect passwords) that the system will accept before locking out that account. The default is 5 and can be set from 1 to 999.

Reset Count After…	This number represents the number of minutes that the system will wait between bad logon attempts before resetting the bad logon count back to 0. For example, if I misenter my password, the bad logon count is set to one. If the reset count is 15 minutes, after 15 minutes, if I do not log on incorrectly again, the bad logon count is set back to 0. The default is 30 minutes, and can be set from 1 to 99,999 minutes (or roughly 70 days, for those of you who couldn't help wondering).
Lockout Duration	You can require an administrator to reset the account after lockout. (This is one of my favorite radio button choices in Windows NT because of its name: "Forever.") You could also specify a length of time for the lockout to be in effect before letting the computer hacker try again. The default for this choice is 30 minutes, and can be set from 1 to 99,999 minutes.
Users Must Log On In	This option will require that the user log in to the system before making password changes. Normally, when a password expires, the user is prompted during logon to change the password. With this option selected, the user will *not* be able to change the expired password, and the administrator will need to reset it. This is useful for short term employee accounts that expire in a specific amount of time to ensure that the employees cannot change the password on their own.

User Rights

As mentioned previously, user rights are *functional* rights and represent functions or tasks that a user or group can perform on a given workstation. Contrast this with *permissions* such as read only, write, and delete,

Ch
6

which reflect resource access rights. User rights include shutting down the computer, formatting a hard disk, backing up files and directories, and so forth.

User rights are granted primarily to local groups. As we will discuss in the next chapter, user rights maintain Access Control Lists (ACLs). Groups and users represented by their SIDs are members of the ACL for each user right. Consequently, there is no way to select an account and see what user rights (or file permissions for that matter) have been assigned to that account because the rights do not "stay" with the account. Table 6.4 highlights the basic user rights and the default groups assigned to each.

Table 6.4 User Rights

User Right	Group(s) Assigned
Access this computer from the network	Administrators, Power Users, Everyone (no Power Users group on domain controllers)
Back up files and directories	Administrators, Backup Operators (Server Operators on domain controllers)
Change the system time	Administrators, Power Users (Server Operators on domain controllers)
Force shutdown from a remote system	Administrators, Power Users (Server Operators on domain controllers)
Load and unload device drivers	Administrators
Log on locally	All built-in groups, including Everyone, except Replicator (all built-in local groups on domain controllers *except* Everyone, Users and Guests)
Manage auditing and security log	Administrators
Restore files and directories	Administrators, Backup Operators (Server Operators on domain controllers)

User Right	Group(s) Assigned
Shut down the system	All built-in groups except Guests and Replicator (all built-in local groups except Everyone, Users and Guests on domain controllers)
Take Ownership of files or objects	Administrators

Accounts assigned to the various user rights can be administered through the User Rights Policy dialog box displayed by choosing <u>U</u>ser Rights from the <u>P</u>olicy menu (see Figure 6.5). Select the user right from the <u>Right</u> drop down list. The default groups assigned this user right will be displayed in the <u>G</u>rant To list box. Choose the <u>A</u>dd button to display the Add Users and Groups dialog box and add user and group accounts to the user right's <u>G</u>rant To list, or choose <u>R</u>emove to delete members from the <u>G</u>rant To list.

FIG. 6.5 ⇒
Log on locally has been selected, and in the Grant To box behind the drop down list, you can see the groups assigned this user right.

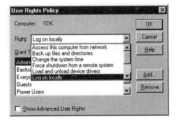

There are advanced rights that can also be displayed by checking that option at the bottom of the User Rights Policy dialog box. These rights are for use primarily by developers. However, there are two advanced user rights which as an administrator on a network you may need to modify from time to time.

Ch
6

Bypass traverse checking	This advanced user right allows the specified user or group accounts to change between directories and navigate directory trees even if permission has been denied to various directories. This might be assigned to Power Users or resource managers.

Log on as a service	This advanced user right is intended for user accounts that are used by certain background application tasks or Windows NT system functions such as Directory Replication. This right allows the service or function to log in as the specified account for the express purpose of carrying out that specific task. No other user needs to be logged in for the task to be performed.

Audit Policy

As stated earlier, auditing for events relating to file and directory access, print access, and so forth, is accomplished by specifying the users or groups whose access you wish to audit. This is done at the file, directory, and print levels. However, auditing for those security events must first be enabled for user and group accounts and that is done through User Manager by selecting Audit from Policies on the menu (see Figure 6.6).

FIG. 6.6 ⇒
This Audit Policy has enabled auditing of failed logon and logoff attempts, unsuccessful file and object access, and any events relating to restart, shutdown, or system processes.

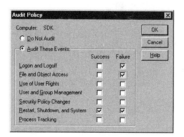

By default, auditing is not enabled because of the additional resources required to monitor the system for related events. There are seven areas for which auditing can be enabled.

Logon and Logoff	Monitors user logon and logoff of the workstation and network connections.

File and Object Access	Monitors user access of files, directories, or printers. This enables the auditing. The users and groups that are audited are set up at the file, directory, and printer level.
Use of User Rights	Monitors when a user right is exercised by a user (such as formatting the hard disk).
User and Group Management	Monitors events relating to user and group management such as the creation of new users, the modification of group membership, or the change of a password.
Security Policy Changes	Monitors changes made to User Rights or Account Policy information.
Restart, Shutdown, System	Monitors events related to these activities.
Process Tracking	Monitors events related to certain process activity such as starting a program, indirect object access, and so on.

Successful and Unsuccessful events can be logged in the Security Log which can be viewed through the Event Viewer, another useful Administrative Tools utility. It is generally not at all useful for you to monitor successful and unsuccessful events for all seven options, even on a server because of the resources involved, and the volume of data that would be collected in the security log. Auditing, however, can be very helpful in troubleshooting events such as unsuccessful logins or unsuccessful file access.

Creating and Managing User Profiles

When we speak of the User Profile in Windows NT 4.0, we are really talking about managing the user's working environment. Through the User Environment Profile dialog box (see Figure 6.7) in User Manager (and User Manager for Domains in the enterprise), various elements of the user's environment can be defined.

Ch
6

FIG. 6.7 ⇒

BrownC's profile
information is
stored on a server
called Kiteserver,
that KITELOG.
BAT will be ex-
ecuted when he
logs on, and that his
personal data folder
is in a share called
Users.

These include the Under Profile Path, which identifies the location of the
Registry files and profile folders for the user, the Logon Script Name,
which identifies the name and optional path of a set of commands that
are executed when the user logs on, and the Home Directory, which
identifies the location of the user's personal data folder.

Home Directory

The Home Directory simply represents a place where the user can routinely save data files. This is usually a folder (directory) that has been
created on a centrally located server in the enterprise network, though
in small workgroups, it may actually be found on the user's local workstation—or not identified at all.

The advantage of placing the home directory on a centrally located
server somewhere in the domain is primarily that of security. By using
NTFS permissions, the users' folders can be secured quite nicely so that
only they (and whomever they determine) can have access to them. In
addition, these folders can then be included in regular server data backups, thus ensuring the availability of the files in the event of accidental
deletion, corruption, or system crashes.

In the Home Directory section of the User Environment Profile dialog box (accessed by viewing the Properties of the user account and choosing Profile), there are two choices: Local Path and Connect To. The first represents the drive and path to an existing home directory folder, such as C:\USERS in which the user's own profile folder can be created. The other represents a UNC (Universal Naming Convention) path that identifies the name of the server that contains an existing home directory share, and a logical drive letter to assign to it that the user can use for saving files in applications, searching, exploring with Explorer, and so on.

Note   A UNC name is very much like a DOS path in that it represents the path through the network to a network resource. In this case, the network resource is a directory that has been "shared" for the creation of a home directory folder for the user. UNC names take the following form:

    \\servername\sharename\path

where *servername* represents the name of the server computer that contains the folder, *sharename* represents the name of the directory that has been made available for use as a resource (shared), and where *path* represents an optional path to a subdirectory or specific file.

In the previous Figure 6.7, the Home Directory will be located on the server called Kiteserver under a directory called Users (which has been shared). You will notice the use of an environmental parameter to identify the path. If I had entered a specific directory name, Windows NT would have created that directory for me if it did not already exist. By using the variable %USERNAME%, Windows NT will create a directory using the username as the directory name. This is particularly useful when using a template for creating large numbers of users. Recall that when you create a new user account by copying an existing account, the User Environment Profile information is also copied. Using %USERNAME% will enable individual user home folders to be created by using each user's username as the directory name. Table 6.5, later in this chapter, displays a list of the environment variables that Windows NT 4.0 can use.

Ch
6

Logon Scripts

If you have had any dealings with networks before, you have encountered a logon script. Logon scripts are simply files that contain a set of network commands which need to be executed in a particular order. Often, as is the case with Novell Netware, logon scripts have a specific command language and structure that should be used. In the case of Windows NT, they are simply batch files and support all the Windows NT command line commands, or in some cases, an executable.

Here is an example of a Windows NT logon script called LOGON.BAT:

```
@echo Welcome to the NT Network!
@echo off
Pause
Net use p:\\server5\database
Net use r:\\server4\budget
Net time \\server1 /set /y
```

The name of the logon script is arbitrary. Windows NT does provide a place for storing logon scripts. In an enterprise setting they are usually placed in the WINNT40\SYSTEM32\REPL\IMPORT\SCRIPTS subdirectory on a domain controller. Since the user uses an available domain controller to gain access to the network, it makes sense that the logon scripts be stored there as well.

The advantage of storing the logon scripts on a domain controller is that through a process called Directory Replication, the scripts can be distributed to *all* the domain controllers in the network. Since a user may authenticate at any one of the domain controllers, this provides a convenient way to ensure that the logon scripts are always available. Also, it provides the administrator with *one* central storage place for the scripts, making maintenance of them easier.

Notice that in the example in Figure 6.7 earlier in this chapter, the entry for the Logon Script Name is simply the batch file name. Windows NT assumes that you will be storing this file in the Scripts subdirectory on the validating server. If you are logging on locally to the workstation, that directory can be found on the local hard drive and Windows NT will look there. If you are logging on to an enterprise network,

Windows NT assumes that the file is in that directory on a domain controller. If the logon script cannot be found, Windows NT will record that fact and proceed with validation. More Environment Variables are shown in Table 6.5.

Table 6.5   Additional Environment Variables for Home Directories and Logon Scripts

Variable	Description
%HOMEDIR%	Returns the logical mapping to the shared folder that contains the user's home directory.
%HOMEDRIVE%	Returns the logical drive mapped to the home directory share.
%HOMEPATH%	Returns the path name of the user's home directory folder.
%HOMESHARE%	Returns the share name of the folder which contains the user's home directory folder.
%OS%	Returns the operating system of the user's computer.
%PROCESSOR_ARCHITECTURE%	Returns the processor's base architecture, such as Intel or MIPS, of the user's computer.

Ch
6

continues

Table 6.5 Continued	
Variable	Description
%PROCESSOR_LEVEL%	Returns the processor type, such as 486, of the user's computer.
%USERDOMAIN%	Returns the name of the enterprise account domain in which the user is validating.
%USERNAME%	Returns the user's logon ID (username).

User Profiles

The User Profile itself represents the user's environment settings such as screen colors, wallpaper, persistent network and printer connections, mouse settings and cursors, shortcuts, personal groups, and Startup programs. These settings are normally saved as part of the Windows NT Registry and loaded when the user logs on to the system.

In Windows NT 3.51 and earlier versions, these settings were kept in the WINNT40\SYSTEM32\CONFIG subdirectory with the other Registry files on the local computer, workstation or server, that the user logged into. The next time that the user logged on, the profile settings were made available and merged into the Registry for that session. If the user moved to another computer, whether the user logged on locally or on the network, a new profile would be created on that computer and saved locally.

Profiles in Windows NT 4.0 are still saved on the local computer at which the user logs on. However, all information relating to the user's profile is saved in a subdirectory structure created in the WINNT40\PROFILES subdirectory which contains the Registry data file as well as directory links to desktop items. An example of this structure is displayed in Figure 6.8.

FIG. 6.8 ⇒

In this view of
Windows Explorer,
we see the
WINNT40\
PROFILES
subdirectory with
the profile folder
structure for
BROWNC ex-
panded. Notice
the Registry file
NTUSER.DAT.

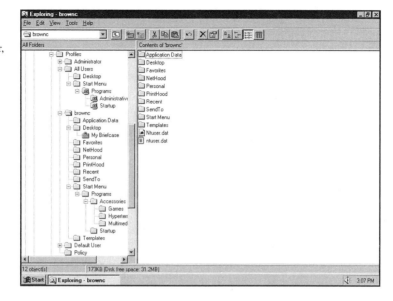

There are three default profile structures created during installation: one
for the Administrator's account, of course; one called *Default User* from
which new user accounts derive their initial environment settings; and
one called *All Users* which are used with the user's profile settings to
assign settings which should be common to all users, such as startup
items and common groups. The directory structure of the user's profile
directory is outlined in Table 6.6.

When the user first logs on, the settings contained in Default User are
used to create that user's own profile folders. In addition, the Registry
data file, called NTUSER.DAT is created and stored in the root of the
user's profile folder (refer to Figure 6.8). As the user modifies the environment by changing settings, creating shortcuts, installing applications,
and adding programs to the Start Menu, Windows NT adds and modifies entries in the appropriate profile folder and updates the Registry
file. For example, if BrownC (profile folders shown in Figure 6.8) added
a shortcut to his desktop for Word 7.0, Windows NT would add an
entry representing the shortcut to Word 7 in the Desktop folder under
WINNT40\PROFILES\BROWNC.

Ch

6

The Registry data file, NTUSER.DAT is actually a cached copy of the Registry subtree HKEY_CURRENT_USER and as we discussed in Chapter 5, "Configuration and the Registry," contains information relating to the user's environment settings such as color schemes, cursors, wallpaper, and so forth.

Table 6.6 Overview of the Profile Folder Directory Structure

Profile Folder	Description
Application	Contains references to application-specific data and is usually modified by the application during installation or when a user modifies a setting for the application.
Desktop	Contains references to shortcuts created on the desktop and the Briefcase.
Favorites	Contains references to shortcuts made to favorite programs and locations.
NetHood	Contains references to shortcuts made to Network Neighborhood items, such as to shared folders.
Personal	Contains references to shortcuts to personal group programs.
PrintHood	Contains references to shortcuts made to print folder items.
Recent	Contains references to items on the computer most recently accessed by the user.
SendTo	Contains references to the last items that documents were "sent to" or copied, such as the A: drive or My Briefcase.
Start Menu	Contains references to program items contained on the Start menu, including the Startup group.
Templates	Contains references to shortcuts made to template items.

Note By default the NetHood, PrintHood, Recent, and Templates folders are hidden from display in Windows Explorer. They can be viewed by choosing View, Options, Show All Files. ■

Server-Based User Profiles

As we have seen, user profile information is stored on the computer(s) that the user logs in on. If a user routinely logs on to several computers, it might be inconvenient for the user to create or modify preferred settings on each computer before beginning to work on that computer. It would be far more efficient if the user's work environment settings "followed" him or her to whatever computer that the user logs into. This type of user is known as the "roaming user," a concept which is a bit disconcerting to me in the workplace, and their profiles are known as server-based, or "roaming" profiles which, perhaps, might be even more disconcerting than the vagabond users. Actually, this type of profile is used more often in organizations to provide a level of consistency among their users' desktops rather than to accommodate roaming users.

Windows NT Workstation 4.0 and Server computers support two types of server-based profiles: Roaming User Profiles and Mandatory User Profiles. They both are user profile settings which have been copied to a centrally located server for access by the user when logging on. The location and name of the profile are identified in the user's User Environment Profile information through User Manager (or User Manager for Domains). When the user logs on to a computer, either a mandatory or roaming profile are downloaded to that computer. Changes made to the roaming profile are updated both on the local computer and the server. The next time the user logs on, whichever copy of the profile is more recent is loaded, and when the user logs off, both are updated again.

The primary difference between mandatory and roaming profiles is that the *mandatory* profile is created for the user and *cannot* be modified by the user.

Ch
6

Key Concept

The user may change environment settings while in a particular session, but those settings are *not* saved back to the mandatory profile. Also, if the mandatory profile is *not* available to the user when logging on, the user will *not* be able to log on.

The roaming profile can be, and is meant to be, modified by the user and follow the user as a convenience.

Creating the Server-Based Profile

Windows NT 4.0 Server no longer provides the User Profile utility that some of you may have been familiar with. Instead, it has built-in management of User Profiles into the System applet in Control Panel. Start the System Applet and select the User Profiles tab.

The User Profiles tab displays the profiles that have been created and stored on that computer. Remember that a profile is created each time a user logs on. If you plan on deleting a user, you should delete the user's profile first through this tab. If you delete the user first, you will see an entry such as the one displayed in Figure 6.9—`Account Deleted`. This is not really such a big deal; if the account is deleted anyway, it is a pretty safe bet that you can delete its profile information. Recall that all settings relating to a user account are linked to the user's SID. Deleting the account deletes the SID and renders all previous settings obsolete.

FIG. 6.9 ⇒

Here we see that there are three user profiles contained on this computer. One of them is for an account that has since been deleted. It should be removed to clean up the Profiles directory on the hard disk.

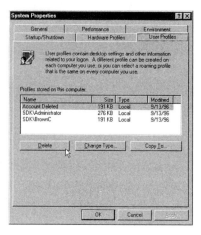

The first step in creating a roaming or mandatory profile is to identify the users or groups which require this type of profile. The Registry file name NTUSER.DAT cannot be changed, and it is this file that will determine whether the profile is mandatory or not. Next, identify the central computer on which you plan to store the users' profiles. This should be a computer that is readily accessible by the users on that network or subnet, particularly if the profiles are mandatory. The directory should then be shared on the network. Within this directory, optionally create subdirectories for the different users or groups which will use various profiles you create.

Caution

If you permit several users or a group of users to use the same roaming profile, remember that that profile *can be modified* by the user. It is possible that multiple users may make multiple changes to the profile. Mandatory profiles are better used for groups of users. Individual roaming users should each have their own roaming "changeable" profile.

Roaming and mandatory profiles are then configured in the following manner:

1. Create a user account (or select an existing account) and make the appropriate changes to that account's work environment settings.

2. Select that account through the User Profiles tab in the System applet in Control Panel and choose Copy To.

3. In the Copy Profile To box enter the UNC name to the share and directory that will contain the profiles, or choose Browse to look for the location.

4. Select Change, and from the Choose User dialog box that is displayed, select the user (Show Users) or groups which you are permitting to use this profile.

5. Choose OK to save the profile and exit the System applet.

Ch
6

If you require the profile to become mandatory, you must use Windows Explorer to select the NTUSER.DAT file and change the extension to NTUSER.MAN.

Next, you must identify the profile file to the user or users in question through the User Manager utility:

1. Open User Manager (or User Manager for Domains).

2. From the User Properties of the user in question, choose Profile to display the User Environment Profile dialog box.

3. In the User Profile Path text box, enter the UNC path to the profile file. For example, if the profile NTUSER.MAN is located in the BROWNC directory in the share PROFILES on the server KITESERVER, you would enter "**\\KITESERVER\ PROFILES\BROWNC\NTUSER.MAN**".

4. Choose OK and exit User Manager.

5. Test the profile by logging on as that user.

Note Throughout this discussion, I have not really distinguished between Windows NT Workstation 4.0 and Server other than referencing both User Manager and User Manager for Domains. This is because server-based profiles are available for use on both Windows NT Workstation 4.0 and Server. A single workstation or server computer that is part of a simple workgroup can just as easily be used to store these profiles and act as the profile "server" as a domain controller, or server participating in a domain could. It is more likely to find the use of server-based profiles in a larger domain network than in a smaller workgroup setting.

A Profile Alternative

On a server or domain controller in an enterprise domain, the System Policy Editor can alternatively, and perhaps more effectively, be used to control user profile settings. This utility was discussed briefly in Chapter 5, "Configuration and the Registry." It is only available on Windows NT servers. Through the System Policy Editor, you can modify the default settings for all users, or copy the settings and modify them by individual user or groups. The policy file is then saved as

NTCONFIG.POL in the WINNT40\SYSTEM32\REPL\IMPORT\ SCRIPTS subdirectory on all validating domain controllers.

Through the System Policy Editor, you can restrict user activity in the Display applet in Control Panel, specify desktop settings such as wallpaper and color schemes; customize desktop folders; create custom folders and Start menu options; restrict use of Run, Find, and Shutdown; and disable editing of the Registry. Combined with computer system policies, applied to the computer at which a user logs on, the administrator can get a finer level of granularity over controlling the user's work environment.

Troubleshooting Accounts, Policies, and Profiles

If you have been reading carefully, you already have the necessary building blocks for understanding and troubleshooting account management. The best tool for learning is to practice. Pay particular attention to user profiles; these can cause you some grief (as pointed out in the notes and cautions).

Most of the problems that you will encounter regarding user and group accounts will have to do with permissions to use resources rather than with the account setup itself. Nevertheless, here are some things to keep in mind.

User Cannot Be Logged On by System

When a user cannot log on, fortunately the message(s) that Windows NT displays to the screen are self-explanatory. Usually they involve the user incorrectly typing their username, or more likely, their password. Usernames are not case-sensitive, but passwords are. Usernames and passwords can both have spaces, but that tends to confuse users more than provide descriptive account names. Be sure to be consistent in your use of usernames. Educate your users in the importance of maintaining the integrity of their passwords, and expect a call every now and then from someone who has forgotten his or her password, or has the caps lock on when their password is in lowercase.

If a user forgets the Administrator password on a local workstation, you have few options. If you created an Emergency Repair Disk during installation, you can restore the SAM database, and thus the original Administrator account and password from it. However, if the Emergency Repair Disk has not been kept up to date, and additional accounts have been created in the meantime, the repair process will restore the *original* SAM database, thus losing all the additional account information. You can see now the importance of securing the Administrator account and password. If you need to, reread the sections in this chapter regarding the default Administrator account and password considerations.

Unable to Access Domain Controllers or Servers

Another possibility that can slow or inhibit a person's ability to log on successfully is the unavailability of a server. If the user is logging on locally, the user is being validated on the local computer for access to resources on that computer. Unless the computer suddenly turns itself off, the user should be able to logon successfully. If the user is validating on an enterprise network domain controller, the domain controller must be accessible to the user or the user may not be able to log on.

For example, if the primary domain controller is down and there is no backup domain controller identified to the network, the user will be unable to log on. If the user logged on successfully at the computer in a previous session, a message may display that the domain controller is unavailable and that the user will be logged on with cached information from the Registry. Any changes that may have been made to your profile since the last session will probably not be available.

You troubleshoot this one, of course, by verifying that the domain controller is up, and that the computer in question has a valid connection to the network. If you are using TCP/IP as your protocol, you will want to check that the computer has a valid IP address and subnet mask, and if routing is involved, a valid default router address.

If the user cannot log on because a mandatory profile cannot be found, there are a couple of things to look at. First check that the path to the profile specified in the user's account properties is correct. Be sure that the share name specified is indeed "shared." Next, as with the domain controller, be sure that the server which contains the profile information is accessible by the user. Look at the same suggestions made in the last paragraph.

Sometimes network-based errors cannot be easily tracked down. For example, everything may seem to be functioning OK, but you just can't seem to access the network. Sometimes the network card can get confused and the best thing to do is to shut down the computer and do a cold boot. A warm boot does not always reset the hardware, in this case the network card.

Other Logon Problems

Other problems may be related to settings made through User Manager for Domains. Recall that in this utility the administrator can additionally add logon hour and workstation restrictions for the user, as well as account expiration. Again, the messages that Windows NT displays are pretty obvious in this regard, and will direct you to the appropriate account property to check and modify.

From Here...

The next chapter will discuss an issue that is of paramount importance to any type of network, and one which we have alluded to but not pursued with great diligence. I am, of course, referring to security. We will next discuss the Windows NT security model and how to apply security to resources and make those resources available to the users and groups we have created.

Ch
6

Taking the Disc Test

 If you have read and understood the material in the chapter, you are ready to test your knowledge. Insert the CD-ROM that comes with this book and run the self-test software as described in Appendix I, "Using the CD-ROM."

Chapter Prerequisite

Before reading this chapter, you should understand the account management concepts discussed in Chapter 6 and be comfortable navigating the Windows NT 4.0 interface, especially Explorer (see Chapter 4). You should also be familiar with the Windows NT 4.0 architecture as described in Chapter 2.

7

Windows NT 4.0 Security Model

So far in our travels through the wonderful world of Windows NT, we have encountered two levels of access security: logon and user rights. Logon security is implemented through the use of user accounts and passwords. User rights, as we saw in the last chapter, are functional in nature and define what activities a user can engage in on a given computer.

In this chapter, we will discuss more thoroughly the Windows NT 4.0 security model. The security model itself applies both to Windows NT Workstation 4.0 and Server, as does the method of applying permissions and sharing resources. Specifically, we will cover the following topics:

◆ Examining Windows NT 4.0 security

◆ Exploring the Windows NT logon process

◆ Examining access tokens and access control lists

◆ Determining access rights to a security object

◆ Determining resource access in the network

◆ Sharing resources and assigning permissions

◆ Troubleshooting security access

Examining the Windows NT 4.0 Security Model

All security provided by Windows NT 4.0 is handled through an executive service known as the *Security Reference Monitor*. When a user logs on, tries to perform a function at the workstation—like formatting a disk—or tries to access a resource, the Security Reference Monitor determines whether and to what extent to allow access to the user. Logon provides security through password protection. User rights are functional in nature and define what actions a user can take at a given workstation, such as shutting down the workstation or formatting a disk. These were discussed in Chapter 6, "Managing Users and Accounts." There are also *permissions*, which define a user's access to network resources. Permissions define what a user can do *to* or *with* a resource, such as delete a print job or modify a file. The terms "rights" and "permissions" are often used interchangeably, and usually refer to resource access. With Windows NT, rights refers to those functional user rights that you can set through User Manager and User Manager for Domains; permissions refers to resource access. This is how I use these terms throughout this book.

There are two types of permissions that can be applied in Windows NT: share-level and resource-level. Share-level permissions define how a user can access a resource that has been made available (shared) on the network. This is a resource that resides some place other than the workstation at which the user is sitting and that the user accesses remotely. The owner or administrator of the resource makes it available as a network resource by sharing it. The owner or administrator of the resource also defines a list of users and groups that can access the resource through the share and determines just how much access to give them.

Resource-level permissions also define a user's access to a resource, but at the resource itself. The owner or administrator of the resource assigns a list of users and groups that can access the resource itself and the level of access to allow. Combined with share-level permissions, the owner and administrator of a resource can provide a high degree of security.

The most common resource-level permissions that you will encounter are those for files and folders. File and folder permissions are only available on NTFS-formatted partitions. If you do not have a partition formatted for NTFS, you will only be able to use the FAT-level properties—read only, archive, system, and hidden. Under NTFS, you get a more robust set of properties including read, write, delete, execute, and change permissions.

Shared devices, such as printers, also provide a means of assigning permissions to use the device—for example, printing to a print device, managing documents on the print device, and so on.

Key Concept

Any resource for which access can be determined is considered to be a security object. In other network operating systems, such as Novell Netware, permissions to use resources are assigned directly to the user or group and stay with the user or group. This is not true with Windows NT. In all cases, it is important to note that permissions are assigned to and stay with the security object and *not* the user. A user's access to a resource is determined at the time the user tries to access it, *not* when the user logs on.

When a user logs on to Windows NT, whether at the local workstation or through a domain controller, the user is granted an access token. Permissions ascribed to an object (resource) reside in an access control list with the object. The Security Reference Monitor compares the user's access token information with that in the access control list and determines what level of access to grant the user. Let's explore these concepts further.

Exploring the Windows NT Logon Process

When a user logs on to Windows NT, the username, password, and point of authentication must be provided. This is part of the Winlogon service that monitors the logon process. The Winlogon service passes this information to the CSR (client\server) subsystem, which in turn passes it to the Security Reference Monitor (see Figure 7.1).

FIG. 7.1 ⇒

Diagram of the Windows NT 4.0 logon process.

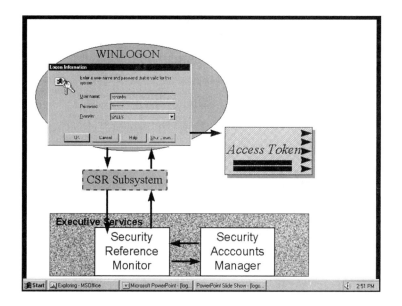

The Security Reference Monitor checks the information entered against the Security Accounts Manager (SAM) database. If the information is accurate, the Security Reference Monitor authenticates the user and returns a valid *access token* back to the CSR subsystem and the Winlogon process. The user now has the ability to access the workstation and resources on the network.

The Account Access Token

Many companies that have secured areas provide access to those areas through an electronic key card. A magnetic stripe on the back of the card contains the user's information, such as a security ID. The card is read by a card reader at the point of entry. Often, the user may also have to enter in a security number or password on a keypad before the door is unlocked.

The access token is a lot like a key card. It contains important security information about the user. This information includes, most importantly, the user's SID. Recall that the SID is the unique security identifier that Windows NT assigned to the user's account when the account was created. All security-related requests made by the user are linked to and matched first and foremost against the user's SID. Other information includes the username and password, group memberships by name and group SIDs, profile location, home directory information, logon hours, and so on.

The access token is used by Windows NT to determine whether a user can gain access to a resource, and how much access to provide.

Local versus Domain Access Tokens

When a user logs on to a local Windows NT workstation participating in a workgroup model, the user's account resides in the local Windows NT workstation's Registry (SAM database). Hence, the user's access token is created on that local Windows NT workstation and can only be used to access resources on that workstation.

When a user logs on to a Windows NT workstation that is a member of a domain, the user's account resides in the domain SAM database on the domain controller. Recall that this type of account is called a domain, or global, account because the user can log on once and access any resource in the network that the account has been given permission to use. Hence, the user's access token is created on the domain controller for that domain and can be used (as it is a global account) to access any resource throughout the enterprise domain that the account has been given permission to use.

Because access to remote resources is determined by examining the SIDs for each account in the ACL with the SIDs listed in the user's access token, the point of logon validation affects the user's ability to access a resource.

Ch
7

In a domain, the user and group accounts are global and can be used in the ACL of any resource in the domain. When the user logs on to the domain, the access token contains the user's SID (and group SIDs per group membership) and is global to the network. Both access tokens and ACLs obtain their SIDs from the same SAM database. Thus, the user can access any resource that has given access permission to any SID contained in the user's access token (to the extent that the permission allows).

In a workgroup model, a user's access token is only good on the local Windows NT workstation. A remote resource's ACL consists of SIDs from the local SAM database on the Windows NT computer on which the resource resides. If the user has an account on that remote computer, the user's SID on that computer is necessarily different (see Chapter 6, "Managing Users and Accounts") from the SID the user gets when he logs on to his own computer. When the user tries to access the remote resource that has been shared in the workgroup, the two SIDs (access token and ACL) do not match and the user is never able to access the resource.

Even if the administrator of the remote computer creates an account for the user, that account has a different SID.

Windows NT uses a process called *pass-through authentication* to validate the user on the remote computer. Windows NT takes the username and password from the user's access token on the local workstation rather than the SID, and "passes it through" to the remote computer. There, the user is, in effect, logged on to the remote computer, and a new access token is created there with the user's account and group SIDs from the remote computer's SAM database. The user can then access resources on that computer to which the ACL grants permission.

This all works great so long as the username and password match on both the local workstation and the remote resource computer. If they do not, the user can still access the resource through pass-through authentication, but has to supply a password as well. The user also has the option of connecting to a remote resource using a different account—that is, an account that is valid on the remote workstation.

Let's look at an example. If Computer1 has BrownC with password ABC, and BrownC wants to access a shared printer on Computer2, the first thing the print administrator must do is add BrownC to the ACL for the printer. However, in a workgroup setting, the administrator of Computer2 can only add members of Computer2's SAM database to the printer's ACL. This means that an account for BrownC must be created on Computer2 and added to the ACL for the printer. If BrownC's account on Computer2 also expects password ABC, then Windows NT uses pass-through authentication to pass "BrownC" and "ABC" from BrownC's access token on Computer1 to the Security Reference Monitor on Computer2 to be authenticated. A new access token is created for BrownC on Computer2. This can be used successfully to access the printer because now the SID for BrownC on Computer2 matches the SID for BrownC in the ACL for the printer.

If the passwords do not match, BrownC can still access the printer, but has to connect to it by supplying the password for his account on Computer2. Similarly, if BrownC does not have an account on Computer2, but knows the username and password for a valid account on Computer2, say VanPeltL, he can connect to the printer by supplying both the username and password that are valid on Computer2.

Examining Access Control Lists

When a key card is read by the card reader, the information on the card is generally checked against a central database to see whether this user has the appropriate level of access to be let in the secured area. The database may indicate that the card holder has full access and allows the door to open; or the database may indicate that the card holder has minimum access and only allows a window in the door to open. If the access token is thought of as the key card for access to secured areas, an *access control list* can be thought of as the card reader database.

An access control list, hereafter referred to as the ACL, is just that—a list of users and groups that have some level of access to the resource. It is

Ch

7

created at the object (resource or share) level and stays with the security object. It consists of user and group account entries that reference the accounts' SIDs rather than the accounts' names. These entries are called Access Control Entries, or ACEs. (An acronym for everything and everything has its acronym!) Each entry has a particular level of permission associated with it, such as read only, full control, or no access.

How ACLs Determine Access

When a user tries to access a resource, the request is passed once again to the Security Reference Monitor. The Security Reference Monitor acts here as the card reader. It checks the SID entries in the access token against the SID entries in the ACL (see Figure 7.2).

FIG. 7.2 ⇒

Diagram of the
security access
process.

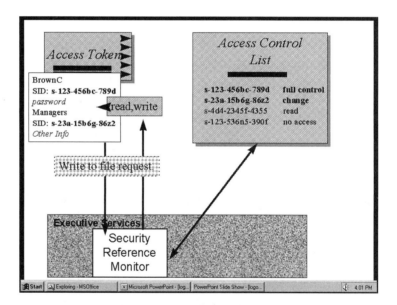

It determines all matches, evaluates the permissions assigned to each matching entry, and calculates an overall permission level for the user which becomes the user's effective access to the resource. It then returns that effective access as a security "handle" to the object—for example, read and write permissions for a file. The security handle becomes part of the access token for as long as the user accesses the object.

Key Concept

As long as the user maintains access to the object, the same security handle is in effect, even if the owner or administrator of the resource changes the user's access. The changed permissions do not take effect for the user until the user releases control of the object and tries to access it again. For example, if BrownC has full access to a file he has opened, and the owner of the file decides to restrict BrownC to read only, BrownC continues to have full control until he closes the file and tries to open it again.

Sharing Resources and Determining Network Access

A resource, such as a folder or printer, is made available as a network resource by sharing the resource. For simplicity, we discuss printer sharing in Chapter 9, "Managing Printers."

Only Power User or Administrator has the ability to share a resource on a workstation or server. In addition, the Server service must be running and the network card operational. If you suspect a problem with the Server service or the network card, a good place to begin troubleshooting is the Event Viewer. Look for any devices or services that failed to start.

Sharing a folder is a relatively simple process. A folder is shared by selecting the file or folder through Windows Explorer or My Computer, right-clicking it, and choosing Sharing, or through the object's properties sheet. Figure 7.3 shows an example of a folder that has been shared.

FIG. 7.3 ⇒

My Documents has been shared with the name Budget. Notice the list of groups and the permissions assigned to each.

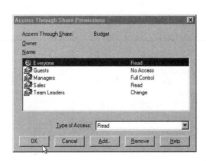

Ch

7

Sharing is enabled by clicking the Shared As option. When you share a folder, the share name defaults to the folder name, but can be changed to be more descriptive for its potential users. You can also indicate the number of users that are allowed to access the share at a time, or accept the default of Maximum Allowed.

 Note Recall that the maximum number of remote connections allowed on a Windows NT workstation is 10. On a server, the number of connections is effectively unlimited, except as defined by the license option chosen.

If you go no further, Windows NT shares this resource to any and all users. The default permission for every shared resource is Everyone with Full Control.

Key Concept

Windows NT's philosophy of sharing resources is to make information readily and easily available. Therefore, the default is to give every network user access to the resource. Hence, the default permission is always Everyone with Full Control.

If you want to add a layer of security to the shared folder, you must choose <u>P</u>ermissions and <u>A</u>dd the appropriate group and user accounts, modifying the permissions as necessary. By doing this, you are creating and modifying the ACL for the folder.

Caution

It is recommended that you either remove the Everyone group and explicitly assign permissions to specific users and groups, or give Everyone the least level of access (Read) to provide a greater level of security. Do not give the Everyone group NO ACCESS. Because every network user is automatically a member of Everyone, giving it NO ACCESS results in locking every user—even the owner and administrator—out of that shared resource.

There are four share-level permissions that you can assign in your ACL. They are defined in Table 7.1.

Table 7.1 Permissions for Shared Folders

Permission	Effect
Read	Displays the folder and file names; allows files to be opened and programs to be run; allows similar access to subfolders.
Change	In addition to read permissions, allows changes to be made to files and folders, including creating and deleting files and folders.
Full Control	Allows complete access to the folder and its files and subfolders, including the ability to take ownership of files and change permissions of files and folders.
No Access	Denies access to the folder and its contents.

Caution

Note that share permissions take effect for users accessing the resource remotely over the network. If the user sits down at the computer that has the folder, and no other permissions have been assigned, the user still has complete access to the folder and its files.

Note If two or more users attempt to access the same file at the same time, the first user is able to modify the file, and the rest see the file in a read-only fashion.

Permissions assigned to a folder also apply to all files and folders within the shared folder. For example, if you give Sales read permissions for the folder DATA, the members of the Sales group also have read permissions for all files and subfolders within DATA.

Ch
7

Effective Permissions

The Security Reference Monitor checks the user's access token against the entries in the ACL, as we have seen. When it identifies a match or matches, it then must determine the permissions to give the user. The effective share permissions are cumulative. The permissions explicitly assigned to a user, as well as permissions assigned to any groups that the user is a member of, are added together, and the highest level of permission is granted to the user. The only exception to this rule is the No Access permission which will always deny access regardless of the other permissions assigned.

For example, suppose BrownC is a member of Managers and Sales. BrownC has been given Change access, Managers has been given Full Control, and Sales has been given Read access to a shared folder. BrownC's effective permissions are Full Control by virtue of his membership in the Managers group.

However, No Access always supersedes any other permission, even Full Control. Using the same example, if BrownC is given No Access explicitly, he is not able to access the shared folder, even though he is a member of the Managers group which has Full Control.

It is important, therefore, that you take sufficient time to plan your shared folders and their permissions. Let's look at the home directory folders as an example. Suppose that users' home directories are created under a share called Users. By default, Users are shared to Everyone with Full Control. This means that all files and folders within Users also give Everyone Full Control. Thus, all network users can see all other users' files in their home directories. This is probably not a good idea.

So how can we fix that? Here is one suggestion. Change the share permissions for Users to remove Everyone and add Administrators with Full Control (or at least read). Share each home directory to the appropriate user explicitly with Full Control and change the users' properties through User Manager appropriately. Now, while Administrators can access everything for security reasons (and because they like the power), each user can access only his own home directory.

Administrative and Hidden Shares

When Windows NT is installed, it creates several shares, called administrative shares, all of which are hidden except for NETLOGON. Hidden shares are shares that exist, but cannot be seen by any user in lists of available shared resources. They are meant to be used either by the operating system for specific tasks and services, such as IPC$ and REPL$, or by an administrator for security access or troubleshooting, such as the root drive shares.

Table 7.2 summarizes these administrative shares.

Table 7.2   Administrative Shares

Share Name	Description
drive$	The root directory of every partition that Windows NT can recognize is assigned an administrative share name consisting of the drive letter followed by the $. Administrators, Server Operators, and Backup Operators have the ability to connect to these shares remotely.
Admin$	This administrative share is used by the operating system during remote administration of the computer, and represents the directory into which the Windows NT system files were installed (such as C:\WINNT40). Administrators, Server Operators, and Backup Operators have the ability to connect to these shares remotely.
IPC$	This administrative share represents the named pipes that are used for communication between programs and systems, and is used by the operating system during remote administration of a computer, and when accessing another computer's shared resources.

continues

Ch

7

Table 7.2 Continued

Share Name	Description
Netlogon	This administrative share is created and used on domain controllers only for authenticating users logging on to the enterprise domain.
Print$	Similar to IPC$, this administrative share provides remote access support for shared printers.
REPL$	This administrative share is created and used on a Windows NT server computer when the Directory Replication service is configured and enabled. It identifies the location of the directories and files to be exported.

With the exception of NETLOGON, hidden shares can be identified by the $ after the share name. As an administrator, you can view all the administrative shares on a computer by starting the Server applet from Control Panel and viewing Shares (or by starting Server Manager on a Windows NT server, viewing a computer's properties, and then its Shares).

You can also create hidden shares yourself by adding the $ to the end of the share name that you enter. This is a way to keep certain shares more secure. The only users that can connect to them are those who know the share name.

Accessing a Shared Folder

There are several ways that a user can access a shared folder (assuming that the user has been given permission to do so). Shares can be accessed by connecting directly to the resource through Network Neighborhood or the Find command, or by mapping a drive letter to a shared folder through My Computer or Windows Explorer.

All four utilities offer a point-and-click method of accessing the resource, which means that you do not necessarily have to know where the resource is exactly. With Network Neighborhood and Find, you do not waste a drive letter on the resource. With My Computer and Windows Explorer, you utilize a drive letter for every mapping you create—and the alphabet is not an unlimited list.

Network Neighborhood

Perhaps the easiest way to connect to a shared folder is to use Network Neighborhood, especially if you only need occasional or short access to the folder and its contents (see Figure 7.4).

FIG. 7.4 ⇒

Network Neighborhood is used here to display the contents of the SDK folder shared on the computer Glemarek.

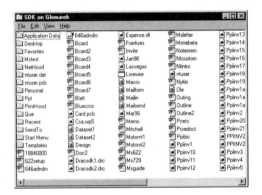

To connect to a shared folder using Network Neighborhood, follow these steps:

1. Double-click Network Neighborhood.

   All members of your workgroup are listed under Entire Network.

2. Double-click the computer that has the shared folder to display a list of its shared folders.

3. Double-click the appropriate share name to see the contents of that folder.

Ch

7

Or, if you participate in a domain:

1. Double-click Network Neighborhood.

   All members of your workgroup are listed under Entire Network.

2. Double-click Entire Network, and then Microsoft Network, to see a list of domains.

3. Select your domain and double-click to see a list of computers in the domain that contain shared folders.

4. Double-click the computer that has the shared folder to display a list of shared folders.

5. Double-click the appropriate share name to see the contents of that folder.

Find Command

The Find command on the Start menu can be used effectively to search for computers that do not show up right away in a browse list like Network Neighborhood displays, or for a specific file or folder in a shared folder whose name you cannot recall.

To find a computer, follow these steps:

1. Choose Start, Find and then Computer from the taskbar.

2. In the Computer Name box, enter the name of the computer that has the shared folder.

3. Choose Find Now. Find displays a window showing the computer it finds.

4. Double-click the computer to display its shared folders.

5. Double-click the appropriate share name to display its contents.

To find a file or folder by name:

1. Choose Start, Find and then Files or Folders from the taskbar.

2. In the Look In box, enter the name of the computer that contains the shared folder. Or, you can choose Browse to

browse the Network Neighborhood entry to find the computer.

3. In the Named box, enter the name of the file or folder that you are looking for.

4. Choose Find Now. Find displays a window with its search results. Double-click the appropriate file or folder to work with it.

 Note All the Find options are available to help narrow your search, such as Date Modified and Advanced. For example, if you are only looking for a folder contained in some share on a computer, use Advanced to narrow the search only to folders. ■

My Computer and Windows Explorer

My Computer can be used to map a network drive to a shared folder on a computer. This is similar to the way logical drives are assigned to Novell Netware resources for those of you who are familiar with that network operating system (see Figure 7.5).

Using Windows Explorer is probably closest to using File Manager in previous versions of Windows NT or Windows for Workgroups. It displays a Map Network Drive dialog box similar to that used with My Computer, and, in fact, they both operate the same way.

FIG. 7.5 ⇒

Here we are making the same connection as in Figure 7.4. Through My Computer, we expand through the Microsoft Network entry to find the computer Glemarek in the workgroup Studygroup, and display its shares.

Ch

7

To map to a shared folder using Network Neighborhood, follow these steps:

1. Right-click My Computer and choose Map Network Drive. Or, you can start Windows Explorer, and choose Tools, Map Network Drive.

2. The next available drive letter is displayed in the Drive box. Select it or make another choice of letter.

3. Double-click the appropriate network entry in the Shared Directories list box to display a browse list of Workgroups and Domains.

4. Double-click the Workgroup or Domain that contains the sharing computer to display a list of computers with shared resources.

5. Double-click the appropriate computer to display its list of shared resources.

6. Select the appropriate shared folder from the list.

Or, if you do not see the computer or folder in the Browse list, but know the name of the computer and share, follow these steps:

1. Right-click My Computer and choose Map Network Drive. Or, you can start Windows Explorer, and choose Tools, Map Network Drive.

2. The next available drive letter is displayed in the Drive box. Select it or make another choice of letter.

3. In the Path box, enter the UNC name to the shared folder using the convention *server**share*, where *server* represents the name of the computer that has the shared folder, and *share* represents the name of the shared folder.

4. Click OK.

Notice in Figure 7.5 that the check box Reconnect at Logon is selected by default. This is known as a persistent connection. If you do not deselect this box, drive H is reconnected to the share every time the user logs in. If this is a resource that the user accesses frequently, then this is a convenient tool. If not, then you are just taking up extra system resources to locate the shared folder, make the connection, and monitor for access.

Note   Mapped drives can be disconnected when no longer needed by right-clicking My Computer and choosing Disconnect Network Drive, or by choosing Tools, Disconnect Network Drive Windows Explorer. Select the drive from the list that you want to disconnect and choose OK. ▪

Also, it may happen that you need to access a resource on a computer on which you do not have a valid user account. This is particularly possible in workgroup configurations, or in the case of administrative access to various workstations or servers. If you know the name and password of a valid user account on that computer (including Guest), you can enter the UNC name in the Path box, as described in step 3 of the preceding list, and then enter the name of the valid account in the Connect As box. Windows NT asks you for the password, if it is required or different from your own, before connecting you to the resource.

Securing Folders and Files with NTFS Permissions

Up to this point, we have discussed how to make resources available to other network users, how to secure those resources that you share on the network, and how you access them. There is another level of security that can be applied to files and folders stored on an NTFS partition. Among the many benefits of formatting a partition as NTFS, Windows NT's own file system, is the ability to assign permissions directly to the file and folder—that is, at the resource level.

Permissions are set for a file or folder by right-clicking the file or folder, displaying its Properties sheet, and selecting the Security tab. Choosing Permissions here displays the file or folders permissions dialog box from which you can make your choices.

Ch

7

Effective File and Folder Permissions

When you assign permissions to a folder or file, you are creating an ACL (Access Control List) for that folder or file, much like you did for the share. The Security Reference Monitor checks the user's access token against the entries in the ACL, as we have seen. When it identifies a match or matches, it then must determine the permissions to give the user. The effective file or folder permissions are cumulative. The permissions explicitly assigned to a user, as well as permissions assigned to any groups that the user is a member of, are added together, and the highest level of permission is granted to the user *at the file or folder level*.

For example, suppose BrownC is a member of Managers and Sales. BrownC has been given Change access to a particular file, Managers has been given Full Control, and Sales has been given Read access to the file. BrownC's effective permissions for that file are Full Control by virtue of his membership in the Managers group.

The only exception to this rule is No Access. No Access always supersedes any other permission, even Full Control. Using the same example, if BrownC is given No Access explicitly, he is not able to access the file, even though he is a member of the Managers group which has Full Control.

Unlike share permissions, which are effective for all files and folders within the share, folder and file permissions are effective only for the immediate folder and its contents, or for an individual file if applied to that file. The permissions for files in a folder, or for subfolders, *can* trickle down, but can also be applied individually. If permissions have been applied to an individual file, the file permission *always* supersedes the folder permission.

For example, if BrownC has been given Read permission for the folder Data, and Change permission to a file budget.doc, BrownC's effective permission for the file budget.doc is Change, even though because of the folder permission he has read permission to all the other files in Data.

As you can see, you have a great deal of discretion and control over the application of permissions to folders, subfolders, and files. It is important, therefore, that you take sufficient time to plan your folder and file permissions. Let's take a different look at the home directory folders as an example. Suppose that users' home directories are created under a share called Users. By default, Users are shared to Everyone with Full Control. If the home folders are on an NTFS partition, you can assign each user the NTFS permission Full Control to his own home folder only while assigning the Everyone group List access to the directory. This effectively restricts access to each folder only to the owner of the folder.

Assigning File and Folder Permissions

There are six individual permissions that can be applied to files and folders. Table 7.3 describes these permissions.

Table 7.3   NTFS File and Folder Permissions

Permission	Folder Level	File Level
Read (R)	Can display folders, attributes, owner, and permissions	Can display files and file data, attributes, owner, and permissions
Write (W)	Can add files and create subfolders, change folder attributes, and display folder owner and permissions	Can change file contents and attributes and display file owner and permissions
Execute (E)	Can make changes to subfolders, and display folder owners' attributes and permissions	Can run executable files, and display file owner, attributes, and permissions
Delete (D)	Can delete a folder	Can delete a file
Change Permission (P)	Can change folder permissions	Can change file permissions
Take Ownership (O)	Can take ownership of a folder	Can take ownership of a file

Ch

7

Files and folders can be assigned these permissions individually or more often by using standard groupings provided by Windows NT security. There are nine standard folder permissions, which include two choices for setting your own custom choice of folder permissions and file permissions to apply to all files in a folder. There are five standard file permissions, which includes an option for setting your own custom choice of file permissions per individual file. Tables 7.4 and 7.5 outline these permissions and what they allow the user to do.

Note that when viewing and setting permissions, Windows NT always displays the individual permissions in parentheses alongside the standard permission. For Folder permissions, the first set of parentheses represents the permissions on the folder, and the second set represents the permissions that apply to files globally, including any new file created in the folder.

Table 7.4 Standard Permissions for Folders

Permission	Access
No Access (None)(None)	Supersedes all other file permissions and prevents access to the file.
List (RX)(Not Specified)	Allows user to view folders and subfolders, and file names within folders and subfolders. List is not available as a valid permission option for files.
Read (RX)(RX)	In addition to List access, user can display file contents and subfolders, and run executable files.
Add (WX)(Not Specified)	User can add files to the folder, but not list its contents. Add is not available as a valid permission option for files.
Add and Read (RWX)(RX)	In addition to Add, user can display the contents of files and subfolders, and run executable files.

Permission	Access
Change (RWXD)(RWXD)	Allows user the ability to display and add files and folders, modify the contents of files and folders, and run executable files.
Full Control (All)(All)	In addition to Change, allows user the ability to modify folder and file permissions and take ownership of folders and files.
Special Directory Access	Allows the selection of any combination of individual permissions (R,W,E,D,P,O) for folder access.
Special File Access	Allows the selection of any combination of individual permissions (R,W,E,D,P,O) for file access.

Table 7.5   Standard Permissions for Files

Permission	Access
No Access (None)	No access is allowed to the file.
Read (RX)	Allows user to display file data and run executable files.
Change (RWXD)	In addition to Read, the user can modify the file contents and delete the file.
Full Control (All)	In addition to Change, the user can modify the file's permissions and take ownership of the file.
Special Access	Allows the selection of any combination of individual permissions (R,W,E,D,P,O) for a file.

Ch

7

Caution
The Folder permission Full Control provides the user an inherent ability to delete files in a folder even if the user is given No Access permission to a specific file. This is done to preserve Posix application support on UNIX systems, for which Write permission on a folder allows the user to delete files in the folder. This can be superseded by choosing the Special Directory Access standard permission and checking all the individual permissions.

Permissions are set for a file or folder by right-clicking the file or folder, displaying its Properties sheet, and selecting the *Security* tab. Choosing Permissions here displays the file or folders permissions dialog box as shown in Figure 7.6 from which you can make your choices.

Notice in the Directory Permissions dialog box shown in Figure 7.6 that there are two Replace choices: Replace Permissions on Sub-directories and Replace Permissions on Existing Files (which is selected by default).

FIG. 7.6 ⇒

The Public folder's permission list (ACL) shows that Administrators has Full Control, Everyone has Read, and Managers has Change. The Type of Access list box displays the standard permission options.

Caution
The effect of Replace Permissions on Existing Files is to change any and all permissions that you set on individual files with the permissions that you set at the folder level. Because this option is selected by default, it is easy to forget when setting permissions at the folder level, and you

can accidentally change permissions on files that you do not want to change. Bottom line: Read all screens carefully.

Choosing Replace Permissions on Subdirectories causes Windows NT to apply the permissions set at this folder level to all subfolders. If Replace Permissions on Existing Files is also left selected, the permissions are applied not only to the subfolders, but to their contents as well.

The Type of Access list box shows all the standard permissions that are available at the folder level, including the two special options, Special Directory Access and Special File Access, from which you can customize your choice of permissions.

As with share permissions, users and groups can be added or removed from the ACL through the Add and Remove buttons.

Determining Access When Using Share and NTFS Permissions

A folder (and its contents) is made accessible across the network by sharing it. As we have discussed, an ACL can be created for the share. This defines which users and group accounts can access the share, and the level of access allowed. We know that the effective permissions are cumulative at the share level.

When NTFS permissions are assigned to individual folders and files, the level of access can be further refined by creating an ACL at the file and folder level. We know that the effective permissions at the file and folder level are also cumulative.

When a user accesses a file or folder protected by NTFS permissions across the network through a share, the Security Reference Monitor determines the cumulative permissions at the share and the cumulative permissions at the file or folder. Whichever permission is *most restrictive* becomes the effective permission for the user.

Ch
7

For example, if BrownC, a member of the Managers group, has been given Read access individually and Change access through the Managers group to a share called Public, then BrownC's effective permission for Public is Change. If BrownC has been given Read access to a file budget.doc (contained in the folder that has been shared as Public) and Full Control through the Managers group, BrownC's effective permission at the file level is Full Control. However, BrownC's net effective permission to budget.doc, when accessing it through the network share, is Change, which is the more restrictive of the two permissions.

Through a shrewd use of share and file\folder level permissions, you can create a very effective security structure for resources stored on your Windows NT workstations and servers.

Understanding the Concept of Ownership

The user who creates a file or folder is noted by Windows NT to be the owner of that file or folder, and is placed in the Creator Owner internal group for that file or folder. A user cannot give someone else ownership of her files or folders. However, a user can give someone the *permission* to take ownership of her files and folders.

The Take Ownership permission is implied through Full Control, but can also be assigned to a user or group through the Special Access permission options. A user that has this permission can take ownership of the file or folder. After ownership has been taken, the new owner can modify the file or folder's permissions, delete the file, and so on. Administrators always have the ability to take ownership of a file or folder.

Taking Ownership

A user who has the Take Ownership permission can take ownership or a folder of file by following these steps:

1. Right-click the folder or file and select Properties.
2. In the Properties sheet, select the Security tab.

3. On the Security tab, choose <u>O</u>wnership. The current owner is displayed.

4. Choose <u>T</u>ake Ownership, and then choose OK.

> **Note**   If any *member* of the Administrators group takes ownership of a file or folder, or creates a file or folder, the owner becomes the Administrators *group*.

Taking ownership of files and folders can be useful, especially when users move around from department to department or position to position, or leave the organization. It provides a way to assign files and folders that are no longer being used by a user to an appropriate replacement.

Copying and Moving Files...and Permissions

When you copy a file from one folder to another, the file assumes the permissions of the target folder. When you move a file from one folder to another, the file maintains its current permissions. This sounds simple enough, except that a move isn't always a move. When you move a file from a folder in one partition to another, you are actually copying the file to the target folder, and then deleting the original file. A move is only a move where permissions are involved when you move a file from a folder in one partition to another folder in the *same* partition.

Troubleshooting Security

The most likely problem that you will have with security will be a user unable to access a resource. There is not much additional advice I can offer besides what has been said. In other words, you must go back and check the share permissions and file and folder permissions. Remember that at the share level, and at the file and folder level, permissions are cumulative. However, when comparing share permissions to file and folder permissions, Windows NT assigns the most restrictive permission to the user.

Ch
7

When changing permissions on a share, file, or folder, the user will not notice the effect of the change until the next time the resource is accessed. This is because of the way Windows NT assigns the permission to the user. Recall that when the user's access token is compared to the ACL, and the effective permission established, the user's access token receives a permission handle to the resource. This handle remains in effect until the user releases the resource.

For example, BrownC has effective permission Change to budget.doc. The owner of budget.doc decides to restrict BrownC to Read. While BrownC has budget.doc open and in use, his effective permission remains Change. When he closes budget.doc and opens it later, his effective permission is Read.

Suppose BrownC has established a logical drive mapping to the Data share and has effective permission Change to the share. The owner of the share changes BrownC's permission to Read. BrownC continues to maintain Change permission to the share until he disconnects from it and reconnects, or until he logs off and logs back on.

Similarly, suppose BrownC is currently a member of the Managers group. BrownC has Read permission to the Data folder but Full Control effective permission through his membership in the Managers group. You take BrownC out of the Managers group to ensure that he only has Read access to the folder. When BrownC accesses the folder, he still has Full Control access to the folder. This is because his access token still maintains that he has membership in the Managers group. Remember that the access token is created during *logon*. Thus, the group change is not effective until BrownC logs off and logs back on.

From Here...

Chapter 8 will take a closer look at the NTFS file system and what benefits it can offer you. Also, we will begin a discussion of disk management through Windows NT 4.0 highlighting the Disk Administrator utility.

Taking the Disc Test

 If you have read and understood the material in the chapter, you are ready to test your knowledge. Insert the CD-ROM that comes with this book and run the self-test software as described in Appendix I, "Using the CD-ROM."

Ch
7

Chapter Prerequisite

Before reading this chapter, you should be familiar with basic disk concepts such as drives, partitions, folders, and files. You should also be comfortable with the security concepts discussed in Chapter 7.

Managing Disk Resources

Throughout the first half of this book, we have examined installation issues, configuration methods and concerns, the Windows NT Registry, account management, and resource security. In the rest of this book, we cover additional management topics such as disk and printer management, application support, network connectivity, and suggestions for tuning Windows NT. As always, we are approaching these topics from the workstation point of view. Nevertheless, concepts discussed here are nearly always applicable within the larger enterprise environment. As before, wherever practical, I will continue to call your attention to specific information relating to Windows NT 4.0 Server, as a point of comparison.

In this chapter, we will:

◆ Discuss partition support and management
◆ Review the Disk Administrator utility

◆ Discuss Windows NT file system support

◆ Consider the effect of long file names

◆ Explore stripe sets and volume sets

◆ Examine Microsoft's Backup and Restore utility

Understanding Partitions

Before a computer can be used effectively, an operating system must be installed. Before an operating system can be installed, the computer's hard disk(s) must be partitioned into the storage space required by the operating system *and* the user, and formatted with a file system supported by the operating system, such as File Allocation Table (FAT).

There are many types of partitions supported by Windows NT Workstation 4.0 and Server. The most common that you will encounter are primary and extended. Others include volume sets and stripe sets. Windows NT 4.0 Server adds fault-tolerant partition options, such as stripe sets with parity and disk mirroring.

In MS-DOS, the *primary* partition contains the boot files needed to start MS-DOS and initialize the system. It is also called the active partition, and it cannot be subdivided any further. Under Windows NT 4.0, a primary partition usually holds the operating system files for Windows NT or an alternate operating system, but can also designate simply another data or application storage place. Up to four primary partitions are supported per physical disk device under Windows NT 4.0. MS-DOS can only recognize one primary partition per physical disk device, and, to dual boot to MS-DOS (or Windows 95), that partition must also be marked as the active partition.

An *extended* partition offers a way to get beyond the four partition limit, and subdivide a partition into more than four logical drives. Consequently, an extended partition usually comprises the remaining free space on a disk after the primary partition is created. Because MS-DOS only recognizes one primary (active) partition per physical disk, logical drives in an extended partition provide a way to support a larger

Ch
8

number of "drives" under MS-DOS. A logical drive is virtually the same as a partition, except that from MS-DOS' and Windows NT's point of view, it is a division *within* a partition. That's logical isn't it? (A little partition humor.) The use of logical drives allows greater control and flexibility for the disk administrator over the storage of applications and data on the physical disk.

There is also the matter of simple arithmetic in the way that Windows NT counts partitions. This becomes more of a concern for Windows NT when the partition scheme changes frequently, or when trouble-shooting with a boot disk among a variety of Windows NT computers because it involves the ARC path to the Windows NT system files.

The ARC path, you may recall from Chapter 3, "Installing Windows NT Workstation 4.0," specifies the physical location of the partition that contains the Windows NT operating system files (the WINNT40 installation directory). Here is an example of an ARC path used by the BOOT.INI file: multi(0)disk(0)rdisk(0)partition(2). According to this path, the WINNT40 directory can be found on the second partition of the first physical drive attached to the first physical controller card. Because the ARC path involves the *physical* path, which includes the controller, disk device, and partition *number*, if partition schemes change frequently, it is possible that the partition *number* of the Windows NT system partition could also change.

Windows NT always counts the active primary partition first, or the first primary partition on each additional physical disk, then other primary partitions from the first to the last physical disk, then the logical drives from first physical disk to last (see Figure 8.1).

Key Concept

Windows NT refers to the partition from which the computer system boots as the *system* partition. This is the partition that, for Windows NT, contains the files that Windows NT uses to boot (NTLDR, NTDETECT.COM, BOOT.INI, NTBOOTDD.SYS, and BOOTSECT.DOS). The partition that contains the Windows NT system files such as NTOSKRNL.EXE (the WINNT40 installation directory) is called the *boot*

continues

continued

partition. In other words, the system partition contains the operating system boot files, and the boot partition is the partition that contains the Windows NT directory. I use this terminology for the remainder of this chapter.

FIG. 8.1 ⇒
In this partition scheme, you see primary, extended, and logical partitions. They are numbered as Windows NT would number them when it boots. Notice that primary partitions are counted before logical drives in an extended partition.

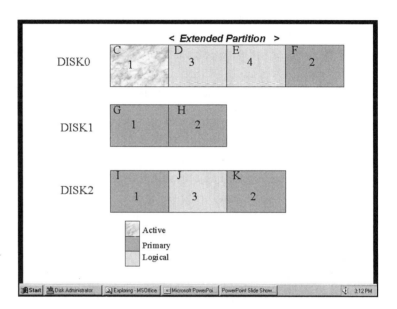

Exploring File System Support in Windows NT 4.0

After the partition scheme has been decided and applied to the physical disk(s), the disk(s) must then be formatted with a file system that the operating system can understand. MS-DOS and Windows 95 support the FAT file system. Windows NT supports FAT and its own NTFS (New Technology File System). All support the CD-ROM file system (CDFS). Windows NT 4.0 does not support Windows 95 FAT32.

Note Previous versions of Windows NT provided support for IBM OS/2's HPFS (High Performance File System). This support is no longer available under Windows NT 4.0. ▪

An Overview of FAT

FAT support under Windows NT is somewhat expanded from that offered under MS-DOS. For example, FAT under Windows NT supports long file names. Here are some characteristics of FAT as supported under Windows NT 4.0:

- FAT is required for the system partition if you intend to dual boot between Windows NT and MS-DOS or Windows 95.

- FAT supports file names of up to 255 characters.

- The file name can have multiple sections, separated by periods and, as such, can be considered multi-qualified. The last section is treated as the file extension.

- File names must begin with an alphanumeric character and can contain any characters, including spaces, but excluding the following:

    ```
    " / \ [ ] : ; | = , ^ ★ ?
    ```

- FAT offers only the traditional file attributes: Read, Archive, System, and Hidden; and, as such, does not provide the range of security that NTFS permissions can.

- Folders in a FAT partition can be shared.

- FAT supports a maximum partition (file) size of 4G.

- FAT is considered most efficient for file access on partitions of less than 400M in size.

- Formatting a partition as FAT requires less than 1M of overhead for the file system.

- The system partition of RISC-based systems must be at least 2M, formatted as FAT.

An Overview of NTFS

NTFS provides the most features and benefits for securing your data. However, it is only recognized by Windows NT computers. Also, your old MS-DOS-based disk utilities most likely do not recognize NTFS-formatted partitions, nor do your MS-DOS- or Windows 95-based applications.

I find that while NTFS is used extensively on Windows NT 4.0 server computers to provide a high level of security and fault tolerance, it is only used on Windows NT 4.0 workstation computers for those end-users that require that level of support, such as developers, network administrators, secure data systems, and so on.

Following are some characteristics of NTFS:

- NTFS supports long file and folder names of up to 255 characters, including extensions.

- File names preserve case, but are not case sensitive, except when using POSIX-based applications for which case-sensitivity is supported.

- File and folder names can contain any characters, including spaces, but excluding the following: " / \ < > : | * ?

- NTFS supports a theoretical partition (file) size of up to 16 exabytes. However, on most hardware, this translates to file size limits of 4G to 64G, and to a functional partition size of up to 2T, due to industry standard limitations of disk sectors.

- NTFS is considered more efficient on partitions larger than 250M.

- Formatting a partition as NTFS requires between 4M and 5M of system overhead, making it impossible to format a floppy disk with NTFS.

- NTFS provides support for built-in file compression. File compression is treated as a file and folder attribute and is enabled through the properties of the file or folder.

- NTFS offers automatic Transaction Tracking, which logs all disk activity and provides a means of recovery in the event of a power failure or system crash.

- NTFS offers automatic Sector Sparing, also called hot fixing, in which so-called bad clusters are determined and marked, and the data contained therein is moved to a new good cluster.

- Through the Services for Macintosh feature on Windows NT 4.0 Server, NTFS provides support for Macintosh files.

◆ NTFS provides the highest level of security for files and folders
through its permission set (see Chapter 7, "Windows NT 4.0
Security Model").

◆ NTFS maintains a separate Recycle Bin for each user.

As you can see, NTFS is quite a robust file system, but perhaps not
always the preferred choice on all workstations.

Converting a FAT Partition to NTFS

It is certainly not necessary to format a partition as NTFS right away, or
during installation. One of the nicest things about NTFS is its capability
to be *applied* to an existing FAT partition.

Windows NT provides a conversion tool that you can use to apply
NTFS to an existing FAT partition. It is called CONVERT.EXE and
can be found in the WINNT40\SYSTEM32 subdirectory. No data is
lost during the conversion process as this is not a reformatting operation. The syntax of the command is as follows. At an MS-DOS prompt,
type:

```
CONVERT D: /FS:NTFS
```

where D: represents the drive letter of the partition to be converted.

If Windows NT is currently accessing the drive in some way—for
example, the pagefile is located on it—or you have the drive window
open through My Computer or Windows Explorer, Windows NT displays a message to that effect and offers to schedule the conversion for
the next boot. If you choose to accept the offer, when Windows NT
boots, it detects that the partition is marked for conversion. It reboots
and performs the conversion, then it reboots again to start the operating
system and lets the user log in.

Considering Long File Names

Both FAT and NTFS under Windows NT 4.0 support long file names
for files and folders. However, not all Microsoft Network clients support
or recognize long file names. For example, MS-DOS and Windows

3.x-based computers and their applications do not recognize long file names. Windows NT has allowed for this variety in operating systems. When you create a file or folder using a long file name to identify it, Windows NT automatically assigns an 8.3 format version of the name. This allows DOS- and Windows-based systems to "see" the files and folders. There are, however, several considerations to keep in mind as you work with long file names.

How 8.3 Names Are Created

The internal algorithm that Windows NT uses to auto-generate an 8.3 name from a long file name is really quite simple within the first four iterations. Windows NT takes the first six characters of the name, minus spaces, and adds a ~ followed by a number increment. Notice the convention followed in this example:

1995 Budget Summary Spreadsheet.XLS	1995Bu~1.xls
1995 Budget Detail Spreadsheet.XLS	1995Bu~2.xls
Budget Overages.DOC	Budget~1.doc

As you can see, the short file name does not give anywhere near the level of description that the long file name does. Do you see another consideration? You probably notice that if several long file names start with the same characters within the first six, the 8.3 versions are identifiable only by the number increment. After the fifth iteration, Windows NT's algorithm performs a name hash retaining the first two characters of the long file name, and generating the remaining characters randomly as shown in this next example:

KiteFlyers Corp Budget - January.XLS	KiteFl~1.XLS
KiteFlyers Corp Budget - February.XLS	KiteFl~2.XLS
KiteFlyers Corp Budget - March.XLS	KiteFl~3.XLS
KiteFlyers Corp Budget - April.XLS	KiteFl~4.XLS
KiteFlyers Corp Budget - May.XLS	Kia45s~1.XLS
KiteFlyers Corp Budget - June.XLS	Ki823x~1.XLS

On a network with a variety of clients that include Windows NT, MS-DOS, and Windows 95, the short names can become a source of confusion for users using those clients and applications that only support and display the short name. Consequently, in a mixed environment, try to keep the long file names unique within the first six characters.

Additional Thoughts on Long Names

Here are some additional considerations to ponder:

◆ When referring to long names at a DOS prompt, most DOS commands require that the name be placed in quotes. For example, if I am copying the file MY BUDGET SPREADSHEET.XLS from C:\Apps to the D:\Data directory, I would need to type it as:

```
COPY "C:\Apps\MY BUDGET SPREADSHEET.XLS" D:\Data
```

◆ Some DOS and Windows 16-bit applications save files by creating a temporary file, deleting the original file, and renaming the temporary file to the original name. This deletes not only the long file name, but also any NTFS permissions associated with the file.

◆ Third-party DOS-based disk utilities that manipulate the FAT can also destroy long file names contained in FAT because they do not recognize those entries as valid DOS files.

◆ The 8.3 version of the long file name can be displayed at a DOS prompt by typing **DIR** **/X** at the prompt.

◆ Every long file name utilizes one FAT directory entry for the 8.3 name (called the alias) and a hidden secondary entry for up to every 13 characters of the long file name. MY BUDGET SPREADSHEET.XLS, for example, uses one FAT directory entry for the 8.3 name—MYBUDG~1.XLS—plus two secondary entries for the long file name (25 characters divided by 13), for a total of three. The FAT root directory has a hard-coded limit of 512 directory entries. It is, therefore, possible to run out of directory entries if using very long file names consistently.

As you can see, if you are supporting a variety of clients in a Windows NT network enterprise, the use of long file names must be duly considered, and if widely used, explained thoroughly to the end-users who will encounter them.

In Chapter 5, "Configuration and the Registry," I made a concerted effort to dissuade you from ever modifying the Registry if a utility is available to you. That having been said, there are occasions in which you can only, or best effect, a change by modifying the Registry. Here is an example of that for your Windows NT 4.0 workstation.

You can prevent the support of long file names on FAT partitions altogether by modifying a Registry entry. Use the Registry Editor to expand the HKEY_LOCAL_MACHINE subtree to the following subkey:

HKEY_LOCAL_MACHINE\SYSTEM\CurrentControlSet\ Control\FileSystem\

Change the parameter setting for Win31FileSystem from 0 to 1. This is particularly useful when several clients are accessing files stored on a central server and there is any chance of confusion among them. They are only able to name files and folders following the 8.3 convention on the FAT partitions.

Exploring File Compression Under NTFS

When a partition is formatted as NTFS, among the features provided is the ability to compress files and folders. Compression is treated as another attribute of the file and folder and is, in fact, enabled through the General Properties for the file or folder. This compression is handled on-the-fly and, like all compression algorithms, while resulting in greater disk capacity, can result in a performance decrease especially across heavy traffic networks.

NTFS compression follows a roughly 2:1 ratio with slightly more for data files and slightly less for executables. In general, compression can be most effective for those files that are not accessed on a regular basis, but that cannot be archived because ready access is required. Good file candidates also are going to be fairly large in size and located on disk partitions whose storage space is at a premium.

Note   NTFS does not support compression on NTFS-formatted partitions whose cluster size is greater than 4K. You can determine cluster size by starting the Windows NT Diagnostics utility in the Administrative Tools group and viewing the specific partition's Properties on the Drives tab. Multiply the bytes per sector by the number of sectors per cluster. ▨

How to Enable Compression

As I said earlier, compression is considered an attribute of the file or folder on an NTFS partition. To enable compression for either a file or a folder, right-click the file or folder and display its Properties sheet. On the General tab, select Compress.

If a folder's Compress attribute is set, then any new files placed in the folder also have their Compress attribute set. Also, for folders, you can choose to apply the Compress attribute down through that folder's subfolders. Disable compression for folders and files by deselecting the Compress attribute.

Windows Explorer can be configured to display compressed files and folders in blue on the screen. You can do this by choosing View, Options and selecting Display Compressed Files and Folders with Alternate Color.

The WINNT40 installation folder and all its files and subfolders can be compressed if disk space is an issue. However, as Windows NT is accessing these folders and files rather frequently, compressing them almost certainly results in a noticeable decrease in performance on that computer. This is especially unwise on a Windows NT 4.0 server computer or domain controller. NTLDR and the current pagefile can never be compressed.

Managing Compression from the Command Prompt

Windows NT provides a command prompt utility called COMPACT.EXE that you can use to enable and disable file and folder compression on NTFS partitions (see Table 8.1). The basic syntax is one of the following:

```
COMPACT /C d:\path\filename
COMPACT /C d:\foldername
        COMPACT /?.
```

Table 8.1 COMPACT.EXE Switches

Switch	Description
/C	Enables compression of specified files and folders.
/U	Disables compression of specified files and folders.
/S	Applies the command to files in the specified folder and to all subfolders.
/A	Displays hidden and system files (omitted by default).
/I	Continues the operation even if errors are encountered. By default, Compact stops when it encounters an error.
/F	Forces compression on all specified files, even if previously marked as compressed. If a file is being compressed when power is lost, the file may be *marked* as compressed without actually *being* compressed.
/Q	Displays summary information about the operation.

Note Like NTFS permissions, when you copy a file from one folder to another, it assumes the compression attribute of the target folder. Similarly, if the file is moved from one folder to another, it retains its compression attribute. Of course, a move is only considered a move when the operation takes place between folders on the same partition.

Managing Disks with Disk Administrator

Now that we've explored partitions and file systems, we'll next take a look at another utility in the Administrative Tools group called *Disk Administrator*.

My favorite way of introducing Disk Administrator is to call it a GUI "FDISK." You should remember the MS-DOS FDISK utility that you used to create the primary and extended partition and logical drives. Disk Administrator does the same for your Windows NT workstation and server, plus a whole lot more. We discuss its capabilities here.

Creating and Managing Partitions

Let's begin with the simplest task, creating a new partition. Recall that you can create up to four primary partitions per physical disk, and one extended partition that can contain many logical drives. Refer to Figure 8.2 as we continue this discussion.

FIG. 8.2 ⇒

This shows a sample Disk Administrator screen to help you interpret the text.

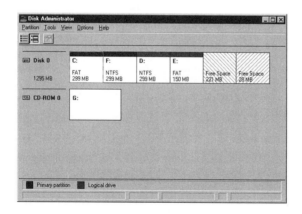

To create a partition, follow these steps:

1. Start Disk Administrator (Start, Programs, Administrative Tools).
2. Click an area of free space on a physical disk.
3. Choose Partition, Create to create a new primary partition. Or, choose Partition, Create Extended to create an extended partition.

4. The Create Primary or Create Extended Partition dialog box displays, showing you the smallest size (2M) and the largest size partition you can create. In the Create Partition of Size text box, enter the size partition you want to create.

5. Click OK. The new primary partition is displayed in Disk Administrator as Unformatted. The new extended partition is set apart from any additional free space with an opposing cross-hatch.

Note If a primary partition already exists, when you create the next 2-4 primary partitions, Windows NT displays a message to the effect that the partition scheme may not be compatible with MS-DOS. This is because MS-DOS cannot recognize more than two primary partitions on the same physical disk. If you dual boot between DOS and Windows NT on the same computer, DOS can only see the primary active partition. Users connecting to your computer through a share will be able to see all your partitions.

After you have created an extended partition, you need to create logical drives within it to store data and other files. You can create a logical drive following the same basic set of steps:

1. Click an area of free space in the extended partition.

2. Choose Partition, Create to create a new logical drive.

3. The Create Logical Drive dialog box displays showing you the smallest size (2M) and the largest size drive you can create. In the Create Logical Drive of Size spin box, enter the size drive you want to create.

4. Click OK. The new logical drive is displayed in Disk Administrator as Unformatted.

The Format Process

The next step, of course, is to format the new primary partition or logical drive. Before you can do that, you must confirm your partition changes to Windows NT. Do this by choosing Partition, Commit Changes Now. Disk Administrator asks that you confirm your changes, and then reminds you to update the Emergency Repair Disk with this new configuration information by using the RDISK.EXE command-line utility. This is discussed in Chapter 12, "Tuning, Optimizing, and Other Troubleshooting Tips," along with other tools for tuning and optimization.

To format the new primary partition or logical drive, follow these steps:

1. Select the partition or drive.

2. Choose Tools, Format. The Format Drive dialog box is displayed. If you are formatting an already formatted drive or partition, the Capacity text box displays its size. Otherwise, it simply says Unknown Capacity.

3. In the File System list box, select either FAT or NTFS.

4. Specify an Allocation Unit Size. Unless you know something different, stick with Default.

5. Enter a Volume Label if you want. The label displays in Disk Administrator and Windows Explorer and helps to make the drive and its contents more descriptive.

6. Select Quick Format if the disk has been previously formatted and you know it is not damaged. Quick Format removes files and does not perform a scan for base sectors before formatting. It is faster, but potentially more risky.

7. Select Enable Compression if you are formatting as NTFS and want to turn the compression attribute on for the entire drive or partition.

8. Choose Start. The dialog box charts the progress of the format operation. Click OK when format is complete, and then choose Close.

Deleting Partitions and Drives

Deleting a partition is as simple as choosing Partition, Delete. Disk Administrator warns you that deleting the partition or drive will irrevocably lose any data stored on the partition. But you already knew that, didn't you? So, always check the contents of a drive or partition before you delete it to ensure that you will not inadvertently lose something valuable—and that you don't have backed up!

Disk Management Extras—Drive Letters, Properties, and Display Options

Besides the format option, Tools (on the menu bar) gives you the ability to assign a specific drive letter to a logical drive or primary partition. By default, Windows NT assigns the next available drive letter to your primary partition or logical drive. Some programs require that a particular drive letter be used for the partition that holds the application files. Or, you can choose to assign drive letters for consistency. Sometimes, a persistent connection to a mapped drive takes up a drive letter that you would prefer to assign to a logical drive or primary partition after you have disconnected.

To assign a drive letter, follow these steps:

1. Select the drive or partition in Disk Administrator.

2. Choose Tools, Assign Drive Letter.

3. In the Assign Drive Letter text box, select the desired drive letter. Only available drive letters are shown. If there is a drive letter you want to use that is currently in use by a persistent connection, disconnect that mapping first to release the drive letter.

You have the option of not assigning a drive letter at all. Because there are a limited number of letters in the alphabet, and some are reserved up front, this option allows you to create additional drives and partitions now, and assign drive letters to them as you need to access them. This kind of activity is not recommended on the average end-user's desktop as it can lead to confusion and possible misplacement or loss of data.

You can quickly display the Properties sheet of any partition or logical drive by selecting that drive and choosing Tools, Properties. From here, you can see usage statistics, change the volume label, run volume scan and defragmentation tools, and view sharing information for the drive.

As you create primary partitions, logical drives, volume sets, and so forth using Disk Administrator, it uses various color codes and cross-hatching to facilitate your interpretation of the disks' partition and formatting schemes. The Options menu includes options for changing

Colors and Patterns used in the legend, whether to show partition and drive sizes to scale through Disk Display, and whether and how to show a specific physical disk only through Region Display. Through Customize Toolbar, you can even create and customize your own icon toolbar to facilitate your most frequent activities.

System, Boot, and Active Partitions

As I mentioned earlier, Windows NT refers to the partition that contains the Windows NT boot files (NTLDR, NTDETECT.COM, NTBOOTDD.SYS, BOOT.INI, and BOOTSECT.DOS) as the system partition, and the partition that contains the WINNT40 installation directory as the boot partition. Only one partition can be marked as active. On MS-DOS computers, this usually referred to the C: drive. In Windows NT, on dual boot computers (booting between both Windows NT 4.0 and MS-DOS or Windows 95), this is probably still the C: drive. However, it *must* be the partition that contains the Windows NT boot files. There might be multiple operating systems on your computer, such as Windows NT 4.0 and UNIX or Windows NT 4.0 and OS/2. Each expects its boot files to be on the partition marked active. You are most likely to find this type of configuration on developer's workstations or test servers.

You use the boot manager utility that comes with the other operating system to mark the Windows NT system partition as the active partition when you want to restart your workstation and boot into Windows NT. When you are in Windows NT and are ready to restart your system and boot into another operating system, use Disk Administrator as your boot manager.

To change the active partition marker, follow these steps:

1. Start Disk Administrator.
2. Select the partition to be marked active (primary partitions only).
3. Choose Partition, Mark Active. Disk Administrator displays a confirmation message that the partition has been marked active and will boot with whatever operating system is on it the next time you restart your system.

The active partition can be spotted if you look very closely in the color bar above the drive letter. The active partition is marked with a star. You can see this better if you choose Options, Colors and Patterns and change the color bar to something other than dark blue.

Creating and Managing Volume Sets

A volume can be thought of as any partition or logical drive on any physical disk that can be accessed as a single unit. In Windows NT, a volume can be a single contiguous area of disk space or a collection of non-contiguous areas of disk space. The latter is called a *volume set*.

A volume set can consist of from 2 to 32 areas of free disk space on one or more physical disk drives. They are combined and treated by Windows NT as though they were one large volume, and can be formatted as either FAT or NTFS. After these areas have been combined, they cannot be split apart. Consequently, deleting any part of a volume set deletes the entire volume set.

You can use volume sets to clean up areas of free space that, by themselves, may not be large enough to be useful, or to create storage areas larger than any one physical disk can provide.

Here are some more fun facts about volume sets:

◆ Volume sets can contain areas of free space from different drive types such as SCSI, ESDI, and IDE.

◆ Data is written to each member of a volume set in turn. That is to say that when one member is filled, then the next member is written to, and so on. Therefore, a volume set really does not improve disk I/O performance.

◆ Windows NT system and boot partitions may not participate in a volume set.

◆ Like NTFS, on workstations that dual boot between Windows
NT and MS-DOS or Windows 95, volume sets are not accessible by MS-DOS or Windows 95.

◆ If any member of a volume set fails, or the disk that a member
resides on fails, the entire volume set is corrupted.

Note   When you choose areas of free space of very disparate sizes,
Disk Administrator sizes each member of the volume set
proportionate to the amount of free disk space selected. For example, if
you choose to create a 50M volume set out of a 10M and 200M area of
free space, you might expect Disk Administrator to use all of the 10M
space for the first member of the volume set, and then 40M from the
remaining 200M free space for the second member of the volume set.
However, Disk Administrator determines, as you see in Figure 8.3, that
proportionate to the size of the free areas selected, the first member is
4M and the remaining is 47M. This same note applies to extended volume
sets. ▨

Creating and Formatting a Volume Set

To create a volume set, follow these steps:

1. Start Disk Administrator.

2. Select from 2 to 32 areas of free disk space by clicking the first,
   and then Ctrl-clicking the rest.

3. Choose Partition, Create Volume Set. The Create Volume Set
   dialog box is displayed showing the smallest size (2M) and
   largest size volume set you can create from your selections.

4. In the Create Volume Set of Total Size text box, enter the *total*
   size you want for the volume set.

5. Choose OK. Disk Administrator displays the new volume set
   similar to the example shown in Figure 8.3.

6. Format the new volume set as FAT or NTFS.

FIG. 8.3 ⇒

In this example, note that the volume set J: consists of two non-contiguous areas of disk space and has been formatted as NTFS.

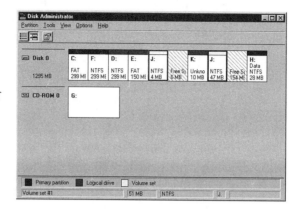

Extending a Volume Set

If you have formatted a partition, logical drive, or volume set as NTFS, and you are running out of space on it, never fear. NTFS-formatted space can be extended into free space without any loss of data and without having to reformat the space. This process is called *extending* the volume set.

This can be particularly helpful in adding extra print spool space to a partition, or allowing for the growth of a database.

To extend a volume set, follow these steps:

1. From Disk Administrator, select the NTFS partition, drive, or volume set.

2. Ctrl-click an area of free space that you want to add on.

3. Choose Partition, Extend Volume Set to display the Extend Volume Set dialog box. The minimum and maximum *total* size for the extended volume is shown.

4. In the Create Volume Set of Total Size text box, enter in the total size you want the volume set to be.

5. Choose OK. Disk Administrator creates what appears to be a volume set and applies NTFS to the new volume set member (see Figure 8.4).

FIG. 8.4 ⇒
Note how drive H
has been extended
from 28M to a
total of 52M.
Because it was
formatted as
NTFS, NTFS is
automatically
applied to the
extended volume.

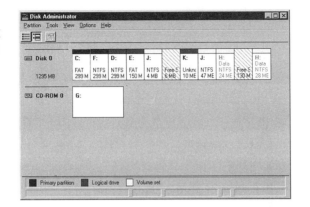

Ch
8

Creating and Managing Stripe Sets

A stripe set in Windows NT is quite similar to a volume set in that
both involve combining areas of free disk space into a single large volume. The similarities end there, however.

A stripe set consists of free space from at least 2 and up to 32 different
physical drives. The area of free space chosen on each disk must be the
same size on each disk. For example, if you have three disks with 100,
200, and 300M of free space each, and you want to combine all three to
create a stripe set, the largest any member can be is the smallest of the
areas of free space, or 100M, providing a total stripe set across all three
disks of 300M (100M×3 disks). Or, I can combine two 200M areas
from the second and third disks to create a total stripe set of size 400M.
It's all just simple arithmetic.

Unlike volume sets, in which the first member gets filled up before the
second member is written, in stripe sets, data is written uniformly in
64K blocks across all members of the stripe set (see Figure 8.5). Because
data can be written concurrently across the physical disks, a stripe set
can result in an overall disk I/O performance increase.

Here are some more fun facts about stripe sets:

◆ Windows NT system and boot partitions can not participate in
a stripe set.

◆ Like NTFS, on workstations that dual boot between Windows NT and MS-DOS or Windows 95, stripe sets are not accessible by MS-DOS or Windows 95.

◆ If any member of a stripe set fails, or the disk that a member resides on fails, the entire stripe set is corrupted.

FIG. 8.5 ⇒

Drive H in this example represents a 600M stripe set distributed across three physical disk drives.

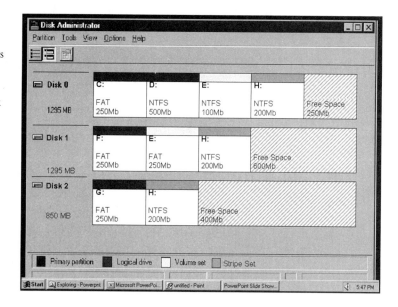

To create a stripe set, follow these steps:

1. From Disk Administrator, select from 2 to 32 areas of free disk space on different physical disks. Click the first area and Ctrl-click the remaining areas. The areas should be of approximately the same size. If not, Disk Administrator sizes the stripe set based on the smallest area of disk space selected.

2. Choose Partition, Create Stripe Set to display the Create Stripe Set dialog box. The minimum and maximum total sizes for the stripe set are shown.

3. In the Create Stripe Set of Size text box, enter the total size stripe set you want.

4. Choose OK. Disk Administrator displays the equal sized members of the stripe set distributed across the physical disks selected.

5. Format the stripe set.

6. Quit Disk Administrator or choose Partition, Commit Changes Now to save your changes in the Registry.

The System Partition and RISC

The system partition on a RISC-based computer must be formatted as FAT because these computers can only boot from FAT. There is no way to protect the system partition in this environment with local security. However, Disk Administrator provides an additional menu choice called Secure System Partition. When this option is selected, only administrators on that computer are able to access the system partition.

Disk Administrator Options on Windows NT 4.0 Server

In addition to the partition, volume set, and stripe set options that you have seen, Disk Administrator on a Windows NT 4.0 server provides additional disk fault-tolerant options. From the menu option Fault Tolerance, you can create stripe sets with parity, also called RAID 5, and disk mirroring, as well as regenerate data lost because of failed stripe sets with parity or mirrored disks.

We are talking about software-based fault tolerance that is built into the Windows NT operating system. When enabled, it places additional stress on the processor for resource management and disk I/O. Also, when a member of a stripe set fails, or a disk mirror fails, Windows NT must be shut down, the drive replaced, and the data regenerated. Hardware-based fault tolerant systems generally allow for hot-changing failed disks without shutting down Windows NT. However, Windows NT's software-based fault tolerance is considerably less expensive than its hardware counterparts. If you are just getting started and need to secure your servers with fault tolerance, this is a good way to go. Look for more information on these options in the *Windows NT 4.0 Server Exam Guide* from Que.

Backing Up and Restoring Data

By now, if you have spent any length of time working with microcomputers, especially within a network environment, you have heard the words "backup and restore" at least once. Perhaps you heard them uttered yourself as in, "Why didn't I...?"

Backing up data and having the ability to recover it is perhaps the most important part of disk management, especially within an enterprise network environment. As companies move faster and closer toward electronic media for conveying information—and in spite of rhetoric to the contrary, believe that it is happening—the backup process has taken on a much more prominent and integral role in securing data.

There are several strategies that one might follow in implementing a backup procedure, and just about as many hardware and software options to choose from. This section is not intended to drive home the importance of developing and implementing a sound backup/restore policy. If you haven't yet been convinced, you will be the first (and last) time that you lose $20,000,000 worth of financial records because the incremental daily backup failed to occur and no one monitored it (as happened to a previous employer of mine).

The purpose of this section is to introduce you to the backup/restore utility included with your installation of Windows NT Workstation 4.0 and Server, explain some terms that Microsoft uses (and that you are apt to encounter on the Workstation exam), and to posit a couple of backup and restore strategies.

Requirements, Terms, and Strategy

The Windows NT Backup utility is designed for use with a Windows NT-compatible tape backup device. To determine whether your tape backup device is compatible, consult—as with any new piece of hardware—the Windows NT 4.0 Hardware Compatibility List (HCL).

The Windows NT Backup utility is meant primarily as a file and folder backup product and does not back up data at the sector level. Consequently, Windows NT's backup utility cannot be used to perform volume recovery. If you need this kind of functionality, or want built-in scheduled backups, and so on, you should review the many third-party backup programs available now for Windows NT. Nevertheless, the Windows NT Backup utility is a fine product, and does allow the backup of the Registry.

The following persons can perform the backup and restore function:

- ◆ Administrator
- ◆ Members of the local Backup Operators group
- ◆ Members of the local Server Operators group
- ◆ Users granted the user right Backup (Restore) Files and Directories
- ◆ Users who have read permission to files and folders

As for strategy, Microsoft promotes the following three areas of consideration when planning your backup procedure:

- ◆ *What do you need to backup?*—Significance of the data.
- ◆ *Where are you backing up from?*—Centrally stored data or locally distributed.
- ◆ *How often do you need to backup?*—Frequency with which the data should be backed up to provide recovery.

The significance of the data is always subjective. For purposes of your strategy, you need to determine how much data is significant so as to plan for the appropriate number of backup devices, right-sized media, location of devices, and so on.

Data stored centrally tends to be easier to maintain than data stored at local computers. For one thing, while you can back up users' data remotely with Windows NT's backup utility or various third-party products, you rely more heavily on the user to either back up his own data or make his computer available for the remote backup, sharing folders, closing files, and exiting applications. The backup of centrally stored data is usually the responsibility of one or two persons who can monitor network usage and ensure that important files are closed and can be backed up regularly.

Key Concept

The obvious recommendation, then, is to store critical files in a central location and always back them up. Files that you cannot live without— including the Registry, especially on the domain controller (SAM and Security databases)—should be backed up regularly, perhaps daily. Files that change infrequently or are of less importance might also be backed up on a regular basis, perhaps weekly. Temporary files and files that are used once and forgotten can probably never be backed up.

Table 8.2 lists some backup terms that Windows NT uses and that you may already be familiar with.

Table 8.2 Backup Types

Term	Effect
Normal	Backs up selected files and folders and sets their archive attribute.
Copy	Backs up selected files and folders but does not set the archive attribute. This option is generally used for creating tape copies outside the regular backup routine.
Incremental	Backs up only selected files and folders that have changed since the last backup, and sets their archive attribute.
Differential	Backs up only selected files and folders that have changed since the last time they were backed up, but does not set their archive attribute.
Daily	Backs up only files and folders that changed that day without setting their archive attribute.

The use of the archive attribute is significant for any backup strategy. The archive attribute indicates whether the file has been previously backed up or not. Let's examine the difference between a differential and incremental backup as an example.

According to Table 8.2, they do precisely the same thing except for setting the archive attribute. The incremental sets it and the differential does not.

Let's say that you have a data folder in which users make frequent contributions and modifications. If you employ an incremental backup each day of the week, starting with a normal backup on Monday, the backup would proceed like this:

Monday   Back up all files and set their archive attribute

Tuesday   Back up all files that are new or have changed since
              Monday and set their archive attribute

Wednesday   Back up all files that are new or have changed since
              Tuesday and set their archive attribute

Thursday   Back up all files that are new or have changed since
              Wednesday and set their archive attribute

Friday   Back up all files that are new or have changed since
              Thursday and set their archive attribute

By the end of the week, you have created five backup tapes, each containing data that changed since the previous day. If data is lost in the folder on Friday, all tapes can be employed to recover the data that is lost because you would not know necessarily which day's data is lost. The backup process is faster, but the restore can potentially take longer.

Now let's back up the same folder using a normal backup on Monday and a differential the rest of the week:

Monday   Back up all files and set their archive attribute

Tuesday   Back up all files that are new or have changed since
              Monday, but do not set their archive attribute

Wednesday	Back up all files that are new or have changed since Monday, but do not set their archive attribute
Thursday	Back up all files that are new or have changed since Monday, but do not set their archive attribute
Friday	Back up all files that are new or have changed since Monday, but do not set their archive attribute

Notice that each day's tape contains files that are new or have changed since the beginning of the week. This backup process takes a little longer, but if data is lost from the folder on Friday, only the Monday and Thursday tapes need be restored because Monday contains all the original data, and Thursday contains everything that has changed since Monday.

Another twist on these strategies is to perform a complete normal or copy backup once every week or every month, and archive that tape off site. By designating a series of tapes in rotation, you can cycle your off-site archive tapes into the regular routine and always maintain a valid and timely recovery system that includes off-site data storage.

Table 8.3 lists some additional terms that Microsoft uses regarding the backup process.

Table 8.3   Backup Terms

Term	Description
Backup Set	The group of files and folders backed up during a backup session. A tape may contain one or more backup sets.
Family Set	The group of tapes that contains files and folders backed up during a single backup session.
Backup Log	The backup text file that the backup utility creates that records details relating to the session, such as the date, type of backup, which files and folders were backed up, and so on.

Term	Description
Catalog	A graphical representation of the backup that is loaded during the restore process and displays the backup sets on a tape, and the files and folders contained in a backup set.

Initiating Backup

The first step in initiating a backup is to determine what you will be backing up (see Figure 8.6). It helps to know ahead of time what files and folders you want to back up, and where they are located. For example, if you are planning on backing up files located in a remote server or a user's workstation, the folder containing the files must first be shared, and then you must connect to that share from the computer that is doing the backup. All files, of course, must be closed because backup cannot operate on open files. After you have made these preparations, you can start the backup utility. Unfortunately, you cannot back up the Registry from a remote computer.

FIG. 8.6 ⇒

Notice, in this backup example, that files and folders on drive D: are selected by a simple point-and-click.

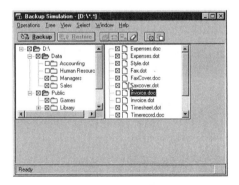

To back up files and folders, follow these steps:

1. Start the Windows NT Backup utility (Start, Programs, Administrative Tools, Backup).

2. In the Backup dialog box, select the drives, folders, or files to be backed up by pointing and clicking the appropriate check boxes.

   Your selections are hierarchical in that if you select a drive or folder, you automatically select its contents and subfolders (see Figure 8.6).

3. Next, choose Operations, Backup, or just click the Backup button to display the Backup Information dialog box shown in Figure 8.7.

4. In the Tape Name text box, enter a name for the tape up to 32 characters. If you are appending to an existing tape, the Tape Name box is not available.

5. Choose the appropriate tape options.

   See Table 8.4 for a description of the tape options.

6. Enter a Description for the backup set you are creating.

7. Choose a Backup Type.

8. In the Log File text box, enter the name and path for the text file you want to use to record details about the backup operation, and select whether you want to capture all backup information (Full Detail); only major operations such as starting, stopping, and failing to open files (Summary Only); or Don't Log at all.

9. Choose OK.

   Backup displays the status of the operation as it takes place and a summary when it is complete. This is shown in Figure 8.8.

10. Choose OK to complete the operation.

11. Store your tape in a safe place.

FIG. 8.7 ⇒

This tape for the files selected on Kite Server includes an incremental backup of the Registry and is restricted to the user that performed the backup.

FIG. 8.8 ⇒

Here you see the statistics compiled for a successful backup of the files and folders selected in Figure 8.6.

Table 8.4   Tape Options

Option	Description
Append	Adds a new backup set to an existing tape.
Replace	Overwrites the data on an existing tape.
Verify after backup	Compares files selected with files backed up and confirms that they are backed up accurately.

continues

Table 8.4 Continued

Option	Description
Backup Registry	In addition to the files selected, copies the Registry to the backup set. (At least one file in the volume containing the Registry must have been selected for the Registry to be backed up successfully.)
Restrict Access	Only Administrators, Backup Operators, or the user that performed the backup is allowed access to the backup set for purposes of recovery.
Hardware Compression	If the tape drive supports data compression, select this option to enable it.

Initiating a Restore

The restore process is much the same as the backup process, but in reverse. The same rules apply regarding who can perform the operation, and your restore strategy pretty much depends on what type of backup strategy you implemented. Refer to the two backup examples outlined earlier in the section "Requirements, Terms, and Strategy."

Also, as with backup, the first step in initiating a restore is to determine what you will be restoring. You will make good use of the backup logs created during the backup process to determine which files and folders you want to restore, on what backup set they are located, and where you need to restore them to. For example, if you are planning on restoring files to a remote server or a user's workstation, you must connect to the appropriate drive on that computer. Unfortunately, the Registry cannot be restored to a remote computer.

To restore files and folders, follow these steps:

1. Start the Windows NT Backup utility.

2. The Tapes window displays the name of the tape in the device and information regarding the first backup set on the tape.

3. To see additional backup sets, load the tape catalog by choosing Operations, Catalog. The Catalog Status dialog box is displayed.

4. Choose OK when the process completes. A new window with the tape's name is displayed.

5. In this window, select the appropriate backup set to load its catalog.

6. Next, select the drives, folders, and files to be restored by selecting the appropriate check boxes. Your selections are hierarchical in that if you select a drive or folder, you automatically select its contents and subfolders.

7. Next, choose Operations, Restore, or just click the Restore button to display the Restore Information dialog box, shown in Figure 8.9.

8. In the Restore to Drive text box, the original drive and path are displayed, or select an Alternate Path.

9. Select the appropriate restore option. See Table 8.5 for a description of the three options.

10. Enter the name and path for the text file you want to use to record details about the restore operation in the Log File text box, and select whether you want to capture all restore information (Full Detail), only major operations, such as starting, stopping, and failing to restore files (Summary Only), or Don't Log at all.

11. Choose OK. Restore displays the status of the operation as it takes place and a summary when it is complete, as shown in Figure 8.10.

12. Choose OK to complete the operation.

FIG. 8.9 ⇒
This operation restores the selected files and folders to the original D: drive, as well as the Registry, and maintains the original permission settings.

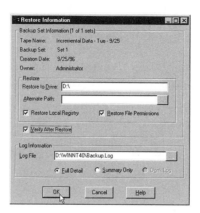

FIG. 8.10 ⇒
Here are the summary statistics for the restore operation you began in Figure 8.9.

Table 8.5 Restore Options

Option	Description
Restore Registry	Restores the local Registry to the target computer.
Restore Permissions	Restores the NTFS permissions to the files as they are recovered. If this option is not selected, files assume the permissions of the target folder. If you restore to a different computer, be sure that you have valid user and group accounts or your permissions may be inaccurate.
Verify After Restore	Compares files selected with files restored and confirms that they are restored accurately.

Ch
8

Troubleshooting Backup and Restore

You are not likely to encounter any problems with the Backup utility provided you are using a supported tape device and have the appropriate level of permission to perform the operation, either by virtue of membership in the Administrators, Backup Operators, or Server Operators group, by assignment of the Backup (Restore) Files and Directories user right, or through Read permission to the files and folders.

If you have chosen to log the backup and restore operations, any exceptions to the process, such as open files that couldn't be backed up, are duly recorded there. You can use that file to troubleshoot what did and did not get backed up, where it was backed up from, what backup set it can be found in, and so on.

Also, you should review the catalog for the selected backup set before restoring files. Corrupted files and folders are highlighted with a red X. Obviously, you should probably not restore these.

Scheduling a Tape Backup

Windows NT provides a command-line backup utility that you can use in combination with Windows NT's AT command to schedule a tape backup operation. To accomplish this, you need to create a batch file that contains the backup command syntax, and then use the AT command to schedule the batch file to run.

The basic backup command syntax is as follows:

```
NTBACKUP BACKUP path\filenames options
```

where path\filenames indicates the location of and selected files, and options are any selected from Table 8.6.

Table 8.6   NTBACKUP Options

Option	Description
/A	Adds (appends) the backup set to the existing tape.
/b	Backs up the local Registry.
/d "text"	Adds a description for the backup set.

continues

Table 8.6 Continued

Option	Description
/e	Creates a summary log rather than a detail log.
/l *filename*	Assigns a file name to the backup log other than the default.
/r	Restricts access to Administrators, Backup Operators, Server Operators, or users who perform the backup.
/t *type*	Indicates the *type* of backup (*Copy, Incremental, Differential, Daily*) other than the default *Normal*.
/v	Verifies that files were backed up accurately.
/hc:*on/off*	Turns on or off hardware compression for tape devices that support the option.

If you need to connect to a remote share to back up files, begin the batch file with a connection to that remote share using the following syntax:

```
CMD /C net use d: \\server\share
```

where d: represents the logical drive mapping, and \\server\share the UNC path to the remote share. At the end of the batch file, include the same line with a /d at the end to disconnect from the share.

Following is an example of a batch file called DATABACK.BAT; it connects to a share called DATA on server ACCT1, does an incremental backup of the files in that share, the Registry, restricts access, and verifies the backup:

```
CMD /C NET USE M: \\ACCT1\DATA
NTBACKUP M: /a /t Incremental /b /r /v
CMD /C NET USE M: /D
```

To use the AT command to schedule this batch file, the Scheduler Service must be running. Use the Services applet in Control Panel to enable and configure this service.

The AT command uses the following syntax:

```
AT \\computer time options batchfilename
```

where `computer` represents a remote computer (otherwise the local computer is assumed), `time` indicates the 24-hour time hour:minute (00:00) notation for the operation to take place, `options` are as described in Table 8.7, and `batchfilename` indicates the command or batch file that you want to execute.

For example, if you want to schedule your ACCT1 backup to occur at 11:00 PM every weekday, the AT command would look like this:

```
AT 23:00 /every:M,T,W,Th,F DATABACK.BAT
```

Table 8.7   AT Command Options

Option	Description
/delete	Cancels a scheduled command by the ID number assigned to it.
/interactive	Lets the job interact with the currently logged on user.
/every:*date*	Runs the command on the specified day(s) of the week (M,T,W,Th,F,S,Su) or one or more days of the month using numbers (1-31). Default is the current day.
/next:*date*	Runs the command on the next occurrence of the day(s) specified or one or more days of the month.

Troubleshooting Disk Management

As with all the troubleshooting sections so far in this book, if you have read the material and understand it, and have taken the opportunity to experiment with the utilities discussed, you already have the basic tools you need to troubleshoot most problems. Here are a few more considerations.

Saving Disk Configurations

When you have made changes to the partition and format scheme on your computer, it is important to update that information. Of course, the current Registry settings are updated. However, if you are using the Emergency Repair Disk as a recovery tool, then you must remember to update it. You can do so by running the RDISK command at the command line. This updates the Emergency Repair information with any Registry changes including the disk configuration.

You can also choose Partition, Configuration, Save from the Disk Administrator menu bar to save assigned drive letters, volume sets, stripe sets, stripe sets with parity, and mirror sets to a blank disk or the Emergency Repair Disk. This can be particularly useful when planning migrations, software upgrades, and so on.

Other Considerations

If Windows NT fails to recognize a drive, it is most likely an incompatibility problem or driver problem. Always check the HCL before upgrading any hardware on your Windows NT 4.0 computer. Detected hardware errors are listed in the Registry in the key: HKEY_LOCAL_MACHINE\Hardware.

Corrupted files and folders should generally be deleted and good versions restored from your most recent backup. Worst cases require that you reformat the disk and then restore from backup.

When dual booting to MS-DOS, running some third-party MS-DOS-based utilities that modify the FAT entries can result in corruption or loss of data in Windows NT, especially if long file names are in use. Don't use these utilities to avoid file corruption or loss, or disable long file name support for FAT partitions.

1G IDE disk drives that follow the EIDE standard have a BIOS limit of 1024 cylinders, which restricts Windows NT's capability to access all of the available storage space on these disks. Either the BIOS needs to be able to get around the limit through sector translation or relative cluster addressing, or Windows NT needs to be able to communicate with the disk's controller. Windows NT currently supports Western Digital 1003-compatible controllers.

From Here...

Next up on our agenda is a trip through the wonderful world of network printing—still an adventure after all these years. Before you journey on, be sure to try the review questions and lab for this chapter.

Taking the Disc Test

 If you have read and understood the material in the chapter, you are ready to test your knowledge. Insert the CD-ROM that comes with this book and run the self-test software as described in Appendix I, "Using the CD-ROM."

Chapter Prerequisite

Before reading this chapter,
you should be familiar with the
Windows NT 4.0 architecture
as described in Chapter 2. You
should also be comfortable
navigating in Windows NT 4.0
(see Chapter 4).

Managing Printers

This chapter will introduce you to the Windows NT 4.0 printing process. There have been a couple significant changes from Windows NT 3.51 to Windows NT 4.0 that will serve to enhance the management process for you. As with previous topics, the concepts and procedures discussed in this chapter apply to both workstation and server installations. Also, since Windows NT is predominantly a network-based operating system, we will concentrate on network-related issues regarding the Windows NT 4.0 printing process.

The following four topics will be covered:

◆ Introducing and examining the Windows NT 4.0 print process

◆ Exploring print process components

◆ Managing the print process

◆ Discussing troubleshooting techniques

Introducing and Examining the Windows NT 4.0 Print Process

In the past, printing has been an adventurous prospect not only on the local desktop, but also across the network. It still is. However, great effort has been made among operating system developers and printer manufacturers to streamline the process and facilitate management of the print process, particularly on the network.

Microsoft has been especially mindful of the problems associated with network printing and has throughout its history tried to enhance the process. For example, every MS-DOS application generally requires its own print driver to be loaded in order for that application to successfully talk with a given printing device. With Windows, Microsoft introduced a single set of print drivers that could be used with all Windows applications. In other words, Windows required the installation of one driver which all its applications would use instead of a driver for each application.

Windows NT follows this same concept—one driver that can be used by all applications running under Windows NT. It takes the concept a step further in version 4.0, however, by not requiring a driver for every installation of Windows NT, as we will see shortly.

First, let's explore some terminology that we will use throughout this chapter, and that you will encounter as you read through materials published by Microsoft and others.

When we speak of a printer in Windows NT 4.0, we are referring to the print driver. The actual hardware box that does the printing is called the print device. The print request is called the print job and can be sent to either a local print device connected directly to the user's local computer, or a remote print device which is attached to or managed by another computer on the network.

The printer interacts with the print device to ensure that the print device receives a print job that has been formatted appropriately for that device. The printer also provides the print management interface from which print jobs can be viewed and manipulated. You could call it, therefore, the print queue as well since it does display the status of jobs that have been spooled for that print device.

Once a print device has been made available to users on the network, any valid Microsoft network client (Windows NT, DOS, Windows 95, Windows for Workgroups, Windows 3.1, LAN Manager 2.x, Netware, Macintosh) and even OS/2 and UNIX clients are able to direct print jobs to that device.

When you make a print device available as a remote printer, you are not actually sharing the device itself. Rather, you are sharing the printer, that is to say, the management interface. A given print device might have several printers associated with it, each with a different set of characteristics, priorities, or permissions. We will explore this concept further later in this chapter.

Windows NT 4.0 Print Process

When an application makes a print request, the print process begins. One of the innovative things Microsoft has done with Windows NT regards its Windows NT (all versions) and Windows 95 clients. While clients need a print driver to process print requests, these clients *do not require* that a print driver be installed locally. Instead, Windows NT checks to see whether a local driver exists. If it does not, or if its version is older than that on the print server, then the print server downloads a copy of the print driver to the client computer where it is cached for that session. If the client's driver is newer, then the newer local driver is used.

This allows the printing administrators the ability to provide a greater number and variety of print devices easily to their clients without worrying about running around and installing a bunch of drivers on everyone's computer. Pretty slick, huh?! Figure 9.1 gives a graphic representation of the print process.

FIG. 9.1 ⇒

The Windows NT 4.0 Print Process for Windows NT and Windows 95 Clients.

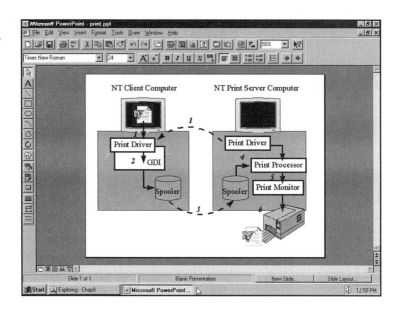

Step 1.   When an application makes a request for printing on a print device attached to a print server, the client computer checks to see whether it has a local print driver installed. If it does not, or if the local copy is older than the copy on the print server, the print server sends a copy of the print driver to the client. The print driver is loaded into memory on the client computer.

Step 2.   The *GDI* component of the client operating system creates a print job in enhanced metafile format. This is sometimes called a journal file, and represents the print job formatted to print on most any print device type, such as HPPCL, or PostScript. It is sent to the local spooler.

Step 3.   The local *Spooler* service makes an RPC connection to the corresponding service on the print server (not unlike your mapping a logical drive) and copies the print job there. The bulk of the print process now continues on the print server.

Step 4.   The print job is routed to the appropriate *print processor* where the print job is further rendered into a format compatible for the specific print device. This is usually referred to as a RAW file. If a *separator page* has been requested, then it is attached to the beginning of the print job.

Step 5.   The print job is then passed to the appropriate *print monitor* which controls access to print devices, directs jobs to the correct port, monitors status of the job, and so on.

Step 6.   The *print device* receives the print job from the print monitor and generates the final print product.

Printing from other clients is essentially the same except that the appropriate print driver must be installed on that local computer. The fully formatted RAW print job file is generated locally and routed to the print server spooler. Since no further rendering is needed, a separator page is added if required and the print monitor sends the print job to the print device.

Windows NT 4.0 supports MS-DOS-based applications and Windows-based applications. In general, these applications will take advantage of the Windows NT print driver and print successfully. Some MS-DOS applications which produce graphic print output, however, will probably require that the print driver native to that application be installed for that application. It is safe to say that if the print output from MS-DOS or Windows-based applications is not correct, you will need to install an application-specific driver.

Exploring Print Process Components

There are four basic components of the print process that I have introduced: print driver, spooler, print processor, and print monitor. We'll now explore each in more detail.

Print Driver

As I said earlier, the print driver interacts with the print device to allow applications to generate printed output. It also provides the graphic interface through which the print device and queue can be managed. The print driver consists of three pieces—two DLLs and what is called a characterization data file.

The *printer graphics driver DLL* converts the print job output from an application into a print device-ready format.

The *printer interface driver DLL* provides the interactive management screen through which the print jobs and the print device can be manipulated.

The *characterization data file* provides information concerning device-specific characteristics of the print device, such as the amount of memory, internal cartridges, additional form trays, and so on.

Print Spooler

The print spooler actually refers to the spooler service running in Windows NT 4.0. It is responsible for making a connection to the spooler on a remote print server. It tracks print jobs, sending them to the appropriate ports and assigning them an appropriate print priority.

You could consider the spooler to be the print queue for the Windows NT print process. As such, the spooler can get "stuck" if a print job hangs, or the system crashes, or some other such thing. If a print job hangs, or the spooler does not seem to be responding, you must purge the spooler. This is actually quite easy, although all jobs in the spooler will also be purged.

Since the spooler is a Windows NT service, it can be controlled through the Services applet in Control Panel. Simply select the spooler service from the list, choose STOP, and then choose START. This will effectively purge any print jobs waiting in the spooler.

Note It is always preferable to use the printer interface to try to pause or delete a problem job rather than stopping and starting the spooler service so as not to lose any other jobs in queue. ▪

By default, print job files are spooled to the WINNT40\SYSTEM32\ SPOOL\PRINTERS directory. Depending on the size of the partition, as well as the number and size of the print jobs spooled there, it is indeed possible to run out of disk space due to SPOOL folder capacity.

Tip

The folder compression attribute discussed in Chapter 8, "Managing Disk Resources," could be used here to compress the spool files and conserve disk space. However, keep in mind that compression does add additional overhead to your system and could, with large print files, result in a performance decrease.

If this were an NTFS partition, you could use Disk Administrator to *extend* the volume into available free space (you see, there *is* a good reason for doing it). Windows NT also provides a Registry entry through which you can modify the location of the SPOOL folder globally for all printers, as well as for individual printers.

Use Registry Editor to select the HKEY_LOCAL_MACHINE subtree and expand through to find the following key:

    SYSTEM\CurrentControlSet\Control\Print\Printers

Look for a parameter entry called DefaultSpoolDirectory and modify its value to correspond to the new spool location. This change will affect *all* printers installed on the computer.

On the next level below the Printer key, you will find an entry for each printer you created on the computer. Each of these also has a SpoolDirectory entry that, if modified, will change the spool location just for that printer.

As you can see, when you plan your installation of Windows NT 4.0, especially if your installation will be a server, or provide server-related activities such as print serving, you need to allow for enough disk space for those activities as well.

Print Processor

The print processor is responsible for carrying out any further formatting or rendering of the print job required for the specific printer to understand it. The default print processor for Windows NT 4.0 is WINPRINT.DLL. It recognizes and renders the print job types listed in Table 9.1.

Table 9.1 WINPRINT.DLL Print Job Types

Type	Description
Raw Data	The most common print job type. It represents a print job that has been fully rendered and ready for the specific print device, such as PostScript.
Enhanced Metafile (EMF)	Portable format that can be used with any print device.
Text	Represents a print job rendered with raw unformatted ASCII text and minimal control codes (linefeeds, carriage returns).
PSCRIPT1	Used on Windows NT servers running services for Macintosh, it represents PostScript code from a Macintosh client destined for a non-PostScript print device on a Windows NT print server.

Print Monitor

Where the spooler tracks the location of the job and ensures that the print job reaches the appropriate destination, the Windows NT 4.0 print monitor is responsible for tracking the status of the print job. It controls the stream of jobs to the printer ports, sends the job to its destination print device, releases the port when finished, returns print device messages like "out of paper" or "out of toner," and notifies the spooler when the print device has completed the generation of print output.

Table 9.2 outlines the print monitors supplied by Windows NT 4.0. The print monitor installed will depend on the print driver that you are using, the print device type, such as PostScript, HPPCL, or DEC, as well as the network protocol used to direct print traffic.

Table 9.2 Windows NT 4.0 Print Monitors

Print Monitor	Description
LOCALMON.DLL	Monitors print jobs targeted for print devices connected to local ports.
HPMON.DLL	Monitors print jobs targeted for Hewlett-Packard network print devices. The DLC protocol must be installed on the print server, and the printer "port" identified by supplying the print device's hardware address.
SFMMON.DLL	Monitors Macintosh print jobs routed using AppleTalk protocol to network print devices.
LPRMON.DLL	Monitors print jobs targeted for print devices communicating through the TCP/IP protocol, such as UNIX print devices and print spooler services.

continues

Ch
9

Table 9.2 Continued

Print Monitor	Description
DECPSMON.DLL	Monitors print jobs targeted for DEC's Digital PrintServer and other DEC print devices. Either the DECnet protocol or TCP/IP may be used to communicate with these print devices. Obtains the DECnet protocol from DEC (Digital Equipment Corporation).
LEXMON.DLL	Monitors print jobs targeted for Lexmark MarkVision print devices using DLC, TCP/IP, or IPX to communicate.
PJLMON.DLL	Monitors print jobs targeted for any bi-directional print device that uses the PJL (Printer Job Language) standard, such as the HP LaserJet 5Si.

More About LPD Devices

The Line Printer Port print monitor (LPRMON.DLL) is loaded when the TCP/IP Printing Support is installed on the print server. It is designed to facilitate the routing and tracking of print jobs destined for network-ready print devices that communicate using the TCP/IP protocol, or print devices that are connected to UNIX-based computers

Windows NT provides two command line utilities for directing and monitoring print jobs targeted for UNIX host printers called LPR.EXE and LPQ.EXE. If you are familiar with the UNIX environment, you probably have used these commands before.

To direct a print job to a UNIX host print device, open a command prompt window and enter the command:

LPR -S IP address of UNIX host -P Printer Name file name

where *IP address of UNIX host* is the TCP/IP address of the printer or host computer to which the printer is attached, *printer name* is the shared name of the printer and *file name* is the name of the print job that you are directing.

To receive queue information on the print server, enter the command:

LPQ -S IP address of UNIX host -P Printer Name -l

Keep in mind that LPR and LPQ command switches are case-sensitive.

Managing the Print Process

In this section, we will learn how to create and share printers, set their characteristics and properties, assign security, manage print jobs, and other fun printer stuff.

Creating a Printer

Now recall our definition of a printer: When we speak of a *printer* in Windows NT 4.0, we are referring to the *print driver*, the interface through which we interact with the print device and from which we can monitor and manipulate print jobs.

The first step in creating a printer is to ensure that the print device is compatible with Windows NT 4.0. This information can be verified in the Hardware Compatibility List (HCL).

As you might also expect, only certain users have the ability to create printers and share them on the network. Administrators, of course, have this ability by default. However, members of the Print Operators and Server Operators groups on domain controllers, and Power Users group members on any other Windows NT workstation or computer can perform this task as well.

The advantage of using something like the Print Operators group can be summed up in one glorious word: Delegation. Recall from our discussion in Chapter 6, "Managing Users and Accounts," regarding the tasks and rights granted the different built-in groups. Print Operators, for example, allows its members to create and manage printers, but not perform any other administrative tasks. This can be particularly useful for administering remote print servers.

Printers are created and connected using the Add Printer Wizard, accessible through the Printers folder in My Computer or Start, Settings, Printers. Let's walk through the process of creating a new printer that is connected to our local computer. Our local computer (workstation or server) will act as a print server for users on our network (workgroup or domain-based).

To create a new printer follow these steps:

1. From the Printers folder start the Add Printers Wizard by double-clicking Add Printer (see Figure 9.2).

FIG. 9.2 ⇒

Add Printer Wizard dialog box.

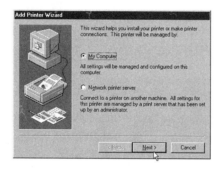

2. If the printer is connected directly to this computer, keep the default setting My Computer. Network printer server will be used later to connect to a remote printer. Choose Next.

3. Select the port that the printer is attached to (see Figure 9.3). Use Configure Port to modify transmission retry or baud settings of the designated port. If the print device is a network printer, or is identified through a hardware or IP address, choose Add Port to provide that information, select or add the appropriate print monitor, or load another or third-party print monitor. You also have the option of enabling a printer pool. Printer pools and their benefits will be discussed later in this chapter. Choose Next.

4. The list of print driver options has grown tremendously and so has Microsoft's support (see Figure 9.4). Microsoft has very wisely divided the on-screen listing into choices of device manufacturer and print device. If the device you are installing is not represented in the list, and you have an OEM disk with the

Windows NT-compatible driver on it, choose <u>H</u>ave Disk to install it. Choose <u>N</u>ext.

FIG. 9.3 ⇒

In the ports dialog box, we've indicated that the print device is attached to LPT1.

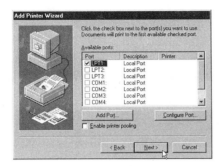

FIG. 9.4 ⇒

Here we have indicated that we want to install the print driver for the HP LaserJet 4.

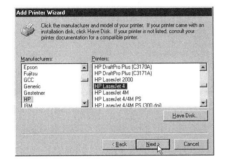

5. Enter a printer name that is descriptive of the print device (see Figure 9.5). This is the name that print administrators will use to identify the printer. Also, if the printer is being installed for local use, identify it as the default printer for use by applications if you like. The first installed printer will always be designated as the default. Choose <u>N</u>ext.

FIG. 9.5 ⇒

Our printer name will remain the default name of the print device and will be the default print device for applications run on this computer.

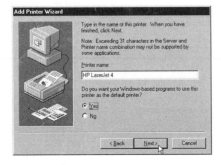

Ch

9

6. If you want to share the printer now, you can do so by selecting Shared, but you can always share it later, especially if you are not clear on how to set the printer permissions. Enter a Share Name that will be descriptive for the users who will connect to this printer (see Figure 9.6).

FIG. 9.6 ⇒

This printer has been shared using the name ACCT-HP4. Note that Windows 95 has been identified as a client that will print to this printer.

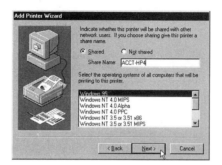

Also, in the list box on the lower portion of this dialog box, you will see a list of alternate driver platforms that you can support with this printer. For example, if Windows 95 clients will be accessing this printer, and you want to download the driver to each client rather than installing it separately on every Windows 95 client, then select Windows 95 from the list. Windows NT will be prompting you later for the Windows 95 source files, however, so be sure to have them ready. Again, you can always modify this later.

Choose Next.

7. The wizard asks whether or not you would like to print a test page to the print device. This is usually a good idea, especially if you are identifying a network print device through a hardware or IP address. Choose Finish.

8. As Windows NT installs the print driver, you will note the various driver files, DLLs, monitor files, and so forth, being loaded. If asked, supply the path to the location of the Windows NT source files.

9. As the installation completes, the wizard adds an icon to represent the printer in the Printer folder (see Figure 9.7), and asks

whether the test page printed successfully. If it did, you are done. If it did not, you have the opportunity to go back and modify your settings. The new printer icon is your access to the print manager for that printer, its jobs, and its print device(s).

FIG. 9.7 ⇒

Notice the new HP LaserJet 4 icon created in Printers, and the print manager window that it displays.

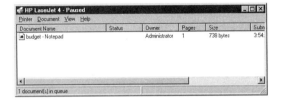

Sharing and Securing a Printer

If you chose not to share the printer while you were installing it, you can do so later. As I mentioned before, it is probably not always a good idea to share a printer without knowing how you will secure it. The default permission for shared printers, as you probably guessed, allows everyone to print to it. Not adequately securing the printer can be particularly embarrassing if the printer is the Graphics Department's expensive network-connected color laser print device, and your users from all over the network are printing party invitations or banners on it. Even if you did share it during installation, your next step should be to secure it.

To share a printer:

1. Display the printer properties (right-click, then choose Properties).

2. Select the Sharing tab.

3. Enter a user-friendly share name. This is the name that users will see when they are determining which printer to connect to. Make it descriptive and informative (within eight characters).

4. Optionally, choose to install an alternate platform printer driver if needed.

5. Choose OK. The printer will now be shared.

> **Note** Printer share names, as is true with all share names, must remain within the eight-character range in order for non-Windows NT and Windows 95 clients to be able to see the name. If your name is longer than eight characters, some network clients may not be able to connect to the printer. ▪

Setting Permissions for the Shared Printer

Recall that when sharing folders, you have the option of setting permissions of the share. These interact with any NTFS permissions set on the files and folders to produce an effective permission for the user. There are no permissions that you can set directly on a printer share. Instead, permissions are set on the printer itself. There are four permissions that can be used to secure a printer in Windows NT 4.0:

♦ *No Access* means just that, as always. Regardless of whatever permission you have been assigned through group membership, if you get No Access explicitly or through a group, you will not be able to access the printer to print *or* view the print jobs.

♦ *Print* permission is the default permission for the Everyone group. It allows users to connect to the printer, send print jobs to the printer, and manage their own print jobs—such as delete, pause, resume, or restart print jobs owned by the user.

♦ *Manage Documents* allows all the permissions of Print, and extends job management to *all* print jobs.

♦ *Full Control,* in addition to the permissions allowed for Manage Documents, lets the user modify printer settings, enable or disable sharing, delete printers, and modify permissions.

Like file and folder permissions, the permission list is actually the Access Control List (ACL) for the printer. By default, Administrators and Power Users are given Full Control on Windows NT workstations and servers, and Administrators, Print Operators, and Server Operators have Full Control on Windows NT domain controllers. On all Windows NT computers, Everyone has Print permission and Creator Owner has Manage Documents. Recall that the Creator Owner group is a special internal group that Windows NT uses to identify the owner of a file, folder, or in this case, a print job. By assigning it the Manage Documents permission, you are in effect saying that only the owner of any given print job has the ability to pause, delete, resend, or cancel it.

To secure a printer:

1. Display the printer properties (right-click and choose Properties).
2. Select the Security tab.
3. Choose Permissions to display the permissions dialog box. The current ACL for the printer is displayed in the Name list box (see Figure 9.8).

FIG. 9.8 ⇒

In the printer permissions for HP LaserJet 4, the Everyone group has been removed and the Developers group has been added with Print permission.

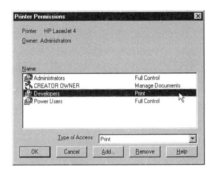

4. Modify the access of the current ACL entries by selecting the entry and choosing a Type of Access; or Remove entries from the list (like Everyone, Print); or choose Add to add user and group accounts from the local or domain SAM database.
5. Choose OK to save the permissions.

Auditing and Taking Ownership of the Printer

As with files and folders, access to a printer can be audited provided auditing has been enabled in User Manager. The audit events are saved as part of the Security log which can be viewed through the Event Viewer utility (see Figure 9.9).

Auditing for the printer can be configured by selecting Auditing from the Security tab of the printer's properties. Recall that you audit the activities of specific users and groups regarding the printer rather general access to the printer.

FIG. 9.9 ⇒

Users who are members of the Developers and Managers groups that access this printer to print will be recorded in the Security log of the Event Viewer.

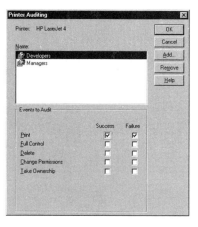

In the Printer Auditing dialog box, select <u>A</u>dd to display the account database. Select the users and groups for whom you want to record printer activity. In the Printer Auditing dialog box, select the activities you wish to audit.

> **Caution**
> Auditing places additional strain on resources and the processor. It is designed as a troubleshooting technique rather than as a reporting tool.

As with files and folders, the user who creates the printer becomes the owner of the printer. If for some reason that user is no longer able to manage the printer, you can take ownership of it like you might take ownership of a file or folder. Remember that ownership must be taken; it cannot be bestowed.

Members of the Administrators, Print Operators, Server Operators, and Power Users groups have the ability to take ownership of a printer. Also, any other user or group that has been given Full Control permission for the printer can take ownership of that printer.

To take ownership of the printer, select <u>O</u>wnership from the Security tab on the printer's property sheet and choose <u>T</u>ake Ownership.

Working with Printer Properties

You were undoubtedly lured to explore the other properties tabs while sharing and securing your printer. Let's explore them further.

General Tab

As seen in Figure 9.10, the General tab gives you the option of entering a descriptive comment about the printer, such as who can use it, what options it provides, and so on. Also, you can enter a descriptive location of the printer. This is useful when users are browsing for printers, viewing print manager screens, or receiving device-specific messages.

FIG. 9.10 ⇒

A comment and descriptive location have been added. When users view the printers, or receive device-specific messages, they will see the location as well.

Here, you also have the ability to identify a Separator Page, alternate Print Processor, and print a Test Page.

Separator pages, sometimes called banner pages, identify and separate print output by printing a page before the document that indicates who submitted the document and the date and time it printed. However, they also have the function of switching a printer between modes. Windows NT provides three separator pages located in WINNT40\ SYSTEM32, as shown in Table 9.3.

Table 9.3 Windows NT 4.0 Separator Pages

Separator File	Description
SYSPRINT.SEP	Causes a page to print before each document and is compatible with PostScript print devices.
PCL.SEP	Causes the device to switch to PCL mode for HP devices and prints a page before each document.
PSCRIPT.SEP	Causes the device to switch to PostScript mode for HP devices and does not print a page before each document.

Separator pages are text files and can be created and saved with an SEP extension in the WINNT40\SYSTEM32 directory using any text editor. Control characters that you can use to customize a separator page include \N which returns the name of the user who sent the document, \D which returns the date the document was printed, \T which returns the time the document was printed, and \H*nn* which sets a printer-specific control sequence based on a specified hexadecimal ASCII code.

Note More information about creating custom separator pages can be found in the online Books that come on the Windows NT Workstation and server CD. Just start up Books, choose Find, and search for "separator."

Print Processor lets you specify an alternate print processor for the print device and port, and modify the job types it creates to accommodate your applications. For example, WINPRINT offers five default print job types, including RAW, the default, RAW (FF appended), and RAW (FF auto). Let's say that the application that sends jobs to a particular printer always leaves the last page stuck in the printer. It is not adding a form feed to the end of the document. You might choose RAW (FF appended) to force a form feed on the end of any document sent to the printer, or RAW (FF auto) to let the print processor decide.

Ports Tab

The Ports tab is used for a number of different activities. First, you can use it to see which port the printer and print device is associated with and what kind of print device it is.

However, you could also change the port associated with a given printer. For example, if the LPT1 port has failed, and you move the print device to the LPT2 port, you need only change the port designation here rather than create a new printer.

On another note, you could also use the port associations listed here to redirect print output from one printer to another. For example, if the printer stalls for some reason, perhaps because of a failed port, or broken printer, or problem print job, you can redirect the output of the printer from the current printer to, perhaps, a remote printer (see Figure 9.11). It would be prudent to test this type of redirection before implementing it. If the spooling has been done in extended metafile format (EMF), the print job will print correctly. If not, the remote print device needs to be identical to the printer you are redirecting from.

FIG. 9.11 ⇒

Here the HP 4 has been redirected from LPT1 to a remote printer on a server named Glemarek.

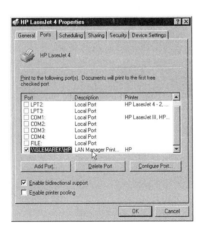

Use Add Port to add additional ports, such as a network port IP address for an LPD-enabled print device. For example, if you need to redirect print jobs from an existing printer to a network printer, use Add Port to add the remote printer to the list of ports, then select it from the list on the Ports tab. Use Delete Port to delete ports that you no longer need.

Ch
9

Use <u>C</u>onfigure Port to modify the transmission retry value, COM port settings, and so on.

When the print device associated with the printer you installed supports the sending of setting and status information back to the printer, we say it provides *bidirectional* support. Any extra information about the print process that you can get will be helpful. If the print device supports this feature, select <u>E</u>nable bidirectional support.

Print Pools

Perhaps the most useful activity you can perform with ports is the creation of a *print pool.* A print pool represents one printer associated with two or more print devices. In other words, the same printer driver and management window are used to interact with two or more print devices that are compatible with that printer driver. This type of arrangement is particularly efficient on a network with a high volume of printing. Print jobs sent to the pool will print on the next available print device, thus reducing the time jobs stay in queue. In addition, you only need to manage one printer rather than several.

For example, as you see in Figure 9.12, three print devices are available for use on the computer. An HP 4 is connected to LPT1 and LPT2, and an HP LaserJet III is connected to COM1. I could create a separate printer for each print device. However, this doesn't stop users from favoring one printer over another. They may, for example, rarely send to the HPIII printer because of its slower performance. Consequently, print jobs may get stacked up on the other two printers.

FIG. 9.12 ⇒

Three printers have been configured as a print pool in this example.

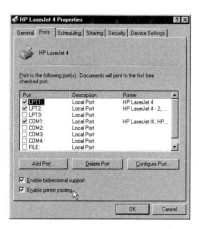

By associating one printer with all three devices, users have only one shared printer choice to make and their print jobs will be serviced by the next available print device. However, the user will not know on which printing device the job printed.

To set up a print pool:

1. Choose Enable printer pooling on the Ports tab.
2. Check off the ports connected to the print devices you want as part of the pool.

As you can see, this is a very straightforward process.

> ### Caution
> Be sure that the print device you associate with the printer driver in the pool supports that print device. If it does not, print output may be unintelligible. For example, while the HP LaserJet 4 printer driver is downward-compatible with an HP LaserJet III print device, it will definitely not support an HP LaserJet 5Si. The print driver, then must be compatible with the print devices in the print pool.

Print pools can be combined with other printers to produce a variety of output control options for the print manager. Suppose I create three shared printers—one each for Developers, Accountants, and Managers. I have set up the permissions so that members of each group can only print to their specified printer. However, it is important that Managers' print jobs get printed as quickly as possible.

I can make the Managers' printer into a print pool by associating it with the other two print devices. Now, Developers and Accountants each have one print device that services their print jobs, but Managers' print jobs can be printed on any of three, i.e., the next available print device.

Scheduling Tab

The Scheduling tab, besides allowing you to define when the printer can service jobs, lets you set a priority for the printer and define additional spool settings as well as shown in Figure 9.13. All three of these option settings will help the crafty print manager to further refine how and when print jobs are serviced.

FIG. 9.13 ⇒

This printer will begin sending print jobs to the print device after 10:00 PM. It will also wait until the entire job has been spooled before it sends it, and will print jobs that have finished spooling ahead of jobs that are still spooling.

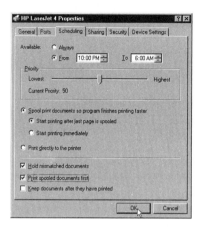

Defining when the printer can service jobs is fairly straightforward. Select Available: From and select the time range you want. Print jobs sent to this printer will still be spooled, but will not print until the designated time.

For example, suppose that you have a color laserjet print device to which several different groups of users send print jobs. One group, Graphics, tends to send very large graphic files that cause the other group's print jobs to wait in the spooler. You could create a separate printer for that print device and assign only the Graphics group print access. Then, you could set the printing time to print at off-peak hours. The Graphics group's print jobs will then wait in queue until the print time for their printer is reached.

Priority

When you set a priority for a printer, you are really setting a priority for all print jobs received by that printer. The printer priority can be set from 1 (lowest) to 99 (highest).

Setting a priority really only makes sense when you want documents sent to the *same* print device to have different priorities on that device. The key to making the priority effective is to associate two or more printers with the *same* print device. This is the exact opposite of a print pool in which *one* printer is associated with *two or more* print devices.

Once you have created and associated the printer with two or more print devices (reread the caution under Print Pools), set a priority for each from the Scheduling tab by using the sliding bar under <u>P</u>riority.

Let's use the same example I posited for Print Pools. I have three groups: Managers, Developers, and Accountants. They all are using the same HP LaserJet 5Si network print device. Accountants tend to send large spreadsheets to the HP5Si, but Developers send pretty hefty blocks of code. Managers always want their documents to print as soon as possible.

I create three *printers* and associate each with the *same* HP LaserJet 5Si print device. I will set permissions so that each group can only print to their respective printer. I will also set the priority for each printer as follows:

99 (highest) for the printer used by Managers

50 (medium) for the printer used by Accountants

1 (lowest) for the printer used by Developers

Whether my Developers let me get away with this is a separate discussion. Nevertheless, I have accomplished my task. Since the Managers' printer has been given the highest priority, their print jobs will print ahead of Accountants and Developers. Likewise, since the Accountants' printer has been given a medium priority, their print jobs will print ahead of Developers. Since the Developers' printer has the lowest priority, their print jobs will always wait until Managers' and Accountants' jobs finish printing.

Note Priorities will not affect a job that has begun printing. If a Developer's print job has begun printing, the Manager's print job will wait until it is finished. However, any subsequent Developer's print job will wait until Managers' and Accountants' print jobs have completed.

Other Spool Options

There are several cool options that you can use to determine how jobs are spooled, and in combination with print pools and priorities, will give the print administrator many options for affecting how, when, and where print jobs are printed.

The first is Spool Print Documents So Program Finishes Printing Faster. This is the default, and simply means that print requests will be spooled to a file rather than sent directly to the printer, resulting in a faster return to the application for the user. The other option is to Print Directly to the Printer. In this case, the print job is not spooled. It decreases printing time because the rendered print job is sent directly to the print device. However, the user will wait until the print job is complete before control is returned to the application.

If you choose Spool Print Documents, you have two "suboptions" to consider. The default, Start Printing Immediately, indicates that the print job will be sent to the print device for printing as soon as enough information has been spooled. Printing, of course, will be faster overall. The other option, Start Printing After Last Page Is Spooled, indicates that the print job will not be sent to the print device for printing until the entire job has been spooled. When used with printers of different priorities, this option can be effectively used to prevent large documents from "hogging" the print device. Smaller documents will be printed first, because they will be spooled first.

Did you ever experience the problem of sending a legal size print job to a print device that only had a letter size tray? The print job hangs up at the print device. Hold Mismatched Documents is designed to prevent that from happening by comparing the format of the print job with the configuration of the printer. If they do not match, the print job will be held in queue and not allowed to print while other print jobs in the queue will proceed.

Print Spooled Documents First allows print jobs that have completed spooling to print ahead of those that are still spooling, even if their priority is lower. When used with the option Start Printing After Last Page Is Spooled, it virtually assures that smaller print jobs will print ahead of larger print jobs. If there are no print jobs finished spooling, larger jobs will print ahead of smaller jobs.

When a print job finishes printing, the spooler deletes the print job from the queue, thus from the printer management window. If you would like to keep the document in queue to see its "complete" status, or to keep open the option of resubmitting the job, or to redirect it to another printer if it prints incorrectly, choose Keep Documents After They Have Printed. After the print job is completed, it will be held in the spooler rather than be deleted, and its status will be displayed. For example, if you have an end-of-month report that is difficult to reproduce that you would like to resubmit, use this option to keep the job in the spooler. On the other hand, the jobs remain in the spooler directory taking up space and it becomes the responsibility of the print administrator to remove these jobs when they are no longer needed—consider this option seriously before selecting it.

Device Settings Tab

You will use the Device Settings tab to assign forms to paper trays, indicate the amount of memory installed in the print device, specify font cartridges, and configure other device-specific settings such as soft font or halftone.

Configuring these options is as easy as selecting the option you wish to configure, and choosing a setting from the list box displayed in the lower portion of the dialog box. The options that are available, and their settings, will depend on the print device and the printer you installed to manage it. For example, while an HP LaserJet 4 only has one paper tray, an HP LaserJet 5Si may have several, including an envelope feed. The Device Settings tab will reflect these device features.

> **Note** Some printers offer page protection as a feature, and this option will be displayed on the Device Settings tab. Page protection ensures that the print device prints each page in memory before creating the output page. If you regularly send print jobs whose pages are composed of complex text and graphics, enabling this option will help ensure that the print device will print the page successfully rather than possibly breaking the page up as it prints it.

Managing the Printer and Its Documents

Double-clicking a printer icon in the Printers folder displays its print management window. There are four menu options to choose from, Printer, Document, View, and Help. View and Help are fairly self-explanatory. You will spend most of your time with Printer and Document.

From Printer, you can pause the printer, change the default printer for the computer, manage sharing and permissions, purge all documents from the spooler, and, of course, manage printer properties. In addition, you can set document defaults that apply to all print jobs sent to the printer. Among the options that can be set are the paper size, paper tray, number of copies, orientation, and resolution settings.

From Document, you can pause, resume, restart, and cancel print jobs. Each print job also has individual properties which can be set much like the properties for the printer itself.

Document Properties

Individual print jobs can have their properties set just like printers, though there aren't as many. However, the most important options—such as scheduling a time and priority for the job—are available (see Figure 9.14). Only users who have Full Control or Manage Documents permissions, or the owner of the document, can modify the print job's properties.

Display a print job's properties by highlighting the document in the printer management window and selecting Document, Properties.

The General tab displays statistics about the print job such as its size, number of pages, its owner, and when it was submitted. In addition, you can specify a user account to send a message to when the print job is complete.

FIG. 9.14 ⇒
The BUDGET
document is scheduled to print between 12 midnight
and 1:30 AM
with the highest
priority.

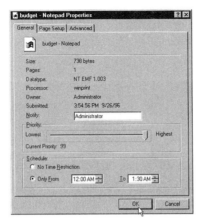

Ch

9

You can set an individual priority for the job here like you did for the printer. However, the priority selected here overrides the printer priority. Thus, if there is one particular large print job that has been sent to a low-priority printer that needs to be printed as soon as possible, you can set its priority higher.

Finally, a time range within which the document can be printed can be set for the individual print job. Using Figure 9.13 as an example, the BUDGET document is a large job that has been sent to the low-priority printer Developer's printer. Other jobs have undoubtedly been sent to the Managers' and Accountants' printers which have higher priorities. BUDGET's individual property settings ensure that it will print with the highest priority between 12:00 midnight and 1:30 AM.

The Page Setup and Advanced tab let you set additional options for the particular document such as the paper size, paper tray, number of copies, orientation, and resolution settings.

Troubleshooting Printing

Let's start this discussion with some basic troubleshooting steps to follow when the printing process fails; steps that I am certain most of you have followed in the past. The following bullets outline this troubleshooting checklist:

◆ Check to see if the print device is turned on and online.

◆ Check to see whether the print device connection is good. Swap out cables, check the network card, IP address, and so on.

◆ Verify that the printer driver installed is compatible with the print device.

◆ Confirm that the printer is available and has been selected. Verify that sharing has been enabled and that the permissions allow printing to take place for the users affected.

◆ Verify that the appropriate print port has been selected and configured by printing a test page.

◆ Monitor network traffic in the case of remote printing to verify that print jobs are being routed correctly and not being dropped.

◆ Check the amount of disk space available for spooling. Recall that the default spool directory is WINNT40\SYSTEM32\ SPOOL. The installation partition often only contains the Windows NT files and is kept purposefully small. If there is not enough space for the spooled files, printing will fail. Either add more disk space (extend the partition if it is NTFS) or move the spool directory to a disk with adequate space through the Registry. You could also turn on compression for the spool directory. However, this could have a negative effect on printing performance for large print jobs.

   ▶ **See** "Print Spooler," **p. 290**

◆ Determine whether the printing problem is due to a specific application error, or occurs with all applications. Some MS-DOS and Windows 16-bit applications may require their own print drivers installed to successfully print their documents.

◆ Resubmit the print job to print to a file and then copy the file to a printer port. If the job prints successfully, the problem may be related to the spooler or transmission process. If not, the problem is probably related to the application or printer driver.

Another source of help for troubleshooting printing problems is the built-in Windows NT Help program. It also provides a set of troubleshooting steps and tips to help resolve printing-related problems. Access help for printing problems by following these steps:

1. Select Help, Help Topics from the menu of any window opened through My Computer or Network Neighborhood.

2. Choose the contents tab on the Help dialog box.

3. Double-click the contents entry titled Troubleshooting.

4. Select the topic, If You Have Trouble Printing.

5. Find the problem you are having and click it.

6. Help will guide you through a series of questions and suggestions to help resolve the problem.

7. Exit Help when you are finished by closing the Help window.

Additional Considerations

As noted earlier, you are most likely to experience problems due to inadequate disk space, incorrect port or address settings, or restrictive permissions. Also, recall that most older MS-DOS-based applications, and some Windows-based applications, require that their own printer driver be installed. Be sure to consider these possibilities as well when troubleshooting.

Windows-based applications will print just like they did under Windows. Settings saved in WIN.INI and/or CONFIG.SYS are copied into the Windows NT Registry and will be used for these applications printing under Windows NT. Applications that produce PostScript-specific graphics will probably print incorrectly or not at all. If no default printer has been selected, these applications will produce an out-of-memory error message when loading or not allow selection of fonts.

If print jobs stall in a printer, or no one is able to print to it any longer, the spooler has probably stalled. The spooler can be purged of its documents and restarted by stopping and restarting the spooler service accessed through the Services applet in Control Panel. Stopping and restarting the spooler service will purge *all* documents in the spooler, so caution should be used.

Ch
9

If your print server and clients happen to be of different or mixed platforms, and you still want the print server to download the appropriate driver to all the Windows NT workstations, you need to install the appropriate platform drivers on the print server. A given print server may have multiple platform drivers installed for just this purpose.

For example, suppose that your print server is a RISC-based DEC Alpha computer. The Windows NT clients connecting to shared printers on the print server are Intel-based computers. You need to install the Windows NT 4.0 Alpha printer driver in order for the print server to interact successfully with the print device. However, you cannot download the Alpha driver to the Windows NT Intel clients. You could go around to each of the clients and install the Intel drivers on each. An easier solution is to also install the Intel platform driver on the print server. When an Intel client accesses the shared printer, the Intel driver will be downloaded to it. The Alpha print server, in turn, will use the Alpha driver to manage the print job on the print device.

From Here...

In the next chapter, we will look at the subsystem architecture that Windows NT uses to run applications more closely. In particular, we will discuss just how Windows NT does run those MS-DOS- and Windows-based applications you hear so much talk about.

Before you proceed, though, how about reviewing what you've learned in this chapter. Take the review test and try out the lab exercises. See you again in Chapter 10!

Taking the Disc Test

 If you have read and understood the material in the chapter, you are ready to test your knowledge. Insert the CD-ROM that comes with this book and run the self-test software as described in Appendix I, "Using the CD-ROM."

Chapter Prerequisite

Before reading this chapter, you should be familiar with the Windows NT 4.0 architecture as described in Chapter 2.

10

Running Applications Under Windows NT 4.0

In this next chapter, we will explore how applications run under Windows NT 4.0. This is not development-oriented material, but rather an overview of how the Windows NT subsystems support applications running under Windows NT. In particular, we will review the subsystem architecture and some key points about application support, and give particular focus to MS-DOS and Windows 16-bit applications and how they are supported under Windows NT 4.0.

Topics covered in this chapter include:

◆ Reviewing the Windows NT 4.0 subsystem architecture

◆ Examining Windows NT support for MS-DOS-based applications

◆ Examining Windows NT support for 16-bit Windows applications

◆ Examining WIN32 application support

◆ Reviewing OS/2–based application support

◆ Reviewing POSIX–based application support

◆ Considerations for troubleshooting applications

Reviewing the Windows NT 4.0 Subsystem Architecture

As we noted in Chapter 2, "Understanding Microsoft Windows NT 4.0," an integral part of any understanding of Windows NT is a discussion of the internal architecture of the Windows NT operating system. As you will recall, the Windows NT 4.0 architecture consists of two primary processing areas: *User* or *Application mode* and *Kernel* or *Privileged Processor mode*.

The User mode, as it implies, provides operating system support primarily for user applications and the environment, which is what we are concerned with in this chapter. The Kernel mode provides operating system support for just about everything else including kernel processing, memory management, hardware access, and so forth. These are referred to collectively as the *Executive Services*.

User (Application) Mode

The User mode of the operating system provides application processing and logon support. There are four subsystems that run in User mode (see Figure 10.1). The OS/2 and POSIX subsystems provide environment support for OS/2 1.x applications and POSIX applications respectively. The Security subsystem is loaded at boot time and is used solely for managing the Windows NT logon process.

FIG. 10.1 ⇒
Basic Windows
NT 4.0 Architec-
ture Model show-
ing application
support sub-
systems.

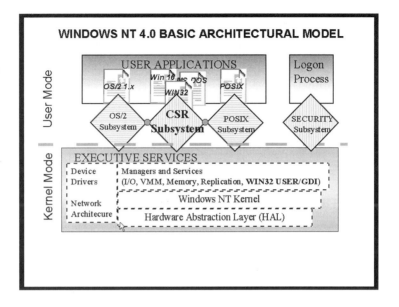

WINDOWS NT 4.0 BASIC ARCHITECTURAL MODEL

The primary subsystem, which is also loaded at boot time, is CSR, the Client/Server subsystem. CSR supports both 32-bit Windows and Win95 applications, as well as 16-bit DOS and Windows applications. It also provides graphics-based support to the environment subsystems and support to any other applications that are not written for the Windows NT application interface, error handling, or shutdown process.

Any application program calls from the two environment subsystems (OS/2 and POSIX) that read/write to the display are forwarded to the CSR subsystem. Any other calls to drivers, or other executive services are communicated directly to the Kernel mode.

Recall from Chapter 2, that in Windows NT version 3.51, the USER and GDI portions of the operating system were included in what was then called the WIN32 subsystem. The USER is the window manager and responds to user input on the screen. The GDI processes graphics primitives such as pixels, lines, fills, and so on. The GDI also performs graphics rendering for print files.

If an application needed either of these two for processing, it would have to create an IPC (InterProcess Communication) connection to it. This would involve a context switch from User mode to Kernel mode (ring 0 to ring 3 of the processor), as well as 64K buffering. Then, another context switch would take place back to User mode. This, obviously, involves some time and decreases overall performance.

Windows NT 4.0 moves the USER, GDI, and graphics device drivers into the Kernel mode as part of the Executive Services. This move significantly improves application performance by eliminating the 64K buffer, and leaving only a kernel transition, such as, one context switch. The benefit can be seen particularly in those applications that involve direct draw to the screen such as Pinball, as well as in multimedia applications such as Quicktime.

Kernel (Privileged Processor) Mode

Kernel mode provides support for all major operating system functions. For example, it controls access to memory and the execution of privileged instructions. All Kernel mode processes run in the protected mode of the processor, ring 0. As such, the applications running in User mode are effectively buffered from direct access to hardware. Thus, 16-bit applications that are designed to access hardware directly will not run successfully under Windows NT.

The Kernel mode consists of three main parts:

◆ The *Executive Services* is the largest part of Kernel Mode and provides support for window management and graphics device interaction, processes, threads, memory management, I/O, IPC, and security. It is here that most Windows NT services and process managers execute. It is also here where device driver support is provided, including Windows NT's network architecture support drivers, protocols, and so forth.

◆ The Windows NT *Kernel* provides support for thread scheduling and context switching, synchronization among services and processes in the Executive, multiprocessor load balancing, and exception and interrupt handling.

◈ The *HAL* provides hardware platform support. It isolates specific platform details from the Executive and the Windows NT Kernel. It is largely due to the HAL that those 16-bit applications that like to talk directly to hardware are unable to run.

Examining WIN32-Based Application Support

Each application written to the WIN32 API is offered the full benefit of OpenGL graphics support, OLE (across both WIN32 and WIN16 applications), DirectX, multithreading, and multiprocessing.

Every WIN32-based application has one or more threads of execution associated with it. Each thread is independent of the other process threads and can be processed concurrently. Further, through Windows NT's Virtual Memory Manager, each WIN32-based application is given its own memory space of up to 2G. By virtue of multithreading and virtual memory addressing, it is almost impossible for one WIN32-based application to interfere with or cause another to fail.

Ch
10

A Word About OpenGL and DirectX

OpenGL is an industry standard programming interface in which Microsoft participates, that allows applications to produce high-quality two- and three-dimensional color graphics. However, while other OpenGL implementations such as UNIX support VGA 256-color - graphics, Windows NT 4.0 supports VGA 16-color mode.

Windows NT offers five 3D screen savers which conform to the OpenGL standard. They are 3D FlowerBox, 3D Flying Objects, 3D Maze, 3D Pipes, and 3D Text. Because they require additional processor resource to manage, they are not recommended on computers that require processor resource for integral applications.

DirectX further adds to the robustness of multimedia support by providing accelerated video and audio support for multimedia

continues

continued

applications as well as network interaction between the applications through regular network interface or dial-up access. Where OpenGL gets its performance through dedicated processors on video cards, DirectX gets its performance through direct access to the multimedia device.

The next time you play 3D Pinball, think OpenGL and DirectX.

WIN32 applications are source-compatible across platforms. That means that the version of a WIN32 application that runs on an Intel computer will not run on the Dec Alpha. The application must be specifically re-compiled for that platform.

MS-DOS-based applications are sensitive to the DOS memory model requiring 640K for application support, 384K for upper memory driver loading, and expanded and extended memory addresses. Windows 95 and Windows NT 4.0 use a flat memory model discarding those distinctions in address. The MS-DOS application, however, needs that security blanket. What is there to do?

Like Windows before it, Windows NT 4.0 generates a *virtual DOS machine (NTVDM)* within which the MS-DOS-based application will load and run. This NTVDM essentially reproduces the MS-DOS environment configuration determined by the PIF and expected by the application to run successfully.

Every NTVDM that is created is given one thread of execution. As such, it is independent of all other threads, and if the NTVDM should fail, only its one process thread is affected. No other Windows NT application will be affected by the failed NTVDM.

The NTVDM is supported by four elements in Windows NT 4.0. When the MS-DOS application is loaded, the NTVDM is created first by the NTVDM.EXE. It emulates and manages the DOS environment for the application based in part on the PIF settings for the application. Two more files are loaded, NTIO.SYS and NTDOS.SYS, which emulate the two MS-DOS system files that provide basic operating system functions to the application. Finally, because MS-DOS applications want to interact with basic hardware directly, but cannot under the Windows NT architecture, virtual device drivers are supplied for application interaction with the keyboard and mouse, printer, video, and other ports.

On RISC-based systems, an additional IEU or Instruction Execution Unit is loaded with the NTVDM to emulate the Intel 486 processor for the application. Thus for all practical purposes, the MS-DOS-based application thinks it is running in its native DOS when in reality it is being faked out by the NTVDM.

Configuring the NTVDM

The NTVDM is configured through the PIF created for each MS-DOS application. Remember, regardless of whether you create one or not, Windows NT will always load a PIF for an MS-DOS-based application even if only the default settings. Therefore, it is to your advantage to create a PIF which more accurately determines memory and other needs of the MS-DOS application.

There have been two major changes to the PIF editor from its earlier Windows and Windows NT versions. In Windows NT 4.0, the PIF settings have been implemented as properties of the MS-DOS application and can be accessed by right-clicking the program executable. So you see, Windows NT will always use PIF settings to generate the NTVDM.

The PIF settings themselves have not changed dramatically from earlier versions (see Figure 10.2), so I will not go into each one in great detail. However, I will review the general areas that can affect the application's NTVDM environment.

Ch
10

FIG. 10.2 ⇒

We can see the six tabs for setting PIF properties for the DOS Editor, including an application-specific autoexec and config file.

The MS-DOS applications properties sheet consists of six tabs, six environmental areas that you can affect: General, Program, Font, Memory, Screen, and Misc.

◆ *General* settings include an informational display of the application path and size, created, modified, and last accessed date, and its DOS attributes (Read, Archive, Hidden, and System). You can set the attributes on this tab.

◆ *Program* lets you affect the icon and name that are associated with the application, the path and executable, the working directory, and whether to run it maximized, minimized, or in a normal window. Perhaps the most significant addition to the PIF settings is the option of creating and naming, through the Windows NT button on this page, autoexec and config files that are specific to the application.

Under Windows 3.x, because Windows is a DOS-based application whose core runs in conventional memory, you pretty much have to have managed your DOS environment before loading Windows. When a DOS application is loaded in Windows, Windows creates its virtual machine by "cloning" the DOS environment. That means that before Windows is loaded, you have to have looked at all the DOS applications that might run under Windows, and have loaded drivers high to provide the best common denominator environment that would suit Windows and the DOS applications it would need to support.

Windows NT 4.0 uses a flat memory model with no autoexec.bat or config.sys and no references to convential, upper, or high memory, so there is no DOS environment to clone for the NTVDM. However, Windows NT does provide default autoexec.NT and config.NT files that you can choose to modify if you wish. Most of the settings one usually makes in these files are addressed by a PIF setting. However, if you do have a particular TSR that you want to run, or a particular device driver that you want loaded, you can do it *for each individual application.* You can create as many different autoexec and config files as you wish and reference them in each application's properties. This provides you with far greater control over how the application will perform under Windows NT than you ever had under Windows.

◆ *Misc* includes setting background operation options, idle processing time, termination warning, and reserved shortcut keys.

Taken altogether, perhaps you can understand my earlier statement that the MS-DOS-based application might indeed experience a performance increase running under Windows NT 4.0. It certainly should not run any worse.

Caution

Remember that any MS-DOS-based application that interacts directly with hardware, such as modem dial out programs or disk management utilities, will not run under Windows NT because those functions are isolated from the application through the HAL.

Examining Win 16 Application Support

Windows-based 16-bit applications are also supported under the Windows NT 4.0 Win32 API. Recall that Windows runs in conventional memory and uses extended memory for application support. Since Windows requires MS-DOS to run, it should seem logical that Windows applications also require an NTVDM to run successfully under Windows NT 4.0.

Just as the NTVDM is designed to emulate the MS-DOS environment for MS-DOS-based applications, the NTVDM for Win 16 applications also is designed to emulate the Windows environment. Windows NT provides an addition to NTVDM called *WOW*. WOW stands for *Win16 on Win32* which is a 32-bit user mode program that allows the 16-bit Windows application to run in the WIN32 environment. And, it *is* a pretty cool concept.

When 16-bit applications run in Windows 3.1, they make 16-bit calls to various Windows 3.1 functions and DLLs. Windows NT 4.0, on the other hand, uses 32-bit functions and DLLs. The WOW intercepts these 16-bit calls, translates them into 32-bit calls, and passes them on to WIN32, and vice versa. This process is called *thunking*. Even though I joke about the term in classes, it does provide a great aural and, for some people, visual picture of the process. Lest you feel that this process results in a performance degradation, any loss in performance through the translation function is more than compensated for by the increased performance gained by WIN32 processes.

So it is the WOW that provides 16-bit Windows applications with the non-preemptive multitasking environment within which they expect to run. In addition to the four NTVDM support files, there are five additional files that support the WOW.

WOWEXEC.EXE and *WOW32.DLL* provide Windows 3.1 environment emulation. KRNL386.EXE, GDI.EXE, and USER.EXE correspond to the same files in Windows 3.1 and manage the thunking process for each one's specific function set.

> **Caution**
> As with MS-DOS-based applications, Win 16 applications which require direct interaction with hardware through DLLs, DOS interrupts, or virtual device drivers will not run successfully under Windows NT 4.0.

When a Win 16 application starts, Windows NT creates a single NTVDM within which *all* subsequent Win 16 applications will also run, again just as they do in Windows 3.1. The NTVDM itself has one process thread associated with it which is preemptively multitasked with all other Windows NT processes and their threads. Win 16 applications are non-preemptively multitasked (time-sliced) within the NTVDM. Consequently, it stands to reason that if one Win 16 application fails— since they all share the same NTVDM, *all* Win 16 applications in the NTVDM can also be affected. However, a failed Windows NTVDM will not affect any other WIN32 functions or their threads.

Of course, this would also be true in the same scenario running under Windows 3.1, so nothing lost, nothing gained. However, there must be some benefit in the NTVDM scenario, and the answer is in *multiples*.

Managing Win 16 Applications with Multiple NTVDMs

It is possible under Windows NT 4.0 to run each Win 16 application in its own NTVDM and thus in its own memory space. This would give each Win 16 application effectively its own process thread.

As you might expect, this eliminates the concern that a so-called "poorly behaved" Win 16 application could adversely affect the others. Also, since running each Win 16 application in its own memory space gives each its own process thread, even if one Win 16 application is busy, the others will be accessible. In fact, Win 16 applications that tended to bog down Windows because of processor or resource memory requirements may actually experience a performance boost when run in their own memory space. Here's what I mean.

Most everyone who has worked with Windows 3.1 applications has at one time received an "out of memory error" due to lack of resource memory (called resource heaps). There is a limited amount of resource memory allocated in Windows 3.1. An application lovingly referred to as a resource "hog" could easily use up most of the available resource memory space just for its own functions. When competing for resources with other applications, one often runs out of resource memory space prompting the "out of memory error" and subsequent system hang.

When you run the same application in its own memory space under Windows NT 4.0, the application is still a resource hog. However, it no longer has to compete with the other Win 16 applications. Thus, it should run as well, or better than it did under Windows 3.1.

Giving the Win 16 Application Its Own Space

There are three ways that you can start a 16-bit Windows application in its own memory space. You can issue a command line command to execute it in its own memory space; you can make the selection through the Start, Run dialog box for that application or its properties (see Figure 10.3); and you can modify the application's run association through Windows Explorer.

FIG. 10.3 ⟹
CONVERT.EXE is a Win 16 application that can be run in a separate memory space by modifying the properties of its shortcut, or from the Start, Run dialog box as shown.

To start a 16-bit Windows application in its own memory space from the command line:

1. Open the MS-DOS Command Prompt window.

2. Enter: **START /SEPARATE** *path/executable* indicating the location and file name of the application's executable file.

To start a 16-bit Windows application in its own memory space from the Start menu:

1. Choose Start, Run.

2. Enter the path to the Win 16 application executable file.

3. Select the option Run in Separate <u>M</u>emory Space.

To configure the application to *always* start in its own memory space:

1. Create a shortcut for the application on the desktop or the Start menu.

2. View the properties of the shortcut.

3. On the Shortcut tab, select Run in Separate <u>M</u>emory Space.

To modify the 16-bit Windows application's run association:

1. Find the application executable through Windows Explorer.

2. Choose <u>V</u>iew, <u>O</u>ptions.

3. Choose the file type for the application and select <u>E</u>dit.

4. Select open from the <u>A</u>ctions list and double-click or choose <u>E</u>dit.

5. In the Appl<u>i</u>cation Used to Perform Action text box, modify the entry to include the following immediately in front of the entry: CMD /C STAR /SEPARATE entry.

6. Choose OK twice and exit from the properties sheet.

Key Concept

While each Win 16 application can be run in its own memory space, only one NTVDM may have multiple Win 16 applications running in it. For example, if I wish to run Word 6, Excel 5, PowerPoint 4, and Access 2 simultaneously, I could run each in its own memory space using any of the methods described. I could also run Word and Excel together in one memory space, and PowerPoint and Access in individual memory spaces. However, I cannot run Word and Excel in one NTVDM and PowerPoint and Access in another. Only one multiple application WOW NTVDM may be running per session.

Considerations

If all the Win 16 applications are well-behaved, OLE and DDE are fully supported among them. If the applications are not well-written or rely on running in shared memory to exchange data, then OLE and DDE-based functions may fail. These applications will have to be run together in one NTVDM in order to provide this level of information exchange.

Caution

Each Win 16 application that is run in its own memory space creates a new NTVDM. Each time an NTVDM is created, it requires up to 2M of additional pagefile space depending on the memory configuration of your system and 1M of additional RAM. This can have an overall negative impact on performance, especially on computers where RAM and disk space is a premium.

Note On Windows NT Workstation 4.0, the WOW environment for the Windows NTVDM is loaded automatically when Windows NT is booted though the NTVDM is not. This reduces start-up time when launching Win 16 applications. On Windows NT 4.0 Server, the WOW is loaded on demand, that is, when the 16-bit Windows application is started. This is an optimization technique designed to improve server performance. If you consider that you don't usually use Windows NT Server to run 16-bit Windows applications, this makes a world of sense.

You can view the WOWEXEC and NTVDM processes loading and the percent of processor time each is commanding by starting the Windows NT Task Manager (right-click the taskbar and choose Task Manager) and selecting the Processes tab. ▪

Reviewing OS/2-Based Application Support

The OS/2 subsystem supports only 1.x–based applications on Intel-based computers. There is no OS/2 subsystem support for any other platform at this time. Some OS/2 applications are considered *bound* applications. That means that the application prefers to be run in the OS/2 subsystem, but can be forced to run in an NTVDM instead. If the application is *bound*, then it can be run in an NTVDM on any platform by issuing the *forcedos* command followed by the executable at the command prompt.

The OS/2 subsystem is not loaded at Windows NT boot time. It is only loaded when an OS/2 1.x application is executed and is supported by the files OS2.EXE, OS2SRV.EXE, and OS2SS.EXE. It communicates with the Windows NT Executive Services through the CSR subsystem for screen-oriented I/O and graphics rendering. When the application is closed, the OS/2 subsystem files will remain in memory until the system is restarted, or until the memory space is needed by another activity.

Microsoft now offers an add-on subsystem to provide support for OS/2 1.x Presentation Manager applications. This add-on replaces the default OS/2 subsystem support files with updated versions and additional files. The additional files that support this add-on include: PMSHELL.EXE, the Presentation Manager desktop interface; PMNTDD.SYS, the Windows NT support device driver; PMSPOOL.EXE, the Presentation Manager Print Manager utility; and PMCPL.EXE, the Presentation Manager Control Panel. When an OS/2 1.x Presentation Manager application is started, the add-on subsystem creates a separate desktop for the Presentation Manager desktop interface.

Configuring the OS/2 Subsystem

OS/2 subsystem configuration information is stored in the Windows NT Registry. Under OS/2, applications are run based on driver, environment, and other information supplied either in the OS/2 CONFIG.SYS file or the STARTUP.CMD file. The first time the OS/2 subsystem is invoked, it will look for these two files to determine its environment and other settings, then add the information to the Windows NT Registry. Subsequent loads of the subsystem use the Registry entries to create the CONFIG.SYS file. Subsystem support file information is stored in

Ch **10**

> HKEY_LOCAL_MACHINE\SYSTEM\CurrentControlSet\ Control\Session Manager\SubSystems.

CONFIG.SYS and STARUP.CMD information is stored in

> HKEY_LOCAL_MACHINE\SOFTWARE\Microsoft\ OS/2 Subsystem For NT\1.0\Config.sys and OS2.ini.

The best way to affect the OS/2 environment before the subsystem is ever loaded is to create an appropriate CONFIG.SYS or STARUP.CMD for the application(s) that you want to support. When the subsystem loads, it will update the Registry. To modify it afterwards, either modify the appropriate Registry entries or start an OS/2 application and modify the CONFIG.SYS file created with an OS/2-based text editor.

Reviewing POSIX-Based Application Support

POSIX is an application standard created for UNIX-based operating systems that meet United States Federal Information Processing Standard 151. Hence, you're most likely to come across these applications in a government office or an underground silo somewhere. POSIX applications that require access to file system resources under Windows NT can only do so on an NTFS partition. POSIX applications that do not require such access can run under any file system.

NTFS provides compliance with the POSIX.1 Library of function calls. For example, NTFS preserves case-sensitive naming for POSIX applications, i.e., README.TXT and readme.txt in the same directory are two *different* files under POSIX.1 Library compliance.

Like the OS/2 subsystem, the POSIX subsystem is only loaded when a POSIX application is started. It communicates with the Windows NT Executive Services through the CSR subsystem for screen-oriented I/O and graphics rendering. When the application is closed, the POSIX subsystem files will remain in memory until the system is restarted, or until the memory space is needed by another activity.

The POSIX subsystem is supported by three components. PSXSS.EXE is the main support file for the subsystem. POSIX.EXE tracks and manages interaction between the subsystem and the Windows NT Executive. PSXDLL.DLL is concerned with providing application support to PSXSS.EXE.

Unlike OS/2 1.x applications, POSIX applications can run on other platforms such as RISC or PowerPC. However, it is necessary to obtain the version of the application compiled for that platform. POSIX applications are source-compatible in this regard.

Considerations for Troubleshooting Application-Related Issues

Most of the problems that you are likely to experience regarding application support under Windows NT 4.0 have already been addressed in one way or another in this chapter, and generally are the result of some incompatibility on the part of the program, or lack of memory, and so on. I'll recap these here:

◆ MS-DOS or Windows-based applications that interact directly with hardware through interrupt calls or virtual device drivers, such as disk utilities or memory managers, will not function successfully or at all under Windows NT 4.0. Recall that these hardware requests are designed to be handled by the Kernel Mode of the operating system, particularly the microkernel and the HAL. The CSR subsystem will simply block these calls from the application.

◆ WIN32 and POSIX applications will only run on the platform for which they have been compiled. Intel versions will not run successfully on a RISC-platform computer.

◆ OS/2 applications that can be forced to run in an NTVDM (bound applications) can be run on other hardware platforms. OS/2 1.x Presentation Manager applications cannot run natively in Windows NT 4.0. However, they are supported with the Presentation Manager Subsystem add-on product.

◆ A new NTVDM is created for each MS-DOS-based application that you run under Windows NT 4.0. A new WOW NTVDM is created for every Win 16 application run in its own memory space. Each NTVDM requires up to 2M additional pagefile space and 1M RAM. On a computer where RAM and disk space are at a premium, running too many NTVDMs can result in the system running out of RAM or disk space and freezing up. Monitor the use of RAM closely when running multiple NTVDMs.

Ch
10

◆ By default, all Win 16 applications run in the same WOW NTVDM. If any of the Win 16 applications hang or fail, the others may also be affected. Resource memory is distributed among all the Win 16 applications. If one or more applications over-utilize the resource memory, the result can be an "out of memory" message and the NTVDM could fail. One solution would be to run the application(s) in question in their own WOW NTVDM, keeping in mind the last bullet point regarding RAM and disk space.

In addition to these reminders, there are three additional tools for your consideration when dealing with application support: thread priority, responsiveness, and the Task Manager.

Thread Priority

Recall that every application or process that executes under Windows NT 4.0 has at least one execution thread associated with it. A thread is a basic unit of code to which the processor can assign processing time. Every NTVDM is given one thread.

The Windows NT kernel assigns thread priorities based on the type of activity associated with the thread. Priority levels range from 0 (lowest) to 31 (highest). In general, user mode activities such as application execution are given a "normal" priority of 7, while Kernel mode activities such as those relating to the operating system (I/O management, memory allocation, and so on) are given a 16 or higher.

An application can be forced to start with a higher or lower priority from the command prompt using the following syntax:

```
START /startoption executable
```

Where *startoption* represents one of four possibilities—described in Table 10.1—and *executable* represents the path and file name of the application file.

Table 10.1   Priority Start Options from the Command Line

Start Option	Sets to This Priority Level
/LOW	Base priority 4, three below normal
/NORMAL	Base priority 7
/HIGH	Base priority 13, six above normal
/REALTIME	Base priority 24, same level as kernel mode functions; available only to Administrators, can result in overall decrease of performance to operating system tasks

Once an application is started with a different priority, Windows NT will still balance priority loads on the processor on its own, and the application may eventually be returned to a priority closer to normal. Some developers also build priority preferences into the application threads. These can also affect overall performance of threads.

Note   The Windows NT 4.0 Resource Kit contains a process thread viewer called PVIEWER through which you can monitor thread activity, alter priorities, and terminate threads. You have a greater degree of control over how the threads can be managed than you would with the task manager utility. This is strictly a "use at your own risk" utility that is, like most Resource Kit utilities, *not* supported by Microsoft.

Modifying Application Responsiveness

As noted in the last section on priorities, the Windows NT kernel will manage and balance priority loads on the processor. When dealing with application threads, whether the application is running in the foreground or background will affect the priority level of the application's thread(s). Windows NT provides a utility in the Control Panel System applet through which you can adjust how Windows NT changes the priority based on foreground and background activity. A change here affects *all* applications whereas the Start command option affected a particular application.

Ch
10

The *Performance* tab on the System applet properties sheet provides three settings that affect foreground application responsiveness:

◆ *Maximum* gives the application a 2 level priority boost from 7 to 9 when the application is running in the foreground. Background applications continue to run at the normal level of 7. This is the default setting for foreground responsiveness.

◆ The *middle* setting boosts the priority level of a foreground application by 1 level from 7 to 8, again leaving the background applications at the normal level. Set the priority to the middle setting when it is not critical that foreground applications receive additional CPU consideration. You might play Solitaire while your database is being sorted with this setting, but you would probably not work on your budget spreadsheet at the same time without putting the setting back to Maximum.

◆ *None* leaves the foreground and background settings both at the normal level. In other words, Windows NT will not adjust processor time given to the application based on whether it is running in the foreground or the background. This might be a good setting to use on a Windows NT server on which you need to occasionally use a utility. The utility should not at all decrease performance of the activities of connected clients.

Task Manager

Windows NT contains a utility which I alluded to earlier that displays basic information about processes currently running on your system. It is called the *Windows NT Task Manager* and can be accessed by right-clicking the taskbar and selecting Task Manager. The Task Manager offers three areas of information for your consideration and tracking: Applications, Processes, and Performance. At the bottom of the Task Manager window is a statistics bar that shows the total number of processes running, and total CPU and RAM usage.

The Applications tab displays a list of the applications currently running on the computer, and their status. If an application has failed or is hung, its status entry will reflect that state. Use this tab to End Tasks, especially those that have failed or hung, Switch to other application windows, or load another application by selecting New Task. Choosing New Task actually brings up the Run dialog box in which you can enter the path and file name of the application executable, and choose to run Win 16 applications in their own memory space.

The Processes tab displays a list of user and Kernel mode processes that are running. If your Win 16 application and MS-DOS-based applications are not displayed here, select Options, Show 16-bit Tasks from the menu to include them. This is generally selected by default. You can end any process by selecting the process and choosing End Process. You can also right-click any process to end the process or to change the priority of the process. These are "use at your own risk" options and should only be used to terminate or alter the priority of a process that you know is application-related (*not* kernel-related) and that has become unresponsive or bound to a processor.

The default screen lists the process name and ID number assigned by the Windows NT kernel, the percentage of CPU usage and CPU time that each process commands, and the amount of RAM used by the process. However, there are nine additional columns that you can use to customize the display screen. To access these, choose View, Select Columns.

Additional choices include Memory Usage Delta, Page Faults (the number of requests for data from the page file or disk), Page Faults Delta, Virtual Memory Size (size of the virtual address space currently in use by the process), Paged Pool (number of bytes of data that can be paged to the pagefile), Non-Paged Pool (number of bytes of data that cannot be paged to the pagefile but must remain in memory), Base Priority (normal, low, high), Handle Count, and Thread Count.

The Performance tab is not a cover charge for using Task Manager. Rather, it offers a dynamic graphic overview of the CPU and RAM usage for the current session, as well as summary totals for threads,

Ch
10

handles, commit limits (physical plus virtual memory), and kernel memory. If you have multiple processors in the computer you can choose to show each processor in its own graph.

Note When the Task Manager is running, it places a CPU usage icon at the far right end on the task bar. It will graphically display CPU usage, and right-clicking it will display the percent of CPU usage at that point in time.

Also, clicking the column header above each column of data will sort that column's data alternatively from greatest to lowest, and from lowest to greatest.

From Here...

Up to this point we have been staying pretty close to home, meaning our computers. Though we have talked about network issues, we have not yet explored Windows NT network architecture. The next chapter, titled "Network Connectivity and Remote Support," will tackle this area of Windows NT Workstation 4.0.

Taking the Disc Test

If you have read and understood the material in the chapter, you are ready to test your knowledge. Insert the CD-ROM that comes with this book and run the self-test software as described in Appendix I, "Using the CD-ROM."

Chapter Prerequisite

Before reading this chapter, you should be familiar with basic networking concepts. Refer to Appendix G, "Networking Basics."

11

Network Connectivity and Remote Support

This chapter will review the Windows NT 4.0 network architecture including the protocols supported by NT 4.0, a brief overview of TCP/IP, and the newest advantages of this release. This chapter also reviews the function of services related to network activity, client support for NetWare networks, and remote access support. This is not meant to be an exhaustive discussion; instead, we'll focus on networking as it pertains to the Windows NT Workstation 4.0.

Topics to be covered include:

◆ Exploring the Windows NT 4.0 networking model

◆ Examining NetBEUI, NWLink, and TCP/IP

◆ Reviewing Workstation and Server services

- ◆ Introducing the browser service
- ◆ Configuring and installing network options
- ◆ Becoming a member of a domain
- ◆ Understanding dial-up networking and remote access service
- ◆ Introducing peer Web services

Exploring the Windows NT 4.0 Networking Model

As discussed in Chapter 2, networking capabilities are fully integrated into Windows NT Workstation 4.0 and Server. Network support is supplied for Microsoft network clients, such as Windows 95 and Windows for Workgroups, and also for Apple Macintosh clients (through Services for Macintosh on the Windows NT Server), NetWare clients and servers (through a variety of NetWare connectivity products for both Windows NT Workstation 4.0 and Server, but primarily for the Server), and TCP/IP systems, such as Internet connectivity and UNIX hosts. In addition, dial-in capabilities are also supported and fully integrated.

The Windows NT 4.0 network architecture is positioned as part of the executive services running in kernel mode. In fact, the Windows NT 4.0 network architecture is itself a three-tiered model that is an integrated part of the Windows NT executive service called the I/O Manager (see Figure 11.1). The I/O Manager is primarily responsible for determining whether a request for resource access is locally or remotely directed. If it is remotely directed, the request enters the layers of the network model.

The three layers are the *File System* or *Redirector* Layer, the *Protocol* Layer, and the *NIC* or *Adapter* Layer. Each layer is separated, but bound by a *boundary* or *transmission* interface through which the request must pass to get to each layer.

FIG. 11.1 ⇒

Windows NT 4.0
Networking
Model.

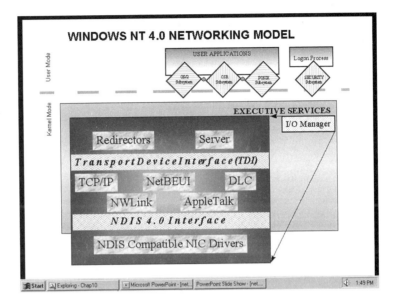

Comparing the OSI Model to Windows NT's Network Model

Some of you may be familiar with the Open Systems Interconnection (OSI) network model created by the International Organization for Standards (ISO). This is a seven-layer model that begins with the Application and concludes at the Physical layers. The seven layers of the OSI model are Application, Presentation, and Session, corresponding to the File System layer in Windows NT's model; Transport and Network, corresponding to the Protocol layer in Windows NT's model; and Data Link and Physical, corresponding to the NIC layer in Windows NT's model.

Microsoft decided to simplify the model and path the requests took through the layers by synthesizing it into three layers connected by two boundary interfaces.

Ch

11

Once the request is made, a path to the location of the resource is established by finding the most appropriate "path" through the layers of the client computer, through the network connection, and up through the layers of the server computer—the computer that has the resource.

These paths through the layers are known as the bindings for that computer. The established connection between a client and server computer is called the interprocess communication or IPC mechanism that enables data to flow between the computers. This type of interaction is often referred to as Distributed Processing. A computer may have several bindings to various protocols to enable the establishment of various IPC mechanisms for different networking platforms, such as NetWare IPX or UNIX TCP/IP. Some of these mechanisms are outlined in Table 11.1.

Table 11.1   IPC Connections

Type of Connection	Description
Named Pipes	A two-way connection channel that guarantees data is sent, received, and acknowledged by both computers.
Mailslots	A one-way connection channel in which data is sent with no acknowledgment of receipt. NetBIOS broadcasts are examples of a mailslot IPC connection.
Windows Sockets	A Windows application-based programming interface (API) that enables two-way acknowledged data transfer between the computers and provides communications support with NetWare Loadable Modules (NLMs).
NetBIOS	Another application-based programming interface (API) that enables two-way acknowledged data transfer between the computers.

Type of Connection	Description
Distributed Component Object Model (DCOM)	A new IPC model in Windows NT 4.0 that enables the distribution of processes across multiple servers in the Windows NT network for the purpose of optimizing access and performance of network-based programs.

Now take a look at the various components of the Windows NT 4.0 network architecture.

File System Layer

The *File System Layer* is also known as the *Redirector* layer because the Windows NT I/O Manager determines where to "redirect" the request for the resource in this layer. If the request is for a local resource, a file on an NTFS partition, the request is kept local and directed to the appropriate file system, in this case, to NTFS on the partition.

If the request is for a resource on another computer in the network, the request must be "redirected" to that *remote* location. As you learned, the remote location might be on another Windows NT workstation or server, therefore, the I/O Manager will redirect the request to Windows NT's own built-in network redirector, RDR.SYS, also known as the workstation service. Every Windows NT computer, whether workstation or server, has a workstation service configured to load and run automatically upon booting Windows NT. Every Windows NT computer has the capability of making, and does make, requests for resources on other computers.

However, the request could be for a resource on a NetWare server or a UNIX host; therefore, the request must be "redirected" accordingly. In the case of NetWare, this involves loading another redirector that can interpret requests meant for a NetWare server and find the appropriate binding and IPC connection to send the message. On a Windows

Ch
11

NT Workstation, this additional redirector is the Client Services for NetWare service (CSNW) that comes with Windows NT Workstation 4.0 as an installable service. Other network redirectors may need to be obtained from the network manufacturer.

Protocol Layer

Protocols are responsible for creating the packets of information sent from one computer to another across the network connection. Various networks support or require specific protocols when communicating with a computer in that network. UNIX hosts require TCP/IP, for example, while NetWare networks prefer IPX/SPX.

Windows NT 4.0 supports five protocols. *TCP/IP* is a routable protocol supporting enterprise networking and NetBIOS connections, and is used to connect to the Internet and UNIX hosts. *NWLink IPX/SPX* is Microsoft's 32-bit implementation of IPX/SPX. It also is routable and supports enterprise networking among Windows NT network clients, as well as connection to Novell servers. *NetBEUI* is a fast, efficient, but non-routable protocol used within smaller networks and thus is not well-suited for enterprise networking. *Data Link Control (DLC)* protocol is used to provide connection support to SNA mainframe computers and network-connected printers. *AppleTalk* is used primarily on Windows NT 4.0 Server computers providing remote access support for Apple Macintosh computers through Services for Macintosh. TCP/IP, NWLink, and NetBEUI will be examined in more detail in the next section.

Windows NT 4.0 supports the installation of one or more protocols in each Windows NT computer.

Network Adapter (NIC) Layer

The *Network Adapter* layer is the hardware layer consisting of the NDIS 4.0-compatible network interface card (NIC) drivers that initialize and manage communications through the hardware device connected to the network. Windows NT 4.0 supports the installation of one or more network interface cards in each Windows NT computer provided that the card is compatible with Windows NT (read: on the HCL) and has an NDIS 4.0-compatible driver available to support it.

Transport Device Interface

The *Transport Device Interface (TDI)* is a boundary interface between the Redirector layer and protocols. It provides a common programming interface that any redirector can use to build a path (bind) to any and all appropriate installed protocols. This enables the redirectors to remain independent of the protocols installed and makes it extremely easy (and attractive) for network manufacturers to write redirectors for Windows NT. The TDI provides the translation necessary to enable the redirector to "talk" successfully with the protocol. This is called "binding" the redirector to a protocol.

NDIS 4.0 Interface

The NDIS 4.0 boundary interface does for network cards what the TDI does for redirectors. It provides a common programming interface between the protocols and the NICs. Protocols are written to communicate with the NDIS 4.0 interface. NIC drivers are also written to communicate with the NDIS 4.0 interface. Consequently, only one set of drivers needs to be written for either a protocol or an NIC. In other models, each protocol would require drivers to communicate with every NIC installed in a computer. This is no longer necessary in Windows NT 4.0. As with the TDI interface, this makes it attractive and easy to write protocol and card drivers to work with Windows NT.

Ch

11

Benefits of TDI and NDIS 4.0

The ultimate benefit from this model is that the TDI and NDIS 4.0 interfaces do all the work of finding the appropriate path for a resource request out on the network. They provide the "bindings" between the layers. As a result, you can install any number of compatible protocols, redirectors, and NICs in a given Windows NT computer. TDI and NDIS 4.0 will neatly manage communications among them.

Furthermore, each network card can have multiple protocols bound to it. Thus, your Windows NT workstation can "talk" with any computer on the network running any of your installed protocols. For example, it would be possible for your computer to have two NICs installed on your Windows NT 4.0 workstation. One NIC could use the NetBEUI protocol to communicate with computers on one subnet, while the other NIC could use TCP/IP to communicate with computers on another subnet. You can access resources on computers in either subnet with this arrangement.

As the administrator, you have the ability to fine-tune these bindings, even turn them off if they're not being used. You will explore this ability in a later section in this chapter.

Examining NetBEUI, NWLink, and TCP/IP

Of the five communication protocols supported by Windows NT 4.0, three are most likely to be used for computer-to-computer communications: NetBEUI, NWLink, and TCP/IP. In the last section, you briefly reviewed each. Here you will look at them in a bit more detail as they relate to Windows NT networking.

NetBEUI

As stated earlier, NetBEUI is a fast, efficient networking protocol used mostly for small, single subnet LANs, rather than large, multiple subnet WANs since NetBEUI is not a routable protocol.

This protocol relies heavily on network broadcast messages to find and complete IPCs and thereby provide communications between computers. Subsequently, NetBEUI LANs have a relatively high level of broadcast traffic. Think of a broadcast as a computer calling out its name with a request for a specific computer, or a response to another computer's request.

NetBEUI has no configuration parameters in Windows NT 4.0.

NWLink IPX/SPX Compatible Transport

NWLink IPX/SPX Compatible Transport is Microsoft's 32-bit NDIS 4.0-compatible implementation of the IPX/SPX protocol and enables Windows NT 4.0 computers to establish connections with other computers or networks running IPX/SPX (such as NetWare networks). NWLink supports the NetBIOS over IPX and Windows Sockets APIs described in the last section.

Being an IPX/SPX compatible protocol, NWLink enables any computer running IPX/SPX, such as NetWare client computers, to communicate with client/server applications running on Windows NT computers. For example, NetWare clients running IPX/SPX could interact with a SQL database running on a Windows NT 4.0 server which is using NWLink as its networking protocol.

NWLink is configurable on Windows NT 4.0. There are three options that may be set on Windows NT computers. They are the frame type, the network number, and, new to Windows NT 4.0 servers, the Routing Information Protocol (RIP).

The network adapter card formats the data packet for transmission on the network. A number of factors determine how this packaging occurs as the request passes through the layers of the Windows NT network model. One of the factors is the network protocol. NWLink requires that a frame type associated with the topology of the network be part of the packet format. The data packet can then only be serviced by computers formatted for the same frame type.

NWLink supports Ethernet II, 802.2, 802.3, and SNAP for Ethernet topologies; 802.5 and SNAP for Token Ring; and 802.2 and SNAP for FDDI (Fiber Distributed Data Interface). NetWare networks default to 802.3 for versions 3.11 and older and 802.2 for versions 3.12 and later.

Windows NT computers using NWLink will by default automatically detect the frame type being used on the network topology and switch to this frame type. This is particularly useful if you are not sure what frame type is being used. However, if multiple frame types are detected, for example, there are both NetWare 3.11 and 3.12 servers on the network, then NWLink *defaults* to 802.2.

Ch
11

Key Concept

Since NWLink defaults to 802.2 when multiple frame types are detected on the network, it is possible that communications will not take place among some of the computers—those with differing frame types. If this is true on your network, you need to manually configure NWLink to recognize multiple frame types and include them in the packet format for your network.

Configuring NWLink Frame Types

If you need to configure your Windows NT 4.0 computer to recognize multiple frame types, the method is somewhat different for workstations and servers.

On a Windows NT 4.0 server, you can make your selections from the frame type list on the General tab for NWLink properties.

However, on a Windows NT 4.0 workstation, the change must be made in the NT Registry. Start the Registry Editor and expand to find the following key:

> HKEY_LOCAL_MACHINE\System\CurrentControlSet\Services\
> Nwlinkipx\NetConfig*network adapter card1*

where *network adapter card1* is the entry for your network adapter card. Look for the parameter *PktType*. This is a multi-string parameter set to *ff* for autodetecting frame types. Specify multiple frame types by removing *ff* and adding the appropriate values for each frame type, each on its own line in the string editor dialog box, according to the following legend:

0	Ethernet II
1	Ethernet 802.3
2	Ethernet 802.2
3	Ethernet SNAP
4	ArcNet

Another parameter that sometimes needs to be set in the network properties for NWLink is the network number. The IPX machine address is made up of two parts: one is the network address, the other is the node address. They are normally represented as DEADDEAD: 00000000. The network number represents the internal network number used for Windows NT and identifies the computer to the network by assigning a logical hexadecimal address to the network interface card. The default is 00000000. In general, especially if you only have one network interface card installed, you will not need to change the default. However, if you have installed multiple network interface cards in your computer or are communicating with services such as SQL or SNA whose applications may require such identification, then you will need to provide a network address for each network interface card installed.

New to Windows NT 4.0 is the ability to enable your Windows NT server to act as an IPX router. This is done by enabling the RIP (Routing Information Protocol) setting for NWLink. This enables the Windows NT server to broadcast IPX routing information such as network addresses to other IPX routers, thus enabling IPX/SPX communications packets to be easily transmitted from one IPX subnet to another. If you have multiple network cards installed in your Windows NT server connected to different subnets, you can enable RIP for each and let the Windows NT server route between the cards.

Ch
11

TCP/IP Protocol

There are mountains of books, magazine articles, Web sites, and friends of friends you can obtain some excellent (and poor) information from about TCP/IP and Internet communications. This section is to relate TCP/IP as it applies to Windows NT Workstation 4.0.

As you know, TCP/IP is *the* communications protocol of the '90s. Well, it *is* the Internet communications protocol, and it is the default protocol choice selected during your installation of Windows NT Workstation 4.0 and Server.

TCP/IP is designed with the enterprise network in mind. Originally developed by the United States Department of Defense and subsequently endorsed by certain educational institutions as a research data sharing mechanism, TCP/IP is network-independent and eminently routable. It does not matter what network operating system you may use internally within your organization. If you use TCP/IP to connect to the Internet, you can communicate with any other organization's network that is also connected to the Internet through TCP/IP.

In addition, on a Windows NT 4.0 computer, with at least two network interface cards, each card can receive its own IP address, and the computer can then be configured to act as an IP router. A Windows NT 4.0 computer configured in this way is referred to as a multi-homed computer.

TCP/IP is a suite of protocols, each designed to handle a specific element of network communications. For example, the *IP* part of TCP/IP stands for Internet Protocol and provides addressing and routing functions. The *TCP* part stands for Transmission Control Protocol and provides connection-oriented guaranteed packet delivery with error checking. Also included in the suite are Windows Sockets, NetBIOS over TCP/IP, *UDP* (User Datagram Protocol) providing connectionless broadcast communications, *ARP* (Address Resolution Protocol) resolving the IP address of a computer to the hardware address of its network interface card, and SNMP (Simple Network Management Protocol) providing network management data required by Management Information Base (MIB) program servers.

TCP/IP comes with a variety of built-in and add-on utilities supplied in the Windows NT 4.0 installation of this protocol. These are used to support data transfer and troubleshooting. Some of these are described in Table 11.2.

Table 11.2 TCP/IP Utilities

Utility	Description
PING	Tests and verifies communications between IP addresses.
IPCONFIG	Displays current TCP/IP settings associated with the computer such as IP address, default gateway address, subnet mask, and WINS server address.

Utility	Description
FTP	Provides a bidirectional file transfer mechanism between two TCP/IP configured computers.
Telnet	Provides a terminal emulation mechanism to another TCP/IP host computer running a Telnet host program.
Internet Explorer	A GUI interface designed to facilitate searching for and locating data on the Internet.
Finger	Retrieves configuration information from another computer running TCP/IP.

Of these utilities, two are of particular value as a troubleshooting device.

Use *PING* (Packet Internet Groper—a wonderful name) to verify that the IP address information, especially to routers and remote hosts, is correct and the routers and hosts can be contacted. At a command prompt, you would type **PING** followed by the IP address of the other host or router. If the connection is made, PING responds with four "reply from" messages from the other host.

Use *IPCONFIG* to verify address parameters associated with a particular host computer. For example, if I want to see what my computer's current IP address and subnet mask is, I can type **IPCONFIG** at a command prompt and the information will display. IPCONFIG offers several command line switches that display with a description when you type **IPCONFIG /?** at a command prompt. The */ALL* switch will additionally display hardware address information, DHCP and WINS address information.

The three most important pieces of information you need to provide when configuring TCP/IP are the IP address, the subnet mask, and the default gateway address.

The *IP address*, of course, is the address of your computer (called a host) on the network. It is a 32-bit address more commonly displayed as a four-part decimal address separated by dots, for example, 121.132.43.5.

Ch
11

Each host address must be unique in the network and each host *must* have an address.

The *subnet* mask is used to identify the IP addresses of one network from those of other networks. It is also used within an organization to identify networks (often referred to as subnets) within the organization from other networks connected by routers. It does so by blocking out, or "masking" a portion of the address by performing a binary "and" of the IP address with the subnet mask. All the addresses associated with a specific subnet mask resolve to the same result when the calculation is performed. Those that do not are not considered part of the local network.

When a data packet is sent to another computer within a subnet, the IP address of the source and target hosts along with the subnet mask determine that the data packet remains within the subnet. Further address and name resolution then takes place to ensure that the data packet arrives at its destination. Likewise, when a data packet is destined for a target host on another subnet, the subnet mask is used to determine that the target host address is not on this subnet. As a result, the data packet is sent to a router configured to send the data packet along to its appropriate subnet destination.

The *Default Gateway* address is the specific router to which these "non-subnet" packets are sent for further address resolution. Routers maintain lists of subnet addresses and masks to which they are connected to facilitate the sending of packets from one subnet to another. Routers themselves may have default gateways for data packets whose address and subnet mask information is not in the router's table.

Through the combination of IP addresses, subnet masks, and routers, a data packet can take one of possibly several routes to get from here to there successfully, even if a router is down along the way. This is partially why the entity is referred to as the "Web." It is a web-like network of routers through which data packets can "ping-pong" like balls in a pinball machine, but with a more determined direction rather than just a random pattern. Web primarily refers to the HTML\HTTP protocol used by the World Wide Web and references the links that connect Web pages like threads of a spider's web.

IP Address Considerations

You can see the significance of having the appropriate, unique addresses and subnet masks identified for each computer on the network. An inaccurate IP address or subnet mask can result in communications failure all the way around.

Further, if a computer is moved from one subnet to another, all the address information must be adjusted to correspond with the new location. The old TCP/IP parameters configured on that computer will likely not apply to the new subnet. This requires a high level of documentation and attention to the details of your network.

Windows NT does provide a Server service that can provide the appropriate TCP/IP configuration data to a computer automatically foregoing the need to configure each computer itself. It is available for all Microsoft Windows NT, Windows 95, Windows for Workgroups and MS-DOS clients (with an appropriate add-on) and is called *Dynamic Host Configuration Protocol*, or *DHCP*. DHCP is a Windows NT Server service only and is not available for Windows NT workstations.

The DHCP service enables you to create and maintain a range of IP addresses available for a subnet, along with the appropriate subnet mask information, default gateway information, and other IP information options. Currently, Microsoft DHCP clients accept and use the following additional information options:

◆ DNS Server, which specifies a list of Domain Name System (DNS) servers available to the client listed in order of preference, and with at least one IP address referenced.

◆ WINS Server (NetBIOS Name Server—NBNS), which specifies a list of RFC 1001/1002 NBNS name servers listed in order of preference, and with at least one IP address referenced.

◆ NetBIOS Node Type, which allows configuration of NetBIOS node type options as described in RFC 1001/1002. These include B-node, P-node, M-node, and H-node.

Ch

11

◆ NetBIOS Scope ID, which specifies the scope parameter for the client as described in RFC 1001/1002.

When a client configured to use DHCP is booted, it requests its IP configuration parameters from the DHCP server. The DHCP server then assigns it an address from its pool of addresses and also provides it with the supplementary information (subnet mask, et al).

This effectively eliminates the need for you to closely monitor the configuration parameters of each computer. For example, if the computer moves from one subnet to another, when it boots it merely asks the DHCP server on that subnet for its address information. It is, in effect, oblivious to the fact that it has moved. The current assigned address information for any given computer can be obtained by using the IPCONFIG command at that computer.

Another address-related component essential to successful communication between computers is the NetBIOS name of the computers. The computer name that you assigned during Windows NT installation is the NetBIOS name of the computer. This is the name that is broadcast when the computer is booted, and the name that you see when browsing for resources. This is also the name you generally use to establish connections between computers using TCP/IP rather than typing in an IP address.

When you attempt to establish communications using a computer's NetBIOS name, for example, mapping a network drive through Windows Explorer, TCP/IP needs to be able to resolve that name to that computer's IP address. If the computer you are mapping to is on the same subnet, this resolution takes place as a NetBIOS name broadcast. However, if the computer you are mapping to is on a different subnet, a NetBIOS name broadcast will not resolve the address. Another method must be used. This has generally been done through a name and address table known as an LMHOSTS file that is maintained on *every* computer in the network. No, TCP/IP doesn't maintain the list, *you* do as the administrator. You can see the compounded mess that ensues when a computer moves.

There are several ways that the list can be dynamically maintained on a "host name" server. Windows NT provides another server-based service that collects and maintains NetBIOS names, and provides name to address resolution. It is called *Windows Internet Name Service*, or *WINS* for short.

WINS eliminates the need for separate host files on each computer by compiling name and address information in its own database. When a request for name to address resolution is made on the network, WINS responds to it by providing the information it has collected to the requesting computers.

You will learn more about DHCP and WINS as you continue your education process with Windows NT 4.0 Server. I mention them here, because Windows NT 4.0 workstations are compatible with, and often are configured to use, these services, and you are likely to see references to them on the Windows NT Workstation 4.0 exam.

Configuring and Installing Network Options

Ch
11

Network-based options are installed, configured, and maintained through the Network applet in Control Panel also accessible through the Network Neighborhood properties (see Figure 11.2). There are five tabs included with the network applet, three of which are of particular interest to our current discussion. They are Protocols, Adapters, and Bindings, the three of interest to us here, and Identification and Services.

The *Protocols* tab displays a list of the currently installed network protocols. Choosing Add displays a list of all the protocols that are available for installation through Windows NT, or through an OEM disk. You can Remove protocols from the computer and Update a protocol driver. Protocols are configured during installation of the protocol, or by selecting the protocol from the list and choosing Properties. For example, notice the TCP/IP configuration parameters displayed in

Figure 11.2. I can specify the usual required IP address and subnet mask, but I can also specify Domain Name Service parameters, location of the WINS server, and configure IP routing. I can determine whether the IP information is obtained from a DHCP server, and I can even specify IP configuration by network adapter card.

FIG. 11.2 ⇒

The Network applet showing the Protocols tab and the properties window for the TCP/IP protocol.

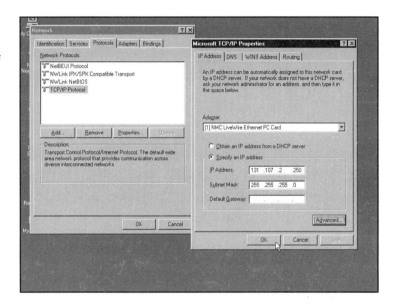

The *Adapters* tab shown in Figure 11.3 displays the installed network adapter cards. Again, by choosing Add, Windows NT displays a list of all supported adapter cards for which Windows NT supplies an NDIS-compatible driver. You can also install a card using a manufacturer-supplied driver provided it is NDIS-compatible. You can Remove and Update drivers as well. Network adapter card drivers are configured during installation of the card, or by selecting the card from the list and choosing Properties. Settings associated with the card will be displayed in a dialog box similar to that displayed in Figure 11.3. Settings such as IRQ level, DMA base, I/O base, and transceiver type can be viewed and modified here.

The *Bindings* tab displays in a graphic format the "paths" that network-bound communications can take to complete their tasks. Arranged like Windows Explorer, you can easily expand through a protocol or service to see what that protocol or service is bound to. For example, one can see in Figure 11.4 that an application using NetBIOS will

communicate with the network through NWLink NetBIOS that is
bound to NWLink IPX/SPX, or through NetBEUI to other computers running NWLink or NetBEUI.

FIG. 11.3 ⇒

Through the
Adapters tab
you can see and
configure adapter
card settings.

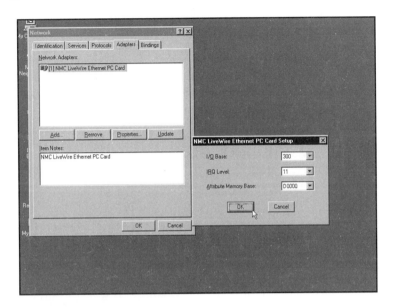

FIG. 11.4 ⇒

Here are some of
the bindings for
NetBIOS and
Workstation.

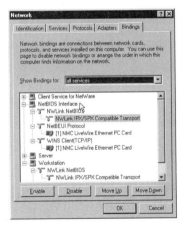

Ch

11

As you can also see from the available buttons on the Bindings tab, you
can enable or disable bindings and change their order. If you think of
network bindings as being a path that a communications request can
take, all enabled bindings are possibilities and Windows NT will check
each one to find the best path to take. Further, it will search the paths
in the order it encounters them. Therefore, you can improve network

performance somewhat by moving the "paths" most likely to be taken up in the list so that they are encountered and chosen ahead of the others, or by disabling paths that are infrequently used.

For example, suppose that you can communicate with several computers throughout your network using TCP/IP and NWLink. Some of the computers have only NWLink, but most use TCP/IP or both. You most frequently communicate with the computers using TCP/IP. If NWLink appears ahead of TCP/IP in the bindings list, Windows NT will have to check the NWLink binding first before choosing TCP/IP (which it usually winds up choosing anyway since you most frequently talk with the TCP/IP computers.) If you move the bindings for TCP/IP ahead of NWLink, then for those computers that you most frequently talk with using TCP/IP, Windows NT only has to check the first binding for TCP/IP and never go any further.

As another example, say that you maintain an archive computer on your subnet that you use to back up data once a month using NetBEUI. There is no particular reason to leave the binding for NetBEUI active since you only use it once a month. It is taking up resource, and very probably sending out many broadcast messages that can affect network traffic. In this case, you could disable the binding for NetBEUI and enable it only when you need to use the protocol to communicate with the archive computer.

The *Identification* tab displays the current computer (NetBIOS) name and workgroup or domain that the computer participates in. You can change either setting through the Change button. You'll explore this in more detail later in this chapter.

The *Services* tab displays Windows NT services that are currently installed on the computer. Recall that services are programs and processes that are added to the Executive Services portion of the Windows NT operating system which perform specific tasks. For example, if I wanted my Windows NT 4.0 workstation to be able to log in to a NetWare server, I need to install Client Services for NetWare on my computer. I would add that service through the Services tab by selecting Add and choosing it from the list of available services.

There are three services that you will look at in particular next. They are Workstation, Server, and Computer Browser.

Reviewing Workstation and Server Services

The *Workstation* and *Server services* are both integral to our ability to share and access resources on the network. You may recall earlier the reference to the redirector that determines which network and binding a resource request is meant for. The Windows NT 4.0 redirector file is RDR.SYS and is more commonly called the Workstation service. In addition to accessing network resources, the Workstation service provides the ability to log on to a domain, connect to shared folders and printers, and access distributed applications. It is your "outgoing" pipe to the Windows NT network.

The "incoming" pipe is the Server service. The Server service enables the creating and sharing of network resources such as printers and folders. It also accepts incoming requests for resource access, directs the request to the appropriate resource (or file system such as NTFS), and forwards resources back to the source computer.

Try to put the whole process together then. A request for a Windows NT network resource is made and sent to the I/O manager on a computer. The I/O manager determines that the request is not for a local resource and sends it to the appropriate network redirector, in this case the Workstation service. Through the redirector and the bindings, the appropriate protocol is chosen and packet created and sent through the network interface card out onto the network.

The request is received by the target computer (determined by NetBIOS name, or IP address, or NWLink hardware address, or frame type, and so on). It is serviced by the Server service on the target computer that determines which resource is required and where it is located (local printer, NTFS folder, and so on) and directs it there. Once the access control list for the resource determines the effective access to the resource, the appropriate resource response (printer driver, file, and so on) is forwarded back through the now established IPC connection to the client computer.

Ch

11

Two additional components play a part in determining name and redirector resolution for network requests. The *Multiple Universal Naming Provider (MUP)* enables the client computer to browse for and request network resources by their UNC name. Recall this is the syntax in which a resource path is established by naming the server and share name for the resource. For example, a folder shared as DATA on server ACCT1 can be accessed by mapping a network drive in Windows Explorer to **\\ACCT1\DATA**—its UNC name. Along with the MUP, the *Multiple Provider Router (MPR)* ensures that on computers with multiple redirectors to multiple networks, requests for network resources are routed to the appropriate network redirector. Once a connection has been established to a network, it is cached for that session and the MRP provides the "route" again for additional requests for that network.

Introducing the Computer Browser Service

The *Computer Browser* service is an interesting Windows NT service over which you have about as much control as watching the sun rise in the east. Well, you have a little more control than that, but not much.

Computer Browser's primary mission in life is to provide lists of network servers and their resources to waiting clients (see Figure 11.5). For example, when you choose Tools, Map Network Drive in Windows Explorer, the bottom of the dialog box displays a list of networks detected, domains and workgroups, computers in each that have shared resources, and finally the resources shared on each computer. This list is collected, maintained, and provided by the Computer Browser service.

Browser lists are maintained on specific computers called browsers. There are various types of browsers, each with a specific role to play in the process. These are described in Table 11.3.

FIG. 11.5 ⇒

The Computer
Browser Service
creates and main-
tains the list of
computers and
shared resources
that is displayed
when mapping a
network drive.

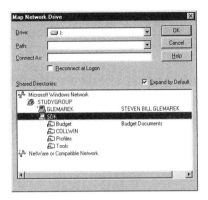

Table 11.3 Browser Computer Types and Roles

Type	Role
Master Browser	This browser computer compiles and maintains the master list of computers and their shared resources. Every workgroup or domain subnet has its own master browser. It distributes copies of its list to backup browsers, or to a domain master browser if applicable, on a periodic basis.
Domain Master Browser	This browser computer is always the primary domain controller (PDC) in a domain-based enterprise network. It compiles and maintains an enterprise-wide list of network resources collected from all the master browsers in the domain, as well as from other domain master browsers for other domains in the enterprise. It distributes copies of its list to the master browsers in the domain, as well as to other domain master browsers on a periodic basis.

continues

Table 11.3 Continued

Type	Role
Backup Browser	This browser computer gets a copy of the master list from a master browser in its workgroup or domain subnet that it distributes to client computers on request (as when mapping a network drive through Windows Explorer).
Potential Browser	These are all computers that have not yet assumed a browser role, but have the potential of becoming a backup or master browser.
Non-Browser	These are computers that have been configured to never become a browser computer of any role.

It is important to realize that there is a finite number of computers that assume a particular browser role. Every domain has one domain master browser. Every workgroup or domain subnet has one master browser and at least one backup browser. For every 32 computers in a workgroup or domain, an additional backup browser is configured. It is equally important to remember that these browser roles are determined with virtually *no* input from you.

Browser Elections

Computers assume their browser roles through an election process. If you check your Event Viewer's system log first thing in the morning, you will notice several entries relating to the browser. Closer inspection will show that these are actually browser election events in which your Windows NT workstation participated.

Examine first the presidential election process—simplified a great deal. Several people want to be elected president. They each publish their criteria which they feel makes them appropriate for the office. They are whittled down in primaries, and decided in a general election.

Once the president is elected, he or she names members to the Cabinet based on their qualifications. They are often chosen from among those who ran for president.

The browser election process is quite similar. When computers boot up, they announce their criteria to become a browser computer. Of course, they'd like to be a master browser. The master browser is determined by the computer with the highest criteria—the best credentials for the job. For example, a primary domain controller will *always* become a domain master browser, because being a PDC is about the coolest thing you can do in a domain. (You get the idea.)

Criteria which decide browser roles include the operating system type and version, its current browser role—master browser, backup browser, or potential browser; the server type—primary domain controller, secondary domain controller, or member server; and length of time it has been a browser. For example, if you are already a master browser, you are not likely to resign that role unless a truly more appropriate computer comes along. If all else is equal, the computer with the lexically lower name becomes the browser.

So these election packets are broadcast on the network and received by a browser. Their criteria are compared and those with lower criteria are discarded and the process continued until a master browser is elected. The master browser then assigns one or more computers the role of backup browser, again based on election criteria.

If the master browser should become unavailable, the backup browser detects that and forces another election to determine the new master browser.

Configuring Browsers

As I said previously, you have little control over the election process. In fact, the most you can do is make some determinations for your Windows NT computer as to whether it should participate in the election process or not. There is no utility provided in Windows NT—for example, in Control Panel—to effect these modifications. This being the case, the configuration must be done in the Registry.

Ch
11

The Registry key you are looking for is HKEY_LOCAL_MACHINE\System\CurrentControlSet\Services\Browser\Parameters. Look for a parameter entry called MaintainServerList. By default, this entry will be set to Auto. This means that the computer will participate in the election process and could become a master or backup browser. You can set this value to No to have it never become a browser. This is convenient for laptop computers or computers which are frequently shut down and restarted. You can also set this value to Yes which indicates that it should always try to become at least a backup browser.

Another parameter that you can add to the registry key is PreferredMasterBrowser. This can be set to either 1 (yes) or 0 (no). If set to Yes, then this computer is given an election boost to master browser among computers where the criteria is essentially the same. If set to No, the computer will never become a master browser.

How Does Browsing Work?

The browser process is really quite simple, and on a certain level, elegant. When computers boot, or share a resource, they announce themselves to the master browser. Computers announce themselves once a minute for the first five minutes after booting, then every twelve minutes thereafter. The master browser compiles a list of computers and their available resources and sends a copy of the list to the backup browser(s) approximately once every 15 minutes.

When a client computer requests a list of resources, it actually begins by asking the master browser for a list of backup browsers in the computer's workgroup or domain subnet. Then the client asks the first available browser for a list of network computers and subsequently for a list of shared resources.

If a computer sharing resources is shutdown normally, it announces that fact to the master browser which then takes it off the list. At the next announcement interval, the updated list is distributed to the backup browser(s) (and domain master browser). However, if the computer crashes, loses power, or is powered off without shutting down, the master browser is not notified. The master browser will wait for three announcement periods (12×3=36 minutes) until it revises its list. At the next announcement interval, it then updates the list.

This means that you could wait for a half-hour or longer before the browse list you see is updated. In the meantime, the computer still remains on the list, and you won't know it is down until you try to double-click it and the system seems to take forever to respond with a message like `Path to computer not found`.

Similarly, backup browsers contact the master every 15 minutes and announce that they are shutting down. However, if they crash, the master browser again won't know for three announcement periods, or in this case, up to 45 minutes. This can pose a performance problem for your users who rely on browse lists to make connections. Since clients get the list from the backup browser; if there are two and one crashes, the master browser won't select another for up to 45 minutes. All browse list requests are now being serviced by just one backup browser, and it can get backed up with requests.

What can you do about this? Nothing. This process is strictly internal. But you should be aware of the timing issues involved both when computers become unavailable, and when they become first available, or make additional resources available.

When a computer is booted, or you share a new resource on a computer, that computer or resource may not be listed right away in the browse list. This is because the browse list is cached and not updated immediately by the master browser (up to 15 minutes, remember?). This does not mean, however, that the computer or its resources are not available.

Key Concept

The Browser service is only a list provider and does not affect the availability or unavailability of network resources. A computer and its resources can always be accessed by using its UNC name either through a **net use** command at a command prompt, or through the Path box when mapping a network drive.

Ch
11

Browsing and browser elections can sometimes adversely affect network traffic with the number of announcements made. Under certain circumstances, it may be advisable to disable the Computer Browser service altogether. For example, if your user's network resource access is predetermined through System Profiles or login scripts and they never map their own connections, then disable the service. You will eliminate the traffic associated with the service and improve network response. Remember, the Computer Browser service is only a list provider. It does not affect access to a resource.

Becoming a Member of a Domain

In Chapter 2, "Understanding Microsoft Windows NT 4.0," you learned the various models of network computing available with Windows NT, and compared workgroup computing with domain computing. When you participate in a workgroup, you are part of a logical grouping of computers that may or may not share resources with each other and for which there is no single point of logon or authentication. Recall that every computer in the workgroup (workstation or server) maintains its own account database. When a user logs on at a computer, that user is authenticated on that local workstation and receives an access token for resource use on that local workstation.

As your network grows and as workgroups merge together, it may become appropriate to migrate to a domain or enterprise model. Recall that a domain centralizes account information in one or more domain controllers. Thus users have a single point of logon. They can log on to the domain from any computer that participates in the domain, be authenticated by a domain controller for the domain, and receive an access token that can be used to access any resource available within the domain.

You can switch your computer's participation from workgroup computing to a domain through the Identification tab in the Network applet accessible through Control Panel (or through the properties of Network Neighborhood). In order for your Windows NT computer to join a domain, it must have a computer account created for it on the domain controller. This can be done ahead of time by a domain administrator, or during the change process by providing the name and password of a valid administrator's account.

Note Only Windows NT Workstation computers require a computer account in a Windows NT domain. Other Windows NT network clients do not.

Caution
Be sure that the computer name you are using is unique in the domain you are joining. If it is not, you can run into some serious connection problems in the domain. If you need to change your computer name to make it unique, modify the entry in the Computer Name text box in the Change dialog box.

As you can see in Figure 11.6, choosing the Change button on the Identification tab displays an Identification Changes dialog box. Select the Domain option and enter the name of the domain your computer is joining. If the computer account for your computer has already been created, choose OK and wait for Windows NT to confirm that you have successfully joined the domain.

Ch
11

FIG. 11.6 ⟹

This computer is about to join the Kiteflyers domain by using the administrator's account from that domain to create a computer account for it there.

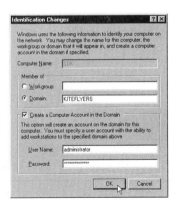

If you do not have a computer account already created, but know the name and password of a valid administrator account for the domain, select the option Create a Computer Account in the Domain. Enter the administrator account name in the User Name text box, and the valid password in Password. Then choose OK.

Once the computer account has been created for your computer, you can move back and forth between a workgroup and a domain. However, you cannot be a member of both simultaneously.

Understanding Dial-Up Networking and Remote Access Services

What is commonly referred to as Remote Access Services (RAS) in Windows NT 4.0 actually consists of two basic components which share some common elements: Dial-Up Networking services which are installed on a Windows NT 4.0 workstation and Remote Access Service services which, when installed on a Windows NT 4.0 workstation, support 1 inbound dial-in connection, and when installed on a Windows NT 4.0 server, support up to 256 inbound dial-in connections.

RAS provides the Windows NT network with standardized WAN-based remote access support. *Dial-Up Networking* is the service a client computer uses to connect to remote network resources through a RAS server. Through RAS, clients using Dial-Up Networking can access network resources through regular telephone lines (Public Switched Telephone Networks, or PSTN) using a modem, through X.25 connections using a packet-switching protocol (X.25 PAD) and an X.25 adapter, or through digital ISDN connections with an ISDN adapter installed at both the client and server computers.

Both SLIP (Serial Line Internet Protocol) and PPP (Point-to-Point Protocol) can be used to establish connections to RAS servers. *SLIP* is an older standard for establishing remote connections which provides little security. While it supports TCP/IP, it cannot take advantage of DHCP, thereby requiring a static IP address assigned to the client. Also, it does not support IPX/SPX or NetBEUI.

PPP, on the other hand, does support several protocols in addition to TCP/IP, can use DHCP and WINS to assign IP addresses and resolve names, and takes advantage of Windows NT's security features. Besides

IPX/SPX (which gives remote Windows NT clients using Client Services for NetWare (CSNW) the ability to dial into NetWare servers) and NetBEUI, PPP supports PPTP (Point-to-Point Tunneling Protocol), AppleTalk, DECnet, and Open Systems Interconnection (OSI).

PPP support on RAS servers enables remote clients to dial-in using any PPP-compliant dial-in software with a protocol enabled on the server side, but must provide at least the level of security that the RAS service is configured to require. Correct protocol, or for that matter another vendor's dial-in software, can gain access to any domain resource as if they were directly connected to the network.

In addition to PPP, Windows NT 4.0 has introduced the PPP Multilink Protocol based on the IETF standard RFC 1717. On computers that have multiple modems, X.25 or ISDN adapters, each with its own analog or digital communications line installed, PPP Multilink Protocol enables them to be combined into logical groups that increases the bandwidth for transmissions. For example, a Windows NT 4.0 workstation with two 14.4 modems and two phone lines can use PPP Multilink Protocol to create one 28.8 logical connection to a RAS server also using PPP Multilink.

In order for this to be effective, the workstation and the server must both have the same number of communications lines and connections available.

The RAS Server can act as a *de facto* router for the network. When RAS is installed on a Windows NT 4.0 server it automatically integrates whatever protocols have been installed on the server. The RAS administrator can enable gateway services for any or all of the network protocols installed on the server. For example, if NetBEUI, NWLink, and TCP/IP have been installed, the RAS gateway can be enabled for any or all of these. This effectively enables a remote client using any one of these protocols to not only access the RAS server, but to access network resources located anywhere in the domain using any of the three protocols installed on the RAS server to get there. RAS on the server can also act as IP and IPX routers to link LANs and WANs together.

Ch
11

Indeed, just about every function that a client computer enjoys while directly connected to an Ethernet or Token Ring network, it will also enjoy, though in decreased line speed, through dial-in networking to a RAS server.

Introducing Point-to-Point Tunneling Protocol

If an organization maintains access to the Internet either directly or through an Internet provider, its users can gain access to their organization's network through the Internet using a new network technology supplied by Microsoft in Windows NT 4.0—*Point-to-Point Tunneling Protocol (PPTP)*.

Clients using PPTP on their Windows NT 4.0 workstations can connect securely to a RAS server in their company network either directly through the Internet—if they are themselves directly connected—or through their local Internet provider. This is known as Virtual Private Networking, or VPN. A VPN provides the ability to "tunnel" through the Internet or other public network to connect to a remote corporate network without sacrificing security. Their transmissions are encrypted and secure, and usually less costly than modem, X.25, or ISDN connections. Because the RAS server can act as a gateway to the company network, you need only have one RAS server connected to the Internet.

Key Concept

PPTP supports multi-protocol encapsulation. This means that dial-up networking clients can use any protocol for their PPP connection. PPTP encapsulates the PPP packet within IP packets and sends it across the Internet using TCP/IP, making it possible to use the Internet as a NetBEUI or IPX/SPX backbone. The client and RAS server must be using TCP/IP only to access the Internet.

When PPTP is provided by the user's Internet provider, the Virtual Private Network support is completely transparent to the user. VPN is enabled when the user connects to his or her provider.

When PPTP is configured on the user's workstation through the Network Properties dialog box, the user can connect to any Internet provider, even those that do not provide PPTP in their points of presence. In addition to installing PPTP, the user creates a phone book entry for the VPN including the IP address of the PPTP server in the corporate network that he or she is connecting to in place of the phone number entry.

The Virtual Private Network uses RAS security. When the user connects through PPTP, the user account is validated in the Windows NT domain database just as though he or she was directly connected to the network. In addition, through RAS, the username, password, and data can all be additionally encrypted. On the PPTP server side, PPTP filtering can be enabled to only allow PPTP-enabled users to connect to the PPTP server through the Internet. It also supports the use of firewalls to screen access to the network.

RAS Security

RAS actually implements several additional security features over and above what Windows NT offers. RAS of course supports Windows NT's domain security requiring a dial-in user to authenticate using the domain account database before resource access can take place. The RAS server also maintains an ACL which identifies which domain users have permission to dial in.

In addition to this, however, RAS enables all logon information and data transmitted to be further encrypted, an especially nice feature when using public telephone lines for dial-in. Auditing can be enabled to track remote connection processes such as logging on and dialing back users.

RAS servers can be configured to use callbacks to provide an extra layer of security. When a client calls in, the RAS server can be configured to call back the client at a predefined number, such as to a particular office location, or at a user-defined number, perhaps a hotel room or client site.

Ch

11

Note Callback to hotel rooms may be tricky given that most hotel phones are routed through a hotel operator making callback unusable. Some hotels, however, are now providing data access lines with separate phone numbers. ▓

RAS servers support the addition of third-party security hosts and firewalls. Firewalls screen incoming and outgoing access to network computers through the use of passwords or security codes.

When connecting through PPTP, the RAS server must have a connection to the Internet either directly or through a firewall allowing connections to the PPTP port. This can become a security issue since the computer is left relatively open to packets other than PPTP. Fortunately, PPTP provides a security feature called "filtering" which when enabled, *disables* all other protocols from using the network adapter that provides PPTP connection to the Internet.

Installing and Configuring RAS and Dial-Up Networking

If you intend to use your Windows NT 4.0 workstation to dial into a RAS server, you need only install and configure Dial-Up networking. This could have been done during Windows NT installation, or later through the Dial-Up Networking program in Accessories.

If you intend to dial into your Windows NT 4.0 workstation, you need to install RAS services on the workstation and configure it for dial-in. For example, if you want to be able to dial into your office desktop from home, install RAS services on the office desktop Windows NT computer.

Since the most likely configuration for a Windows NT 4.0 workstation is as a dial-in client, this chapter will concentrate on that aspect of configuring remote access. However, an overview of the RAS services setup will be presented.

Understanding and Configuring TAPI

Dial-Up Networking is a TAPI-compliant application in Windows NT 4.0. *TAPI* stands for *Telephony Application Programming Interface*, and provides a set of standards for communications programs to manage and control data, voice, and fax dial-up functions such as establishing calls, answering and hanging up, transferring calls, holding, conferencing, and other common phone system functions.

Among the dialing properties configurable for TAPI-compliant applications are phone book entries, area and country codes, outside line access, calling card data (encrypted, of course), and line control codes such as disabling call waiting.

These TAPI properties are configured through the Telephony applet in Control Panel, on the My Locations tab. The options here are fairly self-explanatory as you can see in Figure 11.7.

FIG. 11.7 ⇒

Here are some typical TAPI location settings.

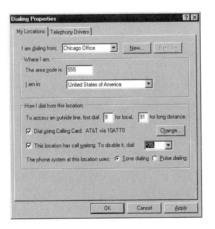

Ch

11

Choose or enter a descriptive name for your calling location in I Am Dialing From. Choose New to add additional locations. In the Where I Am section of the dialog box, enter your area code and country. In the How I Dial From this Location section specify the number you must dial (if any) to reach an outside local line or to place a long distance call. Select the Calling Card option if you are using a calling card to charge the call, and Change to specify the calling card, the call number, and any rules applicable for the card. If you need to disable call-waiting, you can choose to disable it here by specifying the line code to do so. Finally, indicate whether the phone uses Tone or Pulse dialing.

Dial-Up Networking

TAPI properties are used to configure the location you are dialing from. The Dial-Up Networking program lets you configure the phone book entry of the location you are dialing to. It establishes the connection and monitors the call.

The Dial-Up Networking program is accessed through the Accessories group. The first time you access it, a dial-up wizard will prompt you for the first phone book entry. You need to provide a descriptive name for the entry, whether you are calling the Internet or a non-Windows NT server and how to deal with that, and the country code, area code, and phone number of the target location. Subsequent access will display the Dial-Up Networking dialog box that you see in Figure 11.8.

FIG. 11.8 ⇒

Dial-Up Networking Dialog Box showing modification options available.

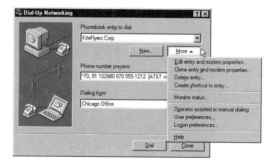

You can select a phone book entry from the Phonebook Entry to Dial list or create a New entry. The phone number for the entry is displayed using any TAPI location properties you specified for the Dialing From location.

The More button displays a list of additional options for modifying the dial-up data. For example, the Edit Phonebook Entry option not only lets you modify the basic entries, but also specify the dial-up access type (SLIP, PPP, PPTP) and protocols of the target server, dial-up scripts that you wish executed, and the level of security you wish to use for this connection (see Figure 11.9).

FIG. 11.9 ⇒
For this dial-up entry, the highest level of security possible is chosen. You are using Microsoft authentication with the current user's account and password and additionally encrypting data transmitted during this session.

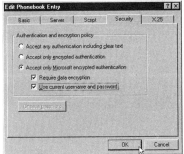

You can specify parameters relating to redial attempts, and callback options through the More, Logon Preferences option. Through More, User Preferences, you can enable the autodial feature. Autodial automatically associates the phone book entry used to map to a network resource. When the resource mapping is reestablished at the next logon, the appropriate RAS server is called automatically.

Choose Dial, finally to dial out and establish the connection with the target location. Once the connection has been made and any authentication has taken place, in the case of Windows NT RAS servers, you now have access to network resources to which you have been given permission.

Configuring RAS on the Server

On the server side of things, RAS is configured as a Windows NT service. As such, it is selected and installed through the Services tab of the Network applet accessible through Control Panel or the Network Neighborhood properties. Recall that a Windows NT service is installed like any other protocol or adapter. Choose Add, select the service from the list of available services, and choose OK. You will be prompted for modem selection and configuration, as well as RAS setting configuration. Windows NT must be shut down and restarted for the Registry to be updated, the bindings to be put into effect, and the new service to start.

Ch
11

Note Follow these same steps to configure RAS services on your Windows NT 4.0 workstation if you intend to use it as a dial-in server. ▮

Once RAS has been installed, it can be selected from the list of services on the Services tab and its <u>P</u>roperties configured. You have the option of configuring the RAS server to act as a dial out or dial in server only, or to accept both. Depending on the dialing option you choose, you can specify which protocol to use for dial out, or to accept through dial-in. As you can see in Figure 11.10, clients dialing in using TCP/IP will be able to access the entire network and will receive their IP address from a DHCP server as well. Notice, too that Microsoft authentication has been selected. Only clients whose dial-up networking has been configured to use Microsoft authentication will be able to access this server.

FIG. 11.10 ⟹

This server has been configured for both dial out and dial in. All protocols have been enabled for both.

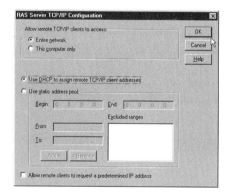

Encryption settings are also set for dial-in clients.

 ## Key Concept

The encryption setting you select for dial-in clients (refer to Figure 11.10) represents the level of encryption that the *client* is configured to use rather than what the server uses. For example, if the Windows NT workstation client's Dial-Up Networking is configured to use Microsoft authentication, that client can access any RAS server configured to accept *any authentication, encrypted authentication, or Microsoft encrypted authentication.* Conversely, if the client is configured to use clear-text, but the RAS server is configured to accept only Microsoft authentication, that client will *not* be able to establish a connection with the RAS server.

Each of the network protocol options can be configured similarly to the way they are configured for the computer itself. For example, the IPX option lets you specify a range of network numbers to assign to the clients as they dial-in. TCP/IP options include a range of IP addresses assigned by the RAS server, or IP addresses assigned by a DHCP server. All three protocols include the option (selected by default) to enable gateway access to the entire network. If you want to restrict dial-up access to the RAS server only, you must disable gateway access for each protocol.

Troubleshooting Considerations

Troubleshooting either RAS or Dial-Up Networking is largely a matter of checking settings, phone numbers, dial access codes, etc. In addition, always check the Event Viewer for events related to Remote Access Service or Dial-Up Networking as the descriptions of the events usually is quite good for pointing you to the root of the problem.

The authentication options can be used as a troubleshooting mechanism. If a client is having difficulty establishing a connection, you can set the server option to the lowest security setting: allow *any* authentication. If the client can establish a connection with that setting, try again with the next highest security option, and so forth, until the connection fails. This indicates at what level of security the client is configured, and at what level of security he or she must be set at.

Finally, a log file that tracks PPP connections can be enabled through the Windows NT Registry. Look for the key HKEY_LOCAL_MACHINE\ System\CurrentControlSet\Services\Rasman\PPP. Here look for the parameter *Logging* and change its value to "1." Setting this value to "2" initiates a "verbose" mode and will cause Windows NT to record even more detailed information. Windows NT will create the text file PPP.LOG, record PPP session information in it, and store it in the

Ch
11

WINNT40\SYSTEM32\RAS directory. The information contained in the log includes the time the PPP packet was sent, the protocol used, such as LCP, the packet type, length, and ID, and the port connected to.

Windows Messaging

A new feature of Windows NT Workstation 4.0 and Server is the Windows Messaging client (Microsoft Exchange 4.0). This is a universal inbox client that can create, send, receive, and organize electronic mail. While it is optimized for use with Microsoft Exchange Server and other Microsoft Exchange clients, it can be used with other mail systems and client software.

To install Windows Messaging, double-click the Inbox icon on the desktop to initiate the installation wizard. You will need to know the location of the mail server and its post office in order to fully complete the installation. Once Windows Messaging is installed, its intuitive interface and Help files will guide you through any additional setup and configuration that needs to take place.

Introducing Peer Web Services

Microsoft has long established the goal of improving Internet access, developing utilities to facilitate the implementation of Internet and intranet services, and the inclusion of Internet and intranet development tools in its future product rollouts.

Most people are now familiar with the Internet—the global network of computers communicating using a common protocol (TCP/IP) whose main interface is the World Wide Web (WWW) service.

The term *intranet*, however, may be new to some of you. Basically, it is an internal Internet-like system used to communicate and publish information using Internet technology such as HTTP and FTP.

With Windows NT 4.0, Microsoft has introduced two new products designed to provide Windows NT 4.0-based computers the ability to develop and publish resources and services such as home pages, FTP services, and Web services. For Windows NT 4.0 Server, Microsoft has included the *Internet Information Server (IIS)*. For Windows NT Workstation 4.0, it has included *Peer Web Services (PWS)*.

Both provide publishing and access services through *Hypertext Transfer Protocol (HTTP)*, *File Transfer Protocol (FTP)*, and *Gopher* service on Windows NT networks using the TCP/IP protocol. They offer the ability to publish files, create links to other files and Internet sites, provide security for resources using the Windows NT security system, and full integration with SQL server, SNA, and other BackOffice applications. The primary difference between IIS and PWS is in the intended audience. IIS is optimized for heavy volume usage while PWS is optimized for departmental or workgroup-sized traffic.

Both products are installed on their respective Windows NT 4.0 installations through the Services tab of the Network applet. Be sure you have the Windows NT 4.0 source CD available as well as enough disk space (about 3.5M if you install everything). You'll also need an NTFS partition to secure data accessed through IIS or PWS. Since the installation and configuration proceeds pretty much the same for both IIS and PWS, this discussion will focus on PWS, a Windows NT Workstation 4.0 book.

Ch
11

Installation Process for PWS

When you begin the installation process for Peer Web Server, you will be presented with seven component options (see Figure 11.11). These are described in Table 11.4.

FIG. 11.11 ⇒
Microsoft Peer
Web Services
Setup dialog box
with all options
selected for
installation.

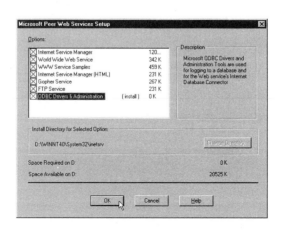

Table 11.4 PWS Component Options

Component	Function
Internet Service Manager	Provides an administration interface for managing PWS services such as WWW or FTP.
World Wide Web Service	Provides a WWW publishing service for the Windows NT 4.0 workstation.
WWW Service Samples	Sample HTML files that can be used as models to create your own.
Internet Service Manager (HTML)	Provides additional HTML browsing services to the Internet Service Manager enabling you to manage the services through the browser.
Gopher Service	Provides a Gopher publishing service for the Windows NT 4.0 workstation.
FTP Service	Provides a file transfer publishing service for the Windows NT 4.0 work-station.
ODBC Drivers and Administration	Enables access and adminis-tration of ODBC-based applications (like SQL databases) from the WWW Service.

Note In addition to installing the ODBC Drivers and Administration for PWS, you will need to set up the ODBC drivers and data sources through the ODBC applet in Control Panel if you want to provide access to ODBC databases through PWS. Before configuring the ODBC options, close all ODBC applications first.

Select the appropriate components and continue. Windows NT will create a directory called WINNT40\SYSTEM32\INETSRV unless you tell it otherwise.

Next, the PWS setup indicates the drive and directory structures it will create for each of the component services you selected on the boot partition. Either change them to point to a different NTFS partition, or simply accept the defaults. Windows NT will create the directories and install the components for you.

After the installation has completed, you will notice a new folder beneath the Administrative Tools group folder on the Start menu called *Microsoft Peer Web Services*. Through this folder, you can gain access to the Internet Service Manager utilities, the Key Manager to secure data transmissions to selected servers through the use of security keys, the PWS setup utility to add, modify, or remove components, and a demonstration program.

You will use the Internet Service Manager (ISM) to configure the PWS services. Through ISM you can manage remote servers, specify user connection, log on and authenticate parameters, specify home directories, log server activity, and secure access through keys for each component service. You can also provide welcome and exit messages for the FTP service.

If you are using WWW service to publish files and other data through PWS, you can use the built-in Internet Explorer program to navigate, access, and browse that data. You simply redirect it to look at your PWS home page.

Ch
11

Providing Connectivity to NetWare Servers

Windows NT provides many options for connecting Windows NT network clients to a NetWare network. Most of these are server-based services which are described briefly in Table 11.5. However, the service covered here is *Client Services for NetWare (CSNW)*.

Table 11.5 Windows NT 4.0 Server NetWare Connectivity Services

Service for NetWare	Description
Gateway Service for NetWare (GSNW)	This service connects the Windows NT 4.0 server to a NetWare server via a service account established on the NetWare server. Trustee rights and permissions are administered at the NetWare server. Through a gateway service, NetWare file and print resources can be shared to Windows NT network clients. Consequently, any Windows NT network client that needs occasional access to a NetWare resource can do so by accessing the gateway share.
File and Print Service (FPNW)	This add-on service effectively makes a Windows NT 4.0 server look like a NetWare server to NetWare client computers. NetWare clients can log in to, attach to, and access resources on a Windows NT 4.0 server just as they would do with a NetWare server. This is handy when migrating users from a NetWare environment to a Windows NT environment.

Service for NetWare	Description
Directory Service Manager (DSMN)	This add-on service enables NetWare accounts to be copied to and managed by a single Windows NT domain controller with changes propagated back out to the NetWare servers as required.
Migration Tool for NetWare	This utility lets you merge NetWare account and group information into the Windows NT account database. It also lets you migrate any or all of the NetWare system volumes to an NTFS partition preserving all rights and permissions assigned through NetWare.

Client Services for NetWare (CSNW), together with NWLink IPX/SPX Compatible Protocol, provide basic file and print access to NetWare 3.x and 4.x servers on your Windows NT 4.0 workstation. It supports NetWare Core Protocol as well as NetWare's Directory Services (NDS) which enables shared resources to be organized into a tree-like hierarchy.

CSNW is installed and configured like most service—through the Services tab of the Network applet. Once the service is installed, Windows NT will add a CSNW applet icon to Control Panel. Through this applet, you can choose a preferred NetWare server to connect to during logon.

 Key Concept

The Windows NT WINLOGON process will pass the Windows NT username and password on to the preferred NetWare server for authentication there. You will be logging in to both the Windows NT network *and* a NetWare server.

This implies—and rightly so—that the user should have a valid login account on the NetWare server that matches the Windows NT username, and to be completely transparent, the passwords should also be matched exactly. A lot of administration can be involved, but Windows NT does provide DSMN just for this purpose (see Table 11.5).

This does not mean, however, that you cannot maintain separate passwords, or even nonmatching user accounts on the NetWare server. If the password or username does not match, the user will receive an error message when logging into the Windows NT 4.0 workstation to the effect that you could not be validated on the preferred NetWare server. The CSNW applet in Control Panel lets you set the preferred server setting to "none." Setting the preferred server to "none" means that the user will not be validated on a NetWare server during the logon process to Windows NT. The user, however, can always connect to a NetWare resource on a server that the user has been accessed through Windows Explorer or Network Neighborhood. Both offer the option of mapping a network drive to a resource *as a specific user*. By specifying the name of a valid user account on the NetWare server, and confirming the password, the user can access any resource that has been allowed access. Follow these steps to map a network drive as a specific user through Windows Explorer:

1. Start Windows Explorer by choosing Start, Programs, Windows Explorer.

2. Select Tools, Map Network Drive to display the Map Network Drive dialog box.

3. Select a drive letter that you wish to assign to this mapping from the Drive list box.

4. Enter the path to the NetWare server and resource you wish to access in the Path text box.

5. In the Connect As text box, enter the name of the NetWare user account that you wish to log in with and choose OK.

6. Windows NT will prompt you for the password. Enter the correct password and choose OK. Windows NT will connect you to the directory and add the mapped drive to your Explorer window.

Follow these steps to map a network drive as a specific user through Network Neighborhood:

1. Right-click the Network Neighborhood icon on the desktop to display the shortcut menu.
2. Select Map Network Drive from the menu.
3. Enter the path to the NetWare server and resource you wish to access in the Path text box.
4. In the Connect As text box, enter the name of the NetWare user account that you wish to log in with and choose OK.
5. Windows NT will prompt you for the password. Enter the correct password and choose OK. Windows NT will connect you to the directory and add the mapped drive to your Explorer window.

The CSNW applet in Control Panel also lets you select a default NDS tree and context to define the default NDS name and position of the user name you will use to log in. All resources in the default tree specified can then be accessed without further password prompts.

Print options that can be defined include adding a form feed at the end of a print job sent to a NetWare print queue, receive a notification when printing is completed, and include a banner page with each print job.

New to Windows NT 4.0 is the ability for CSNW to interpret and execute NetWare login scripts. Select this option if you want the NetWare login script to execute.

Once Client Services for Netware is installed, you will notice a new entry for NetWare networks in your browse lists. Expand this entry to see available NetWare servers that you can map to. When mapping to a resource on a NetWare server, if your Windows NT account matches the NetWare server account, you can connect just like you would to a Windows NT resource—just point and click. However, if the NetWare server account is different, use the Connect As text box to enter the logon id of the valid NetWare account to complete the connection.

Ch
11

Note In order for your Windows NT user account to have administrator privileges on the NetWare server—become a NetWare Admin account, you must have given your NetWare user account supervisory equivalence on the NetWare server. You accomplish this through NetWare's interface utilities, such as Syscon.

Troubleshooting Networking

If you encounter network-related difficulties, they are more likely due to traffic problems, protocol incompatibilities, or hardware failures than anything else. Troubleshoot your Windows NT network like you would troubleshoot any other network. A good network traffic analysis tool would be beneficial for the network administrator, such as the Windows NT Network Monitor utility that comes with Windows NT 4.0 Server (and which is briefly described in Chapter 12, "Tuning, Optimizing, and Other Troubleshooting Tips").

If you experience a network problem after the first installation of Windows NT workstation, or after installing an adapter card, double-check the adapter settings. You may recall from Chapter 3, "Installing Windows NT Workstation 4.0," that Windows NT uses the default factory settings for most network interface cards. As a result, if you did not change the settings, your card may not be properly configured for the network.

Performance Monitor (also described in Chapter 12, "Tuning, Optimizing, and Other Troubleshooting Tips") also provides objects and counters relating to the protocols installed, as well as to the workstation and Server services. For example, for each protocol installed on a Windows NT 4.0 workstation (or server), you can chart total bytes/sec, session time-outs and retries, frame bytes sent and received, packets sent and received, and adapter failures. TCP/IP object counters become available when the SNMP service is installed.

Other tips I can offer include double-checking protocol configuration options. For example, be sure that the TCP/IP address and subnet mask are correct, and that the IP address is unique. If using WINS, be sure that the correct address to these servers has been configured for the workstation. Recall that NWLink auto-detects the network frame type. If multiple frame types are detected, it will simply default to 802.2 which may restrict access to certain resource servers. If necessary, determine what frame types are in use on the network, and manually configure NWLink to recognize them.

Check the Services applet in Control Panel and the Event Viewer to see if any network-related services failed to start, and why. If the workstation service is not running, you cannot connect to network resources. Similarly, if the Server service is not running, you cannot share resources or service network requests.

From Here...

The final stop on our journey through the NT universe is on planet Optimizing with its twin moons Tuning and Troubleshooting. Throughout the book, you encountered tuning, optimizing, and troubleshooting issues as they related to the topics at hand. This final chapter will look at some additional considerations and tools to help you administer your Windows NT 4.0 workstations in particular.

Ch
11

Taking the Disc Test

 If you have read and understood the material in the chapter, you are ready to test your knowledge. Insert the CD-ROM that comes with this book and run the self-test software as described in Appendix I, "Using the CD-ROM."

12

Tuning, Optimizing, and Other Troubleshooting Tips

You have reached the final leg of your journey through Windows NT Workstation 4.0. A lot of ground has been covered, but there are still a few things to discuss.

This chapter covers topics that can loosely be termed tuning and optimization related. Otherwise, they might be termed "miscellaneous stuff that didn't quite fit in anywhere else." Virtual Memory Manager will be examined more closely as will the use of pagefiles. You'll review the use of Event Viewer and Windows Diagnostics as troubleshooting tools. There is also an introduction to the Performance Monitor utility and you will examine how it can be used to track system, and to a certain extent, network performance.

Topics to be covered specifically in this chapter include:

◆ Understanding virtual memory management

◆ Exploring and optimizing pagefile usage

◆ Using the Event Viewer to troubleshoot Windows NT

◆ Exploring the Windows NT Diagnostics Utility

◆ Monitoring system performance with Performance Monitor

◆ Reviewing the Emergency Repair process

◆ Creating and using a Windows NT boot disk

◆ Reviewing system recovery options

Understanding Virtual Memory Management

One of the Executive Services managers is the Virtual Memory Manager. The memory architecture of Windows NT 4.0 is a 32-bit, demand-based, flat, linear model. This model allows the Virtual Memory Manager to provide each process running in Windows NT up to 4G of memory—generally far more than the amount of physical RAM installed in most computers.

Those readers who remember Windows' swap file model will recall that there are two types of swap files: permanent and temporary. Both swap files manage available RAM in 4K pieces using an internal Windows algorithm called the LRU (Least Recently Used). Essentially, the LRU determines that the piece of code in memory that was least recently accessed by a process is liable to be swapped to disk when more RAM is needed for a current process. On computers with the minimal required RAM is Windows, there could be a considerable amount of swapping that takes place. The main difference between permanent and temporary swap files is that a permanent swap file has a preallocated amount of space reserved on the disk. Temporary swap files begin at 2M and then "grow" as needed to a predetermined amount. Thus, while a permanent swap file provides better swap performance because space is always there and available, it also reduces the amount of available disk storage. Similarly, while temporary swap files do not reduce the amount of disk storage available up front, more resource is expended to find additional storage space when the swap file needs to "grow."

Windows NT combines the "best" of these swap files. The Windows NT pagefile (*PAGEFILE.SYS*) is created when Windows NT is installed. It generally defaults to an initial, preallocated size (*à la* permanent swap files) of 12-plus physical RAM, and a maximum size of three times physical RAM (depending on the amount of disk space available). For example, on a computer with 16M of physical RAM, the default initial pagefile size would be 28M (12+16M) and the maximum size would be about 48M (3*16M). Windows NT will boot with the initial size pagefile available. The pagefile subsequently grows as applications are loaded and demands for physical RAM increase.

Windows NT maps memory addresses in 4K blocks, or *pages*. The virtual memory address space can accommodate up to 1,048,576 pages, or 4G of addresses. It is important to realize that while Windows NT allows virtual addressing of up to 4G of memory, the Virtual Memory Manager will allocate up to 2G of *virtual* storage for *each* application. The other 2G is allocated for all system (kernel mode) processing.

The Virtual Memory Manager addresses application memory as follows (see Figure 12.1):

1. When an application is loaded, the Virtual Memory Manager assigns it virtual memory addresses in its own virtual memory space.

2. Next, it maps available physical RAM to the virtual memory addresses. The mapping is transparent to the application.

3. As the data is needed by the application, it calls for the virtual memory addresses.

4. The Virtual Memory Manager moves those pages on demand into available locations in physical RAM.

Ch

12

FIG. 12.1⟹

Windows NT 4.0
Virtual Memory
Model.

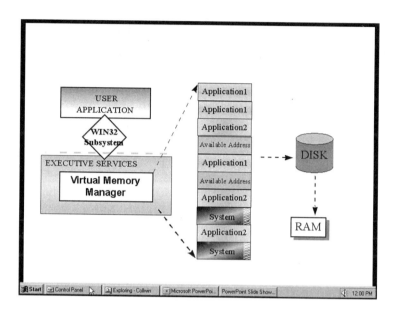

Key Concept

This process of assigning virtual addresses to the application effectively hides the organization of physical RAM from the application. The various pages of the application may wind up in noncontiguous space in physical RAM, but as the Virtual Memory Manager provides the addresses, this isn't a problem—because the organization of physical RAM is hidden. In this way, Windows NT makes the most efficient use of available physical RAM, and provides an overall performance increase for application processing.

Exploring and Optimizing Pagefile Usage

The default size of the paging file (PAGEFILE.SYS) created by Windows NT during installation is 12M + physical RAM. Thus, if you have 16M of RAM installed, the initial pagefile size will be 28M. The minimum size the pagefile can be is 2M, and the maximum tends to be about 3×physical RAM (see Figure 12.2).

FIG. 12.2⇒

This computer must have 32M of RAM installed since the pagefile initial size is 44M (12+32). You also see from Space Available, that there is not enough room on the D drive for the maximum pagefile size.

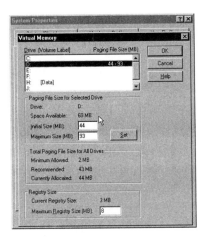

Even though the minimum can be 2M, when planning your computer configuration, you should plan so that the total memory commitment (physical RAM + pagefile) to Windows NT and its processes is at least 22M. This is considered minimum for Windows NT 4.0. Windows NT, as a rule, will take 10M of physical RAM for its own use (kernel mode operations) upon booting. Therefore, to determine the minimum size pagefile that can support Windows NT on a given system, use the following formula: **(RAM - 10M) + pagefile = 22M**. For example, on a computer with 16M of RAM, the minimum pagefile size should be no less than 16M: **(16M - 10M) + 16M (pagefile) = 22M**. Similarly, on a computer with 32M of RAM or more, no pagefile is necessarily needed: **(32M - 10M) + 0 = 22M**. If Windows NT does not consider the pagefile to be properly sized, it will display a message to that effect upon every boot, and display the Virtual Memory dialog box so that you can fix the pagefile size.

Ch
12

Caution

These are considered minimum calculations only and do not necessarily represent an optimal operating environment on a heavily used workstation or server. It is strongly suggested that you maintain the sizes Windows NT recommends for the pagefile.

During installation, Windows NT will look for a disk partition large enough to hold the pagefile it creates. This is often the same as the installation (boot) partition, but it may be another formatted partition.

Since the pagefile is apt to be "hit" quite often by the system, it should make sense to maintain it on a hard disk that is not itself "hit" frequently by other processes. The boot partition contains the Windows NT system files and, as such, is accessed frequently by the operating system quite apart from the pagefile. Keeping the pagefile on the same partition as the Windows NT system files can result in an overall decrease in disk performance due to excessive I/O on that one disk drive.

Therefore, an optimization suggestion for the pagefile, which will also improve overall disk performance, is to move the pagefile to a partition on a different disk drive. This effectively eliminates the competition for disk I/O between system file and pagefile requests.

Moving the Pagefile to Another Disk

All pagefile configuration takes place through the Virtual Memory dialog box (see Figure 12.3).

FIG. 12.3⇒

The pagefile is being prepared to move from the D drive to the F drive in this example. The next step is to delete the current pagefile from the D drive.

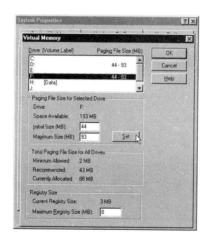

To move the pagefile to another disk:

1. Start the System applet in Control Panel, and switch to the Performance tab.

2. The Virtual Memory section shows the current total page file size for all disk volumes. Select <u>C</u>hange. The Virtual Memory dialog box is displayed.

3. In the <u>D</u>rive list box, note the location of the current pagefile and its initial and maximum sizes.

4. Highlight the drive on which you want to place the pagefile. In the Paging File Size for Selected Drive section of the dialog box, be sure that the Space Available on the selected drive will accommodate the pagefile size needs.

5. In the <u>I</u>nitial Size box enter the initial size of the pagefile. This should be at least as large as the original initial size you noted in step 3.

6. In the Ma<u>x</u>imum Size box enter the maximum size of the pagefile. This should be at least as large as the original maximum size you noted in step 3.

7. Choose <u>S</u>et.

8. In the <u>D</u>rive list box, highlight the drive that contains the original pagefile.

9. In the <u>I</u>nitial Size box delete the size entry.

10. In the Ma<u>x</u>imum Size box delete the size entry.

11. Choose <u>S</u>et.

12. Choose OK. Windows NT will prompt you to restart the system to effect the changes.

Right-Sizing the Pagefile

When Windows NT boots it loads the initial pagefile. As additional page space is needed, the Virtual Memory Manager adds to, or expands, the pagefile to accommodate the need. Of course, every time the pagefile needs to grow, additional disk I/O is expended to find and allocate the space and write the pages.

The pagefile will grow and shrink within the range specified, but it is important to note that it is not cleaned up in any way. It will only

Ch

12

shrink, for example, when the pages at the end of the pagefile are no longer needed or deleted.

While you can use Windows Explorer to monitor the size of the pagefile, the size shown for the pagefile stored on an NTFS volume will probably be inaccurate. This is because in NTFS, file size is not updated while the file is open. It is only update when it is closed. Of course, the pagefile is always opened to its initial size when Windows NT boots.

There is a way around this phenomenon. Try to delete the pagefile through Windows Explorer. You will get a message to the effect that the file is in use by another process (of course Windows NT). Now refresh Windows Explorer, or type **dir** at a command prompt to display the correct pagefile size.

If you are running several large applications simultaneously, which is quite probable on a Windows NT server, and on power users' work-stations, determine what the "expanded" size of the pagefile is. Then modify the pagefile size so that the initial size matches the expanded size. This way you are starting with a "right-sized" pagefile and can eliminate the disk I/O involved with expanding the pagefile. *Voilà!* You will have increased performance all the way around.

To change the pagefile size:

1. Start the System applet in Control Panel, and switch to the Performance tab.

2. The Virtual Memory section shows the current total page file size for all disk volumes. Select Change. The Virtual Memory dialog box is displayed.

3. In the Drive list box, highlight the drive that contains the pagefile whose size you wish to change.

4. In the Initial Size box enter the new initial size.

5. In the Maximum Size box enter a new maximum size if necessary.

> **Caution**
>
> If you have increased the initial size, you should increase the maximum size proportionately. Be sure that the drive can accommodate the increased sizes specified.

6. Choose Set.

7. Choose OK. Windows NT will prompt you to restart the system to effect the changes.

Creating Multiple Pagefiles

Another optimization technique is to create multiple pagefiles, for example, one on each physical disk drive. Unlike Windows 3.1 and Windows for Workgroups, you are not restricted to only one pagefile. In fact, if the computer's disk controller supports contiguous disk I/O, creating a pagefile on each disk can significantly improve disk performance (see Figure 12.4).

FIG. 12.4⇒

In this example, three page files have been created on three different disk drives (D, F, and J) to improve overall performance and alleviate the lack of disk space for the maximum pagefile size on drive D.

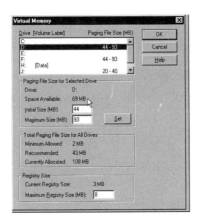

Windows NT writes pages to the pagefile separately. Two writes are allowed to be outstanding for each pagefile. The pagefile with the most free space is always written to first. Thus, placing a pagefile on each disk drive effectively distributes pagefile requests across all available pagefiles on all disk drives.

Ch
12

From another point of view, if you determine that the original pagefile is not large enough, or cannot expand sufficiently due to lack of disk space, creating an additional pagefile can help alleviate the demand of the original pagefile. Because room now exists for "expansion," system performance is improved.

Key Concept

The performance of the pagefile and accompanying disk I/O is directly related to the performance of your applications and any other system processes due to the way virtual memory maps physical addresses to virtual addresses. If an application makes a request for RAM and there is not enough available, the Virtual Memory Manager moves the least recently used pages from RAM to the pagefile to accommodate the application's request. If the pagefile performance is poor, the application's performance will ultimately reflect that. If the pagefile's ability to react to the page request is prompt, the application's performance will be enhanced.

To create multiple pagefiles:

1. Start the System applet in Control Panel, and switch to the Performance tab.

2. The Virtual Memory section shows the current total page file size for all disk volumes. Select Change. The Virtual Memory dialog box is displayed.

3. In the Drive list box, note the location of the current pagefile and its initial and maximum sizes.

4. Highlight the drive on which you wish to place the additional pagefile. In the Paging File Size for Selected Drive section of the dialog box, be sure that the Space Available on the selected drive will accommodate the pagefile size needs.

5. In the Initial Size box enter the initial size of the pagefile. Since Windows NT writes to the pagefile with the most free space, you should probably size all your pagefiles with the same initial size, though that is not required.

6. In the Maximum Size box enter the maximum size of the pagefile. Since Windows NT writes to the pagefile with the most free space, you should probably size all your pagefiles with the same maximum size, though that is not required.

7. Choose Set.

8. Repeat steps 4–7 for each additional pagefile you wish to create.

9. Choose OK. Windows NT will prompt you to restart the system to effect the changes.

Using Event Viewer to Troubleshoot Windows NT

Any events generated by the Windows NT operating system, missing an application, or security auditing are collected in log files that can be viewed with the Event Viewer utility. The failure of a driver to load, a stalled service, an unsuccessful logon, or the corruption of a database file are typical events that are recorded by Windows NT and can be viewed through Event Viewer in one of three log files. The System Log records events generated by the operating system such as failed drivers, disk space limits, pagefile errors, and so on. The Application Log records events generated by applications such as corrupted temporary files or resource allocation errors. The Security Log records events relating to audit events that only Administrators can view. Auditing is enabled through User Manager and then configured for files, folders, and printers through their properties. Events, such as the successful writing of a file or the failed attempt to delete a folder, are recorded in the security log (see Figure 12.5).

There are three types of System and Application Log errors and two types of Security Log errors that are recorded. These are described in Table 12.1.

Ch
12

FIG. 12.5⇒

Sample System Log
showing the event
detail for a Stop
Error.

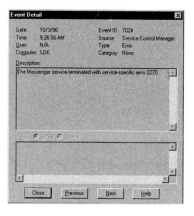

Table 12.1   Event Log Entry Types

Event Type	Description
Information	Denoted by a blue "i" icon, it represents that an infrequent but significant event has taken place, such as a Browser election, or successful synchronization of domain controllers.
Warning	Denoted by a yellow "!" icon, it represents an event that may or may not be significant, but could lead to future concerns, such as low disk space, or unexpected network error.
Error	Denoted by a red "stop sign" icon, it represents a significant problem that has, or could lead to, a service failure or loss of data, such as a driver failing to load.
Success Audit	Denoted by a "key" icon, this security log event represents an audited security event that was successful, such as a successful logon or access to a printer.
Failure Audit	Denoted by a "lock" icon, this security log event represents an audited security event that was unsuccessful, such as an attempt to delete a file to which one did not have access.

The Event Viewer is one of the Administrative Tools utilities and can be accessed by selecting Start, Programs, Administrative Tools, Event Viewer. The default view is the System log. By default, events are listed in descending time order from most recent to least recent.

Each entry records the icon type of the event, the date and time it oc-curred, the source of the event (usually related to a service or function), a category or classification (such as Logon and Logoff or Policy Change), an event number (to be referenced when speaking with a Microsoft product support representative for security logs), the name of the user involved, and the computer on which the event occurred.

More detail can be obtained about each entry by double-clicking the entry (refer to Figure 12.5). Besides a hexadecimal display of the event frame, the event detail also provides a brief description of the problem. This description usually points you in the right direction for trouble-shooting, but might be nothing more than another error code that you can look up in the Windows NT Resource Kit or provide to a Microsoft product support representative. Nevertheless, the recorded events can be useful to track down the cause of a problem.

For example, many services maintain dependencies on other services, not unlike many a dysfunctional family. If one service in the depen-dency fails to start, or otherwise perform its task, the dependent services may also fail or not perform their tasks. This usually manifests itself at boot time with the message "Dependency or service failed to start." This message, in and of itself, is not terribly informative; however, the Event Viewer is.

To troubleshoot this message, start the Event Viewer and look for the first EventLog entry (an information entry) for the approximate time and date that the error occurred. The stop message right above it will likely be the source of the error.

Note   Service dependencies can be viewed through the Services tab in the Windows NT Diagnostics utility. ▮

Ch
12

The event logs by default, are 512K in size and only keep seven days worth of events. This means that when the event log grows to 512K in size, or after seven days' data has been collected, the oldest events are eligible to be dropped from the log if the space is needed.

You can change these defaults through the Log, Log Settings menu option. You can change the size of the log and the number of days' worth of data stored for each individual log. Rather than saving a specified number of day's data, you could choose to overwrite events as needed, or not to overwrite events at all. If you choose not to overwrite events, the Event Viewer will collect data up to the specified size and then stop, requiring the administrator to manually clear the log. Because the event logs can grow rapidly, especially if auditing has been enabled, it is not recommended that you change the default size significantly unless disk space is not of concern to you.

As you grow accustomed to using the Event Viewer to track events, you will become more familiar with the Source and Category entries. The View menu option allows you to change the order of all events displayed in the log, Find a specific entry by event type, source, category, and so forth, and to Filter Events.

The Filter dialog box allows you to select events to display by specific or range of date and time, type, by source, category, user, computer, and event id. For example, if I just wanted to see all stop events, I could use the filter to select only Error event types and deselect the other types. Or, if I wanted to see errors relating to service management, I could select Error event types as above, and also select Service Control Manager as the Source type as shown in Figure 12.6.

FIG. 12.6⇒

The same Event Viewer system log as seen in Figure 12.5 has been filtered to display only error messages whose source is the Service Control Manager.

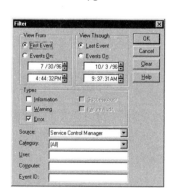

Exploring the Windows NT Diagnostics Utility

Windows NT Diagnostics is an enhanced and GUI version of Microsoft's MS–DOS–based MSD (Microsoft Diagnostics). This cool utility gives detailed information culled directly from the Windows NT Registry relating to system configuration (see Figure 12.7). This version actually provides a greater level of detail than previous Windows NT or Windows versions. You can even print out the information screens. It is accessed through the Administrative Tools group.

FIG. 12.7⇒

The Windows NT Diagnostics is used to view the status of services running on the computer, and to determine the dependencies of the Messenger service that has stopped.

Windows NT Diagnostics provides nine tabs of data relating to your system's configuration.

The Version tab displays general information about this installation of Windows NT such as to its build and version number, and who it is registered to.

The System tab displays more details about the BIOS installed on the computer, and of each processor installed. It also specifies what type of HAL has been installed.

Ch

12

Key Concept

Recall that the HAL performs the majority of application-to-hardware calls. Sometimes, certain models of computers require a BIOS-specific

continues

continued

> HAL for hardware interaction to be successful. If you experience a hardware failure on a specific model computer for an application that runs successfully under Windows NT on other models of computer, find out what HAL has been installed, and contact the manufacturer to see if it has a BIOS-specific HAL for that model computer.

The Display tab shows BIOS information, adapter settings, video memory allocation, and driver data. Again, this can be helpful when trying to determine compatibility problems.

The Drives tab displays a list of logical drives on the computer by type (floppy, CD-ROM, local) or by drive letter. Any drive's properties can be displayed by selecting the drive and choosing the Properties button at the bottom of the Windows NT Diagnostics utility window. From here you can determine the amount of free space left on the disk, as well as sector and cluster size.

The Memory tab gives detailed statistics concerning RAM, kernel memory, commit memory (RAM+pagefile), and pagefile size and usage.

The Services tab shows a list of Windows NT services and devices available and their current status. While the status of the service or device cannot be affected here, more detail about them can be viewed. By selecting an entry and choosing the Properties button at the bottom of the Windows NT Diagnostics window, you can view general information and service and process flags, as well as dependencies this service or device has on other services or devices. Going back to the Event Viewer example, if a service fails due to a dependency, but you are not sure what other services it depends on, you can use Windows NT Diagnostics to find out. Now you know what else to look for, either in Event Viewer, or Services or Devices in Control Panel.

Through the Resources tab you can view summarized or detailed properties for IRQ settings, I/O port addresses, DMA channels, and memory addresses. In addition, you can view a summary of all these by device. To get really technical, you can view the same information as it relates to HAL resource usage.

The Environment tab displays both system and user environment variables such as ComSpec and Temp, respectively, and their current values.

Finally, Network provides general information about the network configuration for the computer, such as the user access level, domain you're participating in, the current user, and where the user was validated. In addition, you can view transport data, session settings (such as session time out and buffer size), network frame statistics for the given session (such as bytes received and sent), SMBs (system message blocks) sent and received, open network sessions, and failed sessions.

All in all, you get a lot of bang for your buck with Windows NT Diagnostics. It can be a useful informational tool when troubleshooting or gathering statistics about your computer. And you can print out of it, as well!

Monitoring System Performance with Performance Monitor

Windows NT 4.0 contains a performance tracking tool called Performance Monitor, which collects data about system resources and presents them in a graphical chart-based format. This section serves as an introduction to Performance Monitor and how it can be used as a troubleshooting utility.

The Performance Monitor treats system resources as *objects* with characteristics, or *counters*. Multiple occurrences of an object and counter, or variations on them, are called *instances*. For example, the processor is an object that can be monitored. It has counters that can be charted, such as the total percent of processor usage, the percent of the processor used by the kernel mode, and so on. If there are multiple processors, you can track each processor's total percent of usage, and so on, for each instance of the processor.

With Performance Monitor, you can also create and view log files, view summary statistics, and create system alerts based on monitored values.

Ch
12

Performance Monitor is used primarily for two purposes: creating baselines of performance and monitoring aberrations from the baseline, i.e., troubleshooting.

Key Concept

It does you no good as an analyst to turn on Performance Monitor to monitor system activity once a problem has been detected if you have no "normal" baseline of activity against which to measure the problem.

There are about 20 objects, each with numerous counters, available by default. Every additional protocol, service, driver, and in some cases application, you install on your Windows NT workstation or server will likely add additional objects and counters to the list. The number of instances varies greatly with each object. However, there are four specific objects that are of particular concern when troubleshooting your system: processor, process, disk, and memory.

This is not to say other objects aren't important to monitor. These are simply the objects most often looked at first to determine aberrations from the baseline and bottlenecks in the system. After all, if the system is running with poor performance, it is likely slowing due to poor performance at the processor (too many I/O requests for its power), in memory (not enough to handle all address requests), on disk (not enough disk space or excessive paging), or with the process itself (an application that overuses resources.

Configuring Performance Monitor

Performance Monitor can be found with the other Administrative Tools. Here are the basic steps to follow when configuring a Performance Monitor chart:

1. From the taskbar, select Start, Programs, Administrative Tools, Performance Monitor.

2. Choose Edit, Add to Chart to display the Add to Chart dialog box.

3. In the Computer text box, type or browse for the computer you wish to monitor. If you have a valid administrator's account,

or participate in a domain in which you are a domain administrator, you can monitor other Windows NT computers remotely.

4. Select the Object that you want to monitor.

5. As you select an object, the Counter list will display counters associated with the chosen object that you can chart. Select the counter that you wish to track. Select multiple counters by clicking the first and Ctrl, then clicking the others.

6. If you are unsure about what a counter measures, select Explain to display descriptive text about the counter.

7. If appropriate, choose an Instance for each object counter.

8. Modify the legend characteristics as you desire (Color, Scale, Width, and line Style.)

9. Choose Add to add the counter(s) to the chart window.

10. Repeat steps 3–9 for any additional objects you wish to monitor.

11. Choose Done when you are finished.

Performance Monitor, by default, displays a line chart that charts activity for every second in time. These defaults can be modified by selecting Options, Chart to display the Chart Options dialog box.

Most of the options in the Chart Options dialog box are self explanatory. However, note the Update Time section. The Periodic Interval is set to 1 second, the default. If you want to capture information in smaller or larger time intervals, modify the value accordingly. The value you enter will affect the Graph Time value on the Statistics bar at the bottom of the graph itself. At a setting of 1 second, it will take 100 seconds to complete one chart pass in the window. A setting of 2 seconds will take 200 seconds to make a complete pass. A setting of .6 seconds will take 60 seconds, or one minute, to complete a pass.

To save chart settings for future use, such as for creating a chart to compare against baseline activity, choose File, Save Chart Settings. The chart settings can then be loaded later to monitor system activity as designed.

Ch
12

Creating a Monitor Log

As was mentioned before, charting values really is ineffective unless you have some baseline values against which you can compare activity. Object counter values can be collected and saved in a log file.

To create a log file:

1. Start Performance Monitor.

2. Choose View, Log to display the log window.

3. From Edit, choose Add to Log. Select all the objects whose data you wish to capture and choose Add. This will cause the log to record activity for every counter associated with each object. Choose Done when you are finished.

4. From Options, choose Log.

5. Enter a name for the log file and a directory to save it in, and set the Periodic Update interval if you desire.

6. Choose Start Log to begin recording system activity.

7. Monitor the file size counter (shown in bytes) until the file grows as large as you like, or simply use your watch to collect data over a specific period of time.

8. When you have collected the desired amount of data, choose Options, Log and select Stop Log.

9. Choose Options, Log and select Save to save the log file.

To view the contents of a log file:

1. Start Performance Monitor.

2. Choose View, Chart to display the chart window.

3. Choose Options, Data From to display the Data From dialog box.

4. Choose Log File and enter the path and file name of the log file, or browse for it. Choose OK.

5. Choose Edit, Add to Chart. The only objects listed will be those you captured in the log file. Select the object, and the appropriate counters for each, for which you want to view chart values and Add them to the chart. A static chart view will be created.

6. Adjust the time view of the chart by choosing Edit, Time Window from the menu and make your adjustment.

Note There is no facility in Performance Monitor to print out charts. However, you can press Print Screen to capture a chart window to the clipboard, and then paste it into a word processing document and print it that way. You could also export the data to an Excel spreadsheet and use it's utilities to create graphs and analyze the data. ■

Network Monitor Utility

The Server installation of Windows NT 4.0 includes yet another useful monitoring utility called Network Monitor. Network Monitor is used to capture, filter, and analyze network traffic. Just like Performance Monitor, so-called "normal" traffic can be captured and saved to compare to unusual network traffic conditions.

Network Monitor offers such statistical information as the percent of network utilization, frames sent and received per second, bytes sent and received per second, and broadcasts and multicasts per second.

This information is shown both in summary format and on a frame-by-frame basis, indicating in great detail the type of packet, protocol, computers, and data involved in that particular frame.

This is a subset of the Network Monitor utility that comes bundled with Microsoft System Management Server.

Ch
12

Objects to Monitor

The four basic objects to monitor, especially when creating a baseline of "normal" system activity are processor, process, logical disk, and memory. Here are some specific counters that can be useful to chart for each.

Processor Object

The processor object monitors processor usage by the system. There are four counters that you may want to chart.

%Processor Time—shown in Figure 12.8—tracks the total processor usage and gives a picture of just how busy the processor is. This counter, in and of itself, is not enough to tell you what is driving the processor to this level of usage, but it does help to indicate whether the problem or bottleneck is related in any way to the processor. %User Time and %Privileged Time defines processor usage by displaying what percentage of the total usage pertains to user mode (application) and kernel mode (operating system) activities, respectively. Again, these do not indicate what specific activities are driving the percentages. These three, in general, should remain below 75–80 percent depending on computer use. For example, you would expect these values to be lower on a desktop computer, but consistently high on a server running Microsoft Systems Management Server.

FIG. 12.8⇒

The total percent of processor usage for the computer is shown here. Note there is only one processor installed, so there is only one instance to track.

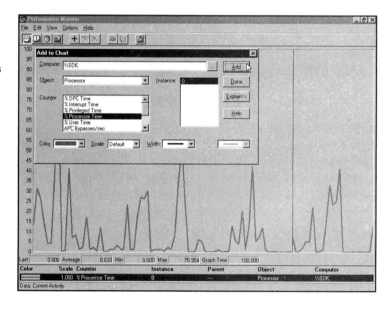

Interrupts/Sec tracks the number of device interrupt requests from hardware devices, such as network cards or disk controllers, serviced by the processor. The number of requests considered optimum will vary from processor to processor. For example, you would expect a Pentium to handle perhaps three times as many requests as a 486 processor. In general, the higher the number (greater than 1000 suggested for 486) the more likely the problem is hardware-related. One would next monitor queue lengths for various suspected hardware devices such as the disk controller or network card. Optimally, there should only be one request waiting in queue. Queue lengths greater than 2 indicate which device is the likely culprit and may need to be replaced or upgraded.

> ## Caution
> Processor object counters, as with all object counters, should never be monitored alone. As pointed out above, the mere indication of activity beyond the norm does not in itself point to the processor as the focus of the problem. Use these, and the other object counters recommended, to draw attention to a problem. Then add additional object counters to help pinpoint and troubleshoot the problem.

Process Object

For every service that is loaded and application that is run, a process is created by Windows NT and monitored by Performance Monitor. Each process is considered an instance in this case, and each object instance has several counters that can be charted.

Notice that the %Processor Time can be tracked for each process instance (see Figure 12.9). This is how you can determine which specific process is driving the processor to higher than normal usage.

FIG. 12.9⇒

The Performance Monitor (perfmon in the legend—the white chart line) is driving the total percent of processor usage. You can also see from the dotted chart line (NTVDM in the legend) when the screen capture program took the snapshot of this chart and contributed to an overall increase in processor usage.

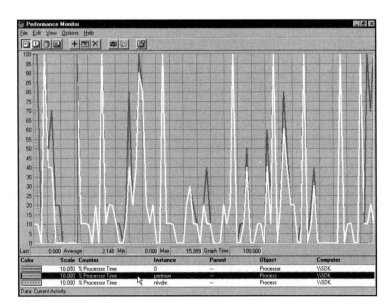

Ch
12

Another useful process counter is the Working Set. This counter actually tracks the amount of RAM required by the process and can be used to help determine when additional RAM is necessary.

Memory Object

Perhaps the most common problem encountered on heavily used computers is inadequate RAM for the processes to perform at their optimum rates. There are two memory counters that can be of particular service to you.

Commit Limit indicates the number of bytes that can be written (committed) to the pagefile without extending, or growing, it. As this number falls, the pagefile is more likely to grow. Use this counter to help you determine whether you need to "right-size" your pagefile (review the section in this chapter about right-sizing pagefiles).

Pages/Sec indicates the number of pages requested by an application or other process that were not in RAM and had to be read from disk. In itself, this value should remain rather low—less than 5 is recommended. Multiply this counter's average value by that of the Logical Disk object's Avg. Disk sec/Transfer counter. This counter indicates the average number of seconds for each disk I/O. The resulting value shows the percent of disk I/O used by paging. Microsoft suggests that if this value consistently exceeds 10 percent, then paging is excessive and you probably need more RAM. The actual threshold will be based on the function of the particular computer. You might expect more paging to occur on a SQL server than on a desktop, for example.

Consider that you have determined that paging is excessive by multiplying the Memory object's Pages/Sec counter by the Logical Disk object's Avg. Disk sec/Transfer counter and got a value of 20 percent. You presume that you need additional RAM. But how much?

You have also been tracking the %Processor Time for the processor as a whole, and for several suspect processes, and you note three that really push the processor.

For each process, also monitor that process' Working Set counter. Recall that this is the amount of RAM required by the process. Make note of the amount of RAM used by each process. Now, terminate one of the processes. Check the percent of disk I/O used by paging. Has it dropped below the acceptable threshold (10 percent, as recommended by Microsoft)? If so, then the amount of RAM required by that application is the minimum amount of additional RAM to add to your computer. If not, terminate another application and check the results again. Keep doing this until the pagefile I/O drops to an acceptable level, and add up the working set values for the terminated processes. The total represents the minimum amount of RAM to add to your computer. Programmers often round this value up to the nearest multiple of four.

Disk Objects

There are actually two objects related to disk activity: physical disk and logical disk.

The Physical Disk object counters track activity related to the disk drive as a whole, and can be used to determine whether one disk drive is being used more than another for load-balancing purposes. For example, if the activity of a disk is particularly high due to operating system requests and pagefile I/O, then you might want to move the pagefile to a disk which is being underutilized, especially if the disk controller can write to each disk concurrently. The number of instances will be the number of physical drives installed on the computer.

The Logical Disk object counters track activity related to specific partitions on each disk and can be used to locate the source of activity on the disk, i.e., on what partition the pagefile is located. The number of instances will be the number of partitions created by drive letter.

Both objects have pretty much the same group of counters for tracking activity. Four of these counters in particular can be useful.

One counter, Avg. Disk sec/Transfer, you saw when reviewing Memory object counters. It shows the average amount of time for disk I/O to complete and can be used with the Memory object's Pages/sec counter to determine whether paging is excessive.

Disk Queue Length represents the number of requests for disk I/O waiting to be serviced. This number should generally be less than 2. Consistently high numbers indicate that the disk is being overutilized, or should be upgraded to a faster access disk.

Ch

12

Disk Bytes/sec indicates the number of bytes of data that are transferred during disk I/O. The higher the average value, the more efficient the performance.

%Disk Time represents the amount of time spent servicing disk I/O requests. A consistently high number, of course, indicates that the disk is being heavily used. You may choose to determine which processes are driving this usage and partition or move the applications to a less heavily used disk to load-balance disk activity.

These counter values, used with the others previously discussed, can help you determine bottlenecks and possible courses of action to alleviate problems.

Key Concept

Disk object counters, while they are visible in the Add to Chart dialog box, are not enabled by default. This is because the resource required to monitor disk activity is, itself, rather demanding. Disk object monitoring must be enabled before any charting can take place, otherwise your chart will always display a flat line graph.

Enable disk monitoring by typing the following command at a DOS command prompt:

> `DISKPERF -Y \\computername` where \\computername optionally references a remote computer whose disk activity you wish to monitor.

When you are finished capturing your data, type:

> `DISKPERF -N \\computername` to disable disk monitoring.

Reviewing the Emergency Repair Process

The Emergency Repair Disk is usually created during the NT installation process (see Chapter 3, "Installing Windows NT Workstation 4.0"). However, it can be created (and updated) at any time by running the Windows NT command `RDISK.EXE` at the Windows NT command prompt.

The Emergency Repair Disk contains setup information relevant to your installation of Windows NT, including the location of source files and computer configuration, disk configuration, and security information from the registry, including the SAM database. It can be used to replace corrupted or missing boot files, recover account information, and restore Windows NT to the master boot record of the computer boot partition if it has been modified.

To use the Emergency Repair disk you must first boot the computer using a Windows NT Startup disk. This disk was created during the Windows NT installation process, unless you chose to do a diskless installation (see Chapter 3, "Installing Windows NT Workstation 4.0").

Tip

If you do not have a Windows NT Startup Disk, but have access to the original installation files, you can create one by accessing the installation file directory and typing the command: **WINNT /O** at a command prompt (refer to Chapter 3, "Installing Windows NT Workstation 4.0," for a complete discussion of this and other installation switches). Be sure to have three disks available and label them as instructed.

Initiating the Repair Process

From the Startup menu, choose <u>R</u>epair. The repair process offers four options:

Ch
12

1. Inspect Registry Files. This option prompts the user for replacement of each registry file, including System and SAM.

Caution

The security files on the Emergency Repair Disk overwrite the security files in the Registry. If you have created or modified accounts, but did not update the Emergency Repair data with the changes, you will lose the new and modified information when you perform the repair process. For this reason, this is *not* the best way to recover damaged security or account information. A backup will be much more useful in maintaining the integrity of existing account entries.

2. Inspect Startup Environment. This option checks the BOOT.INI file for an entry for Windows NT. If it doesn't find one, it adds one for the next boot attempt.

3. Verify Windows NT System Files. This option verifies whether the Windows NT system files match those of the original installation files. For this option you will need to have access to the original installation files. This option also looks for, and verifies, the integrity of the boot files.

Tip

If you updated Windows NT with a service pack, you will need to reinstall the service pack after initiating a repair.

4. Inspect Boot Sector. This option checks the MBR for NTLDR. If it is missing or corrupt, it will restore the boot sector.

If you know specifically which file is missing or corrupt, you can replace the file directly from the source files using the NT EXPAND ★utility. At a Windows NT prompt type **EXPAND -R** followed by the compressed file name. If Windows NT is inoperable on your system, use another Windows NT system to expand the file and then copy it to your computer.

Keep the Emergency Repair information up-to-date by running the RDISK utility after every major configuration change, or after modifying or creating accounts or setting permissions. On a Windows NT workstation, this information is not likely to change frequently, and the Emergency Repair information can be kept on a secure diskette. However, on a Windows NT server, particularly a domain controller, the account database itself is likely to exceed the capacity of the disk many times. Windows NT does keep a copy of the Emergency Repair information in the subdirectory WINNT40\REPAIR. However, in the event of a disk failure, that will not do you much good. As noted in the previous caution, it is best in this situation to have established a regular backup routine, which includes the Registry from which you can more reliably recover lost information.

Creating and Using a Windows NT Boot Disk

Another useful tool to have in your troubleshooting toolkit is a Windows NT boot disk. This is not a disk formatted with NTFS. Rather, it is a disk that has been formatted under Windows NT that has copies of the boot files on it.

When you format a disk under Windows NT, Windows NT creates a boot sector on that disk that references NTLDR. Through Windows Explorer, set your view options to show all files and folders, particularly hidden files. Copy the appropriate boot files from the root directory of the active system partition of your computer to this disk and, *voilà*, you have a Windows NT boot disk. This disk can be used in any number of Windows NT computers because it is not unique to each installation. The only file you may need to modify, for obvious reasons, is the BOOT.INI file because it references the location of the Windows NT system files (boot partition) by ARC path (see Chapter 3, "Installing Windows NT Workstation 4.0").

The boot files you will want to copy to the Windows NT boot disk include: NTLDR, NTDETECT.COM, BOOT.INI, BOOTSECT .DOS, and NTBOOTDD.SYS (if your system boots through a SCSI controller). In addition, it is recommended that you copy the NTOSKRNL.EXE file from the WINNT40 system directory. You now have all the files you need to easily replace missing or corrupt boot files.

Tip

You can format a disk from My Computer. Right-click the A drive icon and select <u>F</u>ormat. Make the appropriate selections and choose OK.

Reviewing System Recovery Options

On rare occasions your Windows NT 4.0 workstation may experience a stop error that causes the system to halt and Windows NT to be restarted. This is a difficult problem to troubleshoot, since you cannot do anything at that time except restart Windows NT.

Windows NT does provide a recovery utility in which you can specify how Windows NT should handle such an error. Its options can be set through the Startup/Shutdown tab of the System applet in Control Panel. There are four recovery options that can be set. These options are not enabled by default on Windows NT Workstation 4.0, but they are enabled by default on Windows NT 4.0 Server.

The first option is perhaps the most useful, given our discussion in this chapter, and that is Write an Event to the System Log. This, of course, causes the stop error to be recorded in the System Log and viewed through Event Viewer.

The next option is to Send an Administrative Alert to all administrators that the stop error has occurred, and on what computer it occurred. This is useful if the stop error is intermittent.

You can choose to Write Debugging Information *to* a specified or the default dump file. This writes all memory registers to the pagefile. In order for this to work, the pagefile must be at least as large as physical RAM, and it must reside on the boot partition (Windows NT system file partition). When Windows NT restarts, this information is copied to a specified dump file (WINNT40\MEMORY.DMP by default). This file can be used by Microsoft Technical Support or with the DUMPEXAM.EXE program supplied on the Windows NT CD-ROM to debug the problem.

Finally, choose Automatically Reboot to restart the computer automatically after the stop error occurs—extremely handy on server installations.

From Here...

Well, there's no where to go but up from here. All the topics you are likely to encounter on the Windows NT Workstation 4.0 Exam have been covered, and then some! Even if you do not take the exam, you will have learned quite a bit about Windows NT 4.0 in general concept, and Windows NT Workstation 4.0 in particular. If you're planning on continuing your certification in Windows NT 4.0, or for the Microsoft Certified System Engineer, you'll want to get the next books in this series: *Windows NT 4.0 Server Exam Guide* and *Windows NT 4.0 Enterprise Exam Guide*.

Taking the Disc Test

 If you have read and understood the material in the chapter, you are ready to test your knowledge. Insert the CD-ROM that comes with this book and run the self-test software as described in Appendix I, "Using the CD-ROM."

Ch
12

Lab Exercises

Chapter 2—Lab Exercises

The best way to become familiar with the installation process is to install Windows NT Workstation 4.0 a few times and pay close attention to what is happening. Later in this book, you will need at least two computers running Windows NT Workstation 4.0 in order to understand the way Windows NT handles access security. If you have two computers available, install one using the *Custom* option and the other using *Typical*. I have included the Preparation Checklist once again in this section. Double-check your hardware configuration against the checklist before beginning setup. Then follow the process as outlined in Chapter 2. I have included specific instructions in the steps outlined in the exercise. As you proceed with installation, *be sure to read each screen for your own edification.*

PREPARATION CHECKLIST

Read all Windows NT documentation files.

Assess system requirements.

Assess hardware compatibility. Refer to the Hardware Compatibility List.

Assess necessary drivers and configuration data:

• Video	Display Type, Adapter and chipset type
• Network	Card type, IRQ, I/O Address, DMA, Connector, and so on.
• SCSI Controller	Adapter and chipset type, IRQ, bus type
• Sound/Media	IRQ, I/O Address, DMA
• I/O Ports	IRQ, I/O Address, DMA
• Modems	Port, IRQ, I/O Address, Modem Type

Back up your current configuration and data files.

What type of initial setup will be performed (you may need three blank formatted disks before running setup)?

Where are the installation files located?

What partition will Windows NT system files be installed on?

What file system will you install?

Will you create an Emergency Repair Disk (if so, you need one blank disk available before running setup)?

What is your installation CD Key?

What is the unique computer name?

What is the workgroup or domain name that the computer joins?

Network connection data: IP addresses, IPX card numbers, and so on.

What time zone is the computer located in?

Recommended Computer Configuration

◆ At least 2 486/66 or higher computers with 16M RAM.

◆ Working network connection between these computers.

◆ If you are part of a larger network, try to have your computer isolated into its own network. If you cannot, be sure to inform your network administrator of what you intend to do so that you can both take all necessary precautions to preserve security on the network.

◆ FAT formatted C: Primary Partition.

◆ At least 300M Free Space on same or other drive.

◆ Two or more physical disk drives to demonstrate disk striping.

◆ CD-ROM drive for installation.

◆ Optional four blank formatted disks—three for startup and one for emergency repair.

◆ One printer attached to either computer.

Exercise 1—Setting Up Your Computers for This Book's Labs

1. If you have your own installation CD and a compatible CD-ROM, run setup from the CD. If you are accessing the installation files over the network, you must make a connection to the installation directory first. Connect as you normally would on your network, or else consult with your network administrator for appropriate access.

2. If you have four formatted blank 3.5" disks available (three for startup and one for emergency repair) run **WINNT.EXE** from the installation directory and follow the directions on the screen. If you choose not to create the startup disks, run **WINNT /B**.

Labs

> **Note** If you are installing Windows NT on a RISC-based system, be sure to create a minimum 2M FAT partition and a large enough system partition for Windows NT before starting setup. Then, follow the guidelines outlined in the Notes and Sidebars of Chapter 2 relating to RISC installations. ▨

3. Press Enter to install Windows NT.

4. If you have any additional storage devices other than what Windows NT detects, add them.

5. Verify that your basic hardware settings are correct and press Enter.

6. Create a 250M partition out of the free space during installation, format it as FAT, and install the Windows NT system partition there in a directory called **WINNT40**.

7. Let Windows NT do an exhaustive scan of your disk drive and then reboot the computer.

8. For your first installation, choose Custom. For your second, choose Typical. Read all screens as you go along. Explore all buttons. It is impossible to create an exercise for all possible permutations that one might encounter, so it is up to you to explore.

9. When prompted for the User and Company Name, use your own.

10. When prompted for a Computer name use:

    COMPUTER1 for the first installation and **COMPUTER2** for the second, and so on for additional installations. You may, of course name the computers anything you like. Future labs will refer to these suggested names. Just remember to substitute your own. If you are part of a larger network, be sure that your computer names are unique.

11. Enter **studynt** as your password just as it appears in lowercase. Again, you may choose your own password. Just don't forget it!

12. If you receive a message regarding the floating point error, do not choose the workaround.

13. If you have a formatted disk handy, create the Emergency Repair Disk. Remember that you can create it later.

14. Look at all the Optional Component lists and sublists to understand your choices. Install as many additional options as you like. Install at least the recommended options that Windows NT displays. If you are low on disk space, deselect games and other unessential accessories.

15. Let Windows NT detect your network card, or if you have an OEM driver disk, install your card from the disk.

16. Deselect TCP/IP and select NETBEUI as your protocol. Also keep the default Network Services and Bindings.

17. You will create a workgroup called **STUDYGROUP**. As before, you can call the workgroup anything you like as long as you remember what you called it for future exercises, and as long as it does not conflict with any other workgroup on your network.

18. Enter the appropriate date and time zone values.

19. Select the appropriate settings for your monitor.

20. Complete the installation and let Windows NT restart the system.

OPTIONAL EXERCISE

Follow the instructions in the Troubleshooting section of Chapter 2, and run the NTHQ utility to see how it works. Log and print a report.

Chapter 3—Lab Exercise

Labs

There is no better practice at getting acquainted with the new Windows NT 4.0 interface than by trying out the new features, exploring ALL object property sheets and having fun. Here is an exercise that uses all the more significant features of the interface. You will need one blank formatted disk.

Exercise—Navigating the Interface—Taskbar, Explorer, Shortcuts, and Briefcase

1. Start Windows Help, and click the Contents tab.

2. From the topic list choose HOW TO, then Change Windows Settings, then Change Taskbar Settings. Following the directions, make it so the taskbar does not display on top of all other windows.

3. Open My Computer. Select Options from the View menu and choose the option that replaces previous windows.

4. Right-click the A: drive icon and drag it to the desktop. Choose Create shortcut from the pop-up menu.

5. Open the C: drive icon. From the File menu choose New and create a new folder called LAB2.

6. From the Start menu choose Programs, then Accessories, and start the WordPad program.

7. Create a file called MEMO.DOC with the following text:

   This is the first draft of my memo.

8. From the File menu choose Save As. Use its browse feature to find the LAB2 directory and save the MEMO.DOC file there. Minimize WordPad.

9. Open Windows Explorer and select the LAB2 directory. Right-click the file and drag it to the Briefcase icon on the desktop. Choose Create Synch Copy from the pop-up menu.

10. Place the formatted blank disk in the A: drive.

11. Drag the Briefcase from the desktop to the A: drive shortcut icon.

12. Move your mouse to the bottom of the screen until the taskbar appears. Select WordPad. Open the MEMO.DOC file in the Briefcase on the A: drive. Add the following text and save the file:

    This is the second draft of my memo.

13. Open the A: drive shortcut icon and drag the briefcase back to the desktop.

14. Open the Briefcase and choose Update from the Briefcase menu option. Notice the window that displays the documents that have changed, and the suggestion to update the older document.

15. Choose Update All. Close Briefcase.

16. Start WordPad and open the MEMO.DOC file in the LAB2 directory. Verify that it has been updated.

17. Start the Find program. From the Advanced tab, search for all files on the C: drive containing the following text: "first draft." In the results window, verify that both copies appear.

Chapter 4—Lab Exercises

The best way to review the applets in Control Panel is to spend time with each one reviewing what each accomplishes. There is no better exercise that I can recommend. However, here are a couple that you can safely try that involve the Registry.

Exercise 1—Using Control Panel to Configure Windows NT

1. Use Control Panel to modify the wallpaper on your computer to LEAVES.BMP, and change your Wait mouse pointer to the animated cursor BANANA.ANI. Note that these changes take effect immediately.

2. Close Control Panel and open the Registry Editor (ex: Start\ RUN\REGEDT32.EXE).

3. Click in the HKEY_CURRENT_USER subtree window to make it active.

4. Select View, Find Key and search for "cursors." When the Cursors key is found, close the Find dialog box and select the Cursors key. Notice that the Wait cursor parameter on the right side of the window shows that BANANA.ANI has been selected.

Labs

5. Change the Wait value from BANANA.ANI to HORSE.ANI by double-clicking the Wait value and typing in **HORSE.ANI** (using the appropriate path).

6. Choose Edit\Add Value and enter the value name **APPSTARTING** with a data type of REG_SZ, choose OK and enter the file name and path to DINOSAUR.ANI.

7. Use Find Key again to find the WALLPAPER key. Were you able to? Recall that wallpaper is a feature of the desktop. Search for DESKTOP.

8. Select the DESKTOP key and view the right side of the window for entries related to wallpaper. You should find two: WALLPAPER and TILEWALLPAPER.

9. Modify the WALLPAPER entry (currently LEAVES.BMP) to WINNT40\FURRYD~1.BMP (check the path for this file before making the change—hint: use Find).

10. Modify the TileWallpaper entry to the value 1.

11. Close the Registry. When do these changes take effect? Log off and then log back on and see if the changes have taken effect. If not, shut down and restart.

Exercise 2—Using the Registry

1. Open the Registry Editor.

2. Click in the HKEY_LOCAL_MACHINE subtree window to make it active.

3. Expand through the SOFTWARE hive to find the WINLOGON key: SOFTWARE\Microsoft\Windows NT\Current Version\Winlogon.

4. Double-click the parameter *Legal Notice Caption* on the right side of the window and enter the caption "**Legal Notice.**"

5. Double-click the parameter Legal Notice Text and enter the following: "**Unauthorized access will be punished!**"

6. Choose <u>E</u>dit, Add <u>V</u>alue and enter the value name **DontDisplayLastUserName** with a data type of REG_SZ, choose OK and enter the value **1** for "yes."

7. Close the Registry. When do these changes take effect? Log off and then log back on and see if the changes have taken effect. If not, shut down and restart.

Exercise 3—Using the Registry, Part 2

1. Open the Registry Editor and make the HKEY_USERS subtree window active.

2. Expand through the .DEFAULT key to find DESKTOP: .DEFAULT\Control Panel\Desktop.

3. Modify the Wallpaper entry with the value LEAVES.BMP and the TileWallpaper entry to 1. This will change the default wallpaper that displays on booting Windows NT.

4. Close the Registry. When do these changes take effect? Log off and then log back on and see if the changes have taken effect. If not, shut down and restart.

Exercise 4—System Policy Editor

If you have access to a Windows NT 4.0 Server (domain controller), and have a valid user account that you can use to log on with from your workstation, complete this exercise. You must be able to log on to that server from your workstation, have the System Policy Editor tool installed on your workstation, and have administrative rights to create System Policies.

1. Log in to the server as Administrator from your workstation.

2. Start the System Policy Editor. (Choose Start, Programs, Administrative Tools, System Policy Editor).

3. If an existing NTCONFIG.POL file exists in WINNT40\ SYSTEM32\REPL\IMPORT\SCRIPTS, open it. Otherwise, select File, New Profile.

4. Choose Edit, Add User and enter your valid user account.

Labs

5. Double-click your new user icon to display the policies.

6. Select Desktop, click the Wallpaper check box, and enter the path and file name to your favorite wallpaper in the lower part of the window (for example, WINNT40\leaves.bmp).

7. Select System, Restrictions and check Disable Registry Editing Tools.

8. Choose Shell, Restrictions, and check Remove Run Command from Start menu and Don't Save Settings at Exit.

9. Close the policy and save it as NTCONFIG.POL in the WINNT40\SYSTEM32\REPL\IMPORT\SCRIPTS subdirectory.

10. Log off and log back on as the user account whose policy you modified. You should note the changes that have taken effect: The wallpaper should now be LEAVES, you should be unable to run REGEDT32, you should not have Run as a Start menu option and any changes you make to the environment, for example colors, cursors, will not be saved.

11. Log back on as Administrator and make further changes to experiment or delete the policy.

Chapter 5—Lab Exercises

These exercises are most helpful if you have two computers available.

Exercise 1—Creating Users and Groups

Complete this exercise on both workstations if you have two.

1. Using Notepad, create the following logon script called KITE.BAT and save it in the WINNT40\SYSTEM32\ REPL\IMPORT\SCRIPTS subdirectory.

   @echo Welcome to the Kite Flyers network!

   @echo off

   Pause

2. Use User Manager to create the following user accounts on both workstations. Require each to change their password when they log on (check User Must Change Password at Next Logon). In the Profiles button for each, enter the KITE.BAT logon script you created in step 1, and enter the following home directory: **c:\users\%USERNAME%**, using the drive in which you installed Windows NT and that contains the USERS directory.

New Users

Username	Full Name	Description	Password
BrownC	Charles Brown	Chairperson	password
VanPeltL	Lucille VanPelt	Secretary General	password
BumsteadD	Dagwood Bumstead	Marketing Manager	password
Dilbert	Dilbert	MIS Manager	password

3. Create the following group accounts:

Group Name	Description	Members
Managers	Kite Flyers Management Team	BrownC VanPeltL BumsteadD Dilbert
Marketing	Marketing Team	BumsteadD
MIS	MIS Team	Dilbert

4. Create the following template accounts. Require the user to change the password at the next logon. Choose the Groups button, remove the Users group for each and add in the corresponding group you created in step 3 (Sales for SalesTemp,

Labs

Marketing for MarketingTemp, MIS for MISTemp). Choose the Profile button for each and enter in the login script you created (kite.bat) and the following home directory: c:\users\%USERNAME%, using the drive in which you installed Windows NT that contains the USERS directory (use Windows Explorer to confirm it).

Username	Full Name	Description	Password
SalesTemp	Sales Template	Sales Representative	stemplate
MarketingTemp	Marketing Template	Account Manager	mtemplate
MIStemp	MIS Template	System Analyst	itemplate

5. Create the following accounts by copying the appropriate template you created in step 4. Notice what elements of the template account are copied (description, password options, group and profile information) and which you need to fill in (username, full name, password).

    Sales

    FlagstonL, Lois Flagston, password

    BumsteadB, Blondie Bumstead, password

    Marketing

    Dogbert, Dogbert, password

    MIS

    GatesB, William Gates, password

    BaileyB, Beetle Bailey, password

6. Use Windows Explorer to confirm that the home directories for each account were created.

Exercise 2—Managing User Profiles

Complete this exercise from Computer1.

1. Log on as GatesB. Change the password as instructed. Modify your environment settings by changing the screen colors, adding a wallpaper, and creating a shortcut to Solitaire on the desktop.

2. Log off and log on again as Administrator.

3. Use Windows Explorer to find the WINNT40\PROFILES directory. Notice the new subdirectory structure for GatesB with the file NTUSER.DAT in the GATESB subdirectory. Expand GATESB to find the Desktop subdirectory and notice the shortcut to Solitaire located there.

4. Find the WINNT40\PROFILES\Default User subdirectory. Expand it to display the Desktop subdirectory. Create a shortcut here for Solitaire (right-click and drag the Solitaire icon from WINNT40\SYSTEM32). Also, rename the NTUSER.DAT file in Default User to NTUSER.OLD and copy the NTUSER.DAT file from GATESB.

5. Create a new user called PAT with no password and no password options selected.

6. Log on as PAT. Notice that the Solitaire shortcut and the environment settings became part of PAT's profile. This will be true not only for each new user you create, but also for any previous user who has not yet logged on for the first time, and thus created his or her own profile.

7. Log back on as Administrator. Use Windows Explorer to delete the NTUSER.DAT file from WINNT40\PROFILES\Default User and rename NTUSER.OLD back to NTUSER.DAT.

Labs

Exercise 3—Managing User Profiles—Part 2

1. Use Windows Explorer to create a new directory called Profiles in the root directory of Computer2. Right-click it and select Sharing, choose Shared As, and select OK. (If you do not have two computers installed, complete this exercise from the same computer and adjust the directions accordingly.)

2. On the first computer, start User Manager. Delete the account PAT. Create a new user account called MEG with no password and no password options selected. Choose Profile and in User Profile Path enter the following: **\\Computer2\profiles\ntuser.dat**.

3. Start the System applet from the Control Panel and switch to the User Profiles tab. You will note an entry for Account Deleted. This was PAT that you deleted in step 2. Select this entry and choose Delete and Yes.

4. In the list, select the entry for GATESB and choose Copy To.

5. In the Copy Profile To text box enter **\\computer2\profiles**, or choose Browse to find the directory in Network Neighborhood. In Permitted to Use, select Change and choose MEG from the list (be sure to select Show Users). Choose OK and exit from System.

6. Log on as MEG. Notice that MEG received her profile from the second computer and that her environment settings match GATESB.

7. On the first computer, log off and log back in again as Administrator. Open the properties for MEG in User Manager and change the profile file reference from NTUSER.DAT to NTUSER.MAN.

8. Log in as MEG. Notice that you are unable to log in because you have referenced a mandatory profile that does not exist.

9. Log back in as Administrator. Delete the account MEG.

Chapter 6—Lab Exercises

This set of labs will be most effective if you use both computers, and if you have one NTFS partition created on each computer. Also, this lab depends on your having completed all exercises from Chapter 5.

If you do not currently have an NTFS partition, but have an existing FAT partition that you can convert to NTFS (other than the boot partition), use the following steps to convert it to NTFS:

1. Open a DOS prompt window.

2. At the prompt, type **CONVERT D: /FS:NTFS**, where D: represents the letter of the partition that you are converting.

3. Press Enter. If there are any files in use by Windows NT on that partition such as the pagefile, you will see a message to the effect that you must reboot for the conversion to take effect. Do so. Otherwise, Windows NT will convert the partition when you press Enter.

If you do not have a partition that you can convert, but do have at least 50M of free disk space available, you can use Disk Administrator to create an NTFS partition. Follow these steps.

1. Start Disk Administrator. If this is the first time you are starting this utility, click OK to start the message.

2. Click the free disk space available in the graphic screen provided.

3. From Partition on the menu choose Create.

4. Specify the total size of the partition and choose OK. It should be at least 50M, but can be no smaller than 10M.

5. Choose Partition, Commit Changes Now.

6. From Tools, choose Format and NTFS.

7. When format is complete, exit Disk Administrator.

Labs

Exercise 1—Using Shares—Part 1

Log on as Administrator.

1. Using Windows Explorer, create the following folders and files on both computers in the NTFS partition. Place a couple lines of text in each file. (You don't need to get fancy now.)

\TOOLS	DOOM.TXT	(Create new text file)
	BUDGET97.DOC	(Create new Wordpad file)
\TOOLS\DATA	MEMO.DOC	
	WELCOME.TXT	

2. Share TOOLS as TOOLS.

3. Remove Everyone from the ACL for the share and add the Managers group with Change, and the Sales group with Read.

4. Create a new user called SimpsonB on Computer1. Add this user to the Sales group on Computer1.

5. Log on as SimpsonB on Computer1.

6. Using Network Neighborhood, access the TOOLS share on Computer2. Can you access it? Windows NT should tell you that you do not have a valid account or password on Computer2. Recall that in a workgroup environment, you must either create a valid account for every user that needs access to shared resources on a computer, or be able to connect as a valid user.

7. Create the account SimpsonB on Computer2 using the same password as you did on Computer1. Make this account a member of the Sales group on Computer2.

8. On Computer1, access the TOOLS share again. Your access should now be successful because you have a valid account on Computer2 that matches the username and password of the account on Computer1. Disconnect from the share.

9. On Computer2, change SimpsonB's password to something else.

10. On Computer1, right-click Network Neighborhood and choose Map Network Drive.

11. Choose the TOOLS share from the list displayed, or type in the path **\\Computer2\TOOLS**.

12. In the Connect As box, enter SimpsonB, and choose OK. Windows NT will request the password for SimpsonB on Computer2. Enter it to gain access to the share. If you know the name and password of a valid user account on another computer, you can access the share on that computer.

Exercise 2—Using Shares—Part 2

1. On Computer1, log on as BrownC.

2. Connect to the TOOLS share on Computer2.

3. Open the file DOOM.TXT and make a change to the file and close it.

4. Log off, and log in as BumsteadB.

5. Connect to the TOOLS share on Computer2.

6. Open the file DOOM.TXT and make a change to the file. Can you save the file? Note that Windows NT will not let you save changes made to the file because BumsteadB is a member of the Sales group which has been given Read access to the file. Do not close the file.

7. On Computer2, make BumsteadB a member of the Managers group.

8. On Computer1, try to access the file and save changes again. Can you do it? Note that you will not be able to save your changes because BumsteadB's access token for the file still reflects the old group membership.

Labs

9. Close the file, and try to access it again and save changes. Could you do it? Disconnect from the share and reconnect, modify the file and save the changes. Were you successful? Note for yourself at which point after group membership changes that the change took effect.

Exercise 3—Hidden Shares

1. Share the DATA folder on Computer2 as DATA$. Give only Managers Change permission to the share.

2. Log on as BrownC on Computer1.

3. Using Network Neighborhood, look for the DATA share in the list of shares for Computer2. You should not see it since the $ makes it a hidden share.

4. Right-click Network Neighborhood, and choose Map Network Drive. In the path box type **\\Computer2\DATA$** and choose OK. You should have been able to access the share.

5. Modify the file MEMO.DOC and save your changes.

6. Disconnect from the share and log off.

Exercise 4—File and Folder Permissions

Log on to both computers as Administrator and make the following changes:

◆ Modify the NTFS permissions for the TOOLS folder. Remove Everyone and add Managers with Read and Administrators with Full Control.

◆ Modify the NTFS permissions for the DATA folder. Remove Everyone and add Sales with Change and MIS with Add.

1. Log on to Computer1 as BrownC.

2. Use Windows Explorer to expand the NTFS partition. Open the file BUDGET97.DOC in TOOLS and modify it.

3. Can you save your changes? Note that the NTFS permission for Managers is Read. Since BrownC is a member of Managers, he also gets Read access to the file and therefore cannot save changes.

4. Log off and log back on as Dilbert, a member of the MIS and Managers group.

5. Use Windows Explorer to access the DATA folder. Since MIS has only Add permission, you cannot access the DATA folder.

6. Use Notepad to create a document called DILBERT.TXT. Try to save it in the DATA folder. (Access denied.) Try to save it in the TOOLS folder. (You only have READ access, so you can't write a file to this folder.) Save it in the root directory of the NTFS partition.

7. Open a DOS prompt window. At the prompt, copy the file DILBERT.TXT from the root of the NTFS partition to the TOOLS\DATA directory. Note that you *can* do this since you have ADD permission to the DATA folder.

8. Log off.

Exercise 5—File and Folder Permissions—Part 2

1. Log on as BrownC.

2. Access the TOOLS share on Computer2.

3. Open the file DOOM.TXT and modify it.

4. Save your changes. Can you do it? Not this time. The share permission is Change for Managers, and the NTFS permission is Read for Managers. When accessing a resource through a share, the more restrictive of the permissions will become the effective permissions. Thus, your effective permission is Read and you cannot save changes.

5. Log on as Administrator on Computer2.

Labs

6. Change the NTFS permission for Managers on TOOLS to Full Control.

7. On Computer1, reconnect to the share and try to modify and save the file again. This time you can since the effective permission is Change (the more restrictive of the share permission—Change—and the NTFS permission—Full Control).

8. As BrownC, create a new file called BrownC.TXT in the TOOLS directory on Computer2.

9. Log off.

10. As Administrator on Computer2, change the NTFS permission for managers on TOOLS to Change.

Exercise 6—File and Folder Permissions—Part 3

1. Log on as Dilbert on Computer2.

2. Locate the TOOLS folder on Computer2.

3. Locate the file BrownC.TXT and display its Security properties (right-click, Properties, Security).

4. Choose Ownership to see that BrownC is the owner.

5. Can you take ownership of the file? No, because you only have Change permission.

6. Log off and log back on as Administrator.

7. Add Dilbert to the ACL for the file BrownC.TXT with the NTFS Special Access Take Ownership permission.

8. Log on as Dilbert again, and try to take ownership of the file. This time you can, because you have the permission to do so. Verify that Dilbert is now the owner of BrownC.TXT

Chapter 7—Lab Exercises

These exercises are designed for computers which have two physical disk drives, and at least 100M of free space outside of an extended partition on one or more drives. If you have less, or if the free space includes an area of an extended partition, you will need to modify the exercise according to your configuration.

Exercise 1—Using Disk Administrator

1. Start Disk Administrator.

2. Select an area of free space.

3. Choose Partition, Create and create a new primary partition of 20M.

4. Create another primary partition of 50M.

5. Commit the changes.

6. Change the drive letter for the 50M partition to X and the 20M partition to Y through Tools, Assign Drive Letter.

7. Format drive Y as FAT and drive X as NTFS.

8. Close Disk Administrator and save your changes.

Exercise 2—Using Compression

1. Start Windows Explorer.

2. Select drive Y and create a new folder called TRUMP.

3. Copy WINNT256.BMP from the WINNT40 directory into TRUMP.

4. Look at the properties sheet for the file. Is their a Security tab? Is their a Compress attribute on the General tab? (No! It's a FAT partition!)

5. Copy the folder and its file from drive Y to drive X.

6. Look at the file's properties sheet again. Is their a Security tab and Compress attribute option? (Yes! It's an NTFS partition!)

7. Enable the compress attribute for the file and choose apply. What is its compressed size?

8. Close Windows Explorer.

9. Open a DOS Prompt window (choose Start, Programs, DOS Prompt).

Labs

10. At the prompt, type **CONVERT Y: /FS:NTFS**, and press Enter. Windows NT will proceed to convert the partition from FAT to NTFS. (If it tells you to restart, do so.)

11. Start Windows Explorer.

12. Select drive Y and look at the properties of the file in TRUMP. You should now see the Security tab and Compress attribute option since the partition is now NTFS.

Exercise 3—Using Volume Sets

1. Start Disk Administrator.

2. Select drive Y and delete it. Note the confirmation message.

3. Select that area of free space (20M) and the remaining free space on the drive.

4. Choose Partition, Create Volume Set. Note the change in legend information indicating the new volume set.

5. Commit your changes, assign it drive letter Y, and format the volume set as FAT.

6. Close Disk Administrator.

7. Start Windows Explorer and select drive Y. Can you tell that it is a volume set? (No! Not even through properties!) Windows NT treats the volume set as a single drive.

8. Copy X:\TRUMP to Y.

9. Close Windows Explorer and start Disk Administrator.

10. Select the second member of Y and choose Partition, Delete. Note the confirmation message, and delete it. What did you delete? (The entire volume set.)

11. Close Disk Administrator and start Windows Explorer.

12. Confirm that drive Y is gone.

Exercise 4—Extended Volume Sets

1. Start Disk Administrator.

2. Select any FAT partition on your computer, and an area of free space on the same or another drive.

3. Choose Partition, Extend Volume Set from the menu. Can you do it? (No! You cannot extend FAT partitions!)

4. Select the NTFS partition drive X and an area of free space on the same drive or another drive.

5. Choose Partition, Extend Volume set. Can you do it? (Yes! You can extend NTFS partitions!) What else do you notice? (The extended set is automatically formatted as NTFS.)

6. Delete drive X. Notice that if you delete any member of the extended volume set, you delete the entire volume set.

Exercise 5—Using Stripe Sets

(Only if you have at least two physical disks with free space on each.)

1. Start Disk Administrator.

2. Select an area of free space on one disk and an area of free space on another. (If you have additional disks, select free space on these as well.)

3. Choose Partition, Create Stripe Set.

4. Create the largest stripe set that you are allowed.

5. Notice in Disk Administrator how the stripe set is evenly distributed across the free space on the disks.

6. Delete the stripe set.

Exercise 6—Backup and Restore

(Only if you have a working tape drive attached to your computer.)

1. Use Disk Administrator to create a 50M NTFS partition (drive Z).

Labs

2. Use Windows Explorer to create a folder called BITMAPS in it and copy the bitmap files from the WINNT40 directory to BITMAPS.

3. Insert a new tape in the tape backup device.

4. Start Backup (choose Start, Programs, Administrative Tools, Backup).

5. Select the Z drive and check the check box in front of it to select all its contents. Double-click it to verify that the bitmap folder and all its files have been selected.

6. Choose BACKUP. Enter a tape name, select Verify Files, keep all other defaults and proceed.

7. When backup is complete, exit the utility.

8. Use Notepad to view the BACKUP.LOG file created in the WINNT40 directory.

9. Start Windows Explorer.

10. Select drive Z and delete the BITMAPS folder.

11. Start Backup. The existing tape will be displayed in the window with the backup set you created listed.

12. If you appended to an existing tape, select Operations, Catalog to find and load the backup set for the BITMAPS files and folder. Otherwise, double-click the backup set in the tapes window to load the catalog for the backup set.

13. Select all files from the backup set including the BITMAPS folder.

14. Choose RESTORE and keep all defaults. Be sure the restore path is pointing to drive Z.

15. After the restore completes, exit the utility.

16. Start Windows Explorer and verify that the files and folder have been restored.

Chapter 8—Lab Exercises

This lab requires that you have one printer attached to one of your computers and assumes it is connected to Computer1. Installing

Windows 95 print drivers is also an option if you have the Windows 95 CD-ROM handy.

Exercise 1—Creating a Printer

Even if you have installed your printer already, complete this exercise on Computer1. Pay close attention to the screens and messages and options available to you. Refer to the chapter text to highlight and clarify screens.

1. Start the Add Printer Wizard. (Choose My Computer, Printers, Add Printer.)

2. You will install the printer on your local computer. Choose My Computer.

3. Select the port that your print device is attached to.

4. Select the manufacturer and model of the print device connected to your computer.

5. Set this to be your print default.

6. Call it Managers Printer and share the printer as NTPRINT. If you have the Windows 95 source CD-ROM available, select Windows 95 from the list of additional print drivers to support.

7. Print a test page to verify your configuration works.

8. If necessary, enter the appropriate path to the Windows NT source files to complete installation.

Exercise 1A—Optional

If you have a network TCP/IP printer available that you can use and are allowed to manage, be sure to add the TCP/IP protocol to your computer and repeat Exercise 1. For step 3, choose Add Port and select local port. Enter in the IP address of the network printer.

Labs

Exercise 2—Connecting to a Network Printer

1. On Computer2, start the Add Printer Wizard.

2. This time, choose Network Printer Server to connect to the printer you just created on Computer1.

3. From the Connect to Printer browse screen, expand through the Microsoft Windows Network entries to find the printer you created on Computer1 called NTPRINT and select it.

   OR

   Type in the UNC path to the printer as follows:

   \\COMPUTER1\NTPRINT

4. Make this the default printer on Computer2.

5. Complete the installation. A network printer icon will be displayed in the Printers folder.

6. Use Notepad to create and save a short text document called PRINT.TXT. Suggested content: If you can read this, printing was successful.

7. Print PRINT.TXT to the network printer you just connected to. Was printing successful? (Yes.)

8. On Computer1, open the NTPRINT print manager window and pause the shared printer.

9. Resubmit PRINT.TXT on Computer2.

10. In the NTPRINT window, select the PRINT.TXT print job and explore the Document Properties. Schedule the job to print at the next half-hour.

11. Resume the printer and wait until the next half-hour to see your print job print.

Exercise 3—Managing Printer Properties

1. On Computer1, open the NTPRINT properties sheet and select the Scheduling tab.

2. Set the priority to the highest setting (99).

3. On the Security tab choose Permissions.

4. Remove Everyone and add Managers with Print permission.

5. Close NTPRINT properties.

6. Create another printer for the same print device on the same port. Call it Staff Printer and share it as STAFFPRT.

7. After it is created, open its properties and select the Scheduling tab.

8. Set the priority to the lowest setting (1).

9. On the Security tab choose Permissions.

10. Remove Everyone and add MIS with Print permission.

11. Close STAFFPRT properties.

12. Make Dilbert a member of the Power Users group on Computer1.

13. Log on to Computer1 as a Manager account—Dilbert.

14. Open both NTPRINT and STAFFPRT windows. Pause NTPRINT and STAFFPRT.

15. Create a text document called TESTP1.TXT with the text "This is a test print - 1" and print to NTPRINT. You should see it queued up in the NTPRINT window.

16. On Computer2, log on as GatesB.

17. Connect to STAFFPRT and make it default.

18. Create a text document called Staffp1.TXT with the text "This is a staff test print - 1" and print to STAFFPRT. You should see it queued up in the STAFFPRT window on Computer1.

19. Create two more documents on Computer1 (TESTP2.TXT and TESTP3.TXT with similar text) and on Computer2 (Staffp2.TXT and Staffp3.TXT with similar text) and print them to their respective printers. You will see them queued up.

20. Resume STAFFPRT then NTPRINT. In what order did the print jobs print? Chances are that since STAFFPRT was resumed first, its low priority STAFFp1.TXT job was sent to the print device ahead of TESTP1.TXT. Nevertheless, before any other staff jobs print, the Managers' jobs will print first since their print queue associated with the same printer has a higher priority than staff print jobs.

If your computer had a previous printer setup, restore it as your default now if you like.

Chapter 9—Lab Exercises

Portions of this lab require that you have installed at least two 16-bit Windows 3.1 applications. These might be earlier versions of Microsoft Office, or even your favorite Windows games.

Exercise 1—Running DOS and Windows 16-Bit Applications

1. Right-click the taskbar and start the Task Manager. Choose View, Select Columns, Base Priority. Resize the Task Manager window so that you can see the Base Priorities column.

2. Switch to Processes. Unless you started a Win 16 application earlier, you will see no entries for NTVDM.

3. Choose Start, Run and start the MS-DOS application EDIT.COM. This is the 16-bit MS-DOS Editor and comes with Windows NT in the WINN40\SYSTEM32 directory.

4. Switch back to Task Manager and notice the addition of a new NTVDM entry. Notice the amount of memory allocated for it and its priority.

5. Start one of your Windows 16-bit applications.

6. Switch back to Task Manager and notice a new NTVDM entry with subentries for the application and the WOWEXEC.EXE. Notice also its Memory Usage and CPU Usage and priority.

7. Start another Windows 16-bit application. Make a mental note of the speed with which it loaded. Since it is being loaded into an existing WOW NTVDM, it will load rather quickly.

8. Switch back to Task Manager and notice its subentry in the WOW NTVDM, as well as the memory and CPU changes.

9. Close the DOS application and both of the Win 16 applications, and note the changes in Task Manager. The WOW

NTVDM remains loaded against the event of a new Win 16 application starting, but the closed application entries have been removed.

10. Leave Task Manager running.

Exercise 2—Running 16-Bit Windows Applications in Their Own Memory Space

1. Start both of the Win 16 applications.

2. Switch to Task Manager and notice the WOW NTVDM sub-entries. On the Performance tab, note the total physical RAM in use.

3. Close one of the Win 16 applications and notice the change in physical RAM.

4. Create a shortcut on your desktop for the Win 16 application you closed. Right-click it and display its properties. On the Shortcut tab select Run in Separate Memory Space.

5. Start the Win 16 application from its shortcut. Notice that it takes a little longer to load than in the last exercise. This is because Windows NT must create a new WOW NTVDM for this application.

6. Switch back to Task Manager and confirm that a new WOW NTVDM has been created. Note its memory, CPU and priority statistics.

7. Switch to the Task Manager Performance tab and note the total physical RAM in use. It is noticeably higher than when both applications ran in the same WOW NTVDM.

8. Close each Win 16 application and monitor the decrease in physical RAM used. How many WOW NTVDM entries remain on the Processes tab? (One.)

Exercise 3—Managing Process Priorities

1. Start Pinball from Start, Programs, Accessories, Games. If it is not available, load it through the Add Programs applet in

Labs

Control Panel. (A quick way to activate a Pinball game and notice changes in this exercise is to run a demo game from the Game menu.)

2. Switch to Task Manager and find its entry. Notice its priority is set to Normal.

3. Close Pinball. Open a DOS Command Prompt window.

4. Start Pinball with a low priority by typing:

   START /LOW PINBALL

5. Switch to Task Manager and verify that Pinball is running with low priority. Pinball itself should appear to be running a bit sluggishly, though on fast Pentium systems the change may not be noticeable.

6. On the Processes tab in Task Manager, right-click the Pinball entry and choose Set Priority. Change it to normal. Switch to the Performance tab and arrange Pinball so that you can see part of the Performance charts in the background. Notice that the charts continue to record data while you play Pinball.

7. Switch to Task Manager. On the Processes tab, right-click Pinball and change its priority to high. Switch to the Performance tab and arrange the screens as before. Notice that the chart ceases to record, or records very slowly while you play Pinball in the foreground.

8. Close Pinball and Task Manager.

Chapter 10—Lab Exercises

Exercise 1—Managing Network Properties

Complete this exercise from both Computer1 and Computer2.

1. Start the Network applet from Control Panel (or right-click Network Neighborhood and view its Properties).

2. Select the Adapters tab to view your installed network adapter card.

3. Select the adapter card from the list and choose Properties. Note the properties of your adapter.

4. Close the adapter properties window and select the Bindings tab. Record the bindings for NetBEUI under NetBIOS, Workstation, and Server.

5. Select the Protocols tab and note that only NetBEUI is installed (unless you did something that I didn't tell you to do in another lab).

6. Choose Add, and select TCP/IP protocol from the network protocols list. Be sure to have the source CD-ROM available. When prompted, enter the drive and path to the source files.

7. After the protocol is installed, choose OK. Windows NT will prompt you for TCP/IP protocol settings. For Computer1, enter **121.132.4.1** with subnet mask 255.255.255.0, and for Computer2, enter **121.132.4.2** with subnet mask 255.255.255.0. (If you are connected to your company network and are using TCP/IP, use your company's recommended IP address and subnet mask, if appropriate. If you have a DHCP server available, and can use it, configure the computers to obtain their IP addresses from the DHCP server.)

8. Restart Windows NT when prompted. After Windows NT reboots, open the Network applet again.

9. On the Bindings tab, note the additional bindings for TCP/IP. Record these and compare them against the NetBEUI bindings. Notice that both bindings are bound to the Workstation and Server service. This means that you can connect to network resources on any server using NetBEUI or TCP/IP, and that your computer can service requests from any computer using NetBEUI or TCP/IP.

10. At a command prompt, enter the command IPCONFIG. What information is displayed? (IP address, subnet mask, and default gateway) Record the information.

Labs

11. Now enter the command **IPCONFIG /ALL**. What additional information is displayed? (Host, DNS, node and other Windows NT IP configuration parameters, and the description and physical address of the adapter card.) Record the adapter information.

12. At the command prompt, PING the other computer's address. For example, on Computer1 type: **PING 121.132.4.1**. You should receive four "Reply from..." messages indicating that communication is established between the computers.

13. Through Windows Explorer, map a network drive to a resource on Computer2. You should be successful. Disconnect the mapping.

14. In the Network applet on Computer1, select the Protocols tab and remove NetBEUI. Restart Windows NT when prompted.

15. After Windows NT reboots, use Windows Explorer to map a drive to the same resource on Computer2. You should be successful. Why? (Windows NT used TCP/IP to establish the connection. Computer2 has both NetBEUI and TCP/IP installed.) Disconnect the mapping.

16. In the Network applet on Computer2, select the Protocols tab and display the properties for TCP/IP.

17. Change the subnet mask to 255.255.0.0. Restart Windows NT when prompted.

18. When Computer2 reboots, use Windows Explorer on Computer1 to map a drive to the same resource on Computer2. You should be unsuccessful this time. Why? (Even though both computers are using TCP/IP and are on the same subnet, they have different subnet masks and so are treated as though they were on different subnets. Therefore, they cannot communicate with each other.)

19. At a command prompt, try the PING command again. You should be unsuccessful (for the same reason as in step 18).

20. Change the subnet mask on Computer2 back to 255.255.255.0. After the computer reboots, verify that communications can be established between the computers. (Use PING and Windows Explorer.)

21. Reinstall NetBEUI on Computer1. Restart Windows NT when prompted.

Exercise 2—Workstation Bindings

1. In the Network applet on Computer1, select the Bindings tab and expand the Workstation bindings. Highlight Workstation in the list and choose Disable to disable its bindings. Choose OK and restart Windows NT when prompted.

2. When Computer1 reboots, you will probably receive a service message error. Use Event Viewer to note which service failed to start (Workstation), and what other services dependent on it also failed to start (Computer Browser, Messenger).

3. Use Network Neighborhood to locate Computer2. Were you successful? (No, because the Workstation service is used to perform this network request, and its bindings have been disabled.)

4. Use Network Neighborhood to locate Computer1. Were you successful? (Yes. Connect to a shared folder on Computer1 and copy a file to your desktop.) Were you successful? Yes. Why? (The Server service on Computer1 handles requests for resources from other computers. These bindings are still enabled, so Computer1 can't browse the network, but it can still share its own resources. This tactic can be used to optimize bindings and improve network performance for Windows NT computers which only need to make their resources available to other computers, but not establish connections of their own.)

5. Reenable the Workstation bindings on Computer1 and restart Windows NT when prompted.

Labs

Exercise 3—Using RAS

To complete this exercise, you must have either a null modem cable to connect to the COM1 port on both computers, or modems installed in both computers and a separate working phone line and number for each.

Perform these steps on both computers. Log on as Administrator.

1. Start the Network Applet and select the Services tab.

2. Choose Add and select Remote Access Service from the list. Be sure to have the source files ready and provide Windows NT with the installation path when prompted.

3. The New Modem Wizard will appear. If you are using a modem, let Windows NT detect it. Otherwise, choose to select it yourself, and pick Dial-Up Networking Serial Cables Between 2 PCs. As you continue through the wizard, choose COM1, specify your country and area code and finish the modem installation.

4. Next, you will need to configure the COM port. In the RAS Setup dialog box, choose the COM port from the list and select Configure. On Computer1 choose Dial Out only and on Computer2 select Dial Out and Receive calls. Then choose OK.

5. Select the Network button and verify that all protocols are selected for both computers. For each protocol on Computer2 under server settings, be sure that the Entire Network option is selected. For TCP/IP, select Use Static Address Pool and enter 121.132.4.100 and 121.132.4.110 as the beginning and ending addresses.

6. Choose OK and complete RAS installation. Choose NO when asked if you want to enable NetBIOS Broadcast Propagation. Restart Windows NT when prompted.

7. After Windows NT reboots, start the Remote Access Admin program on Computer2 (from the Administrative Tools folder).

8. Choose Users, Permissions, Grant All to grant permission to all users.

9. On Computer1, start the Dial-Up Networking program from Accessories. Create a phonebook entry for Computer2 (be creative). Leave the phone number blank if using a null modem cable, or the actual phone number if you are configured with modems and separate phone lines.

10. Disconnect Computer1's network cable connection.

11. Connect the null modem cable to the COM1 port on both computers.

12. Restart Windows NT on Computer1. When the logon box appears, select Logon using Dial-Up Networking. Select the phonebook entry you created for Computer2 as your dial-up number and choose Dial. If prompted for a password, enter the appropriate password for your account. RAS will connect you to Computer2.

13. Use Windows Explorer to connect to a resource on Computer2. Were you successful? (Yes. You are connected using RAS.)

14. Note the connection statistics recorded in the Remote Access Admin utility on Computer2.

15. Start the Dial-Up Networking program again and choose Hang Up.

16. Remove RAS from both computers by starting the Network Applet, selecting Remote Access Service from the Services tab and choosing Remove, answering Yes to the warning message. Restart Windows NT when prompted.

17. Reconnect Computer1 to the network and remove the null modem cable from both computers.

Exercise 4—NetWare Connectivity

Complete this exercise if you have access to a NetWare server. Create an account on your Windows NT Workstation that matches your account and password on the NetWare server. Make this account a member of the Administrators local group on your Windows NT workstation.

1. Start the Network applet on Computer1. On the Protocols tab, select Add and choose NWLink from the list. Be sure to have the source files available. On the Services tab select Add and choose Client Services for NetWare from the list. Choose OK and restart Windows NT when prompted.

2. When Windows NT restarts, log on as the Windows NT account you created to match the account on the NetWare server. You will be prompted for a preferred NetWare server. Select the NetWare server that you have access to. And choose OK. You will be logged in to the NetWare server.

3. Start the newly added CSNW applet in Control Panel. Review the options that are available. If your NetWare server is version 4.x, enter any NDS information that is appropriate.

4. From Windows Explorer, choose Tools, Map Network Drive. Notice the new entry for NetWare or Compatible Network. Expand this entry and find your server in the list.

5. Expand the server entry and select a directory that you have access to. Connect to it. If there is another server on which you have an account, select it from the list, choose a folder, and in the Connect As box, enter the logon ID for that NetWare server. CSNW will complete the connection, no doubt asking you for a password for that server.

6. Disconnect from both NetWare servers.

7. In the CSNW applet, set the preferred server to <NONE>.

Exercise 5—Installing Peer Web Services

Complete this exercise from Computer1 logged on as Administrator.

1. Start the Network applet, select the Services tab, choose Add, and select Peer Web Services from the list. Be sure to have the source files available.

2. Select all options except ODBC drivers.

3. Accept all other defaults and complete setup. Restart Windows NT when prompted.

4. When Windows NT reboots, check the Services applet to see what additional services have been installed. (FTP Publishing, Gopher Publishing, WWW Publishing Services.)

5. From Windows Explorer, check the Windows NT system file partition for the INETPUB folder. Share it as INETPUB. Find the WINNT40\SYSTEM32\INETSRV\IISADMIN folder and copy it to INETPUB.

6. Start the Internet Explorer. Read the start up document. In the Address box enter **\\COMPUTER1\INETPUB\WWWROOT\Default.htm**. This will display one of the sample Web page documents that were installed. Browse through it clicking the hypertext links to display other documents. Be careful!! Some of those links are designed to connect you directly to Microsoft's Web site on the Internet. If you do not have Internet access, don't select these. (Hint: As you place your mouse pointer over a link, its target is displayed in the status line at the bottom of the Internet Explorer window.)

7. Start the Internet Explorer on Computer2. In the Address window, enter **\\COMPUTER1\INETPUB\WWWROOT\Default.htm**. You are using Computer1 as if it were an intranet publishing site for your workgroup. Pretty cool, huh?!

8. From either computer, enter the address **\\COMPUTER1\INETPUB\IISADMIN\HTMLDOCS\iisdocs.htm**. This is the Installation and Planning Guide for Peer Web Services where you can, as they say on television, "learn more about it!" Happy surfing!

Labs

Chapter 11—Lab Exercises

Exercise 1—Optimizing Virtual Memory

This exercise assumes that you have at least two physical disk drives installed and formatted on your computer.

1. Start Windows NT Diagnostics and determine how much RAM you have installed on your computer.

2. Start the System applet from Control Panel and switch to the Performance Tab. Choose Virtual Memory.

3. Note the location, initial, and maximum sizes of the pagefile. Verify that the pagefile is 12 + physical RAM (on some computers this may be 11 + physical RAM because of the way BIOS reads memory addresses).

4. Change the pagefile size so that the initial and maximum values are half what they were.

5. Restart the computer. You may receive a message that the pagefile is inadequately sized for the computer. If so, Windows NT will display the virtual memory window. If not, open it again.

6. Change the pagefile size back to what it was. Restart your computer and verify that the error message (if any) has gone away.

7. Open the virtual memory window again and create a second pagefile on another disk. Make it the same size as the original page file. (If you can, continue with steps 8–10. Otherwise skip to step x.)

8. Remove the original pagefile (select it and delete its initial and maximum values, and choose SET).

9. Restart Windows NT. Your computer should have started just fine. Windows NT is using the new pagefile you created on the other disk drive.

10. Open the virtual memory window again and create the original pagefile again.

11. Restart Windows NT. Your computer should start just fine. Windows NT now has two pagefiles to use and will write to each concurrently if your computer's disk controller supports it.

12. Delete the second pagefile and leave only the original. Restart Windows NT.

Exercise 2—Using Event Viewer to Troubleshoot

1. Use the Services applet in Control Panel to change the startup value for the Messenger Service to Manual.

2. Restart Windows NT. You should receive the message: "At least one service or driver failed to start."

3. Start Event Viewer and look for the first Eventlog entry for the approximate time you restarted Windows NT. Look at the message for the first Stop error right above it. This entry tells you that the Messenger service failed to start.

4. Use Services in Control Panel to set the Messenger Service startup value back to Automatic and restart the computer.

5. The error message should not now occur.

Exercise 3—Viewing Audit Events

1. If you haven't already, start User Manager. From Policy, Audit, enable auditing for successful and failed Logons and Logoffs.

2. Log on to the workstation as BrownC with the wrong password.

3. Try again with the correct password.

4. Log off and log back on as Administrator.

5. Start the Event Viewer and switch to the Security Log.

6. Locate, or filter if you wish, Logon/Logoff entries.

7. Find the entry for the incorrect password (hint: look for the "lock" icon). What information does it provide you? (Reason for the failure, the user account involved, and the workstation on which the logon attempt took place among other things.)

Labs

8. Review the entries for the successful logons.

9. Close Event Viewer.

Exercise 4—Performance Monitor

1. At a command prompt type: **DISKPERF -Y**.

2. If your computer has more than 16M RAM installed, modify the boot.ini file so that you only boot with 16M of RAM:

   To the line under [Operating Systems] that contains the location of the NT 4.0 workstation system files add the switch: /MAXMEM:16. (Remember, Boot.ini is a read-only file.)

3. Shut down and restart Windows NT to enable the Performance Monitor disk objects and their counters.

4. Start the Windows Explorer utility and Pinball.

5. Start the Performance Monitor from the Administrative Tools group and add the following objects and counters to a new chart:

6. Track the values of each of the counters you added to the chart especially noting the working set values for Performance Monitor, Windows Explorer, and Pinball (about 2.2M, 175K, and 184K, respectively). Note also the Commit Limit for the pagefile (will vary). Hint: Press CTRL+H to highlight each line graph.

7. Switch to Explorer and create a new folder called PERFMON. Switch to Pinball and start the demo game.

8. Track the activity of the chart again and note the average values for each of the counters in the chart. Note any significant changes. In particular you should have noticed a spike for %Processor Time for the processor and each of the three processes driven proportionately as each one performed its activity (creating the folder, running the demo game, updating the chart with the new statistics). Notice the flurry in disk counter activity initially, and then how it settles once the actions were performed. Notice, too, the increased amount

of memory required by Pinball and Performance Monitor to correspond with their activities. Multiply Pages/Sec and Avg. Disk sec/Transfer to obtain the percent of Disk I/O related to pagefile activity. It will be well below Microsoft's suggested 10% threshold.

9. Switch to Windows Explorer. Copy the files only from the WINNT40 directory into the Perfmon folder. While the copy is taking place, switch to the Performance Monitor and note the Pages/Sec and Avg. Disk sec/Transfer. These have all peaked at or near the top of the scale. Multiply the average value for each together to obtain a percentage. This should be just over 10% and indicates that for this activity, the percent of disk I/O related to pagefile activity was greater than Microsoft's recommended 10%. If this was consistently above 10%, you might consider adding more RAM.

10. Open the BOOT.INI file and remove the /MAXMEM:16 switch. Restart Windows NT.

11. If you have more than 16M RAM installed, repeat steps 4-9 and note the differences (all disk values and %processor times should be less, though they will vary depending on the amount of additional RAM you have).

12. Close Windows Explorer and Pinball.

Exercise 5—Performance Monitor Logs

1. With Performance Monitor still running, select View from the menu, then LOG. Choose Add to Log and add each of the following objects to the log: Logical Disk, Memory, Process, Processor. Then choose Done.

2. Select Options from the menu, then choose LOG. Enter PERF1.LOG for the log name and save it in the PERFMON folder. Set the interval to 1 second and choose Start Log.

3. Start Pinball and run the demo. Start Windows Explorer and create a new folder called PERFMON2. Copy everything from Perfmon into Perfmon2.

Labs

4. Switch to Performance Monitor. Wait another minute, then select Options, LOG, then Stop Log. Save the log file.

5. Select File, New Chart to clear and reset the chart view for new values.

6. Select Options, Data From. Under Log File, find and select the PERF1.LOG file you just created. Choose OK.

7. Select Edit, Add to Chart. Note the entries listed represent those you collected during the log process. Add the following objects and counters to the chart as you did before. This time, the chart will represent static data collected from the log.

Object	Processor	Instance
Processor	%Processor Time	0
Process	%Processor Time	Perfmon, Explorer, Pinball
Process	Working Set	Perfmon, Explorer, Pinball
Memory	Commit Limit	N/A
Memory	Pages/Sec	N/A
Logical Disk	Avg. Disk sec/ Transfer	pagefile drive
Logical Disk	%Disk Time	pagefile drive

8. Note the average values for each during the log period.

9. Use Edit, Time Window to change the time range to show only the period of peak activity. Note how the average values change.

10. Close Performance Monitor.

11. Use Windows Explorer to delete the folders Perfmon and Perfmon2.

Glossary

A

access time   If a file is executable, the last time it was run, otherwise, the last time the file was read or written to.

access-control entry (ACE)   An entry in an access-control list that defines a set of permissions for a group or user.

access-control list (ACL)   A list containing access-control entries. An ACL determines the permissions associated with an object, which can be anything in a Win32 environment.

ACE   See *access-control entry*.

ACK   Short for **acknowledgment**. A control character sent to another computer in a conversation. Usually used to indicate that transmitted information has been received correctly when using a communications protocol, such as Xmodem.

ACL See *access-control list*.

active window The window the user is currently working with. Windows identifies the active window by highlighting its title bar and border.

Advanced Program-to-Program Communications (APPC) A method of interprogram communication, usually used by applications intended for use with IBM SNA-based networks.

Advanced Research Project Agency (ARPA) The agency responsible for the formation of the forerunner to the Internet. See *Defense Advanced Research Projects Agency*.

agent Software that runs on a client computer for use by administrative software running on a server. Agents are typically used to support administrative actions, such as detecting system information or running services.

Alerter Service A Windows NT Executive service that notifies selected users or computers of system generated administrative alerts.

American National Standards Institute (ANSI) A standards-making organization based in the United States of America.

American Standard Code for Information Interchange (ASCII) A scheme that assigns letters, punctuation marks, and so on, to specific numeric values. The standardization of ASCII enabled computers and computer programs to exchange data.

ANSI See *American National Standards Institute*.

ANSI character set An 8-bit character set used by Microsoft Windows that enables you to represent up to 256 characters (0–255) using your keyboard. The ASCII character set is a subset of the ANSI set. See *American National Standards Institute*.

API See *application programming interface*.

APPC See *Advanced Program-to-Program Communications*.

application   A computer program that is designed to do some specific type of work. An application is different from a utility that performs some type of maintenance (such as formatting a disk).

application programming interface (API)   An API is a list of supported functions. Windows NT 4.0 supports the MS-DOS API, Windows API, and Win32 API. If a function is a member of the API, it is said to be a supported or documented function. Functions that make up Windows, but are not part of the API are referred to as *undocumented* functions.

ARPA   See *Advanced Research Project Agency*.

ASCII   See *American Standard Code for Information Interchange*.

ASCII character set   A 7-bit character set widely used to represent letters and symbols found on a standard U.S. keyboard. The ASCII character set is identical to the first 128 characters in the ANSI character set.

association   The process of assigning a filename extension to a particular application. When an extension has been associated with an application, Windows NT 4.0 will start the application when you choose to open the file from the Windows Explorer. Associations are critical to the concept of document-centric computing.

attributes   A characteristic of a file that indicates whether it is hidden, system, read only, archive, or compressed.

Audio Video Interleaved (AVI)   The format of the full-motion video files used by Windows NT 4.0.

Audit Policy   A definition of the type of security related events that will be recorded by the Event Viewer.

authentication   The validation of a user's access to a computer or domain by either the local computer (local validation) or a backup domain controller for the domain that the user is accessing.

AUTOEXEC.BAT   A file in the root directory of the boot disk that contains a list of MS–DOS commands that are automatically executed when the system is started. Autoexec.bat can be created by either the user or the operating system. Windows NT 4.0 Setup examines the Autoexec.bat file looking for configuration information such as user environment variables.

auxiliary audio device   Audio devices whose output is mixed with the Musical Instrument Digital Interface (MIDI) and waveform output devices in a multimedia computer. An example of an auxiliary audio device is the compact disc audio output from a CD-ROM drive.

AVI   See *Audio Video Interleaved.*

B

background window   Any window created by a thread other than the thread running in the foreground.

Backup Domain Controller   The NT controller server that performs the validation of user logon requests. The Backup Domain Controller obtains a copy of the master account database for the domain from the Primary Domain Controller.

Basic Input/Output System (BIOS)   The bootstrap code of a PC. The low-level routines that support the transfer of information between the various parts of a computer system, such as memory, disks, and the monitor. Usually built into the machine's read-only memory (ROM). The BIOS can have a significant effect on the performance of the computer system.

batch program   A file that contains one or more commands that are executed when you type the file name at the command prompt. Batch programs have the .BAT extension.

App

A

binding   The process that links a protocol driver and a network adapter driver.

BIOS   See *Basic Input/Output System*.

BIOS enumerator   In a Plug and Play system, the BIOS enumerator is responsible for identifying all of the hardware devices on the computer's motherboard.

bit   Short for **binary digit**, the smallest unit of data a computer can store. Bits are expressed as 1 or 0.

bitmap   Originally, an array of bits, but now expanded to include arrays of bytes or even 32-bit quantities that specify the dot pattern and colors that describe an image on the screen or printed paper.

BMP   The extension used for Windows bitmap files.

Boot Loader   This defines the location of the NT boot and system files.

Boot Partition   The partition that contains the NT system files.

Bootstaro Protocol (BOOTP)   This is an internetworking protocol that is used to configure TCP/IP networks across routers.

branch   A segment of the directory tree, representing a directory and any subdirectories it contains.

browse   To look through a list on a computer system. Lists include directories, files, domains, or computers.

buffer   A temporary holding place reserved in memory, where data is held while in transit to or from a storage device or another location in memory.

buffering   The process of using buffers, particularly to or from I/O devices such as disk drives and serial ports.

bus enumerator   A driver responsible for building the hardware tree on a Plug and Play system.

byte   8 bits.

C

Card Services   A protected-mode VxD, linked with the PCMCIA bus drivers. Card Services passes event notifications from socket services to the PCMCIA bus driver, provides information from the computer's cards to the PCMCIA bus driver, and sets up the configuration for cards in the adapter sockets.

cascading menu   A menu that is a submenu of a menu item. Also known as a hierarchical menu. The menus accessed via the Windows NT 4.0 Start Button are cascading menus.

CCITT   See *International Telephone and Telegraph Consultative Committee.*

CD-DA   See *Compact Disc-Digital Audio.*

CD-ROM   See *Compact Disc Read-Only Memory.*

CD-ROM/XA   See *Compact Disc-Read-Only Memory Extended Architecture.*

CD-XA   See *Compact Disc-Extended Architecture.*

CDFS   See *Compact Disc File System.*

central processing unit (CPU)   The computational and control unit of a computer; the device that interprets and executes instructions. The CPU or microprocessor, in the case of a microcomputer, has the ability to fetch, decode, and execute instructions and to transfer information to and from other resources over the computer's main data-transfer path, the bus. The CPU is the chip that functions as the "brain" of a computer.

character   A letter, number, punctuation mark, or a control code. Usually expressed in either the ANSI or ASCII character set.

character mode   A mode of displaying information on the screen, where all information is displayed using text characters (as opposed to graphical symbols). MS-DOS applications run in character mode.

check box   In the Windows NT 4.0 interface, a square box that has two or three states, and is used by the user to select an option from a set of options. A standard check box is a toggle, with two states: checked and unchecked. A three-state check box has an additional state: disabled (grayed).

class   For OLE, a data structure and the functions that manipulate that data structure. An object is a member of a class. For hardware, a grouping of devices and buses for the purpose of installing and managing devices and device drivers, and allocating the resources used by them. The Windows NT 4.0 hardware tree is organized by device class.

clear-to-send   A signal sent from one computer to another in a communications conversation to indicate readiness to accept data.

client   A computer that accesses shared network resources provided by another computer, called a server. See also *server*.

code names   A name assigned to conceal the identity or existence of something or someone. The code name for Microsoft Windows NT 4.0 was "SUR," which sometimes appears as an identifier in several places in the released product, including hardware setup files. The next major release of Windows NT is code named "Cairo."

codec   *Co*mpression/*de*compression technology for digital video and stereo audio.

COMMAND.COM   The command processor for MS-DOS. Windows NT 4.0 loads its version of Command.com (compatible with MS-DOS version 5.0) to process commands typed in MS-DOS mode, or in an MS-DOS prompt.

communications protocol   The rules that govern a conversation between two computers that are communicating via an asynchronous connection. The use of a communications protocol ensures error-free delivery of the data being communicated.

communications resource A device that provides a bidirectional, asynchronous data stream. Examples include serial and parallel ports, and modems. Applications access the resource through a service provider.

Compact Disc File System (CDFS) Controls access to the contents of CD-ROM drivers.

Compact Disc-Digital Audio (CD-DA) An optical data-storage format that provides for the storage of up to 73 minutes of high-quality digital-audio data on a compact disc. Also known as Red Book audio or music CD.

Compact Disc-Extended Architecture (CD-XA) See *Compact Disc-Read-Only Memory Extended Architecture (CD-ROM/XA)*.

Compact Disc-Read-Only Memory (CD-ROM) A form of storage characterized by high capacity (roughly 600 megabytes) and the use of laser optics rather than magnetic means for reading data.

Compact Disc-Read-Only Memory Extended Architecture (CD-ROM/XA) An extended CD-ROM format developed by Philips, Sony, and Microsoft. CD-ROM/XA format is consistent with the ISO 9660 (High Sierra) standard, with further specification of ADPCM (adaptive differential pulse code modulation) audio, images, and interleaved data.

Computer Browser Service This Executive Service identifies those NT that have resources available for use within a Workgroup or Domain.

computer name A unique name that identifies a particular computer on the network. Microsoft networking uses NetBIOS names, which can have up to 15 characters, and cannot contain spaces.

CONFIG.SYS An ASCII text file that contains configuration commands. Used by MS-DOS, OS/2, and Windows NT 4.0 to load real-mode device drivers.

Configuration Manager   One of three central components of a Plug and Play system (one for each of the three phases of configuration management). The configuration managers drive the process of locating devices, setting up the hardware tree, and allocating resources.

context menu   The menu that is displayed at the location of a set menu that is displayed when you right click. It is called the context menu because the contents of the menu depend upon the context it is invoked in.

Control Panel   The primary Windows NT 4.0 configuration tool. Each option that you can change is represented by an icon in the Control Panel window.

Controller   See *Domain Controller.*

conventional memory   The first 640KB of memory in your computer, used to run real-mode MS-DOS applications.

cooperative multitasking   A form of multitasking in which threads cooperate with each other by voluntarily giving up control of the processor. *Contrast: preemptive multitasking.*

CPU   See *central processing unit.*

crash   A serious failure of the software being used.

CTS   See *clear-to-send.*

cursor   A bitmap whose location on the screen is controlled by a pointing device, such as a mouse, pen, or trackball. See also *bitmap.*

D

DARPA   See *Defense Advanced Research Projects Agency.*

data frame   The structured packets into which data is placed by the Data Link layer.

datagram   A packet of information and delivery data that is routed on a network.

DDE   See *Dynamic Data Exchange.*

default   An operation or value that the system assumes, unless the user makes an explicit choice.

Defense Advanced Research Projects Agency (DARPA)   An agency of the U.S. Department of Defense that sponsored the development of the protocols that became the TCP/IP suite. DARPA was previously known as ARPA, the Advanced Research Project Agency, when ARPANET was built.

desktop   The background of your screen, on which windows, icons, and dialog boxes appear.

destination directory   The directory to which you intend to copy or move one or more files.

device   A generic term for a computer component, such as a printer, serial port, or disk drive. A device frequently requires its own controlling software called a device driver.

device contention   The method that Windows NT 4.0 uses to allocate access to peripheral devices when multiple applications are attempting to use them.

device driver   A piece of software that translates requests from one form into another. Most commonly, drivers are used to provide a device-independent way to access hardware.

device ID   A unique ASCII string created by enumerators to identify a hardware device and used to cross-reference data about the device stored in the Registry.

device node   One o the data structures that make up the hardware tree; a device node is built by the Configuration Manager into memory at system startup. Device nodes contain information about a given device, such as the resources it is using.

DHCP   See *Dynamic Host Configuration Protocol.*

dialog box   The type of window that is displayed by Windows NT 4.0 when user input is needed. Usually contains one or more buttons, edit controls, radio buttons, and drop-down lists.

dial-up networking   Formerly known as **remote access service (RAS)**, it provides remote access to networks. Dial-up networking allows a remote user to access their network. Once connected, it is as if the remote computer is logically on the network—the user can do anything that he or she could do when physically connected to the network.

DIP switch   Short for **Dual In-line Package switch**. Used to configure hardware options, especially on adapter cards.

Direct Memory Access (DMA)   A technique used by hardware adapters to store and retrieve information from the computer's RAM memory without involving the computer's CPU.

directory   Part of a structure for organizing your files on a disk. A directory can contain files and other directories (called subdirectories).

Directory Replication Service   This service provides a means of copying a directory and file structure from a source NT server to a target NT server or workstation.

disk caching   A method to improve performance of the file system. A section of memory is used as a temporary holding place for frequently accessed file data. Windows NT 4.0 dynamically allocates its disk cache.

disk operating system (DOS)   See *MS-DOS*.

DLL   See *dynamic-link library*.

DMA   See *Direct Memory Access*.

DMA channel   A channel for DMA transfers that occur between a device and memory directly, without involving the CPU.

DNS   See *Domain Name Service*.

DNS name servers   The servers that hold the DNS name database, and supply the IP address that matches a DNS name in response to a request from a DNS client. See also *Domain Name Service*.

dock   To insert a portable computer into a base unit. Cold docking means the computer must begin from a power-off state and restart before docking. Hot docking means the computer can be docked while running at full power.

docking station   The base computer unit into which a user can insert a portable computer, to expand it to a desktop equivalent. Docking stations usually include drives, expansion slots, AC power, network and SCSI connections, and communication ports.

document   Whatever you work with in an application.

domain   For DNS, a group of workstations and servers that share a single group name. For Microsoft networking, a collection of computers that share a security context and account database stored on a Windows NT Server domain controller. Each domain has a unique name. See also *Domain Name System*.

Domain Controller   The Windows NT Server computer that authenticates domain logons and maintains a copy of the security database for the domain.

Domain Name System (DNS)   A static, hierarchical name service for TCP/IP hosts. Do not confuse DNS domains with Windows NT domains.

DOS   See *Microsoft Disk Operating System*.

DOS Protected Mode Interface (DPMI)   A technique used to allow MS-DOS based applications to access extended memory.

dpi   Short for **dots per inch**. A measurement of the resolution of a monitor or printer.

DPMI   See *DOS Protected Mode Interface*.

drag and drop   To select one or more files, drag them to an application, and drop them there.

DRAM   See *Dynamic Random-Access Memory*.

Dynamic Data Exchange (DDE)   A form of interprocess communication (IPC) implemented in the Microsoft Windows family of operating systems. DDE uses shared memory to exchange data. Most DDE functions have been superseded by OLE.

Dynamic Host Configuration Protocol (DHCP)   A protocol for automatic TCP/IP configuration that provides static and dynamic address allocation and management.

dynamic random-access memory (DRAM)   A computer's main memory.

dynamic-link library (DLL)   File functions compiled, linked, and saved separately from the processes that use them. Functions in DLLs can be used by more than one running process. The operating system maps the DLLs into the process' address space when the process is starting up or while it is running. Dynamic-link libraries are stored in files with the .DLL extension.

E

Eform   See *electronic mail form*.

EISA   See *Extended Industry Standard Architecture*.

electronic mail (e-mail)   A message in an electronic mail system.

electronic mail form (Eform)   A programmed form used to send e-mail in an electronic mail system.

electronic messaging system (EMS)   A system that allows users or applications to correspond using a store-and-forward system.

e-mail   See *electronic mail*.

EMM   See *Expanded Memory Manager*.

EMS   See *Expanded Memory Specification; Electronic Messaging System*.

encapsulated PostScript (EPS)   A file format used to represent graphics written in the PostScript page description language.

enumerator   A Plug and Play device driver that detects devices below its own device node, creates unique device the IDs, and reports to the Configuration Manager during startup.

environment variable   A symbolic variable that represents some element of the operating system, such as a path, a file name, or other literal data. Typically used by batch files, environment variables are created with the SET command.

EPROM   See *Erasable Programmable Read-Only Memory.*

EPS   See *encapsulated PostScript.*

EPS file   A file containing code written in the Encapsulated PostScript printer programming language. Often used to represent graphics for use by desktop publishing applications.

Erasable Programmable Read–Only Memory (EPROM)
A computer chip containing non–volatile memory. It can be erased (for reprogramming) by exposure to an ultraviolet light.

event   An action or occurrence to which an application might respond, such as mouse clicks, key presses, mouse movements, or a system event. System events are any significant occurrence that may require user notification, or some other action by an application.

expanded memory   Memory that complies with the Lotus-Intel-Microsoft Expanded Memory specification. Used by MS-DOS based spreadsheet applications.

Expanded Memory Manager (EMM)   The device driver that controls access to expanded memory.

Expanded Memory Specification (EMS)   The specification that controls and defines Expanded Memory. Also known as the Lotus-Intel-Microsoft (LIM) specification, after the three major companies that designed it.

Extended Industry Standard Architecture (EISA)   An enhancement to the bus architecture used on the IBM PC/AT, which allows the use of 32-bit devices in the same type of expansion slot used by an ISA adapter card. EISA slots and adapters were formerly common in server computers, but have been mostly replaced with PCI slots.

extended memory   Memory that occupies physical addresses above the 1 megabyte mark.

Extended Memory Manager (XMM)   The MS-DOS device driver that provides access to XMS memory.

Extended Memory Specification (XMS)   The specification for the application program interfaces that allow an application to access and use extended memory.

F

family name   The name of a given font family. Windows employs five family names—*Decorative, Modern, Roman, Script,* and *Swiss.* A sixth family name, *Dontcare,* specifies the default font. See also *font family.*

FAT   See *file allocation table.*

FAT file system   A file system based on a file allocation table. Windows NT 4.0 uses a 32-bit implementation called VFAT. See *file allocation table, virtual file allocation table.*

FIFO   See *First In, First Out.*

file   A collection of information stored on a disk, and accessible using a name.

file allocation table (FAT)   A table or list maintained by some operating systems to keep track of the status of various segments of disk space used for file storage. See also *virtual file allocation table.*

file attribute   A characteristic of a file that indicates whether the file is read only, hidden, system, archived, a directory, or normal.

file sharing   The ability of a network computer to share files or directories on its local disks with remote computers.

file system   In an operating system, the overall structure in which files are named, stored, and organized.

file time   A 64-bit value representing the number of 100-nanosecond intervals that have elapsed since January 1, 1601.

file transfer program (FTP)   A utility defined by the TCP/IP protocol suite, used to transfer files between dissimilar systems.

file transfer protocol (FTP)   The standard method of transferring files using TCP/IP. FTP allows you to transfer files between dissimilar computers, with preservation of binary data, and optional translation of text file formats.

First In, First Out (FIFO)   Used to describe a buffer, where data is retrieved from the buffer in the same order it went in.

floppy disk   A disk that can be inserted and removed from a disk drive.

focus   The area of a dialog box that receives input. The focus is indicated by highlighted text or a button enclosed in dotted lines.

folder   In Windows Explorer, a container object, that is, an object that can contain other objects. Examples include disk folders, the fonts folder, and the printers folder.

font   A collection of characters, each of which has a similar appearance. For example, the Arial font.

font family   A group of fonts that have similar characteristics.

font mapper   The routine within Windows that maps an application's request for a font with particular characteristics to the available font that best matches those characteristics.

frame   See *data frame*.

free space   Unused space on a hard disk.

friendly name   A human-readable name used to give an alternative to the often cryptic computer, port, and sharenames. For example, "Digital 1152 Printer In The Hall" as opposed to "HALLPRT."

FTP   See *file transfer program, file transfer protocol*.

G

gateway   A computer connected to multiple networks, and capable of moving data between networks using different transport protocols.

GDI   See *graphics device interface*.

graphical user interface (GUI)   A computer system design in which the user interacts with the system using graphical symbols, tools and events, rather than text-based displays and commands, such as the normal Windows NT 4.0 user interface.

graphics device interface (GDI)   The subsystem that implements graphic drawing functions.

GUI   See *graphical user interface*.

H

handle   An interface (usually a small black square) added to an object to enable the user to move, size, reshape, or otherwise modify the object.

hardware branch   The hardware archive root key in the Registry, which is a superset of the memory-resident hardware tree. The name of this key is Hkey_Local_Machine\Hardware.

hardware tree   A record in RAM of the current system configuration, based on the configuration information for all devices in the hardware branch of the Registry. The Hardware tree is created each time the computer is started or whenever a dynamic change occurs to the system configuration.

high memory area (HMA)   A 64K memory block located just above the 1 MB address in a Virtual DOS Machine (VDM). Originally made possible by a side effect of the 80286 processor design, the memory is usable when the A20 address line is turned on.

High-Performance File System (HPFS)   File System primarily used with OS/2 operating system version 1.2 or later. It supports long file names but does not provide security. Windows NT 4.0 does not support HPFS.

Hive   A discrete body of Registry information, usually stored in a single disk file.

HKEY_CLASSES_ROOT   The Registry tree that contains data relating to OLE. This key is a symbolic link to a subkey of HKEY_LOCAL_MACHINE\SOFTWARE.

HKEY_CURRENT_USER   The Registry tree that contains the currently logged in user's preferences, including desktop settings, application settings and network connections. This key maps to a subkey of HKEY_USERS.

HKEY_LOCAL_MACHINE   The Registry tree that contains configuration settings that apply to the hardware and software on the computer.

HKEY_USERS   The Registry tree that contains the preferences for every user that ever logged onto this computer.

HMA   See *high memory area.*

home directory   A directory that is accessible to a particular user and contains that user's files and programs on a network server.

host   Any device that is attached to the internetwork and uses TCP/IP.

host ID   The portion of the IP address that identifies a computer within a particular network ID.

host name   The name of an internet host. It may or may not be the same as the computer name. In order for a client to access resources by host name, it must appear in the client's HOSTS file, or be resolvable by a DNS server.

host table   The HOSTS and LMHOSTS files, which contain mappings of known IP addresses mapped to host names.

HOSTS file   A local text file in the same format as the 4.3 Berkeley Software Distribution (BSD) UNIX /etc/hosts file. This file maps host names to IP addresses. In Windows NT 4.0, this file is stored in the \WINNT directory.

hotkey   Keystrokes used in place of mouse clicks.

HPFS   See *High-Performance File System.*

I

I/O addresses   One of the critical resources used in configuring devices. I/O addresses are used to communicate with devices. Also known as **port**.

I/O bus   The electrical connection between the CPU and the I/O devices. There are several types of I/O buses: ISA, EISA, SCSI, VLB, and PCI.

I/O device   Any device in or attached to a computer that is designed to receive information from, or provide information to the computer. For example, a printer is an output-only device, while a mouse is an input-only device. Other devices, such as modems, are both input and output devices, transferring data in both directions. Windows NT 4.0 must have a device driver installed in order to be able to use an I/O device.

ICMP   See *Internet control message protocol.*

icon   A small bitmap (usually 16×16 pixels or 32×32 pixels) that is associated with an application, file type, or a concept.

IEEE   See *Institute of Electrical and Electronic Engineers.*

IETF   See *Internet Engineering Task Force.*

IFS   See *installable file system.*

IHV   See *independent hardware vendor.*

independent hardware vendor (IHV)   A manufacturer of computer hardware. Usually used to describe the makers of add-on devices, rather than makers of computer systems.

Industry Standard Architecture (ISA)   A computer system that is built on the Industry Standard Architecture is one that adheres to the same design rules and constraints that the IBM PC/AT adhered to.

INF file   A file, usually provided by the manufacturer of a device, that provides the information that Windows NT 4.0 Setup needs in order to set up a device. INF files usually include a list of valid logical configurations for the device, the names of driver files associated with the device, and other information.

INI files   Initialization files used by Windows-based applications to store configuration information. Windows NT 4.0 incorporates .INI files into its Registry when upgrading from previous versions of Windows.

installable file system (IFS)   A file system that can be installed into the operating system as needed, rather than just at startup time. Windows NT 4.0 can support multiple installable file systems at one time, including the file allocation table (FAT) file system and NTFS, network redirectors and the CD-ROM file system (CDFS).

instance   A particular occurrence of an object, such as a window, module, named pipe, or DDE session. Each instance has a unique handle that distinguishes it from other instances of the same type.

Institute of Electrical and Electronic Engineers (IEEE)   An organization that issues standards for electrical and electronic devices.

Integrated Services Digital Network (ISDN)   A digital communications method that permits connections of up to 128Kbps. ISDN requires a special adapter for your computer. An ISDN connection is available in most areas of the United States for a reasonable cost.

internal command   Commands that are built-in to the COMMAND.COM file.

International Organization for Standardization (ISO)   The organization that produces many of the world's standards. Open Systems Interconnect (OSI) is only one of many areas standardized by the ISO.

International Telephone and Telegraph Consultative Committee (CCITT)   International organization that creates and publishes telecommunications standards, including X.400. The initials CCITT actually stand for the real name of the organization, which is French.

Internet   The worldwide interconnected wide-area network, based on the TCP/IP protocol suite.

Internet control message protocol (ICMP)   A required protocol in the TCP/IP protocol suite. It allows two nodes on an IP network to share IP status and error information. ICMP is used by the ping utility.

Internet Engineering Task Force (IETF)   A consortium that introduces procedures for new technology on the Internet. IETF specifications are released in documents called Requests for Comments (RFCs).

Internet group names   A name known by a DNS server that includes a list of the specific addresses of systems that have registered the name.

Internet protocol (IP)   The Network layer protocol of TCP/IP, responsible for addressing and sending TCP packets over the network.

interprocess communications (IPC)   A set of mechanisms used by applications to communicate and share data.

interrupt   An event that disrupts normal processing by the CPU, and results in the transfer of control to an interrupt handler. Both hardware devices and software can issue interrupts—software executes an INT instruction, while hardware devices signal the CPU by using one of the interrupt request (IRQ) lines to the processor.

interrupt request level (IRQL) Interrupts are ranked by priority. Interrupts that have a priority lower than the processor's interrupt request level setting can be masked (ignored).

interrupt request lines (IRQ) Hardware lines on the CPU that devices use to send signals to cause an interrupt. Normally, only one device is attached to any particular IRQ line.

IP See *Internet protocol*.

IP address Used to identify a node on a network and to specify routing information on an internetwork. Each node on the internetwork must be assigned a unique IP address, which is made up of the network ID, plus a unique host ID assigned by the network administrator. The subnet mask is used to separate an IP address into the host ID and network ID. In Windows NT 4.0, you can either assign an IP address manually, or automatically using DHCP.

IP router A system connected to multiple physical TCP/IP networks that can route or deliver IP packets between the networks. See also *gateway*.

IPC See *interprocess communications*.

IPX/SPX Internetworking Packet eXchange/Sequenced Packet eXchange. Transport protocols used in Novell NetWare networks. Windows NT 4.0 includes the Microsoft IPX/SPX compatible transport protocol (NWLINK).

IRQ See *interrupt request level*.

IRQL See *interrupt request lines*.

ISA See *Industry Standard Architecture*.

ISDN See *Integrated Services Digital Network*.

ISO See *International Organization for Standardization*.

ISO Development Environment (ISODE)   A research tool developed to study the upper layer of OSI. Academic and some commercial ISO products are based on this framework.

ISODE   See *ISO Development Environment*.

K

KB   Standard abbreviation for kilobyte; equals 1024 bytes.

Kbps   Kilobits per second

Kernel   The Windows NT 4.0 core component responsible for implementing the basic operating system functions of Windows NT 4.0 including virtual memory management, thread scheduling, and File I/O services.

L

LAN   See *local area network*.

legacy   Hardware and device cards that don't conform to the Plug and Play standard.

link   A connection at the LLC layer that is uniquely defined by the adapter's address and the destination service access point (DSAP). Also, a connection between two objects, or a reference to an object that is linked to another.

list box   In a dialog box, a box that lists available choices. For example, a list of all files in a directory. If all the choices do not fit in the list box, there is a scroll bar.

LLC   See *logical link control*.

LMHOSTS file   A local text file that maps IP addresses to the computer names of Windows networking computers. In Windows NT 4.0, LMHOSTS is stored in the WINNT directory.

local area network (LAN)   A computer network confined to a single building or campus.

local printer   A printer that is directly connected to one of the ports on your computer, as opposed to a network printer.

localization   The process of adapting software for different countries, languages, or cultures.

logical drive   A division of an extended partition on a hard disk, accessed using a drive letter.

logical link control (LLC)   One of the two sub-layers of the Data Link layer of the OSI reference model, as defined by the IEEE 802 standards. See Logical Link Control (LLC) Sublayer in Chapter 15 for more information.

login   The process by which a user is identified to the computer in a Novell NetWare network.

logon   The process by which a user is identified to the computer in a Microsoft network.

logon script   In Microsoft networking, a batch file that runs automatically when a user logs into a Windows NT Server. Novell networking also uses logon scripts, but they are not batch files.

M

MAC   See *media access control.*

MAC address   The address for a device as it is identified at the media access control layer in the network architecture. MAC addresses are usually stored in ROM on the network adapter card, and are unique.

mailslot   A form of interprocess communications used to carry messages from an application on one network node to another. Mailslots are one-way.

mailslot client   A process that writes a message to a mailslot.

mailslot server   A process that creates and owns a mailslot and can read messages from it. See also *process.*

management information base (MIB)   A set of objects used by SNMP to manage devices. MIB objects represent various types of information about a device.

mandatory user profile   This represents a user environment profile that cannot be changed by the user. If the profile is unavailable, the user will be unable to log on to the NT enterprise.

map   To translate one value into another.

MAPI   See *Messaging Application Programming Interface.*

mapped I/O, or mapped file I/O   This is the file I/O that is performed by reading and writing to virtual memory that is backed by a file.

MB   Standard abbreviation for megabyte, or 1,024 kilobytes.

MDI   See *multiple document interface.*

media access control (MAC)   The lower of the two sublayers of the data-link layer in the IEEE 802 network model.

Media Control Interface (MCI)   High-level control software that provides a device-independent interface to multimedia devices and media files. MCI includes a command-message interface and a command-string interface.

memory   A temporary storage area for information and applications.

memory object   A number of bytes allocated from the heap.

message   A structure or set of parameters used for communicating information or a request. Every event that happens in the system causes a message to be sent. Messages can be passed between the operating system and an application, different applications, threads within an application, and windows within an application.

message loop   A program loop that retrieves messages from a thread's message queue and dispatches them.

Messaging Application Program Interface (MAPI)   A set of calls used to add mail-enabled features to other Windows-based applications. One of the WOSA technologies.

metafile   A collection of structures that stores a picture in a device-independent format. (There are two metafile formats—the enhanced format and the Windows format.)

MIB   See *management information base.*

Microsoft Disk Operating System (MS-DOS)   The dominant operating system for personal computers from the introduction of the IBM Personal Computer until the introduction of Windows 95 and Windows NT 4.0.

MIDI   See *Musical Instrument Digital Interface.*

minidriver   The part of the device driver that is written by the hardware manufacturer, and provides device-specific functionality.

MS-DOS   See *Microsoft Disk Operating System.*

MS-DOS-based application   An application designed to run under MS-DOS. Windows NT 4.0 supports most MS-DOS based applications except those that communicate directly to hardware devices.

multiple document interface (MDI)   A specification that defines the standard user interface for Windows-based applications. An MDI application enables the user to work with more than one document at the same time. Microsoft Word is an example of an MDI application. Each of the documents is displayed in a separate window inside the application's main window.

multitasking   The process by which an operating system creates the illusion that many tasks are executing simultaneously on a single processor. See *cooperative multitasking* and *preemptive multitasking.*

multithreading   The ability of a process to have multiple, simultaneous paths of execution (*threads*).

Musical Instrument Digital Interface (MIDI)   A standard protocol for communication between musical instruments and computers.

N

name registration   The way a computer registers its unique name with a name server on the network, such as a WINS server.

name resolution   The process used on the network to determine the address of a computer by using its name.

named pipe   A one-way or two-way pipe used for communications between a server process and one or more client processes. A server process specifies a name when it creates one or more instances of a named pipe. Each instance of the pipe can be connected to a client. Microsoft SQL Server clients use named pipes to communicate with the SQL Server.

NBF transport protocol   NetBEUI frame protocol. A descendant of the NetBEUI protocol, which is a Transport layer protocol, not the programming interface NetBIOS.

NCB   See *network control block.*

NDIS   See *network device interface specification.*

NetBEUI transport   NetBIOS (Network Basic Input/Output System) Extended User Interface. A transport protocol designed for use on small subnets. It is not routable, but it is fast.

NetBIOS interface   A programming interface that allows I/O requests to be sent to and received from a remote computer. It hides networking hardware from applications.

NetBIOS over TCP/IP   The networking module that provides the functionality to support NetBIOS name registration and resolution across a TCP/IP network.

network   A group of computers and other devices that can interact by means of a shared communications link.

network adapter driver   Software that implements the lower layers of a network, providing a standard interface to the network card.

network basic input/output system (NetBIOS)   A software interface for network communication. See *NetBIOS interface*.

network control block (NCB)   A structured memory used to communicate with the NetBIOS interface.

Network DDE DSDM service   The Network DDE DSDM (DDE share database manager) service manages shared DDE conversations. It is used by the Network DDE service.

Network DDE service   The Network DDE (dynamic data exchange) service provides a network transport and security for DDE conversations. Network DDE is supported in Windows NT 4.0 for backward compatibility, as most of its functions are superseded by OLE.

network device driver   Software that coordinates communication between the network adapter card and the computer's hardware and other software, controlling the physical function of the network adapter cards.

network device interface specification (NDIS)   In Windows networking, the interface for network adapter drivers. All transport drivers call the NDIS interface to access network adapter cards.

network directory   See *shared directory*.

Network File System (NFS)   A service for distributed computing systems that provides a distributed file system, eliminating the need for keeping multiple copies of files on separate computers. Usually used in connection with UNIX computers.

network ID   The portion of the IP address that identifies a group of computers and devices located on the same logical network. Separated from the Host ID using the subnet mask.

Network Information Service (NIS)   A service for distributed computing systems that provides a distributed database system for common configuration files.

network interface card (NIC)   An adapter card that connects a computer to a network.

network operating system (NOS)   The operating system used on network servers, such as Windows NT Server or Novell NetWare.

network provider   The Windows NT 4.0 component that allows Windows NT 4.0 to communicate with the network. Windows NT 4.0 includes providers for Microsoft networks and for Novell NetWare networks. Other network vendors may supply providers for their networks.

network transport   This can be either a particular layer of the OSI Reference Model between the network layer and the session layer, or the protocol used between this layer on two different computers on a network.

network–interface printers   Printers with built-in network cards, such as Hewlett-Packard laser printers equipped with Jet Direct cards. The advantage of network-interface printers is that they can be located anywhere on the network.

New Technology file system (NTFS)   The native file system used by Windows NT 4.0 which supplies file and directory security, sector sparing, compression, and other performance characteristics.

NIC   See *network interface card.*

NIS   See *Network Information Service.*

NOS   See *network operating system.*

NTFS   See *Windows NT file system.*

O

Object Linking and Embedding (OLE)   The specification that details the implementation of Windows objects, and the interprocess communication that supports them.

object   A particular instance of a class. Most of the internal data structures in Windows NT 4.0 are objects.

OCR   See *Optical Character Recognition.*

OEM   See *original equipment manufacturer.*

OLE   See *Object Linking and Embedding.*

Open Systems Interconnect (OSI)   The networking architecture reference model created by the ISO.

operating system (OS)   The software that provides an interface between a user or application and the computer hardware. Operating system services usually include memory and resource management, I/O services, and file handling. Examples include Windows NT 4.0, Windows NT, and UNIX.

Optical Character Recognition (OCR)   A technology that is used to generate editable text from a graphic image.

original equipment manufacturer (OEM)   Software that is sold by Microsoft to OEMs only includes the operating system versions that are preloaded on computers before they are sold.

OS   See *operating system.*

OSI   See *Open Systems Interconnect.*

P

PAB   See *personal address book.*

packet   A transmission unit of fixed maximum size that consists of binary information representing both data, addressing information, and error-correction information, created by the data-link layer.

page   A unit of memory used by the system in managing memory. The size of a page is computer-dependent (the Intel 486 computer, and therefore, Windows NT 4.0, uses 4K pages).

page map   An internal data structure used by the system to keep track of the mapping between the pages in a process' virtual address space, and the corresponding pages in physical memory.

paged pool   The portion of system memory that can be paged to disk.

paging file   A storage file (pagefile.sys) the system uses to hold pages of memory swapped out of RAM. Also known as a swap file.

parity   Refers to an error-checking procedure in which the number of 1s must always be the same (either even or odd) for each group of bits transmitted without error. Also used in the main RAM system of a computer to verify the validity of data contained in RAM.

partition   A partition is a portion of a physical disk that functions as though it were a physically separate unit. See also system partition.

partition table   The partition table contains entries showing the start and end point of each of the primary partitions on the disk. The partition table can hold four entries.

password   A security measure used to restrict access to computer systems. A password is a unique string of characters that must be provided before a logon or an access is authorized.

path   The location of a file or directory. The path describes the location in relation to either the root directory, or the current directory, for example, C:\WINNT\System32. Also, a graphic object that represents one or more shapes.

PCI   See *peripheral component interconnect*.

PCMCIA   See *Personal Computer Memory Card International Association*.

performance monitoring   The process of determining the system resources an application uses, such as processor time and memory. Done with the Windows NT 4.0 Performance Monitor.

Peripheral Component Interconnect (PCI)   The local bus being promoted as the successor to VL. This type of device is used in most Intel Pentium computers and in the Apple PowerPC Macintosh.

persistent connection   A network connection that is restored automatically when the user logs on. In Windows NT 4.0, persistent connections are created by selecting the Reconnect at Logon checkbox.

personal address book (PAB)   One of the information services provided with the Microsoft Exchange client included with Windows NT 4.0. It is used to store the name and e-mail address of people you correspond with.

Personal Computer Memory Card International Association (PCMCIA)   The industry association of manufacturers of credit-card sized adapter cards (PC cards).

PFF   See *printer file format.*

PIF   See *program information file.*

pixel   Short for **picture element**, a dot that represents the smallest graphic unit of measurement on a screen. The actual size of a pixel is screen-dependent, and varies according to the size of the screen and the resolution being used. Also known as *pel.*

platform   The hardware and software required for an application to run.

Plug and Play   A computer industry specification, intended to ease the process of configuring hardware.

Plug and Play BIOS   A BIOS with responsibility for configuring Plug and Play cards and system board devices during system power-up, provides runtime configuration services for system board devices after startup.

p-node   A NetBIOS implementation that uses point-to-point communications with a name server to resolve names as IP addresses.

Point-to-Point Protocol (PPP)   The industry standard that is implemented in dial-up networking. PPP is a line protocol used to connect to remote networking services, including Internet Service Providers. Prior to the introduction of PPP, another line protocol, SLIP, was used.

pointer   The arrow-shaped cursor on the screen that follows the movement of a mouse (or other pointing device) and indicates which area of the screen will be affected when you press the mouse button. The pointer may change shape during certain tasks.

port   The socket that you connect the cable for a peripheral device to. See *I/O address*.

port ID   The method TCP and UDP use to specify which application running on the system is sending or receiving the data.

Postoffice   The message store used by Microsoft Mail to hold the mail messages. It exists only as a structure of directories on disk, and does not contain any active components.

PostScript   A page-description language, developed by Adobe Systems, Inc., that offers flexible font capability and high-quality graphics. PostScript uses English-like commands to control page layout and to load and scale fonts.

PPP   See *Point-to-Point Protocol*.

preemptive multitasking   A multitasking technique that breaks time up into timeslices, during which the operating system allows a particular program thread to run. The operating system can interrupt any running thread at any time. Preemptive multitasking usually results in the best use of CPU time, and overall better perceived throughput. See also *cooperative multitasking*.

primary partition   A primary partition is a portion of a physical disk that can be marked for use by an operating system. There can be up to four primary partitions (or up to three, if there is an extended partition) per physical disk. A primary partition cannot be subpartitioned.

print device   Refers to the actual hardware device that produces printed output.

print monitor   Keeps track of printers and print devices. Responsible for transferring information from the print driver to the printing device, including any necessary flow control.

print provider   A software component that allows the client to print to a network printer. Windows NT 4.0 includes print providers for Microsoft networks and Novell networks.

printer driver The component that translates GDI objects into printer commands.

printer fonts Fonts that are built into your printer.

priority class A process priority category (high, normal, or idle) used to determine the scheduling priorities of a process' threads. Each priority class has five levels. See also *thread*.

private memory Memory owned by a process, and not accessible by other processes.

privileged instruction Processor-privileged instructions have access to system memory and the hardware. Privileged instructions can only be executed by Ring 0 components.

process The virtual address space, code, data, and other operating system resources, such as files, pipes, and synchronization objects that make up an executing application. In addition to resources, a process contains at least one thread that executes the process' code.

profile A set of data describing a particular configuration of a computer. This information can describe a user's preferences (user profile) or the hardware configuration. Profiles are usually stored in the Registry; for example, the key HKEY_USERS contains the profiles for the various users of the computer.

program file A file that starts an application or program. A program file has an .EXE, .PIF, .COM, or .BAT file name extension.

program information file (PIF) Windows NT 4.0 stores information about how to configure the VM for running MS-DOS applications in PIF files.

Programmable Read-Only Memory (PROM) A type of integrated circuit usually used to store a computer's BIOS. PROM chips, once programmed, can only be read from, not written to.

PROM See *Programmable Read-Only Memory*.

properties The dialogs that are used to configure a particular object in Windows NT 4.0.

protocol   A set of rules and conventions by which two computers pass messages across a network. Protocols are used between instances of a particular layer on each computer. Windows NT 4.0 includes NetBEUI, TCP/IP, and IPX/SPX-compatible protocols. See also *communications protocol*.

provider   The component that allows Windows NT 4.0 to communicate with the network. Windows NT 4.0 includes providers for Microsoft and Novell networks.

R

RAM   See *random-access memory*.

random-access memory (RAM)   The RAM memory in a computer is the computer's main memory, where programs and data are stored while the program is running. Information stored in RAM is lost when the computer is turned off.

read-only   A device, document, or file is read-only if you are not permitted to make changes to it.

read-write   A device, document, or file is read-write if you can make changes to it.

reboot   To restart a computer. To reboot a Windows NT 4.0 computer, click the Start Button, choose Shutdown, and then choose Restart Your Computer.

redirector   The networking component that intercepts file i/o requests and translates them into network requests. Redirectors (also called network clients) are implemented as installable file system drivers in Windows NT 4.0.

REG_BINARY   A data type for Registry value entries that designates binary data.

REG_DWORD   A data type for Registry value entries that designates data represented by a number that is 4 bytes long.

REG_SZ A data type for Registry value entries that designates a data string that usually represents human readable text.

Registry Windows NT 4.0's and Windows NT's binary system configuration database.

Registry Editor (REGEDT32.EXE) A utility supplied with Windows NT 4.0 that allows the user to view and edit Registry keys and values.

Registry key A Registry entry that can contain other Registry entries.

remote access service (RAS) An NT Executive service that provides remote networking access to the NT Enterprise for telecommuters, remote users system administrators, and home users. (See *dial-up networking*.)

remote administration The process of administrating one computer from another computer across a network.

remote initiation program load (RIPL) A technique that allows a workstation to boot by using an image file on a network server instead of a disk.

remote procedure call (RPC) An industry-standard method of interprocess communication across a network. Used by many administration tools.

Requests for Comments (RFCs) The official documents of the Internet Engineering Task Force that specify the details for protocols included in the TCP/IP family.

requirements The conceptual design and functional description of a software product, and any associated materials. Requirements describe the features, user interface, documentation, and other functionalities the product will provide.

resource Windows resources include icons, cursors, menus, dialog boxes, bitmaps, fonts, keyboard-accelerator tables, message-table entries, string-table entries, version data, and user-defined data. The resources used by an application are either part of the system, or private resources stored in the application's program file. Also, a part of a computer system that can be assigned to a running process, such as a disk drive, or memory segment.

RFC   See *Requests for Comments*.

RID   See *relative identifier*.

RIP   See *routing information protocol*.

RIPL   See *remote initiation program load*.

ROM BIOS   See *Read-Only Memory Basic Input/Output System*.

ROM   See *read-only memory*.

root directory   See *directory tree*.

router   A computer with two or more network adapters, each attached to a different subnet. The router forwards packets on a subnet to the subnet that they are addressed to.

routing   The process of forwarding packets until they reach their destination.

routing information protocol (RIP)   A protocol that supports dynamic routing. Used between routers.

RPC   See *remote procedure call*.

RPC server   The program or computer that processes remote procedure calls from a client.

S

SAM Database   The registry database that contains the user and group account information, as well as user account policies. It is managed by the User Manager or User Manager for Domains utility.

screen buffer   A memory buffer that holds a representation of an MS–DOS VM's logical screen.

screen saver   Pictures or patterns that appear on your screen when your computer has not been used for a certain amount of time. Originally intended to protect the monitor from damage, modern screen savers are used mostly for their entertainment value.

scroll   To move through text or graphics (up, down, left, or right) in order to see parts of the file that cannot fit on the screen.

scroll arrow   An arrow on either end of a scroll bar that you use to scroll through the contents of the window or list box.

scroll bar   A bar that appears at the right or bottom edge of a window or list box whose contents are not completely visible. The scroll bar consists of two scroll arrows and a scroll box, which you use to scroll through the contents.

scroll box   In a scroll bar, a small box that shows where the information currently visible is, relative to the contents of the entire window.

SCSI   See *Small Computer System Interface*.

Security ID (SID)   The unique randomly generated alphanumeric identifier assigned by NT when a new user, group, trust, or other security object is created.

sequence number   Sequence numbers are used by a receiving node to properly order packets.

Serial Line Internet Protocol (SLIP)   The predecessor to PPP, SLIP is a line protocol supporting TCP/IP over a modem connection. SLIP support is provided for NT 4.0. See also *Point-to-Point Protocol*.

server   A computer or application that provides shared resources to clients across a network. Resources include files and directories, printers, fax modems, and network database services. See also *client*.

server message block (SMB)   A block of data that contains a work request from a workstation to a server, or that contains the response from the server to the workstation. SMBs are used for all network communications in a Microsoft network.

server service   An Executive Service that makes resources available to the workgroup or domain for file, print, and other RPC services.

service   A process that performs a specific system function and often provides an application programming interface (API) for other processes to call. Windows NT 4.0 services Computer Browser, Server, and Workstation.

session   A layer of the OSI reference model that performs name recognition and the functions needed to allow two applications to communicate over the network. Also, a communication channel established by the session layer.

share   In Microsoft networking, the process of making resources, such as directories and printers, available for network users.

share name   The name that a shared resource is accessed by on the network.

shared directory   A directory that has been shared so that network users can connect to.

shared memory   Memory that two or more processes can read from and write to.

shared network directory   See *shared directory*.

shared resource   Any device, data, or program that is used by more than one other device or program. Windows NT 4.0 can share directories and printers.

sharepoint   A shared network resource, or the name that one is known by.

shell   The part of an operating system that the user interacts with. The Windows NT 4.0 shell is Windows Explorer.

shortcut key   A combination of keys that result in the execution of a program, or selection of an option, without going through a menu.

shut down   The process of properly terminating all running programs, flushing caches, and preparing the system to be powered off.

signaled   One of the possible states of a mutex.

SIMM   See *Single In-Line Memory Module*.

Simple Mail Transfer Protocol (SMTP)   The application layer protocol that supports messaging functions over the Internet.

Simple Network Management Protocol (SNMP)   A standard protocol for the management of network components. Windows NT 4.0 includes an SNMP agent.

Single In-Line Memory Module (SIMM)   One of the types of RAM chips.

SLIP   See *Serial Line Internet Protocol*.

Small Computer System Interface (SCSI)   A standard for connecting multiple devices to a computer system. SCSI devices are connected together in a daisy chain, which can have up to seven devices (plus a controller) on it (pronounced "scuzzy").

SMB   See *server message block*.

SMTP   See *Simple Mail Transfer Protocol*.

SNMP   See *Simple Network Management Protocol*.

socket   A channel used for incoming and outgoing data defined by the Windows Sockets API. Usually used with TCP/IP.

socket services   The protected-mode VxD that manages PCMCIA sockets adapter hardware. It provides a protected-mode PCMCIA

Socket Services 2.x interface for use by Card Services. A socket services driver is required for each socket adapter.

source directory   The directory where files in a copy or move operation start out in.

spooler   A scheduler for the printing process. It coordinates activity among other components of the print model and schedules all print jobs arriving at the print server.

static VxD   A VxD that is loaded at system startup.

string   A sequence of characters representing human-readable text.

subdirectory   A directory within a directory.

subkey   A Registry key contained within another Registry key. All Registry keys are subkeys except for the six top-level keys.

subnet   On the Internet, any lower network that is part of the logical network identified by the network ID.

subnet mask   A 32-bit value that is used to distinguish the network ID portion of the IP address from the host ID.

swap file   A special file on your hard disk that is used to hold memory pages that are swapped out of RAM. Also called a paging file.

syntax   The order in which you must type a command and the elements that follow the command.

system directory   The directory that contains the Windows DLLs and drivers. Usually c—\windows\system.

system disk   A disk that contains the files necessary to start an operating system.

system partition   The volume that contains the hardware-specific files needed to load Windows NT 4.0.

T

TAPI   See *Telephony Application Program Interface*.

TCP/IP transport   Transmission Control Protocol/Internet Protocol. The primary wide area network (WAN) transport protocol used on the worldwide Internet, which is a worldwide internetwork of universities, research laboratories, military installations, organizations, and corporations. TCP/IP includes standards for how computers communicate and conventions for connecting networks and routing traffic, as well as specifications for utilities.

TCP   See *Transmission Control Protocol*.

TDI   See *transport driver interface*.

Telephony Application Program Interface (TAPI)   An API that enables applications to control modems and telephony equipment in a device-independent manner. TAPI routes application function calls to the appropriate "Service Provider" DLL for a modem.

telnet   The application layer protocol that provides virtual terminal service on TCP/IP networks.

Terminate and Stay-Resident (TSR)   A technique, used by MS-DOS applications, that allows more than one program to be loaded at a time.

text file   A file containing only ASCII letters, numbers, and symbols, without any formatting information except for carriage return/linefeeds.

thread   The basic entity to which the operating system allocates CPU time. A thread can execute any part of the application's code, including a part currently being executed by another thread (re-entrancy). Threads cannot own resources; instead, they use the resources of the process they belong to.

thread local storage   A storage method in which an index can be used by multiple threads of the same process to store and retrieve a different value for each thread. See also *thread*.

thunking   The transformation between 16-bit and 32-bit formats, which is carried out by a separate layer in the VDM.

time-out   If a device is not performing a task, the amount of time the computer should wait before detecting it as an error.

toolbar   A frame containing a series of shortcut buttons providing quick access to commands, usually located below the menu bar, although many applications provide "dockable" toolbars, which may be moved to different locations on the screen.

Transmission Control Protocol (TCP)   A connection-based protocol, responsible for breaking data into packets, which the IP protocol sends over the network. This protocol provides a reliable, sequenced communication stream for internetwork communication.

Transmission Control Protocol/Internet Protocol (TCP/IP)   The primary wide area network used on the worldwide Internet, which is a worldwide internetwork of universities, research laboratories, military installations, organizations, and corporations. TCP/IP includes standards for how computers communicate and conventions for connecting networks and routing traffic, as well as specifications for utilities.

transport driver interface (TDI)   The interface between the session layer and the network layer, used by network redirectors and servers to send network-bound requests to network transport drivers.

transport protocol   Defines how data should be presented to the next receiving layer in the networking model and packages the data accordingly. It passes data to the network adapter card driver through the NDIS Interface, and to the redirector through the Transport Driver Interface.

TrueType fonts   Fonts that are scaleable and sometimes generated as bitmaps or soft fonts, depending on the capabilities of your printer. TrueType fonts can be sized to any height, and they print exactly as they appear on the screen. They are stored as a collection of line and curve commands, together with a collection of hints that are used to adjust the shapes when the font is scaled.

trust relationship   A security relationship between two domains in which the resource domain "trusts"the user of a trusted account domain to use its resources. Users and groups from a trusted domain can be given access permissions to resources in a trusting domain.

TSR   See *Terminate and Stay-Resident.*

U

UDP   See *user datagram protocol.*

UMB   See *Upper Memory Block.*

UNC   See *universal naming convention.*

Unimodem   The universal modem driver used by TAPI to communicate with modems. It uses modem description files to control its interaction with VCOMM.

uninterruptible power supply (UPS)   A battery operated power supply connected to a computer to keep the system running during a power failure.

universal naming convention (UNC)   Naming convention, including a server name and share name, used to give a unique name to files on a network. The format is as follows:

\\servername\sharename\path\filename

UPS   See *uninterruptible power supply.*

UPS service   A software component that monitors an uninterruptible power supply, and shuts the computer down gracefully when line power has failed, and the UPS battery is running down.

usability   A determination of how well users can accomplish tasks using a software product. Usability considers the characteristics of a product such as software, manuals, tutorials, help, and so on.

user account   Refers to all the information that identifies a user to Windows NT 4.0, including user name and password, group membership, and rights and permissions.

user datagram protocol (UDP)   The transport protocol offering a connectionless-mode transport service in the Internet suite of protocols. See *Transport Control Protocol*.

user name   A unique name identifying a user account in Windows NT 4.0. User names must be unique, and cannot be the same as another user name, workgroup, or domain name.

V

value entry   A parameter under a key or subkey in the Registry. A value entry has three components: name, type, and value. The value component can be a string, binary data, or a DWORD.

VCPI   See *virtual control program interface*.

VDM   See *virtual DOS machine*.

VFAT   See *virtual file allocation table*.

virtual DOS machine (VDM)   A virtual machine provides a complete MS-DOS environment and a character-based window in which to run an MS-DOS based application. Every MS-DOS application runs in its own VDM.

virtual file allocation table (VFAT)   See also *file allocation table*.

virtual machine (VM)   An environment created by the operating system in memory. By using virtual machines, the application developer can write programs that behave as though they own the entire computer. This leaves the job of sorting out, for example, which application is receiving keyboard input at the moment, to Windows NT 4.0.

virtual memory   The technique by which Windows NT 4.0 uses hard disk space to increase the amount of memory available for running programs.

visual editing   The ability to edit an embedded object in place, without opening it into its own window. Implemented by OLE.

VL   Local bus standard for a bus that allows high-speed connections to peripherals, which preceded the PCI specification. Due to limitations in the specification, usually only used to connect video adapters into the system. Also known as VESA bus.

VM   See *virtual machine*.

volume   A partition that has been formatted for use by the file system.

VxD   Virtual device driver. The x represents the type of device—for example, a virtual device driver for a display is a VDD and a virtual device driver for a printer is a VPD.

W

wild card   A character that is used to represent one or more characters, such as in a file specification. The question mark (?) wild card can be used to represent any single character, and the asterisk (★) wild card can be used to represent any character or group of characters that might match that position in other file names.

Win32 API   The 32-bit application programming interface used to write 32-bit Windows based applications. It provides access to operating systems and other functions.

window handle   A 32-bit value that uniquely identifies a window to Windows NT 4.0.

window name   A text string that identifies a window for the user.

Windows Internet Name Service (WINS)   A name resolution service that resolve Windows networking computer names to IP addresses in a routed environment. A WINS server handles name registrations, queries, and releases.

App
A

Windows NT   The portable, secure, 32-bit preemptive-multitasking member of the Microsoft Windows Operating system family. Windows NT server provides centralized management and security, advanced fault tolerance, and additional connectivity. Windows NT Workstation provides operating system and networking functionality for computers without centralized management.

Windows NT file system (NTFS)   The native file system used by Windows NT. Windows NT 4.0 can detect, but not use, NTFS partitions.

WINS   See *Windows Internet Name Service.*

Wizard   A Windows NT 4.0 tool that asks you questions and performs a system action according to your answers. For example, you can use the Add Printer Wizard to add new printer drivers or connect to an existing network printer.

workgroup   A collection of computers that are grouped for viewing purposes, but do not share security information. Each workgroup is identified by a unique name. See also *domain.*

workstation service   This is the NT computer's redirector. It redirects requests for network resources to the appropriate protocol and network card for access to the server computer.

WYSIWYG   Stands for "What You See Is What You Get."

X

X.121   The addressing format used by X.25 base networks.

X.25   A connection-oriented network facility.

x86-based computer   A computer using a microprocessor equivalent to an Intel 80386 or higher chip. Only x86-based computers can run Windows NT 4.0.

X.400   An international messaging standard, used in electronic mail systems.

XModem/CRC   A communications protocol for transmitting binary files that uses a cyclic redundancy check (CRC) to detect any transmission errors. Both computers must be set to transmit and receive eight data bits per character.

XMS   See *Extended Memory Specification.*

B

Certification Checklist

In addition to a resource like this book, this list of tasks tells you what you need to know to get on with the certification process.

Get Started

Once you have decided to start the certification process, you should use the following list as a guideline for getting you started:

1. Get the Microsoft Roadmap to Education and Certification. (See "The Certification Roadmap" sidebar at the end of this appendix.)
2. Use the Roadmap Planning Wizard to determine *your* certification path.

3. Take the Windows NT 4.0 Assessment Exams located on the CD that accompanies this book to determine your competency level. For Microsoft products other than Windows NT 4.0, you can use the Assessment Exams located on the Roadmap to get a feel for the type of questions that appear on the exam. (See "Assessment Exams" in Appendix C.)

Get Prepared

Getting started is one thing, but getting prepared to take the certification exam is a rather difficult process. The following guidelines will help you prepare for the exam:

1. Use the training materials listed in the Planning Wizard:

    • Microsoft Online Institute (MOLI). (See "The Microsoft Online Training Institute," in Appendix C.)

    • Self-Paced Training (See "Self-Paced Training," in Appendix C.)

    • Authorized Technical Education Center (ATEC). (See "Training Resources," in Appendix C.)

    • Additional study materials listed in the Roadmap

2. Review the Exam Study Guide in Appendix C.

3. Review the Exam Prep Guide on the Roadmap.

4. Gain experience with Windows NT 4.0.

Get Certified

Call Sylvan Prometric at 1-800-755-EXAM to schedule your exam at a location near you. (See "How Do I Register for the Exam?" in Appendix C; and Appendix D, "Testing Tips.")

Get Benefits

Microsoft will send your certification kit approximately 2–4 weeks after passing the exam. This kit qualifies you to become a Microsoft Certified Professional. (See "Benefits Up Close and Personal," in the Introduction to this book.)

The Certification Roadmap

The Microsoft Roadmap to Education and Certification is an easy-to-use Windows-based application that includes all the information you need to plan a successful training and certification strategy. The roadmap:

App
B

- Provides comprehensive information on the requirements for Microsoft Certified Professional certifications, with detailed exam topic outlines and preparation guidelines.

- Includes detailed outlines and prerequisites for Microsoft courses that are related to specific certification exams, helping you determine which courses teach the skills you need to meet your certification goals.

- Includes information on related Microsoft products and services.

- Helps you create a personal training and certification plan and print a to-do list of required certification activities.

You can request the Roadmap from Microsoft. In the U.S. and Canada, call 1-800-636-7544. Outside the U.S. and Canada, contact your local Microsoft office.

Or you can download it at the following online addresses:

- The Internet: **ftp://ftp.microsoft.com/Services/MSEdCert/E&CMAP.ZIP**

- The Microsoft Network (MSN): Go To MOLI, Advising Building, E&C Roadmap.

- Microsoft TechNet: Search for "Roadmap" and install from the built-in setup link.

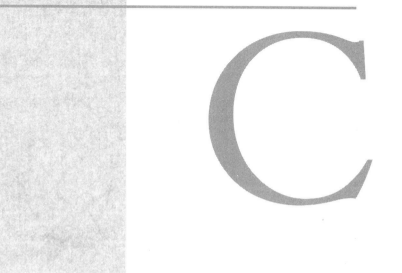

How Do I Get There from Here?

Becoming certified requires a certain level of commitment. The information in this appendix will answer some of the questions you may have about the certification process.

What Will I Be Tested On?

You should be able to apply your knowledge and experience with Windows NT 4.0 to perform the following tasks:

- Plan for and install Windows NT Workstation 4.0.
- Install software or hardware and run applications.
- Answer "how-to" questions from users.

- ◆ Tune and optimize your Windows NT Workstation 4.0.
- ◆ Customize the Windows NT Workstation 4.0 system and user environments.
- ◆ Install, manage, and configure the network components of Windows NT Workstation 4.0.
- ◆ Create and manage user accounts.
- ◆ Create, manage, and secure local resources.
- ◆ Troubleshoot systems and solve user hardware or software problems.
- ◆ Recommend software products, versions, or upgrades.
- ◆ Collect requests for additional software features and functions.

To successfully complete the Windows NT Workstation 4.0 Exam, you need, according to Microsoft, "A comprehensive understanding of Microsoft Windows NT Workstation 4.0 concepts and procedures, and you should be able to analyze what you know about Microsoft Windows NT Workstation 4.0 to synthesize configuration, optimization, and troubleshooting decisions and situations."

Analysis Is Good, but Synthesis Is Harder

Microsoft Certified Professional exams test for specific cognitive skills needed for the job functions being tested. Educational theorists postulate a hierarchy of cognitive levels, ranging from the most basic (knowledge) up to the most difficult (evaluation), and a set of skills associated with each level:

- ◆ *Knowledge* is the lowest cognitive level at which you can identify, define, locate, recall, state, match, arrange, label, outline, and recognize items, situations, and concepts. Questions that ask for definitions or recitation of lists of characteristics test at this level.

◆ *Comprehension*, the level built immediately upon knowledge, requires that you translate, distinguish between, give examples, discuss, draw conclusions, estimate, explain, indicate, and paraphrase, rather than simply play back answers learned by rote.

◆ *Application* is the level at which hands-on activities come into play. Questions at this level ask you to apply, calculate, solve, plot, choose, demonstrate, design a procedure, change, interpret, or operate.

◆ *Analysis*, one of the top three levels, requires a thorough grounding in the skills required at lower levels. You operate at this level when you analyze, state conclusions, detect logic errors, compare and contrast, break down, make an inference from, map one situation or problem to another, diagnose, diagram, or discriminate.

◆ *Synthesis* (which is harder than analysis) requires some creativity and the ability to rebuild and reintegrate what may have been disassembled during analysis. This level requires you to construct a table or graph, design, formulate, integrate, generalize, predict, arrange, propose, tell in your own words, or show the relationship between.

◆ *Evaluation*, the highest cognitive level, is based on all the skills accumulated at lower levels. At this level, you assess, apply standards, decide, indicate fallacies, weigh, show the relationship between, summarize, look at situations and tell what is likely to occur, or make a judgment.

App
C

Exam Objectives

The following list of objectives defines the specific skills Microsoft wants the exam to measure. As you review the list, you can see the level at which the Windows NT Workstation 4.0 exam tests your knowledge and ability to implement, maintain, and troubleshoot the operating system. When an objective or item on the exam includes a verb or verb phrase associated with a given cognitive level (see the preceding section, "Analysis Is Good, but Synthesis Is Harder"), it is asking you to perform at that cognitive level.

For example, the exam objective "Choose when to use Windows NT Workstation 4.0 in a workgroup or domain environment" asks you to perform at the Analysis level because it asks you to make a determination between two network communication models. It's a good idea to be prepared to be tested at the Analysis level or higher for each objective.

You should review the following objectives and be able to apply the listed skills to the tasks described earlier in the section "What Will I Be Tested On?"

Planning

You will be tested for the following planning skills:

- ◈ Create unattended installation files.
- ◈ Choose when to use Windows NT Workstation 4.0 or other Microsoft operating systems, such as Windows NT Server 4.0 or Windows 95, for a given situation.
- ◈ Plan strategies for sharing and securing resources.
- ◈ Choose the appropriate file system (NTFS, FAT, HPFS, Security, Multiple-boot) to use in a given situation.
- ◈ Choose when to use Windows NT Workstation 4.0 in a workgroup or domain environment.

Installation and Configuration

You will be tested for your understanding of the installation process, as well as the various methods and tools available to configure the Windows NT system and user environment. Specific topics include:

◆ Install Windows NT Workstation 4.0 on an Intel platform from a compact disc, using WINNT and WINNT32 with setup switches, a uniqueness data file (UDF), and a boot disk.

◆ Set up a multiple-boot system between Windows NT Workstation and Server 4.0, Windows NT Workstation 4.0 and MS-DOS, and Windows NT Workstation 4.0 and Windows 3.0 and 95 through the installation process, and modifying the boot.ini file.

◆ Deinstall Windows NT Workstation 4.0 in a given situation.

◆ Install, configure, and remove hardware components such as network adapters, SCSI devices, tape devices, UPS, multimedia, display, keyboard, and mouse.

◆ Use the Control Panel applications to configure the Windows NT Workstation 4.0 system and user environments by creating user profiles, creating and managing hardware profiles, configuring telephony, adding and removing programs, starting and stopping services, and changing the computer or domain name.

◆ Upgrade to Windows NT Workstation 4.0 from Windows NT 3.x Workstation, MS-DOS, and Windows 95.

◆ Configure automated or unattended server-based installation for wide-scale deployment by creating an Unattended.txt file and a UDF, using the Sysdiff utility, as well as joining a domain.

App
C

Managing Resources

You will be tested on your ability to manage file and print resources, and to create and manage user and group accounts. Specific topics include:

◆ Create and manage local user accounts and local group accounts including user rights and account policies.

◆ Set up and modify user profiles.

◆ Set up shared folders and permissions.

◆ Set permissions on NTFS partitions, folders, and files, including changing ownership and establishing file and directory auditing.

◆ Install, configure, and share local and network printers, and connect to remote network printers.

Connectivity

You will be tested for your understanding of Windows NT 4.0 Networking and interoperability issues, including:

◆ Add and configure the network components of Windows NT Workstation 4.0, such as services and protocols.

◆ Use various methods to access network resources such as UNC support, fully qualified domain name support, the Connect As option when mapping a network drive, and Novell NetWare support.

◆ Implement Windows NT Workstation 4.0 as a client in a NetWare environment, taking into consideration Novell Directory Services (NDS), NetWare Admin, and NetWare login scripts.

◆ Use various configurations to configure Windows NT Workstation as a TCP/IP client such as DHCP, WINS, and DNS.

◆ Connect to a Microsoft Exchange client.

◆ Configure and install Dial-Up Networking for RAS multilink, Point-to-Point Tunneling Protocol (PPTP), and Internet access.

◆ Configure peer Web services for the intranet as well as implement security for an intranet Web site.

Running Applications

You will be tested for your understanding of the application subsystem support provided in Windows NT Workstation 4.0, specifically:

◆ Start applications on Intel and RISC platforms for OS/2, POSIX, MS-DOS, Win32, and Windows 16-bit applications.

◆ Start applications at various priorities.

Monitoring and Optimization

You will be tested on your ability to track and optimize system performance using a variety of tools. Specific topics include:

◆ Monitor system performance by using various tools such as the Performance Monitor, Network Monitor, and Task Manager.

◆ Identify and resolve a given performance problem such as isolating CPU, network, disk, and memory bottlenecks.

◆ Optimize system performance in various areas such as the hard disk through compression, file placement, file system choices, virtual memory paging file, and foreground and background responsiveness.

App
C

Troubleshooting

You will be tested on your understanding of basic Windows NT 4.0 concepts, processes, and functions, and your ability to choose the correct course of action to resolve problem situations. Specific topics include:

◆ Choose the appropriate course of action to take when the boot process fails such as creating a boot disk, modifying the boot process, maintaining the Emergency Repair Disk, and when to use Last Known Good.

◆ Choose the appropriate course of action to take when a print job fails.

◆ Choose the appropriate course of action to take when the installation process fails.

◆ Choose the appropriate course of action to take when an application fails, including using Task Manager.

◆ Choose the appropriate course of action to take when a user cannot access a resource.

◆ Modify the Registry using the appropriate tool such as Regedit, Regedt32, and System Policy Editor.

◆ Implement advanced techniques to resolve various problems such as configuring a memory dump, and using the Event Log service and Network Monitor.

What Kinds of Questions Can I Expect?

The Windows NT Workstation 4.0 Certification exam includes two types of multiple choice items: single-answer and multiple-answer.

Single-Answer, Multiple-Choice Item

A single-answer, multiple-choice item presents a problem and a list of possible answers. You must select the best answer to the given question from a list. Each answer is preceded by an OptionButton control.

Example:

You will be supporting a group of 10 account executives all running Windows NT Workstation on their computers. Occasionally, each account executive will need to share files with some or all of the other account executives. Two of the account executives have printers that all of them will use. You do not expect the group to grow by any more than five more persons. Which computing model will best meet their needs?

a) The Workgroup Model

b) The Single Domain Enterprise Model

c) The Master Domain Enterprise Model

d) The Complete Trust Enterprise Model

Your response to a single-answer, multiple-choice item is scored as either correct (1 or more points) or incorrect (0 points).

The answer to the above question is **a)** The Workgroup Model.

Multiple-Answer, Multiple-Choice Item

A multiple-answer, multiple-choice item presents a problem and a list of possible answers. You must select the best answer to the given question from a list. The question is often (but not always) followed by a phrase indicating the number of correct answers, such as "Pick two." Each answer is preceded by a CheckBox control.

Example:

Which of the following is part of the Kernel mode of the Windows NT architecture? (Select three.)

App
C

    a) WIN32 Subsystem

    b) HAL

    c) Executive Services

    d) Device Driver support

Your response to a multiple-answer, multiple-choice item is also scored as either correct (1 or more points) or incorrect (0 points). Your response scores all points only if all the correct answers are selected.

The answer to the above question is **b)** HAL; **c)** Executive Services; and **d)** Device Driver support.

How Should I Prepare for the Exam?

It's simple: The best way to prepare for the Windows NT Workstation 4.0 Certified Exam is to study, learn, and master Windows NT Workstation 4.0. If you'd like a little more guidance, Microsoft recommends these specific steps:

    1. Identify the objectives you'll be tested on. (See "Exam Objectives" earlier in this appendix.)

2. Assess your current mastery of those objectives.

3. Practice tasks and study the areas you haven't mastered.

Following are some tools and techniques, in addition to this book, that may offer a little more help.

Assessment Exams

Microsoft provides self-paced practice, or assessment exams, that you can take at your own computer. Assessment exams let you answer questions that are very much like the items in the actual certification exams. Your assessment exam score doesn't necessarily predict what your score will be on the actual exam, but its immediate feedback lets you determine the areas requiring extra study. And the assessment exams offer an additional advantage: They use the same computer-based testing tool as the certification exams, so you don't have to learn how to use the tool on exam day.

An assessment exam exists for almost every certification exam. You can find a complete list of available assessment exams in the Certification Roadmap.

Microsoft Resources

A number of useful resources available from Microsoft are:

◆ *Windows NT Workstation 4.0.* A key component of your exam preparation is your actual use of the product. Gain as much real-world experience with Windows NT 4.0 as possible. As you work with the product, study the online and printed documentation, focusing on areas relating to the exam objectives.

◆ *Microsoft TechNet, an information service for support professionals and system administrators.* If you're a TechNet member, you receive a monthly CD full of technical information.

Note To join TechNet, refer to the TechNet section in the Microsoft Education and Certification Roadmap (see "The Certification Roadmap" sidebar in Appendix B). ■

◆ *The Microsoft Developer Network, a technical resource for Microsoft developers.* If you're a member of the Developer Network, you can receive information on a regular basis through the Microsoft Developer Network CD, *Microsoft Developer Network News,* or the Developer Network Forum on CompuServe.

Note To join the Microsoft Developer Network, refer to the Microsoft Developer Network section in the Roadmap. ■

◆ *The Windows NT Workstation 4.0 Exam Preparation Guide, a Microsoft publication that provides important specifics about the Windows NT Workstation 4.0 test.* The Exam Preparation Guide is updated regularly to reflect changes and is the source for the most up-to-date information about Exam 70-73.

Note The exam preparation guide can change at any time without prior notice, solely at Microsoft's discretion. Before you register for an exam, make sure that you have the current exam preparation guide by contacting one of the following sources:

App
C

- *Microsoft Sales Fax Service.* Call 800-727-3351 in the United States and Canada. Outside the U.S. and Canada, contact your local Microsoft office.
- *CompuServe.* **GO MSEDCERT**, Library Number 5.
- *Internet.* Anonymous FTP to **ftp.microsoft.com**, /Services/ MSEdCert/Certification/ExamPreps.
- *Sylvan Prometric.* Call 800-755-EXAM in the U.S. and Canada. Outside the U.S. and Canada, contact your local Sylvan office. ■

Microsoft Online Training Institute (MOLI)

The Microsoft Online Training Institute (MOLI) on The Microsoft Network (MSN) is an interactive learning and information resource where Learning Advisors (instructors) pair their expert knowledge, guidance, and motivation with electronic self-study materials.

You may access MOLI at its main Classroom Building site on the Internet at **http://moli.microsoft.com**.

You enroll in a class, pay a small tuition fee (to cover the cost of materials and the Learning Advisor's time and expertise), and then receive a shortcut to the classroom. As a student, you can participate in class by interacting with a Learning Advisor and fellow students online via Exchange (e-mail), bulletin boards, forums, or other online communication services available through MSN. You control your own time by studying when and where you choose, working at your own speed, and attending the virtual "class" as often or as little as you want.

Only students enrolled in a class can participate in its online chat sessions and view the contents of the classroom, such as courseware and other materials provided by the Learning Advisor. In addition to MOLI campus resources, you have access to several other resources:

◆ The Assignments BBS give you access to courseware assignments, test questions that measure subject-matter comprehension, chapter review guides, lab assignments, and information about certification exam topics. You can take advantage of these resources anytime.

◆ One or more chat sessions per week allow you to supplement class courseware, interact with other classmates to solve real-life situations, and get expert advice.

◆ The Notes BBS lets students download and play files, tips and tools, and resources available through Microsoft.

Self-Paced Training

If you prefer to learn on your own, you can obtain Microsoft Official Curriculum training (as well as non-Microsoft Official Curriculum courses) in self-paced formats. Self-paced training kits are available through courses offered on the Microsoft Online Training Institute with materials available in book, computer-based training (CBT), and mixed-media (book and video) formats.

Microsoft Approved Study Guides, such as this book, are self-paced training materials developed by Independent Courseware Vendors (ICVs) to help you prepare for Microsoft Certified Professional exams. The Study Guides include both single self-paced training courses and series of training courses that map to one or more MCP exams.

Self-training kits and study guides are often available through Microsoft authorized training centers, or you can purchase them where books from Microsoft Press are sold.

Other Online Resources

Both MSN and CompuServe (**GO MECFORUM**) provide access to technical forums for open discussions and questions about Microsoft products. Microsoft's World Wide Web site (**http:\\www.microsoft. com**) also allows you to access information about certification and education programs.

Training Resources

Microsoft product groups have designed training courses to support the certification process. The Microsoft Official Curriculum is developed by Microsoft course designers, product developers, and support engineers to help you prepare for MCP exams.

Authorized Technical Education Centers (ATECs), such as Productivity Point International, are approved by Microsoft to provide training on Microsoft products and related technologies. By enrolling in a course taught by a Microsoft Solution Provider ATEC, you receive high-end technical training on the design, development, implementation, and support of enterprise-wide solutions using Microsoft operating systems, tools, and technologies.

You also may take MOC courses via face-to-face training offered by Microsoft Authorized Academic Training Program (AATP) institutions. AATP schools use authorized materials and curriculum designed for the Microsoft Certified Professional program and deliver Microsoft authorized materials, including the Microsoft Official Curriculum, over an academic term.

Administering Microsoft Windows NT 4.0, course number 803, and *Supporting Microsoft Windows NT 4.0-Core Technologies*, course number 687, available from Microsoft authorized training institutions, may help you prepare for the exam. Course 803 lasts three days and Course 687 is five days long.

App
C

For a referral to an AATP or Productivity Point ATEC in your area, call 800-SOLPROV.

Suggested Reading and Internet Sites

When you're looking for additional study aids, check out the books and online sites listed in Appendix F, "Suggested Reading."

How Do I Register for the Exam?

Registering for the Windows NT Workstation 4.0 certification exam is simple:

1. Contact Sylvan Prometric at (800) 755-EXAM, with the examination number (70-73), your Social Security number, and a credit card.

2. Complete the registration procedure by phone. (Your SSN becomes the ID attached to your private file; the credit card takes care of the $100 test fee.) Request contact information for the testing center closest to you.

3. After you receive the registration and payment confirmation letter from Sylvan Prometric, call the testing center to schedule your exam. When you call to schedule, you'll be provided with instructions regarding the appointment, cancellation procedures, ID requirements, and information about the testing center location.

You can verify the number of questions and time allotted for your exam at the time of registration. You can schedule exams up to six weeks in advance, or as late as one working day ahead, but you must take the exam within one year of your payment. To cancel or reschedule your exam, contact Sylvan Prometric at least two working days before your scheduled exam date.

 Note At some locations, same-day registration (at least two hours before test time) is available, subject to space availability. ▧

D

Testing Tips

You've mastered the required tasks to take the exam. After reviewing and re-reviewing the exam objectives, you're confident that you have the skills specified in the exam objectives. You're ready to perform at the highest cognitive level. And it's time to head for the testing center. This appendix covers some tips and tricks to remember.

Before the Test

◆ Wear comfortable clothing. You want to focus on the exam, not on a tight shirt collar or a pinching pair of shoes.

◆ Allow plenty of travel time. Get to the testing center 10 or 15 minutes early; nothing's worse than rushing in at the last minute. Give yourself time to relax.

◆ If you've never been to the testing center before, make a trial run a few days before to make sure that you know the route to the center.

◆ Carry with you at least two forms of identification, including one photo ID (such as a driver's license or company security ID). You will have to show them before you can take the exam.

Remember that the exams are closed-book. The use of laptop computers, notes, or other printed materials is not permitted during the exam session.

At the test center, you'll be asked to sign in. The test administrator will give you a Testing Center Regulations form that explains the rules that govern the examination. You will be asked to sign the form to indicate that you understand and will comply with its stipulations.

When the administrator shows you to your test computer, make sure that:

◆ The testing tool starts up and displays the correct exam. If a tutorial for using the instrument is available, you should be allowed time to take it.

Note If you have any special needs, such as reconfiguring the mouse buttons for a left-handed user, you should inquire about them when you register for the exam with Sylvan Prometric. Special configurations are not possible at all sites, so you should not assume that you will be permitted to make any modifications to the equipment setup and configuration. Site administrators are *not* permitted to make modifications without prior instructions from Sylvan.

◆ You have a supply of scratch paper for use during the exam. (The administrator collects all scratch paper and notes made during the exam before you leave the center.) Some centers are now providing you with a wipe-off board and magic marker to use instead of paper. You are not permitted to make any kind of notes to take with you, due to exam security.

♦ Some exams may include additional materials, or exhibits. If any exhibits are required for your exam, the test administrator will provide you with them before you begin the exam and collect them from you at the end of the exam.

♦ The administrator tells you what to do when you complete the exam.

♦ You get answers to any and all of your questions or concerns before the exam begins.

As a Microsoft Certification examination candidate, you are entitled to the best support and environment possible for your exam. If you experience any problems on the day of the exam, inform the Sylvan Prometric test administrator immediately.

During the Test

The testing software lets you move forward and backward through the items, so you can implement a strategic approach to the test.

1. Go through all the items, answering the easy questions first. Then go back and spend time on the harder ones. Microsoft guarantees that there are no trick questions. The correct answer is always among the list of choices.

2. Eliminate the obviously incorrect answer first to clear away the clutter and simplify your choices.

3. Answer all the questions. You aren't penalized for guessing, so it can't hurt.

4. Don't rush. Haste makes waste (or substitute the cliché of your choice).

After the Test

When you have completed an exam:

◆ The testing tool gives you immediate, online notification of your pass or fail status, except for beta exams. Because of the beta process, your results for a beta exam are mailed to you approximately 6-8 weeks after the exam.

◆ The administrator gives you a printed Examination Score Report indicating your pass or fail status and your exam results by section.

◆ Test scores are automatically forwarded to Microsoft within five working days after you take the test. If you pass the exam, you receive confirmation from Microsoft within two to four weeks.

If you don't pass a certification exam:

◆ Review your individual section scores, noting areas where your score must be improved. The section titles in your exam report generally correspond to specific groups of exam objectives.

◆ Review the exam information in this book; then get the latest Exam Preparation Guide and focus on the topic areas that need strengthening.

◆ Intensify your effort to get real-world, hands-on experience and practice with Windows NT 4.0.

◆ Try taking one or more of the approved training courses.

◆ Take (or retake) the Windows NT 4.0 Assessment Exam.

◆ Call Sylvan Prometric to register, pay, and schedule the exam again.

Contacting Microsoft

Microsoft encourages feedback from exam candidates, especially suggestions for improving any of the exams or preparation materials.

To provide program feedback, to find out more about Microsoft Education and Certification materials and programs, to register with Sylvan Prometric, or to get other useful information, check the following resources.

 Note Outside the United States or Canada, contact your local Microsoft office or Sylvan Prometric testing center. ▪

Microsoft Certified Professional Program

(800) 636-7544

For information about the Microsoft Certified Professional program and exams, and to order the Microsoft Roadmap to Education and Certification.

Sylvan Prometric Testing Centers

(800) 755-EXAM

To register to take a Microsoft Certified Professional exam at any of more than 700 Sylvan Prometric testing centers around the world.

Microsoft Sales Fax Service

(800) 727-3351

For Microsoft Certified Professional Exam Preparation Guides and Microsoft Official Curriculum course descriptions and schedules.

Education Program and Course Information

(800) SOLPROV

For information about Microsoft Official Curriculum courses, Microsoft education products, and the Microsoft Solution Provider Authorized Technical Education Center (ATEC) program, where you can attend a Microsoft Official Curriculum course.

Microsoft Certification Development Team

Fax: (206) 936-1311

To volunteer for participation in one or more exam development phases or to report a problem with an exam, address written correspondence to:

Certification Development Team
Microsoft Education and Certification
One Microsoft Way
Redmond, WA 98052

Microsoft TechNet Technical Information Network

(800) 344-2121

For support professionals and system administrators. (Outside the U.S. and Canada, call your local Microsoft subsidiary for information.)

Microsoft Developer Network (MSDN)

App
E

(800) 759-5474

The official source for software development kits, device driver kits, operating systems, and information about developing applications for Microsoft Windows® and Windows NT.

Microsoft Technical Support Options

(800) 936-3500

For information about the technical support options available for
Microsoft products, including technical support telephone numbers and
Premier Support options. (Outside the U.S. and Canada, call your local
Microsoft subsidiary for information.)

Microsoft Online Institute (MOLI)

(800) 449-9333

For information about Microsoft's new online training program.

F

Suggested Reading

Titles from Que

Que Corporation offers a wide variety of technical books for all levels of users. Following are some recommended titles, in alphabetical order, that can provide you with additional information on many of the exam topics and objectives.

While some of the titles recommended are geared specifically toward Windows NT Server 4.0, many of the fundamental concepts of Windows NT are the same for both Workstation and Server. For a fuller understanding of these concepts, a Server-based book will be just as instructive as a Workstation-based book.

Note The final version of Windows NT Workstation 4.0 and Server were released in late August, 1996. Books with a publisher's date earlier than this were probably written based on the Beta versions of the Windows NT 4.0 software. This caution should by no means discourage you from considering these books for purchase, nor is it meant to reflect badly on the authorship or content especially where Windows NT concepts are concerned. However, the final versions of software sometimes introduce subtle changes in look and feel that may not exactly match a description given in any book.

Tip
To order any books from Que Corporation or other imprints of Macmillan Computer Publishing (SAMS, New Riders Publishing, Ziff-Davis Press, and others), call 800-428-5331, visit Macmillan's Information SuperLibrary on the World Wide Web (**http://www.mcp.com**), or check your local bookseller.

Using Windows NT Workstation 4.0

Author: Paul Samna, et. al.

ISBN: 0-7897-0673-3

Windows NT 4.0 Installation and Configuration Handbook

Author: Jim Boyce

ISBN: 0-7897-0818-3

Windows NT Workstation 4.0 Advanced Technical Reference

Author: Jim Boyce, et. al.

ISBN: 0-7897-0863-9

Windows NT Workstation 4.0 Internet and Networking Handbook

Author: Robert Bruce Thompson

ISBN: 0–7897–0817–5

Other Titles

Complete Guide to Windows NT 4.0 Workstation, by Peter Norton and John Paul Mueller (SAMS; ISBN: 0–672–30901–7)

Inside Windows NT Workstation 4, by Kathy Ivens (New Riders Publishing; ISBN: 1–56205–661–1)

Inside Windows NT Server 4, by Drew Heywood (New Riders Publishing; ISBN: 1–56205–649–2)

Windows NT 4 Server Unleashed, by Jason Garms, et. al. (SAMS Publishing; ISBN: 0–672–30933–5)

App

F

Networking Basics

Understanding Networking

Networks provide a method for computers to communicate with one another to share resources. In the early days of computing, prior to the availability of networks, when someone wanted to share the information stored in a file with someone else, he or she had to copy the file to some form of media, such as a disk or tape, and physically carry that media to the other person. This process eventually became known as a *Sneaker-Net*.

Sneaker-Net worked for a while, but eventually people were spending more of their day walking around than actually working.

The next development was the use of asynchronous communication equipment to transfer files from one computer to another directly.

This had several drawbacks, the most significant being speed, and the fact that a communication utility had to be running, to the exclusion of any actual work-related application, while the file was being transferred.

The first true networks were proprietary networks connecting minicomputers and mainframes.

Examining the ISO OSI Model

In 1983, the International Standards Organization (ISO) defined a model for networking called the *Open Systems Interconnection (OSI) reference model*. The model describes the flow of information between the physical network and applications.

Networking vendors use the OSI model as a guideline to develop real world systems.

The OSI reference model defines the communication between the computers in a network as a series of *layers* (see Figure G.1). Each layer implements a particular functionality, such as routing (network layer) or frame construction (data-link layer). Layers logically communicate with their counterpart on other computers, but in actuality, each layer provides services to the layer above it, and uses the services of the layer below it. The lower layer shields the layers above it from having to know, or deal with, the details handled by the lower layers.

The OSI reference model, like other models, is a set of abstract guidelines only. Actual network implementations may implement a single functional layer in several software layers, or implement many functional layers in a single software component.

The OSI reference model defines seven layers. The layers are usually pictured with the Physical layer at the bottom, and the Application layer at the top.

FIG. G.1⇒

The layers of the OSI reference model.

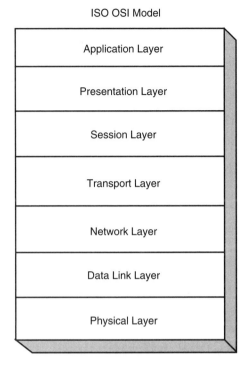

ISO OSI Model

The Seven ISO OSI Layers

Each of the layers communicates with its adjacent layers through an *interface*. The sets of rules that the layers use to communicate logically with their counterpart on the other computer in a conversation are called *protocols*.

As data passes through each of the layers, from the Application Layer down to the Physical Layer, it is wrapped with layer-specific information, and passed to the next lower layer, which wraps its own information around the outside of the data, and so on.

On the recipient computer, each layer removes its layer-specific information before passing the data up to the next layer.

App

G

There are seven layers, from bottom to top, as discussed in the following sections:

- Physical
- Data-Link
- Network
- Transport
- Session
- Presentation
- Application

Physical Layer

The Physical layer defines the methods used to transfer the bitstream that makes up the data across a physical network. It defines the interfaces (electrical, optical, and so on) to the network cable. The Physical layer carries the signals generated by all of the higher layers directly to its counterpart on the remote computer.

The Physical layer defines the complete configuration of all of the physical parts of the network, including cabling type, pin configurations, signal encoding, and so on. It deals with bits only, and does not impose any meaning on the bitstream, although it does ensure that a one bit is received as a one bit, and not a zero bit. Transmission speed, modulation, and encoding are all defined by this layer.

Data-Link Layer

The Data-Link layer converts the bitstream received from the Physical layer into data *frames*, or *packets*. A packet is an organized structure that can contain data. The packet contains error-correction information in the form of a CRC to ensure that the frame is received properly. The upper layers are guaranteed error-free transmission through this layer.

Usually, the Data-Link layer relies on acknowledgments from its counterpart to ensure that a frame was received. If a frame is not acknowledged, the Data-Link layer normally retransmits the frame.

The frame also contains the sender ID and destination ID for the frame.

The Data-Link layer establishes the logical link between two network nodes, and handles frame sequencing and frame traffic control.

Network Layer

The Network layer addresses messages and translates logical addresses and names into physical addresses. It is also responsible for routing packets from the source computer to the destination computer. It determines the route based on a number of criteria, including network conditions and service priorities.

The Network layer is also responsible for dealing with problems on the network, including network congestion. If the destination computers cannot handle packets as large as the sending computer, the Network layer on the sending computer will break the packets up into smaller packets. The packets will be reassembled by the Network layer on the receiving computer.

Transport Layer

The primary function of the Transport layer is to ensure that messages are delivered to the higher layers without errors, and in the proper sequence, with no losses. This layer also packages messages for efficient transfer—short messages will be combined into larger ones, and large messages may be split into smaller messages. The Transport layer on the receiving computer unpacks the messages into their original form.

The Transport layer also provides session multiplexing—it can multiplex several message streams into a single logical link, and separate them on the receiving node. (Multiplexing refers to any technique that allows multiple message streams to share a logical link.)

Session Layer

The Session layer enables applications on two computers to talk to each other by establishing a conversation called a *session*. This layer handles name recognition and other functions that permit two applications to communicate with each other over the network.

The Session layer places checkpoints in the data stream. Checkpoints provide a means of synchronizing the data stream on both computers.

App
G

In the event of a network failure, only the data after the last received checkpoint will need to be re-sent. This layer also controls which side of a conversation is permitted to transmit and for how long.

Presentation Layer

The primary responsibility of the Presentation layer is to translate applications data into a commonly recognized intermediate format for transmission across the network. On the receiving side, the Presentation layer translates the intermediate format back into the original format.

The network redirector operates at this layer. A *redirector* redirects reads and writes to a server on the network.

Other services of the Presentation layer can include data compression, data encryption, character set translation, and other conversions.

Application Layer

The Application layer enables application processes to access network services. Application layer services directly support user applications such as file transfer, messaging, or database access.

Tip
You can remember the order of the OSI layers by using the mnemonic device: **P**lease **D**o **N**ot **T**rust **S**ales **P**eople **A**lways.

IEEE 802 Model

The Institute of Electrical and Electronic Engineers developed another network model to address the proliferation of LAN products that was beginning to take place in early 1980. This project, named 802, was in development at roughly the same time that the ISO was working on the OSI reference model, resulting in a compatible model.

One key difference between the IEEE committee and the ISO committee is that the IEEE committee was made up of networking vendor representatives from companies who had products to sell. In some instances, the IEEE standard was driven by *products* rather than the other way around.

Most of today's networks comply with the IEEE 802 standards. The IEEE 802 standards, including 802.2 (LLC), 802.3 (Ethernet), and 802.5 (Token Ring) are standards that can actually be implemented, whereas the OSI reference model is a more general abstract set of guidelines.

The key difference between the OSI reference model and the IEEE 802 standard lies in the Data-Link layer. The IEEE felt that more detail was needed at this layer, and decided to further divide the layer into two sublayers, the *Media Access Control (MAC)* layer and the *Logical Link Control (LLC)* layer (see Figure G.2).

FIG. G.2⇒

The IEEE 802 standard divides the Data-Link layer into two sublayers.

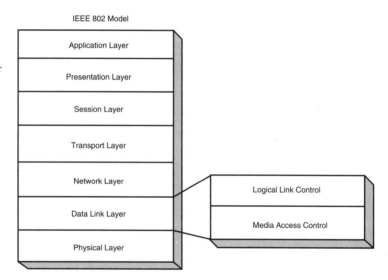

IEEE 802 Model

- Application Layer
- Presentation Layer
- Session Layer
- Transport Layer
- Network Layer
- Data Link Layer
- Physical Layer

- Logical Link Control
- Media Access Control

Media Access Control (MAC) Sublayer

The MAC sublayer is the lower of the two sublayers defined by the IEEE. It provides shared access to the computer's network adapter cards. It talks to the network adapter card directly, and is responsible for error-free delivery of packets across the network.

Logical Link Control (LLC) Sublayer

The upper sublayer of the Data-Link layer is the Logical Link Control layer. It is responsible for link establishment and control, frame sequencing and acknowledgment, and provides Service Access Points (SAPs) that are used to transfer information to higher layers.

App
G

Understanding Network Topologies

The *topology* of a LAN describes the way it is arranged. There are three topologies in current use—ring, bus, and star. Topology is usually used to refer to the logical arrangement, rather than a physical one. For example, the IBM Token Ring network is logically and electrically a ring, but wired physically in a star shape. It's also common for large networks to be hybrids of two or more topologies.

Ring

Nodes in a ring topology (see Figure G.3) are connected, one to the other, in a closed loop. Although usually physically wired in a star shape, the ring is electrically a complete circuit. Messages may pass though one or more other computers before reaching their destination.

FIG. G.3⇒

Ring Topology.

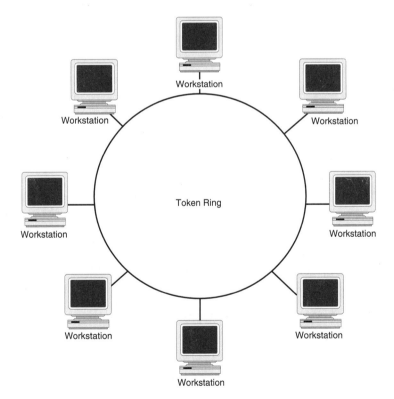

A token-passing access method is used with ring topologies. The only example of an IEEE 802-compliant ring topology is a token-ring network.

Bus

Nodes in a bus topology (see Figure G.4) are connected to a central cable, known as a trunk, or bus. The ends of the cable are each connected to a terminator, which is a resistor that typically matches the characteristic impedance of the cable.

FIG. G.4⇒

Bus Topology.

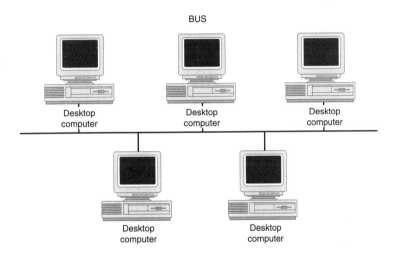

There are two methods commonly used to connect the nodes to the bus. The first, used more often with Thin Ethernet networks, uses T-shaped BNC connectors. One side of the T is connected to the node's network adapter card, and the other two are connected to two cables (or one cable and a terminator) that make up the bus.

The second method, more common with Thick Ethernet networks, places a transceiver on the trunk cable, which is connected to the AUI port on the node's network adapter card with a drop-down cable.

Examples of networks with a bus topology are 10Base2, 10Base5, and Arcnet.

App
G

Star

Nodes in a star topology (see Figure G.5) are connected to a central wiring concentrator, or *hub*. A hub usually acts as an electrical *repeater*, regenerating the signals received from transmitting nodes and sending them to all of the other nodes.

10BaseT is the best example of a star topology network.

FIG. G.5⇒

Star topology.

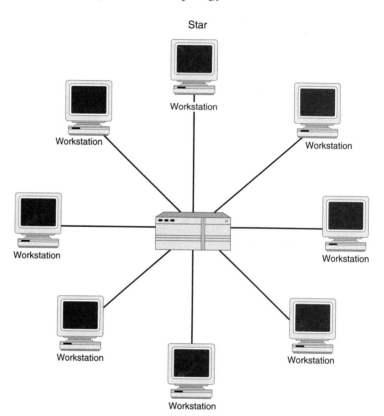

Understanding Architectures

The architecture of a network is determined by its topology, media access method, and transmission media.

Token Ring

IEEE standard 802.5 defines the token-ring network access method. It uses the ring topology, although it is physically shaped like a star.

Token-ring networks use a token-passing access method. A token is a special bit pattern which is passed around the ring from computer to computer. When a computer possesses the token, it has the right to transmit on the network. After it transmits its data, the computer places the token back on the ring so that the next computer has a chance to transmit.

The token-ring access method is non-competitive, meaning that computers do not have to compete for access to the cable; they merely have to wait their turn. The token-ring standard does impose a maximum limit on how much data a computer may transmit at one time, to ensure that the token is passed on fairly. In fact, a computer that holds the token for too long will be partitioned out of the network by the central Multistation Access Unit (MAU).

The first token ring network was designed by E. E. Newhall in 1969. The first commercial support for a token-ring network began with an IBM presentation to the IEEE 802 project in March 1982.

IBM announced the IBM Token Ring Network in 1984, and its design was approved as ANSI/IEEE 802.5 in 1985. Key to the design was the IBM Cabling System, which was based on shielded twisted pair (a later design allowed the use of unshielded twisted pair) cable that connected from the network adapter card to a wall socket, with a centralized hub, a Multistation Access Unit (MAU) located in a centralized location.

The token ring network cabling is distinguished by a unique genderless connector. (A genderless connector can connect to any replica of itself, rather than having a corresponding part, as a plug and socket do.) The self-shorting design of the connector, coupled with the redundant data path available in the cable, ensures that the ring can remain electrically complete, even if a wire breaks, or a computer is turned off. In the former case, the redundant path is automatically switched in by the

App

G

MAU; in the latter, the cabling to the computer is removed from the ring by the MAU and reinserted when the computer is turned on. You can recognize a token ring connector because it is the largest of the connectors used in networking, a roughly cubical shape, about 1.25" on a side.

The original token ring network used a transmission speed of 4Mbps; it was later adapted to 16Mbps. All network cards on the ring must be configured at the same speed.

Each computer can be up to 100 meters from the MAU when using shielded twisted-pair cable, or 45 meters when using unshielded cable. Cables must be at least 2.5 meters in length.

There can be up to 33 MAUs on a ring, each supporting a maximum of 260 computers with shielded twisted-pair cable.

Token rings are most efficient on heavily loaded networks that have a lot of traffic.

Ethernet

The precursor of the Ethernet network was a wide area network called ALOHA that was developed at the University of Hawaii in the late 1960s. It was the first network to use the Carrier-Sense Multiple Access with Collision Detection (CSMA/CD) access method.

Unlike the token-passing method, which is noncompetitive, computers using the CSMA/CD access method compete for a chance to transmit on the cable. A computer that wants to transmit follows several steps:

1. The computer checks the cable to see if a carrier (a transmission signal) is already present. If one is, it waits a random amount of time and tries again (Carrier-Sense).

2. If there is no carrier present, the computer assumes that the cable is available to it. *Other computers may be accessing the cable at the same time* (Multiple Access).

3. The computer transmits its data, and listens for a double carrier. If a double carrier is found, then a collision has occurred.

A collision is caused by another computer starting to transmit at the same time (Collision Detection).

4. If a collision is detected, both computers will wait a random amount of time, and begin with step 1 again.

Xerox Corporation started experimenting with CSMA/CD networks in 1972 and, by 1975, introduced its first Ethernet product, a 2.94Mbps system that could connect over 100 computers on a 1-kilometer-long cable.

The success of the first Ethernet led to Xerox, Intel Corporation, and Digital Equipment Corporation drawing up a standard for the 10Mbps Ethernet, which was used as the basis of the IEEE 802.3 specification. The product complies with most, but not all, of the 802.3 specification.

There are three different types of cable supported by Ethernet networks —thick coaxial cable (ThickNet, or 10base5), thin coaxial cable (ThinNet or 10base2), and unshielded twisted-pair (10baseT).

The 10base5 specification is for baseband communications over thick cabling. The maximum physical segment length is 500 meters. Baseband communications refers to communications where the cable is dedicated to a particular type of signal. The alternative, broadband, refers to communications where multiple signals are multiplexed over a single cable. An example of broadband communications is cable television.

The 10base2 specification is for baseband communications over thin (RG-58) coaxial cabling. The maximum physical segment length is 185 meters.

The 10baseT specification uses baseband communications over unshielded twisted-pair cable. The maximum physical segment length is 100 meters between the workstation and a wiring concentrator, or hub.

ThickNet (10Base5)

Thick, or Standard Ethernet uses a thick cable. The IEEE designation is 10Base5, because it is a 10Mbps, baseband network with a maximum segment length of 500 meters.

10Base5 uses a bus topology to support up to 100 nodes per trunk segment. A node is a workstation, repeater, or bridge. (A bridge is a device that connects two different network segments, passing only traffic destined for another segment. A repeater electrically connects two or more segments, regenerating the signals to each of them.)

Each trunk segment is terminated by resistors at each end. Transceivers are placed along the trunk, and a drop cable attaches to the AUI port on the workstation network adapter cards. Drop cable length is not considered in calculating the length of the trunk cable. As many as five backbone segments can be connected using repeaters.

ThickNet requires a minimum of 2.5 meters between connections on the trunk segment. Drop cables are usually made from shielded-pair cable, and have a maximum length of 50 meters.

ThickNet is typically used to support the network backbone for a building because of its greater resistance to electrical interference and longer segment length.

ThinNet (10Base2)

The 10Base2 network runs over thin, relatively inexpensive coaxial cable (RG-58). The IEEE designation is 10Base2 because it transmits at 10Mbps over a baseband cable for a maximum distance of approximately 200 meters (actually 185 meters).

10Base2 uses a bus topology to support up to 30 nodes per segment.

Each segment is terminated by resistors at each end. Instead of using external transceivers, 10Base2 transceivers are contained on the network adapter card and a T connector is used to connect the cable to the card. There must be at least 0.5 meters of cable between adapters.

As many as five cable segments can be combined using repeaters, giving 10Base2 a maximum of 150 computers per logical segment.

10Base2 was designed to be economical, and easy to set up. Many small networks use 10Base2; in fact, Microsoft used to bundle Windows for Workgroups with 10Base2 adapters and cable.

Twisted-Pair (10BaseT)

The most popular form of Ethernet in use today is best known by its IEEE designation, 10BaseT.

10BaseT runs over unshielded twisted-pair cable, similar to that used by ordinary telephone systems. It is designated 10BaseT by the IEEE because it transmits at 10Mbps over a baseband cable for a maximum distance of 100 meters from the wiring hub. Cables must be at least 2.5 meters in length.

10BaseT is wired in a star topology, but it uses a bus system between the adapter card and the hub, which acts as a repeater.

ArcNet

ArcNet (Attached Resource Computer Network) is a proprietary token-passing bus network developed by Datapoint Corporation. It transmits at 2.5Mbps, although later versions support rates up to 20Mbps.

ArcNet is a proprietary network, predating the IEEE 802 project. It bears some resemblance to 802.4, but 802.4 describes a broadband network, while ArcNet is a baseband network. ArcNet can use either a bus or star technology over coaxial cable. Star configurations use active or passive hubs. Active hubs regenerate the signals, whereas passive hubs simply divide the signals up.

Understanding Transport Protocols

Transport protocols enable you to route information and network requests over LANs and WANs. (A LAN is a Local Area Network, intended to interconnect nodes in the same building or campus, whereas a WAN, or Wide Area Network, can be worldwide.)

App

G

NetBEUI

The NetBEUI protocol stack (a stack is a particular implementation of a protocol) was designed by Microsoft and IBM for use with IBM's PC Network product which was introduced in 1985. At that time, most people expected LANs to consist of small departmental workgroups that would be connected to mainframes via gateways. In fact, the PC Network hardware could only support a maximum of 72 workstations.

NetBEUI was optimized for use in this environment. One consequence of this optimization is the fact that NetBEUI is not routable.

NetBEUI uses the NetBIOS interface at the top, and NDIS at the bottom (see Figure G.6).

FIG. G.6⇒
How NetBEUI fits into the OSI/IEEE networking models.

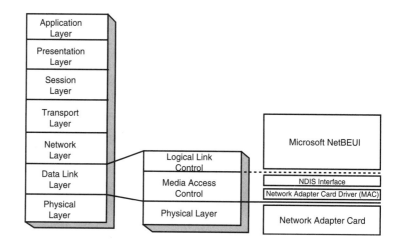

IPX/SPX

IPX was designed by Novell as a routable transport protocol, based on Xerox XNS.

The Microsoft version, IPX/SPX-compatible protocol, is completely compatible with Novell's version, but is a fully 32-bit implementation. The Microsoft implementation includes an optional NetBIOS interface which is required to use resource sharing with Microsoft networks.

TCP/IP

The Transmission Control Protocol/Internet Protocol (TCP/IP) is a suite of protocols designed specifically for wide area networks. It was first developed in 1969 as part of an experiment called the ARPANET, whose purpose was to interconnect the networks that were used by the contractors and universities doing research for the U.S. Department of Defense.

XNS

XNS was the original transport protocol developed by Xerox for use with Ethernet. It is an ancestor of the Novell IPX protocol.

Understanding MAC Drivers

A *MAC driver* is a driver located at the MAC sublayer. It provides support for data transmission to and from the network adapter, as well as managing the adapter itself. MAC drivers are also known as network adapter card drivers.

Understanding Interface Specifications

Device drivers at the MAC and LLC sublayers move data received by the Physical layer up to the other OSI layers.

Until the development of the NDIS standard in 1989, most transport protocol implementations were tied to a proprietary MAC-level interface. Supporting these proprietary interfaces meant that network adapter card manufacturers had to write drivers for each proprietary interface in order to support a variety of network operating systems.

NDIS

In 1989, Microsoft and 3Com developed a joint standard that defined an interface for communicating between the MAC sublayer and

App
G

transport protocol drivers on layers 3 and 4 of the OSI model. This standard, the *Network Device Interface Specification (NDIS)*, is designed to create an environment where any transport protocol can talk to any network adapter card driver without either one knowing anything about the other.

The initial communication channel between the protocol driver and the MAC driver is established through a process called *binding*, in which the *Protocol Manager* establishes the connection between the MAC and transport protocol drivers.

NDIS also permits a single network adapter to support multiple protocol drivers, as well as supporting multiple network adapters. The Protocol Manager is responsible for routing network requests to the appropriate driver.

ODI

Novell's version of an architecture that enables the use of multiple LAN drivers and protocols is called the *Open Data-Link Interface (ODI)* specification.

There are two parts to an ODI stack. The first, the *Multiple Link Interface Driver (MLID)*, is a network adapter specific driver, and the second, the *Link Support Layer (LSL)*, provides the interface to the transport protocols.

H

Internet Resources for Windows NT

Microsoft's Windows operating system series (Windows 95, Windows NT Workstation 4.0, Windows NT Server 4.0) has become quite popular. The amount of new information and programs that becomes available each day is staggering. If you don't want to wait for the next super book or next month's magazine, you can go online to get new information. You can get a lot of information through commercial online services such as CompuServe, America Online, or The Microsoft Network (MSN). You'll find more variety, and potentially more useful information, on the Internet, however.

That's where this appendix comes in. It points you to some of the best resources on the Internet for Windows NT information and programs, earlier versions as well as version 4.0. Keep in mind that there are hundreds of Internet sites for each Windows NT site that you find in this appendix. I didn't include most of them because they contain links to the other sites. The result is a Web of Windows NT pages, all linked together, that contain nothing but links.

This appendix teaches you about:

◆ *FTP Servers.* It's usually easier to find shareware programs on the World Wide Web, but this sample of FTP sites collects so many programs in a few areas that they're worth checking out.

◆ *Mailing lists.* Sometimes it's easier to let the information you want come to you, instead of going out onto the Internet to look for it. Mailing lists deliver information directly to your mailbox.

◆ *World Wide Web.* There's little doubt that the Web is the hottest resource on the Internet. You find a variety of Web pages dedicated to Windows NT, including personal and corporate Web pages.

On the Web

You can find shortcuts to the Internet address described here at Que's Web site at

http://www.quecorp.com

FTP Servers

The FTP servers in this section contain large collections of Windows NT shareware programs. They are all well organized, so you can quickly find the program you're looking for. Note that most of these sites are indexed by **Shareware.com**.

Tip

If you don't have an FTP client, you can use your Web browser to access FTP servers. Type **ftp://** followed by the FTP address in your Web browser's address bar.

Microsoft

FTP address: **ftp://ftp.microsoft.com**

This is the place to look for updated drivers, new files for Windows NT, and sometimes free programs. My favorite part of this FTP site are the KnowledgeBase articles that answer common questions about most of Microsoft's programs. If you're having trouble finding your way around, look for a file called DIRMAP.TXT, which tells you what the different folders have in them. Here's what you find under each of the folders on this site:

- ◆ **/BUSSYS.** Files for business systems, including networking, mail, SQL Server, and Windows NT. Here you can find some KnowledgeBase links specific to Windows NT. The KnowledgeBase entries related to Windows NT reflect all versions of Windows NT.

- ◆ **/DESKAPPS.** Files for all of Microsoft's desktop applications, including Access, Excel, PowerPoint, Project, and Word. You can also find information for the Home series, including games and Works.

- ◆ **/DEVELPR.** The place to look if you're a developer. There are folders for Visual C++, Visual Basic, various utilities, the Microsoft Developer Network, and more. If you subscribe to the *Microsoft Systems Journal*, check here to find the source code for articles.

- ◆ **/KBHELP.** Microsoft's KnowledgeBase folder. A *knowledge base*, in this context, is a help file that contains common questions and answers about Microsoft products. This folder contains one self-extracting, compressed file for each Microsoft product. There is not a lot of information here as yet about Windows NT 4.0. However, this is still a good area to keep scanning for the latest data.

◆ **/SOFTLIB.** The folder to check out if you're looking for updated drivers, patches, or bug fixes. This folder contains more than 1,500 files, though, so you need to check out INDEX.TXT to locate what you want.

◆ **/PEROPSYS.** This folder is for personal operating systems. If you're looking for back issues of WINNEWS, look in the **WIN_NEWS** folder. There are other folders relating to all versions of Windows, MS-DOS, and Microsoft hardware.

◆ **/SERVICES.** Contains information about TechNet, Microsoft educational services, sales information, and so on.

Note   Many of the folders on the Microsoft FTP site have two files that you should read: README.TXT and INDEX.TXT.

README.TXT describes the type of files you find in the current folder and any subfolders. It also may describe recent additions and files that have been removed.

INDEX.TXT describes each file in the folder. It's a good idea to search for the file you want in INDEX.TXT before trying to pick it out of the listing. Note that Microsoft's site is constantly changing, so you'll want to check back here often. ▨

Walnut Creek

FTP address: **ftp://ftp.cdrom.com**

I consider myself lucky to get on this FTP site. It's incredibly popular. Walnut Creek sells CD-ROMs that are packed with freeware and shareware programs. Files from these CD-ROMs are available from the Walnut Creek FTP site, too. The interesting folders under /PUB/ WINNT that you should check out are:

alpha

incoming

intel

> **Tip**
> This site is usually very crowded. If you get onto this site, don't let yourself get disconnected by taking a coffee break—it could be a while before you get on again.

Mailing Lists

Windows NT-related mailing lists keep your mailbox full of messages. There's a lot of noise generated by these lists, but you can find a lot of gems, too. This section describes two of the most popular ones: **DevWire** and **WinNews**.

Microsoft DevWire

This is for Windows programmers. You'll find news and product information, such as seminar schedules and visual tool release schedules. To subscribe, send an e-mail to **DevWire@microsoft.nwnet.com** with **subscribe DevWire** in the body of your message.

Microsoft WinNews

This weekly newsletter keeps you up-to-date on the latest happenings at Microsoft. You also find product tips and press releases. To subscribe, send an e-mail to **enews99@microsoft.nwnet.com** and type **subscribe winnews** in the body of your message.

World Wide Web

The explosive growth of Windows NT Web pages is evident if you search for the keyword **Windows NT** using Yahoo!, WebCrawler, Excite, or Lycos. You can find thousands of Web pages dedicated to

Windows NT, some from the corporate community such as Microsoft or Symantec. Many more exist from individuals who want to make their mark on the world by sharing what they know about Windows NT.

The Web pages in this section are only a start. Many contain links to other Windows NT sites. Before you know it, your Windows NT favorite places list will grow tremendously.

Microsoft Corporation

URL address: **http://www.microsoft.com**

Microsoft's Web site contains an amazing amount of information about its products, services, plans, job opportunities, and more. You can find the two most useful Windows NT Web pages by clicking the Products link or the Support link.

Here's what you find on each:

◆ *Products link.* This Web page contains links for most Microsoft products, including Windows NT. You find links to Microsoft pages for Windows 95, Office, BackOffice, Windows NT Workstation, and more. The bulletin board on this page also contains the latest information about Microsoft products.

◆ *Support link.* The Support Desktop Web page provides access to the Microsoft KnowledgeBase, which you can use to search for articles based on keywords that you specify. It also contains links to the Microsoft Software Library and Frequently Asked Questions (FAQ) Web pages.

 On the Web

This site is best viewed with Microsoft's Internet Explorer. You can get your own copy of Internet Explorer at **http://www.microsoft.com/windows/ie/ie.htm**.

And it's free, too.

Other Windows NT-Related Web sites that you may want to look into are:

Chancellor and Chancellor Windows NT Resource Site

URL address: **http://www.chancellor.com/ntmain.html**

Info Nederland Windows NT Information Site

URL address: **http://nt.info.nl/english/default.htm**

Windows NT Magazine

URL address: **http://www.winntmag.com**

Windows NT Administration FAQ

URL address: **http://ftech.com/classes/admin/admin.htm**

Using the CD-ROM

Using the Self-Test Software

The tests on this CD-ROM consist of performance-based questions. This means that rather than asking you what function an item would fulfill (knowledge-based question), you will be presented with a situation and asked for an answer that shows your ability to solve the problem.

The program consists of three main test structures:

◆ *Self-Assessment Test*. This would typically be the test you take first. This test is meant to give you a sense of where your strengths and weaknesses are on Windows NT Workstation 4.0. You will get immediate feedback on your answer. It will either be correct and you will be able to go to the next question, or it will be incorrect and the system will recommend what part of the study guide to research and you will be prompted to try again.

♦ *Chapter-End Test.* After reading a chapter from the study guide you will have the option to take a mini-test consisting of questions relevant only to the given chapter. You will get immediate feedback on your answer as well as an indication of what subsection to find the answer should your response be incorrect.

♦ *Mastery Test.* This is the big one. This test is different from the two others in the sense that feedback is not given on a question-by-question basis. It simulates the exam situation, so you will give answers to all questions and then get your overall score. In addition to the score, for all wrong answers, you will get pointers as to where in the study guide you need to study further. You will also be able to print a report card featuring your test results.

All test questions are multiple choice offering four possible answers. The answers are all labeled A, B, C, and D. There will always be either one or two alternatives representing the right answer; thus, a right answer might be "A & D" or any other combination.

Equipment Requirements

To run the self-test software, you must have at least the following equipment:

♦ IBM-compatible PC I386

♦ Microsoft DOS 5.0

♦ Microsoft Windows 3.x

♦ 4M of RAM

♦ 256-color display adapter

♦ Double-speed CD-ROM drive

To take full advantage of the software and run it at a more acceptable speed, however, the following equipment is recommended:

- IBM-Compatible I486 DX
- Microsoft Windows 3.1 or better
- 8M of RAM
- 256-color display adapter or better
- Quad speed CD-ROM drive

App
I

Running the Self-Test Software

The self-test software runs directly from the CD-ROM, and does not require you to install any files to your hard drive. After you have followed these simple start-up steps, you will find the software very intuitive and self-explanatory.

If you are using Windows 3.x, Windows NT 3.x, or Windows for Workgroups:

1. Insert the disk in your CD drive.
2. Choose File, Run in Windows Program Manager, click Browse, and select the letter of your CD drive (typically D). Double-click the file name dtique95.exe and the self-test program will be activated.

If you are using Windows 95 or Windows NT 4.0:

1. Insert the disk in your CD drive.
2. Click the Start button on the Windows taskbar, select Run, and click Browse. Select My Computer and double-click dtique95.exe.

As soon as "dtique95" executes, you will be in the program and will just need to follow instructions or click your selections.

J

Sample Tests

Using the Self-Tests

The tests in this appendix contain performance-based questions designed to test your problem-solving capabilities. The questions are divided into three main test structures:

◆ *Self-Assessment Test.* This would typically be the test you take first. This test is meant to give you a sense of where your strengths and weaknesses are on Windows NT Workstation 4.0.

◆ *Chapter-End Test.* After reading a chapter from the study guide you will have the option to take a mini-test consisting of questions relevant only to the given chapter. These questions are listed in order of the chapters in this book.

◆ *Mastery Test.* This test simulates the exam situation, so you will give answers to all questions and then get your overall score.

All test questions are either True/False or multiple-choice type offering four possible answers. The answers are all labeled A, B, C, and D. There will always be several alternatives representing the right answer; thus, a right answer might be "A & D," "B, C, D," "A, B, C, D" or any other combination.

Note These questions are also included on the CD-ROM that accompanies this book. See Appendix I, "Using the CD-ROM," for information on how to access these questions and run the software included with the CD.

Self-Assessment Test

Note The answers to these questions can be found in order at the end of this section. The resource line following each question number is the section of that chapter in the book where information regarding that question is located. ■

Question #1
Resource: Chapter 3, "Mass Storage Device Configuration"

You have begun the setup process and have been queried for mass storage devices. Setup presents you with a blank list of devices, but you know that you have a 1.2G IDE drive installed.

    A. IDE devices are detected but generally not displayed in the list.

    B. Windows NT has incorrectly identified your devices. Press F3 to exit setup and double-check your drive configuration.

    C. Type **S** to add the drive configuration to the list.

    D. Exit setup and run NTHQ to verify hardware detection.

Question #2
Resource: Chapter 7, "Examining Access Control Lists"

The permission list defining access to a resource resides:

    A. With the resource and is called the Access Control List.

    B. With the user and is called the User Rights Policy.

    C. With the user and is called the Access Control List.

    D. With the resource and is called the User Rights Policy.

Question #3
Resource: Chapter 11, "Introducing Peer Web Services"

Your company has implemented an intranet for publishing corporate data and to provide access to database information. Your company is international, and users from all locations will be accessing the intranet. Which service is the best choice for implementing publishing services?

App

J

A. Peer Web Services

B. Internet Information Server Services

C. Internet Explorer Services

D. TCP/IP Protocol Services

Question #4

Resource: Chapter 8, "Creating and Managing Volume Sets" and "Creating and Managing Stripe Sets"

Which of the following statements are true regarding Volume Sets and Stripe Sets? Choose all that apply.

A. Stripe sets can contain the system partition and volume sets cannot.

B. Stripe sets must combine areas of equal size while volume sets can combine areas of any size.

C. Stripe sets cannot contain the system partition and volume sets can.

D. Stripe sets write to all members of the set concurrently while volume sets fill each member of the set in turn.

Question #5

Resource: Chapter 4, "Help Topics—Bookmark"

There is a particular Help topic that you frequent. Is there a way to quickly access it when you open Help?

A. Annotate the topic and then browse annotations when you start Help.

B. Annotate the topic, then use Find to find all help documents with your annotation.

C. Create a bookmark. When you start Help, access the page by selecting the bookmark.

D. You cannot mark a page in Help.

Question #6

Resource: Chapter 3, "Installing Windows NT Networking"

What network information is necessary for you to supply during the Network portion of the Setup Wizard?

A. Network Protocols, Network Services, Network Bindings, Network Card settings, Network Model

B. Network Protocols, Network Card Settings, Workgroup or Domain membership

C. Computer Name, Network Card Settings, Workgroup or Domain membership

D. Windows NT self-detects all network settings.

Question #7

Resource: Chapter 10, "Examining Win 16 Application Support"

Which of the following statements accurately describes a Win 16 application running under Windows NT 4.0?

A. All Win 16 applications run in the same NTVDM by default.

B. All Win 16 applications are non-preemptively multitasked within the NTVDM.

C. 16-bit calls are translated into 32-bit calls through a process called thunking.

D. WOW emulates the Windows 3.1 memory environment for Win 16 applications.

Question #8

Resource: Chapter 6, "Group Management in Domains"

What are the differences between a local group and a global group? Choose all that apply.

A. Local groups can be created on workstations, servers, and domain controllers, while global groups can only be created and maintained on a domain controller.

B. Local groups can contain local users, domain users, and global groups, while global groups can contain only users from their domain.

C. Local groups can contain local users, domain users, global groups, and other local groups, while global groups can contain only users from their domain.

D. Local groups can be used for managing resources only on the local computer, while global groups can be used to manage resources on any computer that participates in the domain.

Question #9

Resource: Chapter 11, "NWLink IPX/SPX Compatible Protocol"

Your Windows NT 4.0 workstations must connect to both Windows NT 4.0 servers and NetWare servers. Your NetWare servers are of all versions. You have installed NWLink IPX/SPX Compatible Protocol on the workstations along with CSNW to allow communications with the NetWare servers. You find during testing that your Windows NT workstations can connect to some of the NetWare servers, but not all of them. The NWLink protocol settings look like this:

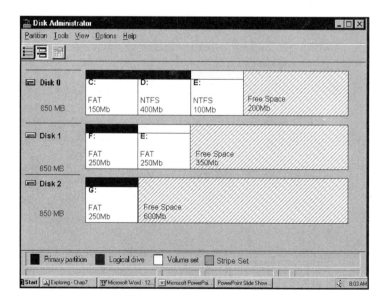

How can you troubleshoot this situation?

    A. Check the network for multiple frame types and configure NWLink to recognize them all.

    B. Do nothing with the protocol settings. Check the network card connections to the network.

    C. Modify the frame types on the NetWare servers to autodetect.

    D. Give each Windows NT 4.0 workstation a network number.

Question #10

Resource: Chapter 9, "Priority"

There is one high-speed network print device connected to the print server in MIS. MIS Managers and Project Leaders should always be able to print to this printer regardless of who else has submitted print jobs. Help Desk staff should be able to print ahead of Developers. What will best accomplish this task?

    A. Create three printers, each associated with the device, and assign the appropriate groups access only to their printer. Give the Managers' printer a priority of 1, Help Desk's printer a priority of 50, and Developers a priority of 99.

    B. Create three printers, each associated with the device, and assign the appropriate groups access only to their printer. Give the Managers' printer a priority of 99, Help Desk's printer a priority of 50, and Developers a priority of 1.

    C. Create three printers, each associated with the device, and assign the appropriate groups access only to their printer. Make the Managers' printer a printer pool by associating it with each print device.

    D. Create three printers associated with the device and assign the appropriate groups access only to their printer. Make each printer a printer pool by associating it with each print device.

Question #11

Resource: Chapter 9, "Troubleshooting Printing"

Which of the following steps is appropriate to take when troubleshooting a failed print job?

App

J

A. Verify that the appropriate print port has been defined and configured by printing a test page.

B. Delete and re-create the printer.

C. Determine whether the print device is online and connected.

D. Resubmit the print job to a file and then copy the file to a printer port to see if it is successful.

Question #12

Resource: Chapter 5, "Boot Process for RISC-based Computers"

While looking at the files on my RISC-based computer, I notice that NTLDR, NTDETECT.COM, and BOOT.INI are missing. What impact will this have on the boot process on this computer?

A. The boot process relies on these files to govern the Boot and Load Phases. Missing or corrupt files will result in error messages and failed boots.

B. It will have no impact on the boot process because RISC-based computers do not rely on these files.

C. The BOOT.INI is not an essential file. Windows NT will look for the default Windows NT system directory.

D. NTLDR is always needed to direct the boot process. NTDETECT.COM and BOOT.INI are not necessary on RISC-based computers.

Question #13

Resource: Chapter 4, "Welcome to Windows NT Workstation 4.0"

The correct way to shut down Windows NT is to: (Choose three)

A. Press Ctrl+Alt+Del on the keyboard, then choose Shutdown in the Windows NT Security dialog box.

B. Choose Shutdown from the Start menu and then Restart the computer.

C. Choose Shutdown from the Start menu and then shut down the computer.

D. Press Ctrl+Alt+Del on the keyboard and then power off the computer.

Question #14

Resource: Chapter 3, "Partition Configuration"

You must preconfigure your installation drive before starting setup.

    A. True

    B. False

Question #15

Resource: Chapter 2, "The Recordset"

Which of the following are characteristics of NTFS? Choose three.

    A. Transaction tracking

    B. File and directory level permissions

    C. Auto-defragmentation of files

    D. Data compression

App

J

Question #16

Resource: Chapter 5, "The System Policy Editor"

There are several temporary employees who will work on two different shifts during the summer. They will log on to the network using different workstations each day. However, they need to have the same desktop configuration and should not be able to modify settings such as display choices, and so on. What is the easiest way to accomplish this?

    A. Windows NT does not provide for this level of control in this version.

    B. Modify the Registry on each workstation that each temporary employee will log on to.

    C. Create a system profile for each user with the appropriate settings.

    D. Create a user account on each workstation for each temporary employee and then modify the appropriate Registry entries for each temporary employee on each workstation.

Question #17

Resource: Chapter 12, "Using Event Viewer to Troubleshoot Windows NT"

What steps need to take place in order to capture and view security related events? Choose all that apply.

A. Switch to the Security Log in Event Viewer.

B. Log on as a Power User.

C. Enable auditing in the User Manager.

D. Configure which security events to audit.

Question #18

Resource: Chapter 6, "Creating a New User"

Under which of the following situations would you disable the user account rather than delete it?

A. JaneD has left the company on maternity leave and plans to return in three months.

B. JohnB has taken an emergency medical leave of absence for possibly six or more months, but hopes to return full-time.

C. JaniceD has left the company to take a job at Microsoft.

D. FrankP has taken a temporary team leader position in another department and will return when the project is completed.

Question #19

Resource: Chapter 7, "Assigning File and Folder Permissions"

You have modified NTFS permissions for the file DOOM.DOC so that Team Leaders have Full Control. For all other files and folders, Team Leaders should have Read access. Using the exhibit, how can you best accomplish this?

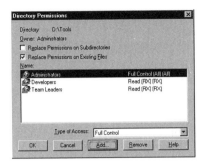

A. Select Replace Permissions on Subdirectories and deselect Replace Permissions on Existing Files.

B. Select Replace Permissions on Subdirectories.

C. Deselect Replace Permissions on Existing Files.

D. Set permissions on each file and folder individually.

Question #20

Resource: Chapter 3, "Formatting the Partition," and sidebar "RISC Partition Formats"

You are installing Windows NT on a RISC-based computer and want to format the Windows NT system partition as NTFS.

A. Create a 2M FAT partition for the Windows NT boot files, and a second partition large enough for the Windows NT system files before starting setup. Select the partition during setup and format it as NTFS.

B. Create a 2M FAT partition for the Windows NT boot files before starting setup. During setup, choose free space, create a partition, and format it as NTFS just as in an Intel installation.

C. Windows NT requires a FAT partition for its system files. You can only format non–system partitions with NTFS.

D. Windows NT does not support NTFS on RISC-based systems.

App

J

Question #21

Resource: Chapter 8, "An Overview of FAT" and "An Overview of NTFS"

Which of the following statements is true regarding FAT and NTFS? Choose all that apply.

- A. FAT supports long file names and so does NTFS.
- B. NTFS supports long file names but FAT does not.
- C. FAT supports a maximum partition size of 4G and NTFS supports a maximum partition size of 16E.
- D. Formatting a partition as FAT requires less than 1M of overhead, while NTFS formatting requires at least 4M.

Question #22

Resource: Chapter 5, "Control Panel" and "Accessibility Options"

Janice is a hearing-impaired account manager who has asked if Windows NT provides any options appropriate for her? What can you do to help?

- A. Select Control Panel, Sounds and increase the volume for system sounds.
- B. Select My Computer, Properties and select the Accessibilities tab to set Sound options.
- C. Select Control Panel, Accessibility Options and set the Sound options.
- D. Windows NT does not provide options for physically challenged persons.

Question #23

Resource: Chapter 9, "Creating a Printer"

Nelson has been selected to assist you as a printing administrator in the Dry Gulch office, because you are unable to travel there frequently, though you'd really like to. What is the minimum level of access you need to give Nelson so that he can perform basic print management tasks such as creating and sharing printers and managing print jobs?

A. Make Nelson a member of the Print Operators local group on his print server.

B. Make Nelson a member of the Server Operator local group on his print server.

C. Make Nelson a member of the Administrators local group on his print server.

D. Give Nelson Full Control permission for each printer on his print server.

Question #24

Resource: Chapter 2, "Workgroup Model"

You will be supporting a group of 10 account executives all running Windows NT Workstation on their computers. Occasionally, each account executive will need to share files with some or all of the other account executives. Two of the account executives have printers that all of them will use. You do not expect the group to grow by any more than five more persons. Which computing model will best meet the group's needs?

A. The Workgroup Model

B. The Single Domain Enterprise Model

C. The Master Domain Enterprise Model

D. The Complete Trust Enterprise Model

Question #25

Resource: Chapter 12, "Reviewing System Recovery Options"

Which of the following recovery options could be useful to troubleshoot an intermittent stop error on a Windows NT 4.0 workstation?

A. Run RDISK at a command prompt.

B. Send an Administrative Alert to the Administrator.

C. Write an event to the System Log.

D. Automatically reboot the computer after the stop error occurs.

App

J

Question #26

Resource: Chapter 10, "Reviewing the Windows NT 4.0 Subsystem Architecture"

Which of the following functions as part of the kernel mode of Windows NT 4.0?

A. CSR Subsystem

B. HAL

C. GDI

D. Thread prioritization

Question #27

Resource: Chapter 2, "Preemptive Multitasking" and "Kernel Mode"

True or False? All Kernel mode processes run in the protected mode of the processor (ring0).

A. True

B. False

Question #28

Resource: Chapter 6, "Creating Server Based Profiles"

There are five summer interns joining the company this year for a three-month period. You want to give them access to the network, but you want to restrict their environment settings to specific programs, colors, and so on. They should not be able to change the settings. What steps are involved?

A. Change the NTUSER.DAT file in the shared directory to NTUSER.MAN.

B. Copy the account through the User Profiles tab in the System applet to a shared directory on a central server.

C. Create a user account and make the appropriate changes to that account's environment settings.

D. Specify the location and file name of the profile in each summer intern's account properties.

Question #29

Resource: Chapter 11, "Configuring Network Options" and "Reviewing Workstation and Server Services"

On your local subnet, you regularly copy data from your Windows NT 4.0 workstations to an archive Windows NT 4.0 workstation using NetBEUI. The archive workstation is not used for any other purpose. How can you optimize the bindings on the archive workstation?

A. Do nothing. Windows NT self-optimizes network bindings.

B. Disable the workstation binding because the archive workstation will never need to establish its own connections with other computers.

C. Disable the server binding because the archive workstation will never need to establish its own connections with other computers.

D. Move the server binding ahead of the workstation binding because the archive workstation responds to network requests rather than making them.

Question 30

Resource: Chapter 11, "File System Layer"

Which Windows NT network model component is responsible for determining where to send a request for resources?

A. File System Layer

B. Transport Device Interface

C. Protocol Layer

D. Network Interface Card Layer

Question #31

Resource: Chapter 8, "Creating and Managing Volume Sets" and "Extending Volume Sets"

You need to extend a FAT partition to allow more space for a growing database. Which option best explains your strategy?

App

J

A. Use Disk Administrator to select the FAT partition and an area of free space and choose Partition, Create Volume Set.

B. Use Disk Administrator to select the FAT partition and an area of free space and choose Partition, Extend Volume Set.

C. Use Disk Administrator to select the FAT partition and an area of formatted space and choose Tools, Combine Volume Sets.

D. You cannot extend the volume.

Question #32

Resource: Chapter 9, "Windows NT 4.0 Print Process"

Which of the following sets of Windows NT network clients do not require print drivers to be installed on the local computer?

A. All Microsoft Network clients

B. Windows NT and Windows 95

C. Windows NT, Windows 95, Windows for Workgroups 3.11

D. Windows NT, Windows 95, LAN Manager v2.x for DOS

Question #33

Resource: Chapter 4, "My Computer" and "Windows Explorer"

Which of the following objects let me browse through my files, folders, drives, and shared network resources?

A. Network Neighborhood

B. My Computer

C. Windows NT Explorer

D. Task Manager

Question #34

Resource: Chapter 5, "Control Panel Services"

Which three of the following four features are a part of the Services applet in Control Panel?

A. Running status

B. Load order

C. Hardware profile assignments

D. Startup options

Question #35

Resource: Chapter 12, "Objects to Monitor, Process Object," "Exploring and Optimizing Pagefile Usage" and "Creating Multiple Pagefiles"

Desiree, a Visual Basic developer, has noticed that her system's performance has decreased since she began work on a large VB application. You have used Performance Monitor to determine that the pagefile usage has increased. You also notice that the pagefile, Windows NT system files, and the VB application are all stored on the same partition. In addition, the working set for the VB application shows that it consistently requires 16M for itself. What solutions can you recommend? Name all that apply.

A. Add more RAM in the computer.

B. Move the pagefile to a disk partition other than the system or application partition.

C. Increase the maximum size for the pagefile.

D. Create multiple page files.

App

J

Question #36

Resource: Chapter 7, "Sharing Resources and Determining Network Access"

The manager of the Accounting department wants to make next year's budget templates available for the staff accountants to review beginning next month. They will be stored on the department resource server called ACCT1 in a folder called BUDGET97. None of the partitions on ACCT1 are formatted with NTFS. How would you make the folder available only to the Accounting department staff?

A. Use User Manager to assign permission to use the folder to the Accountants group.

B. Use User Manager for Domains to assign User Rights to the Accountants group to access the BUDGET97 share.

C. Use the Security tab on the properties sheet for the folder to assign permissions to the Accountants group.

D. Use the Sharing tab on the properties sheet for the folder to assign permissions to the Accountants group.

Question #37

Resource: Chapter 3, "Table 3.1 Windows NT Workstation 4.0 System Requirements"

You are planning to roll out Windows NT Workstation 4.0 to a workgroup that has the following computer configurations. On which computers can you install Windows NT Workstation 4.0 successfully?

- A. 3 386/25, 150M free space, 8M RAM, VGA, Windows 3.1

- B. 2 386/33, 120M free space, 16M RAM, VGA, Windows for Workgroups

- C. 5 486/66DX, 200M free space, 16M RAM, Super VGA, Windows for Workgroups

- D. 2 Pentium/120, 100M free space, 16M RAM, Super VGA, Windows NT 3.51

Question #38

Resource: Chapter 6, "Default User Accounts"

Which of the following statements is true about the default user accounts created in Windows NT Workstation 4.0?

- A. The Administrator account is enabled and can be renamed; the Guest account is enabled and cannot be renamed.

- B. The Administrator account is enabled and cannot be renamed; the Guest account is disabled and cannot be renamed.

- C. The Administrator account is enabled and can be renamed; the Guest account is disabled and can be renamed.

- D. The Administrator account is disabled and cannot be renamed; the Guest account is enabled and can be renamed.

Question #39

Resource: Chapter 2, "Kernel Mode"

Which of the following are part of the Kernel Mode of the Windows NT architecture? Choose three.

A. WIN32 Subsystem

B. HAL

C. Executive Services

D. Device Driver support

Question #40

Resource: Chapter 10, "Examining Support for MS-DOS-based Applications" and "Configuring the NTVDM"

Which of the following statements is true about the NTVDM?

A. Each NTVDM has one thread of operation associated with it.

B. Each NTVDM is designed to emulate the Windows memory environment and provides a set of support files to do so.

C. Each NTVDM is configurable by modifying the properties of the MS-DOS application.

D. Each NTVDM is configurable through one AUTOEXEC.BAT and CONFIG.SYS file that is read when Windows NT boots.

Question #41

Resource: Chapter 6, "Naming Conventions," "Considerations Regarding Passwords," and "Creating a New User"

Which of the following sets of usernames and passwords are acceptable for Windows NT?

	Username	**Password**
A.	First Ass't Comptroller	FirstComp
B.	FirstAsstCompt	1stComp
C.	FirstAss*tCompt	COMP1
D.	AssComp1	123COMPTROLLER1

Question #42

Resource: Chapter 11, "Configuring RAS on the Server"

For security reasons, you want to restrict access for dial-up users only to the RAS server when they dial in, but not restrict their access when at the office. What must you do?

App

J

A. Do nothing. This is the default setting.

B. Disable gateway access for each RAS server network protocol setting.

C. Configure the permissions on each of the resource servers in the network to restrict the users.

D. Configure the dial-in permissions for each user on the RAS server to restrict access to the RAS server.

Question #43

Resource: Chapter 7, "Effective Permissions"

Ned is a member of the Developers group at Springfield Technologies. He has been promoted to team leader for his group. He needs to edit the DOOM.DOC file in the Tools folder, but does not have Write access. What must you do to give Ned access to DOOM.DOC?

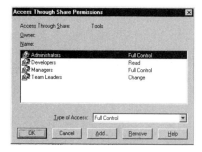

A. Do nothing. The next time Ned logs on, his permissions will change.

B. Change the Developers group permission to Change.

C. Add Ned to the Team Leaders group.

D. Change the Team Leaders group permission to Full Control.

Question #44

Resource: Chapter 8, "Understanding Partitions"

Windows NT calls the active primary partition its:

A. Boot partition

B. System partition

C. Startup partition

D. Extended partition

Question #45

Resource: Chapter 4, "Windows Explorer"

What is the best way to navigate among my files and directories?

A. From the Start menu, choose Programs, Accessories, File Manager.

B. From the Start menu, choose Run and then type **WINFILE.EXE** to start File Manager.

C. From the Start menu, choose Programs, Windows Explorer.

D. From the Start menu, choose Run and then type **PROGMAN.EXE**.

Question #46

Resource: Chapter 2, "Trust Relationships" and "Master Domain"

You have decided to implement an enterprise domain model in which the user accounts are centrally administered, and in which the resources are distributed in their own domains to the various departments that will administer those resources; they will not, however, manage any user accounts. How will you implement the trust relationship?

A. There is no trust relationship involved because this scenario represents a Single Domain Enterprise Model.

B. Each resource domain will trust the account domain.

C. Each domain will trust every other domain.

D. You can only do this in a Workgroup Model.

Question #47

Resource: Chapter 6, "Default Group Accounts"

Everyone should be able to read the files in a certain directory. However, the user who created the file should be able to modify it. What do you need to do?

   A. Do nothing. By default, only the creator of a file has access to it. Windows NT restricts resource access by default.

   B. Give the group Everyone Read access and the Creator Owner group Change access. By default, Windows NT allows everyone complete access to resources.

   C. Give the group Everyone Read access and the Creator Owner group Change access. By default, Windows NT restricts resource access.

   D. Give the group Everyone Read access and the Users group Change access. Windows NT will automatically determine who the owner of the file is and restrict the other users.

Question #48

Resource: Chapter 9, "Print Monitor"

What is the purpose of the print monitor SFMMON.DLL?

   A. SFMMON.DLL monitors Macintosh print jobs routed using AppleTalk protocol to network print devices.

   B. SFMMON.DLL is the System File Manager print monitor that tracks print jobs sent directly to or printed directly from a file.

   C. SFMMON.DLL is the software print job compression DLL that compresses the print job before it is routed from the local print spooler to the print server.

   D. SFMMON.DLL is not a valid print monitor.

Question #49

Resource: Chapter 5, "Control Panel—Mouse" and "Examining the Registry"

Martha wants to modify her mouse pointers. What is the most appropriate procedure for doing this?

A. Choose Control Panel, Mouse and select the pointers through the Pointers tab.

B. Right-click the desktop, choose Properties, and select the Settings tab.

C. Start the Registry Editor, select HKEY_CURRENT_USER, and modify the Cursors subkey.

D. Start the Registry Editor, select HKEY_LOCAL_MACHINE, and modify the System\CurrentControlSet subkey.

Question #50

Resource: Chapter 3, "Troubleshooting Installation and Setup," and "Preparation Checklist"

The three most important tips I can offer a coworker to make a Windows NT installation problem-free are:

A. Create an Emergency Repair Disk. You can use this to restart Windows NT and repair the installation process.

B. Consult the Hardware Compatibility List before starting setup to ensure that all the computer's hardware components have been tested with Windows NT 4.0.

C. Determine whether the computer in question meets all the minimum equipment requirements for a Windows NT installation.

D. Find out all the driver and configuration data specific to devices in the computer, particularly regarding the network card, before starting setup.

Question #51

Resource: Chapter 12, "Understanding Virtual Memory Management"

Which of the following represent characteristics of the Virtual Memory Manager?

A. The Virtual Memory Manager provides up to 2G of storage for each application.

B. The default pagefile size is 12M + physical RAM.

App

J

    C. Application requests for memory are mapped directly into RAM.

    D. The pagefile is created on the partition with the most free space.

Question #52

Resource: Chapter 3, "Upgrading to Windows NT Workstation 4.0—Windows 3.1 and Windows for Workgroups 3.11"

You are installing Windows NT Workstation 4.0 on a computer that needs to support Windows for Workgroups as well. You would like to migrate user and environment settings to Windows NT 4.0. What should you do?

    A. Do nothing. The Windows for Workgroups settings will automatically be migrated to Windows NT 4.0.

    B. Install Windows NT 4.0 in the same directory as Windows for Workgroups. The settings compatible with Windows NT 4.0 will then automatically be migrated. You can continue to boot either to Windows NT or to Windows for Workgroups.

    C. After installing Windows NT 4.0, run the MIGRATE utility from the command prompt.

    D. You cannot migrate those settings from Windows for Workgroups.

Question #53

Resource: Chapter 11, "Benefits of TDI and NDIS 4.0"

Your Windows NT 4.0 workstations must be able to establish connections to resources on NetWare servers and UNIX servers as well as Windows NT 4.0 servers. You need IPX/SPX to communicate with the NetWare servers and TCP/IP to communicate with Windows NT and UNIX servers. What must you do to accomplish this?

    A. Install two network adapters and both NWLink IPX/SPX and TCP/IP on the Windows NT 4.0 workstations. Bind NWLink to one adapter and TCP/IP to the other.

B. Install three network adapters, one for each type of server, and both NWLink IPX/SPX and TCP/IP on the Windows NT 4.0 workstations. Bind NWLink to one adapter and TCP/IP to the other two.

C. Install one network adapter and both NWLink IPX/SPX and TCP/IP on the Windows NT 4.0 workstations. Windows NT will bind both protocols to the same adapter. Enable and disable each binding as necessary when communicating among the various servers.

D. Do nothing. When you install the two protocols, Windows NT will automatically bind them to the network adapter. Nothing else is required for the connections to be established.

Question #54

Resource: Chapter 7, "Understanding the Concept of Ownership"

The person that created DOOM.DOC on server ACCT1 is no longer with the company. Cathy, a member of Team Leaders, will be assuming responsibility for the DOOM project, and needs to become the owner of DOOM.DOC. How can this be accomplished? Choose all that apply.

A. Give Cathy the Take Ownership of Files and Folders User Right on the server ACCT1.

B. Give Cathy the Take Ownership permission on the file DOOM.DOC.

C. Tell Cathy to just take ownership of the file.

D. Give the Team Leaders group the Take Ownership permission for DOOM.DOC.

Question #55

Resource: Chapter 3, "Formatting the Partition"

Which of the following statements does not apply to NTFS?

A. NTFS supports file and directory permissions security and access auditing.

App

J

    B. NTFS supports transaction tracking and sector sparing for data recovery.

    C. NTFS supports file and partition sizes of up to 4G.

    D. NTFS provides file and directory compression.

Question #56

Resource: Chapter 7, "Sharing Resources and Determining Network Access"

The administrator of the Tools shared folder wants to limit access to the folder only to the Developers group. To accomplish this, she gives the Everyone group No Access, and the Developers group Change access. The Developers complain that they cannot access any file in Tools. What else must the administrator do?

    A. Share the files in the Tools folder.

    B. Remove the Everyone group.

    C. Give the Developers group Full Control.

    D. Format the partition as NTFS and assign NTFS permissions in addition to the share permissions.

Question #57

Resource: Chapter 10, "Reviewing the Windows NT 4.0 Subsystem Architecture" and "Examining Win 16 Application Support"

Which of the following functions as part of the user mode of Windows NT 4.0?

    A. CSR Subsystem

    B. HAL

    C. USER

    D. WOW

Question #58

Resource: Chapter 6, "Understanding User Manager" and "Creating a New User"

Your workstations are members of a domain called Titan. You need to create user accounts so that two shifts of temporary employees can log on to the same computer, but only during their shift.

A. Use User Manager for Domains on each local Windows NT workstation to create the temporary accounts and assign each the appropriate logon hours.

B. Use User Manager on each local Windows NT workstation to create the temporary accounts and assign each the appropriate logon hours.

C. Use User Manager for Domains on the domain controller for Titan to create domain accounts for the temporary employees and assign each the appropriate logon hours.

D. Use User Manager on the domain controller for Titan to create domain accounts for the temporary employees and assign each the appropriate logon hours.

Question #59

Resource: Chapter 3, "Table 3.2 Beginning Setup"

Which of the following switches will allow you to install Windows NT without creating the three startup disks?

A. WINNT /B

B. WINNT /O

C. WINNT /OX

D. WINNT /T:c

Question #60

Resource: Chapter 8, "Additional Thoughts on Long Names"

You are deciding whether to support long file names on FAT partitions for your server. You have a variety of client platforms that connect to the server, including MS-DOS and Windows 95. Some of the platforms support older 16-bit applications. Which of the following considerations would you make?

A. There are no significant concerns. All applications support long file names on all platforms in a Microsoft network.

B. Most Microsoft applications will support the long file names, but some older applications save changes by deleting the old file and renaming a temporary file to the original file name. This could corrupt the long file name.

C. Long file names saved in the root of the drive require one directory entry for the alias, and one for up to every 13 characters of the name. Because the root is hard-coded for 512 directory entries, you could run out of entries.

D. If long file name support is disabled for the FAT partition, it is disabled for all partitions on that computer, including NTFS.

Question #61

Resource: Chapter 10, "Managing Win 16 Applications with Multiple NTVDMS"

Mandy is running Pinball, the DOS Editor, Word 6, Excel 5, and Microstomp, a 16-bit, third-party Windows Web surfing program. Microstomp occasionally hangs up due to low resource memory. This affects his other Windows applications. What can you suggest to alleviate this problem?

A. Configure Microstomp to run in its own memory space.

B. Configure each Win 16 application to run in its own memory space.

C. Modify the PIF for Microstomp to increase its resource memory allocation.

D. Modify the PIF for the WOW NTVDM to increase resource memory allocations for all the Windows applications.

Question #62

Resource: Chapter 11, "TCP/IP Protocol"

Which TCP/IP utility would be useful to determine a computer's address settings?

A. Ping

B. IPCONFIG

C. FTP

D. Network Neighborhood

Question #63

Resource: Chapter 4, "Find" and "Start Menu-Documents"

Bill has created an important legal document, but cannot remember where he saved it, or exactly what he called it. However, he knows he created it yesterday. How can you help him?

A. Use Windows Explorer to display all files by their date. Then browse each directory until you find the missing file.

B. From the Start menu, choose Documents. Bill should be able to find his document listed there.

C. From the Start menu, choose Find Files or Folders. On the Date\Time tab enter yesterday's date. Bill should be able to find his file in the Find results window.

D. Take Bill out to lunch.

Question #64

Resource: Chapter 9, "Auditing and Taking Ownership of the Printer"

Rosemarie was the print administrator in Ulan Bator, but has left the country to pursue a career as an opera singer. You need to assign a new print administrator. What will you need to do concerning ownership of the Ulan Bator printers that Rosemarie created and managed?

A. Do nothing. Printers are not owned by a user; they are owned by the system.

B. Make the new print administrator a Print Operator. The new print administrator can then take ownership of the printers in Ulan Bator.

C. Give ownership of the printers to the new print administrator.

D. Give the new administrator Full Control permission over the printers. Full Control automatically assigns ownership to that user.

App

J

Question #65
Resource: Chapter 5, "Control Panel Services"

Which three of the following four features is a part of the Services applet in Control Panel?

    A. Running status

    B. Load order

    C. Hardware profile assignments

    D. Startup options

Question #66
Resource: Chapter 8, "(Backup) Requirements, Terms and Strategy"

Lucy has been appointed the backup coordinator for the network. What must you do to enable her to accomplish this task and still maintain security on the data? Choose all that apply.

    A. Make Lucy a member of the local Backup Operators group on each computer that needs to be backed up.

    B. Make Lucy a member of the Server Operators group on each server computer that needs to be backed up.

    C. Assign Lucy the Backup Files and Directories user right.

    D. Give Lucy Full Control over all files and folders.

Question #67
Resource: Chapter 7, "Examining the Windows NT Security Model"

A user's effective access to a resource is determined by:

    A. Comparing the rights of the user with the permissions assigned through the ACL of the resource.

    B. Comparing the permissions in the access token of the user with the permissions assigned through the ACL of the resource.

    C. Comparing the user and group SID entries in the user's access token with the permissions assigned through the ACL of the resource.

    D. Comparing the user and group SID entries in the user's access token with the user rights listed in the ACL of the resource.

Question #68

Resource: Chapter 10, "Task Manager"

Mandy is running Pinball, the DOS Editor, Word 6, Excel 5, and Microstomp, a 16-bit, third-party Windows Web surfing program. He says that he has configured Microstomp to run in its own memory space. However, it has failed and the other Windows applications are also unresponsive. How can you tell if Microstomp has been configured to run in its own memory space?

A. Start Task Manager and look for a second WOW NTVDM entry with a reference to the Microstomp application on the Processes tab.

B. Display the properties of the shortcut for Microstomp and see whether Run in Separate Memory Space has been selected on the Shortcut tab.

C. Start Task Manager and look for duplicate occurrences of WOWEXEC on the Applications tab.

D. You cannot tell without restarting the application.

Question #69

Resource: Chapter 8, "Converting a FAT Partition to NTFS" and "Requirements, Terms, and Strategy"

A user wants to convert a partition from FAT to NTFS with no loss of data. How would you advise the user to accomplish this task?

A. Use Disk Administrator to select the partition and choose Tools, Format. Then select NTFS.

B. Use the command-line utility CONVERT.EXE to convert the partition.

C. Use the Windows NT Backup utility to back up the partition data to disk. Then format the partition for NTFS and restore the data.

D. You cannot convert a FAT partition to NTFS without loss of data.

App
J

Question #70

Resource: Chapter 5, "Examining the Registry" and "Changing the Default Startup Screen"

I need to add the company's logo to the default Windows NT boot-up screen. From which Registry subtree(s) can I make this modification?

A. HKEY_LOCAL_MACHINE

B. HKEY_CURRENT_USER

C. HKEY_USERS

D. This change can only be done through Control Panel, Service, Startup.

Question #71

Resource: Chapter 2, "Binding Other Controls to the Data Control"

True or False? The File Manager utility is no longer accessible in Windows NT 4.0.

A. True

B. False

Question #72

Resource: Chapter 9, "Print Processor"

If the final print output is corrupted, what print process component should you check?

A. Spooler service on the client computer

B. Spooler service on the print server

C. Print processor on the print server

D. Print monitor on the client computer

Question #73

Resource: Chapter 6, "User Profiles" and "A Profile Alternative"

As you create new users you would like them to assume the same default environment settings, such as common application groups, startup programs, and company logo, as wallpaper. Which steps will achieve this end?

A. Modify the appropriate changes in the Default User and All Users profile folders in WINNT40\Profiles. When a new user is created, that user's profile will begin with the settings from these two.

B. Create a System Policy file that contains the appropriate settings for the Default user and save it in the WINNT40\SYSTEM32\REPL\IMPORT\SCRIPTS subdirectory on the validating computer.

C. Create a template user account and modify the settings for that account. Create new accounts by copying the template.

D. Create a system policy file for each set of users modifying the settings as appropriate for each user.

Question #74

Resource: Chapter 9, "Windows NT 4.0 Print Process"

Jeanette calls to say that her print jobs seem to have stopped running. You check the printer that she sent the jobs to and see that the jobs are stuck in queue. What steps should you take to clear the stuck jobs? Choose all that apply.

A. Select the stuck jobs and choose Document, Cancel.

B. Select Printer, Purge Printer.

C. Use the Control Panel applet Service to stop and restart the Spooler service.

D. Select each stuck job and change its priority.

Question #75

Resource: Chapter 9, "Priority"

There is one high-speed network print device connected to the print server in MIS. MIS Managers and Project Leaders should always be able to print to this printer regardless of who else has submitted print jobs. Help Desk staff should be able to print ahead of Developers. What will best accomplish this task?

App

J

A. Create three printers each associated with the device and assign the appropriate groups access only to their printer. Give the Managers' printer a priority of 1, Help Desk's printer a priority of 50, and Developers a priority of 99.

B. Create three printers each associated with the device and assign the appropriate groups access only to their printer. Give the Managers' printer a priority of 99, Help Desk's printer a priority of 50, and Developers a priority of 1.

C. Create three printers each associated with the device and assign the appropriate groups access only to their printer. Make the Managers' printer a printer pool by associating it with each print device.

D. Create three printers associated with the device and assign the appropriate groups access only to their printer. Make each printer a printer pool by associating it with each print device.

Answer Key

Question	Answer	Question	Answer
1	A	11	A,C,D
2	A	12	B
3	B	13	A,B,C
4	B,D	14	B
5	C	15	B
6	A	16	C
7	A,B,C,D	17	A,C,D
8	A,B,D	18	A,B,D
9	A	19	A
10	B	20	A

Question	Answer	Question	Answer
21	A,C,D	49	A
22	C	50	B,C,D
23	A	51	A,B,D
24	A	52	B
25	B,C,D	53	D
26	B,C,D	54	A,B,D
27	A	55	C
28	A,B,C,D	56	B
29	B	57	A,D
30	A	58	C
31	D	59	A
32	B	60	A,B
33	B,C	61	A
34	C	62	B
35	A,B,D	63	B,C
36	D	64	B
37	C	65	A,C,D
38	A	66	A,B,C
39	B,C,D	67	C
40	A,C	68	A,B
41	B	69	B
42	B	70	C
43	C	71	B
44	B	72	C
45	C	73	A,B
46	B	74	A,B,C
47	B	75	B
48	A		

App
J

Chapter Tests

Note The answers to these questions can be found in order at the end of this section. The resource line following each question number is the section of that chapter in the book where information regarding that question is located.

Chapter 2

Question #02-01
Resource: Chapter 2, "The Recordset"

You have recently installed Windows NT Workstation on Bob's computer. Bob calls to complain that his favorite Windows 3.1 disk optimizer will no longer work. What can you do to help Bob?

    A. Configure the disk optimization program to run in a separate memory space.

    B. Purchase a Windows NT version of the disk optimization program. Older applications that interact with hardware directly will not run successfully under Windows NT.

    C. Create a PIF (Program Information File) for the disk optimization program.

    D. Take Bob out for lunch.

Question #2-02
Resource: Chapter 2, "The Recordset"

Which of the following are characteristics of NTFS? Choose three.

    A. Transaction tracking

    B. File- and directory-level permissions

    C. Auto-defragmentation of files

    D. Data compression

Question #02-03
Resource: Chapter 2, "Connect Property"

Remote Access Service has been implemented on a Windows NT Workstation computer in a workgroup. Several users with laptop computers are intending to dial in to this workstation to access file resources. When they dial in, they complain that only one person at a time can gain access to the workstation. What can you do to help them?

A. Reconfigure the RAS workstation client for multiple dial-in support.

B. Purchase additional modems for the workstation and reconfigure the RAS client for those modems.

C. Install Windows NT Server on a computer in the workgroup and then install the RAS server on that computer.

D. Give each user his own dial-in access ID.

Question #02-04

Resource: Chapter 2, "Binding Other Controls to the Data Control"

True or False? The File Manager utility is no longer accessible in Windows NT 4.0.

A. True

B. False

Question #02-05

Resource: Chapter 2, "Hardware Profiles"

Betty travels a lot for your organization and has the laptop to prove it. When she is at the office, she plugs her laptop in to her desktop docking station. The docking station has its own monitor, keyboard, and mouse, as well as a network card connection to the company LAN. How can you support Betty's multiple hardware profiles?

A. Windows NT does not support multiple hardware profiles.

B. You must install Windows NT on a separate hard disk in the docking station and boot from that disk when the laptop is docked.

C. Create a second hardware profile for the docking station configuration.

D. You don't need to do anything. Windows NT will recognize the changed configuration when the laptop is docked.

App

J

Question #02-06

Resource: Chapter 2, "Workgroup Model"

You will be supporting a group of 10 account executives all running Windows NT Workstation on their computers. Occasionally, each account executive will need to share files with some or all of the other account executives. Two of the account executives have printers that all of them will use. You do not expect the group to grow by any more than five more persons. Which computing model will best meet the group's needs?

    A. The Workgroup Model

    B. The Single Domain Enterprise Model

    C. The Master Domain Enterprise Model

    D. The Complete Trust Enterprise Model

Question #02-07

Resource: Chapter 2, "Enterprise Model" and "Single Domain Model"

The Account Executive group has merged with the Sales and Marketing Group. You are now supporting 50 users. Each has a variety of files and directories to share with other department members. There are two laser printers, one color printer, one scanner, and two network-ready printers. You are the only administrator for the group. What would be the best model to support these users?

    A. The Workgroup Model

    B. The Single Domain Enterprise Model

    C. The Master Domain Enterprise Model

    D. The Complete Trust Enterprise Model

Question #02-08

Resource: Chapter 2, "Trust Relationships" and "Master Domain"

You have decided to implement an enterprise domain model in which the user accounts are centrally administered, and in which the resources are distributed in their own domains to the various departments that will administer those resources; they will not, however, manage any user accounts. How will you implement the trust relationship?

    A. There is no trust relationship involved because this scenario represents a Single Domain Enterprise Model.

    B. Each resource domain will trust the account domain.

    C. Each domain will trust every other domain.

    D. You can only do this in a Workgroup Model.

Question #02-09

Resource: Chapter 2, "Kernel Mode"

Which of the following is part of the Kernel Mode of the Windows NT architecture? Choose three.

    A. WIN32 Subsystem

    B. HAL

    C. Executive Services

    D. Device Driver support

Question #02-10

Resource: Chapter 2, "Preemptive Multitasking" and "Kernel Mode"

True or False? All Kernel mode processes run in the protected mode of the processor (ring0).

    A. True

    B. False

Question #02-11

Resource: Chapter 2, "Windows NT Virtual Memory Management"

Which of the following statements applies to virtual memory management in Windows NT? Choose two.

    A. When an application is loaded, the Virtual Memory Manager assigns it virtual memory addresses in physical RAM.

    B. The pagefile is created each time that Windows NT is booted.

App

J

C. The pagefile defaults to an initial size of 12M + physical RAM, which is preallocated on the disk, and a maximum size of about three times physical RAM.

D. When an application calls for a page from the pagefile, the Virtual Memory Manager adjusts physical RAM so that all pages of the application reside in contiguous address space.

Question #02-12

Resource: Chapter 2, "Exploring New Features of Windows NT 4.0"

Choose three features of Windows NT 4.0.

A. Windows 95 Interface

B. Peer Web Services

C. Plug and Play

D. Hardware Profiles

Chapter 3

Question #03-01

Resource: Chapter 3, "Table 3.1 Windows NT Workstation 4.0 System Requirements"

You are planning to roll out Windows NT Workstation 4.0 to a workgroup that has the following computer configurations. On which computers can you install Windows NT Workstation 4.0 successfully?

A. 3 386/25, 150M free space, 8M RAM, VGA, Windows 3.1

B. 2 386/33, 120M free space, 16M RAM, VGA, Windows for Workgroups

C. 5 486/66DX, 200M free space, 16M RAM, Super VGA, Windows for Workgroups

D. 2 Pentium/120, 100M free space, 16M RAM, Super VGA, Windows NT 3.51

Question #03-02

Resource: Chapter 3, "Executing the Windows NT Workstation 4.0 Startup Process"

Which of the following dialogs take place during the text mode of the Setup process? Choose three.

    A. Detection and configuration of storage devices

    B. Initial hardware verification

    C. Request for network card settings

    D. Choice of file system for the system partition

Question #03-03

Resource: Chapter 3, "Executing the Windows NT Workstation 4.0 Startup Process"

Which of the following dialogs takes place as part of the Setup Wizard?

    A. Personal information

    B. Detection and configuration of storage devices

    C. Request for network card settings

    D. Video display setup

Question #03-04

Resource: Chapter 3, "Table 3.2 Beginning Setup"

Which of the following switches will allow you to install Windows NT without creating the three startup disks?

    A. WINNT /B

    B. WINNT /O

    C. WINNT /OX

    D. WINNT /T:c

Question #03-05

Resource: Chapter 3, "Beginning Setup," sidebar "Setup Executable on RISC-based Systems"

On a RISC-based computer, which of the following statements is true regarding Windows NT installation?

App

J

A. Execute setup from either the CD–ROM or over the network by typing **WINNT32** and any optional switches.

B. You must have a 2M FAT minimum system partition before starting setup.

C. Execute setup only from a CD–ROM by running WINNT / ARC.

D. Run SETUPLDR from the I386 subdirectory on the CD–ROM.

Question #03-06

Resource: Chapter 3, "Mass Storage Device Configuration"

You have begun the setup process and have been queried for mass storage devices. Setup presents you with a blank list of devices, but you know that you have a 1.2G IDE drive installed.

A. IDE devices are detected but generally not displayed in the list.

B. Windows NT has incorrectly identified your devices. Press F3 to exit setup and double-check your drive configuration.

C. Type **S** to add the drive configuration to the list.

D. Exit setup and run NTHQ to verify hardware detection.

Question #03-07

Resource: Chapter 3, "Partition Configuration"

You must preconfigure your installation drive before starting setup.

A. True

B. False

Question #03-08

Resource: Chapter 3, "Partition Configuration"

During the text mode phase, Windows NT displays a dialog box that shows you two drive partitions, and 600M free space on one drive. You would like to install Windows NT on the free space, but only want to use 200M.

A. You must preconfigure the free space before starting setup.

B. You can select the free space during setup, but you cannot change its size.

C. Select the free space and choose ENTER.

D. Select the free space and choose C to create the new partition. Then select the new partition and continue with installation.

Question #03-09

Resource: Chapter 3, "Formatting the Partition"

Which of the following statements does not apply to NTFS?

A. NTFS supports file and directory permissions security and access auditing.

B. NTFS supports transaction tracking and sector sparing for data recovery.

C. NTFS supports file and partition sizes of up to 4G.

D. NTFS provides file and directory compression.

Question #03-10

Resource: Chapter 3, "Formatting the Partition," and "Upgrading to Windows NT Workstation 4.0—Windows and Windows for Workgroups"

You are installing Windows NT Workstation 4.0 on a computer with a previous installation of Windows for Workgroups. You would like to retain that installation and boot to either Windows or Windows NT.

A. You must install Windows NT in a new directory in order to preserve the original installation.

B. Do nothing. Windows NT will automatically install as dual boot in this installation.

C. Create a new partition using FDISK and install Windows NT in that partition.

D. You cannot dual boot between Windows and Windows NT.

Question #03-11

Resource: Chapter 3, "Formatting the Partition," and sidebar "RISC Partition Formats"

App

J

You are installing Windows NT on a RISC-based computer and want to format the Windows NT system partition as NTFS.

A. Create a 2M FAT partition for the Windows NT boot files, and a second partition large enough for the Windows NT system files before starting setup. Select the partition during setup and format it as NTFS.

B. Create a 2M FAT partition for the Windows NT boot files before starting setup. During setup, choose free space, create a partition, and format it as NTFS just as in an Intel installation.

C. Windows NT requires a FAT partition for its system files. You can only format non-system partitions with NTFS.

D. Windows NT does not support NTFS on RISC-based systems.

Question #03-12

Resource: Chapter 3, "Formatting the Partition," and sidebar "Dual Booting Windows NT 4.0 and OS/2"

You are installing Windows NT on a computer that also must support and boot OS/2.

A. Windows NT supports OS/2's High Performance File System (HPFS) so there are no problems installing the Windows NT system files in the same partition as OS/2.

B. Windows NT 4.0 no longer supports HPFS, so you must install Windows NT in another partition. When Windows NT restarts the system, you can use the OS/2 boot manager to manage both partitions.

C. Windows NT 4.0 no longer supports HPFS, so you must install Windows NT in another partition. When Windows NT restarts the system, it will disable the OS/2 boot manager, but you can reenable it by marking the Boot Manager partition active while in Windows NT and restarting the computer.

D. Windows NT and OS/2 cannot coexist on the same computer.

Question #03-13

Resource: Chapter 3, "Windows NT Setup Wizard"

Name the three main phases of the Setup Wizard.

    A. Installing Windows NT Networking

    B. Finishing Setup (Time Zone, Display, and final file copy)

    C. Setup Options

    D. Gathering Information About Your Computer

Question #03-14

Resource: Chapter 3, "Installing Windows NT Networking"

What network information is necessary for you to supply during the Network portion of the Setup Wizard?

    A. Network Protocols, Network Services, Network Bindings, Network Card settings, Network Model

    B. Network Protocols, Network Card Settings, Workgroup or Domain membership

    C. Computer Name, Network Card Settings, Workgroup or Domain membership

    D. Windows NT self-detects all network settings.

Question #03-15

Resource: Chapter 3, "Troubleshooting Installation and Setup," and "Preparation Checklist"

The three most important tips I can offer a coworker to make a Windows NT installation problem-free are:

    A. Create an Emergency Repair Disk. You can use this to restart Windows NT and repair the installation process.

    B. Consult the Hardware Compatibility List before starting setup to ensure that all the computer's hardware components have been tested with Windows NT 4.0.

App

J

    C. Determine whether the computer in question meets all the minimum equipment requirements for a Windows NT installation.

    D. Find out all the driver and configuration data specific to devices in the computer, particularly regarding the network card, before starting setup.

Question #03-16

Resource: Chapter 3, "Troubleshooting Installation and Setup"

You have just completed the text mode portion of Windows NT setup and have rebooted to start the GUI Setup Wizard. Windows NT displays the message `Missing or Corrupt NTOSKRNL`. What should you check?

    A. Check the Hardware Compatibility List to see whether the hard disk is compatible with Windows NT.

    B. Your Installation CD may be corrupted. Contact Microsoft for a replacement CD.

    C. Windows NT may have misdetected the SCSI drive. Boot to DOS and edit the BOOT.INI file changing SCSI to MULTI for this installation and verifying the partition number.

    D. This happens occasionally on SCSI drives. You must reinstall Windows NT.

Question #03-17

Resource: Chapter 3, "Upgrading to Windows NT Workstation 4.0—Windows 95"

You are installing Windows NT Workstation 4.0 on a computer that needs to support Windows 95 as well. You would like to migrate user environment settings from Windows 95 to Windows NT 4.0. What should you do?

    A. Do nothing. The Windows 95 settings will automatically be migrated to Windows NT 4.0.

    B. Install Windows NT 4.0 in the same directory as Windows 95. The settings will then automatically be migrated.

C. After installing Windows NT 4.0, run the MIGRATE utility from the command prompt.

D. You cannot migrate those settings from Windows 95.

Question #03-18

Resource: Chapter 3, "Upgrading to Windows NT Workstation 4.0— Windows 3.1 and Windows for Workgroups 3.11"

You are installing Windows NT Workstation 4.0 on a computer that needs to support Windows for Workgroups as well. You would like to migrate user and environment settings to Windows NT 4.0. What should you do?

A. Do nothing. The Windows for Workgroups settings will automatically be migrated to Windows NT 4.0.

B. Install Windows NT 4.0 in the same directory as Windows for Workgroups. The settings compatible with Windows NT 4.0 will then automatically be migrated. You can continue to boot either to Windows NT or to Windows for Workgroups.

C. After installing Windows NT 4.0, run the MIGRATE utility from the command prompt.

D. You cannot migrate those settings from Windows for Workgroups.

Question #03-19

Resource: Chapter 3, "Unattended Setup"

You are installing several Windows NT Workstation computers that share common characteristics, like network properties. You would like to streamline your installation so that you can reduce your installation time and require minimum user input. Select all necessary steps.

A. Place the Windows NT Workstation installation files on a shared server location.

B. Use Setup Manager to create an answer file for the computers.

C. Run setup with the /U:answer_file and /S:source_directory switches.

D. Run the 32-bit version of setup (Winnt32) with the /B switch.

App

J

Question #03-20

Resource: Chapter 3, "Troubleshooting Installation and Setup"

Frank was using Windows NT Workstation 4.0 to test an application that he is developing. His computer is dual-booting between MS-DOS and Windows NT. He has decided to remove Windows NT Workstation 4.0 from his computer. What steps must he follow to accomplish this? Choose all that apply.

A. Back up the data on the Windows NT installation partition and reformat it.

B. Use a DOS system floppy disk with the SYS.COM utility on it to restore the Master Boot Record on the computer to MS-DOS.

C. Delete the Windows NT boot files and the Windows NT system directories.

D. Boot from the Emergency Repair Disk and restore the Master Boot Record to MS-DOS.

Chapter 4

Question #04-01

Resource: Chapter 4, "Welcome to Windows NT Workstation 4.0"

You need to log on to a Windows NT Workstation 4.0 that another person is using in order to administer a shared resource. What does the other person need to do? Choose two.

A. From the Start menu, choose Shutdown, then select Close All Programs, and log on as a different person.

B. From the Start menu, choose Shutdown, and then select Restart the Computer.

C. Press Ctrl+Alt+Del on the keyboard to shut down Windows NT so you can restart and log on as another person.

D. Press Ctrl+Alt+Del on the keyboard to display the Windows NT Security dialog box, then click Logoff.

Question #04-02

Resource: Chapter 4, "Welcome to Windows NT Workstation 4.0"

The correct way to shut down Windows NT is to: (Choose three)

    A. Press Ctrl+Alt+Del on the keyboard, then choose Shutdown in the Windows NT Security dialog box.

    B. Choose Shutdown from the Start menu and then Restart the computer.

    C. Choose Shutdown from the Start menu and then shut down the computer.

    D. Press Ctrl+Alt+Del on the keyboard and then power off the computer.

Question #04-03

Resource: Chapter 4, "Taskbar"

Which of the following Windows NT 4.0 options will let me switch between open windows? Choose three.

    A. Click the window title in the taskbar.

    B. Press Alt+Tab on the keyboard to select the desired window.

    C. Press Ctrl+Esc to display the Windows NT Task Switcher.

    D. Right-click the taskbar to display the Windows NT Task Manager.

Question #04-04

Resource: Chapter 4, "Windows Explorer"

What is the best way to navigate among my files and directories?

    A. From the Start menu, choose Programs, Accessories, File Manager.

    B. From the Start menu, choose Run and then type **WINFILE.EXE** to start File Manager.

    C. From the Start menu, choose Programs, Windows Explorer.

    D. From the Start menu, choose Run and then type **PROGMAN.EXE**.

App

J

Question #04-05
Resource: Chapter 4, "Shortcuts"

Randy works with a particular budget file almost every day and would like to be able to open it quickly without having to browse through several directories to find it. What is the best solution you can recommend?

A. Tell Randy that a quick open feature is coming in the next release of Windows NT.

B. Create a shortcut to the file and place it on Randy's desktop.

C. Use Windows Explorer to browse for the file so that not as many windows are opened.

D. Use My Computer with the Replace Window option to minimize the number of open windows on the screen.

Question #04-06
Resource: Chapter 4, "My Computer" and "Windows Explorer"

Which of the following objects lets me browse through my files, folders, drives, and shared network resources?

A. Network Neighborhood

B. My Computer

C. Windows NT Explorer

D. Task Manager

Question #04-07
Resource: Chapter 4, "My Briefcase"

Beth frequently travels for your company. She takes several files with her that she works on while making client calls. When she returns, she docks her laptop and then needs to update the copies she keeps on the network. She thinks there must be a better way to keep the files updated. What can you suggest?

A. Create shortcuts to the network files on the laptop's desktop. This way Beth can access the files while she is away, and just update them when she gets back.

B. Copy the files into the Briefcase on Beth's laptop. She will have copies of the files that she can work on while away, and can synchronize them with her work copies when she returns.

C. Use Windows Explorer to copy the laptop copies on top of the network copies.

D. Windows NT automatically updates laptop copies of network files when you dock the laptop. It is called autosynch.

Question #04-08

Resource: Chapter 4, "Find" and "Start Menu–Documents"

Bill has created an important legal document, but cannot remember where he saved it, or exactly what he called it. However, he knows he created it yesterday. How can you help him?

A. Use Windows Explorer to display all files by their date. Then browse each directory until you find the missing file.

B. From the Start menu, choose Documents. Bill should be able to find his document listed there.

C. From the Start menu, choose Find Files or Folders. On the Date\Time tab enter yesterday's date. Bill should be able to find his file in the Find results window.

D. Take Bill out to lunch.

Question #04-09

Resource: Chapter 4, "Using Windows NT Help"

Linda cannot remember how to connect to shared resources on her network. You cannot go to her desk right now because you are currently assisting Bill with his lost file. What quick self-help advice can you give Linda now?

A. Use the Contents tab of Windows Help to find the topic relating to connecting to network shared resources. Click the task-based Help button to open the appropriate dialog box and connect to the resource following the directions in the Help screen.

App

J

B. Use the Properties screen of Network Neighborhood to connect to the shared resource.

C. You can only help her while at her desk.

D. Invite her to join you at lunch with Bill.

Question #04-10

Resource: Chapter 4, "Help Topics-Bookmark"

There is a particular Help topic that you frequent. Is there a way to quickly access it when you open Help?

A. Annotate the topic and then browse annotations when you start Help.

B. Annotate the topic, then use Find to find all help documents with your annotation.

C. Create a bookmark. When you start Help, access the page by selecting the bookmark.

D. You cannot mark a page in Help.

Chapter 5

Question #05-01

Resource: Chapter 5, "Display Properties" and "Control Panel-Display"

Fred would like to modify his desktop wallpaper, screen saver, and screen colors. What two options are available to him?

A. Choose Display from the Control Panel.

B. Right-click the desktop and choose Properties.

C. Right-click My Computer and choose Properties, Display.

D. Choose Start, Programs, Display.

Question #05-02

Resource: Chapter 5, "Control Panel Services"

Which three of the following four features are a part of the Services applet in Control Panel?

A. Running status

B. Load order

C. Hardware profile assignments

D. Startup options

Question #05-03

Resource: Chapter 5, "Exploring the Administrative Tools"

Which Control Panel applet creates and manages accounts?

A. Disk Administrator

B. User Manager

C. Accessibility Options

D. There is no Control Panel Applet that does this.

App
J

Question #05-04

Resource: Chapter 5, "Control Panel" and "Accessibility Options"

Janice is a hearing-impaired account manager who has asked if Windows NT provides any options appropriate for her. What can you do to help?

A. Select Control Panel, Sounds and increase the volume for system sounds.

B. Select My Computer, Properties and select the Accessibilities tab to set Sound options.

C. Select Control Panel, Accessibility Options and set the Sound options.

D. Windows NT does not provide options for physically challenged persons.

Question #05-05

Resource: Chapter 5, "Creating and Managing Hardware Profiles"

Antonio frequently travels for the company and accesses the network on his laptop via modem while on the road. When he is at the office, he docks his laptop at his workstation and uses the network card in the docking station to access the network. How can you facilitate the boot process between these two hardware configurations?

A. Hardware profiles are a feature of Windows 95, not Windows NT 4.0.

B. Create a hardware profile for each configuration—docked and undocked—and set a default timeout value for the most frequently used configuration.

C. Modify the BOOT.INI file and include a boot menu choice for a second hardware configuration using the \PROFILE:filename boot switch.

D. Use Control Panel, Services and create a new profile from the HW Profiles button.

Question #05-06

Resource: Chapter 5, "Control Panel—Mouse" and "Examining the Registry"

Martha wants to modify her mouse pointers. What is the most appropriate procedure for doing this?

A. Choose Control Panel, Mouse and select the pointers through the Pointers tab.

B. Right-click the desktop, choose Properties, and select the Settings tab.

C. Start the Registry Editor, select HKEY_CURRENT_USER, and modify the Cursors subkey.

D. Start the Registry Editor, select HKEY_LOCAL_MACHINE, and modify the System\CurrentControlSet subkey.

Question #05-07

Resource: Chapter 5, "Examining the Registry"

Which of the following hives in HKEY_LOCAL_MACHINE have corresponding directory files in the Windows NT system directory?

A. System

B. Software

C. Hardware

D. Security

Question #05-08

Resource: Chapter 5, "Examining the Registry" and "Changing the Default Startup Screen"

I need to add the company's logo to the default Windows NT boot up screen. From which Registry subtree(s) can I make this modification?

A. HKEY_LOCAL_MACHINE

B. HKEY_CURRENT_USER

C. HKEY_USERS

D. This change can only be made through Control Panel, Service, Startup.

Question #05-09

Resource: Chapter 5, "Understanding the Windows NT Boot Process"

App

J

Which of the following boot files is essential to the Boot Phase of the boot process?

A. NTLDR

B. NTDETECT.COM

C. NTOSKRNL.EXE

D. BOOT.INI

Question #05-10

Resource: Chapter 5, "Boot Process for RISC-based Computers"

While looking at the files on my RISC-based computer, I notice that NTLDR, NTDETECT.COM, and BOOT.INI are missing. What impact will this have on the boot process on this computer?

A. The boot process relies on these files to govern the Boot and Load Phases. Missing or corrupt files will result in error messages and failed boots.

B. It will have no impact on the boot process because RISC-based computers do not rely on these files.

C. The BOOT.INI is not an essential file. Windows NT will look for the default Windows NT system directory.

D. NTLDR is always needed to direct the boot process. NTDETECT.COM and BOOT.INI are not necessary on RISC-based computers.

Question #05-11

Resource: Chapter 5, "BOOT.INI"

The BOOT.INI file on my computer looks like this:

```
[Boot Loader]
timeout=15
default=multi(0)disk(2)rdisk(1)partition(3)\winnt40
[Operating Systems]
multi(0)disk(2)rdisk(1)partition(3)\winnt40="Windows NT
➥4.0 Workstation"
multi(0)disk(2)rdisk(1)partition(3)\winnt40="Windows NT
➥4.0 Workstation [VGA Mode]"
/basevideo
  c:\=MS-DOS
```

What can I infer from this file?

A. The timeout value before Windows NT loads is 15 seconds. Windows NT system files can be found on the third partition of the second physical disk attached to the first controller card.

B. The timeout value before Windows NT loads is 15 seconds and DOS is the default operating system.

C. The timeout value before Windows NT loads is 15 seconds. Windows NT system files can be found on the third partition of the first physical disk attached to the first controller card.

D. The controller card is a SCSI adapter.

Question #05-12

Resource: Chapter 5, "Troubleshooting the Boot Process"

Jonas accidentally deleted the BOOT.INI file from his C: drive. Windows NT has been installed in the WINNT subdirectory on C:. What effect will the missing BOOT.INI have?

A. There will be no noticeable effect on the boot process. Windows NT will boot as always.

B. The BOOT.INI file provides the ARC path information that Windows NT needs to find the Windows NT system files. If it is missing, Windows NT will display a message that it cannot find the NTOSKRNL file and fail to boot.

C. If the BOOT.INI file is missing, Windows NT will not display the boot menu during boot up. Windows NT will look for the Windows NT system files on the boot partition in the default directory name (WINNT).

D. The BOOT.INI file is not needed on RISC-based systems.

Question #05-13

Resource: Chapter 5, "Troubleshooting the Boot Process"

I have booted Windows NT and receive the message:

```
Windows NT could not start because the following file is
missing or corrupt:  \winnt root\system32\ntoskrnl.exe
```

How can I recover this file?

A. Boot with the Emergency Repair Disk and choose Verify Windows NT System Files.

B. Boot with the Windows NT Startup disk, choose Repair, and then Verify Windows NT System Files from the Emergency Repair Disk.

C. Find a working Windows NT computer and use the EXPAND command to expand the compressed version of this file from the installation source directory. Then copy the file to the system directory on the problem computer.

D. Boot with a Windows NT Boot Disk and copy the file from this disk.

App

J

Question #05-14

Resource: Chapter 5, "The System Policy Editor"

There are several temporary employees who will work on two different shifts during the summer. They will log on to the network using different workstations each day. However, they need to have the same desktop configuration and should not be able to modify settings such as display choices, and so on. What is the easiest way to accomplish this?

    A. Windows NT does not provide for this level of control in this version.

    B. Modify the Registry on each workstation that each temporary employee will log on to.

    C. Create a system profile for each user with the appropriate settings.

    D. Create a user account on each workstation for each temporary employee and then modify the appropriate Registry entries for each temporary employee on each workstation.

Chapter 6

Question #06-01

Resource: Chapter 6, "Default User Accounts"

Which of the following statements is true about the default user accounts created in Windows NT Workstation 4.0?

    A. The Administrator account is enabled and can be renamed; the Guest account is enabled and cannot be renamed.

    B. The Administrator account is enabled and cannot be renamed; the Guest account is disabled and cannot be renamed.

    C. The Administrator account is enabled and can be renamed; the Guest account is disabled and can be renamed.

    D. The Administrator account is disabled and cannot be renamed; the Guest account is enabled and can be renamed.

Question #06-02

Resource: Chapter 6, "Default User Accounts"

In an effort to add an extra level of security to your workstation installations, you have been presented with several options. Which option provides the greatest level of security?

A. Create separate user accounts for the end-users at each workstation and make them a member of the local Administrators group; rename the Administrator accounts and change their passwords.

B. Create separate user accounts for the end-users at each workstation; rename the Administrator accounts and change their passwords.

C. Create separate user accounts for the end-users at each workstation; delete the Administrator accounts and create new administrator accounts with different names and passwords.

D. Create separate user accounts for the end-users at each workstation; rename the Administrator accounts and randomly assign one of several predetermined passwords to each account.

Question #06-03

Resource: Chapter 6, "Default Group Accounts"

Your end-users need to be able to create and manage shares on their workstations; however, you do not want them to have the same level of access that an administrator has. What can you do?

A. Add each end-user's account to the local Power Users group on their workstation.

B. Add each end-user's account to the local Administrators group on their workstation.

C. Add each end-user's account to the Account Operator's group on each workstation.

D. Users have the ability to create and manage shares by default.

App
J

Question #06-04

Resource: Chapter 6, "Default Group Accounts"

Everyone should be able to read the files in a certain directory. However, the user who created the file should be able to modify it. What do you need to do?

    A. Do nothing. By default, only the creator of a file has access to it. Windows NT restricts resource access by default.

    B. Give the group Everyone Read access and the Creator Owner group Change access. By default, Windows NT allows everyone complete access to resources.

    C. Give the group Everyone Read access and the Creator Owner group Change access. By default, Windows NT restricts resource access.

    D. Give the group Everyone Read access and the Users group Change access. Windows NT will automatically determine who the owner of the file is and restrict the other users.

Question #06-05

Resource: Chapter 6, "Group Management in Domains"

You have installed 15 Windows NT 4.0 workstations as members of a workgroup. On one of these workstations, you have stored a sales database and a marketing database, and have also shared a color printer. Five of the users are salespersons, five are marketers, and the rest are programmers. The users should be able to access their respective databases, but only the team leaders for sales, marketing, and programmers should be able to access the color printer. Which group strategy is the best?

    A. Create local groups for sales, marketing, and team leaders and assign the appropriate user accounts to the appropriate groups. Then assign permissions for each resource to the appropriate group.

    B. Create global groups for sales, marketing, and team leaders and assign the appropriate user accounts to the appropriate groups. Then assign permissions for each resource to the appropriate group.

C. Create global groups for sales, marketing, and team leaders and assign the appropriate user accounts to the appropriate groups. Following Microsoft's suggested strategy to allow for growth, create local groups for each and assign the global group to the local group. Then assign permissions for each resource to the appropriate local group.

D. Simply assign the appropriate users access to the resources that they need access to.

Question #06-06

Resource: Chapter 6, "Group Management in Domains"

What are the differences between a local group and a global group? Choose all that apply.

A. Local groups can be created on workstations, servers, and domain controllers, while global groups can only be created and maintained on a domain controller.

B. Local groups can contain local users, domain users, and global groups, while global groups can contain only users from their domain.

C. Local groups can contain local users, domain users, global groups, and other local groups, while global groups can contain only users from their domain.

D. Local groups can be used for managing resources only on the local computer, while global groups can be used to manage resources on any computer that participates in the domain.

Question #06-07

Resource: Chapter 6, "Naming Conventions," "Considerations Regarding Passwords," and "Creating a New User"

Which of the following sets of usernames and passwords are acceptable for Windows NT?

Username	**Password**
A. First Ass't Comptroller	FirstComp
B. FirstAsstCompt	1stComp
C. FirstAss*tCompt	COMP1
D. AssComp1	123COMPTROLLER1

Question #06-08

Resource: Chapter 6, "Understanding User Manager" and "Creating a New User"

Your workstations are members of a domain called Titan. You need to create user accounts so that two shifts of temporary employees can log on to the same computer, but only during their shift.

A. Use User Manager for Domains on each local Windows NT workstation to create the temporary accounts and assign each the appropriate logon hours.

B. Use User Manager on each local Windows NT workstation to create the temporary accounts and assign each the appropriate logon hours.

C. Use User Manager for Domains on the domain controller for Titan to create domain accounts for the temporary employees and assign each the appropriate logon hours.

D. Use User Manager on the domain controller for Titan to create domain accounts for the temporary employees and assign each the appropriate logon hours.

Question #06-09

Resource: Chapter 6, "Understanding User and Group Accounts" and "Creating a New User"

Your boss has advised you that BrownC has left the company and asks that you delete his account. Later, your boss hires BrownC back as a consultant and tells you to put his account back on the network. BrownC calls you the next day and informs you gruffly that he can no longer access any of the network resources that he used to. How do you troubleshoot?

A. Use the Registry to set BrownC's SID back to what it was before you deleted his account. He will then be able to access all the old resources.

B. Deleting BrownC's account also deleted his SID. Because security in Windows NT is linked to the user's SID, you will need to reestablish all the network resource access that BrownC used to have.

C. Use the Emergency Repair Disk or your last network backup to copy BrownC's old account back to the Registry.

D. Leave the company and get hired back as a consultant yourself.

Question #06-10

Resource: Chapter 6, "Creating a New User"

Under which of the following situations would you disable the user account rather than deleting it?

A. JaneD has left the company on maternity leave and plans to return in three months.

B. JohnB has taken an emergency medical leave of absence for possibly six or more months, but hopes to return full-time.

C. JaniceD has left the company to take a job at Microsoft.

D. FrankP has taken a temporary team leader position in another department and will return when the project is completed.

Question #06-11

Resource: Chapter 6, "Renaming, Copying, and Deleting Accounts" and "Home Directory"

You are creating multiple user accounts for sales persons, marketers, and programmers. Each set of accounts belongs to the same relative groups (sales users in SALES, marketing users in MARKETING, and programmer users in PROGRAMMERS), uses the same logon scripts (SALES. BAT, MARKET.BAT, PROGRAM.BAT), and saves data in a home directory relative to each group (sales users under USERS\SALES, marketing users under USERS\MARKETERS, programmer users under USERS\PROGRAMMERS). What is the most efficient way to create these users?

App

J

A. Create a separate account for each user. As you create the user, use the %USERNAME% environment variable when specifying the home directory to let Windows NT create it for you.

B. Create a template for each type of user. Make the appropriate choices and entries for groups, logon script, and home directory. Use the %USERNAME% environment variable when specifying the home directory to let Windows NT create them for you. Then create each user by copying the appropriate template.

C. Create all the users without specifying group membership. After they are all created, select each group of users by Ctrl+clicking them and create the appropriate group.

D. You must create each user individually.

Question #06-12
Resource: Chapter 6, "Account Policy"

To provide a greater level of security, you have decided to create an account policy that requires a minimum password length of eight characters, that users change their passwords at least once a month, and does not allow users to use the same password twice in two months. Which Account Policy settings are appropriate?

A. Max Password Age: 60   Min Password Age: 30
   Min Password Length: 8 Password Uniqueness: 2

B. Max Password Age: 30   Min Password Age: 30
   Min Password Length: 8 Password Uniqueness: 6

C. Max Password Age: 30   Min Password Age: 10
   Min Password Length: 8 Password Uniqueness: 6

D. Max Password Age: 60   Min Password Age: 30
   Min Password Length: 8 Password Uniqueness: 1

Question #06-13

Resource: Chapter 6, "Account Policy" and "Audit Policy"

You suspect that someone is trying to log in to various workstations unauthorized. What is the best step you can take to increase security and determine who might be doing this?

    A. Enable Account Lockout in the Account Policy requiring the Administrator to unlock the account.

    B. Enable Account Lockout in the Account Policy requiring the Administrator to unlock the account. Enable auditing of unsuccessful logons and logoffs and monitor these events in the Event Viewer.

    C. Advise users to change their passwords more frequently and not to use obvious passwords.

    D. Increase the minimum password length in Account Policy.

Question #06-14

Resource: Chapter 6, "User Rights"

You want to give a particular user the ability to back up files on a workstation, but not be able to restore files. How can you accomplish this?

    A. Make the user a member of the Backup Operators group on the workstation.

    B. Make the user a member of the Server Operators group on the workstation.

    C. Create a new local group called BACKUP ONLY on the local workstation and make the user a member of it. Assign this new group to the Backup Files and Directories User Right.

    D. Give the user Read Only access to all the files.

Question #06-15

Resource: Chapter 6, "User Profiles" and "A Profile Alternative"

As you create new users you would like them to assume the same default environment settings, such as common application groups, startup programs, and company logo, as wallpaper. Which steps will achieve this end?

App

J

    A. Modify the appropriate changes in the Default User and All Users profile folders in WINNT40\Profiles. When a new user is created, that user's profile will begin with the settings from these two.

    B. Create a System Policy file that contains the appropriate settings for the Default user and save it in the WINNT40\SYSTEM32\ REPL\IMPORT\SCRIPTS subdirectory on the validating computer.

    C. Create a template user account and modify the settings for that account. Create new accounts by copying the template.

    D. Create a system policy file for each set of users modifying the settings as appropriate for each user.

Question #06-16

Resource: Chapter 6, "Creating Server Based Profiles"

There are five summer interns joining the company this year for a three-month period. You want to give them access to the network, but you want to restrict their environment settings to specific programs, colors, and so on. They should not be able to change the settings. What steps are involved?

    A. Change the NTUSER.DAT file in the shared directory to NTUSER.MAN.

    B. Copy the account through the User Profiles tab in the System applet to a shared directory on a central server.

    C. Create a user account and make the appropriate changes to that account's environment settings.

    D. Specify the location and file name of the profile in each summer intern's account properties.

Question #06-17

Resource: Chapter 6, "Troubleshooting Accounts, Policies, and Profiles"

A user is having problems logging on to the network and seeing a variety of messages. Which of the following things would you check to troubleshoot?

A. The user is entering the correct username and password.

B. The username is case-sensitive.

C. The domain controller is up and accessible.

D. The user's account requires a mandatory profile that is accessible.

Chapter 7

Question #07-01

Resource: Chapter 7, "Sharing Resources and Determining Network Access"

The manager of the Accounting department wants to make next year's budget templates available for the staff accountants to review beginning next month. They will be stored on the department resource server called ACCT1 in a folder called BUDGET97. None of the partitions on ACCT1 are formatted with NTFS. How would you make the folder available only to the Accounting department staff?

A. Use User Manager to assign permission to use the folder to the Accountants group.

B. Use User Manager for Domains to assign User Rights to the Accountants group to access the BUDGET97 share.

C. Use the Security tab on the properties sheet for the folder to assign permissions to the Accountants group.

D. Use the Sharing tab on the properties sheet for the folder to assign permissions to the Accountants group.

Question #07-02

Resource: Chapter 7, "Sharing Resources and Determining Network Access" and "Examining the Windows NT Security Model"

The manager of the Accounting department wants to make next year's budget templates available for the staff accountants to review beginning next month. They will be stored on the department resource server

App

J

called ACCT1 in a folder called BUDGET97. None of the partitions on ACCT1 is formatted with NTFS. How would you make the folder available only to the Accounting department staff? Choose all that apply.

A. Share the BUDGET97 directory.

B. Add the Accountants group to the ACL for the share.

C. Remove the Everyone group from the ACL for the share.

D. Give the Accountants group Read and Write permissions at the folder level.

Question #07-03

Resource: Chapter 7, "Examining the Windows NT Security Model"

A user's effective access to a resource is determined by:

A. Comparing the rights of the user with the permissions assigned through the ACL of the resource.

B. Comparing the permissions in the access token of the user with the permissions assigned through the ACL of the resource.

C. Comparing the user and group SID entries in the user's access token with the permissions assigned through the ACL of the resource.

D. Comparing the user and group SID entries in the user's access token with the user rights listed in the ACL of the resource.

Question #07-04

Resource: Chapter 7, "Local versus Domain Access Tokens"

The Sales team workstations participate in a workgroup computing model. Janis recently acquired a laser-quality printer with an envelope feed that the rest of the team will share. Janis has shared the printer with the default permission, but none of the other team members can access the printer. What else must Janis do?

A. Create a group called Sales and assign it the print permission for the printer.

B. Create user accounts for each of the other Sales team members on her workstation.

C. Give the Everyone group the Access Printers Remotely user right on her workstation.

D. Install the printer driver on all the other workstations.

Question #07-05

Resource: Chapter 7, "Examining Access Control Lists"

The permission list defining access to a resource resides:

A. With the resource and is called the Access Control List.

B. With the user and is called the User Rights Policy.

C. With the user and is called the Access Control List.

D. With the resource and is called the User Rights Policy.

Question #07-06

Resource: Chapter 7, "How ACLs Determine Access"

Arlo, a member of the Developers group, is currently editing the file DOOM.DOC in the share Tools. The administrator of the share changes permission to the Developers group from Change to Read. Arlo continues to make changes to the document. What else must the administrator do to restrict Arlo's access?

A. Take Arlo out of the Developers group.

B. Give Arlo No Access explicitly.

C. Disconnect Arlo from the resource.

D. Nothing. Arlo must disconnect from the share and then reconnect before the new permission will take effect.

App

J

Question #07-07

Resource: Chapter 7, "Sharing Resources and Determining Network Access"

The administrator of the Tools shared folder wants to limit access to the folder only to the Developers group. To accomplish this, she gives the Everyone group No Access, and the Developers group Change access. The Developers complain that they cannot access any file in Tools. What else must the administrator do?

A. Share the files in the Tools folder.

B. Remove the Everyone group.

C. Give the Developers group Full Control.

D. Format the partition as NTFS and assign NTFS permissions in addition to the share permissions.

Question #07-08

Resource: Chapter 7, "Effective Permissions"

Ned is a member of the Developers group at Springfield Technologies. He has been promoted to team leader for his group. He needs to edit the DOOM.DOC file in the Tools folder, but does not have Write access. What must you do to give Ned access to DOOM.DOC?

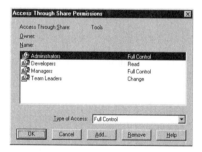

A. Do nothing. The next time Ned logs on, his permissions will change.

B. Change the Developers group permission to Change.

C. Add Ned to the Team Leaders group.

D. Change the Team Leaders group permission to Full Control.

Question #07-09

Resource: Chapter 7, "Sharing Resources and Determining Network Access"

The Tools folder has been shared to the Developers group with Change permission. Doom is a subdirectory under Tools. Team Leaders should have access to Doom with Read permissions. What can you do to accomplish this?

    A. Add Team Leaders to the Tools share with Read permission.

    B. Create a new share called DOOM and give Team Leaders Read permission to it.

    C. Add Team Leaders to the Tools share with Change permission.

    D. Add Team Leaders to the Tools share with No Access and to the Doom subdirectory with Read.

App

J

Question #07-10

Resource: Chapter 7, "Assigning File and Folder Permissions"

The manager of the Accounting department wants to make next year's budget templates available for the staff accountants to review beginning next month. They will be stored on the department resource server called ACCT1 in a folder called BUDGET97 on an NTFS partition. The folder has been shared with the default permission. How would you make the folder's contents available only to the Accounting department staff?

    A. Use User Manager to assign permission to use the folder to the Accountants group.

    B. Use User Manager for Domains to assign User Rights to the Accountants group to access the BUDGET97 share.

    C. Use the Security tab on the properties sheet for the folder to assign permissions to the Accountants group.

    D. Use the Sharing tab on the properties sheet for the folder to also assign permissions to the Accountants group.

Question #07-11

Resource: Chapter 7, "Effective File and Folder Permissions"

The manager of the Accounting department wants to make next year's budget templates available for the staff accountants to review beginning next month. They will be stored on the department resource server called ACCT1 in a folder called BUDGET97 on an NTFS partition. The folder has been shared with the default permission. How would you make the folder's contents available only to the Accounting department staff? Choose all that apply.

A. Change the share permissions to just the Accountants with Change permission.

B. Assign the Accountants group the NTFS permission Change to the BUDGET97 folder.

C. Change the share permission to Everyone with No Access and assign the Accountants group the NTFS permission Change for the BUDGET97 folder.

D. Change the share permission to Everyone with Read and assign the Accountants group the NTFS permission Change for the BUDGET97 folder.

Question #07-12

Resource: Chapter 7, "Determining Access when using Share and NTFS Permissions"

Team Leaders need to be able to modify files contained in the share Tools. While you were on vacation, your trusted sidekick modified the permissions for the share and the folder. The following two figures show what the permissions look like now. Team Leaders complain that they are unable to modify their files. What should you do?

A. Fire your trusted sidekick.

B. Change the Tools NTFS permission for Team Leaders to Change and the share permission to Read.

C. Change the Tools NTFS permission for the Team Leaders to Change.

D. Remove Team Leaders from the ACL for the Tools share.

Question #07-13

Resource: Chapter 7, "Assigning File and Folder Permissions"

You have modified NTFS permissions for the file DOOM.DOC so that Team Leaders have Full Control. For all other files and folders, Team Leaders should have Read access. Using the exhibit, how can you best accomplish this?

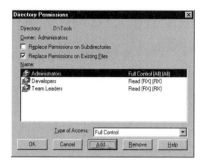

A. Select Replace Permissions on Subdirectories and deselect Replace Permissions on Existing Files.

B. Select Replace Permissions on Subdirectories.

C. Deselect Replace Permissions on Existing Files.

D. Set permissions on each file and folder individually.

Question #07-14

Resource: Chapter 7, "Understanding the Concept of Ownership"

The person that created DOOM.DOC on server ACCT1 is no longer with the company. Cathy, a member of Team Leaders, will be assuming responsibility for the DOOM project, and needs to become the owner of DOOM.DOC. How can this be accomplished? Choose all that apply.

A. Give Cathy the Take Ownership of Files and Folders User Right on the server ACCT1.

B. Give Cathy the Take Ownership permission on the file DOOM.DOC.

C. Tell Cathy to just take ownership of the file.

D. Give the Team Leaders group the Take Ownership permission for DOOM.DOC.

Question #07-15

Resource: Chapter 7, "Troubleshooting Security"

Fred is a member of the Developers group. The Developers group has been given the NTFS permission Full Control to the Tools folder. Fred is changing jobs and has been given No Access to the file DOOM.DOC, which is contained in the Tools folder. Later, Fred logs on and deletes the file DOOM.DOC. Luckily, you can restore the file from your tape backup. How can you prevent Fred from deleting the file again, but still maintain the original level of access for him and the Developers group?

A. Fire Fred.

B. Give the Developers group Special Access with all options selected for the Tools folder. Then give Fred No Access to the file.

C. Give the Developers group Change access at the folder level.

D. Give Fred No Access at the folder level.

Chapter 8

Question #08-01

Resource: Chapter 8, "Creating and Managing Stripe Sets"

Your server is configured as shown in the exhibit. You have a database file that is 325M in size and growing. What is the largest stripe set you can create on your server?

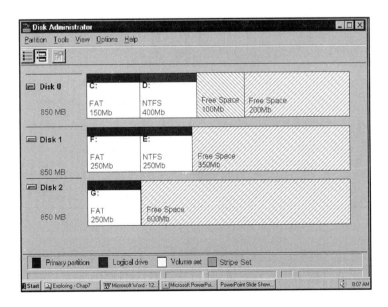

A. 200M

B. 600M

C. 700M

D. 1150M

Question #08-02

Resource: Chapter 8, "Creating and Managing Volume Sets" and "Extending Volume Sets"

You need to extend a FAT partition to allow more space for a growing database. Which option best explains your strategy?

A. Use Disk Administrator to select the FAT partition and an area of free space and choose Partition, Create Volume Set.

B. Use Disk Administrator to select the FAT partition and an area of free space and choose Partition, Extend Volume Set.

C. Use Disk Administrator to select the FAT partition and an area of formatted space and choose Tools, Combine Volume Sets.

D. You cannot extend the volume.

Question #08-03

Resource: Chapter 8, "Extending Volume Sets"

You need to extend a FAT partition to allow more space for a growing database. Choose all steps that apply.

A. Use Disk Administrator to select the partition and an area of free space and choose Partition, Extend Volume Set.

B. Use the Convert utility to convert the FAT partition to NTFS.

C. Set the partition attribute to Compress.

D. Specify the total size of the volume.

Question #08-04

Resource: Chapter 8, "Converting a FAT Partition to NTFS" and "Requirements, Terms, and Strategy"

A user wants to convert a partition from FAT to NTFS with no loss of data. How would you advise the user to accomplish this task?

    A. Use Disk Administrator to select the partition and choose Tools, Format. Then select NTFS.

    B. Use the command-line utility CONVERT.EXE to convert the partition.

    C. Use the Windows NT Backup utility to back up the partition data to disk. Then format the partition for NTFS and restore the data.

    D. You cannot convert a FAT partition to NTFS without loss of data.

App

J

Question #08-05

Resource: Chapter 8, "Creating and Managing Volume Sets" and "Creating and Managing Stripe Sets"

Which of the following statements are true regarding Volume Sets and Stripe Sets? Choose all that apply.

    A. Stripe sets can contain the system partition and volume sets cannot.

    B. Stripe sets must combine areas of equal size while volume sets can combine areas of any size.

    C. Stripe sets cannot contain the system partition and volume sets can.

    D. Stripe sets write to all members of the set concurrently while volume sets fill each member of the set in turn.

Question #08-06

Resource: Chapter 8, "How to Enable Compression"

Wilma has compressed the data files in the QUARRY folder. Later, she moves some of them and other files into another folder so that Betty can access them remotely. Wilma notices that some of the files she moved are compressed and some are not. She calls you for an explanation.

    A. Tell Wilma she is hallucinating.

    B. When you move files from one folder to another on the same partition, the compression attribute stays with the file. This is probably what happened.

    C. The target folder probably had the Compress New Files Only option selected in its properties. Tell Wilma to deselect this option.

    D. The compression attribute always stays with the file.

Question #08-07

Resource: Chapter 8, "Understanding Partitions"

Windows NT calls the active primary partition its:

    A. Boot partition

    B. System partition

    C. Startup partition

    D. Extended partition

Question #08-08

Resource: Chapter 8, "Understanding Partitions"

Windows NT is installed on the D: drive as configured in the exhibit. Which ARC path in the BOOT.INI file accurately represents the location of the installation directory so that Windows NT can boot successfully?

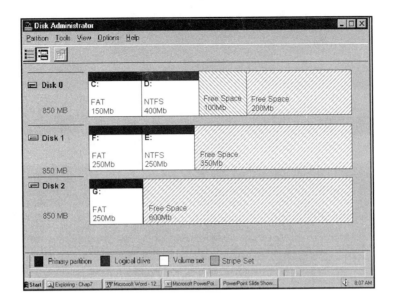

A. multi(0)disk(0)rdisk(0)partition(2)

B. multi(0)disk(0)rdisk(0)partition(5)

C. multi(0)disk(1)rdisk(0)partition(2)

D. multi(0)disk(0)rdisk(1)partition(2)

Question #08-09

Resource: Chapter 8, "An Overview of FAT" and "An Overview of NTFS"

Which of the following statements is true regarding FAT and NTFS? Choose all that apply.

A. FAT supports long file names and so does NTFS.

B. NTFS supports long file names but FAT does not.

C. FAT supports a maximum partition size of 4G and NTFS supports a maximum partition size of 16E.

D. Formatting a partition as FAT requires less than 1M of overhead, while NTFS formatting requires at least 4M.

App

J

Question #08-10

Resource: Chapter 8, "An Overview of NTFS"

Which of the following statements accurately describes NTFS? Choose all that apply.

A. NTFS provides built-in transaction tracking.

B. NTFS supports file compression as a file property.

C. NTFS requires less than 4M of overhead for formatting.

D. NTFS offers file and folder level security.

Question #08-11

Resource: Chapter 8, "Additional Thoughts on Long Names"

You are deciding whether to support long file names on FAT partitions for your server. You have a variety of client platforms that connect to the server, including MS-DOS and Windows 95. Some of the platforms support older 16-bit applications. Which of the following considerations would you make?

A. There are no significant concerns. All applications support long file names on all platforms in a Microsoft network.

B. Most Microsoft applications will support the long file names, but some older applications save changes by deleting the old file and renaming a temporary file to the original file name. This could corrupt the long file name.

C. Long file names saved in the root of the drive require one directory entry for the alias, and one for up to every 13 characters of the name. Because the root is hard-coded for 512 directory entries, you could run out of entries.

D. If long file name support is disabled for the FAT partition, it is disabled for all partitions on that computer, including NTFS.

Question #08-12

Resource: Chapter 8, "Creating and Managing Volume Sets"

Your Windows NT Workstation has two physical disks, each with less than 50M of free space left. What would be the most effective use of this free space?

A. Create a stripe set with parity.

B. Create a volume set out of the remaining free space.

C. Extend the FAT partitions on each disk into the remaining free space.

D. Make each area of free space its own primary partition and format it as NTFS.

Question #08-13

Resource: Chapter 8, "(Backup) Requirements, Terms, and Strategy"

Lucy has been appointed the backup coordinator for the network. What must you do to enable her to accomplish this task and still maintain security on the data? Choose all that apply.

A. Make Lucy a member of the local Backup Operators group on each computer that needs to be backed up.

B. Make Lucy a member of the Server Operators group on each server computer that needs to be backed up.

C. Assign Lucy the Backup Files and Directories user right.

D. Give Lucy Full Control over all files and folders.

Question #08-14

Resource: Chapter 8, "Backing Up and Restoring Data"

You have been asked to implement a backup strategy that backs up all files each Monday to a tape, and then only files that are new or have changed each day since the Monday backup to subsequent tapes on Tuesday through Friday. In addition, on Friday, you must create an archive tape for off-site storage. Which solution will meet this requirement?

A. Perform a normal backup on Monday, then a differential backup Tuesday through Friday. On Friday, perform an additional Copy backup for archival off-site.

B. Perform a normal backup on Monday, then an incremental backup Tuesday through Friday. On Friday, perform an additional Copy backup for archival off-site.

App

J

C. Perform a normal backup on Monday and Friday and an incremental backup each day.

D. Perform a normal backup on Monday and Friday and a differential backup each day.

Question #08-15

Resource: Chapter 8, "(Backup) Requirements, Terms, and Strategy"

You are ready to implement your backup strategy and want to back up files from all Windows NT computers remotely to an archive directory on your local computer. All remote shares have been implemented. What is the best solution?

A. Connect to the shares, start Backup, and select the files and folders to be backed up. Choose Backup and enter the UNC path to the target archive directory in the Backup Path text box.

B. Connect to the shares, start Backup, and choose Operations, Select Target from the menu. Enter the path to the archive directory in the Backup Path text box.

C. Connect to the shares, start Backup and redirect the backup path using the Tools, Options menu.

D. You cannot back up to disk.

Question #08-16

Resource: Chapter 8, "Troubleshooting Backup and Restore"

You need to recover a lost folder for a user. Before you do so, what can you do to minimize errors?

A. Review the backup set catalog for any corrupted files before proceeding with the backup.

B. Review the backup log file to see if any files were missed during the backup process.

C. Select the verify files restore option.

D. Do nothing. Windows NT automatically verifies files while restoring to disk.

Chapter 9

Question #09-01

Resource: Chapter 9, "Windows NT 4.0 Print Process"

Which of the following sets of Windows NT network clients do not require print drivers to be installed on the local computer?

A. All Microsoft Network clients

B. Windows NT and Windows 95

C. Windows NT, Windows 95, and Windows for Workgroups 3.11

D. Windows NT, Windows 95, and LAN Manager v2.x for DOS

Question #09-02

Resource: Chapter 9, "Windows NT 4.0 Print Process"

Which of the following steps applies to the Windows NT 4.0 print process on Windows NT computers? Choose all that apply.

A. The GDI component of the client computer generates an enhanced metafile print job.

B. The bulk of the print process completes in the spooler on the client before forwarding the print job to the print server.

C. The print monitor controls access to the print devices and device ports, and monitors status of the print job.

D. The local printer spooler makes a remote connection to the print server spooler and copies the print job there.

Question #09-03

Resource: Chapter 9, "Windows NT 4.0 Print Process"

Jeanette calls to say that her print jobs seem to have stopped running. You check the printer that she sent the jobs to and see that the jobs are stuck in queue. What steps should you take to clear the stuck jobs? Choose all that apply.

A. Select the stuck jobs and choose Document, Cancel.

B. Select Printer, Purge Printer.

C. Use the Control Panel applet Service to stop and restart the Spooler service.

D. Select each stuck job and change its priority.

Question #09-04
Resource: Chapter 9, "Windows NT 4.0 Print Process"

Several users have called you within the past half-hour to complain that their print jobs are not printing. In fact, they get system messages that tell them that the spooler is not responding. You have verified that the spooler directory partition does not have adequate free space to hold all the print jobs sent to it. What steps should you take to resolve this situation? Choose two.

A. Use the Control Panel applet Services to more frequently stop and restart the Spooler service to keep the print jobs from becoming fragmented.

B. Change the location of the spool directory to a partition with enough disk space by modifying the HKEY_LOCAL_ MACHINE\System\CurrentControlSet\Control\Print\Printers DefaultSpoolDirectory parameter.

C. Change the location of the spool directory to a partition with enough disk space by modifying the HKEY_Current_User\ Control\Print\Printers\Spool SpoolDirectory parameter.

D. If the partition is formatted with NTFS, compress the spool directory.

Question #09-05
Resource: Chapter 9, "Print Processor"

If the final print output is corrupted, what print process component should you check?

A. Spooler service on the client computer

B. Spooler service on the print server

C. Print processor on the print server

D. Print monitor on the client computer

Question #09-06

Resource: Chapter 9, "Print Monitor" and "A Little More About LPD Devices"

Which print monitor is loaded with TCP/IP and tracks print jobs targeted for TCP/IP print hosts?

    A. IPMON.DLL

    B. LPDMON.DLL

    C. LPRMON.DLL

    D. LOCALMON.DLL

Question #09-07

Resource: Chapter 9, "Print Monitor"

What is the purpose of the print monitor SFMMON.DLL?

    A. SFMMON.DLL monitors Macintosh print jobs routed using AppleTalk protocol to network print devices.

    B. SFMMON.DLL is the System File Manager print monitor that tracks print jobs sent directly to or printed directly from a file.

    C. SFMMON.DLL is the software print job compression DLL that compresses the print job before it is routed from the local print spooler to the print server.

    D. SFMMON.DLL is not a valid print monitor.

Question #09-08

Resource: Chapter 9, "A Little More About LPD Devices"

A print job can be routed directly to a UNIX host print device and its status checked using which two command-line utilities?

    A. LPD and LPR

    B. LPD and LPQ

    C. LPR and IPCONFIG

    D. LPR and LPQ

App

J

Question #09-09

Resource: Chapter 9, "Creating a Printer"

Nelson has been selected to assist you as a printing administrator in the Dry Gulch office, because you are unable to travel there frequently, though you'd really like to. What is the minimum level of access you need to give Nelson so that he can perform basic print management tasks such as creating and sharing printers and managing print jobs?

- A. Make Nelson a member of the Print Operators local group on his print server.
- B. Make Nelson a member of the Server Operator local group on his print server.
- C. Make Nelson a member of the Administrators local group on his print server.
- D. Give Nelson Full Control permission for each printer on his print server.

Question #09-10

Resource: Chapter 9, "Sharing and Securing a Printer" and "Setting Permissions for the Shared Printer"

You have created four printers. Each of them will be used by a specific group of users. Name all the steps that are required to successfully make the printer available to the appropriate users.

- A. Share each printer.
- B. Set the share permissions for each printer so that only the appropriate group has access.
- C. Set the printer permissions for each printer so that only the appropriate group has access.
- D. Create a printer pool so that each group can access all the print devices.

Question #09-11

Resource: Chapter 9, "Auditing and Taking Ownership of the Printer"

Rosemarie was the print administrator in Ulan Bator, but has left the country to pursue a career as an opera singer. You need to assign a new print administrator. What will you need to do concerning ownership of the Ulan Bator printers that Rosemarie created and managed?

A. Do nothing. Printers are not owned by a user; they are owned by the system.

B. Make the new print administrator a Print Operator. The new print administrator can then take ownership of the printers in Ulan Bator.

C. Give ownership of the printers to the new print administrator.

D. Give the new administrator Full Control permission over the printers. Full Control automatically assigns ownership to that user.

Question #09-12

Resource: Chapter 9, "Ports Tab"

The print device associated with a particular printer has failed. Several print jobs are waiting in queue in that printer. How can you service these print jobs?

A. Connect to another remote printer. Open the printer manager window for the printer and drag the waiting print jobs to the remote printer manager window.

B. Use the Ports tab properties for the printer to add a port for another remote printer. Deselect the current print port associated with the printer and select the remote port. Resume printing.

C. Do nothing. You must replace the failed print device before printing can resume.

D. Use the Control Panel applet Services to stop the spooler service, configure it to connect to another remote printer, and restart it.

Question #09-13

Resource: Chapter 9, "Print Pools" and "Priority"

There are three downward-compatible print devices connected to the print server in MIS. MIS Managers and Project Leaders should always be able to print to the first available printer. Help Desk staff and Developers should be able to print only to their specified print device. What will best accomplish this task?

    A. Create a printer for each device and assign the appropriate groups access only to their printer. Give the Managers' printer a priority of 1, Help Desk's printer a priority of 50, and Developers a priority of 99.

    B. Create a printer for each device and assign the appropriate groups access only to their printer. Give the Managers' printer a priority of 99, Help Desk's printer a priority of 50, and Developers a priority of 1.

    C. Create a printer for each device and assign the appropriate groups access only to their printer. Make the Managers' printer a printer pool by associating it with each print device.

    D. Create a printer for each device and assign the appropriate groups access only to their printer. Make each printer a printer pool by associating it with each print device.

Question #09-14

Resource: Chapter 9, "Priority"

There is one high-speed network print device connected to the print server in MIS. MIS Managers and Project Leaders should always be able to print to this printer regardless of who else has submitted print jobs. Help Desk staff should be able to print ahead of Developers. What will best accomplish this task?

    A. Create three printers, each associated with the device, and assign the appropriate groups access only to their printer. Give the Managers' printer a priority of 1, Help Desk's printer a priority of 50, and Developers a priority of 99.

B. Create three printers, each associated with the device, and assign the appropriate groups access only to their printer. Give the Managers' printer a priority of 99, Help Desk's printer a priority of 50, and Developers a priority of 1.

C. Create three printers, each associated with the device, and assign the appropriate groups access only to their printer. Make the Managers' printer a printer pool by associating it with each print device.

D. Create three printers associated with the device and assign the appropriate groups access only to their printer. Make each printer a printer pool by associating it with each print device.

Question #09-15

Resource: Chapter 9, "Document Properties"

The printer for a network print device has been configured to print documents at all times. Farley plans to print a large, complex graphics document that he would like completed tomorrow morning. This job will take at least one hour to complete. What can you do to minimize the effect that printing this document will have on other documents in the queue?

A. Select Farley's document and pause it. Resume printing after hours when print jobs are at a minimum.

B. Modify the printer schedule so that it only prints documents after hours.

C. Modify the document schedule for Farley's document so that it only prints between 1:00 a.m. and 3:00 a.m.

D. Do nothing. The printer automatically holds long jobs until short jobs finish spooling and printing.

Question #09-16

Resource: Chapter 9, "Troubleshooting Printing"

Which of the following steps are appropriate to take when trouble-shooting a failed print job?

App

J

A. Verify that the appropriate print port has been defined and configured by printing a test page.

B. Delete and re-create the printer.

C. Determine whether the print device is online and connected.

D. Resubmit the print job to a file and then copy the file to a printer port to see if it is successful.

Question #09-17

Resource: Chapter 9, "Troubleshooting Printing" and "Additional Considerations"

You are using a RISC-based computer as your print server. All your clients are either MS-DOS, Windows for Workgroups, Windows 95, or Windows NT running on Intel-based computers. What must you do to ensure that all your clients can print to the print devices managed by the RISC-based print server?

A. Install both RISC-based and Intel print drivers on the RISC-based print server. Install the appropriate print drivers only on the MS-DOS and Windows for Workgroups computers.

B. Install both RISC-based and Intel print drivers on the RISC-based print server. The client computers will receive the appropriate platform driver from the print server when they make a print request.

C. Install RISC-based print drivers on the RISC-based print server and Intel print drivers on the client computers. Windows NT will do the platform translation.

D. Install the Intel print drivers on the RISC-based print server and RISC-based print drivers on the client computers.

Question #09-18

Resource: Chapter 9, "Introducing and Examining the Print Process" and "Troubleshooting Printing"

There are 300 Windows NT and Windows 95 client computers that print to five printers on a print server. You have received upgraded print drivers for two of the print devices connected to this print server. What must you do to ensure that all clients can continue to access all the print devices?

A. Install the upgraded print drivers on all the clients that need to use those print devices.

B. Install the upgraded print drivers on all the client computers.

C. Install the upgraded print drivers only on the Windows NT client computers.

D. Do nothing. The print server can download the new drivers to the clients the next time they make a print request.

Chapter 10

Question #10-01

Resource: Chapter 10, "Reviewing the Windows NT 4.0 Subsystem Architecture"

Of the following, which functions as part of the Kernel mode of Windows NT 4.0?

A. CSR Subsystem

B. HAL

C. GDI

D. Thread prioritization

Question #10-02

Resource: Chapter 10, "Reviewing the Windows NT 4.0 Subsystem Architecture" and "Examining Win 16 Application Support"

Of the following, which functions as part of the user mode of Windows NT 4.0?

A. CSR Subsystem

B. HAL

C. USER

D. WOW

Question #10-03

Resource: Chapter 10, "User (Application) Mode"

Which two subsystems are loaded when Windows NT boots?

- A. CSR and Security Subsystems
- B. CSR and OS/2 Subsystems
- C. Environment and Security Subsystems
- D. OS/2 and POSIX Subsystems

Question #10-04

Resource: Chapter 10, "Examining WIN32-Based Application Support"

Bernadette obtained a WIN32 application from a friend through e-mail but has not been able to successfully load and run it on her Power PC. You have checked for the usual things—memory, disk space, and so on—and all looks fine. What else can you do?

- A. Run the WIN32 application in its own memory space.
- B. Check the platform for which the application was compiled. Bernadette must use a version compiled for the PowerPC platform.
- C. Shut down and restart Windows NT to free up application resources.
- D. The application may be corrupted. Have Bernadette obtain another copy.

Question #10-05

Resource: Chapter 10, "Examining WIN32-Based Application Support," "Examining Support for MS-DOS-Based Applications," "Examining Win 16 Application Support," and "Considerations for Troubleshooting"

Mandy is running Pinball, the DOS Editor, Word 6, Excel 5, and Microstomp, a 16-bit, third-party Windows Web surfing program. Microstomp has hung up due to low resource memory. What other applications will be affected?

A. All other applications

B. All other applications except the DOS Editor

C. All other applications except Pinball

D. All other applications except Pinball and DOS Editor

Question #10-06

Resource: Chapter 10, "Managing Win 16 Applications with Multiple NTVDMs," "Examining WIN32-Based Application Support," "Examining Support for MS-DOS-Based Applications," "Examining Win 16 Application Support," and "Considerations for Troubleshooting"

Mandy is running Pinball, the DOS Editor, Word 6, Excel 5, and Microstomp, a 16-bit, third-party Windows Web surfing program. Microstomp has been configured to run in its own memory space. Microstomp has hung up due to low resource memory. What other applications will be affected?

A. No other applications

B. No other applications except the DOS Editor

C. No other applications except Pinball

D. No other applications except the other Win 16 applications

Question #10-07

Resource: Chapter 10, "Examining Support for MS-DOS-Based Applications" and "Configuring the NTVDM"

Which of the following statements is true about the NTVDM?

A. Each NTVDM has one thread of operation associated with it.

B. Each NTVDM is designed to emulate the Windows memory environment and provides a set of support files to do so.

C. Each NTVDM is configurable by modifying the properties of the MS-DOS application.

D. Each NTVDM is configurable through one AUTOEXEC.BAT and CONFIG.SYS file that is read when Windows NT boots.

App

J

Question #10-08

Resource: Chapter 10, "Configuring the NTVDM"

Angela has an older MS-DOS program that she needs to run on her Windows NT 4.0 workstation. The application requires a specific environmental variable set and device driver loaded. How can you help Angela configure her program to run successfully?

- A. Configure the program to run in its own memory space.
- B. Create an AUTOEXEC.BAT and CONFIG.SYS with the appropriate settings to load when Windows NT boots.
- C. Create a specific AUTOEXEC and CONFIG for the application and reference it in the applications properties (PIF).
- D. Install the application using the ADD Application applet in Control Panel and reference the environment variable and device driver during installation.

Question #10-09

Resource: Chapter 10, "Examining Win 16 Application Support"

Which of the following statements accurately describes a Win 16 application running under Windows NT 4.0?

- A. All Win 16 applications run in the same NTVDM by default.
- B. All Win 16 applications are non-preemptively multitasked within the NTVDM.
- C. 16-bit calls are translated into 32-bit calls through a process called thunking.
- D. WOW emulates the Windows 3.1 memory environment for Win 16 applications.

Question #10-10

Resource: Chapter 10, "Managing Win 16 Applications with Multiple NTVDMS"

Mandy is running Pinball, the DOS Editor, Word 6, Excel 5, and Microstomp, a 16-bit, third-party Windows Web surfing program.

Microstomp occasionally hangs up due to low resource memory. This affects his other Windows applications. What can you suggest to alleviate this problem?

    A. Configure Microstomp to run in its own memory space.

    B. Configure each Win 16 application to run in its own memory space.

    C. Modify the PIF for Microstomp to increase its resource memory allocation.

    D. Modify the PIF for the WOW NTVDM to increase resource memory allocations for all the Windows applications.

Question #10-11

Resource: Chapter 10, "Managing Win 16 Applications with Multiple NTVDMs—Considerations"

App

J

Bernadette is running Microstomp, which has been configured to run in its own memory space to prevent its affecting other applications when it hangs. When Microstomp ran in the same NTVDM, Bernadette could cut and paste text from Microstomp into her Word 6 documents. Now her pastes and paste links will no longer work. What can she do?

    A. Do nothing. Windows NT does not support OLE and DDE across multiple WOW NTVDMs.

    B. Windows NT does not support OLE and DDE across multiple WOW NTVDMs. Bernadette must run Microstomp in the same WOW NTVDM as the other Windows applications.

    C. Windows NT does not support OLE and DDE across multiple WOW NTVDMs for poorly behaved applications. Bernadette should run Microstomp and Word 6 in the same WOW NTVDM to preserve OLE and DDE for these two applications, and configure the other two Windows applications to each run in its own memory space.

    D. Modify the PIF for Microstomp to support OLE and DDE.

Question #10-12

Resource: Chapter 10, "Configuring the OS/2 Subsystem"

Len occasionally needs to run an OS/2 database program on his Windows NT 4.0 workstation. He configured a CONFIG.SYS prior to running the application for the first time, and the changes took. He now needs to modify the CONFIG.SYS file. He used WordPad to make the changes, but they do not seem to be read by the OS/2 application. What two options do you advise?

A. Use Notepad to modify the CONFIG.SYS file.

B. The OS/2 subsystem obtains information for its CONFIG.SYS file from the Windows NT Registry. Use an OS/2–based text editor to modify the OS/2 CONFIG.SYS after starting the OS/2 application.

C. Use the OSCONFIG command-line utility to update the Windows NT Registry information.

D. Modify the entries in the Windows NT Registry.

Question #10-13

Resource: Chapter 10, "Troubleshooting Considerations"

Mandy has recently upgraded to Windows NT Workstation 4.0 from MS-DOS. When he tries to run his favorite disk optimization utility, the application fails. What do you advise?

A. Reinstall the application under Windows NT so that the Registry can be updated.

B. Modify the application's properties to allow hardware interaction (Advanced tab).

C. Remove the application or dual boot and run it only from DOS. Applications that directly access hardware devices will not run successfully under Windows NT 4.0.

D. Do nothing. You can never run this application.

Question #10-14

Resource: Chapter 10, "Thread Priority"

Bernadette has a math-intensive program that runs calculations while in the background. She wants to work with other program files while this application cranks away, but she does not want to sacrifice its CPU time. What do you advise?

A. Through the Systems applet in Control Panel, set the foreground response time to None. This will let foreground and background applications run at the same base priority level.

B. Through the Systems applet in Control Panel, set the background response time to Maximum. This will increase background base priority 2 levels.

C. From the Start, Run dialog box, start the math-intensive program with the /Realtime switch.

D. Do nothing. You cannot change application priorities.

App
J

Question #10-15

Resource: Chapter 10, "Task Manager"

Len is running Pinball, the DOS Editor, Word 6, Excel 5, and Microstomp, a 16-bit, third-party Windows Web surfing program. He says that he has configured Microstomp to run in its own memory space. However, it has failed and the other Windows applications are also unresponsive. How can you unload Microstomp and try to return control to the other Windows applications?

A. Shut down and restart Windows NT Workstation 4.0.

B. Click the X button in the upper-right corner of the Microstomp window.

C. Start Task Manager, select Microstomp from the list of applications, and choose End Task.

D. Start Task Manager, select the WOW NTVDM entry on the Processes tab, and select End Process.

Question #10-16

Resource: Chapter 10, "Task Manager"

Mandy is running Pinball, the DOS Editor, Word 6, Excel 5, and Microstomp, a 16-bit, third-party Windows Web surfing program. He says that he has configured Microstomp to run in its own memory space. However, it has failed and the other Windows applications are also unresponsive. How can you tell if Microstomp has been configured to run in its own memory space?

    A. Start Task Manager and look for a second WOW NTVDM entry with a reference to the Microstomp application on the Processes tab.

    B. Display the properties of the shortcut for Microstomp and see whether Run in Separate Memory Space has been selected on the Shortcut tab.

    C. Start Task Manager and look for duplicate occurrences of WOWEXEC on the Applications tab.

    D. You cannot tell without restarting the application.

Chapter 11

Question #11-01

Resource: Chapter 11, "Exploring the Windows NT 4.0 Networking Model"

Your Windows NT network will consist of a variety of client computers including Windows NT 4.0 workstations, Windows NT 3.51 workstations, Windows 95, Windows for Workgroups, UNIX, NetWare, and Apple Macintosh. Which of these clients will be able to connect to the Windows NT network? Choose the best answer.

    A. Windows 95, Windows NT 4.0 and 3.51, and Windows for Workgroups

    B. Windows NT 4.0 and 3.51

    C. Windows 95, Windows for Workgroups, Windows NT 4.0 and 3.51, NetWare, and Macintosh

    D. All of them

Question #11-02

Resource: Chapter 11, "File System Layer"

Which Windows NT network model component is responsible for determining where to send a request for resources?

    A. File System Layer

    B. Transport Device Interface

    C. Protocol Layer

    D. Network Interface Card Layer

Question #11-03

Resource: Chapter 11, "Transport Device Interface"

Which Windows NT network model component is responsible for translating the resource request so that the redirector can talk with the protocol?

    A. File System Layer

    B. Transport Device Interface

    C. Protocol Layer

    D. Network Interface Card Layer

App

J

Question #11-04

Resource: Chapter 11, "Benefits of TDI and NDIS 4.0"

Your Windows NT 4.0 workstations must be able to establish connections to resources on NetWare servers and UNIX servers as well as Windows NT 4.0 servers. You need IPX/SPX to communicate with the NetWare servers and TCP/IP to communicate with Windows NT and UNIX servers. What must you do to accomplish this?

    A. Install two network adapters and both NWLink IPX/SPX and TCP/IP on the Windows NT 4.0 workstations. Bind NWLink to one adapter and TCP/IP to the other.

    B. Install three network adapters, one for each type of server, and both NWLink IPX/SPX and TCP/IP on the Windows NT 4.0 workstations. Bind NWLink to one adapter and TCP/IP to the other two.

C. Install one network adapter and both NWLink IPX/SPX and TCP/IP on the Windows NT 4.0 workstations. Windows NT will bind both protocols to the same adapter. Enable and disable each binding as necessary when communicating among the various servers.

D. Do nothing. When you install the two protocols, Windows NT will automatically bind them to the network adapter. Nothing else is required for the connections to be established.

Question #11-05

Resource: Chapter 11, "Protocol Layer" and "Examining NetBEUI, NWLink, and TCP/IP"

Which of the following supported network protocols is required to allow an IPC connection to be established with another Windows NT 4.0 computer? Choose all that apply.

A. NetBEUI

B. NWLink

C. TCP/IP

D. DECnet

Question #11-06

Resource: Chapter 11, "Protocol Layer" and "Examining NetBEUI, NWLink, and TCP/IP"

Which of the following supported network protocols is required to allow an IPC connection to be established with another Windows NT 4.0 computer across a router? Choose all that apply.

A. NetBEUI

B. NWLink

C. TCP/IP

D. DECnet

Question #11-07

Resource: Chapter 11, "NWLink IPX/SPX Compatible Protocol"

Your Windows NT 4.0 workstations must connect to both Windows
NT 4.0 servers and NetWare servers. Your NetWare servers are of all
versions. You have installed NWLink IPX/SPX Compatible Protocol
on the workstations along with CSNW to allow communications with
the NetWare servers. You find during testing that your Windows NT
workstations can connect to some of the NetWare servers, but not all of
them. The NWLink protocol settings look like this:

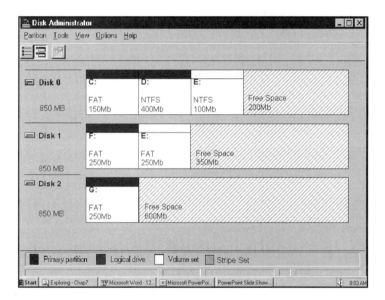

App

J

How can you troubleshoot this situation?

A. Check the network for multiple frame types and configure
NWLink to recognize them all.

B. Do nothing with the protocol settings. Check the network card
connections to the network.

C. Modify the frame types on the NetWare servers to autodetect.

D. Give each Windows NT 4.0 workstation a network number.

Question #11-08

Resource: Chapter 11, "NWLink" and "TCP/IP Protocol"

For which of the following supported network protocols can Windows NT 4.0 Workstation act as a router?

    A. NWLink IPX/SPX

    B. TCP/IP, if the computer is multi-homed

    C. NWLink and TCP/IP

    D. Windows NT Workstation 4.0 cannot route protocols.

Question #11-09

Resource: Chapter 11, "TCP/IP Protocol"

Which TCP/IP utility would be useful to determine a computer's address settings?

    A. Ping

    B. IPCONFIG

    C. FTP

    D. Network Neighborhood

Question #11-10

Resource: Chapter 11, "IP Address Considerations"

You are going to convert your Windows NT network over to the TCP/IP protocol. Your company dynamic is such that when employees change positions within the company, they take their PCs with them. This kind of movement is frequent. What can you do to simplify management of IP addresses for these computers?

    A. Keep good documentation.

    B. There is no easy way to manage this. Each computer requires its own appropriate IP address and subnet mask.

    C. Configure the Windows NT 4.0 workstations to obtain their IP address settings from a DHCP server.

    D. Create an LMHOSTS file for each computer.

Question #11-11

Resource: Chapter 11, "IP Address Considerations"

You have installed TCP/IP on your Windows NT 4.0 workstation and configured its IP address settings. You find that, while you can communicate with other TCP/IP computers on your local subnet, you cannot establish connections with any Windows NT servers on other subnets in your company. What should you check? Choose all that apply.

    A. Subnet mask

    B. Default gateway address

    C. Address settings on the subnet's router

    D. Local IP address

Question #11-12

Resource: Chapter 11, "Configuring Network Options" and "Reviewing Workstation and Server Services"

On your local subnet, you regularly copy data from your Windows NT 4.0 workstations to an archive Windows NT 4.0 workstation using NetBEUI. The archive workstation is not used for any other purpose. How can you optimize the bindings on the archive workstation?

    A. Do nothing. Windows NT self-optimizes network bindings.

    B. Disable the workstation binding because the archive workstation will never need to establish its own connections with other computers.

    C. Disable the server binding because the archive workstation will never need to establish its own connections with other computers.

    D. Move the server binding ahead of the workstation binding because the archive workstation responds to network requests rather than making them.

Question #11-13

Resource: Chapter 11, "Reviewing Workstation and Server Services"

Eunice says that she can connect to resources on other Windows NT computers in her workgroup, but no one can connect to hers. What should you check?

App

J

A. Workstation Service is running

B. Server Service is running

C. Redirector Service is running

D. Frame types match

Question #11-14
Resource: Chapter 11, "Configuring Browsers"

Vern has implemented a workgroup of 10 Windows NT 4.0 workstations and one Windows NT 4.0 server. The server will act as a resource provider and contain common shared folders, workgroup printers, and so on. Vern also wants to ensure that the server is the master browser for the workgroup. What should he do?

A. Do nothing. Windows NT 4.0 servers will become master browsers ahead of Windows NT 4.0 workstations.

B. Configure the Windows NT 4.0 server to become the master browser though the Is Master Browser check box in the Computer Browser Service properties.

C. Change the Browser service parameter MaintainServerList in the Registry to "auto."

D. Change the Browser service parameter MaintainServerList in the Registry to "yes."

Question #11-15
Resource: Chapter 11, "Configuring Browsers"

Vern has implemented a workgroup of 10 Windows NT 4.0 workstations. One of the workstations is used only occasionally by a temporary employee. Vern would like this workstation to default to the master browser for the workgroup for performance reasons. What should he do?

A. Do nothing. Windows NT 4.0 workstations will determine the master browser solely by their browser criteria.

B. Configure the Windows NT 4.0 workstation to become the master browser through the Is Master Browser check box in the Computer Browser Service properties.

C. Change the Browser service parameter MaintainServerList in the Registry to "auto."

D. Add the Browser service parameter PreferredMasterBrowser to the Registry with a value of "yes."

Question #11-16

Resource: Chapter 11, "Configuring Browsers"

You have installed a new color laserjet on a Windows NT 4.0 workstation in a workgroup and shared it with default permissions. Bubba immediately tries to connect to the printer, but cannot find it in his shared printers list. What is the proper course of action?

A. Reinstall the printer and check the permissions.

B. Check the network adapter and protocol settings for the new Windows NT 4.0 workstation.

C. Have Bubba connect to the printer by entering its full UNC name in the path text box.

D. Wait 15 minutes until the workstation announces itself to the master browser.

Question #11-17

Resource: Chapter 11, "Becoming a Member of a Domain"

Windows NT 4.0 has been chosen as the network operating system of choice for your company. There are several small Windows NT 4.0 workstations and Windows 95 workgroups within the company that now need to become part of the company's domain structure. Choose all steps that need to take place.

A. Create computer accounts for each Windows NT 4.0 workstation in the domain.

B. Create computer accounts for each of the Windows 95 workstations in the domain.

C. Check for uniqueness of computer names.

D. Change participation of the Windows NT workstations from the workgroup to the domain through the Identification tab of the Network properties of each computer.

Question #11-18

Resource: Chapter 11, "Understanding Dial-Up Networking and Remote Access Service"

Which communication protocol can be used to establish RAS connections between Windows NT 4.0 workstations and RAS servers? Choose all that apply.

A. SLIP

B. PPP

C. X-Link

D. PPP Multilink

Question #11-19

Resource: Chapter 11, "Understanding Dial-Up Networking and Remote Access Service"

Users in remote offices need to connect through dial-up networking to various resources on the company network. The resource servers use a variety of protocols for various performance reasons. What must you do to ensure that users dialing in can access any resource server that they have been given access to?

A. Assign dial-in permission for each user to each resource server.

B. Install every protocol on every resource server.

C. Install all the protocols on the RAS server only.

D. Install all the protocols on each user's remote computer.

Question #11-20

Resource: Chapter 11, "Introducing Point-to-Point Tunneling"

Flora, the MIS director, wants company employees to be able to access the company's network through their personal Internet providers. However, she has concerns about the security of the company's network from unauthorized Internet access. What is your solution? Choose all that apply.

A. Use Point-to-Point Tunneling on the RAS server.

B. Enable callback security for Internet connections.

C. Connect only the RAS server to the Internet.

D. Enable filtering for PPTP on the RAS server.

Question #11-21

Resource: Chapter 11, "RAS Security"

The marketing department staff travels a lot and dials in to the company network while visiting client offices to obtain product information. Elvira, the marketing director, wants the company to assume the dial-up costs rather than the client. What do you advise?

A. Enable callback security on the RAS server and let the marketer provide the callback number.

B. Enable callback security on the RAS server and specify a number the server should always call back.

C. Do nothing. Charges are always assumed by the RAS server.

D. Select the Reverse Charges option on the RAS server Callback properties.

Question #11-22

Resource: Chapter 11, "Understanding and Configuring TAPI"

The marketing department staff travels a lot and dials in to the company network while visiting client offices to obtain product information. There are several numbers that can be used for dialing in. The marketers do not want to have to take the additional time during their client presentations to configure area code and country code information for each dial-in number. What do you advise?

A. Enable callback security on the RAS server and let the marketer provide the callback number.

B. Have the marketers create a TAPI location before their client call that includes the area code and country code. This location can then be applied to any of the dial-in numbers when Dial-Up networking is loaded.

App

J

C. You must change the country and area codes each time you select a dial-in number.

D. Create separate phone book entries for each area code and country code.

Question #11-23

Resource: Chapter 11, "Configuring RAS on the Server"

For security reasons, you want to restrict access for dial-up users only to the RAS server when they dial in, but not restrict their access when at the office. What must you do?

A. Do nothing. This is the default setting.

B. Disable gateway access for each RAS server network protocol setting.

C. Configure the permissions on each of the resource servers in the network to restrict the users.

D. Configure the dial-in permissions for each user on the RAS server to restrict access to the RAS server.

Question #11-24

Resource: Chapter 11, "Introducing Peer Web Services"

Your company has implemented an intranet for publishing corporate data and to provide access to database information. Your company is international, and users from all locations will be accessing the intranet. Which service is the best choice for implementing publishing services?

A. Peer Web Services

B. Internet Information Server Services

C. Internet Explorer Services

D. TCP/IP Protocol Services

Question #11-25

Resource: Chapter 11, "Introducing Peer Web Services"

Your company has implemented an intranet for publishing corporate data and to provide access to database information. Some of the data is confidential and should not be available for everyone to access. What do you do?

A. Enable PPTP filtering for PWS.

B. Enable PPTP filtering for IIS.

C. Use Windows NT security and Internet Service Manager keys to secure the Web pages.

D. Do nothing. There is no security through Web publishing.

Question #11-26

Resource: Chapter 11, "Providing Connectivity to NetWare Servers"

Your Windows NT 4.0 Workstation clients need to access NetWare servers on a regular basis. What do you need to do to make this process seamless? Choose all that apply.

A. Install NWLink on the Windows NT 4.0 workstations.

B. Install Client Services for NetWare on the Windows NT 4.0 workstations.

C. Select a preferred NetWare server to connect to through the CSNW Control Panel applet.

D. Maintain different user accounts between the NetWare server and the Windows NT workstation.

Chapter 12

Question #12-01

Resource: Chapter 12, "Understanding Virtual Memory Management"

Which of the following represent characteristics of the Virtual Memory Manager?

A. The Virtual Memory Manager provides up to 2G of storage for each application.

B. The default pagefile size is 12M + physical RAM.

App

J

   C. Application requests for memory are mapped directly into RAM.

   D. The pagefile is created on the partition with the most free space.

Question #12-02

Resource: Chapter 12, "Exploring and Optimizing Pagefile Usage"

Desiree, a Visual Basic developer, has noticed that her system's performance has decreased since she began work on a large VB application. You have used Performance Monitor to determine that the pagefile usage has increased and that disk drive itself is being over-utilized. You also notice that the pagefile, Windows NT system files, and the VB application are all stored on the same partition. There are two other disk drives installed on the system. How can you balance disk usage for the VB application and the pagefile?

   A. Move the VB application files to a partition on another disk drive.

   B. Move the VB application files to a partition on another disk drive and move the pagefile to a different partition on another disk drive.

   C. Increase the size of the page file.

   D. Nothing. She must buy more RAM.

Question #12-03

Resource: Chapter 12, "Right-Sizing the Pagefile"

Frederick has recently loaded two more C++ applications to modify on his Windows NT 4.0 workstation. He has noticed that when he boots and loads all his applications, Windows NT takes longer to respond to application requests. You use Performance Monitor and notice that pagefile usage has increased, and that the Commit Limit for the pagefile drops rapidly when the applications are loaded. What is the best solution you can offer Frederick?

   A. Purchase more RAM for Frederick's computer.

   B. Move the pagefile to another disk partition.

C. Increase the initial size of the pagefile so that it doesn't have to grow right away as the applications load.

D. Move the C++ applications to another disk partition.

Question #12-04

Resource: Chapter 12, "Objects to Monitor, Process Object," "Exploring and Optimizing Pagefile Usage," and "Creating Multiple Pagefiles"

Desiree, a Visual Basic developer, has noticed that her system's performance has decreased since she began work on a large VB application. You have used Performance Monitor to determine that the pagefile usage has increased. You also notice that the pagefile, Windows NT system files, and the VB application are all stored on the same partition. In addition, the working set for the VB application shows that it consistently requires 16M for itself. What solutions can you recommend? Name all that apply.

A. Add more RAM in the computer.

B. Move the pagefile to a disk partition other than the system or application partition.

C. Increase the maximum size for the pagefile.

D. Create multiple page files.

Question #12-05

Resource: Chapter 12, "Using Event Viewer to Troubleshoot Windows NT" and "Exploring the Windows NT Diagnostics Utility"

Frederica has received the following message when booting Windows NT: `Dependency or Service failed to start`. She answers OK to the message, but finds that she cannot send any broadcast messages. What two utilities can you use to determine which services are involved in the problem?

A. Control Panel, Services

B. Windows NT Diagnostics

C. Performance Monitor

D. Event Viewer

Question #12-06

Resource: Chapter 12, "Using Event Viewer to Troubleshoot Windows NT"

What steps need to take place in order to capture and view security related events? Choose all that apply.

A. Switch to the Security Log in Event Viewer.

B. Log on as a Power User.

C. Enable auditing in the User Manager.

D. Configure which security events to audit.

Question #12-07

Resource: Chapter 12, "Using Event Viewer to Troubleshoot Windows NT"

Heinrich is receiving intermittent service errors throughout his computing session. You are using the Event Viewer on Heinrich's Windows NT workstation to help pinpoint the errors. However, his System Log is quite full. How can you more easily pinpoint the source of the errors?

A. Use Performance Monitor to track the Services object's Stop Errors counter.

B. Filter the System Log to only show Service Control Manager events.

C. Clear the System Log and record only Service Control Manager events.

D. Shut down and restart Windows NT and record any service error messages.

Question #12-08

Resource: Chapter 12, "Objects to Monitor," "Processor Object"

Which Processor object counter would be useful to determine how much processor time is being utilized by application requests?

A. %Processor Time

B. %User Time

C. %Application Time

D. %Privileged Time

Question #12-09

Resource: Chapter 12, "Objects to Monitor," "Processor Object"

Which Process object counter would be useful in determining the amount of memory required by an application?

A. %Application Memory

B. Commit Limit

C. Working Set

D. Avg. Disk sec\Transfer

Question #12-10

Resource: Chapter 12, "Objects to Monitor," "Memory Object"

Which Memory object counter would help to identify when to right-size the pagefile?

A. %Pagefile

B. Commit Limit

C. Working Set

D. %Disk Time

Question #12-11

Resource: Chapter 12, "Objects to Monitor," "Memory Object"

On your Windows NT 4.0 development workstation, you have concluded that performance as a whole has decreased. You are not sure which process is driving this, but you have noticed that your disk drive has had a lot more activity lately. What objects should you monitor through Performance Monitor to help you troubleshoot this situation?

A. Check the Processor object's %Processor Time counter, determine the percent of disk I/O used for paging through the Memory object's Pages/Sec counter and the Logical Disk object's Avg. Disk sec/Transfer counter, and determine the Process object's Working Set for every process running.

App

J

B. Check the Processor object's %Processor Time counter, and determine the percent of disk I/O used for paging through the Memory object's Pages/Sec counter and the Logical Disk object's Avg. Disk sec/Transfer counter. Track the Process object's %Processor Time counter for every process running to determine which processes are pushing the processor excessively. Check the Working Set counter for these processes in particular.

C. Check the Processor object's %Processor Time counter, determine the percent of disk I/O used for paging through the Logical Disk object's Disk Queue Length counter, and the Process object's Working Set for every process running.

D. Check the Processor object's %User Time counter, determine the percent of disk I/O used for paging through the Logical Disk object's %Disk Time counter, and the Memory object's Commit Limit counter for the pagefile.

Question #12-12

Resource: Chapter 12, "Reviewing the Emergency Repair Process" and "Initiating the Repair Process"

A portion of the Registry has become corrupted on a Windows NT 4.0 workstation. You have an Emergency Repair Disk for that workstation that has been kept up-to-date. How can you use it to restore the Registry? Choose all that apply.

A. Choose Repair and, through the repair process, choose Inspect Registry Files.

B. Boot from a Windows NT boot disk.

C. Insert the Windows NT startup disk and boot the computer.

D. Insert the Emergency Repair Disk and run RDISK.

Question #12-13

Resource: Chapter 12, "Reviewing the Emergency Repair Process" and "Initiating the Repair Process"

A user accidentally used the DOS SYS command to set the master boot record on his Windows NT workstation back to MS-DOS. Now,

Windows NT won't boot. You have an Emergency Repair Disk for that workstation that has been kept up-to-date. How can you use it to restore Windows NT to the master boot record? Choose all that apply.

    A. Boot from a Windows NT boot disk and copy the NTLDR file to the master boot record.

    B. Insert the Windows NT startup disk and boot the computer.

    C. Choose Repair and, through the repair process, choose Inspect Boot Sector.

    D. Insert the Emergency Repair Disk and run RDISK.

Question #12-14

Resource: Chapter 12, "Creating and Using a Windows NT Boot Disk"

You have booted a Windows NT 4.0 workstation and received the message: `Missing or corrupt NTDETECT.COM`. How can you quickly troubleshoot this problem?

    A. Reinstall Windows NT Workstation 4.0 on the computer.

    B. Boot from the Emergency Repair Disk and choose Verify the Windows NT System Files.

    C. Boot from a Windows NT boot disk to determine if you can boot successfully. If so, replace the corrupted file with the working NTDETECT.COM on the Windows NT boot disk.

    D. Boot from a Windows NT boot disk and run RDISK from a command prompt.

Question #12-15

Resource: Chapter 12, "Reviewing System Recovery Options"

Which of the following recovery options could be useful to troubleshoot an intermittent stop error on a Windows NT 4.0 workstation?

    A. Run RDISK at a command prompt.

    B. Send an Administrative Alert to the Administrator.

    C. Write an event to the System Log.

    D. Automatically reboot the computer after the stop error occurs.

App

J

Answer Key

Chapter Tests

Chapter 2

Question	Answer	Question	Answer
02–01	B	02–07	B
02–02	A,B,D	02–08	B
02–03	C	02–09	B,C,D
02–04	B	02–10	A
02–05	C	02–11	A,C
02–06	A	02–12	A,B,D

Chapter 3

Question	Answer	Question	Answer
03–01	C	03–10	B
03–02	A,B,D	03–11	A
03–03	A,C,D	03–12	C
03–04	A	03–13	A,B,D
03–05	B	03–14	A
03–06	A	03–15	B,C,D
03–07	B	03–16	C
03–08	D	03–17	D
03–09	C	03–18	B

Chapter 4

Question	Answer	Question	Answer
04–01	A,D	04–06	B,C
04–02	A,B,C	04–07	B
04–03	A,B,D	04–08	B,C
04–04	C	04–09	A
04–05	C	04–10	C

Chapter 5

Question	Answer	Question	Answer
05-01	A,B	05-08	C
05-02	A,C,D	05-09	A
05-03	D	05-10	B
05-04	C	05-11	C
05-05	B	05-12	C
05-06	A	05-13	B,C,D
05-07	A,B,D	05-14	C

Chapter 6

Question	Answer	Question	Answer
06-01	A	06-10	A,B,D
06-02	D	06-11	B
06-03	A	06-12	C
06-04	B	06-13	B
06-05	A	06-14	C
06-06	A,B,D	06-15	A,B
06-07	B	06-16	A,B,C,D
06-08	C	06-17	A,C,D
06-09	B		

Chapter 7

Question	Answer	Question	Answer
07-01	D	07-09	B
07-02	A,B,C	07-10	C
07-03	C	07-11	A,B
07-04	B	07-12	C
07-05	A	07-13	A
07-06	D	07-14	A,B,D
07-07	B	07-15	B
07-08	C		

App
J

Chapter 8

Question	Answer	Question	Answer
08-01	C	08-09	A,C,D
08-02	D	08-10	A,B,D
08-03	A,B,D	08-11	B,C
08-04	B	08-12	B
08-05	B,D	08-13	A,B,C
08-06	B	08-14	B
08-07	B	08-15	D
08-08	A	08-16	A,B,C

Chapter 9

Question	Answer	Question	Answer
09-01	B	09-10	A,C
09-02	A,C,D	09-11	B
09-03	A,B,C	09-12	B
09-04	B,D	09-13	C
09-05	C	09-14	B
09-06	C	09-15	C
09-07	A	09-16	A,C,D
09-08	D	09-17	A
09-09	A	09-18	D

Chapter 10

Question	Answer	Question	Answer
10-01	B,C,D	10-09	A,B,C,D
10-02	A,D	10-10	A
10-03	A	10-11	C
10-04	B	10-12	B,D
10-05	D	10-13	C
10-06	A	10-14	A
10-07	A,C	10-15	C
10-08	C	10-16	A,B

Chapter 11

Question	Answer	Question	Answer
11-01	D	11-14	A
11-02	A	11-15	D
11-03	B	11-16	C
11-04	D	11-17	A,C,D
11-05	A,B,C	11-18	A,B,D
11-06	B,C	11-19	C
11-07	A	11-20	A,C,D
11-08	B	11-21	A
11-09	B	11-22	B
11-10	C	11-23	B
11-11	A,B,C	11-24	B
11-12	B	11-25	C
11-13	B	11-26	A,B,C

Chapter 12

Question	Answer	Question	Answer
12-01	A,B,D	12-09	C
12-02	B	12-10	B
12-03	C	12-11	B
12-04	A,B,D	12-12	A,C
12-05	B,D	12-13	B,C
12-06	A,C,D	12-14	C
12-07	B	12-15	B,C,D
12-08	B		

App
J

Mastery Test

Note The answers to these questions can be found in order at the end of this section. The resource line following each question number is the section in that chapter in the book where information regarding that question is located. ▪

Question #1
Resource: Chapter 3, "Troubleshooting Installation and Setup," and "Preparation Checklist"

The three most important tips I can offer a coworker to make a Windows NT installation problem-free are:

A. Create an Emergency Repair Disk. You can use this to restart Windows NT and repair the installation process.

B. Consult the Hardware Compatibility List before starting setup to ensure that all the computer's hardware components have been tested with Windows NT 4.0.

C. Determine whether the computer in question meets all the minimum equipment requirements for a Windows NT installation.

D. Find out all the driver and configuration data specific to devices in the computer, particularly regarding the network card, before starting setup.

Question #2
Resource: Chapter 6, "Default User Accounts"

Which of the following statements is true about the default user accounts created in Windows NT Workstation 4.0?

A. The Administrator account is enabled and can be renamed; the Guest account is enabled and cannot be renamed.

B. The Administrator account is enabled and cannot be renamed; the Guest account is disabled and cannot be renamed.

C. The Administrator account is enabled and can be renamed; the Guest account is disabled and can be renamed.

D. The Administrator account is disabled and cannot be renamed; the Guest account is enabled and can be renamed.

Question #3

Resource: Chapter 8, "Converting a FAT Partition to NTFS," and "Requirements, Terms, and Strategy"

A user wants to convert a partition from FAT to NTFS with no loss of data. How would you advise the user to accomplish this task?

A. Use Disk Administrator to select the partition and choose Tools, Format. Then select NTFS.

B. Use the command-line utility CONVERT.EXE to convert the partition.

C. Use the Windows NT Backup utility to back up the partition data to disk. Then format the partition for NTFS and restore the data.

D. You cannot convert a FAT partition to NTFS without loss of data.

Question #4

Resource: Chapter 10, "Reviewing the Windows NT 4.0 Subsystem Architecture"

Which of the following functions as part of the Kernel mode of Windows NT 4.0?

A. CSR Subsystem

B. HAL

C. GDI

D. Thread prioritization

Question #5

Resource: Chapter 11, "Understanding Dial-Up Networking and Remote Access Service"

App
J

Users in remote offices need to connect through dial-up networking to various resources on the company network. The resource servers use a variety of protocols for various performance reasons. What must you do to ensure that users dialing in can access any resource server that they have been given access to?

    A. Assign dial-in permission for each user to each resource server.

    B. Install every protocol on every resource server.

    C. Install all the protocols on the RAS server only.

    D. Install all the protocols on each user's remote computer.

Question #6

Resource: Chapter 12, "Reviewing the Emergency Repair Process," and "Initiating the Repair Process"

A user accidentally used the DOS.SYS command to set the master boot record on his Windows NT workstation back to MS-DOS. Now, Windows NT won't boot. You have an Emergency Repair Disk for that workstation that has been kept up-to-date. How can you use it to restore Windows NT to the master boot record? Choose all that apply.

    A. Boot from a Windows NT boot disk and copy the NTLDR file to the master boot record.

    B. Insert the Windows NT startup disk and boot the computer.

    C. Choose Repair and, through the repair process, choose Inspect Boot Sector.

    D. Insert the Emergency Repair Disk and run RDISK.

Question #7

Resource: Chapter 7, "Local versus Domain Access Tokens"

The Sales team workstations participate in a workgroup computing model. Janis recently acquired a laser quality printer with an envelope feed that the rest of the team will share. Janis has shared the printer with the default permission, but none of the other team members can access the printer. What else must Janis do?

A. Create a group called Sales and assign it the print permission for the printer.

B. Create user accounts for each of the other Sales team members on her workstation.

C. Give the Everyone group the Access Printers Remotely user right on her workstation.

D. Install the printer driver on all the other workstations.

Question #8

Resource: Chapter 2, "Enterprise Model," and "Single Domain Model"

The Account Executive group has merged with the Sales and Marketing Group. You are now supporting 50 users. Each has a variety of files and directories to share with other department members. There are two laser printers, one color printer, one scanner, and two network-ready printers. You are the only administrator for the group. What would be the best model to support these users?

A. The Workgroup Model

B. The Single Domain Enterprise Model

C. The Master Domain Enterprise Model

D. The Complete Trust Enterprise Model

Question #9

Resource: Chapter 9, "Windows NT 4.0 Print Process"

Jeanette calls to say that her print jobs seem to have stopped running. You check the printer that she sent the jobs to and see that the jobs are stuck in queue. What steps should you take to clear the stuck jobs? Choose all that apply.

A. Select the stuck jobs and choose Document, Cancel.

B. Select Printer, Purge Printer.

C. Use the Control Panel applet Service to stop and restart the Spooler service.

D. Select each stuck job and change its priority.

App

J

Question #10

Resource: Chapter 10, "User (Application) Mode"

Which two subsystems are loaded when Windows NT boots?

- A. CSR and Security Subsystems
- B. CSR and OS/2 Subsystems
- C. Environment and Security Subsystems
- D. OS/2 and POSIX Subsystems

Question #11

Resource: Chapter 3, Table 3.2 "Beginning Setup"

Which of the following switches will allow you to install Windows NT without creating the three startup disks?

- A. WINNT /B
- B. WINNT /O
- C. WINNT /OX
- D. WINNT /T:c

Question #12

Resource: Chapter 11, "Understanding and Configuring TAPI"

The marketing department staff travels a lot and dials in to the company network while visiting client offices to obtain product information. There are several numbers that can be used for dialing in. The marketers do not want to have to take the additional time during their client presentations to configure area code and country code information for each dial-in number. What do you advise?

- A. Enable callback security on the RAS server and let the marketer provide the callback number.
- B. Have the marketers create a TAPI location before their client call that includes the area code and country code. This location can then be applied to any of the dial-in numbers when Dial-Up Networking is loaded.

C. You must change the country and area codes each time you select a dial-in number.

D. Create separate phone book entries for each area code and country code.

Question #13

Resource: Chapter 3, "Formatting the Partition," and the sidebar, "Dual Booting Windows NT 4.0 and OS/2"

You are installing Windows NT on a computer that also must support and boot OS/2.

A. Windows NT supports OS/2's High Performance File System (HPFS) so there are no problems installing the Windows NT system files in the same partition as OS/2.

B. Windows NT 4.0 no longer supports HPFS, so you must install Windows NT in another partition. When Windows NT restarts the system, you can use the OS/2 boot manager to manage both partitions.

C. Windows NT 4.0 no longer supports HPFS, so you must install Windows NT in another partition. When Windows NT restarts the system, it will disable the OS/2 boot manager, but you can reenable it by marking the Boot Manager partition active while in Windows NT and restarting the computer.

D. Windows NT and OS/2 cannot coexist on the same computer.

Question #14

Resource: Chapter 4, "Help Topics-Bookmark"

There is a particular Help topic that you frequent. Is there a way to quickly access it when you open Help?

A. Annotate the topic and then browse annotations when you start Help.

B. Annotate the topic, then use Find to find all help documents with your annotation.

App

J

C. Create a bookmark. When you start Help, access the page by selecting the bookmark.

D. You cannot mark a page in Help.

Question #15

Resource: Chapter 11, "Protocol Layer" and "Examining NetBEUI, NWLink, and TCP/IP"

Which of the following supported network protocols is required to allow an IPC connection to be established with another Windows NT 4.0 computer? Choose all that apply.

A. NetBEUI

B. NWLink

C. TCP/IP

D. DECnet

Question #16

Resource: Chapter 3, Table 3.1 "Windows NT Workstation 4.0 System Requirements"

You are planning to roll out Windows NT Workstation 4.0 to a workgroup that has the following computer configurations. On which computers can you install Windows NT Workstation 4.0 successfully?

A. 3 386/25, 150M free space, 8M RAM, VGA, Windows 3.1

B. 2 386/33, 120M free space, 16M RAM, VGA, Windows for Workgroups

C. 5 486/66DX, 200M free space, 16M RAM, Super VGA, Windows for Workgroups

D. 2 Pentium/120, 100M free space, 16M RAM, Super VGA, Windows NT 3.51

Question #17

Resource: Chapter 6, "User Rights"

You want to give a particular user the ability to back up files on a workstation, but not be able to restore files. How can you accomplish this?

A. Make the user a member of the Backup Operators group on the workstation.

B. Make the user a member of the Server Operators group on the workstation.

C. Create a new local group called BACKUP ONLY on the local workstation and make the user a member of it. Assign this new group to the Backup Files and Directories User Right.

D. Give the user Read Only access to all the files.

Question #18

Resource: Chapter 8, "Understanding Partitions"

Windows NT calls the active primary partition its:

A. Boot partition

B. System partition

C. Startup partition

D. Extended partition

Question #19

Resource: Chapter 9, "Ports Tab"

The print device associated with a particular printer has failed. Several print jobs are waiting in queue in that printer. How can you service these print jobs?

A. Connect to another remote printer. Open the printer manager window for the printer and drag the waiting print jobs to the remote printer manager window.

B. Use the Ports tab properties for the printer to add a port for another remote printer. Deselect the current print port associated with the printer and select the remote port. Resume the printer.

App

J

C. Do nothing. You must replace the failed print device before printing can resume.

D. Use the Control Panel applet Services to stop the spooler service, configure it to connect to another remote printer, and restart it.

Question #20

Resource: Chapter 9, "Print Pools" and "Priority"

There are three downward-compatible print devices connected to the print server in MIS. MIS Managers and Project Leaders should always be able to print to the first available printer. Help Desk staff and Developers should be able to print only to their specified print device. What will best accomplish this task?

A. Create a printer for each device and assign the appropriate groups access only to their printer. Give the Managers' printer a priority of 1, Help Desk's printer a priority of 50, and Developers' a priority of 99.

B. Create a printer for each device and assign the appropriate groups access only to their printer. Give the Managers' printer a priority of 99, Help Desk's printer a priority of 50, and Developers' a priority of 1.

C. Create a printer for each device and assign the appropriate groups access only to their printer. Make the Managers' printer a printer pool by associating it with each print device.

D. Create a printer for each device and assign the appropriate groups access only to their printer. Make each printer a printer pool by associating it with each print device.

Question #21

Resource: Chapter 5, "Creating and Managing Hardware Profiles"

Antonio frequently travels for the company and accesses the network on his laptop via modem while on the road. When he is at the office, he docks his laptop at his workstation and uses the network card in the docking station to access the network. How can you facilitate the boot process between these two hardware configurations?

A. Hardware profiles are a feature of Windows 95, not Windows NT 4.0.

B. Create a hardware profile for each configuration—docked and undocked—and set a default timeout value for the most frequently used configuration.

C. Modify the BOOT.INI file and include a boot menu choice for a second hardware configuration using the \PROFILE:filename boot switch.

D. Use Control Panel, Services and create a new profile from the HW Profiles button.

Question #22

Resource: Chapter 3, "Upgrading to Windows NT Workstation 4.0— Windows 3.1 and Windows for Workgroups 3.11"

You are installing Windows NT Workstation 4.0 on a computer that needs to support Windows for Workgroups as well. You would like to migrate user and environment settings to Windows NT 4.0. What should you do?

A. Do nothing. The Windows for Workgroups settings will automatically be migrated to Windows NT 4.0.

B. Install Windows NT 4.0 in the same directory as Windows for Workgroups. The settings compatible with Windows NT 4.0 will then automatically be migrated. You can continue to boot either to Windows NT or to Windows for Workgroups.

C. After installing Windows NT 4.0, run the MIGRATE utility from the command prompt.

D. You cannot migrate those settings from Windows for Workgroups.

App

J

Question #23

Resource: Chapter 3, "Mass Storage Device Configuration"

You have begun the setup process and have been queried for mass storage devices. Setup presents you with a blank list of devices, but you know that you have a 1.2G IDE drive installed.

- A. IDE devices are detected but generally not displayed in the list.
- B. Windows NT has incorrectly identified your devices. Press F3 to exit setup and double-check your drive configuration.
- C. Type **S** to add the drive configuration to the list.
- D. Exit setup and run NTHQ to verify hardware detection.

Question #24

Resource: Chapter 4, "Welcome to Windows NT Workstation 4.0"

The correct way to shut down Windows NT is to: (Choose three)

- A. Press Ctrl+Alt+Del on the keyboard, then choose Shutdown in the Windows NT Security dialog box.
- B. Choose Shutdown from the Start menu and then restart the computer.
- C. Choose Shutdown from the Start menu and then shut down the computer.
- D. Press Ctrl+Alt+Del on the keyboard and then power off the computer.

Question #25

Resource: Chapter 10, "Examining Win 16 Application Support"

Which of the following statements accurately describes a Win 16 application running under Windows NT 4.0?

- A. All Win 16 applications run in the same NTVDM by default.
- B. All Win 16 applications are non-preemptively multitasked within the NTVDM.
- C. 16-bit calls are translated into 32-bit calls through a process called thunking.
- D. WOW emulates the Windows 3.1 memory environment for Win 16 applications.

Question #26

Resource: Chapter 9, "Print Processor"

If the final print output is corrupted, what print process component should you check?

A. Spooler service on the client computer

B. Spooler service on the print server

C. Print processor on the print server

D. Print monitor on the client computer

Question #27

Resource: Chapter 8, "Creating and Managing Stripe Sets"

Your server is configured as shown in the exhibit. You have a database file that is 325M in size and growing. What is the largest stripe set you can create on your server?

App

J

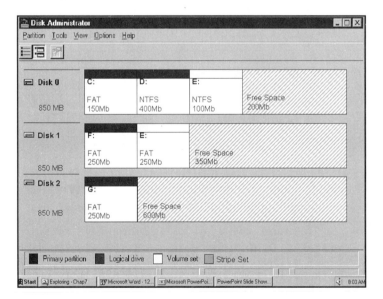

A. 200M

B. 600M

C. 700M

D. 1150M

Question #28

Resource: Chapter 7, "Sharing Resources and Determining Network Access"

The manager of the Accounting department wants to make next year's budget templates available for the staff accountants to review beginning next month. They will be stored on the department resource server called ACCT1 in a folder called BUDGET97. None of the partitions on ACCT1 is formatted with NTFS. How would you make the folder available only to the Accounting department staff?

A. Use User Manager to assign permission to use the folder to the Accountants group.

B. Use User Manager for Domains to assign User Rights to the Accountants group to access the BUDGET97 share.

C. Use the Security tab on the properties sheet for the folder to assign permissions to the Accountants group.

D. Use the Sharing tab on the properties sheet for the folder to assign permissions to the Accountants group.

Question #29

Resource: Chapter 3, "Beginning Setup," and the sidebar, "Setup Executable on RISC-based Systems"

On a RISC-based computer, which of the following statements is true regarding Windows NT installation?

A. Execute setup from either the CD-ROM or over the network by typing **WINNT32** and any optional switches.

B. You must have a 2M FAT minimum system partition before starting setup.

C. Execute setup only from a CD-ROM by running WINNT /ARC.

D. Run SETUPLDR from the I386 subdirectory on the CD-ROM.

Question #30

Resource: Chapter 2, "Hardware Profiles"

Betty travels a lot for your organization and has the laptop to prove it. When she is at the office, she plugs her laptop into her desktop docking station. The docking station has its own monitor, keyboard, and mouse, as well as a network card connection to the company LAN. How can you support Betty's multiple hardware profiles?

    A. Windows NT does not support multiple hardware profiles.

    B. You must install Windows NT on a separate hard disk in the docking station and boot from that disk when the laptop is docked.

    C. Create a second hardware profile for the docking station configuration.

    D. You don't need to do anything. Windows NT will recognize the changed configuration when the laptop is docked.

App

J

Question #31

Resource: Chapter 11, "Exploring the Windows NT 4.0 Networking Model"

Your Windows NT network will consist of a variety of client computers including Windows NT 4.0 workstations, Windows NT 3.51 workstations, Windows 95, Windows for Workgroups, UNIX, NetWare, and Apple Macintosh. Which of these clients will be able to connect to the Windows NT network? Choose the best answer.

    A. Windows 95, Windows NT 4.0 and 3.51, and Windows for Workgroups

    B. Windows NT 4.0 and 3.51

    C. Windows 95, Windows for Workgroups, Windows NT 4.0 and 3.51, NetWare, and Macintosh

    D. All of them

Question #32

Resource: Chapter 10, "Configuring the OS/2 Subsystem"

Len occasionally needs to run an OS/2 database program on his Windows NT 4.0 workstation. He configured a CONFIG.SYS prior to running the application for the first time, and the changes took. He now needs to modify the CONFIG.SYS file. He used WordPad to make the changes, but they do not seem to be read by the OS/2 application. What two options do you advise?

    A. Use Notepad to modify the CONFIG.SYS file.

    B. The OS/2 subsystem obtains information for its CONFIG.SYS file from the Windows NT Registry. Use an OS/2-based text editor to modify the OS/2 CONFIG.SYS after starting the OS/2 application.

    C. Use the OSCONFIG command-line utility to update the Windows NT Registry information.

    D. Modify the entries in the Windows NT Registry.

Question #33

Resource: Chapter 5, "BOOT.INI"

The BOOT.INI file on my computer looks like this:

```
[Boot Loader]
timeout=15
default=multi(0)disk(2)rdisk(1)partition(3)\winnt40
[Operating Systems]
multi(0)disk(2)rdisk(1)partition(3)\winnt40="Windows NT
➥4.0 Workstation"
multi(0)disk(2)rdisk(1)partition(3)\winnt40="Windows NT
➥4.0 Workstation [VGA Mode]"
    /basevideo
      c:\=MS-DOS
```

What can I infer from this file?

    A. The timeout value before Windows NT loads is 15 seconds. Windows NT system files can be found on the third partition of the second physical disk attached to the first controller card.

B. The timeout value before Windows NT loads is 15 seconds and DOS is the default operating system.

C. The timeout value before Windows NT loads is 15 seconds. Windows NT system files can be found on the third partition of the first physical disk attached to the first controller card.

D. The controller card is a SCSI adapter.

Question #34

Resource: Chapter 6, "Understanding User Manager" and "Creating a New User"

Your workstations are members of a domain called Titan. You need to create user accounts so that two shifts of temporary employees can log on to the same computer, but only during their shift.

A. Use User Manager for Domains on each local Windows NT workstation to create the temporary accounts and assign each the appropriate logon hours.

B. Use User Manager on each local Windows NT workstation to create the temporary accounts and assign each the appropriate logon hours.

C. Use User Manager for Domains on the domain controller for Titan to create domain accounts for the temporary employees and assign each the appropriate logon hours.

D. Use User Manager on the domain controller for Titan to create domain accounts for the temporary employees and assign each the appropriate logon hours.

Question #35

Resource: Chapter 11, "IP Address Considerations"

You are going to convert your Windows NT network over to the TCP/IP protocol. Your company dynamic is such that when employees change positions within the company, they take their PCs with them. This kind of movement is frequent. What can you do to simplify management of IP addresses for these computers?

App

J

A. Keep good documentation.

B. There is no easy way to manage this. Each computer requires its own appropriate IP address and subnet mask.

C. Configure the Windows NT 4.0 workstations to obtain their IP address settings from a DHCP server.

D. Create an LMHOSTS file for each computer.

Question #36

Resource: Chapter 2, "The Recordset"

Which of the following are characteristics of NTFS? Choose three.

A. Transaction tracking

B. File and directory level permissions

C. Auto-defragmentation of files

D. Data compression

Question #37

Resource: Chapter 7, "Effective Permissions"

Ned is a member of the Developers group at Springfield Technologies. He has been promoted to team leader for his group. He needs to edit the DOOM.DOC file in the Tools folder, but does not have Write access. What must you do to give Ned access to DOOM.DOC?

A. Do nothing. The next time Ned logs on, his permissions will change.

B. Change the Developers group permission to Change.

C. Add Ned to the Team Leaders group.

D. Change the Team Leaders group permission to Full Control.

Question #38

Resource: Chapter 9, "Print Monitor" and "A Little More About LPD Devices"

Which print monitor is loaded with TCP/IP and tracks print jobs targeted for TCP/IP print hosts?

A. IPMON.DLL

B. LPDMON.DLL

C. LPRMON.DLL

D. LOCALMON.DLL

Question #39

Resource: Chapter 3, "Formatting the Partition"and "Upgrading to Windows NT Workstation 4.0—Windows and Windows for Workgroups"

You are installing Windows NT Workstation 4.0 on a computer with a previous installation of Windows for Workgroups. You would like to retain that installation and boot to either Windows or Windows NT.

A. You must install Windows NT in a new directory in order to preserve the original installation.

B. Do nothing. Windows NT will automatically install as dual boot in this installation.

C. Create a new partition using FDISK and install Windows NT in that partition.

D. You cannot dual boot between Windows and Windows NT.

Question #40

Resource: Chapter 10, "Examining WIN32-based Application Support"

Bernadette obtained a WIN32 application from a friend through e-mail but has not been able to successfully load and run it on her PowerPC. You have checked for the usual things—memory, disk space, and so on—and all looks fine. What else can you do?

App

J

A. Run the WIN32 application in its own memory space.

B. Check the platform for which the application was compiled. Bernadette must use a version compiled for the PowerPC platform.

C. Shut down and restart Windows NT to free up application resources.

D. The application may be corrupted. Have Bernadette obtain another copy.

Question #41

Resource: Chapter 11, "Configuring Browsers"

Vern has implemented a workgroup of 10 Windows NT 4.0 workstations and one Windows NT 4.0 server. The server will act as a resource provider and contain common shared folders, workgroup printers, and so on. Vern also wants to ensure that the server is the master browser for the workgroup. What should he do?

A. Do nothing. Windows NT 4.0 servers will become master browsers ahead of Windows NT 4.0 workstations.

B. Configure the Windows NT 4.0 server to become the master browser through the Is Master Browser check box in the Computer Browser Service properties.

C. Change the Browser service parameter MaintainServerList in the Registry to "auto."

D. Change the Browser service parameter MaintainServerList in the Registry to "yes."

Question #42

Resource: Chapter 12, "Understanding Virtual Memory Management"

Which of the following represent characteristics of the Virtual Memory Manager?

A. The Virtual Memory Manager provides up to 2G of storage for each application.

    B. The default pagefile size is 12M + physical RAM.

    C. Application requests for memory are mapped directly into RAM.

    D. The pagefile is created on the partition with the most free space.

Question #43

Resource: Chapter 12, "Reviewing System Recovery Options"

Which of the following recovery options could be useful to trouble-shoot an intermittent stop error on a Windows NT 4.0 workstation?

    A. Run RDISK at a command prompt.

    B. Send an Administrative Alert to the Administrator.

    C. Write an event to the System Log.

    D. Automatically reboot the computer after the stop error occurs.

App

J

Question #44

Resource: Chapter 4, "Shortcuts"

Randy works with a particular budget file almost every day and would like to be able to open it quickly without having to browse through several directories to find it. What is the best solution you can recommend?

    A. Tell Randy that a quick open feature is coming in the next release of Windows NT.

    B. Create a shortcut to the file and place it on Randy's desktop.

    C. Use Windows Explorer to browse for the file so that not as many windows are opened.

    D. Use My Computer with the Replace Window option to minimize the number of open windows on the screen.

Question #45

Resource: Chapter 9, "Windows NT 4.0 Print Process"

Which of the following sets of Windows NT network clients do not require print drivers to be installed on the local computer?

A. All Microsoft Network clients

B. Windows NT and Windows 95

C. Windows NT, Windows 95, Windows for Workgroups 3.11

D. Windows NT, Windows 95, LAN Manager v2.x for DOS

Question #46

Resource: Chapter 8, "How To Enable Compression"

Wilma has compressed the data files in the QUARRY folder. Later, she moves some of them and other files into another folder so that Betty can access them remotely. Wilma notices that some of the files she moved are compressed and some are not. She calls you for an explanation.

A. Tell Wilma she is hallucinating.

B. When you move files from one folder to another on the same partition, the compression attribute stays with the file. This is probably what happened.

C. The target folder probably had the Compress New Files Only option selected in its properties. Tell Wilma to deselect this option.

D. The compression attribute always stays with the file.

Question #47

Resource: Chapter 6, "Troubleshooting Accounts, Policies, and Profiles"

A user is having problems logging on to the network and seeing a variety of messages. Which of the following things would you check to troubleshoot?

A. The user is entering the correct username and password.

B. The username is case-sensitive.

C. The domain controller is up and accessible.

D. The user's account requires a mandatory profile that is accessible.

Question #48

Resource: Chapter 2, "Windows NT Virtual Memory Management"

Which of the following statements applies to virtual memory management in Windows NT? Choose two.

A. When an application is loaded, the Virtual Memory Manager assigns it virtual memory addresses in physical RAM.

B. The pagefile is created each time that Windows NT is booted.

C. The pagefile defaults to an initial size of 12M + physical RAM, which is preallocated on the disk, and a maximum size of about three times physical RAM.

D. When an application calls for a page from the pagefile, the Virtual Memory Manager adjusts physical RAM so that all pages of the application reside in contiguous address space.

Question #49

Resource: Chapter 11, "Transport Device Interface"

Which Windows NT network model component is responsible for translating the resource request so that the redirector can talk with the protocol?

A. File System Layer

B. Transport Device Interface

C. Protocol Layer

D. Network Interface Card Layer

Question #50

Resource: Chapter 6, "Creating a New User"

Under which of the following situations would you disable the user account rather than deleting it?

A. JaneD has left the company on maternity leave and plans to return in three months.

B. JohnB has taken an emergency medical leave of absence for possibly six or more months, but hopes to return full time.

App

J

C. JaniceD has left the company to take a job at Microsoft.

D. FrankP has taken a temporary team leader position in another department and will return when the project is completed.

Question #51

Resource: Chapter 12, "Objects to Monitor" and "Processor Object"

Which Processor object counter would be useful to determine how much processor time is being utilized by application requests?

A. %Processor Time

B. %User Time

C. %Application Time

D. %Privileged Time

Question #52

Resource: Chapter 12, "Creating and Using a Windows NT Boot Disk"

You have booted a Windows NT 4.0 workstation and received the message: `Missing or corrupt NTDETECT.COM`. How can you quickly troubleshoot this problem?

A. Reinstall Windows NT 4.0 Workstation on the computer.

B. Boot from the Emergency Repair Disk and choose Verify the Windows NT System Files.

C. Boot from a Windows NT boot disk to determine if you can boot successfully. If so, replace the corrupted file with the working NTDETECT.COM on the Windows NT boot disk.

D. Boot from a Windows NT boot disk and run RDISK from a command prompt.

Question #53

Resource: Chapter 11, "Introducing Peer Web Services"

Your company has implemented an intranet for publishing corporate data and to provide access to database information. Some of the data is confidential and should not be available for everyone to access? What do you do?

A. Enable PPTP filtering for PWS.

B. Enable PPTP filtering for IIS.

C. Use Windows NT security and Internet Service Manager keys to secure the Web pages.

D. Do nothing. There is no security through Web publishing.

Question #54

Resource: Chapter 10, "Reviewing the Windows NT 4.0 Subsystem Architecture" and "Examining Win 16 Application Support"

Which of the following functions as part of the user mode of Windows NT 4.0?

A. CSR Subsystem

B. HAL

C. USER

D. WOW

Question #55

Resource: Chapter 3, "Formatting the Partition"

Which of the following statements does not apply to NTFS?

A. NTFS supports file and directory permissions security and access auditing.

B. NTFS supports transaction tracking and sector sparing for data recovery.

C. NTFS supports file and partition sizes of up to 4G.

D. NTFS provides file and directory compression.

Question #56

Resource: Chapter 5, "Examining the Registry"

Which of the following hives in HKEY_LOCAL_MACHINE have corresponding directory files in the Windows NT system directory?

A. System

B. Software

C. Hardware

D. Security

Question #57

Resource: Chapter 9, "Windows NT 4.0 Print Process"

Several users have called you within the past half-hour to complain that their print jobs are not printing. In fact, they get system messages that tell them that the spooler is not responding. You have verified that the spooler directory partition does not have adequate free space to hold all the print jobs sent to it. What steps should you take to resolve this situation? Choose 2.

A. Use the Control Panel applet Services to more frequently stop and restart the Spooler service to keep the print jobs from becoming fragmented.

B. Change the location of the spool directory to a partition with enough disk space by modifying the HKEY_LOCAL_MACHINE\System\CurrentControlSet\Control\Print\Printers DefaultSpoolDirectory parameter.

C. Change the location of the spool directory to a partition with enough disk space by modifying the HKEY_Current_User\Control\Print\Printers\Spool SpoolDirectory parameter.

D. If the partition is formatted with NTFS, compress the spool directory.

Question #58

Resource: Chapter 2, "Kernel Mode"

Which of the following is part of the Kernel mode of the Windows NT architecture? Choose three.

A. WIN32 Subsystem

B. HAL

  C. Executive Services

  D. Device Driver support

Question #59

Resource: Chapter 11, "File System Layer"

Which Windows NT network model component is responsible for determining where to send a request for resources?

  A. File System Layer

  B. Transport Device Interface

  C. Protocol Layer

  D. Network Interface Card Layer

Question #60

Resource: Chapter 6, "Group Management in Domains"

What are the differences between a local group and a global group? Choose all that apply.

  A. Local groups can be created on workstations, servers, and domain controllers, while global groups can only be created and maintained on a domain controller.

  B. Local groups can contain local users, domain users, and global groups, while global groups can contain only users from their domain.

  C. Local groups can contain local users, domain users, global groups, and other local groups, while global groups can contain only users from their domain.

  D. Local groups can be used for managing resources only on the local computer, while global groups can be used to manage resources on any computer that participates in the domain.

Question #61

Resource: Chapter 12, "Exploring and Optimizing Pagefile Usage"

Desiree, a Visual Basic developer, has noticed that her system's performance has decreased since she began work on a large VB application.

You have used Performance Monitor to determine that the pagefile usage has increased and that disk drive itself is being over-utilized. You also notice that the pagefile, Windows NT system files, and the VB application are all stored on the same partition. There are two other disk drives installed on the system. How can you balance disk usage for the VB application and the pagefile?

A. Move the VB application files to a partition on another disk drive.

B. Move the VB application files to a partition on another disk drive and move the pagefile to a different partition on another disk drive.

C. Increase the size of the page file.

D. Nothing. She must buy more RAM.

Question #62

Resource: Chapter 11, "Configuring Browsers"

You have installed a new color laserjet on a Windows NT 4.0 workstation in a workgroup and shared it with default permissions. Bubba immediately tries to connect to the printer, but cannot find it in his shared printers list. What is the proper course of action?

A. Reinstall the printer and check the permissions.

B. Check the network adapter and protocol settings for the new Windows NT 4.0 workstation.

C. Have Bubba connect to the printer by entering its full UNC name in the path text box.

D. Wait 15 minutes until the workstation announces itself to the master browser.

Question #63

Resource: Chapter 9, "Document Properties"

The printer for a network print device has been configured to print documents at all times. Farley plans to print a large, complex graphics document that he would like completed tomorrow morning. This job will take at least one hour to complete. What can you do to minimize the effect that printing this document will have on other documents in the queue?

A. Select Farley's document and pause it. Resume printing after hours when print jobs are at a minimum.

B. Modify the printer schedule so that it only prints documents after hours.

C. Modify the document schedule for Farley's document so that it only prints between 1:00 a.m. and 3:00 a.m.

D. Do nothing. The printer automatically holds long jobs until short jobs finish spooling and printing.

Question #64

Resource: Chapter 3, "Upgrading to Windows NT Workstation 4.0— Windows 95"

You are installing Windows NT Workstation 4.0 on a computer that needs to support Windows 95 as well. You would like to migrate user environment settings from Windows 95 to Windows NT 4.0. What should you do?

A. Do nothing. The Windows 95 settings will automatically be migrated to Windows NT 4.0.

B. Install Windows NT 4.0 in the same directory as Windows 95. The settings will then automatically be migrated.

C. After installing Windows NT 4.0, run the MIGRATE utility from the command prompt.

D. You cannot migrate those settings from Windows 95.

Question #65

Resource: Chapter 4, "Welcome to Windows NT Workstation 4.0"

You need to log on to a Windows NT 4.0 workstation that another person is using in order to administer a shared resource. What does the other person need to do? Choose two.

App

J

A. From the Start menu, choose Shutdown, then select Close All Programs, and log on as a different person.

B. From the Start menu, choose Shutdown, and then select Restart the Computer.

C. Press Ctrl+Alt+Del on the keyboard to shut down Windows NT so you can restart and log on as another person.

D. Press Ctrl+Alt+Del on the keyboard to display the Windows NT Security dialog box, then click Logoff.

Question #66

Resource: Chapter 5, "Display Properties" and "Control Panel-Display"

Fred would like to modify his desktop wallpaper, screen saver, and screen colors. What two options are available to him?

A. Choose Display from the Control Panel.

B. Right-click the desktop and choose Properties.

C. Right-click My Computer and choose Properties, Display.

D. Choose Start, Programs, Display.

Question #67

Resource: Chapter 8, "An Overview of FAT" and "An Overview of NTFS"

Which of the following statements is true regarding FAT and NTFS? Choose all that apply.

A. FAT supports long file names and so does NTFS.

B. NTFS supports long file names but FAT does not.

C. FAT supports a maximum partition size of 4G and NTFS supports a maximum partition size of 16E.

D. Formatting a partition as FAT requires less than 1M of overhead, while NTFS formatting requires at least 4M.

Question #68

Resource: Chapter 7, "Assigning File and Folder Permissions"

The manager of the Accounting department wants to make next year's budget templates available for the staff accountants to review beginning next month. They will be stored on the department resource server called ACCT1 in a folder called BUDGET97 on an NTFS partition. The folder has been shared with the default permission. How would you make the folder's contents available only to the Accounting department staff?

A. Use User Manager to assign permission to use the folder to the Accountants group.

B. Use User Manager for Domains to assign User Rights to the Accountants group to access the BUDGET97 share.

C. Use the Security tab on the properties sheet for the folder to assign permissions to the Accountants group.

D. Use the Sharing tab on the properties sheet for the folder to also assign permissions to the Accountants group.

Question #69

Resource: Chapter 3, "Executing the Windows NT Workstation 4.0 Startup Process"

Which of the following dialogs takes place as part of the Setup Wizard?

A. Personal information

B. Detection and configuration of storage devices

C. Request for network card settings

D. Video display setup

Question #70

Resource: Chapter 11, "NWLink" and "TCP/IP Protocol"

For which of the following supported network protocols can Windows NT Workstation 4.0 act as a router?

App

J

A. NWLink IPX/SPX

B. TCP/IP, if the computer is multi-homed

C. NWLink and TCP/IP

D. Windows NT Workstation 4.0 cannot route protocols.

Question #71

Resource: Chapter 6, "Default Group Accounts"

Everyone should be able to read the files in a certain directory. However, the user who created the file should be able to modify it. What do you need to do?

A. Do nothing. By default, only the creator of a file has access to it. Windows NT restricts resource access by default.

B. Give the group Everyone Read access and the Creator Owner group Change access. By default, Windows NT allows everyone complete access to resources.

C. Give the group Everyone Read access and the Creator Owner group Change access. By default, Windows NT restricts resource access.

D. Give the group Everyone Read access and the Users group Change access. Windows NT will automatically determine who the owner of the file is and restrict the other users.

Question #72

Resource: Chapter 12, "Reviewing the Emergency Repair Process" and "Initiating the Repair Process"

A portion of the Registry has become corrupted on a Windows NT 4.0 workstation. You have an Emergency Repair Disk for that workstation that has been kept up-to-date. How can you use it to restore the Registry? Choose all that apply.

A. Choose Repair and, through the repair process, choose Inspect Registry Files.

B. Boot from a Windows NT boot disk.

C. Insert the Windows NT startup disk and boot the computer.

D. Insert the Emergency Repair Disk and run RDISK.

Question #73

Resource: Chapter 11, "Introducing Peer Web Services"

Your company has implemented an intranet for publishing corporate data and to provide access to database information. Your company is international, and users from all locations will be accessing the intranet. Which service is the best choice for implementing publishing services?

A. Peer Web Services

B. Internet Information Server Services

C. Internet Explorer Services

D. TCP/IP Protocol Services

App

J

Question #74

Resource: Chapter 9, "Priority"

There is one high-speed network print device connected to the print server in MIS. MIS Managers and Project Leaders should always be able to print to this printer regardless of who else has submitted print jobs. Help Desk staff should be able to print ahead of Developers. What will best accomplish this task?

A. Create three printers each associated with the device and assign the appropriate groups access only to their printer. Give the Managers' printer a priority of 1, Help Desk's printer a priority of 50, and Developers' a priority of 99.

B. Create three printers each associated with the device and assign the appropriate groups access only to their printer. Give the Managers' printer a priority of 99, Help Desk's printer a priority of 50, and Developers' a priority of 1.

C. Create three printers each associated with the device and assign the appropriate groups access only to their printer. Make the Managers' printer a printer pool by associating it with each print device.

D. Create three printers associated with the device and assign the appropriate groups access only to their printer. Make each printer a printer pool by associating it with each print device.

Question #75

Resource: Chapter 3, "Troubleshooting Installation and Setup"

You have just completed the text mode portion of Windows NT setup and have rebooted to start the GUI Setup Wizard. Windows NT displays the message `Missing or Corrupt NTOSKRNL`. What should you check?

A. Check the Hardware Compatibility List to see whether the hard disk is compatible with Windows NT.

B. Your Installation CD may be corrupted. Contact Microsoft for a replacement CD.

C. Windows NT may have mis-detected the SCSI drive. Boot to DOS and edit the BOOT.INI file changing SCSI to MULTI for this installation and verifying the partition number.

D. This happens occasionally on SCSI drives. You must reinstall Windows NT.

Question #76

Resource: Chapter 4, "Taskbar"

Which of the following Windows NT 4.0 options will let me switch between open windows? Choose three.

A. Click the window title in the taskbar.

B. Press Alt+Tab on the keyboard to select the desired window.

C. Press Ctrl+Esc to display the Windows NT Task Switcher.

D. Right-click the taskbar to display the Windows NT Task Manager.

Question #77

Resource: Chapter 9, "Print Monitor"

What is the purpose of the print monitor SFMMON.DLL?

    A. SFMMON.DLL monitors Macintosh print jobs routed using AppleTalk protocol to network print devices.

    B. SFMMON.DLL is the System File Manager print monitor that tracks print jobs sent directly to or printed directly from a file.

    C. SFMMON.DLL is the software print job compression DLL that compresses the print job before it is routed from the local print spooler to the print server.

    D. SFMMON.DLL is not a valid print monitor.

Question #78

Resource: Chapter 7, "Assigning File and Folder Permissions"

You have modified NTFS permissions for the file DOOM.DOC so that Team Leaders have Full Control. For all other files and folders, Team Leaders should have Read access. Using the exhibit, how can you best accomplish this?

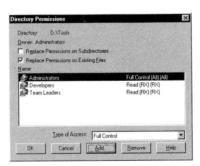

    A. Select Replace Permissions on Subdirectories and deselect Replace Permissions on Existing Files.

    B. Select Replace Permissions on Subdirectories.

    C. Deselect Replace Permissions on Existing Files.

    D. Set permissions on each file and folder individually.

App

J

Question #79

Resource: Chapter 6, "Renaming, Copying, and Deleting Accounts" and "Home Directory"

You are creating multiple user accounts for salespersons, marketers, and programmers. Each set of accounts belongs to the same relative groups (sales users in SALES, marketing users in MARKETING, and programmer users in PROGRAMMERS), uses the same logon scripts (SALES.BAT, MARKET.BAT, and PROGRAM.BAT), and saves data in a home directory relative to each group (sales users under USERS\ SALES, marketing users under USERS\MARKETERS, and programmer users under USERS\PROGRAMMERS). What is the most efficient way to create these users?

    A. Create a separate account for each user. As you create the user, use the %USERNAME% environment variable when specifying the home directory to let Windows NT create it for you.

    B. Create a template for each type of user. Make the appropriate choices and entries for groups, logon script, and home directory. Use the %USERNAME% environment variable when specifying the home directory to let Windows NT create them for you. Then create each user by copying the appropriate template.

    C. Create all the users without specifying group membership. After they are all created, select each group of users by Ctrl+clicking them and create the appropriate group.

    D. You must create each user individually.

Question #80

Resource: Chapter 2, "Workgroup Model"

You will be supporting a group of 10 account executives all running Windows NT Workstation on their computers. Occasionally, each account executive will need to share files with some or all of the other account executives. Two of the account executives have printers that all of them will use. You do not expect the group to grow by any more than five more persons. Which computing model will best meet the group's needs?

A. The Workgroup Model

B. The Single Domain Enterprise Model

C. The Master Domain Enterprise Model

D. The Complete Trust Enterprise Model

Question #81

Resource: Chapter 11, "NWLink IPX/SPX Compatible Protocol"

Your Windows NT 4.0 workstations must connect to both Windows NT 4.0 servers and NetWare servers. Your NetWare servers are of all versions. You have installed NWLink IPX/SPX Compatible Protocol on the workstations along with CSNW to allow communications with the NetWare servers. You find during testing that your Windows NT workstations can connect to some of the NetWare servers, but not all of them. The NWLink protocol settings look like this:

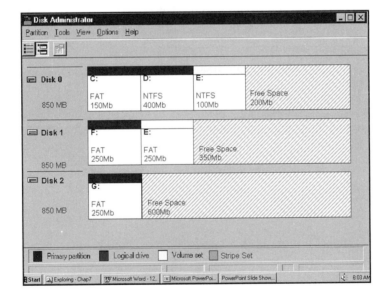

How can you troubleshoot this situation?

A. Check the network for multiple frame types and configure NWLink to recognize them all.

B. Do nothing with the protocol settings. Check the network card connections to the network.

C. Modify the frame types on the NetWare servers to autodetect.

D. Give each Windows NT 4.0 workstation a network number.

Question #82

Resource: Chapter 6, "Default User Accounts"

In an effort to add an extra level of security to your workstation installations, you have been presented with several options. Which option provides the greatest level of security?

A. Create separate user accounts for the end-users at each workstation and make them a member of the local Administrators group; rename the Administrator accounts and change their passwords.

B. Create separate user accounts for the end-users at each workstation; rename the Administrator accounts and change their passwords.

C. Create separate user accounts for the end-users at each workstation; delete the Administrator accounts and create new administrator accounts with different names and passwords.

D. Create separate user accounts for the end-users at each workstation; rename the Administrator accounts and randomly assign one of several predetermined passwords to each account.

Question #83

Resource: Chapter 12, "Objects to Monitor, Memory Object"

Which Memory object counter would help to identify when to right-size the pagefile?

A. %Pagefile

B. Commit Limit

C. Working Set

D. %Disk Time

Question #84

Resource: Chapter 11, "Providing Connectivity to NetWare Servers"

Your Windows NT Workstation 4.0 clients need to access NetWare servers on a regular basis. What do you need to do to make this process seamless? Choose all that apply.

A. Install NWLink on the Windows NT 4.0 workstations.

B. Install Client Services for NetWare on the Windows NT 4.0 workstations.

C. Select a preferred NetWare server to connect to through the CSNW Control Panel applet.

D. Maintain different user accounts between the NetWare server and the Windows NT workstation.

App

J

Question #85

Resource: Chapter 9, "Introducing and Examining the Print Process" and "Troubleshooting Printing"

There are 300 Windows NT and Windows 95 client computers that print to five printers on a print server. You have received upgraded print drivers for two of the print devices connected to this print server. What must you do to ensure that all clients can continue to access all the print devices?

A. Install the upgraded print drivers on all the clients that need to use those print devices.

B. Install the upgraded print drivers on all the client computers.

C. Install the upgraded print drivers only on the Windows NT client computers.

D. Do nothing. The print server can download the new drivers to the clients the next time they make a print request.

Question #86

Resource: Chapter 3, "Installing Windows NT Networking"

What network information is necessary for you to supply during the Network portion of the Setup Wizard?

A. Network Protocols, Network Services, Network Bindings, Network Card settings, and Network Model

B. Network Protocols, Network Card Settings, and Workgroup or Domain membership

C. Computer Name, Network Card Settings, and Workgroup or Domain membership

D. Windows NT self-detects all network settings.

Question #87

Resource: Chapter 4, "Windows Explorer"

What is the best way to navigate among my files and directories?

A. From the Start menu, choose Programs, Accessories, File Manager.

B. From the Start menu, choose Run and then type **WINFILE.EXE** to start File Manager.

C. From the Start menu, choose Programs, Windows Explorer.

D. From the Start menu, choose Run and then type **PROGMAN.EXE**.

Question #88

Resource: Chapter 8, "(Backup)Requirements, Terms, and Strategy"

You are ready to implement your backup strategy and want to back up files from all Windows NT computers remotely to an archive directory on your local computer. All remote shares have been implemented. What is the best solution?

A. Connect to the shares, start Backup, and select the files and folders to be backed up. Choose Backup and enter the UNC path to the target archive directory in the Backup Path text box.

B. Connect to the shares, start Backup, and choose Operations, Select Target from the menu. Enter the path to the archive directory in the Backup Path text box.

C. Connect to the shares, start Backup and redirect the backup path using the Tools, Options menu.

D. You cannot back up to disk.

Question #89

Resource: Chapter 9, "Sharing and Securing a Printer" and "Setting Permissions for the Shared Printer"

You have created four printers. Each of them will be used by a specific group of users. Name all the steps that are required to successfully make the printer available to the appropriate users.

A. Share each printer.

B. Set the share permissions for each printer so that only the appropriate group has access.

C. Set the printer permissions for each printer so that only the appropriate group has access.

D. Create a printer pool so that each group can access all the print devices.

Question #90

Resource: Chapter 7, "Effective File and Folder Permissions"

The manager of the Accounting department wants to make next year's budget templates available for the staff accountants to review beginning next month. They will be stored on the department resource server called ACCT1 in a folder called BUDGET97 on an NTFS partition. The folder has been shared with the default permission. How would you make the folder's contents available only to the Accounting department staff? Choose all that apply.

A. Change the share permissions to just the Accountants with Change permission.

B. Assign the Accountants group the NTFS permission Change to the BUDGET97 folder.

App

J

    C. Change the share permission to Everyone with No Access and assign the Accountants group the NTFS permission Change for the BUDGET97 folder.

    D. Change the share permission to Everyone with Read and assign the Accountants group the NTFS permission Change for the BUDGET97 folder.

Question #91

Resource: Chapter 8, "Creating and Managing Volume Sets" and "Extending Volume Sets"

You need to extend a FAT partition to allow more space for a growing database. Which option best explains your strategy?

    A. Use Disk Administrator to select the FAT partition and an area of free space and choose Partition, Create Volume Set.

    B. Use Disk Administrator to select the FAT partition and an area of free space and choose Partition, Extend Volume Set.

    C. Use Disk Administrator to select the FAT partition and an area of formatted space and choose Tools, Combine Volume Sets.

    D. You cannot extend the volume.

Question #92

Resource: Chapter 7, "Examining the Windows NT Security Model"

A user's effective access to a resource is determined by:

    A. Comparing the rights of the user with the permissions assigned through the ACL of the resource.

    B. Comparing the permissions in the access token of the user with the permissions assigned through the ACL of the resource.

    C. Comparing the user and group SID entries in the user's access token with the permissions assigned through the ACL of the resource.

    D. Comparing the user and group SID entries in the user's access token with the user rights listed in the ACL of the resource.

Question #93
Resource: Chapter 2, "Connect Property"

Remote Access Service has been implemented on a Windows NT Workstation computer in a workgroup. Several users with laptop computers are intending to dial in to this workstation to access file resources. When they dial in, they complain that only one person at a time can gain access to the workstation. What can you do to help them?

    A. Reconfigure the RAS workstation client for multiple dial-in support.

    B. Purchase additional modems for the workstation and reconfigure the RAS client for those modems.

    C. Install Windows NT Server on a computer in the workgroup and then install the RAS server on that computer.

    D. Give each user his own dial-in access ID.

Question #94
Resource: Chapter 10, "Task Manager"

Len is running Pinball, the DOS Editor, Word 6, Excel 5, and Microstomp (a 16-bit, third-party Windows Web surfing program). He says that he has configured Microstomp to run in its own memory space. However, it has failed and the other Windows applications are also unresponsive. How can you unload Microstomp and try to return control to the other Windows applications?

    A. Shut down and restart Windows NT Workstation 4.0.

    B. Click the X button in the upper-right corner of the Microstomp window.

    C. Start Task Manager, select Microstomp from the list of applications, and choose End Task.

    D. Start Task Manager, select the WOW NTVDM entry on the Processes tab, and select End Process.

App

J

Question #95

Resource: Chapter 5, "Examining the Registry" and "Changing the Default Startup Screen"

I need to add the company's logo to the default Windows NT boot up screen. From which Registry subtree(s) can I make this modification?

- A. HKEY_LOCAL_MACHINE
- B. HKEY_CURRENT_USER
- C. HKEY_USERS
- D. This change can only be done through Control Panel, Service, Startup.

Question #96

Resource: Chapter 12, "Objects to Monitor, Process Object," "Exploring and Optimizing Pagefile Usage," and "Creating Multiple Pagefiles"

Desiree, a Visual Basic developer, has noticed that her system's performance has decreased since she began work on a large VB application. You have used Performance Monitor to determine that the pagefile usage has increased. You also notice that the pagefile, Windows NT system files, and the VB application are all stored on the same partition. In addition, the working set for the VB application shows that it consistently requires 16M for itself. What solutions can you recommend? Name all that apply.

- A. Add more RAM in the computer.
- B. Move the pagefile to a disk partition other than the system or application partition.
- C. Increase the maximum size for the pagefile.
- D. Create multiple page files.

Question #97

Resource: Chapter 11, "IP Address Considerations"

You have installed TCP/IP on your Windows NT 4.0 workstation and configured its IP address settings. You find that, while you can communicate with other TCP/IP computers on your local subnet, you cannot establish connections with any Windows NT servers on other subnets in your company. What should you check? Choose all that apply.

   A. Subnet mask

   B. Default gateway address

   C. Address settings on the subnet's router

   D. Local IP address

Question #98

Resource: Chapter 2, "Binding Other Controls to the Data Control"

True or False? The File Manager utility is no longer accessible in Windows NT 4.0.

   A. True

   B. False

Question #99

Resource: Chapter 11, "TCP/IP Protocol"

Which TCP/IP utility would be useful to determine a computer's address settings?

   A. Ping

   B. IPCONFIG

   C. FTP

   D. Network Neighborhood

Question #100

Resource: Chapter 10, "Troubleshooting Considerations"

Mandy has recently upgraded to Windows NT 4.0 Workstation from MS-DOS. When he tries to run his favorite disk optimization utility, the application fails. What do you advise?

   A. Reinstall the application under Windows NT so that the Registry can be updated.

App

J

B. Modify the application's properties to allow hardware interaction (Advanced tab).

C. Remove the application or dual boot and run it only from DOS. Applications that directly access hardware devices will not run successfully under Windows NT 4.0.

D. Do nothing. You can never run this application.

Question #101

Resource: Chapter 5, "Boot Process for RISC-based Computers"

While looking at the files on my RISC-based computer, I notice that NTLDR, NTDETECT.COM, and BOOT.INI are missing. What impact will this have on the boot process on this computer?

A. The boot process relies on these files to govern the Boot and Load Phases. Missing or corrupt files will result in error messages and failed boots.

B. It will have no impact on the boot process because RISC-based computers do not rely on these files.

C. The BOOT.INI is not an essential file. Windows NT will look for the default Windows NT system directory.

D. NTLDR is always needed to direct the boot process. NTDETECT.COM and BOOT.INI are not necessary on RISC-based computers.

Question #102

Resource: Chapter 12, "Using Event Viewer to Troubleshoot Windows NT"

Heinrich is receiving intermittent service errors throughout his computing session. You are using the Event Viewer on Heinrich's Windows NT workstation to help pinpoint the errors. However, his System Log is quite full. How can you more easily pinpoint the source of the errors?

A. Use Performance Monitor to track the Services object's Stop Errors counter.

B. Filter the System Log to only show Service Control Manager events.

C. Clear the System Log and record only Service Control Manager events.

D. Shut down and restart Windows NT and record any service error messages.

Question #103

Resource: Chapter 3, "Partition Configuration"

During the text mode phase, Windows NT displays a dialog box that shows you two drive partitions, and 600M free space on one drive. You would like to install Windows NT on the free space, but only want to use 200M.

A. You must preconfigure the free space before starting setup.

B. You can select the free space during setup, but you cannot change its size.

C. Select the free space and choose ENTER.

D. Select the free space and choose C to create the new partition. Then select the new partition and continue with installation.

Question #104

Resource: Chapter 5, "Control Panel" and "Accessibility Options"

Janice is a hearing-impaired account manager who has asked if Windows NT provides any options appropriate for her? What can you do to help?

A. Select Control Panel, Sounds and increase the volume for system sounds.

B. Select My Computer, Properties and select the Accessibilities tab to set Sound options.

C. Select Control Panel, Accessibility Options and set the Sound options.

D. Windows NT does not provide options for physically challenged persons.

App

J

Question #105

Resource: Chapter 8, "Creating and Managing Volume Sets"

Your Windows NT workstation has two physical disks, each with less than 50M of free space left. What would be the most effective use of this free space?

- A. Create a stripe set with parity.
- B. Create a volume set out of the remaining free space.
- C. Extend the FAT partitions on each disk into the remaining free space.
- D. Make each area of free space its own primary partition and format it as NTFS.

Question #106

Resource: Chapter 8, "Understanding Partitions"

Windows NT is installed on the D: drive as configured in the exhibit. Which ARC path in the BOOT.INI file accurately represents the location of the installation directory so that Windows NT can boot successfully?

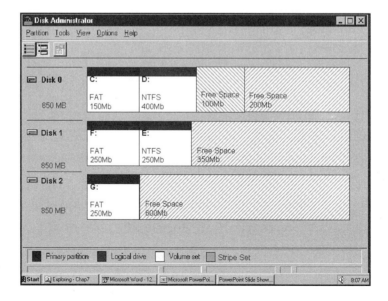

A. multi(0)disk(0)rdisk(0)partition(2)

B. multi(0)disk(0)rdisk(0)partition(5)

C. multi(0)disk(1)rdisk(0)partition(2)

D. multi(0)disk(0)rdisk(1)partition(2)

Question #107

Resource: Chapter 6, "Creating Server Based Profiles"

There are five summer interns joining the company this year for a three-month period. You want to give them access to the network, but you want to restrict their environment settings to specific programs, colors, and so on. They should not be able to change the settings. What steps are involved?

A. Change the NTUSER.DAT file in the shared directory to NTUSER.MAN.

B. Copy the account through the User Profiles tab in the System applet to a shared directory on a central server.

C. Create a user account and make the appropriate changes to that account's environment settings.

D. Specify the location and file name of the profile in each summer intern's account properties.

App

J

Question #108

Resource: Chapter 6, "Account Policy"

To provide a greater level of security, you have decided to create an account policy that requires a minimum password length of eight characters, that users change their passwords at least once a month, and does not allow users to use the same password twice in two months. Which Account Policy settings are appropriate?

A. Max Password Age: 60   Min Password Age: 30

   Min Password Length: 8 Password Uniqueness: 2

B. Max Password Age: 30   Min Password Age: 30

   Min Password Length: 8 Password Uniqueness: 6

C. Max Password Age: 30 Min Password Age: 10

Min Password Length: 8 Password Uniqueness: 6

D. Max Password Age: 60 Min Password Age: 30

Min Password Length: 8 Password Uniqueness: 1

Question #109

Resource: Chapter 7, "Sharing Resources and Determining Network Access"

The administrator of the Tools shared folder wants to limit access to the folder only to the Developers group. To accomplish this, she gives the Everyone group No Access, and the Developers group Change access. The Developers complain that they cannot access any file in Tools. What else must the administrator do?

A. Share the files in the Tools folder.

B. Remove the Everyone group.

C. Give the Developers group Full Control.

D. Format the partition as NTFS and assign NTFS permissions in addition to the share permissions.

Question #110

Resource: Chapter 2, "Trust Relationships" and "Master Domain"

You have decided to implement an enterprise domain model in which the user accounts are centrally administered, and in which the resources are distributed in their own domains to the various departments that will administer those resources; they will not, however, manage any user accounts. How will you implement the trust relationship?

A. There is no trust relationship involved because this scenario represents a Single Domain Enterprise Model.

B. Each resource domain will trust the account domain.

C. Each domain will trust every other domain.

D. You can only do this in a Workgroup Model.

Question #111

Resource: Chapter 10, "Managing Win 16 Applications with Multiple NTVDMS"

Mandy is running Pinball, the DOS Editor, Word 6, Excel 5, and Microstomp, a 16-bit, third-party Windows Web surfing program. Microstomp occasionally hangs up due to low resource memory. This affects his other Windows applications. What can you suggest to alleviate this problem?

A. Configure Microstomp to run in its own memory space.

B. Configure each Win 16 application to run in its own memory space.

C. Modify the PIF for Microstomp to increase its resource memory allocation.

D. Modify the PIF for the WOW NTVDM to increase resource memory allocations for all the Windows applications.

App

J

Question #112

Resource: Chapter 5, "The System Policy Editor"

There are several temporary employees that will work on two different shifts during the summer. They will log on to the network using different workstations each day. However, they need to have the same desktop configuration and should not be able to modify settings such as display choices, and so on. What is the easiest way to accomplish this?

A. Windows NT does not provide for this level of control in this version.

B. Modify the Registry on each workstation that each temporary employee will log onto.

C. Create a system profile for each user with the appropriate settings.

D. Create a user account on each workstation for each temporary employee and then modify the appropriate Registry entries for each temporary employee on each workstation.

Question #113

Resource: Chapter 12, "Objects to Monitor" and "Processor Object"

Which Process object counter would be useful in determining the amount of memory required by an application?

A. %Application Memory

B. Commit Limit

C. Working Set

D. Avg. Disk sec\Transfer

Question #114

Resource: Chapter 11, "Introducing Point to Point Tunneling"

Flora, the MIS director, wants company employees to be able to access the company's network through their personal Internet providers. However, she has concerns about the security of the company's network from unauthorized Internet access. What is your solution? Choose all that apply.

A. Use Point-to-Point Tunneling on the RAS server.

B. Enable callback security for Internet connections.

C. Connect only the RAS server to the Internet.

D. Enable filtering for PPTP on the RAS server.

Question #115

Resource: Chapter 10, "Configuring the NTVDM"

Angela has an older MS-DOS program that she needs to run on her Windows NT 4.0 workstation. The application requires a specific environmental variable set and device driver loaded. How can you help Angela configure her program to run successfully?

A. Configure the program to run in its own memory space.

B. Create an AUTOEXEC.BAT and CONFIG.SYS with the appropriate settings to load when Windows NT boots.

C. Create a specific AUTOEXEC and CONFIG for the application and reference it in the applications properties (PIF).

    D. Install the application using the ADD Application applet in Control Panel and reference the environment variable and device driver during installation.

Question #116

Resource: Chapter 3, "Formatting the Partition," and the sidebar "RISC Partition Formats"

You are installing Windows NT on a RISC-based computer and want to format the Windows NT system partition as NTFS.

    A. Create a 2M FAT partition for the Windows NT boot files, and a second partition large enough for the Windows NT system files before starting setup. Select the partition during setup and format it as NTFS.

    B. Create a 2M FAT partition for the Windows NT boot files before starting setup. During setup, choose free space, create a partition, and format it as NTFS just as in an Intel installation.

    C. Windows NT requires a FAT partition for its system files. You can only format non-system partitions with NTFS.

    D. Windows NT does not support NTFS on RISC-based systems.

App

J

Question #117

Resource: Chapter 4, "Find" and "Start Menu-Documents"

Bill has created an important legal document, but cannot remember where he saved it, or exactly what he called it. However, he knows he created it yesterday. How can you help him?

    A. Use Windows Explorer to display all files by their date. Then browse each directory until you find the missing file.

    B. From the Start menu, choose Documents. Bill should be able to find his document listed there.

    C. From the Start menu, choose Find Files or Folders. On the Date\Time tab enter yesterday's date. Bill should be able to find his file in the Find results window.

    D. Take Bill out to lunch.

Question #118

Resource: Chapter 8, "(Backup)Requirements, Terms, and Strategy"

Lucy has been appointed the backup coordinator for the network. What must you do to enable her to accomplish this task and still maintain security on the data? Choose all that apply.

A. Make Lucy a member of the local Backup Operators group on each computer that needs to be backed up.

B. Make Lucy a member of the Server Operators group on each server computer that needs to be backed up.

C. Assign Lucy the Backup Files and Directories user right.

D. Give Lucy Full Control over all files and folders.

Question #119

Resource: Chapter 8, "Creating and Managing Volume Sets" and "Creating and Managing Stripe Sets"

Which of the following statements are true regarding Volume Sets and Stripe Sets? Choose all that apply.

A. Stripe sets can contain the system partition and volume sets cannot.

B. Stripe sets must combine areas of equal size while volume sets can combine areas of any size.

C. Stripe sets cannot contain the system partition and volume sets can.

D. Stripe sets write to all members of the set concurrently while volume sets fill each member of the set in turn.

Question #120

Resource: Chapter 6, "User Profiles" and "A Profile Alternative"

As you create new users, you would like them to assume the same default environment settings, such as common application groups, startup programs, and company logo, as wallpaper. Which steps will achieve this end?

A. Modify the appropriate changes in the Default User and All Users profile folders in WINNT40\Profiles. When a new user is created, that user's profile will begin with the settings from these two.

B. Create a System Policy file that contains the appropriate settings for the Default user and save it in the WINNT40\SYSTEM32\REPL\IMPORT\SCRIPTS subdirectory on the validating computer.

C. Create a template user account and modify the settings for that account. Create new accounts by copying the template.

D. Create a system policy file for each set of users modifying the settings as appropriate for each user.

Question #121

Resource: Chapter 7, "Examining Access Control Lists"

The permission list defining access to a resource resides:

A. With the resource and is called the Access Control List.

B. With the user and is called the User Rights Policy.

C. With the user and is called the Access Control List.

D. With the resource and is called the User Rights Policy.

Question #122

Resource: Chapter 2, "Preemptive Multitasking," and "Kernel Mode"

True or False? All Kernel mode processes run in the protected mode of the processor (ring0).

A. True

B. False

Question #123

Resource: Chapter 10, "Task Manager"

Mandy is running Pinball, the DOS Editor, Word 6, Excel 5, and Microstomp (a 16-bit, third-party Windows Web surfing program). He says that he has configured Microstomp to run in its own memory space. However, it has failed and the other Windows applications are also unresponsive. How can you tell if Microstomp has been configured to run in its own memory space?

A. Start Task Manager and look for a second WOW NTVDM entry with a reference to the Microstomp application on the Processes tab.

B. Display the properties of the shortcut for Microstomp and see whether Run in Separate Memory Space has been selected on the Shortcut tab.

C. Start Task Manager and look for duplicate occurrences of WOWEXEC on the Applications tab.

D. You cannot tell without restarting the application.

Question #124

Resource: Chapter 11, "Benefits of TDI and NDIS 4.0"

Your Windows NT 4.0 workstations must be able to establish connections to resources on NetWare servers and UNIX servers as well as Windows NT 4.0 servers. You need IPX/SPX to communicate with the NetWare servers and TCP/IP to communicate with Windows NT and UNIX servers. What must you do to accomplish this?

A. Install two network adapters and both NWLink IPX/SPX and TCP/IP on the Windows NT 4.0 workstations. Bind NWLink to one adapter and TCP/IP to the other.

B. Install three network adapters, one for each type of server, and both NWLink IPX/SPX and TCP/IP on the Windows NT 4.0 workstations. Bind NWLink to one adapter and TCP/IP to the other two.

C. Install one network adapter and both NWLink IPX/SPX and TCP/IP on the Windows NT 4.0 workstations. Windows NT will bind both protocols to the same adapter. Enable and disable each binding as necessary when communicating among the various servers.

D. Do nothing. When you install the two protocols, Windows NT
will automatically bind them to the network adapter. Nothing
else is required for the connections to be established.

Question #125

Resource: Chapter 6, "Group Management in Domains"

You have installed 15 Windows NT 4.0 workstations as members of a
workgroup. On one of these workstations, you have stored a sales database and a marketing database, and have also shared a color printer. Five
of the users are salespersons, five are marketers, and the rest are programmers. The users should be able to access their respective databases,
but only the team leaders for sales, marketing, and programmers should
be able to access the color printer. Which group strategy is the best?

A. Create local groups for sales, marketing, and team leaders and
assign the appropriate user accounts to the appropriate groups.
Then assign permissions for each resource to the appropriate
group.

B. Create global groups for sales, marketing, and team leaders and
assign the appropriate user accounts to the appropriate groups.
Then assign permissions for each resource to the appropriate
group.

C. Create global groups for sales, marketing, and team leaders and
assign the appropriate user accounts to the appropriate groups.
Following Microsoft's suggested strategy to allow for growth,
create local groups for each and assign the global group to the
local group. Then assign permissions for each resource to the
appropriate local group.

D. Simply assign the appropriate users access to the resources that
they need access to.

Question #126

Resource: Chapter 12, "Objects to Monitor" and "Memory Object"

On your Windows NT 4.0 development workstation, you have concluded that performance as a whole has decreased. You are not sure

App

J

which process is driving this, but you have noticed that your disk drive has had a lot more activity lately. What objects should you monitor through Performance Monitor to help you troubleshoot this situation?

- A. Check the Processor object's %Processor Time counter, determine the percent of disk I/O used for paging through the Memory object's Pages/Sec counter and the Logical Disk object's Avg. Disk sec/Transfer counter, and determine the Process object's Working Set for every process running.

- B. Check the Processor object's %Processor Time counter, and determine the percent of disk I/O used for paging through the Memory object's Pages/Sec counter and the Logical Disk object's Avg. Disk sec/Transfer counter. Track the Process object's %Processor Time counter for every process running to determine which processes are pushing the processor excessively. Check the Working Set counter for these processes in particular.

- C. Check the Processor object's %Processor Time counter, determine the percent of disk I/O used for paging through the Logical Disk object's Disk Queue Length counter, and the Process object's Working Set for every process running.

- D. Check the Processor object's %User Time counter, determine the percent of disk I/O used for paging through the Logical Disk object's %Disk Time counter, and the Memory object's Commit Limit counter for the pagefile.

Question #127

Resource: Chapter 11, "Becoming a Member of a Domain"

Windows NT 4.0 has been chosen as the network operating system of choice for your company. There are several small Windows NT Workstation 4.0 and Windows 95 workgroups within the company that now need to become part of the company's domain structure. Choose all steps that need to take place.

A. Create computer accounts for each Windows NT 4.0 workstation in the domain.

B. Create computer accounts for each of the Windows 95 workstations in the domain.

C. Check for uniqueness of computer names.

D. Change participation of the Windows NT workstations from the workgroup to the domain through the Identification tab of the Network properties of each computer.

Question #128

Resource: Chapter 9, "Troubleshooting Printing"

Which of the following steps is appropriate to take when troubleshooting a failed print job?

A. Verify that the appropriate print port has been defined and configured by printing a test page.

B. Delete and re-create the printer.

C. Determine whether the print device is online and connected.

D. Resubmit the print job to a file and then copy the file to a printer port to see if it is successful.

Question #129

Resource: Chapter 4, "My Computer" and "Windows Explorer"

Which of the following objects let me browse through my files, folders, drives, and shared network resources?

A. Network Neighborhood

B. My Computer

C. Windows NT Explorer

D. Task Manager

Question #130

Resource: Chapter 9, "Creating a Printer"

Nelson has been selected to assist you as a printing administrator in the Dry Gulch office, because you yourself are unable to travel there

App

J

frequently, though you'd really like to. What is the minimum level of access you need to give Nelson so that he can perform basic print management tasks such as creating and sharing printers and managing print jobs?

A. Make Nelson a member of the Print Operators local group on his print server.

B. Make Nelson a member of the Server Operator local group on his print server.

C. Make Nelson a member of the Administrators local group on his print server.

D. Give Nelson Full Control permission for each printer on his print server.

Question #131

Resource: Chapter 7, "Understanding the Concept of Ownership"

The person that created DOOM.DOC on server ACCT1 is no longer with the company. Cathy, a member of Team Leaders, will be assuming responsibility for the DOOM project, and needs to become the owner of DOOM.DOC. How can this be accomplished? Choose all that apply.

A. Give Cathy the Take Ownership of Files and Folders User Right on the server ACCT1.

B. Give Cathy the Take Ownership permission on the file DOOM.DOC.

C. Tell Cathy to just take ownership of the file.

D. Give the Team Leaders group the Take Ownership permission for DOOM.DOC.

Question #132

Resource: Chapter 7, "Sharing Resources and Determining Network Access"

The Tools folder has been shared to the Developers group with Change permission. Doom is a subdirectory under Tools. Team Leaders should have access to Doom with Read permissions. What can you do to accomplish this?

   A. Add Team Leaders to the Tools share with Read permission.

   B. Create a new share called DOOM and give Team Leaders Read permission to it.

   C. Add Team Leaders to the Tools share with Change permission.

   D. Add Team Leaders to the Tools share with No Access and to the Doom subdirectory with Read.

Question #133

Resource: Chapter 10, "Thread Priority"

Bernadette has a math-intensive program that runs calculations while in the background. She wants to work with other program files while this application cranks away, but she does not want to sacrifice its CPU time. What do you advise?

   A. Through the Systems applet in Control Panel, set the foreground response time to None. This will let foreground and background applications run at the same base priority level.

   B. Through the Systems applet in Control Panel, set the background response time to Maximum. This will increase background base priority 2 levels.

   C. From the Start, Run dialog, start the math-intensive program with the /Realtime switch.

   D. Do nothing. You cannot change application priorities.

Question #134

Resource: Chapter 5, "Troubleshooting the Boot Process"

Jonas accidentally deleted the BOOT.INI file from his C: drive. Windows NT has been installed in the WINNT subdirectory on C:. What effect will the missing BOOT.INI have?

   A. There will be no noticeable effect on the boot process. Windows NT will boot as always.

App

J

B. The BOOT.INI file provides the ARC path information that Windows NT needs to find the Windows NT system files. If it is missing, Windows NT will display a message that it cannot find the NTOSKRNL file and fail to boot.

C. If the BOOT.INI file is missing, Windows NT will not display the boot menu during boot up. Windows NT will look for the Windows NT system files on the boot partition in the default directory name (WINNT).

D. The BOOT.INI file is not needed on RISC-based systems.

Question #135

Resource: Chapter 12, "Using Event Viewer to Troubleshoot Windows NT"

What steps need to take place in order to capture and view security related events? Choose all that apply.

A. Switch to the Security Log in Event Viewer.

B. Log on as a Power User.

C. Enable auditing in the User Manager.

D. Configure which security events to audit.

Question #136

Resource: Chapter 11, "Configuring Browsers"

Vern has implemented a workgroup of 10 Windows NT 4.0 workstations. One of the workstations is used only occasionally by a temporary employee. Vern would like this workstation to default to the master browser for the workgroup for performance reasons. What should he do?

A. Do nothing. Windows NT 4.0 workstations will determine the master browser solely by their browser criteria.

B. Configure the Windows NT 4.0 workstation to become the master browser through the Is Master Browser check box in the Computer Browser Service properties.

C. Change the Browser service parameter MaintainServerList in the Registry to "auto."

D. Add the Browser service parameter PreferredMasterBrowser to the Registry with a value of "yes."

Question #137

Resource: Chapter 11, "Configuring RAS on the Server"

For security reasons, you want to restrict access for dial-up users only to the RAS server when they dial in, but not restrict their access when at the office. What must you do?

A. Do nothing. This is the default setting.

B. Disable gateway access for each RAS server network protocol setting.

C. Configure the permissions on each of the resource servers in the network to restrict the users.

D. Configure the dial-in permissions for each user on the RAS server to restrict access to the RAS server.

Question #138

Resource: Chapter 10, "Examining Support for MS-DOS-based Applications" and "Configuring the NTVDM"

Which of the following statements is true about the NTVDM?

A. Each NTVDM has one thread of operation associated with it.

B. Each NTVDM is designed to emulate the Windows memory environment and provides a set of support files to do so.

C. Each NTVDM is configurable by modifying the properties of the MS-DOS application.

D. Each NTVDM is configurable through one AUTOEXEC.BAT and CONFIG.SYS file that is read when Windows NT boots.

Question #139

Resource: Chapter 3, "Partition Configuration"

You must preconfigure your installation drive before starting setup.

A. True

B. False

App

J

Question #140

Resource: Chapter 5, "Control Panel Services"

Which three of the following four features is a part of the Services applet in Control Panel?

A. Running status

B. Load order

C. Hardware profile assignments

D. Startup options

Question #141

Resource: Chapter 8, "Troubleshooting Backup and Restore"

You need to recover a lost folder for a user. Before you do so, what can you do to minimize errors?

A. Review the backup set catalog for any corrupted files before proceeding with the backup.

B. Review the backup log file to see if any files were missed during the backup process.

C. Select the verify files restore option.

D. Do nothing. Windows NT automatically verifies files while restoring to disk.

Question #142

Resource: Chapter 8, "Extending Volume Sets"

You need to extend a FAT partition to allow more space for a growing database. Choose all steps that apply.

A. Use Disk Administrator to select the partition and an area of free space and choose Partition, Extend Volume Set.

B. Use the Convert utility to convert the FAT partition to NTFS.

C. Set the partition attribute to Compress.

D. Specify the total size of the volume.

Question #143

Resource: Chapter 11, "Configuring Network Options" and "Reviewing Workstation and Server Services"

On your local subnet, you regularly copy data from your Windows NT 4.0 workstations to an archive Windows NT 4.0 workstation using NetBEUI. The archive workstation is not used for any other purpose. How can you optimize the bindings on the archive workstation?

    A. Do nothing. Windows NT self-optimizes network bindings.

    B. Disable the workstation binding because the archive workstation will never need to establish its own connections with other computers.

    C. Disable the server binding because the archive workstation will never need to establish its own connections with other computers.

    D. Move the server binding ahead of the workstation binding because the archive workstation responds to network requests rather than making them.

Question #144

Resource: Chapter 5, "Understanding the Windows NT Boot Process"

Which of the following boot files is essential to the Boot Phase of the boot process?

    A. NTLDR

    B. NTDETECT.COM

    C. NTOSKRNL.EXE

    D. BOOT.INI

Question #145

Resource: Chapter 12, "Right-Sizing the Pagefile"

Frederick has recently loaded two more C++ applications to modify on his Windows NT 4.0 workstation. He has noticed that when he boots and loads all his applications, Windows NT takes longer to respond to

App

J

application requests. You use Performance Monitor and notice that pagefile usage has increased, and that the Commit Limit for the pagefile drops rapidly when the applications are loaded. What is the best solution you can offer Frederick?

A. Purchase more RAM for Frederick's computer.

B. Move the pagefile to another disk partition.

C. Increase the initial size of the pagefile, so that it doesn't have to grow right away as the applications load.

D. Move the C++ applications to another disk partition.

Question #146

Resource: Chapter 11, "Reviewing Workstation and Server Services"

Eunice says that she can connect to resources on other Windows NT computers in her workgroup, but no one can connect to hers. What should you check?

A. Workstation Service is running

B. Server Service is running

C. Redirector Service is running

D. Frame types match

Question #147

Resource: Chapter 5, "Control Panel—Mouse" and "Examining the Registry"

Martha wants to modify her mouse pointers. What is the most appropriate procedure for doing this?

A. Choose Control Panel, Mouse and select the pointers through the Pointers tab.

B. Right-click the desktop, choose Properties, and select the Settings tab.

C. Start the Registry Editor, select HKEY_CURRENT_USER, and modify the Cursors subkey.

D. Start the Registry Editor, select HKEY_LOCAL_MACHINE, and modify the System\CurrentControlSet subkey.

Question #148

Resource: Chapter 9, "Windows NT 4.0 Print Process"

Which of the following steps applies to the Windows NT 4.0 print process on Windows NT computers? Choose all that apply.

A. The GDI component of the client computer generates an enhanced metafile print job.

B. The bulk of the print process completes in the spooler on the client before forwarding the print job to the print server.

C. The print monitor controls access to the print devices and device ports, and monitors status of the print job.

D. The local printer spooler makes a remote connection to the print server spooler and copies the print job there.

Question #149

Resource: Chapter 7, "Determining Access when Using Share and NTFS Permissions"

Team Leaders need to be able to modify files contained in the share Tools. While you were on vacation, your trusted sidekick modified the permissions for the share and the folder. The following two figures show what the permissions look like now. Team Leaders complain that they are unable to modify their files. What should you do?

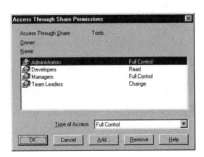

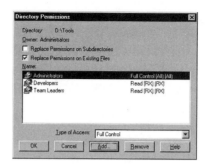

A. Fire your trusted sidekick.

B. Change the Tools NTFS permission for Team Leaders to Change and the share permission to Read.

C. Change the Tools NTFS permission for the Team Leaders to Change.

D. Remove Team Leaders from the ACL for the Tools share.

Question #150

Resource: Chapter 7, "Sharing Resources and Determining Network Access" and "Examining the Windows NT Security Model"

The manager of the Accounting department wants to make next year's budget templates available for the staff accountants to review beginning next month. They will be stored on the department resource server called ACCT1 in a folder called BUDGET97. None of the partitions on ACCT1 is formatted with NTFS. How would you make the folder available only to the Accounting department staff? Choose all that apply.

A. Share the BUDGET97 directory.

B. Add the Accountants group to the ACL for the share.

C. Remove the Everyone group from the ACL for the share.

D. Give the Accountants group Read and Write permissions at the folder level.

Question #151

Resource: Chapter 11, "Protocol Layer" and "Examining NetBEUI, NWLink, and TCP/IP"

Which of the following supported network protocols is required to allow an IPC connection to be established with another Windows NT 4.0 computer across a router? Choose all that apply.

   A. NetBEUI

   B. NWLink

   C. TCP/IP

   D. DECnet

Question #152

Resource: Chapter 6, "Default Group Accounts"

Your end-users need to be able to create and manage shares on their workstations; however, you do not want them to have the same level of access that an administrator has. What can you do?

   A. Add each end-user's account to the local Power Users group on their workstation.

   B. Add each end-user's account to the local Administrators group on their workstation.

   C. Add each end-user's account to the Account Operator's group on each workstation.

   D. Users have the ability to create and manage shares by default.

Question #153

Resource: Chapter 11, "RAS Security"

The marketing department staff travels a lot and dials in to the company network while visiting client offices to obtain product information. Elvira, the marketing director, wants the company to assume the dial-up costs rather than the client. What do you advise?

   A. Enable callback security on the RAS server and let the marketer provide the callback number.

B. Enable callback security on the RAS server and specify a number the server should always call back.

C. Do nothing. Charges are always assumed by the RAS server.

D. Select the Reverse Charges option on the RAS server Callback properties.

Question #154

Resource: Chapter 11, "Understanding Dial-Up Networking and Remote Access Service"

Which communication protocol can be used to establish RAS connections between Windows NT 4.0 workstations and RAS servers? Choose all that apply.

A. SLIP

B. PPP

C. X-Link

D. PPP Multilink

Question #155

Resource: Chapter 9, "Auditing and Taking Ownership of the Printer"

Rosemarie was the print administrator in Ulan Bator, but has left the country to pursue a career as an opera singer. You need to assign a new print administrator. What will you need to do concerning ownership of the Ulan Bator printers that Rosemarie created and managed?

A. Do nothing. Printers are not owned by a user; they are owned by the system.

B. Make the new print administrator a Print Operator. The new print administrator can then take ownership of the printers in Ulan Bator.

C. Give ownership of the printers to the new print administrator.

D. Give the new administrator Full Control permission over the printers. Full Control automatically assigns ownership to that user.

Question #156

Resource: Chapter 8, "Additional Thoughts on Long Names"

You are deciding whether to support long file names on FAT partitions for your server. You have a variety of client platforms that connect to the server, including MS-DOS and Windows 95. Some of the platforms support older 16-bit applications. Which of the following considerations would you make?

    A. There are no significant concerns. All applications support long file names on all platforms in a Microsoft network.

    B. Most Microsoft applications will support the long file names, but some older applications save changes by deleting the old file and renaming a temporary file to the original file name. This could corrupt the long file name.

    C. Long file names saved in the root of the drive require one directory entry for the alias, and one for up to every 13 characters of the name. Because the root is hard-coded for 512 directory entries, you could run out of entries.

    D. If long file name support is disabled for the FAT partition, it is disabled for all partitions on that computer, including NTFS.

Question #157

Resource: Chapter 6, "Account Policy" and "Audit Policy"

You suspect that someone is trying to log in to various workstations unauthorized. What is the best step you can take to increase security and determine who might be doing this?

    A. Enable Account Lockout in the Account Policy requiring the Administrator to unlock the account.

    B. Enable Account Lockout in the Account Policy requiring the Administrator to unlock the account. Enable auditing of unsuccessful logons and logoffs and monitor these events in the Event Viewer.

C. Advise users to change their passwords more frequently and not to use obvious passwords.

D. Increase the minimum password length in Account Policy.

Question #158
Resource: Chapter 6, "Naming Conventions," "Considerations Regarding Passwords," and "Creating a New User"

Which of the following sets of usernames and passwords are acceptable for Windows NT?

Username	Password
A. First Ass't Comptroller	FirstComp
B. FirstAsstCompt	1stComp
C. FirstAss*tCompt	COMP1
D. AssComp1	123COMPTROLLER1

Question #159
Resource: Chapter 6, "Understanding User and Group Accounts" and "Creating a New User"

Your boss has advised you that BrownC has left the company and asks that you delete his account. Later, your boss hires BrownC back as a consultant and tells you to put his account back on the network. BrownC calls you the next day and informs you gruffly that he can no longer access any of the network resources that he used to. How do you troubleshoot?

A. Use the Registry to set BrownC's SID back to what it was before you deleted his account. He will then be able to access all the old resources.

B. Deleting BrownC's account also deleted his SID. Because security in Windows NT is linked to the user's SID, you will need to reestablish all the network resource access that BrownC used to have.

C. Use the Emergency Repair Disk or your last network backup to copy BrownC's old account back to the Registry.

D. Leave the company and get hired back as a consultant yourself.

Answer Key

Question	Answer	Question	Answer
1	B,C,D	28	D
2	A	29	B
3	B	30	C
4	B,C,D	31	D
5	C	32	B,D
6	B,C	33	C
7	B	34	C
8	B	35	C
9	A,B,C	36	A,B,D
10	A	37	C
11	A	38	C
12	B	39	B
13	C	40	B
14	C	41	A
15	A,B,C	42	A,B,D
16	C	43	B,C,D
17	C	44	C
18	B	45	B
19	B	46	B
20	C	47	A,C,D
21	B	48	A,C
22	B	49	B
23	A	50	A,B,D
24	A,B,C	51	B
25	A,B,C,D	52	C
26	C	53	C
27	C	54	A,D

App
J

Question	Answer	Question	Answer
55	C	84	A,B,C
56	A,B,D	85	D
57	B,D	86	A
58	B,C,D	87	C
59	A	88	D
60	A,B,D	89	A,C
61	B	90	A,B
62	C	91	D
63	C	92	C
64	D	93	C
65	A,D	94	C
66	A,B	95	C
67	A,C,D	96	A,B,D
68	C	97	A,B,C
69	A,C,D	98	B
70	B	99	B
71	B	100	C
72	A,C	101	B
73	B	102	B
74	B	103	D
75	C	104	C
76	A,B,D	105	B
77	A	106	A
78	A	107	A,B,C,D
79	B	108	C
80	A	109	B
81	A	110	B
82	D	111	A
83	B	112	C

Question	Answer	Question	Answer
113	C	137	B
114	A,C,D	138	A,C
115	C	139	B
116	A	140	A,C,D
117	B,C	141	A,B,C
118	A,B,C	142	A,B,D
119	B,D	143	B
120	A,B	144	A
121	A	145	C
122	A	146	B
123	A,B	147	A
124	D	148	A,C,D
125	A	149	C
126	B	150	A,B,C
127	A,C,D	151	B,C
128	A,C,D	152	A
129	B,C	153	A
130	A	154	A,B,D
131	A,B,D	155	B
132	B	156	B,C
133	A	157	B
134	C	158	B
135	A,C,D	159	B
136	D		

Index

Check out Que® Books on the World Wide Web
http://www.quecorp.com

As the biggest software release in computer history, Windows 95 continues to redefine the computer industry. Click here for the latest info on our Windows 95 books

Make computing quick and easy with these products designed exclusively for new and casual users

Examine the latest releases in word processing, spreadsheets, operating systems, and suites

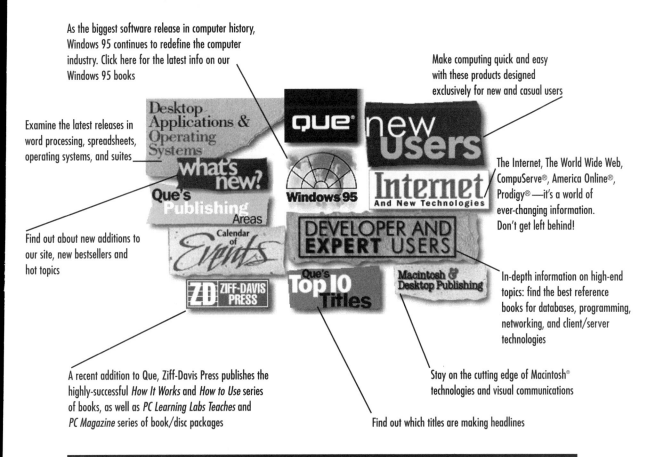

The Internet, The World Wide Web, CompuServe®, America Online®, Prodigy®—it's a world of ever-changing information. Don't get left behind!

Find out about new additions to our site, new bestsellers and hot topics

In-depth information on high-end topics: find the best reference books for databases, programming, networking, and client/server technologies

A recent addition to Que, Ziff-Davis Press publishes the highly-successful *How It Works* and *How to Use* series of books, as well as *PC Learning Labs Teaches* and *PC Magazine* series of book/disc packages

Stay on the cutting edge of Macintosh® technologies and visual communications

Find out which titles are making headlines

With 6 separate publishing groups, Que develops products for many specific market segments and areas of computer technology. Explore our Web Site and you'll find information on best-selling titles, newly published titles, upcoming products, authors, and much more.

- Stay informed on the latest industry trends and products available
- Visit our online bookstore for the latest information and editions
- Download software from Que's library of the best shareware and freeware

Complete and Return this Card
for a *FREE* Computer Book Catalog

Thank you for purchasing this book! You have purchased a superior computer book written expressly for your needs. To continue to provide the kind of up-to-date, pertinent coverage you've come to expect from us, we need to hear from you. Please take a minute to complete and return this self-addressed, postage-paid form. In return, we'll send you a free catalog of all our computer books on topics ranging from word processing to programming and the internet.

Mr. ☐   Mrs. ☐   Ms. ☐   Dr. ☐

Name (first) ☐☐☐☐☐☐☐☐☐☐☐☐ (M.I.) ☐ (last) ☐☐☐☐☐☐☐☐☐☐☐☐☐☐☐☐☐☐☐

Address ☐☐☐☐☐☐☐☐☐☐☐☐☐☐☐☐☐☐☐☐☐☐☐☐☐☐☐☐☐☐☐☐☐☐☐☐☐

City ☐☐☐☐☐☐☐☐☐☐☐☐☐☐☐ State ☐☐ Zip ☐☐☐☐☐ ☐☐☐☐

Phone ☐☐☐ ☐☐☐ ☐☐☐☐ Fax ☐☐☐ ☐☐☐ ☐☐☐☐

Company Name ☐☐☐☐☐☐☐☐☐☐☐☐☐☐☐☐☐☐☐☐☐☐☐☐☐☐☐☐☐☐☐☐☐☐

E-mail address ☐☐☐☐☐☐☐☐☐☐☐☐☐☐☐☐☐☐☐☐☐☐☐☐☐☐☐☐☐☐☐☐☐☐

1. Please check at least (3) influencing factors for purchasing this book.

Front or back cover information on book .... ☐
Special approach to the content .... ☐
Completeness of content .... ☐
Author's reputation .... ☐
Publisher's reputation .... ☐
Book cover design or layout .... ☐
Index or table of contents of book .... ☐
Price of book .... ☐
Special effects, graphics, illustrations .... ☐
Other (Please specify): _____ ☐

2. How did you first learn about this book?

Saw in Macmillan Computer Publishing catalog .... ☐
Recommended by store personnel .... ☐
Saw the book on bookshelf at store .... ☐
Recommended by a friend .... ☐
Received advertisement in the mail .... ☐
Saw an advertisement in: _____ ☐
Read book review in: _____ ☐
Other (Please specify): _____ ☐

3. How many computer books have you purchased in the last six months?

This book only .... ☐   3 to 5 books .... ☐
2 books .... ☐   More than 5 .... ☐

4. Where did you purchase this book?

Bookstore .... ☐
Computer Store .... ☐
Consumer Electronics Store .... ☐
Department Store .... ☐
Office Club .... ☐
Warehouse Club .... ☐
Mail Order .... ☐
Direct from Publisher .... ☐
Internet site .... ☐
Other (Please specify): _____ ☐

5. How long have you been using a computer?

☐ Less than 6 months   ☐ 6 months to a year
☐ 1 to 3 years   ☐ More than 3 years

6. What is your level of experience with personal computers and with the subject of this book?

	With PCs	With subject of book
New	☐	☐
Casual	☐	☐
Accomplished	☐	☐
Expert	☐	☐

Source Code ISBN: 0-7897-0989-9

7. Which of the following best describes your job title?

Administrative Assistant .... ☐
Coordinator .... ☐
Manager/Supervisor .... ☐
Director .... ☐
Vice President .... ☐
President/CEO/COO .... ☐
Lawyer/Doctor/Medical Professional .... ☐
Teacher/Educator/Trainer .... ☐
Engineer/Technician .... ☐
Consultant .... ☐
Not employed/Student/Retired .... ☐
Other (Please specify): _____ ☐

8. Which of the following best describes the area of the company your job title falls under?

Accounting .... ☐
Engineering .... ☐
Manufacturing .... ☐
Operations .... ☐
Marketing .... ☐
Sales .... ☐
Other (Please specify): _____ ☐

Comments: _____
_____
_____

9. What is your age?

Under 20 .... ☐
21-29 .... ☐
30-39 .... ☐
40-49 .... ☐
50-59 .... ☐
60-over .... ☐

10. Are you:

Male .... ☐
Female .... ☐

11. Which computer publications do you read regularly? (Please list)

_____
_____
_____
_____
_____
_____
_____
_____
_____
_____

Fold here and scotch-tape to mail

Before using this disc, please read Appendix I, "Using the CD-ROM," for information on how to install the disc and what programs are included on the disc. If you have problems with this disc, please contact Macmillan Technical Support at (317) 581-3833. We can be reached by e-mail at **support@mcp.com** or on CompuServe at **GO QUEBOOKS**.

License Agreement

By opening this package you are agreeing to be bound by the following:

This software is copyrighted and all rights are reserved by the publisher and its licensers. You are licensed to use this software on a single computer. You may copy the software for backup or archival purposes only. Making copies of the software for any other purpose is a violation of United States copyright laws. THIS SOFTWARE IS SOLD AS IS, WITHOUT WARRANTY OF ANY KIND, EITHER EXPRESSED OR IMPLIED, INCLUDING BUT NOT LIMITED TO THE IMPLIED WARRANTIES OF MERCHANTABILITY AND FITNESS FOR A PARTICULAR PURPOSE. Neither the publisher nor its licensers, dealers, or distributors assumes any liability for any alleged or actual damages arising from the use of this software. (Some states do not allow exclusion of implied warranties, so the exclusion may not apply to you.)

The entire contents of the disc and the compilation of the software are copyrighted and protected by United States copyright laws. The individual programs on these discs are copyrighted by the authors or owners of each program. Each program has its own use permissions and limitations. To use each program, you must follow the individual requirements and restrictions detailed for each. Do not use a program if you do not agree to follow its licensing agreement.

® 201 W. 103rd Street, Indianapolis, IN 46290 (317) 581-3500
Copyright© 1997 by Que® Corporation.

Productivity Point International Training Centers

Call 1-800-848-0980 or go to **http://www.propoint.com/que** for class schedules and registration information.

United States Locations

Arizona
Phoenix

California
Culver City
Fresno
San Francisco
San Diego
Santa Clara

Colorado
Denver

Florida
Boca Raton
Fort Lauderdale
Jacksonville
Maitland
Miami
Tallahassee
Tampa

Georgia
Atlanta

Illinois
Chicago
Deerfield
Hinsdale
Naperville
Rolling Meadows

Indiana
Indianapolis
Mishawaka

Iowa
Cedar Rapids
West Des Moines

Kansas
Overland Park

Kentucky
Florence
Louisville

Louisiana
Baton Rouge
Lafayette
New Orleans

Maine
Portland

Massachusetts
Boston
Marlboro
Newton Lower Falls

Michigan
Ann Arbor
Grand Rapids
Holland
Troy

Minnesota
Bloomington
Minneapolis

Missouri
St. Louis

Nevada
Las Vegas
Reno

New Hampshire
Bedford

New Jersey
Iselin
Mt. Laurel
Parsippany

New York
Melville
New York
Rochester

North Carolina
Durham
Greensboro
Raleigh

Ohio
Cincinnati
Dayton
Dublin
Maumee

Oklahoma
Oklahoma City

Oregon
Portland

Pennsylvania
Allentown
Blue Bell
Camp Hill

Philadelphia
Pittsburgh

Tennessee
Brentwood
Memphis

Texas
Austin
Dallas
Fort Worth
Houston
San Antonio

Utah
Murray
Salt Lake City

Virginia
Alexandria
Glen Allen
Richmond

Washington
Bellevue
Spokane

Washington D.C.

West Virginia
Charleston

Wisconsin
Green Bay
Neenah
Stevens Point
Wausau

Caribbean Locations

Puerto Rico
Hato Rey

Canadian Locations

Alberta
Calgary

British Columbia
Vancouver

Manitoba
Brandon
Thompson
Winnipeg

Ontario
Etobicoke
Hamilton
Kenora
Kitchener
London
Niagara
North Bay
Ottawa
Sarnia
Scarborough
Sudbury
Toronto

Quebec
Montreal

Saskatchewan
Regina
Saskatoon

MCPS and MCSD Certification Requirements

The following exams are currently available for Microsoft Certified Product Specialist and Microsoft Certified Solution Developer certification tracks. For complete details, visit Microsoft's Training and Certification Web site at **http://www.microsoft.com/train_cert/**.

Test #	Exam Name	MCPS[1]	MCSD[2]
70-30	Microsoft Windows 3.1	C	
70-42	Implementing and Supporting Microsoft Windows NT Workstation 3.51	C	
70-43	Implementing and Supporting Microsoft Windows NT Server 3.51	C	
70-48	Microsoft Windows for Workgroups 3.11	C	
70-63	Implementing and Supporting Microsoft Windows 95	C	
70-67	Implementing and Supporting Microsoft Windows NT Server 4.0	C	
70-73	Implementing and Supporting Microsoft Windows NT Workstation 4.0	C	
70-150	Microsoft Windows Operating Systems and Services Architecture I	C	C
70-151	Microsoft Windows Operating Systems and Services Architecture II	C	C
70-38	Microsoft Project 4.0 for Windows	E	
70-39	Microsoft Excel 5.0 for Windows	E	
70-49	Microsoft Word 6.0 for Windows	E	
70-66	Microsoft Word for Windows 95	E	
70-21	Microsoft SQL Server 4.2 Database Implementation	E	
70-24	Developing Applications with C++ Using the Microsoft Foundation Class Library		
70-25	Implementing OLE in Microsoft Foundation Class Applications		E
70-27	Implementing a Database Design on Microsoft SQL Server 6.0		E
70-50	Microsoft Visual Basic 3.0 for Windows—Application Development		E
70-51	Microsoft Access 2.0 for Windows—Application Development		E
70-52	Developing Applications with Microsoft Excel 5.0 Using Visual Basic for Applications		E
70-54	Programming in Microsoft Visual FoxPro 3.0 for Windows		E
70-65	Programming with Microsoft Visual Basic 4.0		E
70-69	Microsoft Access for Windows 95 and the Microsoft Access Developer's Toolkit		E

[1]*Microsoft Certified Product Specialist (MCPS)*

Requires one operating system exam. Additional product specialties listed are electives.

[2]*Microsoft Certified Solution Developer (MCSD)*

Requires two core technology exams and two elective exams.

C − core E = elective

See other side for Microsoft Certified Systems Engineer requirements.

MCSE Certification Requirements

The following exams are currently available for Microsoft Certified Systems Engineer certification tracks. For complete details, visit Microsoft's Training and Certification Web site at **http://www.microsoft.com/train_cert/**.

Test #	Exam Name	MCSE[1] 3.51 Track	MCSE[1] 4.0 Track	NT 3.5 to NT 4.0 Migration Path[2]
70-42	Implementing and Supporting Microsoft Windows NT Workstation 3.51	C		
70-43	Implementing and Supporting Microsoft Windows NT Server 3.51	C		
70-30	Microsoft Windows 3.1	C	C	
70-46	Networking with Microsoft Windows for Workgroups 3.11	C	C	
70-47	Networking with Microsoft Windows 3.1	C	C	
70-58	Networking Essentials	C	C	
70-63	Implementing and Supporting Microsoft Windows 95	C	C	
70-48	Microsoft Windows for Workgroups 3.11		C	
70-73	Implementing and Supporting Microsoft Windows NT Workstation 4.0		C	
70-67	Implementing and Supporting Microsoft Windows NT Server 4.0		C	C
70-68	Implementing and Supporting Microsoft Windows NT Server 4.0 in the Enterprise		C	C
70-12	Microsoft SNA Server	E	E	
70-14	Implementing and Supporting Microsoft Systems Management Server	E	E	
70-21	Microsoft SQL Server 4.2 Database Implementation	E	E	
70-22	Microsoft SQL Server 4.2 Database Administration for Microsoft Windows NT	E	E	
70-26	System Administration of Microsoft SQL Server 6.0	E	E	
70-27	Implementing a Database Design on Microsoft SQL Server 6.0	E	E	
70-37	Microsoft Mail 3.2 for PC Networks—Enterprise	E	E	
70-53	Internetworking Microsoft TCP/IP on Microsoft Windows NT 3.5	E	E	
70-59	Internetworking Microsoft TCP/IP on Microsoft Windows NT 4.0	E	E	
70-75	Implementing and Supporting Microsoft Exchange	E	E	
70-77	Implementing and Supporting Microsoft Internet Information Server	E	E	
70-78	Implementing and Supporting Microsoft Proxy Server 1.0	E	E	

[1]***Microsoft Certified System Engineer (MCSE)***

Requires four operating system exams and two elective exams.

[2]***NT 3.5 to NT 4.0 Migration Path***

MCSEs certified under the Windows NT 3.51 track who wish to upgrade their certification to Windows NT 4.0. Requires two operating system exams.

C = core   E = elective

See other side for Microsoft Certified Product Specialist and Microsoft Certified Solution Developer requirements.